AGENTS OF ATLAS

WRITER
Jeff Parker

PENCILER
Leonard Kirk

INKERS
Kris Justice with **Terry Pallot**

COLORIST
Michelle Madsen

LETTERER
Artmonkeys' Dave Lanphear

COVER ARTIST
Tomm Coker

ASSISTANT EDITOR
Nathan Cosby

EDITOR
Mark Paniccia

Special thanks to **Crusher Hogan, Murray Ward
& Dr. Michael J. Vassallo**

SENIOR EDITOR, SPECIAL PROJECTS
Jeff Youngquist

EDITORS, SPECIAL PROJECTS
Jennifer Grünwald & Mark D. Beazley

ASSISTANT EDITORS
Cory Levine & John Denning

PRODUCTION
Jerry Kalinowski

SENIOR VICE PRESIDENT OF SALES
David Gabriel

BOOK DESIGNER
Patrick McGrath

VICE PRESIDENT OF CREATIVE
Tom Marvelli

EDITOR IN CHIEF
Joe Quesada

PUBLISHER
Dan Buckley

INTRODUCTION

"That would be one kick-ass hotdog stand."

— Ken Hale, the Gorilla Man

I know this is an intro, but maybe you should go ahead and read the story, and then come back to this. I don't want to spoil it, and it may all make more sense once you know where my head was. Go ahead, enjoy.

OK, welcome back. Did you like it? Great. So I was writing *Marvel Adventures Fantastic Four* when editor Mark Paniccia called and asked me to look at a book from the '70s, *What If #9*, featuring the "Secret Avengers." He had just come across it again and couldn't stop thinking, "There's something there." Immediately, I agreed: There *was* something there. The team broke down into archetypes of pulp adventure: A secret agent. A spaceman. A goddess. A gorilla. A robot. A guy who was like *three* guys. OK, they didn't all correlate so well — but one of them could sit this round out. Then, I looked into another character that appears briefly in the story and found out that cartooning legend Bill Everett conveniently left this superstrong Atlantean in a block of ice. A mermaid? This could be the greatest team *ever*.

Then, the hand of Fate and the hand of Paniccia conspired to place artist Leonard Kirk in the mix. Kirk immediately clicked with the story proposal and knew how to pull it off. Yes, it had wacky, over-the-top elements throughout — but under all the pulp trappings, the characters were real people. If we believed in them, readers would too. Even knowing Kirk's track record, we didn't realize his true range until now. Leonard can handle *any* genre of fiction, which comes in handy because we go through so many in our story. He invests something of himself into each of the cast, and they come to life completely. His character designs sing. The Atomic Age of Comics is still evident in the team's look, yet each has a timeless quality. They look like a group that belongs together.

During this planning stage, we went through about thirty names. "Secret Avengers" got claimed for something else, and no word combination could make all of us happy. Then, the obvious occurred: While we have this rare chance to acknowledge the earlier days of Marvel, we should put the company label of the 1950s, Atlas, in there. I called to say this and Assistant Editor Nate Cosby blurted, "Agents of Atlas!" From this point, the arcane and powerful Atlas Foundation began to emerge in full, and the mysterious Mr. Lao stepped out of the shadows. Tomm Coker started turning in iconic cover designs that would give the series a strong presence. Michelle Madsen brought her formidable color design to the House of Ideas (not warned about what unreasonable menaces Leonard and I are with color notes). We all labored over details that may never get noticed, and Kris Justice and Dave Lanphear were saddled with ridiculous windows to bring the final pages together. But it was happening, and it was exciting.

If I can speak for everyone else — and of course I can, because I'm writing the intro! — I think we all realized we were suddenly creating something special, something bigger than our individual efforts might produce. A big part of comic books, some say the biggest element, is wish fulfillment. For my part, I can say it's the driving impulse in *Agents of Atlas*. When Mark called me with his hunch about offbeat characters no one had seen in decades, I went straight for my greatest wish. I had only two weeks earlier given permission for my father to be taken off life support. My days were filled trying to make my deadlines from his house while poring through the artifacts of his whole life, looking through photos of him as a young man. If Ken Hale seeing Jimmy Woo in critical condition at S.H.I.E.L.D.'s Mojave Base has resonance, that's where it came from. I wasn't concerned with what was in vogue in mainstream comics. I wanted full-on, indulgent *escapism*. Wouldn't it be great if that idealistic young FBI agent got another chance at life? Any of us? To hell with the real world where we have to settle for one go-round, this is *comics*. It *could* happen, and *it was going to*.

This story is about returns and second chances, largely brought about by characters who aren't willing to let the past swallow up their old friends. There are moments in history when the right people connect at the right time. Jimmy Woo's secret team was only together for about half a year, 50 years ago. Yet that combination at that point *meant* something. When the reformed killer robot M-11 reappears with no explanation, Ken Hale takes it seriously. And as an immortal gorilla, Ken Hale does not take much seriously. Of course, as our Mr. Lao points out at the end of Book One, nothing returns alone, does it?

Maybe you'll recognize people you know in Jimmy Woo's team, like the winning young leader himself. The incredibly sweet-natured Venus, and the alienated and withdrawn Bob Grayson. The earthy and adventurous Ken Hale. Or the regal, honor-bound Namora. The inscrutable M-11 is probably the model we should all follow in our dealings with others. What little he says gives no insight, but his actions tell Jimmy Woo everything he needs to know about the oddly named "Human Robot." I'm also very fond of the team's unofficial member, Derek Khanata, the rational yet empathetic S.H.I.E.L.D. agent.

The Agents of Atlas took on a life of their own, and here's hoping they keep it. Should I ever find myself in real danger — and in the Marvel universe — I'd certainly welcome the help of any heroes shooting flames or webs. But I think I'd be most happy to see a beam projecting down from a Uranian flying saucer.

Jeff Parker

March 2007

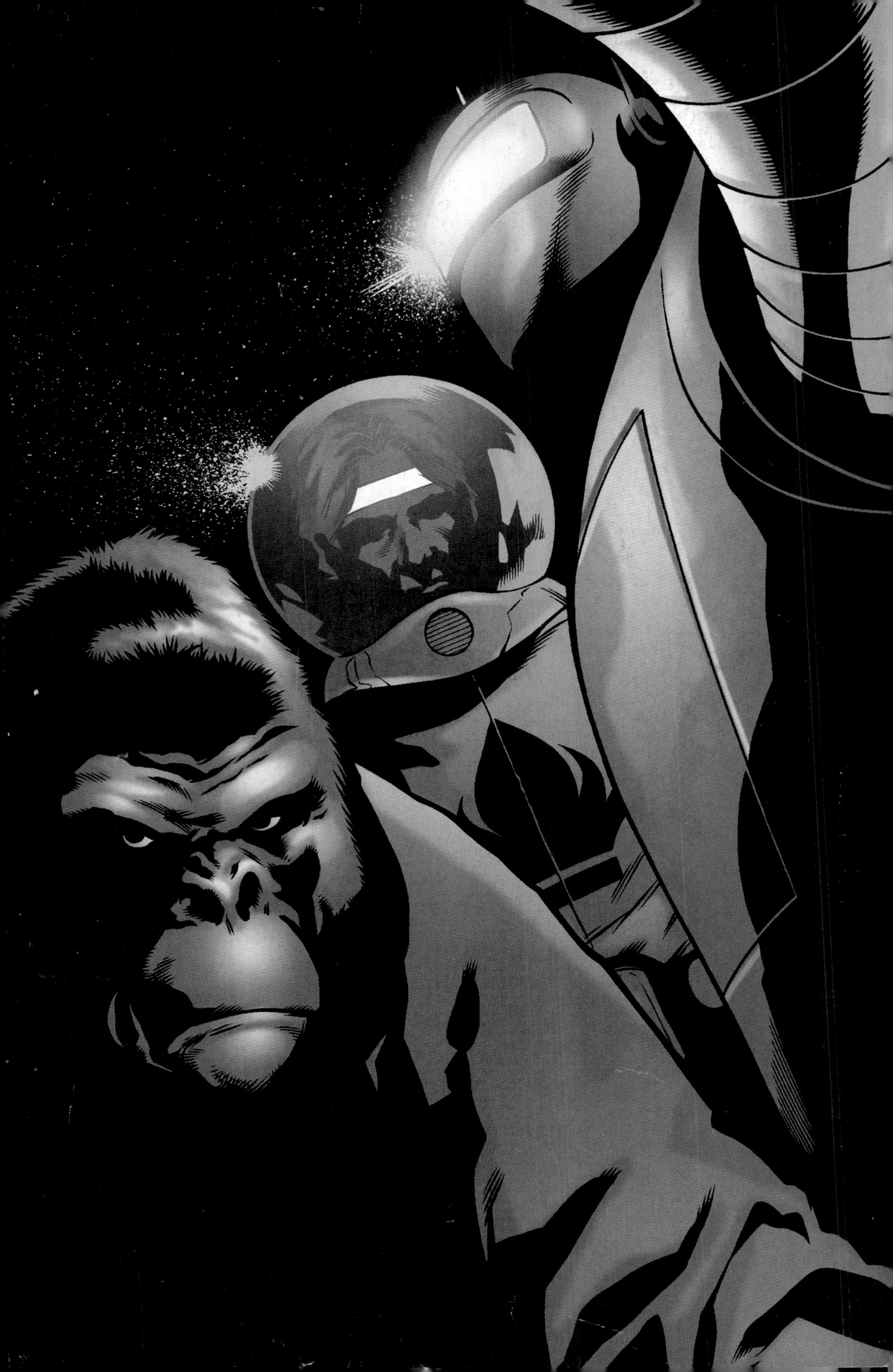

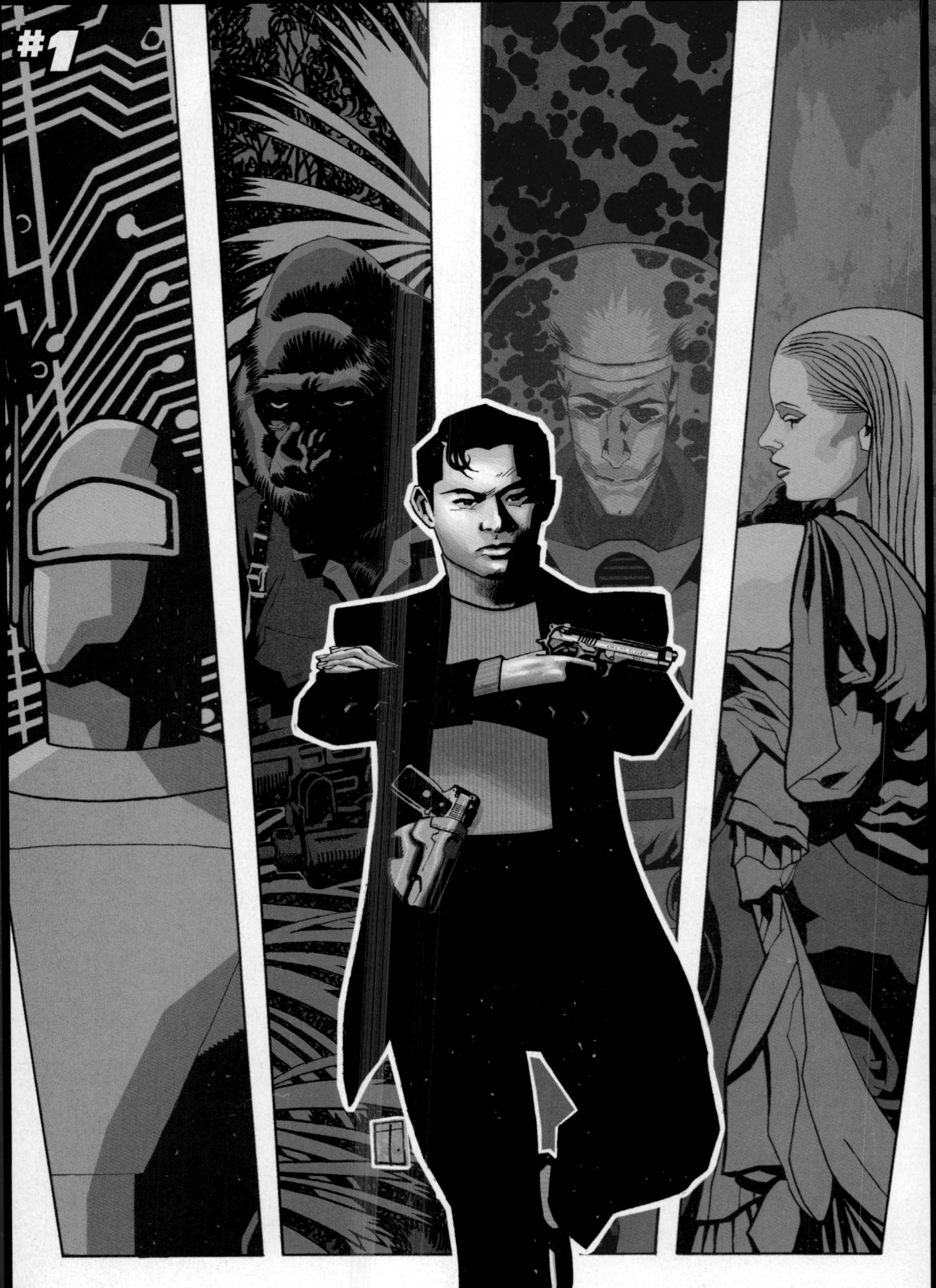
#1

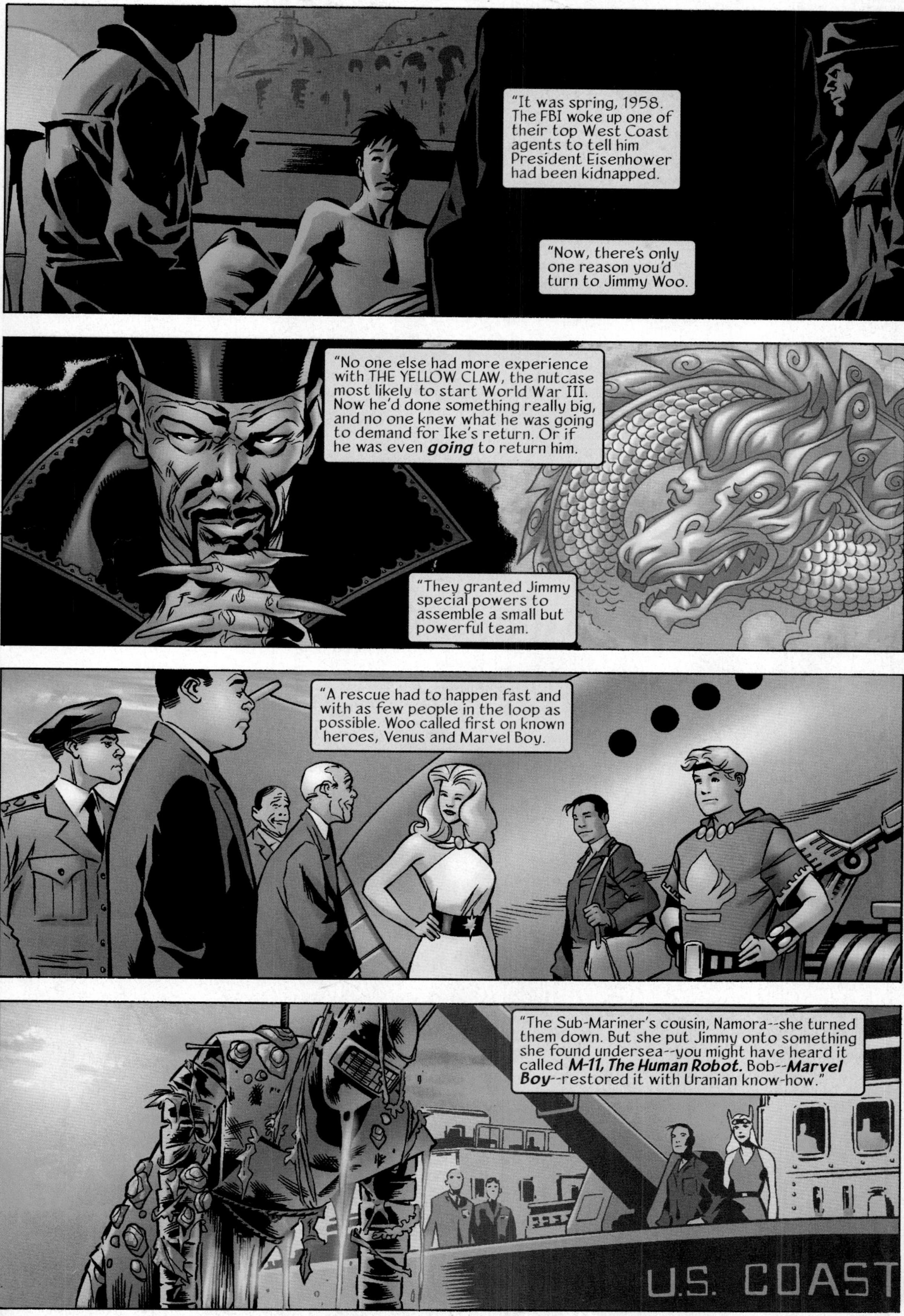
"It was spring, 1958. The FBI woke up one of their top West Coast agents to tell him President Eisenhower had been kidnapped.
"Now, there's only one reason you'd turn to Jimmy Woo.
"No one else had more experience with THE YELLOW CLAW, the nutcase most likely to start World War III. Now he'd done something really big, and no one knew what he was going to demand for Ike's return. Or if he was even ***going*** to return him.
"They granted Jimmy special powers to assemble a small but powerful team.
"A rescue had to happen fast and with as few people in the loop as possible. Woo called first on known heroes, Venus and Marvel Boy.
"The Sub-Mariner's cousin, Namora--she turned them down. But she put Jimmy onto something she found undersea--you might have heard it called ***M-11, The Human Robot.*** Bob--***Marvel Boy***--restored it with Uranian know-how."
U.S. COAST

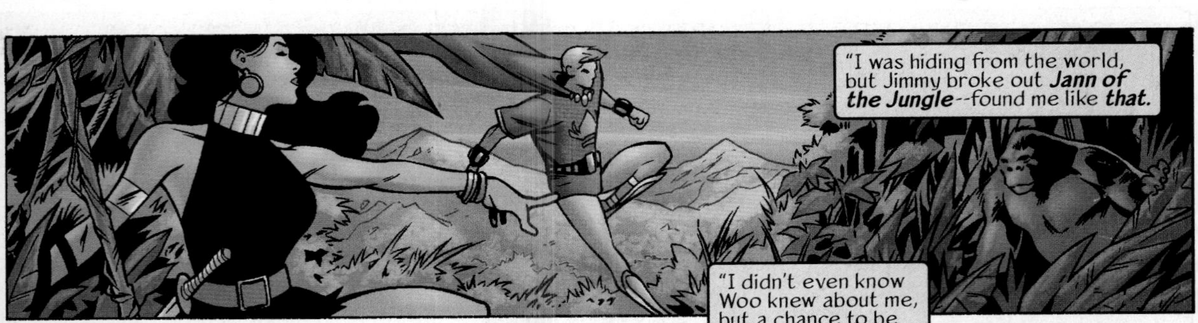
"I was hiding from the world, but Jimmy broke out *Jann of the Jungle*--found me like *that.*
"I didn't even know Woo knew about me, but a chance to be treated like a man?

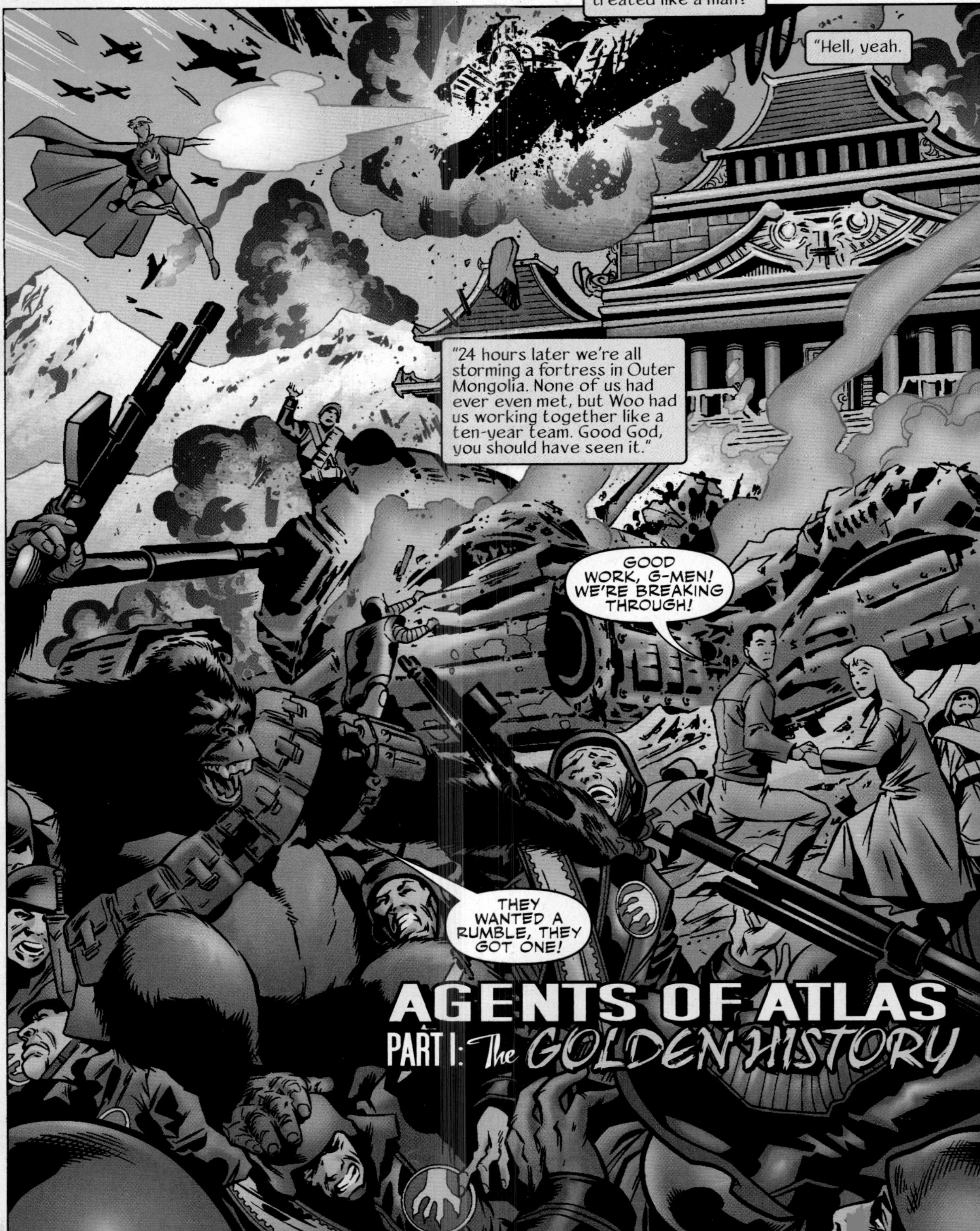
"Hell, yeah.
"24 hours later we're all storming a fortress in Outer Mongolia. None of us had ever even met, but Woo had us working together like a ten-year team. Good God, you should have seen it."
GOOD WORK, G-MEN! WE'RE BREAKING THROUGH!
THEY WANTED A RUMBLE, THEY GOT ONE!
AGENTS OF ATLAS
PART I: The GOLDEN HISTORY

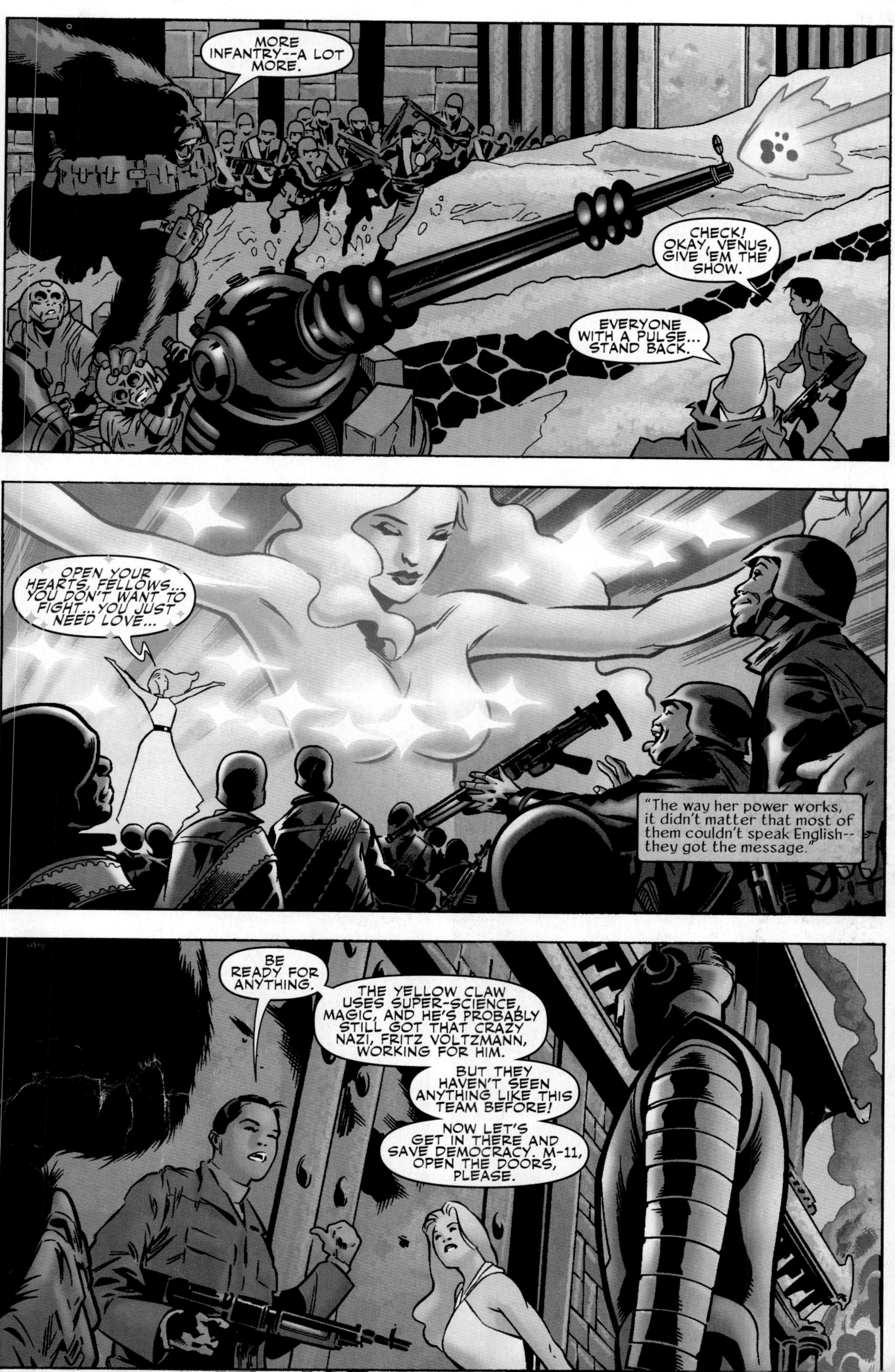
MORE INFANTRY--A LOT MORE.
CHECK! OKAY, VENUS, GIVE 'EM THE SHOW.
EVERYONE WITH A PULSE... STAND BACK...
OPEN YOUR HEARTS, FELLOWS... YOU DON'T WANT TO FIGHT...YOU JUST NEED LOVE...
"The way her power works, it didn't matter that most of them couldn't speak English--they got the message."
BE READY FOR ANYTHING.
THE YELLOW CLAW USES SUPER-SCIENCE, MAGIC, AND HE'S PROBABLY STILL GOT THAT CRAZY NAZI, FRITZ VOLTZMANN, WORKING FOR HIM.
BUT THEY HAVEN'T SEEN ANYTHING LIKE THIS TEAM BEFORE!
NOW LET'S GET IN THERE AND SAVE DEMOCRACY. M-11, OPEN THE DOORS, PLEASE.

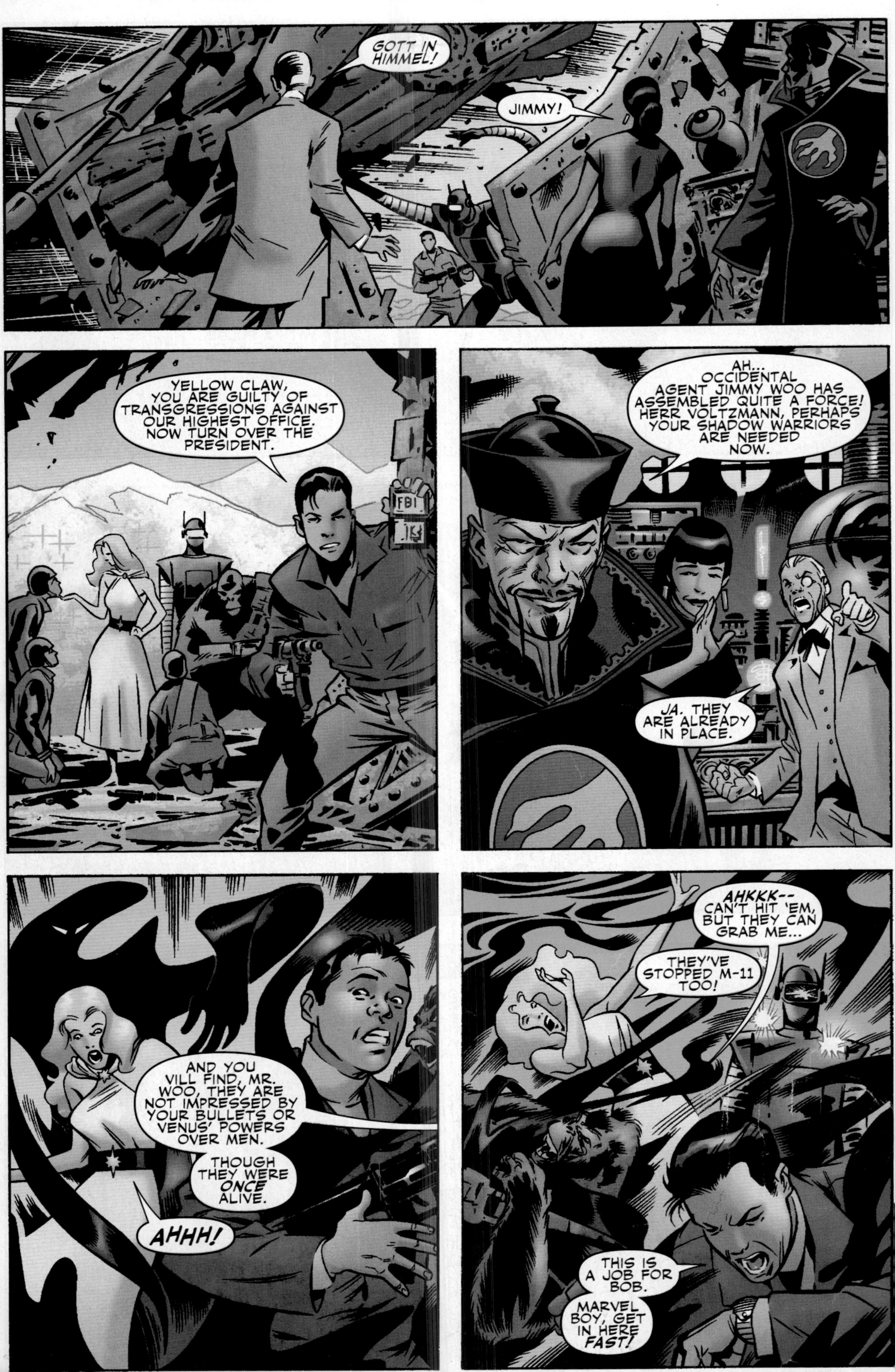
GOTT IN HIMMEL!
JIMMY!
YELLOW CLAW, YOU ARE GUILTY OF TRANSGRESSIONS AGAINST OUR HIGHEST OFFICE. NOW TURN OVER THE PRESIDENT.
FBI
AH... OCCIDENTAL AGENT JIMMY WOO HAS ASSEMBLED QUITE A FORCE! HERR VOLTZMANN, PERHAPS YOUR SHADOW WARRIORS ARE NEEDED NOW.
JA. THEY ARE ALREADY IN PLACE.
AND YOU VILL FIND, MR. WOO, THEY ARE NOT IMPRESSED BY YOUR BULLETS OR VENUS' POWERS OVER MEN.
THOUGH THEY WERE ONCE ALIVE.
AHHH!
AHKKK-- CAN'T HIT 'EM, BUT THEY CAN GRAB ME...
THEY'VE STOPPED M-11 TOO!
THIS IS A JOB FOR BOB.
MARVEL BOY, GET IN HERE FAST!

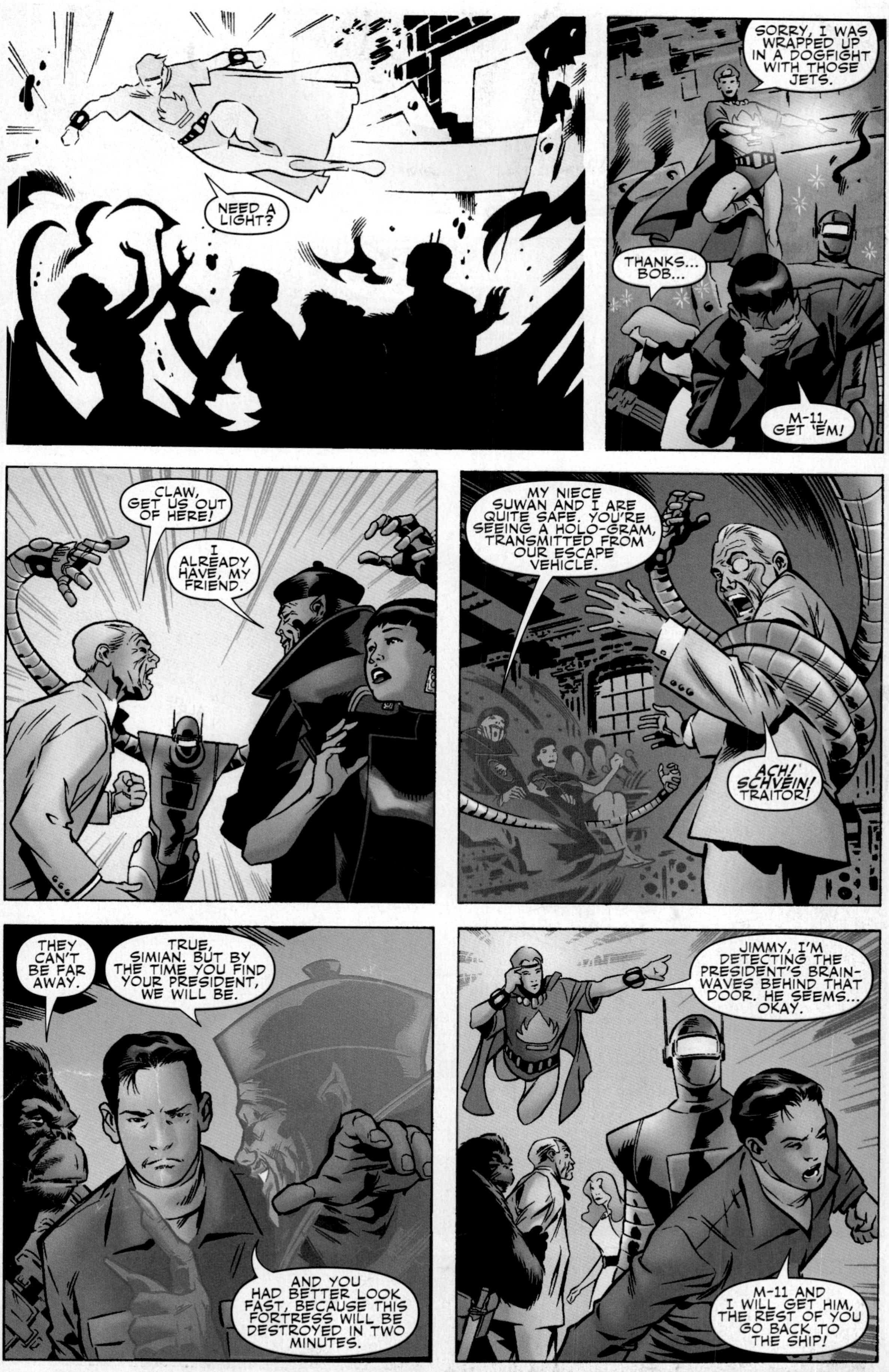
NEED A LIGHT?
SORRY, I WAS WRAPPED UP IN A DOGFIGHT WITH THOSE JETS.
THANKS... BOB...
M-11, GET 'EM!
CLAW, GET US OUT OF HERE!
I ALREADY HAVE, MY FRIEND.
MY NIECE SUWAN AND I ARE QUITE SAFE. YOU'RE SEEING A HOLO-GRAM, TRANSMITTED FROM OUR ESCAPE VEHICLE.
ACH! SCHVEIN! TRAITOR!
THEY CAN'T BE FAR AWAY.
TRUE, SIMIAN. BUT BY THE TIME YOU FIND YOUR PRESIDENT, WE WILL BE.
AND YOU HAD BETTER LOOK FAST, BECAUSE THIS FORTRESS WILL BE DESTROYED IN TWO MINUTES.
JIMMY, I'M DETECTING THE PRESIDENT'S BRAIN-WAVES BEHIND THAT DOOR. HE SEEMS... OKAY.
M-11 AND I WILL GET HIM, THE REST OF YOU GO BACK TO THE SHIP!

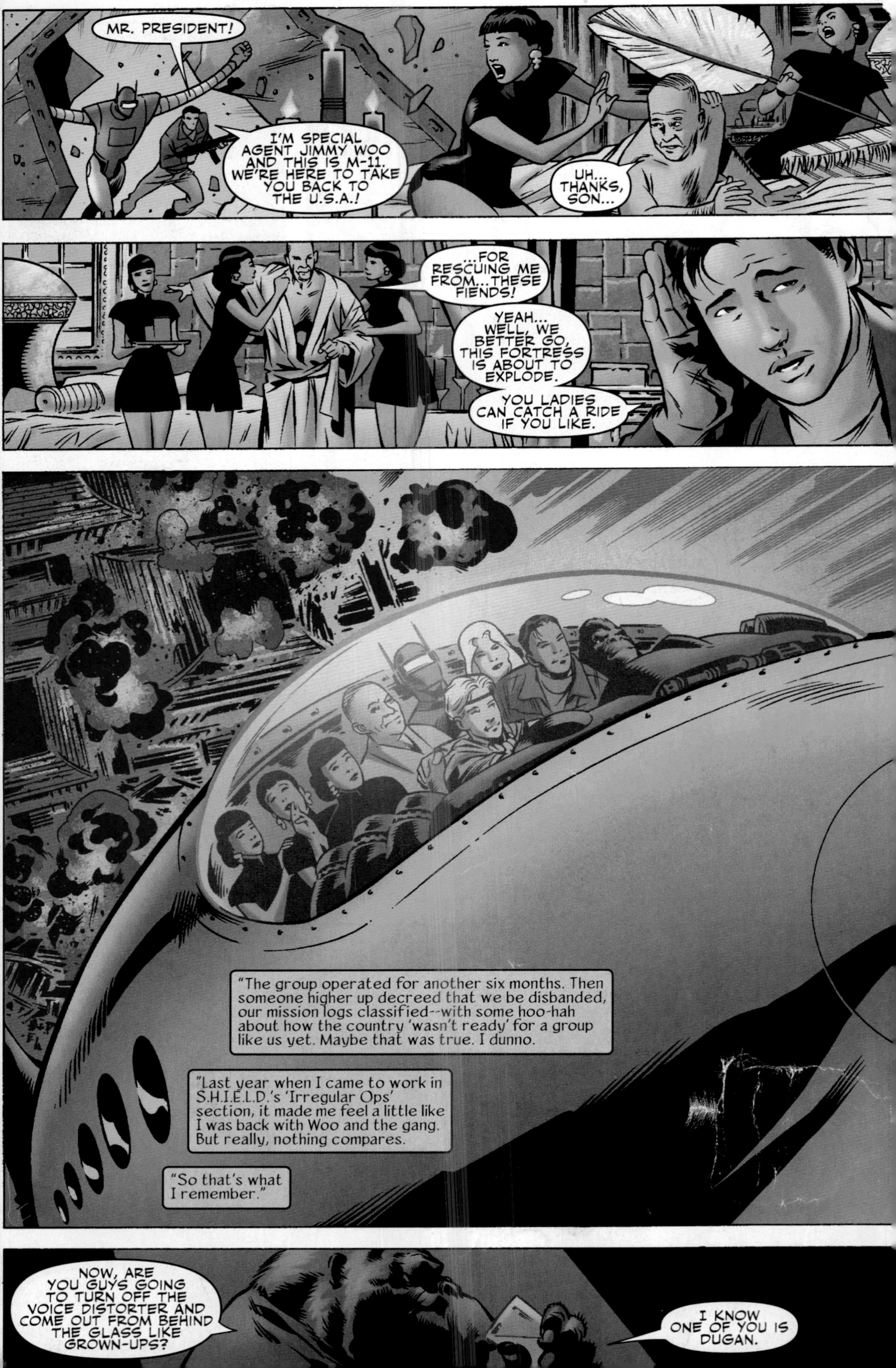
MR. PRESIDENT!
I'M SPECIAL AGENT JIMMY WOO AND THIS IS M-11. WE'RE HERE TO TAKE YOU BACK TO THE U.S.A.!
UH... THANKS, SON...
...FOR RESCUING ME FROM...THESE FIENDS!
YEAH... WELL, WE BETTER GO, THIS FORTRESS IS ABOUT TO EXPLODE.
YOU LADIES CAN CATCH A RIDE IF YOU LIKE.
"The group operated for another six months. Then someone higher up decreed that we be disbanded, our mission logs classified--with some hoo-hah about how the country 'wasn't ready' for a group like us yet. Maybe that was true. I dunno.
"Last year when I came to work in S.H.I.E.L.D.'s 'Irregular Ops' section, it made me feel a little like I was back with Woo and the gang. But really, nothing compares.
"So that's what I remember."
NOW, ARE YOU GUYS GOING TO TURN OFF THE VOICE DISTORTER AND COME OUT FROM BEHIND THE GLASS LIKE GROWN-UPS?
I KNOW ONE OF YOU IS DUGAN.

STANDARD S.H.I.E.L.D. DEBRIEFING, HALE--YOU KNOW THAT. NOW, HOW'D YOU KNOW I WAS THERE?

SMELLED YA.

THIS IS AGENT DEREK KHANATA. HE'S HEADING THIS INVESTIGATION.

MISTER HALE.

YOUR ACCOUNT LINES UP WITH WHAT WE LEARNED FROM THE FBI FILE, SEALED UNTIL YESTERDAY. TILL THEN, WE KNEW NOTHING ABOUT YOUR TEAM.

THEY MUST HAVE BEEN PRETTY PROUD OF US, HUH? LOOK, IF S.H.I.E.L.D. IS MAD THAT I DIDN'T MENTION MY SERVICE RECORD--

NO, WE KNOW YOU WEREN'T ALLOWED TO TALK ABOUT IT. THIS AIN'T ABOUT YOU. IT'S ABOUT JIMMY WOO.

SUBDIRECTOR JAMES WOO

WOO'S BEEN WITH US SINCE THE '60'S. WORKED IN DIRECTORATE FOR THE LAST EIGHT YEARS.

EXTREMELY RELIABLE...UP UNTIL 48 HOURS AGO.

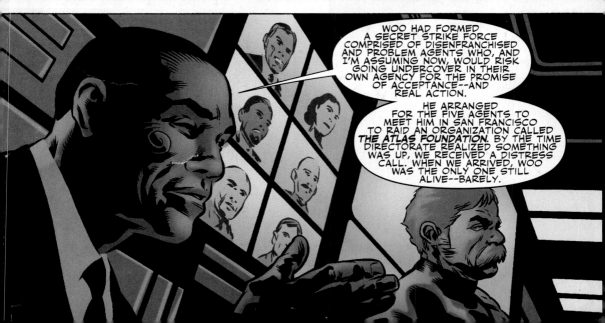

WOO HAD FORMED A SECRET STRIKE FORCE COMPRISED OF DISENFRANCHISED AND PROBLEM AGENTS WHO, AND I'M ASSUMING NOW, WOULD RISK GOING UNDERCOVER IN THEIR OWN AGENCY FOR THE PROMISE OF ACCEPTANCE--AND REAL ACTION.

HE ARRANGED FOR THE FIVE AGENTS TO MEET HIM IN SAN FRANCISCO TO RAID AN ORGANIZATION CALLED THE ATLAS FOUNDATION. BY THE TIME DIRECTORATE REALIZED SOMETHING WAS UP, WE RECEIVED A DISTRESS CALL. WHEN WE ARRIVED, WOO WAS THE ONLY ONE STILL ALIVE--BARELY.

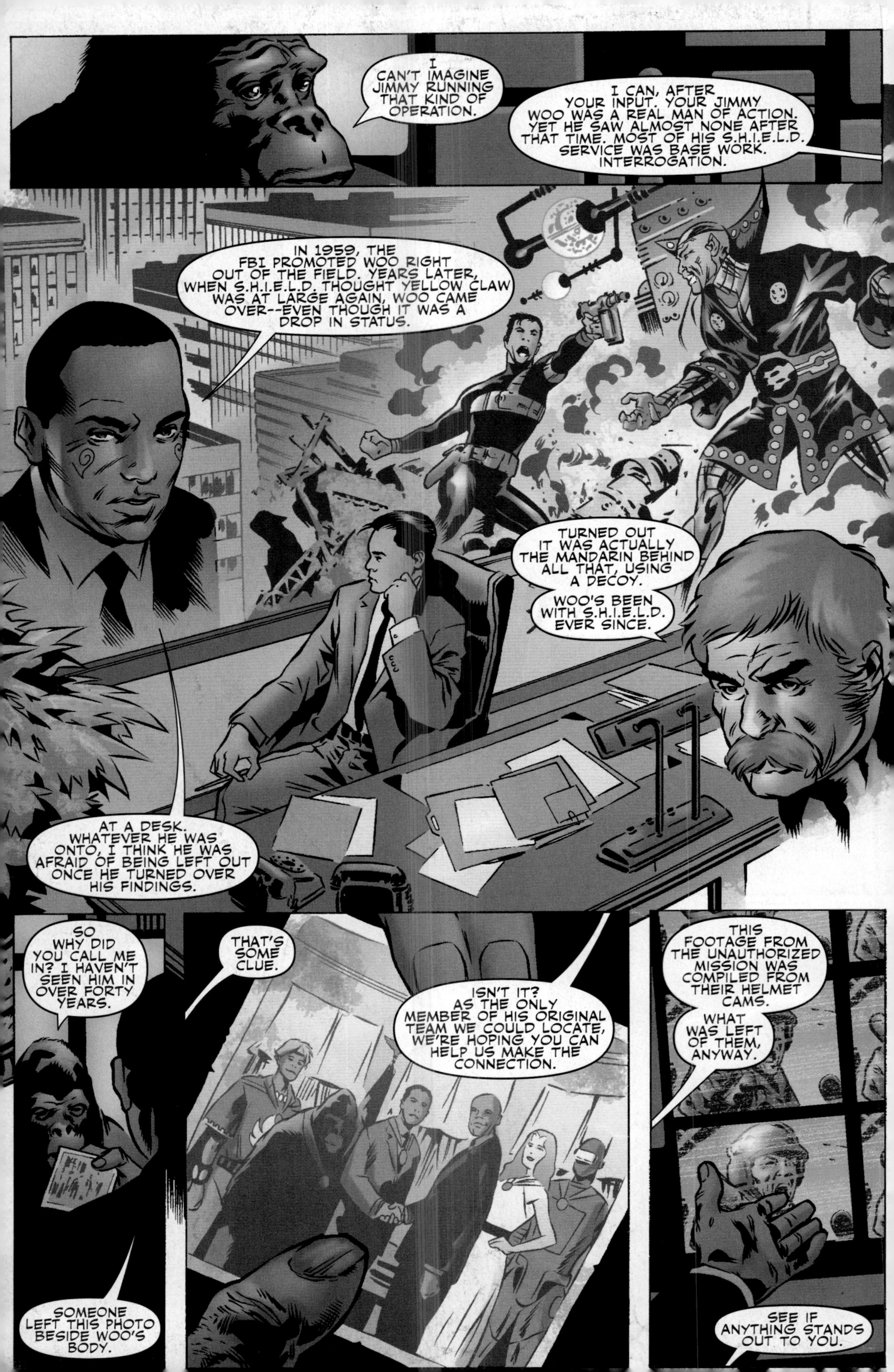

I CAN'T IMAGINE JIMMY RUNNING THAT KIND OF OPERATION.
I CAN, AFTER YOUR INPUT. YOUR JIMMY WOO WAS A REAL MAN OF ACTION. YET HE SAW ALMOST NONE AFTER THAT TIME. MOST OF HIS S.H.I.E.L.D. SERVICE WAS BASE WORK. INTERROGATION.
IN 1959, THE FBI PROMOTED WOO RIGHT OUT OF THE FIELD. YEARS LATER, WHEN S.H.I.E.L.D. THOUGHT YELLOW CLAW WAS AT LARGE AGAIN, WOO CAME OVER--EVEN THOUGH IT WAS A DROP IN STATUS.
TURNED OUT IT WAS ACTUALLY THE MANDARIN BEHIND ALL THAT, USING A DECOY.
WOO'S BEEN WITH S.H.I.E.L.D. EVER SINCE.
AT A DESK. WHATEVER HE WAS ONTO, I THINK HE WAS AFRAID OF BEING LEFT OUT ONCE HE TURNED OVER HIS FINDINGS.
SO WHY DID YOU CALL ME IN? I HAVEN'T SEEN HIM IN OVER FORTY YEARS.
SOMEONE LEFT THIS PHOTO BESIDE WOO'S BODY.
THAT'S SOME CLUE.
ISN'T IT? AS THE ONLY MEMBER OF HIS ORIGINAL TEAM WE COULD LOCATE, WE'RE HOPING YOU CAN HELP US MAKE THE CONNECTION.
THIS FOOTAGE FROM THE UNAUTHORIZED MISSION WAS COMPILED FROM THEIR HELMET CAMS.
WHAT WAS LEFT OF THEM, ANYWAY.
SEE IF ANYTHING STANDS OUT TO YOU.

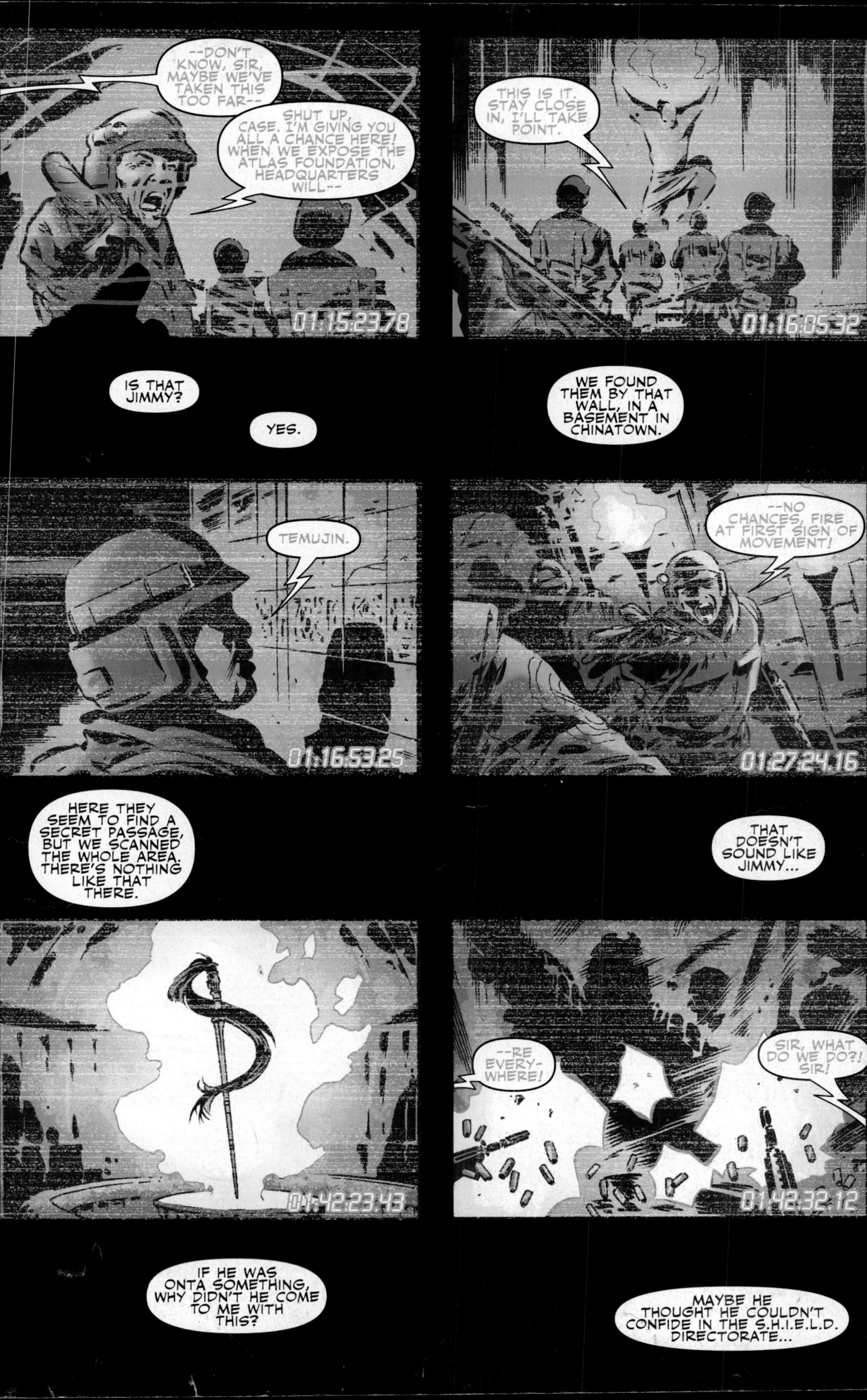
--DON'T KNOW, SIR, MAYBE WE'VE TAKEN THIS TOO FAR--
SHUT UP, CASE. I'M GIVING YOU ALL A CHANCE HERE! WHEN WE EXPOSE THE ATLAS FOUNDATION, HEADQUARTERS WILL--
01:15:23.78
THIS IS IT. STAY CLOSE IN, I'LL TAKE POINT.
01:16:05.32
IS THAT JIMMY?
YES.
WE FOUND THEM BY THAT WALL, IN A BASEMENT IN CHINATOWN.
TEMUJIN.
01:16:53.25
--NO CHANCES, FIRE AT FIRST SIGN OF MOVEMENT!
01:27:24.16
HERE THEY SEEM TO FIND A SECRET PASSAGE, BUT WE SCANNED THE WHOLE AREA. THERE'S NOTHING LIKE THAT THERE.
THAT DOESN'T SOUND LIKE JIMMY...
01:42:23.43
--RE EVERY-WHERE!
SIR, WHAT DO WE DO?! SIR!
01:42:32.12
IF HE WAS ONTA SOMETHING, WHY DIDN'T HE COME TO ME WITH THIS?
MAYBE HE THOUGHT HE COULDN'T CONFIDE IN THE S.H.I.E.L.D. DIRECTORATE...

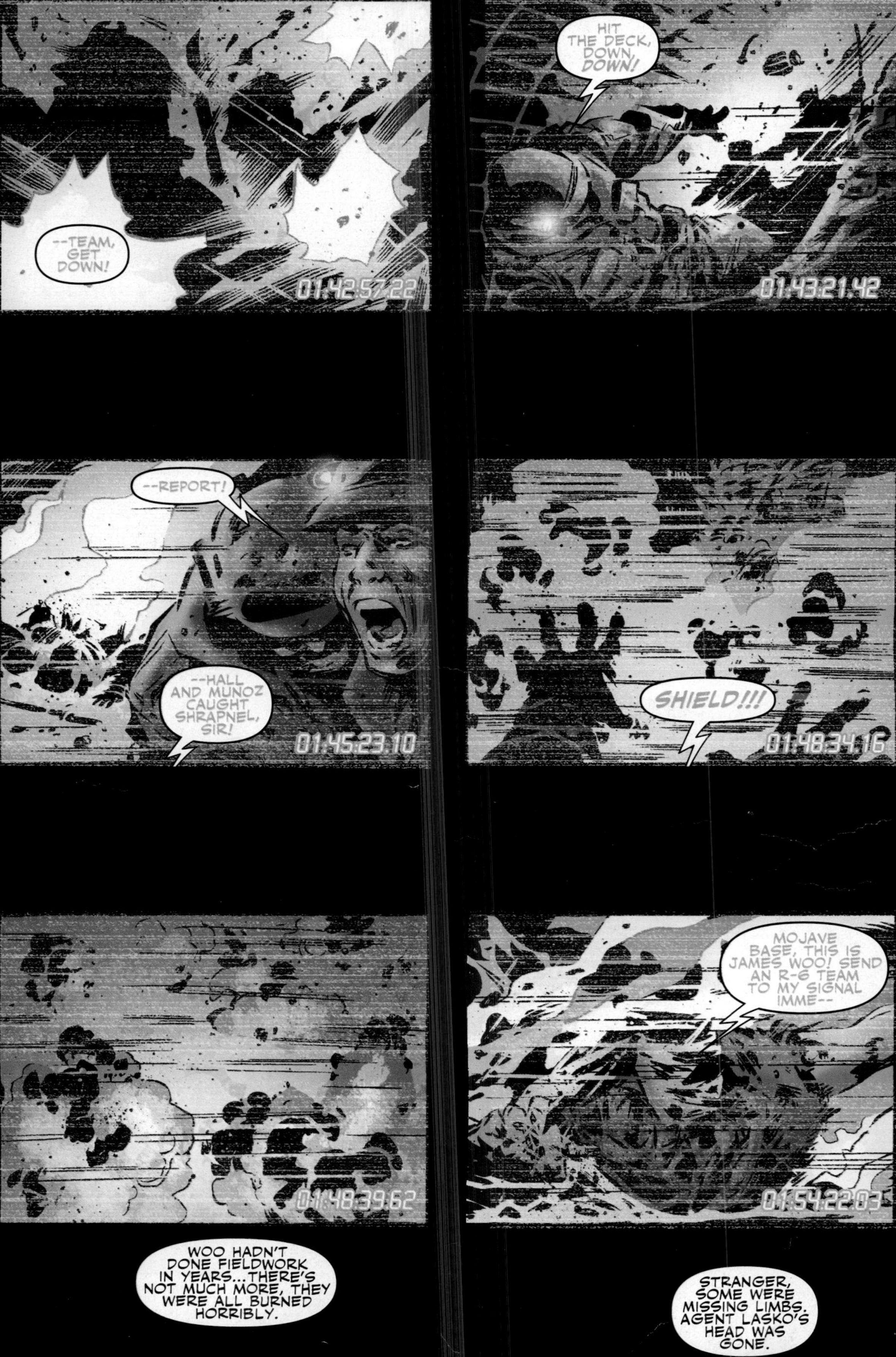
--TEAM, GET DOWN!
01:42:57.22
HIT THE DECK, DOWN, DOWN!
01:43:21.42
--REPORT!
--HALL AND MUNOZ CAUGHT SHRAPNEL, SIR!
01:45:23.10
SHIELD!!!
01:48:34.16
01:48:39.62
MOJAVE BASE, THIS IS JAMES WOO! SEND AN R-6 TEAM TO MY SIGNAL IMME--
01:54:22.03
WOO HADN'T DONE FIELDWORK IN YEARS... THERE'S NOT MUCH MORE, THEY WERE ALL BURNED HORRIBLY.
STRANGER, SOME WERE MISSING LIMBS. AGENT LASKO'S HEAD WAS GONE.

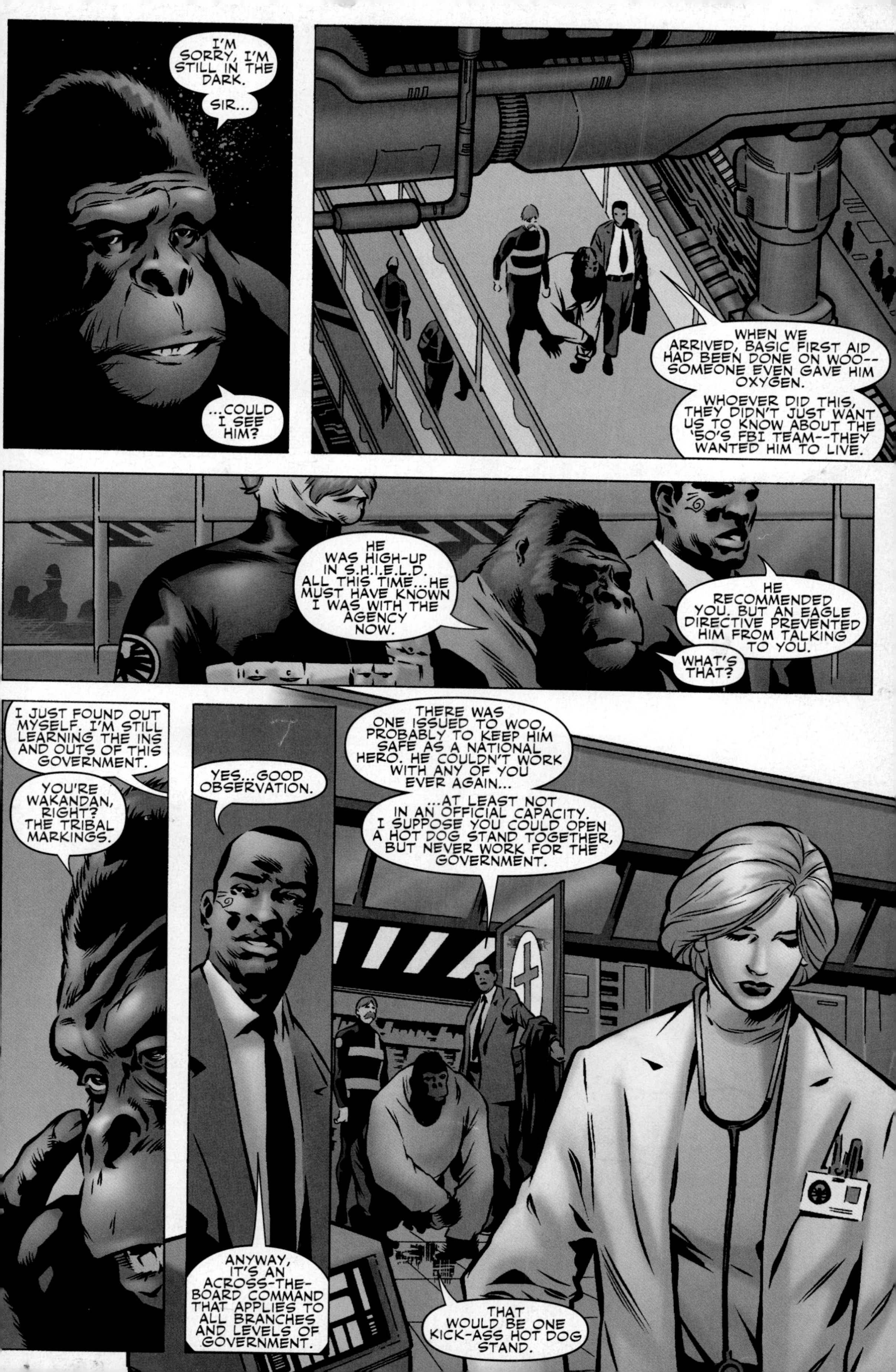
I'M SORRY, I'M STILL IN THE DARK.
SIR...
...COULD I SEE HIM?
WHEN WE ARRIVED, BASIC FIRST AID HAD BEEN DONE ON WOO-- SOMEONE EVEN GAVE HIM OXYGEN.
WHOEVER DID THIS, THEY DIDN'T JUST WANT US TO KNOW ABOUT THE '50'S FBI TEAM--THEY WANTED HIM TO LIVE.
HE WAS HIGH-UP IN S.H.I.E.L.D. ALL THIS TIME...HE MUST HAVE KNOWN I WAS WITH THE AGENCY NOW.
HE RECOMMENDED YOU. BUT AN EAGLE DIRECTIVE PREVENTED HIM FROM TALKING TO YOU.
WHAT'S THAT?
I JUST FOUND OUT MYSELF. I'M STILL LEARNING THE INS AND OUTS OF THIS GOVERNMENT.
YOU'RE WAKANDAN, RIGHT? THE TRIBAL MARKINGS.
YES...GOOD OBSERVATION.
THERE WAS ONE ISSUED TO WOO, PROBABLY TO KEEP HIM SAFE AS A NATIONAL HERO. HE COULDN'T WORK WITH ANY OF YOU EVER AGAIN...
...AT LEAST NOT IN AN OFFICIAL CAPACITY. I SUPPOSE YOU COULD OPEN A HOT DOG STAND TOGETHER, BUT NEVER WORK FOR THE GOVERNMENT.
ANYWAY, IT'S AN ACROSS-THE-BOARD COMMAND THAT APPLIES TO ALL BRANCHES AND LEVELS OF GOVERNMENT.
THAT WOULD BE ONE KICK-ASS HOT DOG STAND.

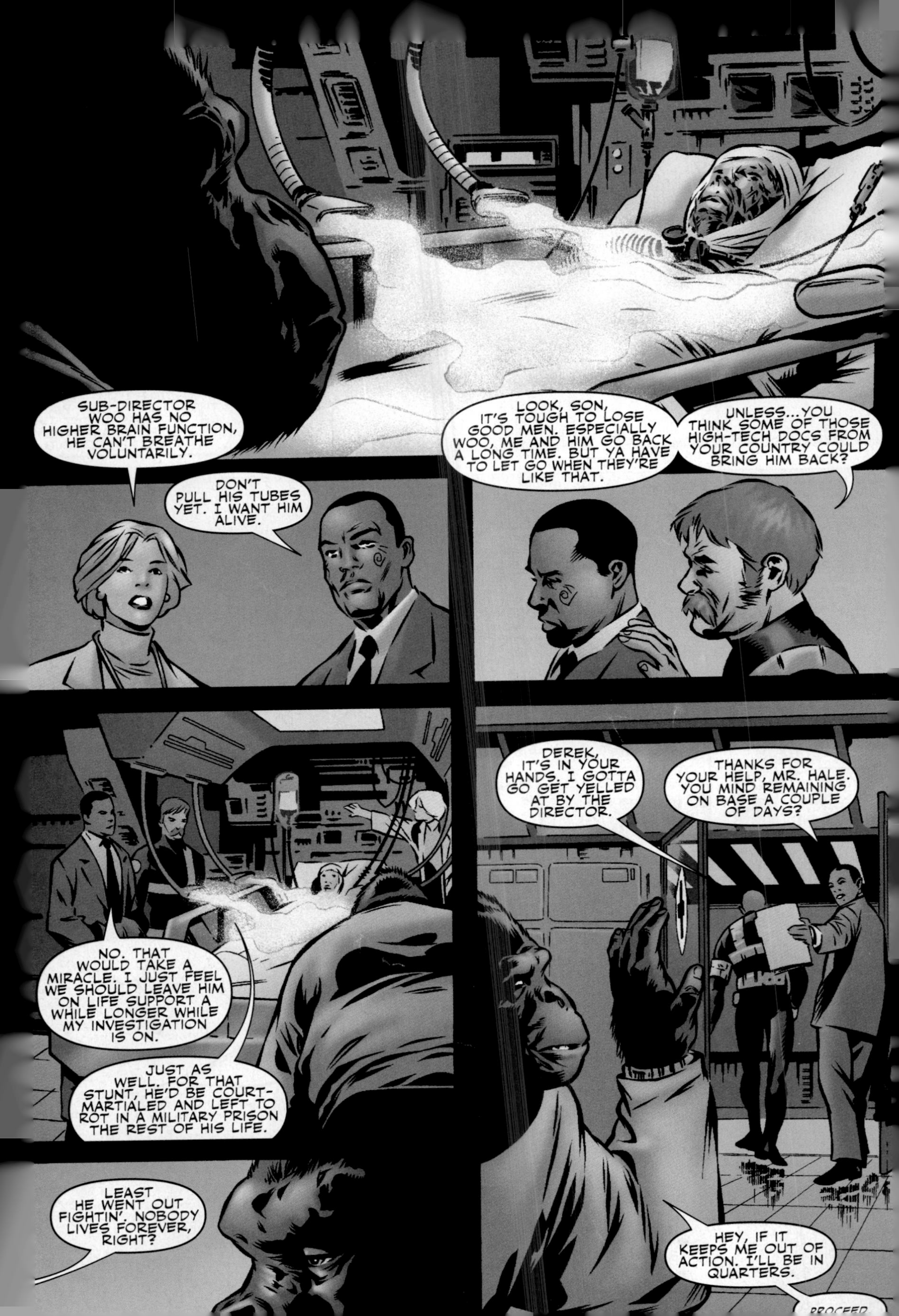
SUB-DIRECTOR WOO HAS NO HIGHER BRAIN FUNCTION, HE CAN'T BREATHE VOLUNTARILY.
DON'T PULL HIS TUBES YET. I WANT HIM ALIVE.
LOOK, SON, IT'S TOUGH TO LOSE GOOD MEN. ESPECIALLY WOO, ME AND HIM GO BACK A LONG TIME. BUT YA HAVE TO LET GO WHEN THEY'RE LIKE THAT.
UNLESS...YOU THINK SOME OF THOSE HIGH-TECH DOCS FROM YOUR COUNTRY COULD BRING HIM BACK?
NO. THAT WOULD TAKE A MIRACLE. I JUST FEEL WE SHOULD LEAVE HIM ON LIFE SUPPORT A WHILE LONGER WHILE MY INVESTIGATION IS ON.
JUST AS WELL. FOR THAT STUNT, HE'D BE COURT-MARTIALED AND LEFT TO ROT IN A MILITARY PRISON THE REST OF HIS LIFE.
DEREK, IT'S IN YOUR HANDS. I GOTTA GO GET YELLED AT BY THE DIRECTOR.
THANKS FOR YOUR HELP, MR. HALE. YOU MIND REMAINING ON BASE A COUPLE OF DAYS?
LEAST HE WENT OUT FIGHTIN'. NOBODY LIVES FOREVER, RIGHT?
HEY, IF IT KEEPS ME OUT OF ACTION. I'LL BE IN QUARTERS.
PROCEED

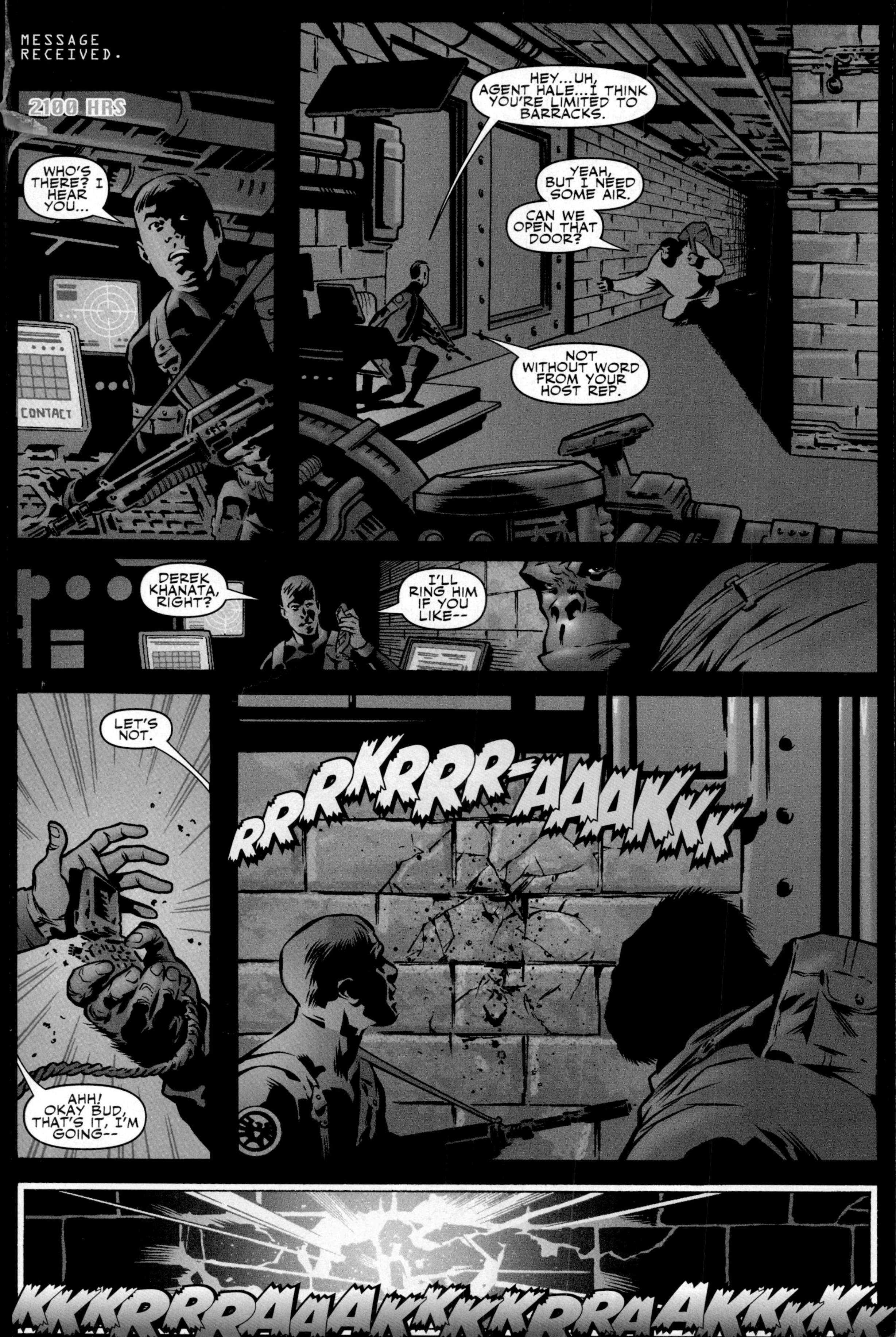
MESSAGE RECEIVED.
2100 HRS
WHO'S THERE? I HEAR YOU...
CONTACT
HEY...UH, AGENT HALE...I THINK YOU'RE LIMITED TO BARRACKS.
YEAH, BUT I NEED SOME AIR.
CAN WE OPEN THAT DOOR?
NOT WITHOUT WORD FROM YOUR HOST REP.
DEREK KHANATA, RIGHT?
I'LL RING HIM IF YOU LIKE--
LET'S NOT.
AHH! OKAY BUD, THAT'S IT, I'M GOING--
RRRKRRR-AAAKKK
KKKRRRAAAKKKKRRAAKKKK

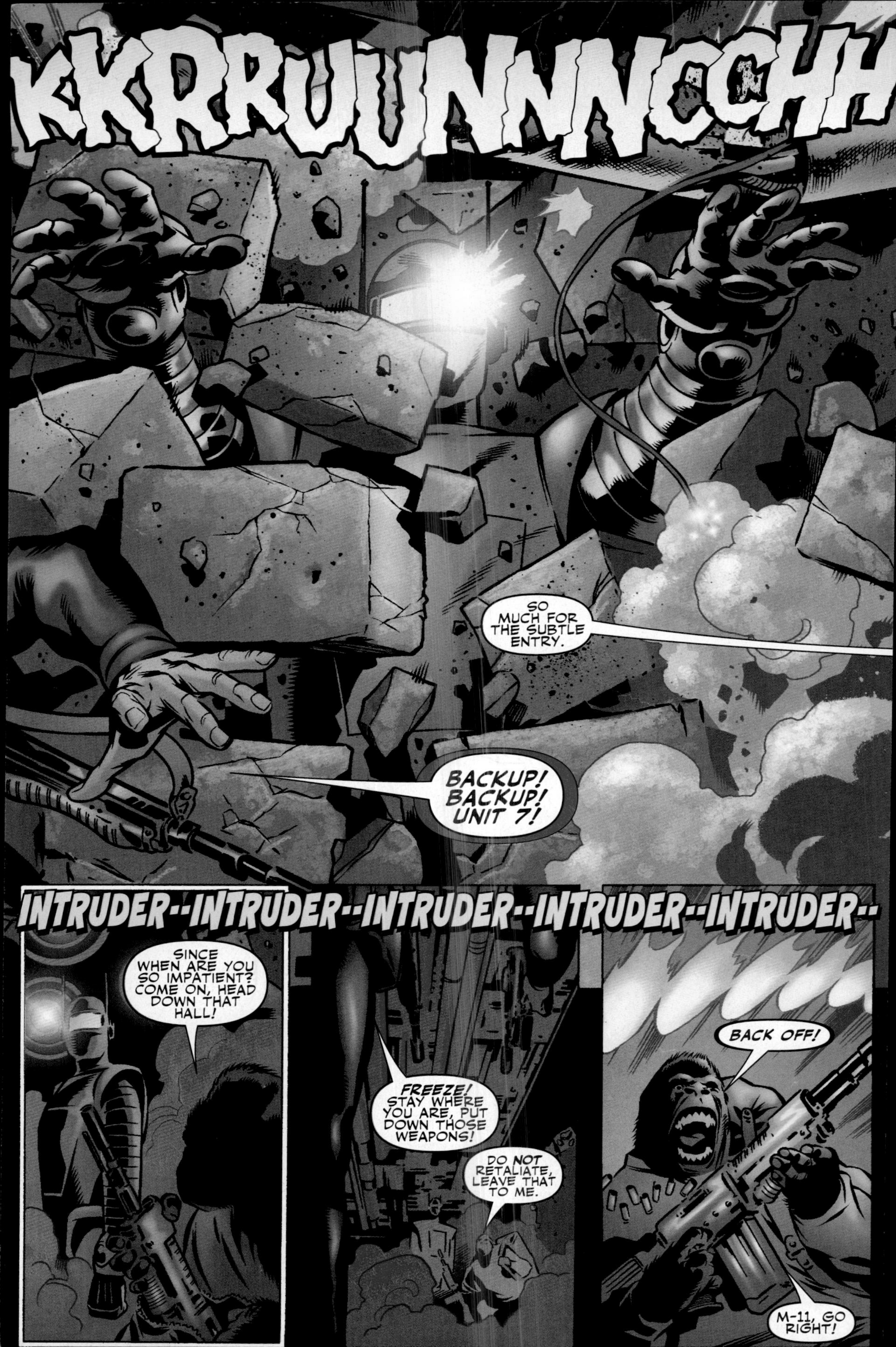
KKRRUUNNNCCHH
SO MUCH FOR THE SUBTLE ENTRY.
BACKUP! BACKUP! UNIT 7!
INTRUDER--INTRUDER--INTRUDER--INTRUDER--INTRUDER--
SINCE WHEN ARE YOU SO IMPATIENT? COME ON, HEAD DOWN THAT HALL!
FREEZE! STAY WHERE YOU ARE, PUT DOWN THOSE WEAPONS!
DO NOT RETALIATE, LEAVE THAT TO ME.
BACK OFF!
M-11, GO RIGHT!

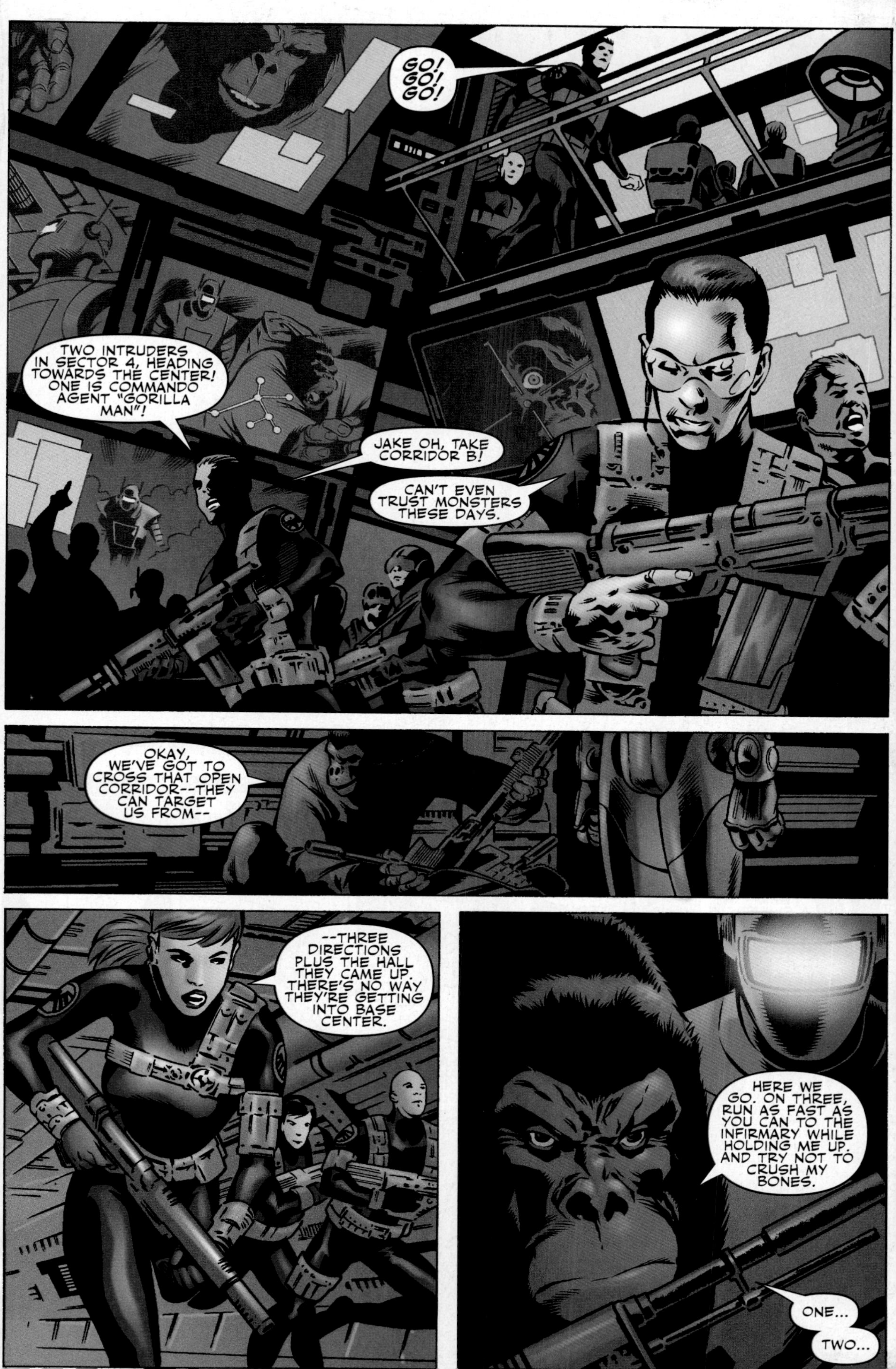
GO! GO! GO!
TWO INTRUDERS IN SECTOR 4, HEADING TOWARDS THE CENTER! ONE IS COMMANDO AGENT "GORILLA MAN"!
JAKE OH, TAKE CORRIDOR B!
CAN'T EVEN TRUST MONSTERS THESE DAYS.
OKAY, WE'VE GOT TO CROSS THAT OPEN CORRIDOR--THEY CAN TARGET US FROM--
--THREE DIRECTIONS PLUS THE HALL THEY CAME UP. THERE'S NO WAY THEY'RE GETTING INTO BASE CENTER.
HERE WE GO. ON THREE, RUN AS FAST AS YOU CAN TO THE INFIRMARY WHILE HOLDING ME UP. AND TRY NOT TO CRUSH MY BONES.
ONE...
TWO...

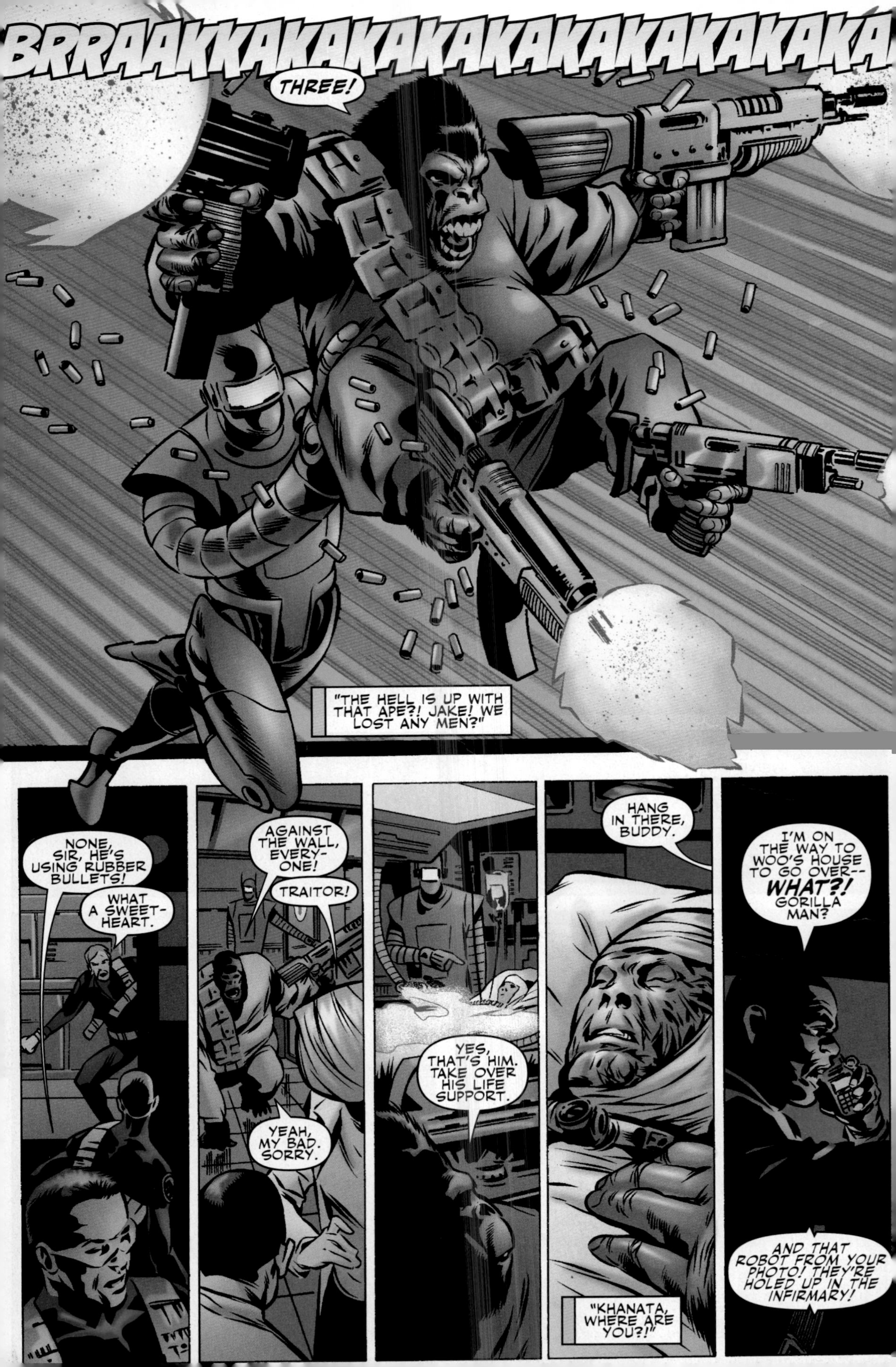
BRRAAKKAKAKAKAKAKAKAKAKAKA
THREE!
"THE HELL IS UP WITH THAT APE?! JAKE! WE LOST ANY MEN?"
NONE, SIR, HE'S USING RUBBER BULLETS!
WHAT A SWEET-HEART.
AGAINST THE WALL, EVERY-ONE!
TRAITOR!
YEAH, MY BAD. SORRY.
YES, THAT'S HIM. TAKE OVER HIS LIFE SUPPORT.
HANG IN THERE, BUDDY.
"KHANATA, WHERE ARE YOU?!"
I'M ON THE WAY TO WOO'S HOUSE TO GO OVER-- WHAT?! GORILLA MAN?
AND THAT ROBOT FROM YOUR PHOTO! THEY'RE HOLED UP IN THE INFIRMARY!

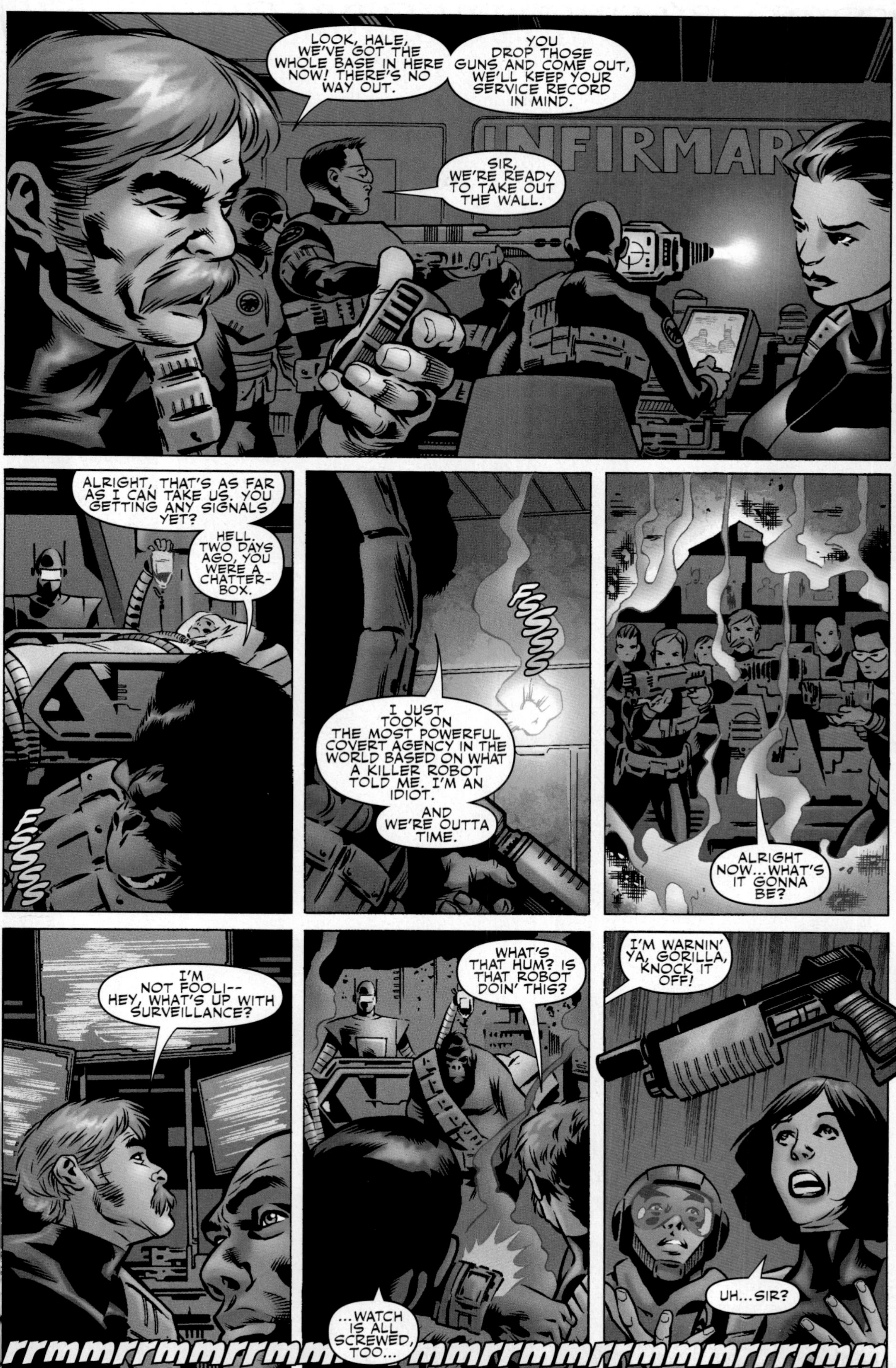
LOOK, HALE, WE'VE GOT THE WHOLE BASE IN HERE NOW! THERE'S NO WAY OUT.
YOU DROP THOSE GUNS AND COME OUT, WE'LL KEEP YOUR SERVICE RECORD IN MIND.
INFIRMARY
SIR, WE'RE READY TO TAKE OUT THE WALL.
ALRIGHT, THAT'S AS FAR AS I CAN TAKE US. YOU GETTING ANY SIGNALS YET?
HELL. TWO DAYS AGO, YOU WERE A CHATTER-BOX.
FSSSS
FSSSS
I JUST TOOK ON THE MOST POWERFUL COVERT AGENCY IN THE WORLD BASED ON WHAT A KILLER ROBOT TOLD ME. I'M AN IDIOT.
AND WE'RE OUTTA TIME.
ALRIGHT NOW...WHAT'S IT GONNA BE?
I'M NOT FOOLI-- HEY, WHAT'S UP WITH SURVEILLANCE?
WHAT'S THAT HUM? IS THAT ROBOT DOIN' THIS?
...WATCH IS ALL SCREWED, TOO...
I'M WARNIN' YA, GORILLA, KNOCK IT OFF!
UH...SIR?
rrmmmrrmmmrrmm
mmmrrmmmrrmmmmrrrrmm

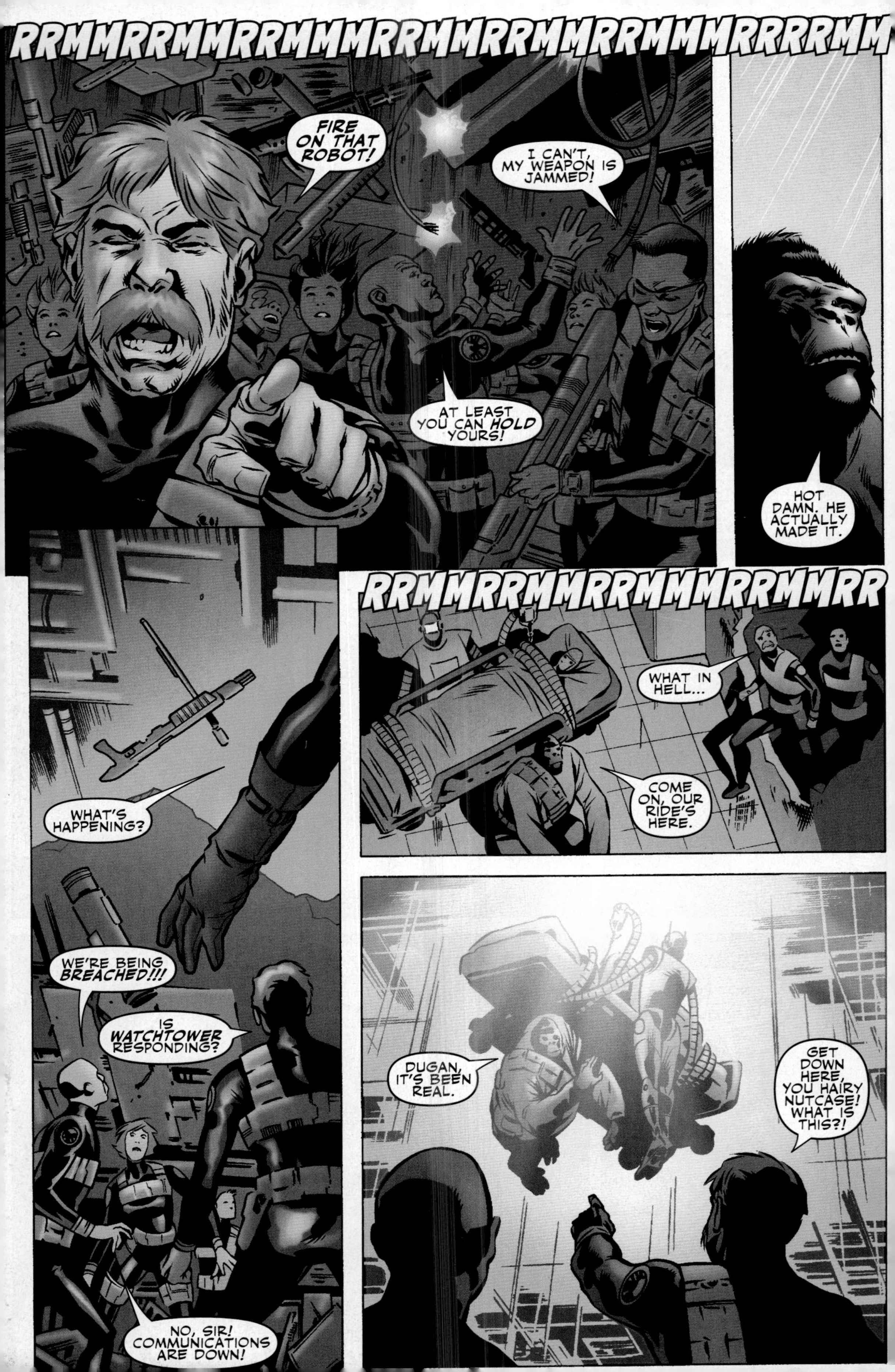
RRMMRRMMRRMMMRRMMRRMMRRMMMRRRRMM
FIRE ON THAT ROBOT!
I CAN'T, MY WEAPON IS JAMMED!
AT LEAST YOU CAN HOLD YOURS!
HOT DAMN. HE ACTUALLY MADE IT.
WHAT'S HAPPENING?
WE'RE BEING BREACHED!!!
IS WATCHTOWER RESPONDING?
NO, SIR! COMMUNICATIONS ARE DOWN!
RRMMRRMMRRMMMRRMMRR
WHAT IN HELL...
COME ON, OUR RIDE'S HERE.
DUGAN, IT'S BEEN REAL.
GET DOWN HERE, YOU HAIRY NUTCASE! WHAT IS THIS?!

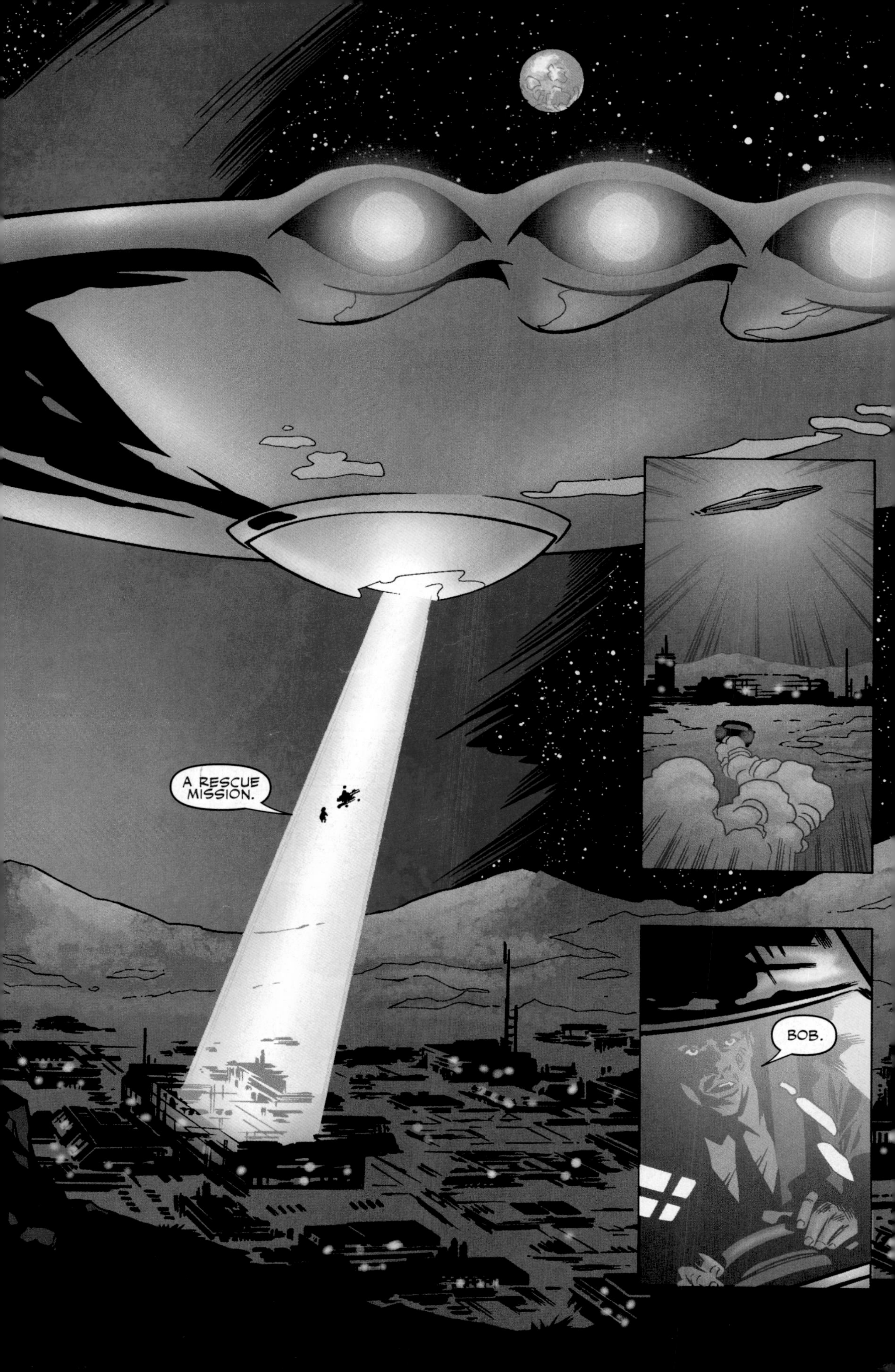
A RESCUE MISSION.
BOB.

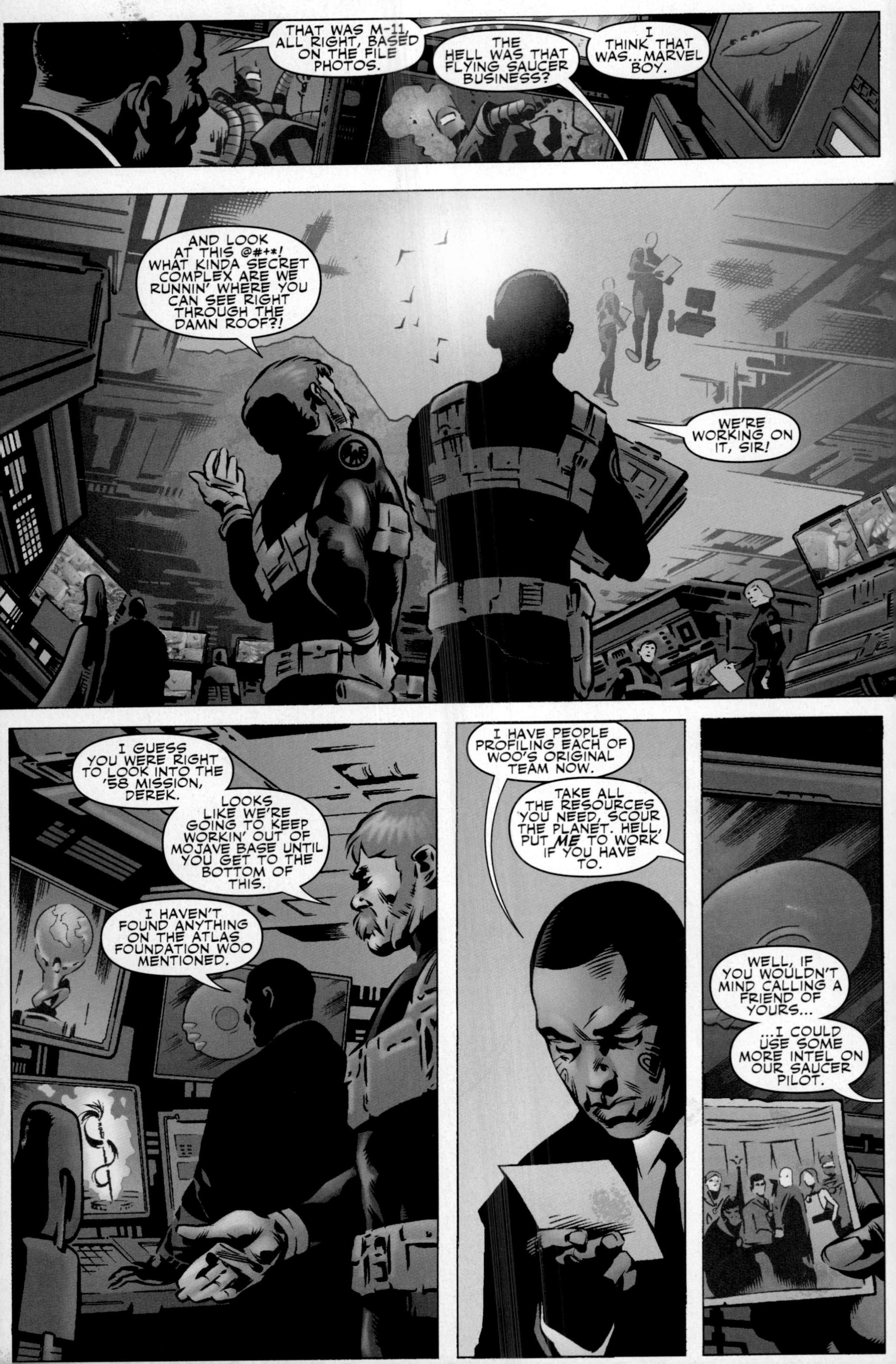
THAT WAS M-11, ALL RIGHT, BASED ON THE FILE PHOTOS.
THE HELL WAS THAT FLYING SAUCER BUSINESS?
I THINK THAT WAS...MARVEL BOY.
AND LOOK AT THIS @#+*! WHAT KINDA SECRET COMPLEX ARE WE RUNNIN' WHERE YOU CAN SEE RIGHT THROUGH THE DAMN ROOF?!
WE'RE WORKING ON IT, SIR!
I GUESS YOU WERE RIGHT TO LOOK INTO THE '58 MISSION, DEREK.
LOOKS LIKE WE'RE GOING TO KEEP WORKIN' OUT OF MOJAVE BASE UNTIL YOU GET TO THE BOTTOM OF THIS.
I HAVEN'T FOUND ANYTHING ON THE ATLAS FOUNDATION WOO MENTIONED.
I HAVE PEOPLE PROFILING EACH OF WOO'S ORIGINAL TEAM NOW.
TAKE ALL THE RESOURCES YOU NEED, SCOUR THE PLANET. HELL, PUT ME TO WORK IF YOU HAVE TO.
WELL, IF YOU WOULDN'T MIND CALLING A FRIEND OF YOURS...
...I COULD USE SOME MORE INTEL ON OUR SAUCER PILOT.

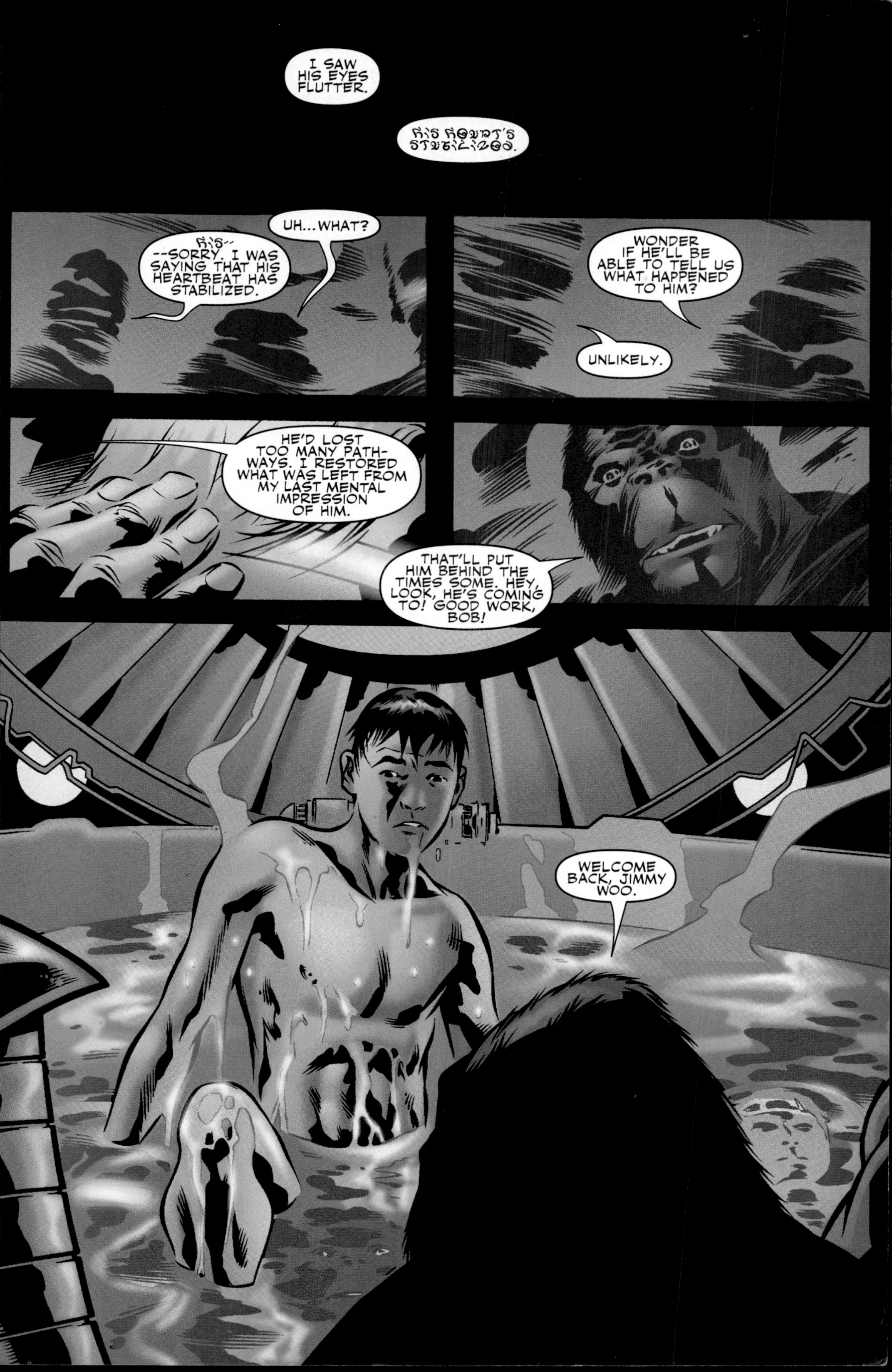
I SAW HIS EYES FLUTTER.
UH...WHAT?
--SORRY. I WAS SAYING THAT HIS HEARTBEAT HAS STABILIZED.
WONDER IF HE'LL BE ABLE TO TELL US WHAT HAPPENED TO HIM?
UNLIKELY.
HE'D LOST TOO MANY PATH-WAYS. I RESTORED WHAT WAS LEFT FROM MY LAST MENTAL IMPRESSION OF HIM.
THAT'LL PUT HIM BEHIND THE TIMES SOME. HEY, LOOK, HE'S COMING TO! GOOD WORK, BOB!
WELCOME BACK, JIMMY WOO.

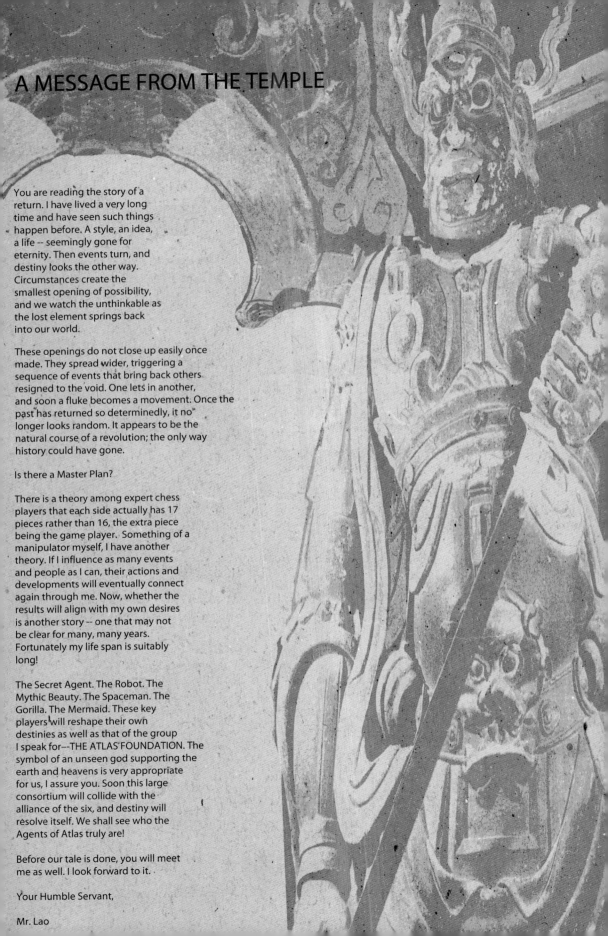

A MESSAGE FROM THE TEMPLE

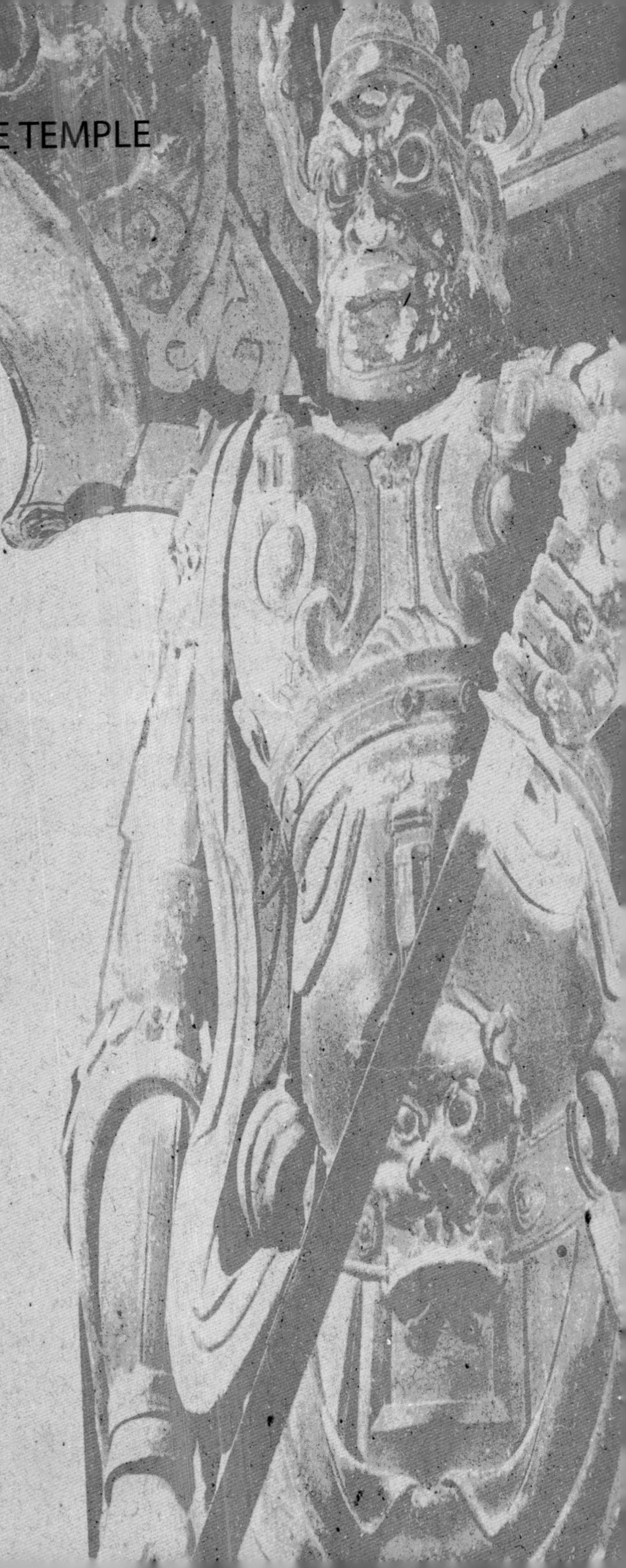

You are reading the story of a return. I have lived a very long time and have seen such things happen before. A style, an idea, a life -- seemingly gone for eternity. Then events turn, and destiny looks the other way. Circumstances create the smallest opening of possibility, and we watch the unthinkable as the lost element springs back into our world.

These openings do not close up easily once made. They spread wider, triggering a sequence of events that bring back others resigned to the void. One lets in another, and soon a fluke becomes a movement. Once the past has returned so determinedly, it no longer looks random. It appears to be the natural course of a revolution; the only way history could have gone.

Is there a Master Plan?

There is a theory among expert chess players that each side actually has 17 pieces rather than 16, the extra piece being the game player. Something of a manipulator myself, I have another theory. If I influence as many events and people as I can, their actions and developments will eventually connect again through me. Now, whether the results will align with my own desires is another story -- one that may not be clear for many, many years. Fortunately my life span is suitably long!

The Secret Agent. The Robot. The Mythic Beauty. The Spaceman. The Gorilla. The Mermaid. These key players will reshape their own destinies as well as that of the group I speak for--THE ATLAS FOUNDATION. The symbol of an unseen god supporting the earth and heavens is very appropriate for us, I assure you. Soon this large consortium will collide with the alliance of the six, and destiny will resolve itself. We shall see who the Agents of Atlas truly are!

Before our tale is done, you will meet me as well. I look forward to it.

Your Humble Servant,

Mr. Lao

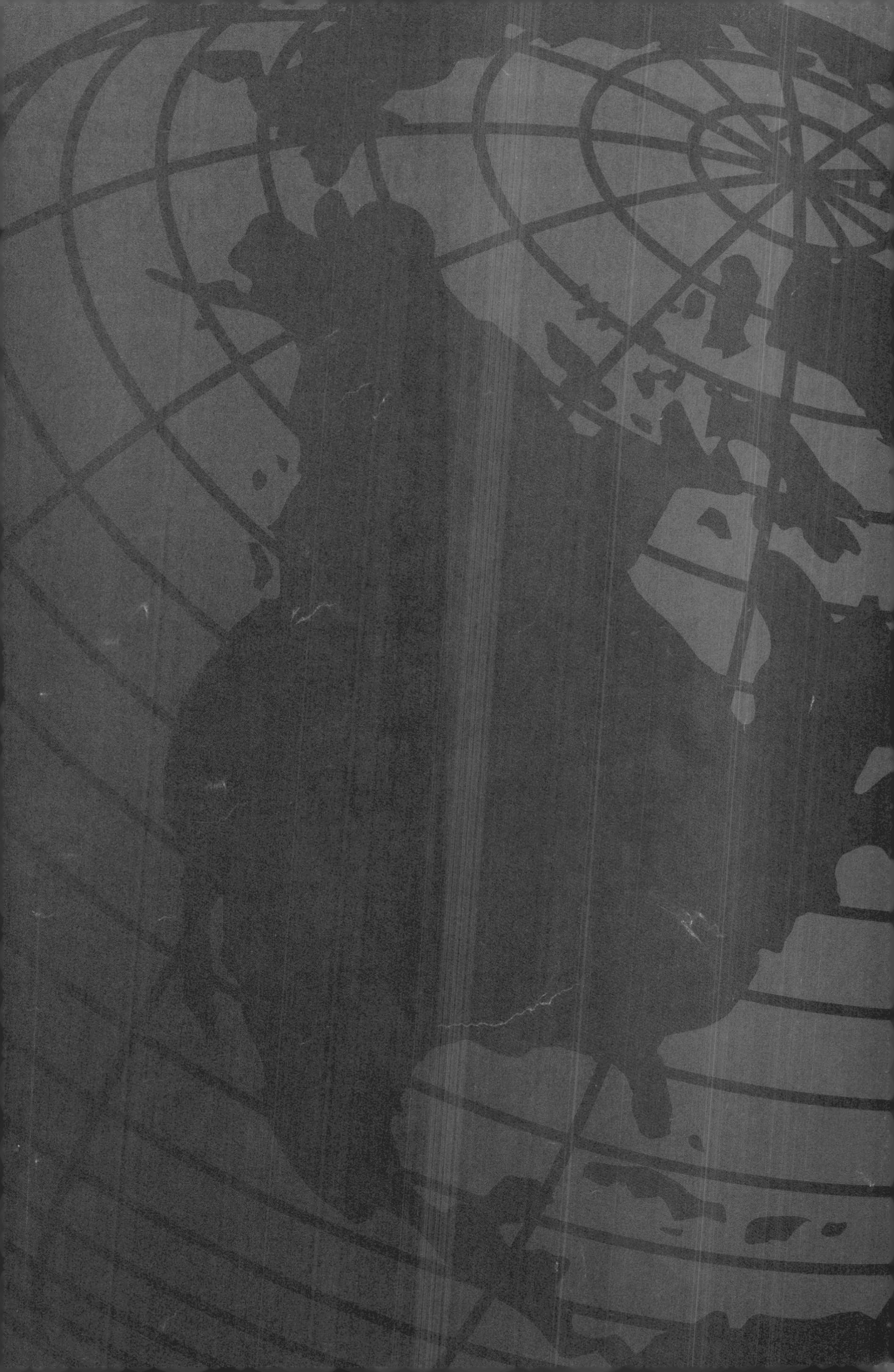

#2

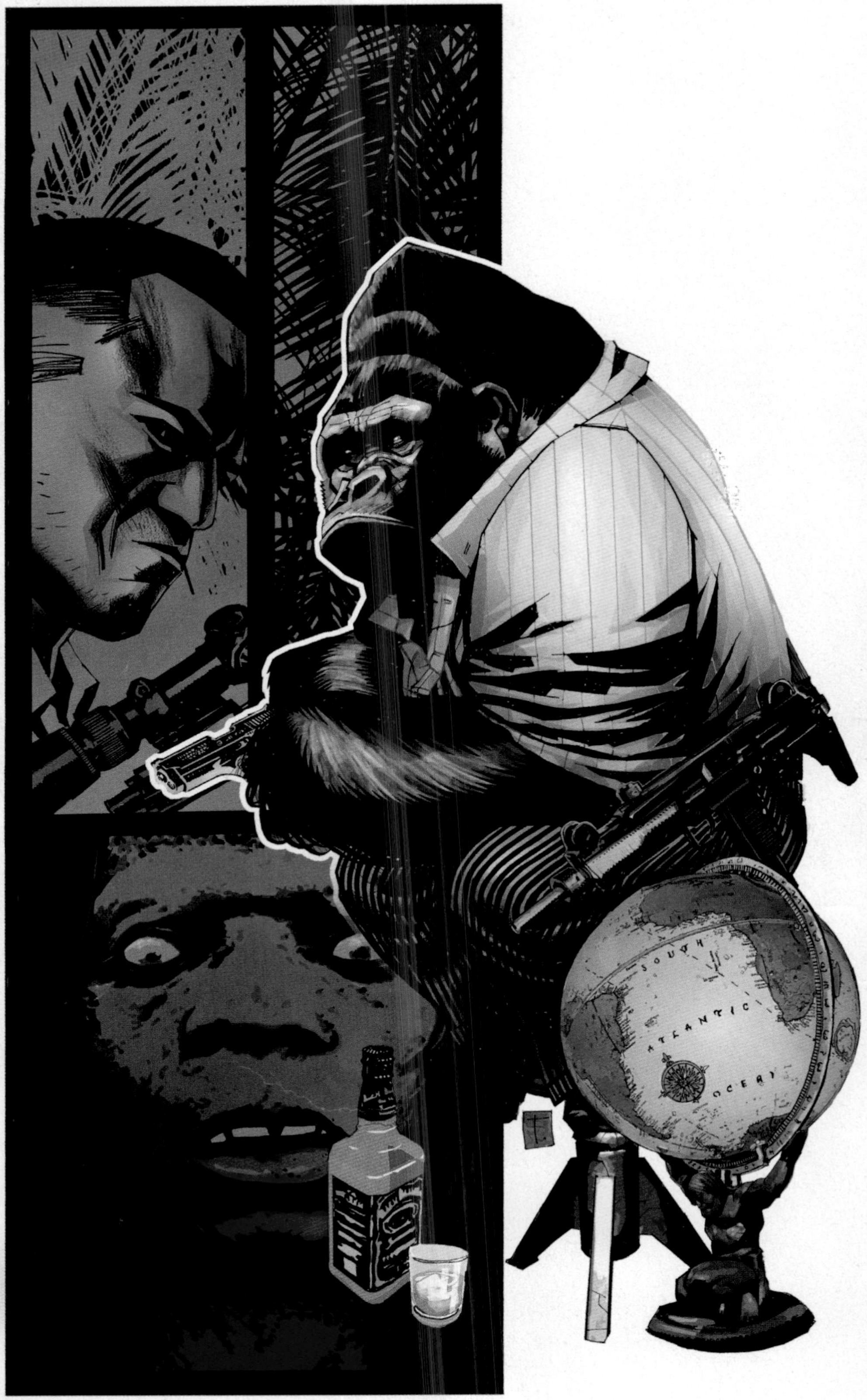
SOUTH
ATLANTIC

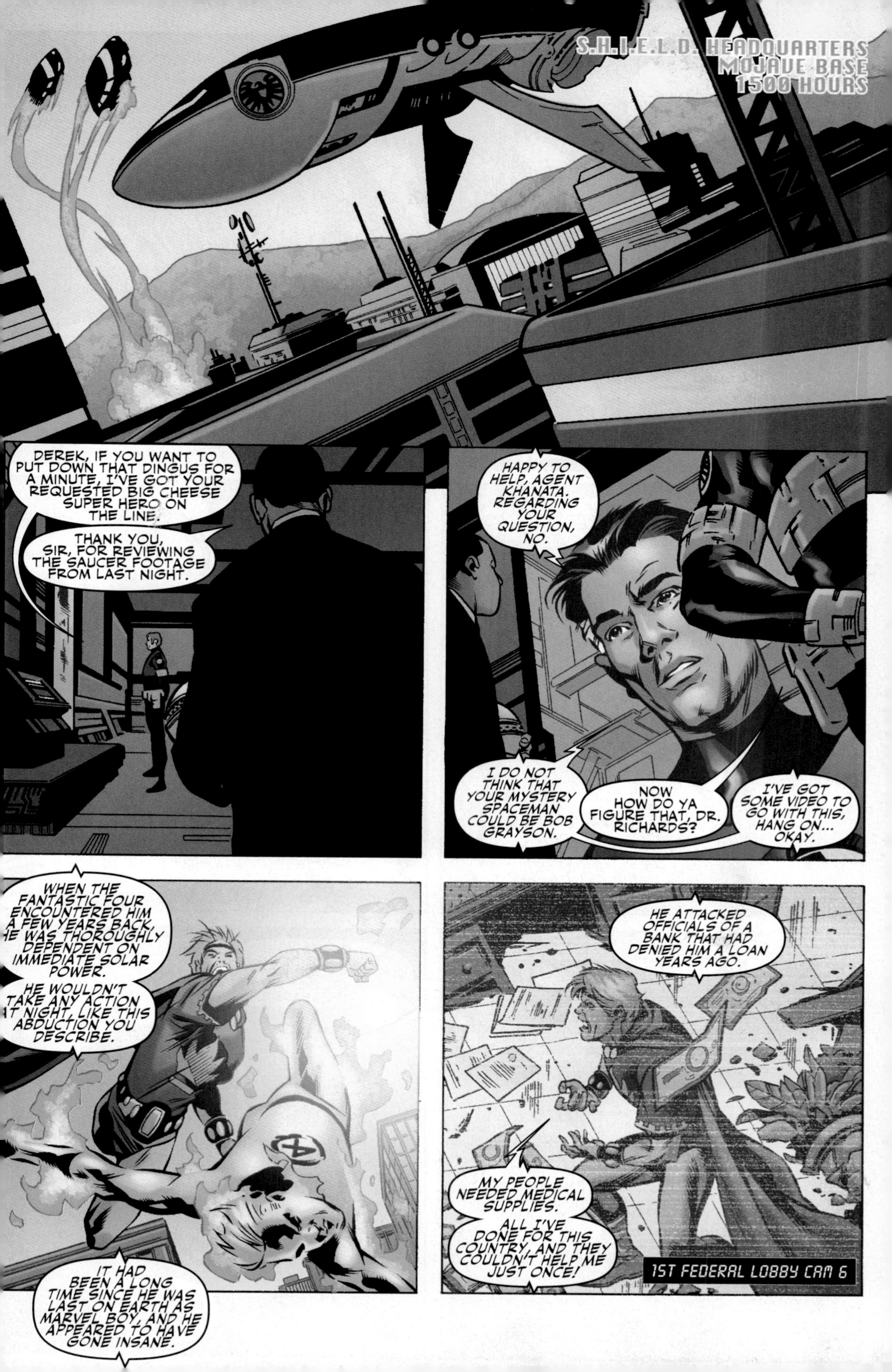

S.H.I.E.L.D. HEADQUARTERS
MOJAVE BASE
1500 HOURS
DEREK, IF YOU WANT TO PUT DOWN THAT DINGUS FOR A MINUTE, I'VE GOT YOUR REQUESTED BIG CHEESE SUPER HERO ON THE LINE.
THANK YOU, SIR, FOR REVIEWING THE SAUCER FOOTAGE FROM LAST NIGHT.
HAPPY TO HELP, AGENT KHANATA. REGARDING YOUR QUESTION, NO.
I DO NOT THINK THAT YOUR MYSTERY SPACEMAN COULD BE BOB GRAYSON.
NOW HOW DO YA FIGURE THAT, DR. RICHARDS?
I'VE GOT SOME VIDEO TO GO WITH THIS, HANG ON... OKAY.
WHEN THE FANTASTIC FOUR ENCOUNTERED HIM A FEW YEARS BACK, HE WAS THOROUGHLY DEPENDENT ON IMMEDIATE SOLAR POWER.
HE WOULDN'T TAKE ANY ACTION AT NIGHT, LIKE THIS ABDUCTION YOU DESCRIBE.
IT HAD BEEN A LONG TIME SINCE HE WAS LAST ON EARTH AS MARVEL BOY, AND HE APPEARED TO HAVE GONE INSANE.
HE ATTACKED OFFICIALS OF A BANK THAT HAD DENIED HIM A LOAN YEARS AGO.
MY PEOPLE NEEDED MEDICAL SUPPLIES.
ALL I'VE DONE FOR THIS COUNTRY, AND THEY COULDN'T HELP ME JUST ONCE!
1ST FEDERAL LOBBY CAM 6

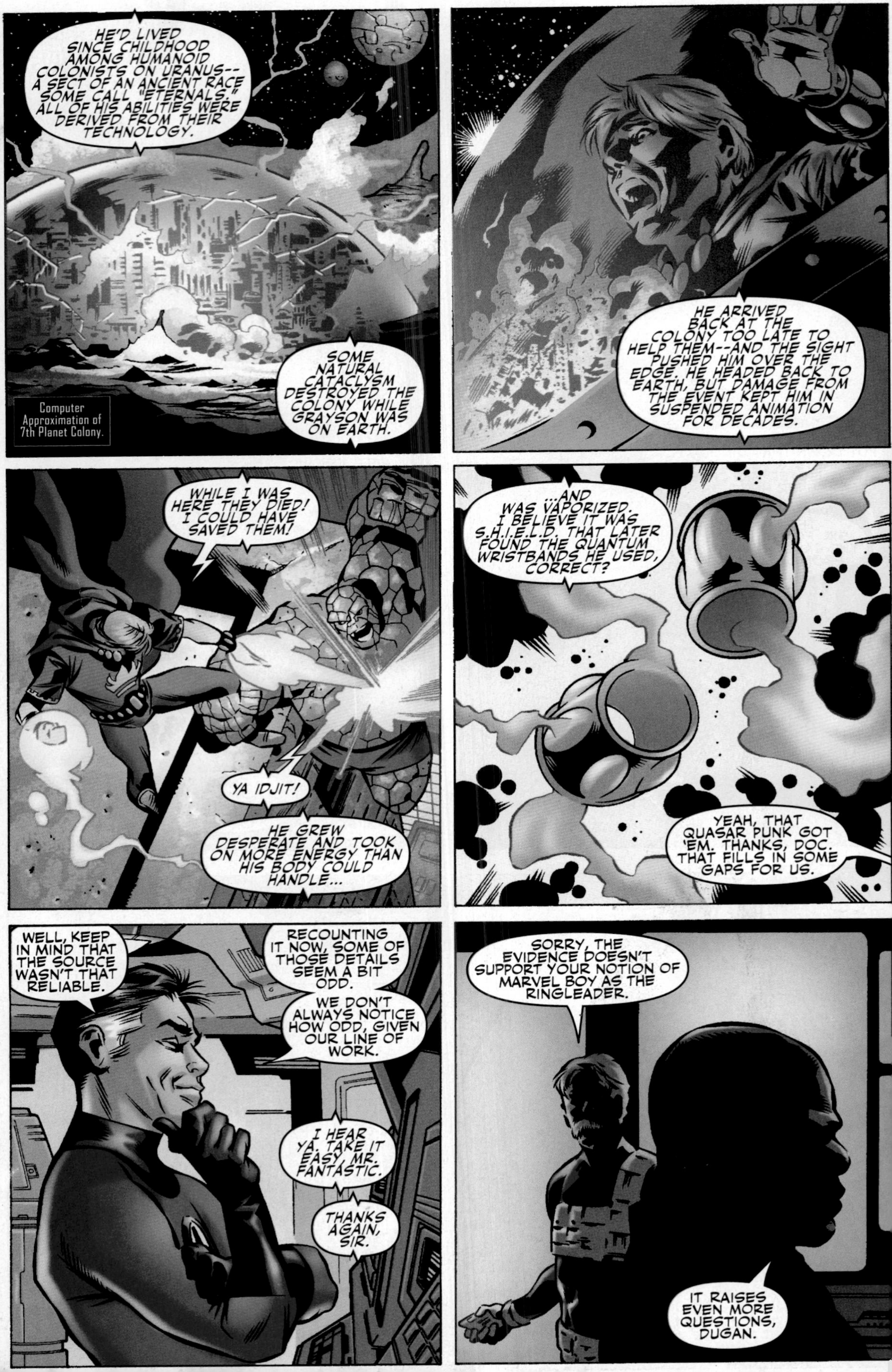
HE'D LIVED SINCE CHILDHOOD AMONG HUMANOID COLONISTS ON URANUS-- A SECT OF AN ANCIENT RACE SOME CALL "ETERNALS." ALL OF HIS ABILITIES WERE DERIVED FROM THEIR TECHNOLOGY.
SOME NATURAL CATACLYSM DESTROYED THE COLONY WHILE GRAYSON WAS ON EARTH.
Computer Approximation of 7th Planet Colony.
HE ARRIVED BACK AT THE COLONY TOO LATE TO HELP THEM--AND THE SIGHT PUSHED HIM OVER THE EDGE. HE HEADED BACK TO EARTH, BUT DAMAGE FROM THE EVENT KEPT HIM IN SUSPENDED ANIMATION FOR DECADES.
WHILE I WAS HERE THEY DIED! I COULD HAVE SAVED THEM!
YA IDJIT!
HE GREW DESPERATE AND TOOK ON MORE ENERGY THAN HIS BODY COULD HANDLE...
...AND WAS VAPORIZED. I BELIEVE IT WAS S.H.I.E.L.D. THAT LATER FOUND THE QUANTUM WRISTBANDS HE USED, CORRECT?
YEAH, THAT QUASAR PUNK GOT 'EM. THANKS, DOC. THAT FILLS IN SOME GAPS FOR US.
WELL, KEEP IN MIND THAT THE SOURCE WASN'T THAT RELIABLE.
RECOUNTING IT NOW, SOME OF THOSE DETAILS SEEM A BIT ODD.
WE DON'T ALWAYS NOTICE HOW ODD, GIVEN OUR LINE OF WORK.
I HEAR YA. TAKE IT EASY, MR. FANTASTIC.
THANKS AGAIN, SIR.
SORRY, THE EVIDENCE DOESN'T SUPPORT YOUR NOTION OF MARVEL BOY AS THE RINGLEADER.
IT RAISES EVEN MORE QUESTIONS, DUGAN.

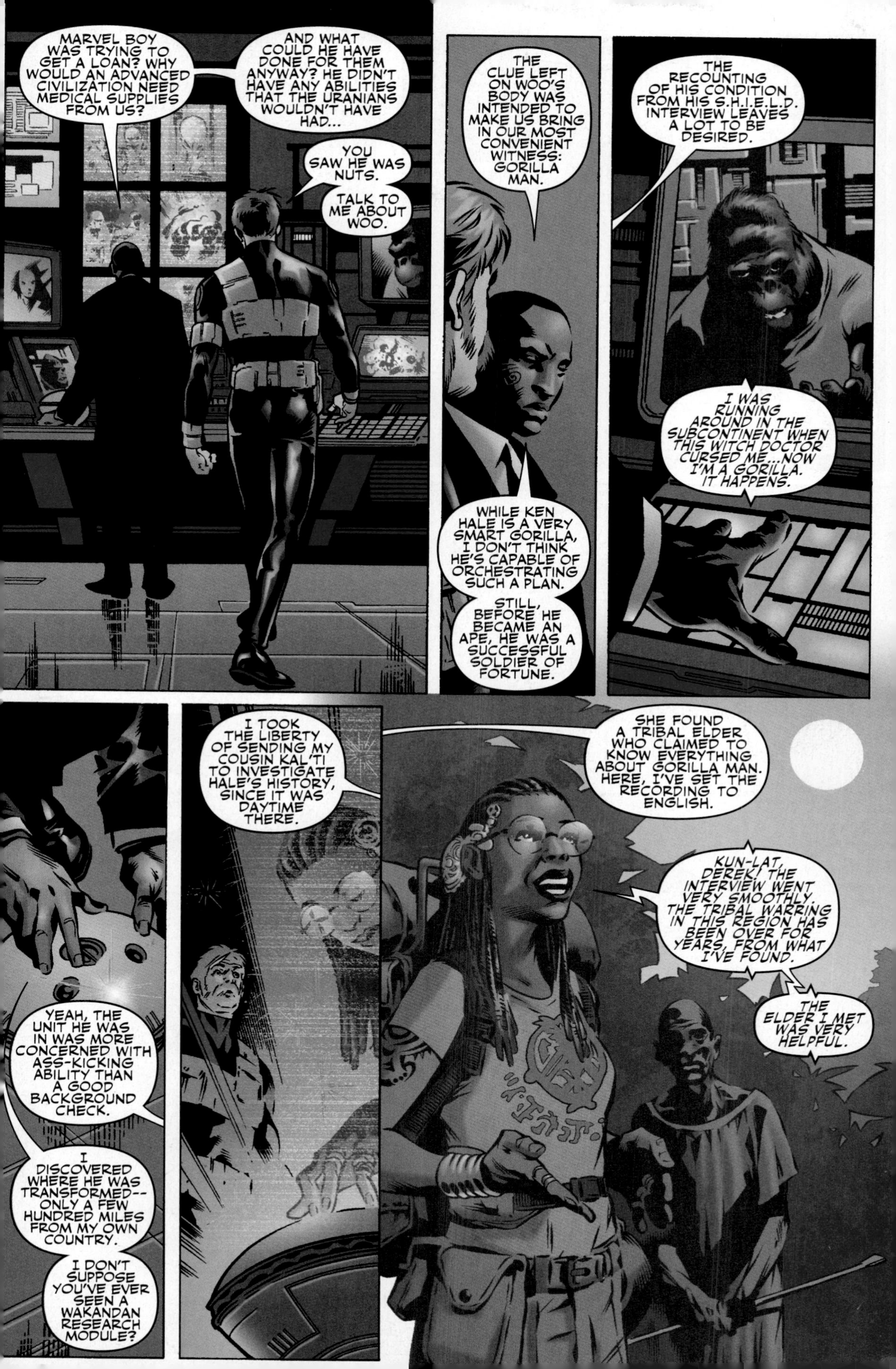
MARVEL BOY WAS TRYING TO GET A LOAN? WHY WOULD AN ADVANCED CIVILIZATION NEED MEDICAL SUPPLIES FROM US?
AND WHAT COULD HE HAVE DONE FOR THEM ANYWAY? HE DIDN'T HAVE ANY ABILITIES THAT THE URANIANS WOULDN'T HAVE HAD...
YOU SAW HE WAS NUTS.
TALK TO ME ABOUT WOO.
THE CLUE LEFT ON WOO'S BODY WAS INTENDED TO MAKE US BRING IN OUR MOST CONVENIENT WITNESS: GORILLA MAN.
WHILE KEN HALE IS A VERY SMART GORILLA, I DON'T THINK HE'S CAPABLE OF ORCHESTRATING SUCH A PLAN.
STILL, BEFORE HE BECAME AN APE, HE WAS A SUCCESSFUL SOLDIER OF FORTUNE.
THE RECOUNTING OF HIS CONDITION FROM HIS S.H.I.E.L.D. INTERVIEW LEAVES A LOT TO BE DESIRED.
I WAS RUNNING AROUND IN THE SUBCONTINENT WHEN THIS WITCH DOCTOR CURSED ME...NOW I'M A GORILLA. IT HAPPENS.
YEAH, THE UNIT HE WAS IN WAS MORE CONCERNED WITH ASS-KICKING ABILITY THAN A GOOD BACKGROUND CHECK.
I DISCOVERED WHERE HE WAS TRANSFORMED-- ONLY A FEW HUNDRED MILES FROM MY OWN COUNTRY.
I DON'T SUPPOSE YOU'VE EVER SEEN A WAKANDAN RESEARCH MODULE?
I TOOK THE LIBERTY OF SENDING MY COUSIN KAL'TI TO INVESTIGATE HALE'S HISTORY, SINCE IT WAS DAYTIME THERE.
SHE FOUND A TRIBAL ELDER WHO CLAIMED TO KNOW EVERYTHING ABOUT GORILLA MAN. HERE, I'VE SET THE RECORDING TO ENGLISH.
KUN-LAT, DEREK! THE INTERVIEW WENT VERY SMOOTHLY. THE TRIBAL WARRING IN THIS REGION HAS BEEN OVER FOR YEARS, FROM WHAT I'VE FOUND.
THE ELDER I MET WAS VERY HELPFUL.

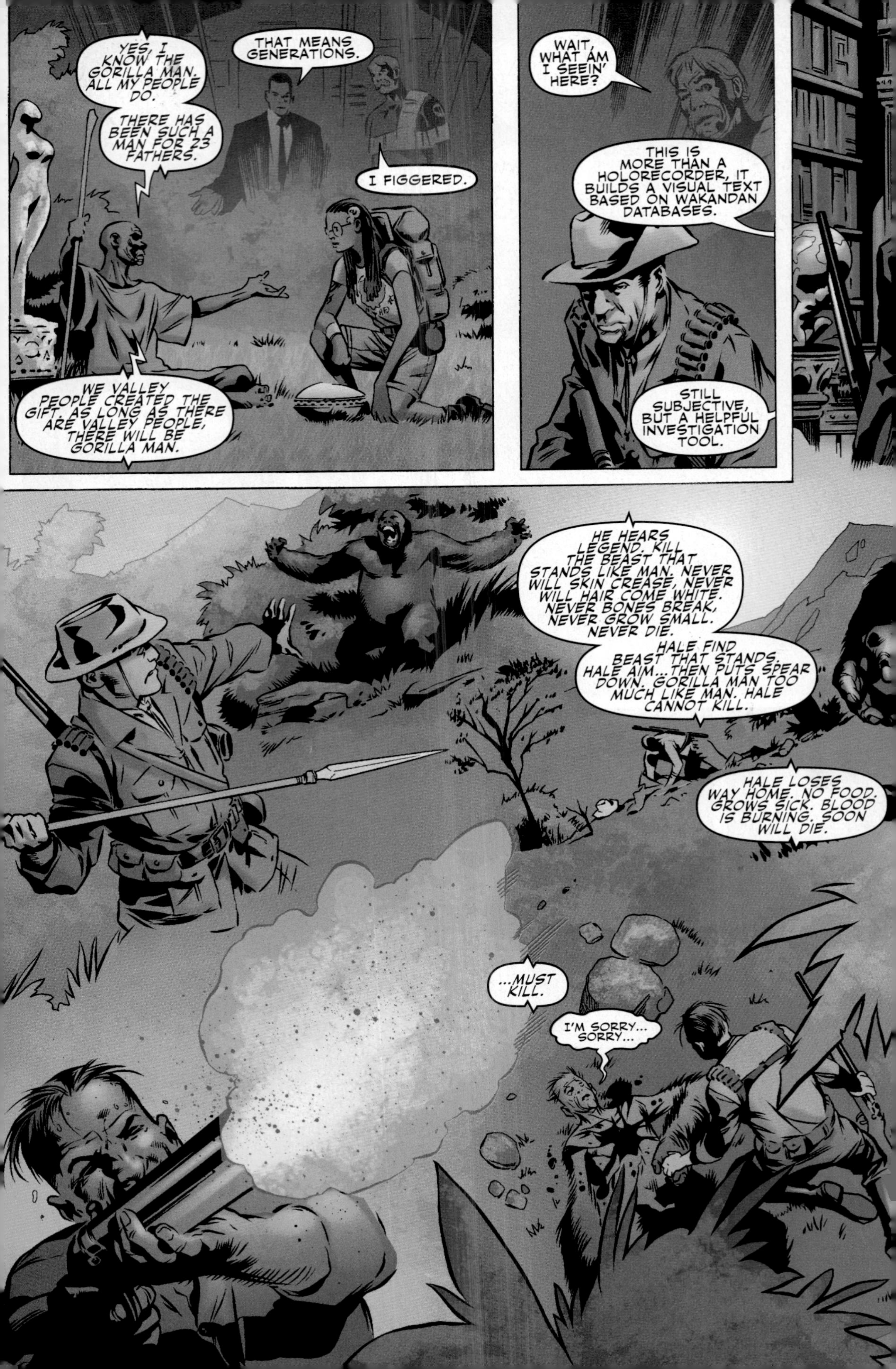
YES, I KNOW THE GORILLA MAN. ALL MY PEOPLE DO.
THERE HAS BEEN SUCH A MAN FOR 23 FATHERS.
THAT MEANS GENERATIONS.
I FIGGERED.
WE VALLEY PEOPLE CREATED THE GIFT. AS LONG AS THERE ARE VALLEY PEOPLE, THERE WILL BE GORILLA MAN.
WAIT, WHAT AM I SEEIN' HERE?
THIS IS MORE THAN A HOLORECORDER, IT BUILDS A VISUAL TEXT BASED ON WAKANDAN DATABASES.
STILL SUBJECTIVE, BUT A HELPFUL INVESTIGATION TOOL.
HE HEARS LEGEND. KILL THE BEAST THAT STANDS LIKE MAN. NEVER WILL SKIN CREASE, NEVER WILL HAIR COME WHITE. NEVER BONES BREAK, NEVER GROW SMALL. NEVER DIE.
HALE FIND BEAST THAT STANDS. HALE AIM...THEN PUTS SPEAR DOWN. GORILLA MAN TOO MUCH LIKE MAN. HALE CANNOT KILL.
HALE LOSES WAY HOME. NO FOOD. GROWS SICK. BLOOD IS BURNING. SOON WILL DIE.
...MUST KILL.
I'M SORRY... SORRY...

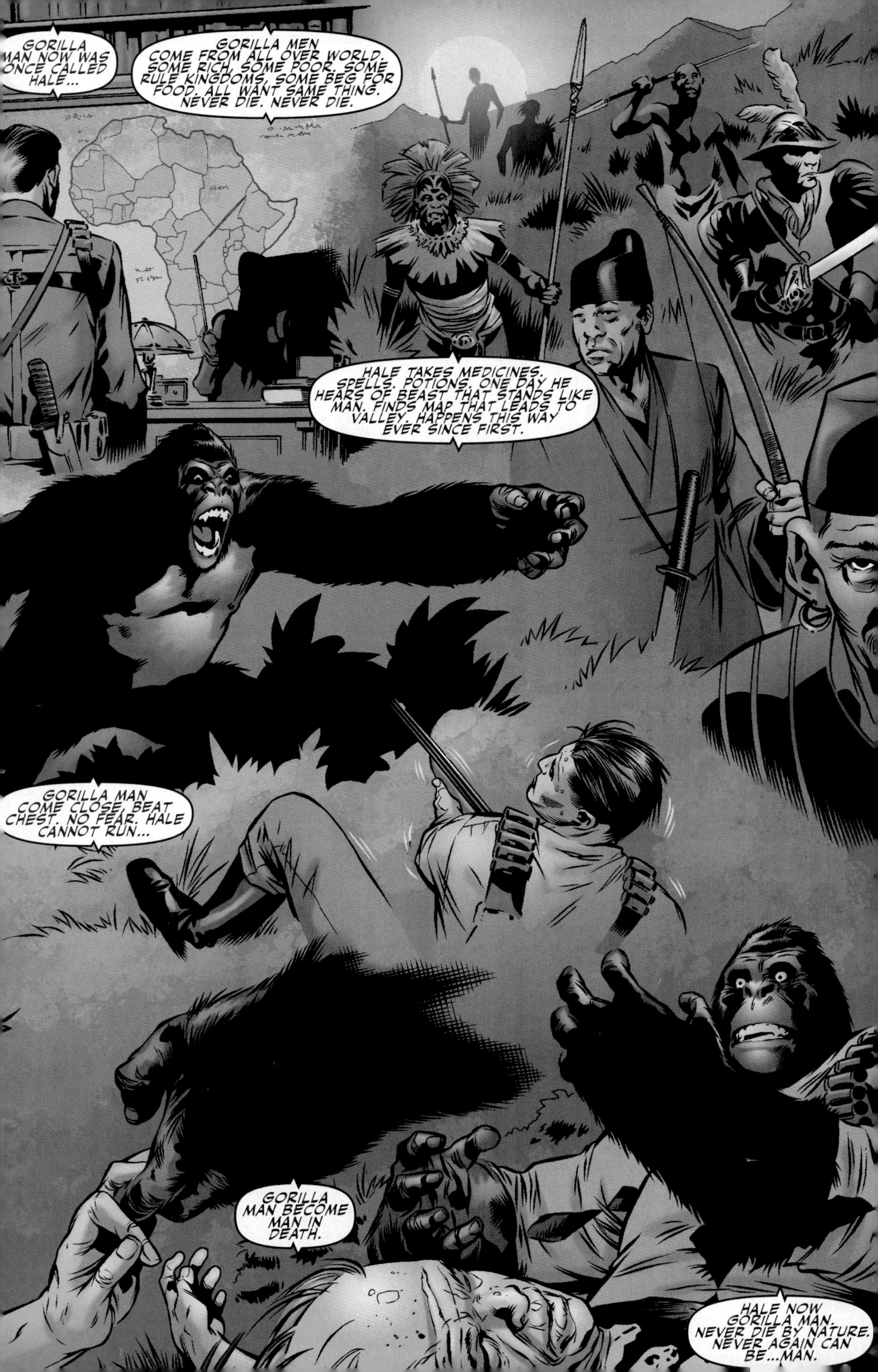
GORILLA MAN NOW WAS ONCE CALLED HALE...
GORILLA MEN COME FROM ALL OVER WORLD. SOME RICH, SOME POOR. SOME RULE KINGDOMS, SOME BEG FOR FOOD. ALL WANT SAME THING. NEVER DIE. NEVER DIE.
HALE TAKES MEDICINES. SPELLS. POTIONS. ONE DAY HE HEARS OF BEAST THAT STANDS LIKE MAN. FINDS MAP THAT LEADS TO VALLEY. HAPPENS THIS WAY EVER SINCE FIRST.
GORILLA MAN COME CLOSE, BEAT CHEST. NO FEAR. HALE CANNOT RUN...
GORILLA MAN BECOME MAN IN DEATH.
HALE NOW GORILLA MAN. NEVER DIE BY NATURE. NEVER AGAIN CAN BE...MAN.

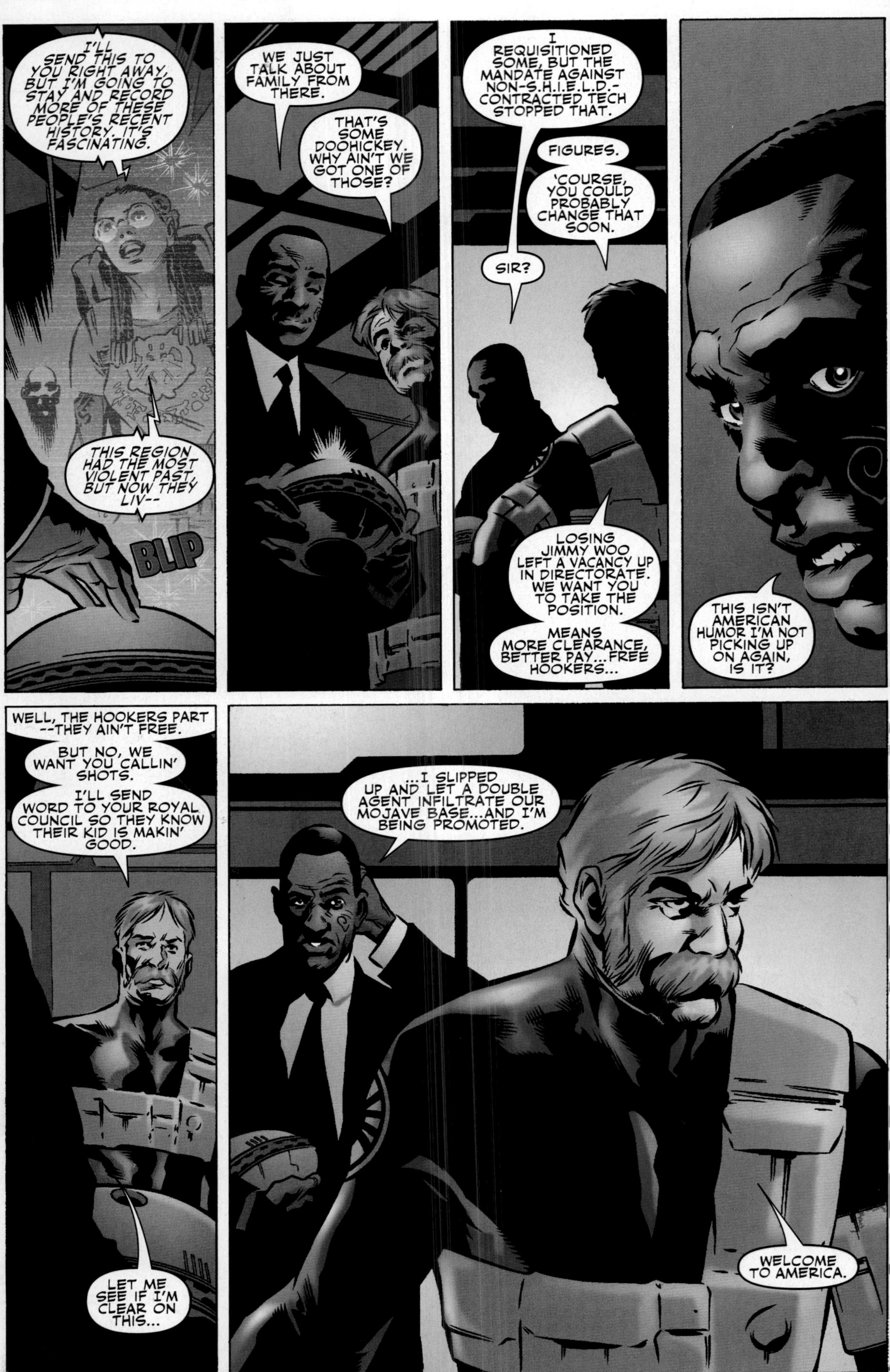
I'LL SEND THIS TO YOU RIGHT AWAY, BUT I'M GOING TO STAY AND RECORD MORE OF THESE PEOPLE'S RECENT HISTORY. IT'S FASCINATING.
THIS REGION HAD THE MOST VIOLENT PAST, BUT NOW THEY LIV--
BLIP
WE JUST TALK ABOUT FAMILY FROM THERE.
THAT'S SOME DOOHICKEY. WHY AIN'T WE GOT ONE OF THOSE?
I REQUISITIONED SOME, BUT THE MANDATE AGAINST NON-S.H.I.E.L.D.-CONTRACTED TECH STOPPED THAT.
FIGURES.
'COURSE, YOU COULD PROBABLY CHANGE THAT SOON.
SIR?
LOSING JIMMY WOO LEFT A VACANCY UP IN DIRECTORATE. WE WANT YOU TO TAKE THE POSITION.
MEANS MORE CLEARANCE, BETTER PAY...FREE HOOKERS...
THIS ISN'T AMERICAN HUMOR I'M NOT PICKING UP ON AGAIN, IS IT?
WELL, THE HOOKERS PART --THEY AIN'T FREE.
BUT NO, WE WANT YOU CALLIN' SHOTS.
I'LL SEND WORD TO YOUR ROYAL COUNCIL SO THEY KNOW THEIR KID IS MAKIN' GOOD.
LET ME SEE IF I'M CLEAR ON THIS...
...I SLIPPED UP AND LET A DOUBLE AGENT INFILTRATE OUR MOJAVE BASE...AND I'M BEING PROMOTED.
WELCOME TO AMERICA.

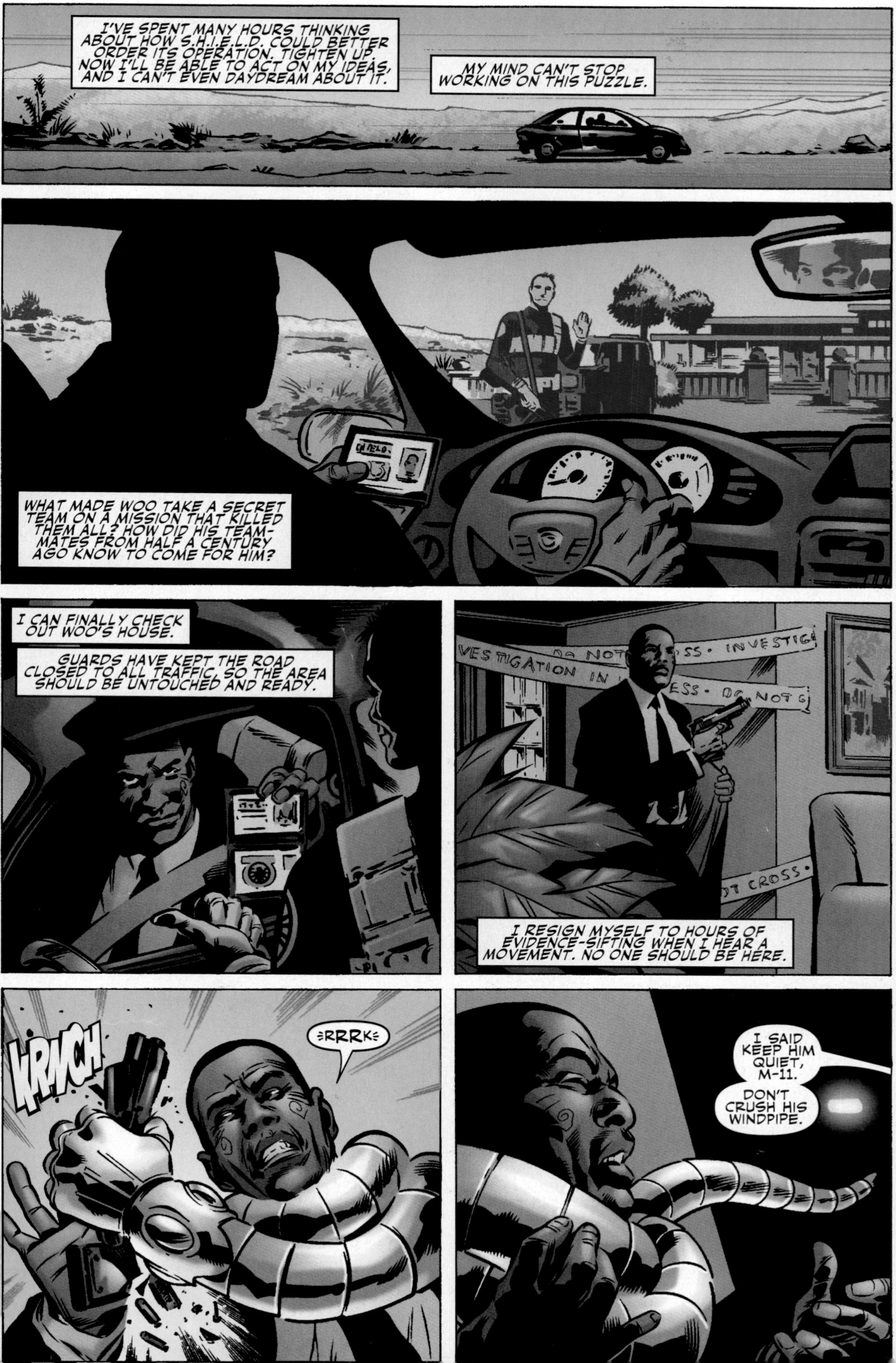
I'VE SPENT MANY HOURS THINKING ABOUT HOW S.H.I.E.L.D. COULD BETTER ORDER ITS OPERATION. TIGHTEN UP. NOW I'LL BE ABLE TO ACT ON MY IDEAS, AND I CAN'T EVEN DAYDREAM ABOUT IT.
MY MIND CAN'T STOP WORKING ON THIS PUZZLE.
WHAT MADE WOO TAKE A SECRET TEAM ON A MISSION THAT KILLED THEM ALL? HOW DID HIS TEAM-MATES FROM HALF A CENTURY AGO KNOW TO COME FOR HIM?
I CAN FINALLY CHECK OUT WOO'S HOUSE.
GUARDS HAVE KEPT THE ROAD CLOSED TO ALL TRAFFIC, SO THE AREA SHOULD BE UNTOUCHED AND READY.
I RESIGN MYSELF TO HOURS OF EVIDENCE-SIFTING WHEN I HEAR A MOVEMENT. NO ONE SHOULD BE HERE.
KRUNCH
RRRK
I SAID KEEP HIM QUIET, M-11.
DON'T CRUSH HIS WINDPIPE.

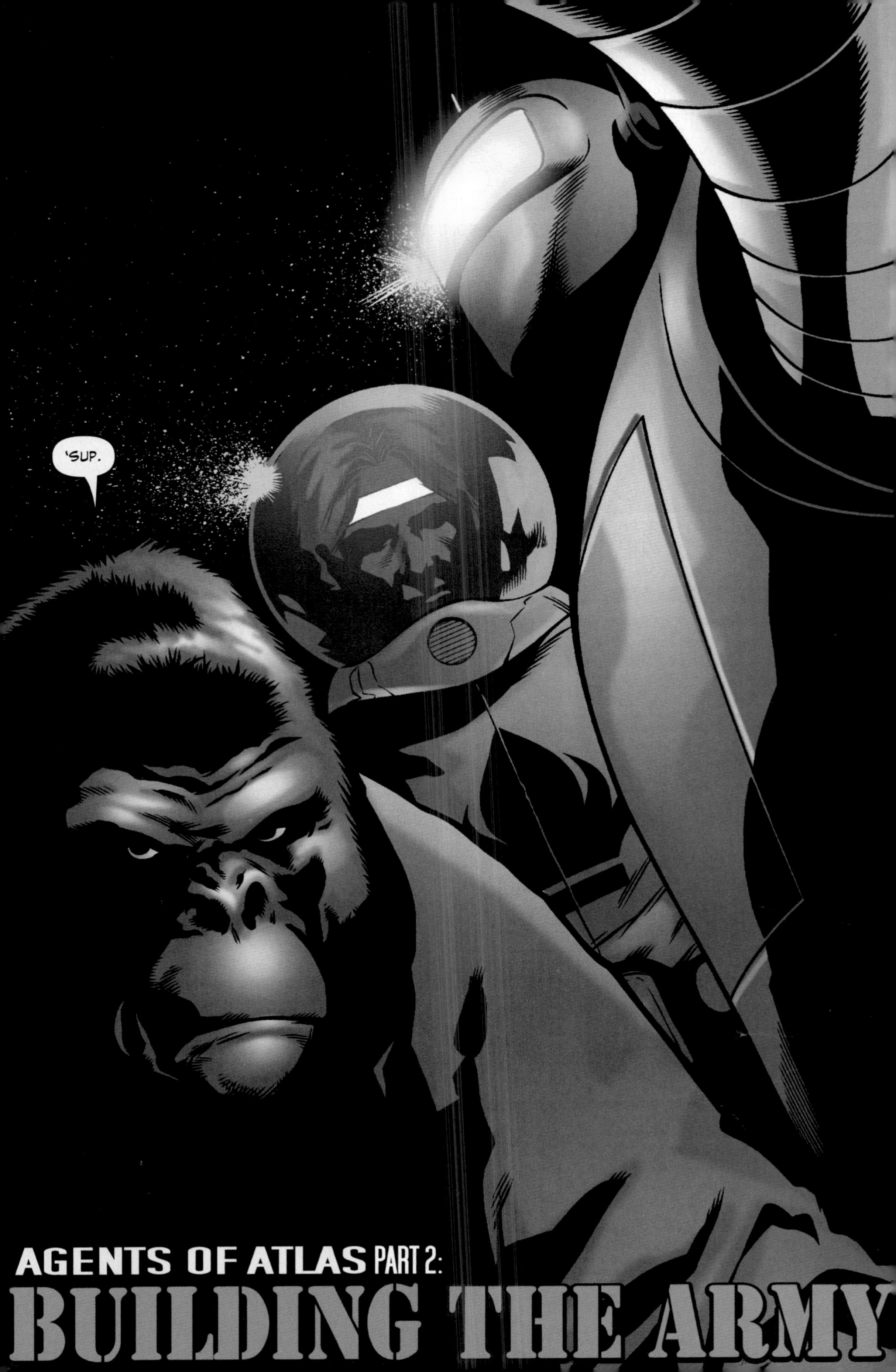
'SUP.
AGENTS OF ATLAS PART 2:
BUILDING THE ARMY

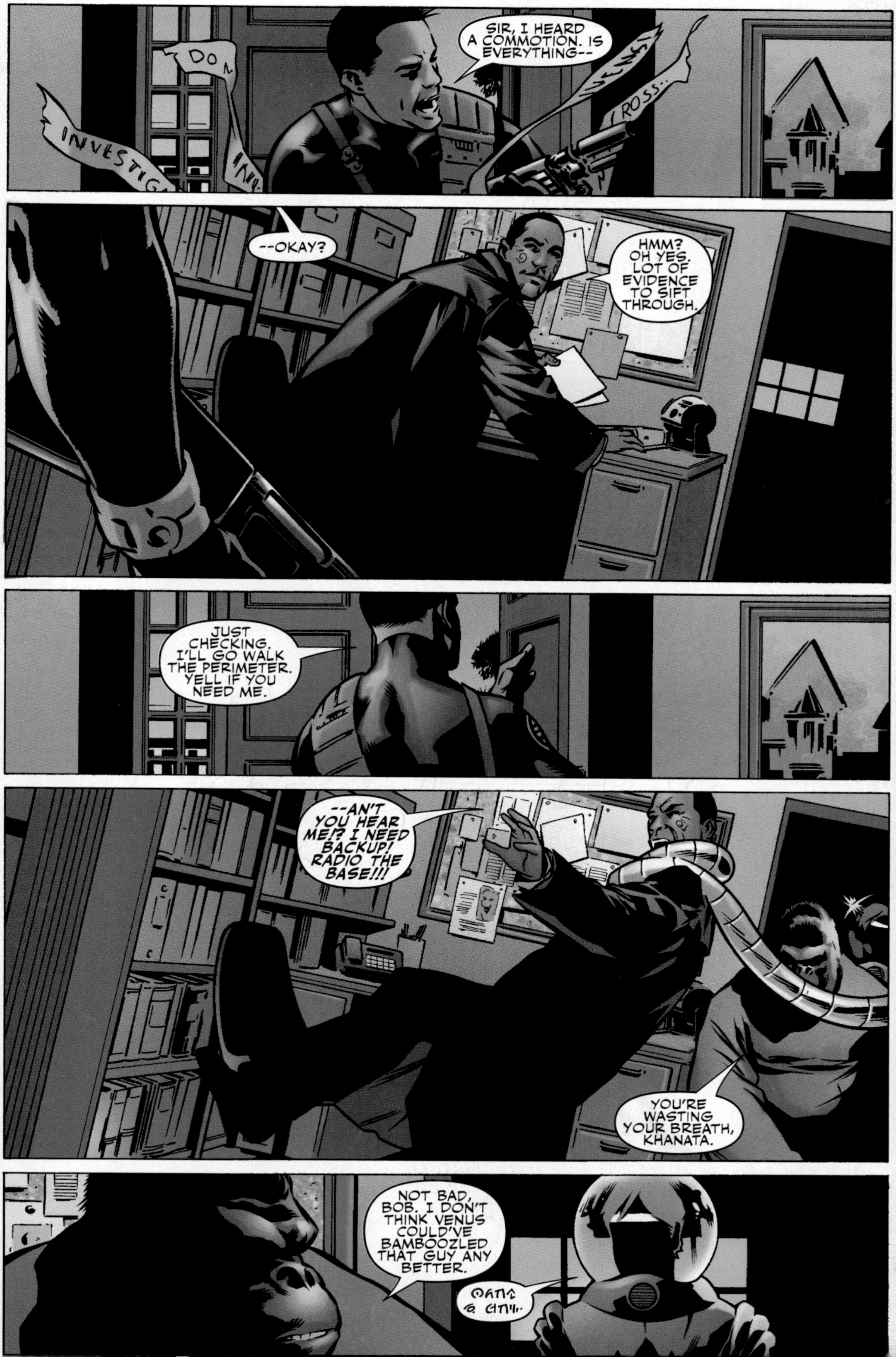
SIR, I HEARD A COMMOTION. IS EVERYTHING--
--OKAY?
HMM? OH YES. LOT OF EVIDENCE TO SIFT THROUGH.
JUST CHECKING. I'LL GO WALK THE PERIMETER. YELL IF YOU NEED ME.
--AN'T YOU HEAR ME!? I NEED BACKUP! RADIO THE BASE!!!
YOU'RE WASTING YOUR BREATH, KHANATA.
NOT BAD, BOB. I DON'T THINK VENUS COULD'VE BAMBOOZLED THAT GUY ANY BETTER.

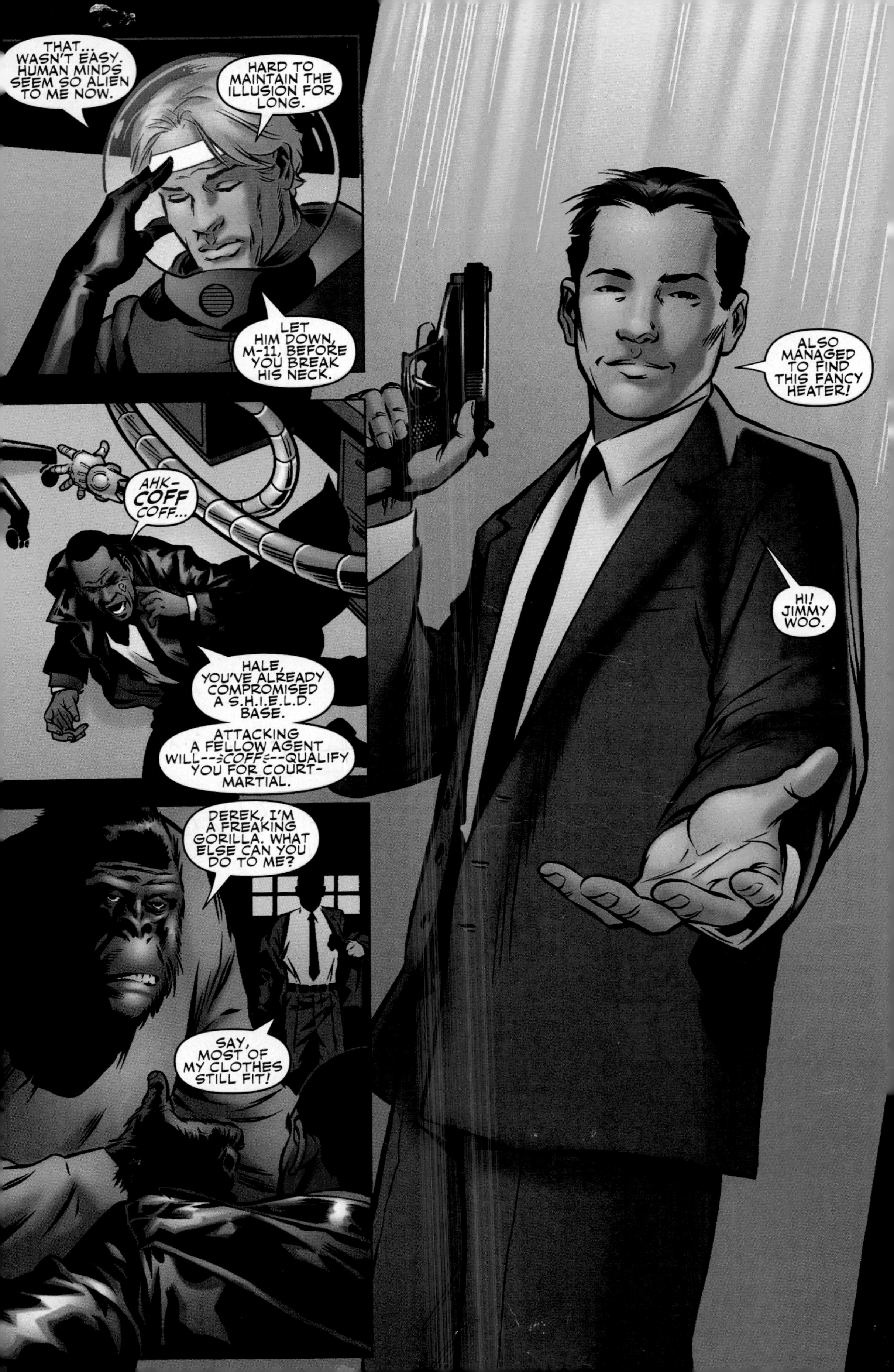
THAT... WASN'T EASY. HUMAN MINDS SEEM SO ALIEN TO ME NOW.
HARD TO MAINTAIN THE ILLUSION FOR LONG.
LET HIM DOWN, M-11, BEFORE YOU BREAK HIS NECK.
AHK-COFF COFF...
HALE, YOU'VE ALREADY COMPROMISED A S.H.I.E.L.D. BASE.
ATTACKING A FELLOW AGENT WILL--COFF--QUALIFY YOU FOR COURT-MARTIAL.
DEREK, I'M A FREAKING GORILLA. WHAT ELSE CAN YOU DO TO ME?
SAY, MOST OF MY CLOTHES STILL FIT!
ALSO MANAGED TO FIND THIS FANCY HEATER!
HI! JIMMY WOO.

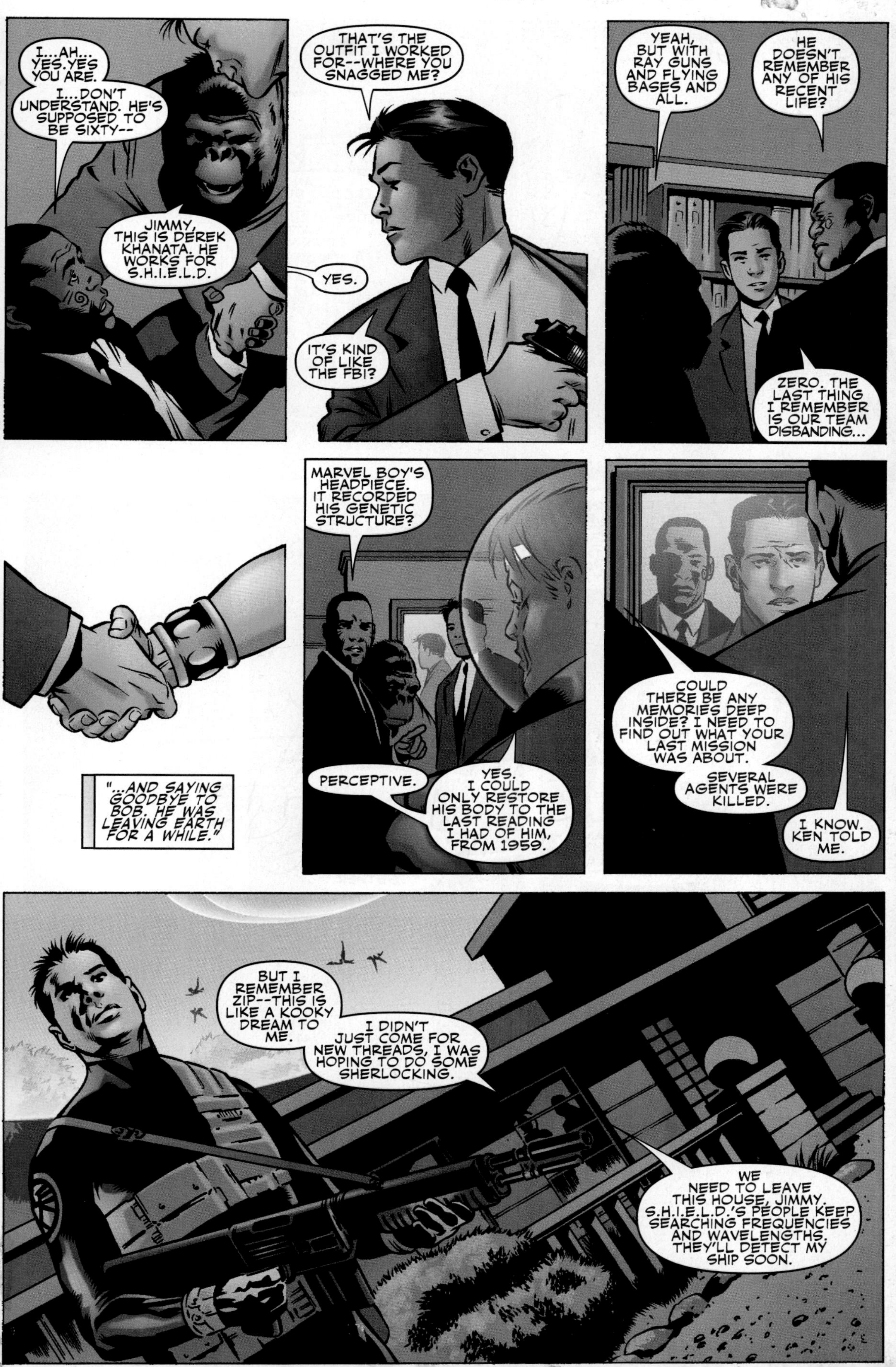
I...AH... YES. YES YOU ARE.
I...DON'T UNDERSTAND. HE'S SUPPOSED TO BE SIXTY--
JIMMY, THIS IS DEREK KHANATA. HE WORKS FOR S.H.I.E.L.D.
THAT'S THE OUTFIT I WORKED FOR--WHERE YOU SNAGGED ME?
YES.
IT'S KIND OF LIKE THE FBI?
YEAH, BUT WITH RAY GUNS AND FLYING BASES AND ALL.
HE DOESN'T REMEMBER ANY OF HIS RECENT LIFE?
ZERO. THE LAST THING I REMEMBER IS OUR TEAM DISBANDING...
"...AND SAYING GOODBYE TO BOB. HE WAS LEAVING EARTH FOR A WHILE."
MARVEL BOY'S HEADPIECE. IT RECORDED HIS GENETIC STRUCTURE?
PERCEPTIVE.
YES. I COULD ONLY RESTORE HIS BODY TO THE LAST READING I HAD OF HIM, FROM 1959.
COULD THERE BE ANY MEMORIES DEEP INSIDE? I NEED TO FIND OUT WHAT YOUR LAST MISSION WAS ABOUT.
SEVERAL AGENTS WERE KILLED.
I KNOW. KEN TOLD ME.
BUT I REMEMBER ZIP--THIS IS LIKE A KOOKY DREAM TO ME.
I DIDN'T JUST COME FOR NEW THREADS, I WAS HOPING TO DO SOME SHERLOCKING.
WE NEED TO LEAVE THIS HOUSE, JIMMY. S.H.I.E.L.D.'S PEOPLE KEEP SEARCHING FREQUENCIES AND WAVELENGTHS. THEY'LL DETECT MY SHIP SOON.

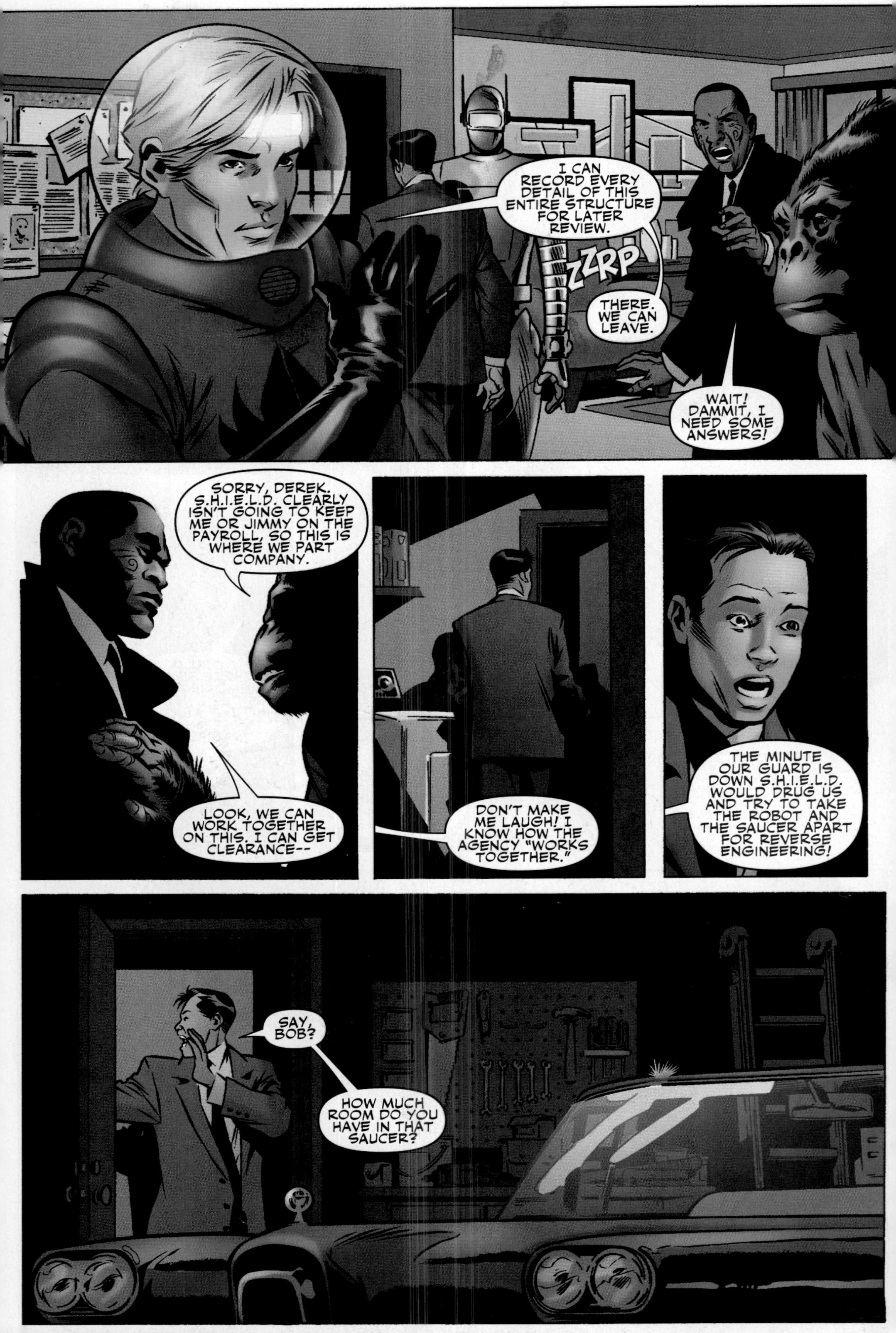
I CAN RECORD EVERY DETAIL OF THIS ENTIRE STRUCTURE FOR LATER REVIEW.
ZZRP
THERE. WE CAN LEAVE.
WAIT! DAMMIT, I NEED SOME ANSWERS!
SORRY, DEREK. S.H.I.E.L.D. CLEARLY ISN'T GOING TO KEEP ME OR JIMMY ON THE PAYROLL, SO THIS IS WHERE WE PART COMPANY.
LOOK, WE CAN WORK TOGETHER ON THIS. I CAN GET CLEARANCE--
DON'T MAKE ME LAUGH! I KNOW HOW THE AGENCY "WORKS TOGETHER."
THE MINUTE OUR GUARD IS DOWN S.H.I.E.L.D. WOULD DRUG US AND TRY TO TAKE THE ROBOT AND THE SAUCER APART FOR REVERSE ENGINEERING!
SAY, BOB?
HOW MUCH ROOM DO YOU HAVE IN THAT SAUCER?

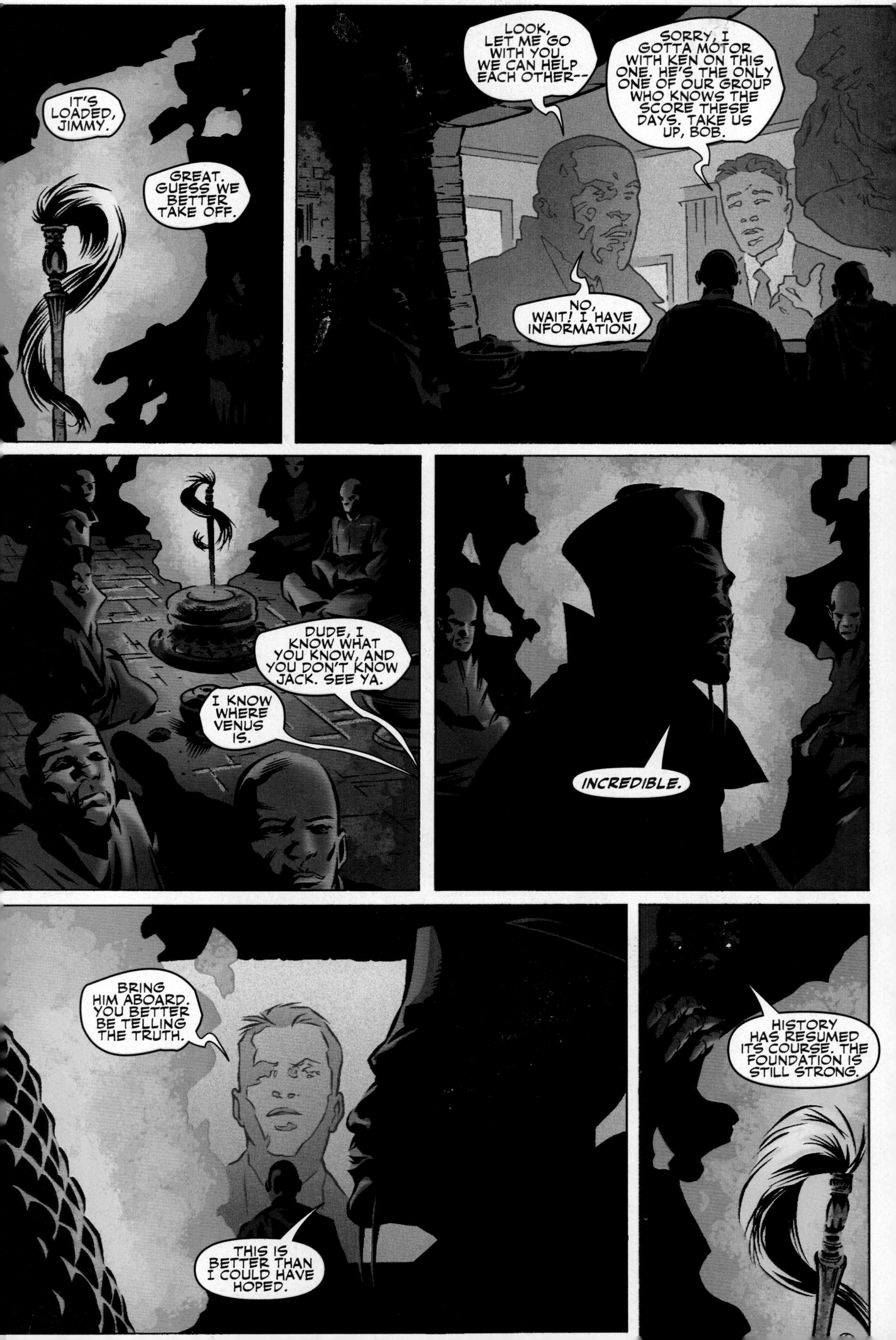
IT'S LOADED, JIMMY.
GREAT. GUESS WE BETTER TAKE OFF.
LOOK, LET ME GO WITH YOU. WE CAN HELP EACH OTHER--
SORRY, I GOTTA MOTOR WITH KEN ON THIS ONE. HE'S THE ONLY ONE OF OUR GROUP WHO KNOWS THE SCORE THESE DAYS. TAKE US UP, BOB.
NO, WAIT! I HAVE INFORMATION!
DUDE, I KNOW WHAT YOU KNOW, AND YOU DON'T KNOW JACK. SEE YA.
I KNOW WHERE VENUS IS.
INCREDIBLE.
BRING HIM ABOARD. YOU BETTER BE TELLING THE TRUTH.
THIS IS BETTER THAN I COULD HAVE HOPED.
HISTORY HAS RESUMED ITS COURSE. THE FOUNDATION IS STILL STRONG.

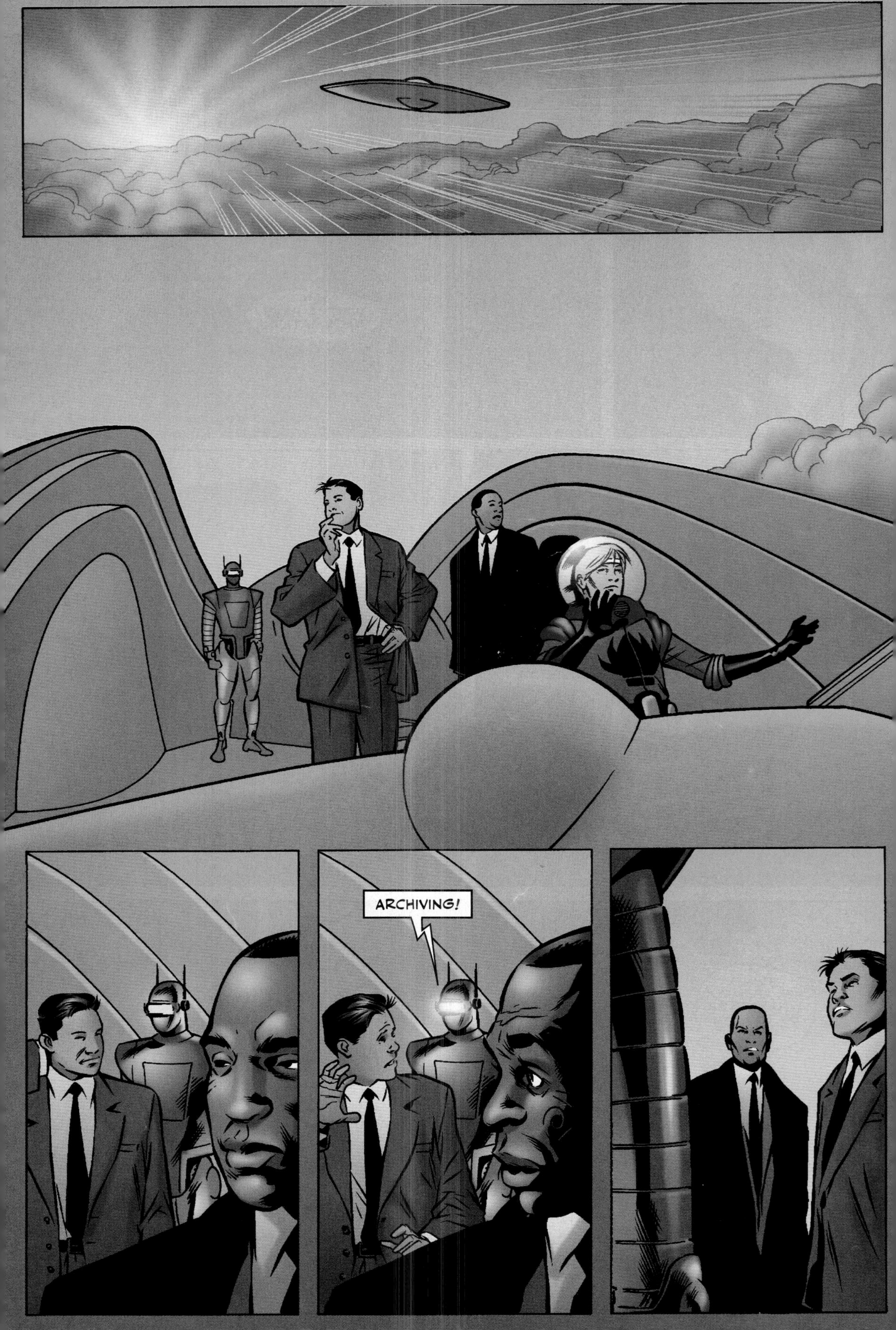
ARCHIVING!

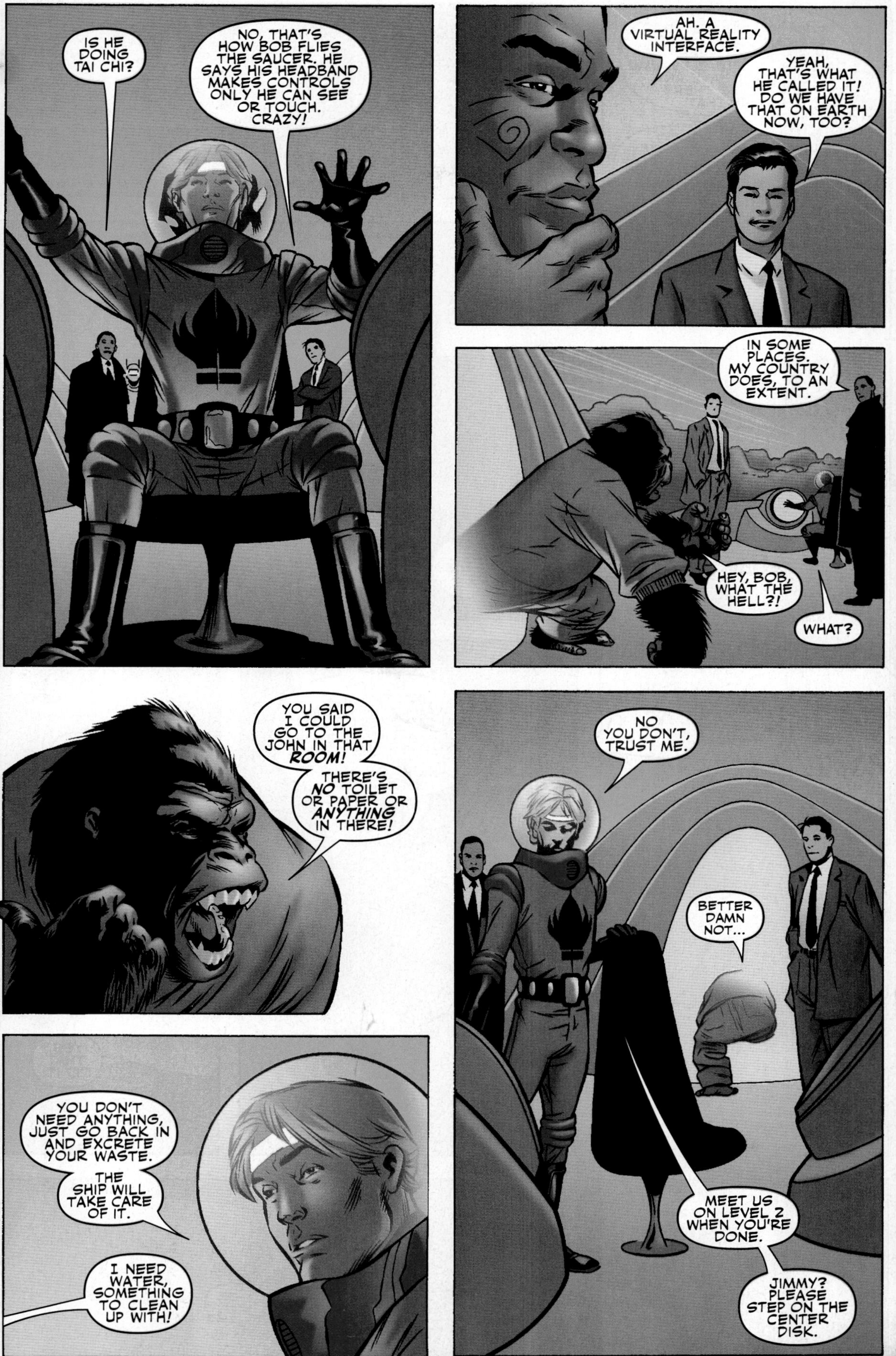
IS HE DOING TAI CHI?
NO, THAT'S HOW BOB FLIES THE SAUCER. HE SAYS HIS HEADBAND MAKES CONTROLS ONLY HE CAN SEE OR TOUCH. CRAZY!
AH. A VIRTUAL REALITY INTERFACE.
YEAH, THAT'S WHAT HE CALLED IT! DO WE HAVE THAT ON EARTH NOW, TOO?
IN SOME PLACES. MY COUNTRY DOES, TO AN EXTENT.
HEY, BOB, WHAT THE HELL?!
WHAT?
YOU SAID I COULD GO TO THE JOHN IN THAT *ROOM*!
THERE'S *NO* TOILET OR PAPER OR *ANYTHING* IN THERE!
YOU DON'T NEED ANYTHING, JUST GO BACK IN AND EXCRETE YOUR WASTE.
THE SHIP WILL TAKE CARE OF IT.
I NEED WATER, SOMETHING TO CLEAN UP WITH!
NO YOU DON'T, TRUST ME.
BETTER DAMN NOT...
MEET US ON LEVEL 2 WHEN YOU'RE DONE.
JIMMY? PLEASE STEP ON THE CENTER DISK.

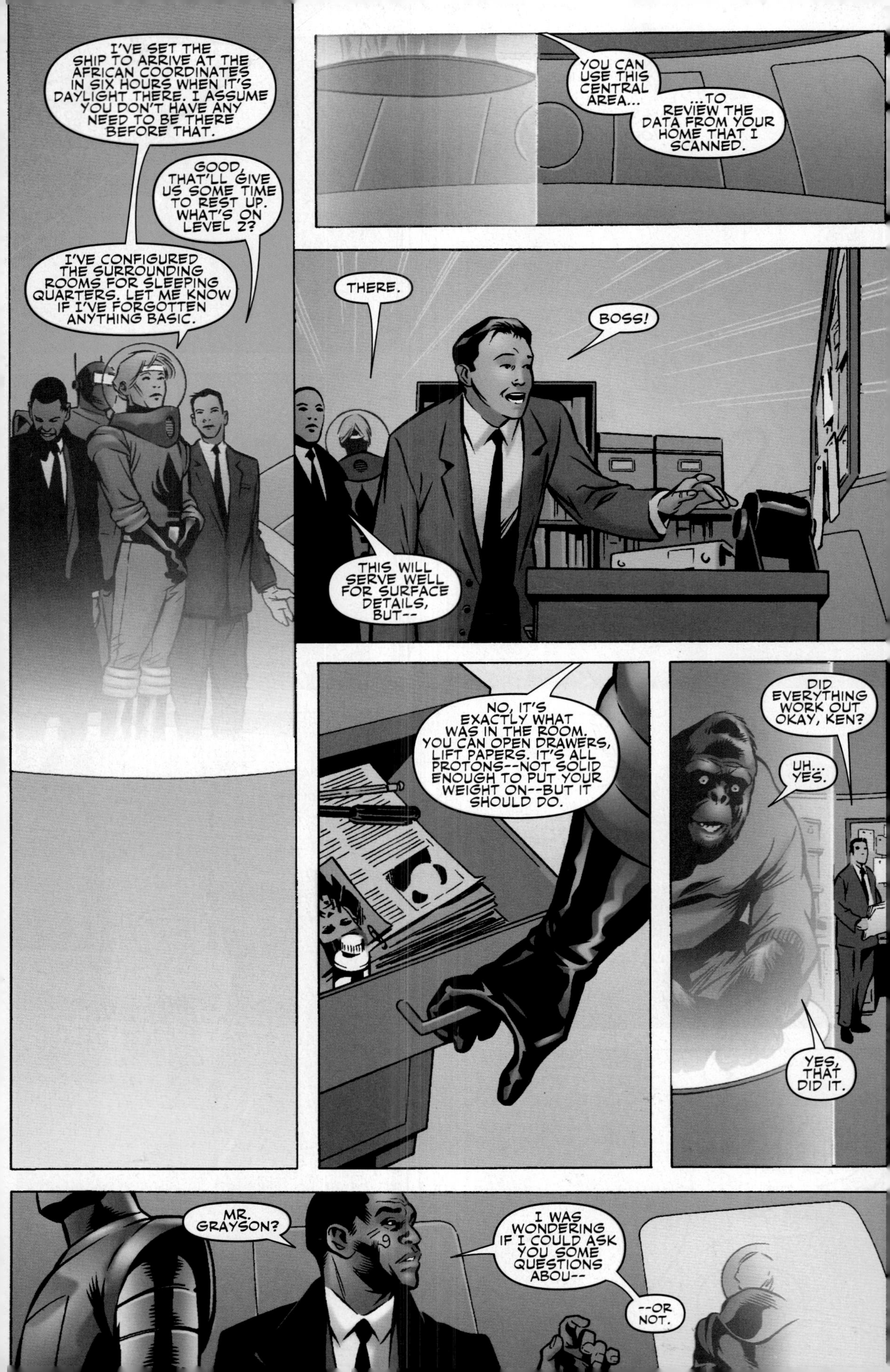
I'VE SET THE SHIP TO ARRIVE AT THE AFRICAN COORDINATES IN SIX HOURS WHEN IT'S DAYLIGHT THERE. I ASSUME YOU DON'T HAVE ANY NEED TO BE THERE BEFORE THAT.
GOOD, THAT'LL GIVE US SOME TIME TO REST UP. WHAT'S ON LEVEL 2?
I'VE CONFIGURED THE SURROUNDING ROOMS FOR SLEEPING QUARTERS. LET ME KNOW IF I'VE FORGOTTEN ANYTHING BASIC.
YOU CAN USE THIS CENTRAL AREA...
...TO REVIEW THE DATA FROM YOUR HOME THAT I SCANNED.
THERE.
BOSS!
THIS WILL SERVE WELL FOR SURFACE DETAILS, BUT--
NO, IT'S EXACTLY WHAT WAS IN THE ROOM. YOU CAN OPEN DRAWERS, LIFT PAPERS. IT'S ALL PROTONS--NOT SOLID ENOUGH TO PUT YOUR WEIGHT ON--BUT IT SHOULD DO.
DID EVERYTHING WORK OUT OKAY, KEN?
UH... YES.
YES, THAT DID IT.
MR. GRAYSON?
I WAS WONDERING IF I COULD ASK YOU SOME QUESTIONS ABOU--
--OR NOT.

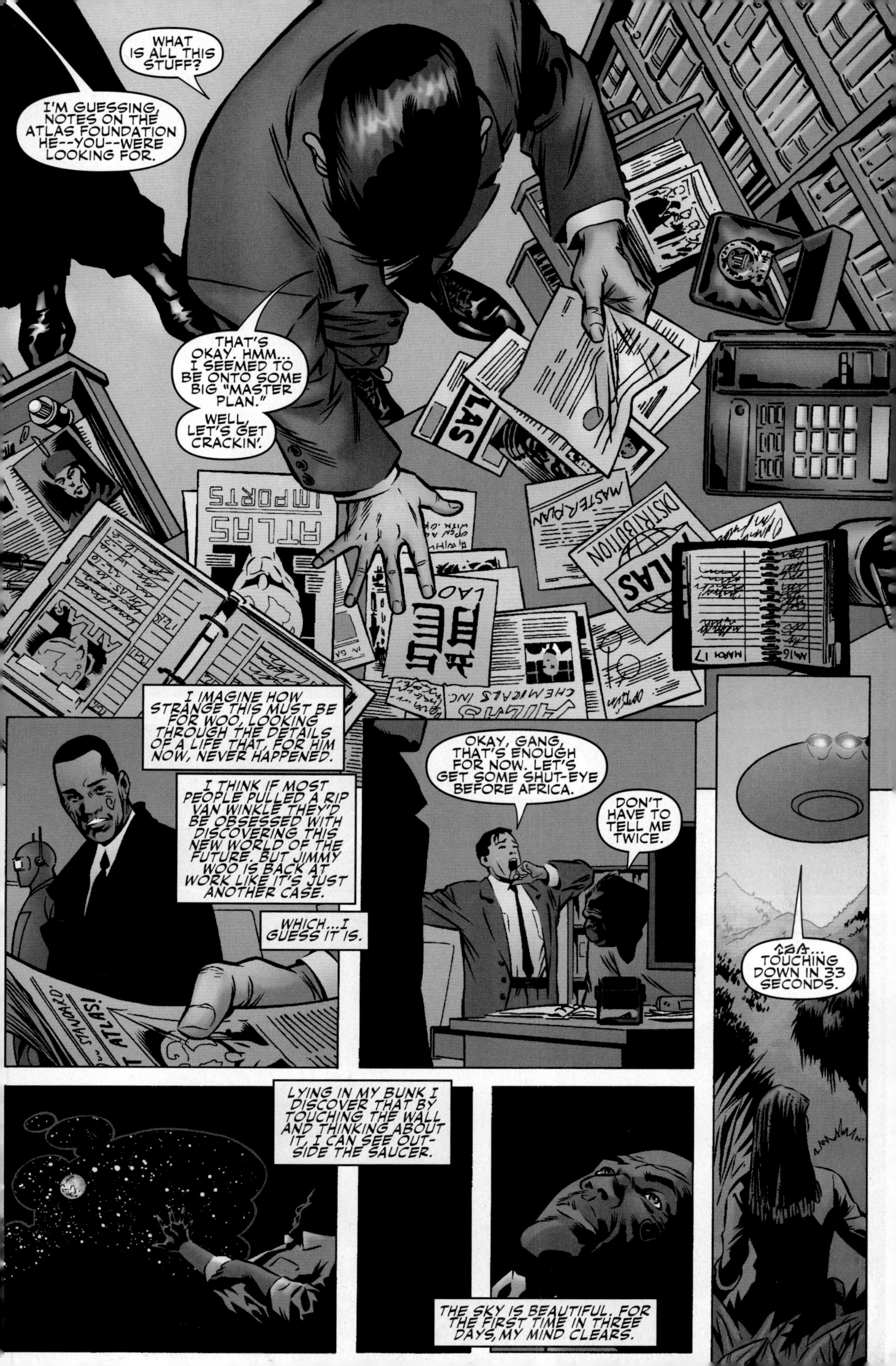
WHAT IS ALL THIS STUFF?
I'M GUESSING, NOTES ON THE ATLAS FOUNDATION HE--YOU--WERE LOOKING FOR.
THAT'S OKAY. HMM... I SEEMED TO BE ONTO SOME BIG "MASTER PLAN."
WELL, LET'S GET CRACKIN'.
ATLAS IMPORTS
MASTER PLAN
DISTRIBUTION
ATLAS
I IMAGINE HOW STRANGE THIS MUST BE FOR WOO, LOOKING THROUGH THE DETAILS OF A LIFE THAT, FOR HIM NOW, NEVER HAPPENED.
I THINK IF MOST PEOPLE PULLED A RIP VAN WINKLE THEY'D BE OBSESSED WITH DISCOVERING THIS NEW WORLD OF THE FUTURE. BUT JIMMY WOO IS BACK AT WORK LIKE IT'S JUST ANOTHER CASE.
WHICH...I GUESS IT IS.
OKAY, GANG, THAT'S ENOUGH FOR NOW. LET'S GET SOME SHUT-EYE BEFORE AFRICA.
DON'T HAVE TO TELL ME TWICE.
TOUCHING DOWN IN 33 SECONDS.
LYING IN MY BUNK I DISCOVER THAT BY TOUCHING THE WALL AND THINKING ABOUT IT, I CAN SEE OUT-SIDE THE SAUCER.
THE SKY IS BEAUTIFUL. FOR THE FIRST TIME IN THREE DAYS, MY MIND CLEARS.

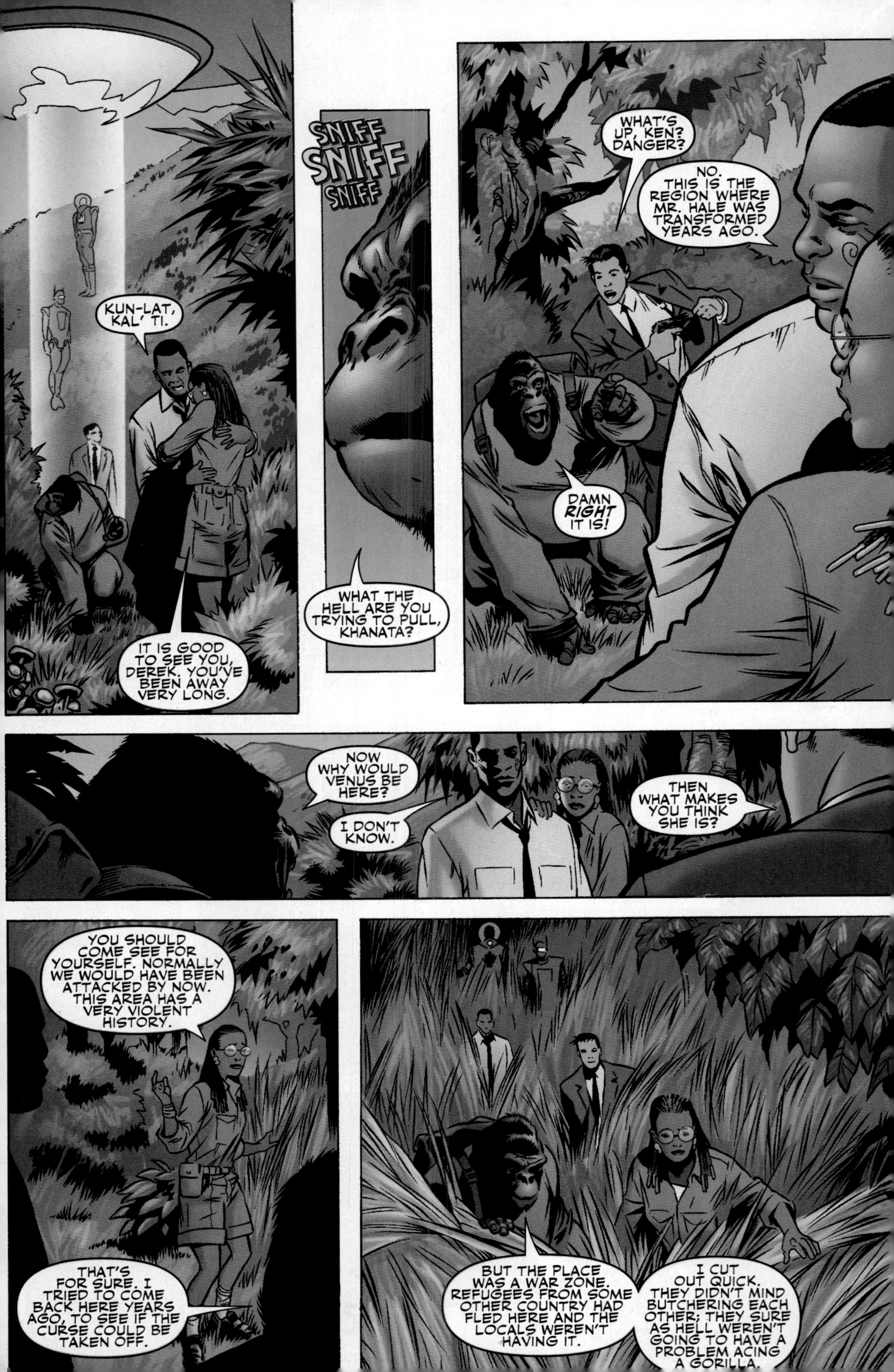
KUN-LAT, KAL' TI.
IT IS GOOD TO SEE YOU, DEREK. YOU'VE BEEN AWAY VERY LONG.
SNIFF SNIFF SNIFF
WHAT THE HELL ARE YOU TRYING TO PULL, KHANATA?
WHAT'S UP, KEN? DANGER?
NO. THIS IS THE REGION WHERE MR. HALE WAS TRANSFORMED YEARS AGO.
DAMN RIGHT IT IS!
NOW WHY WOULD VENUS BE HERE?
I DON'T KNOW.
THEN WHAT MAKES YOU THINK SHE IS?
YOU SHOULD COME SEE FOR YOURSELF. NORMALLY WE WOULD HAVE BEEN ATTACKED BY NOW. THIS AREA HAS A VERY VIOLENT HISTORY.
THAT'S FOR SURE. I TRIED TO COME BACK HERE YEARS AGO, TO SEE IF THE CURSE COULD BE TAKEN OFF.
BUT THE PLACE WAS A WAR ZONE. REFUGEES FROM SOME OTHER COUNTRY HAD FLED HERE AND THE LOCALS WEREN'T HAVING IT.
I CUT OUT QUICK. THEY DIDN'T MIND BUTCHERING EACH OTHER; THEY SURE AS HELL WEREN'T GOING TO HAVE A PROBLEM ACING A GORILLA.

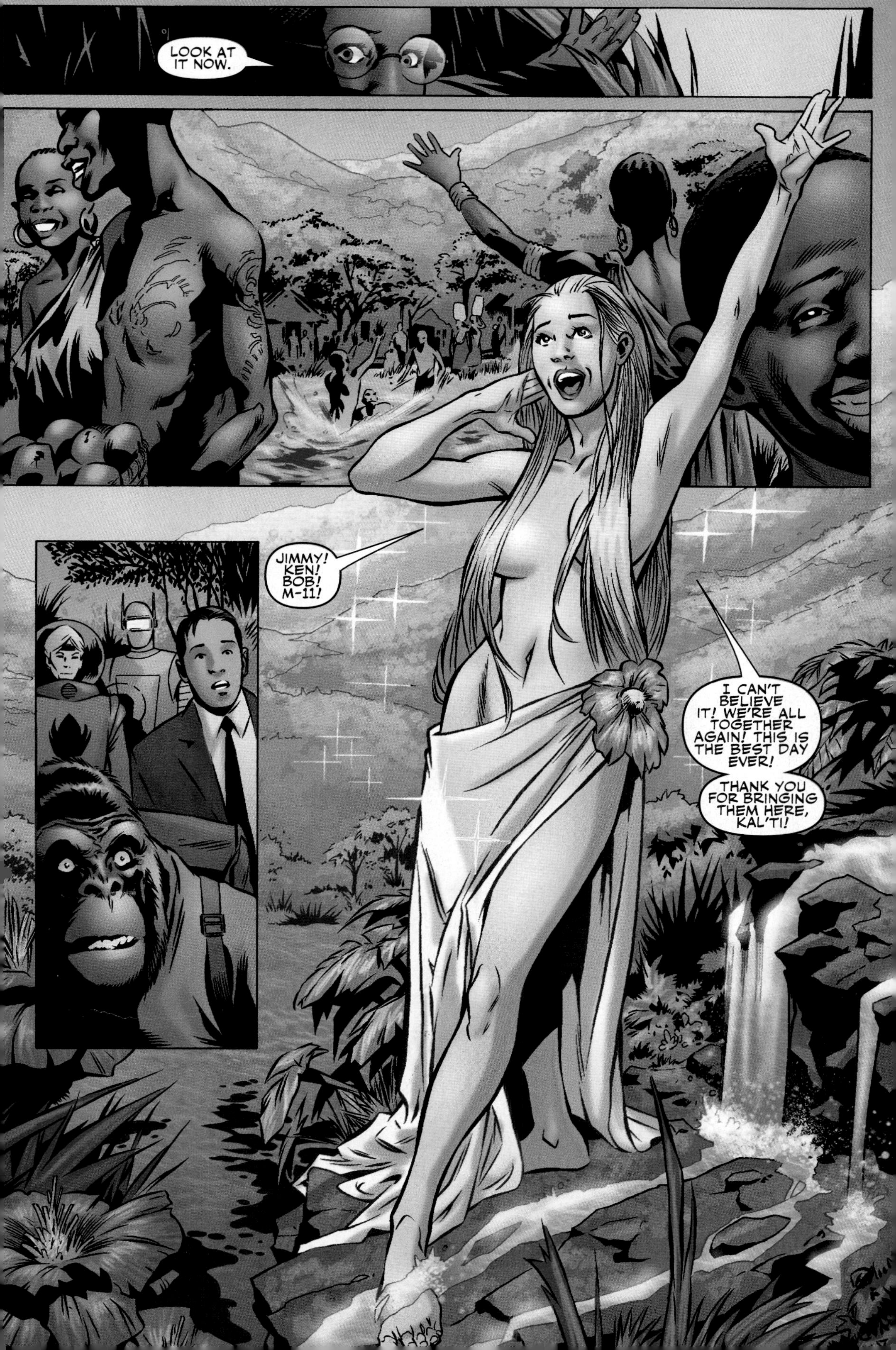
LOOK AT IT NOW.
JIMMY! KEN! BOB! M-11!
I CAN'T BELIEVE IT! WE'RE ALL TOGETHER AGAIN! THIS IS THE BEST DAY EVER!
THANK YOU FOR BRINGING THEM HERE, KAL'TI!

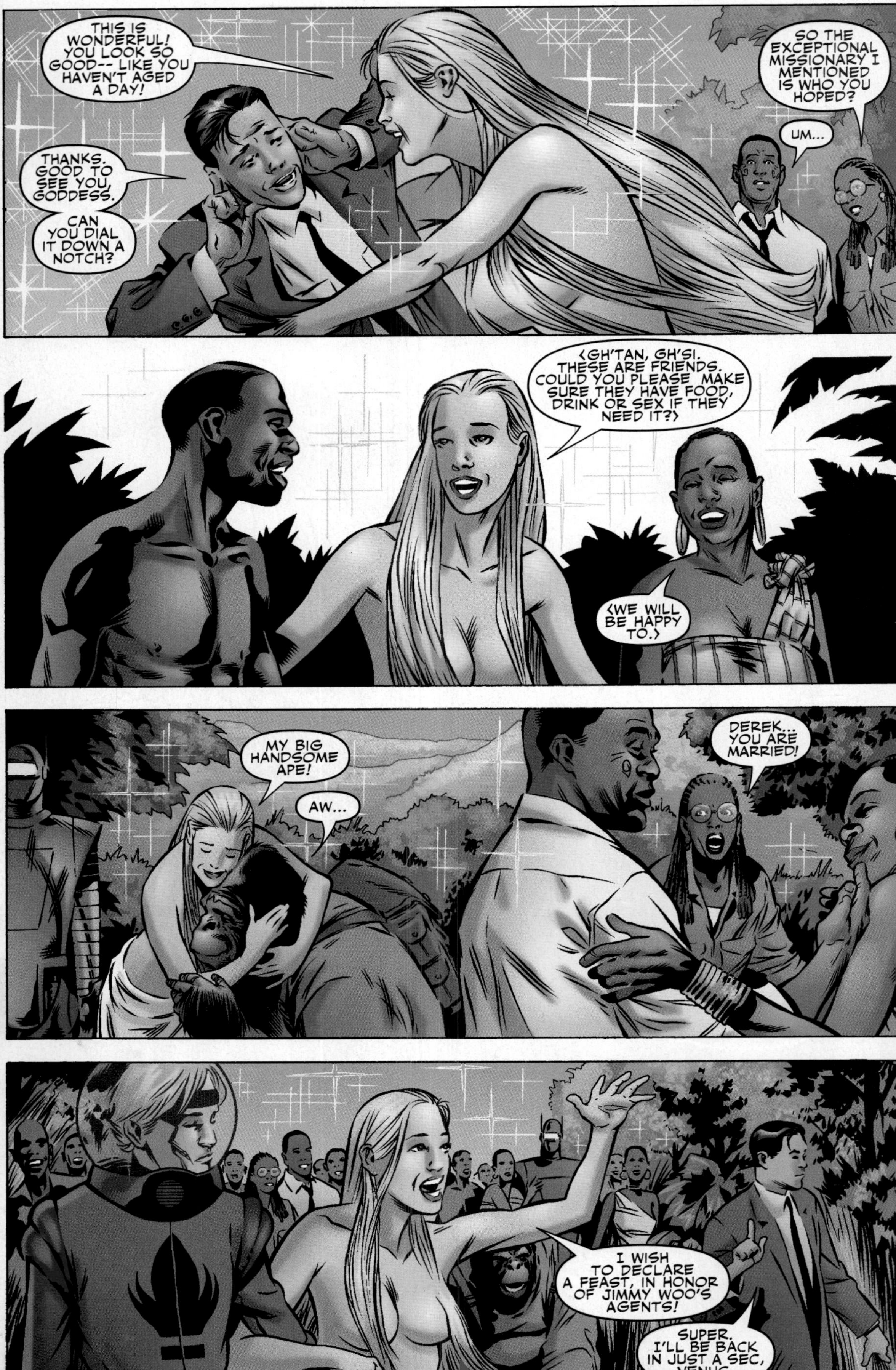
THIS IS WONDERFUL! YOU LOOK SO GOOD-- LIKE YOU HAVEN'T AGED A DAY!
THANKS. GOOD TO SEE YOU, GODDESS.
CAN YOU DIAL IT DOWN A NOTCH?
SO THE EXCEPTIONAL MISSIONARY I MENTIONED IS WHO YOU HOPED?
UM...
<GH'TAN, GH'SI. THESE ARE FRIENDS. COULD YOU PLEASE MAKE SURE THEY HAVE FOOD, DRINK OR SEX IF THEY NEED IT?>
<WE WILL BE HAPPY TO.>
MY BIG HANDSOME APE!
AW...
DEREK... YOU ARE MARRIED!
I WISH TO DECLARE A FEAST, IN HONOR OF JIMMY WOO'S AGENTS!
SUPER. I'LL BE BACK IN JUST A SEC, VENUS.

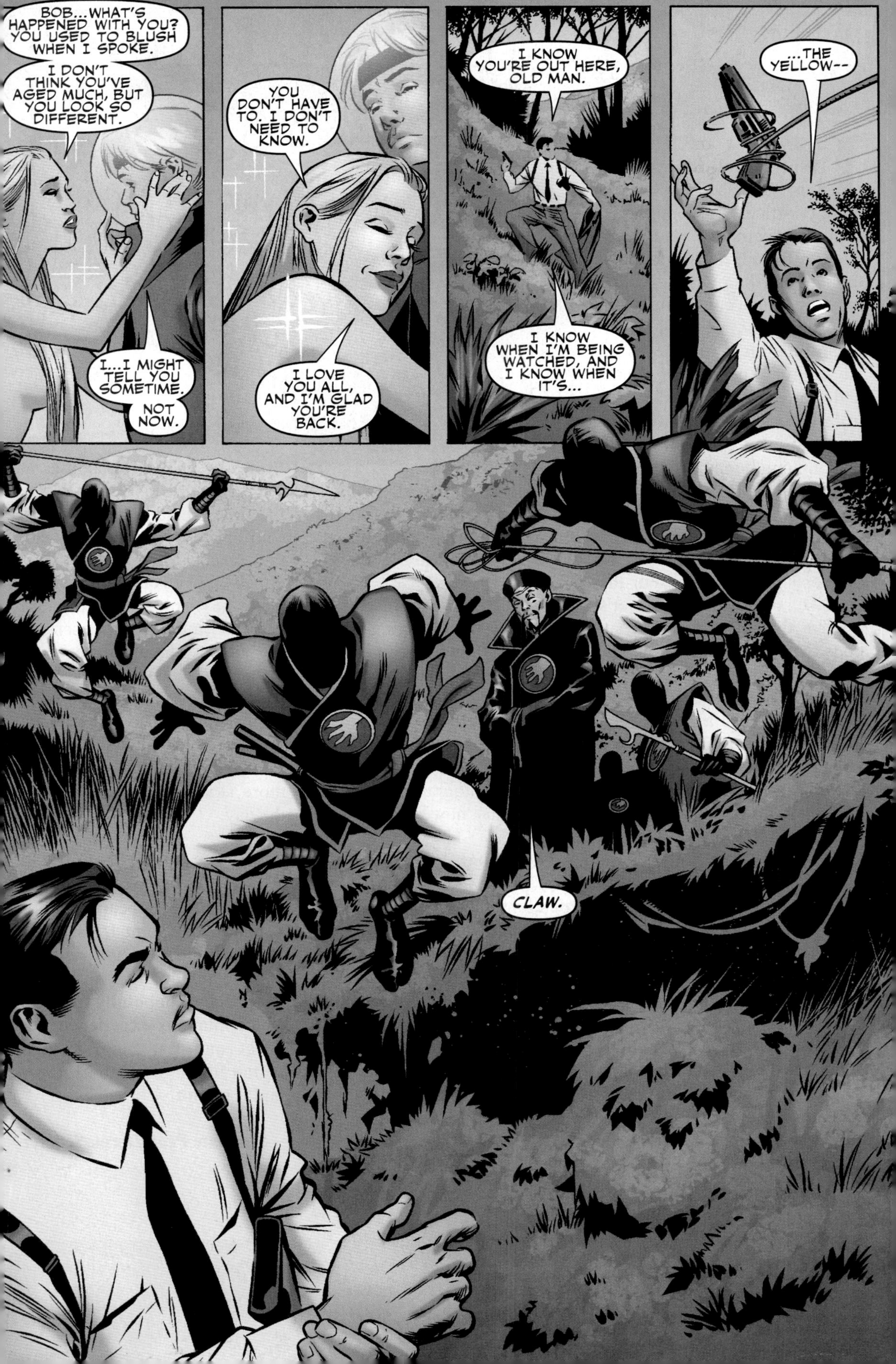
BOB...WHAT'S HAPPENED WITH YOU? YOU USED TO BLUSH WHEN I SPOKE.
I DON'T THINK YOU'VE AGED MUCH, BUT YOU LOOK SO DIFFERENT.
I...I MIGHT TELL YOU SOMETIME.
NOT NOW.
YOU DON'T HAVE TO. I DON'T NEED TO KNOW.
I LOVE YOU ALL, AND I'M GLAD YOU'RE BACK.
I KNOW YOU'RE OUT HERE, OLD MAN.
I KNOW WHEN I'M BEING WATCHED, AND I KNOW WHEN IT'S...
...THE YELLOW--
CLAW.

THE GODS WALK AMONG US

In 1958 at the Hunter's Point Naval Shipyard in San Francisco, I was a young officer susceptible to beautiful women. I had never been affected as profoundly, though, as when I saw a young lady riding in a convertible with a gorilla and a robot. I would later find this woman was an adventurer known as Venus, and many testify that she was in fact the actual deity who had given up many godly powers to walk among humans.

Some of her behavior was perplexing; primarily that Venus would show herself to ordinary humans at all. For the purpose of speculation, let's assume that the Greco-Roman gods were, in fact, real beings. By all accounts, they rarely interacted directly with mortals, preferring to use a go-between of some sort. At times the gods would speak to mortals through statues in their likeness, or through nature, such as animals with traits reflective of them.

Later I found some unreliable accounts of her living in Europe, but nothing concrete until 1948, when she came to New York City. She was in fact working as an editor for the popular magazine, *Beauty*, for publisher Whitney Hammond, under the name Victoria Starr. Searching a paper trail revealed the unfortunate middle name Nutley, which to me seemed an odd choice until one considers her frame of reference may be far different from that of

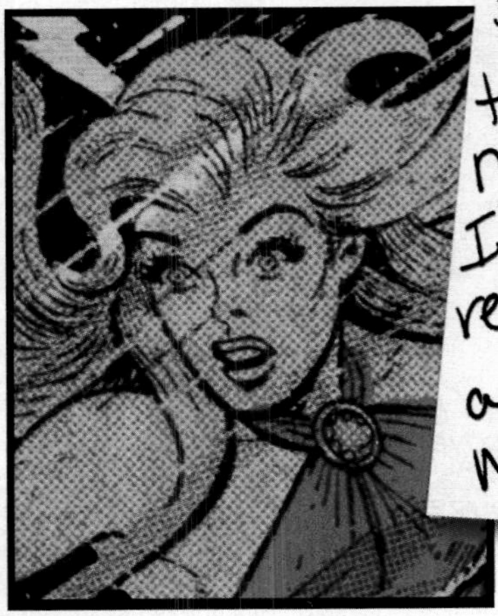

Dugan—
this is the only
noteworthy writing
I've found on the woman
requested so far, from
a Literature Professor.
More coming, I hope.
—Coover

a modern woman. It is likely given her whimsical nature that the name is based on the initials, VNS, a winking sobriquet.

A trait that confuses the records is the changing of her hair color*, which apparently happens at regular intervals. I suspected at first this was due to subjective viewing, as many eyewitnesses could be rendered unreliable upon exposure to Venus. Photographs gathered support this, however.

An interview with the Dutch pop band, Shocking Blue, mentions that they based their 1969 chart-topping hit "Venus" (later covered by Bananarama) on a real woman traveling in their home city. I note this because Venus also seems to be an expert on world languages, soon mastering the local tongue wherever she goes.

Given my chosen life in academia, I was particularly surprised to run across a Vicki Starr in the early 1970's, a Professor of the Humanities at Pepperdine University**. By the time I made it to Southern California to follow this lead, the teacher in question had already moved on. I suspect this was the same Starr because campus interviews described the faculty member as more concerned with organizing peace rallies than in following a curriculum. The rallies were far more peaceful than other anti-war gatherings of the time, more akin to the "love-ins" of the day.

In my upcoming book I will provide documentation of all the possible appearances of Venus to the point I lost track of her in the late 20th-century. Many claim that this work is all in service of hopefully meeting the woman to experience her effect one last time, a final hurrah for an old man. I never said it wasn't.

–Associate Prof. Derek Schiller

*While it would be easy enough for Venus to dye her hair red, blonde, or brunette, one of the pictures- and many accounts- portray her with shimmering silver hair. I've not been made aware of any tonsorial tincture or pigment capable of creating this particular hue.

** An intriguing detail I found while going through her class roster (she only taught two semesters) was the presence of a student named Nita Prentiss. News from the recent catastrophe in Stamford, Connecticut reveal that name as being used by the young Atlantean heroine known as Namorita or Kymaera. The discrepancy in years would seem to refute this until one remembers that Merpeople age at a far slower rate than surface dwellers. That one heroine would have studied under another in a non-adventuring context is of interest, I think.

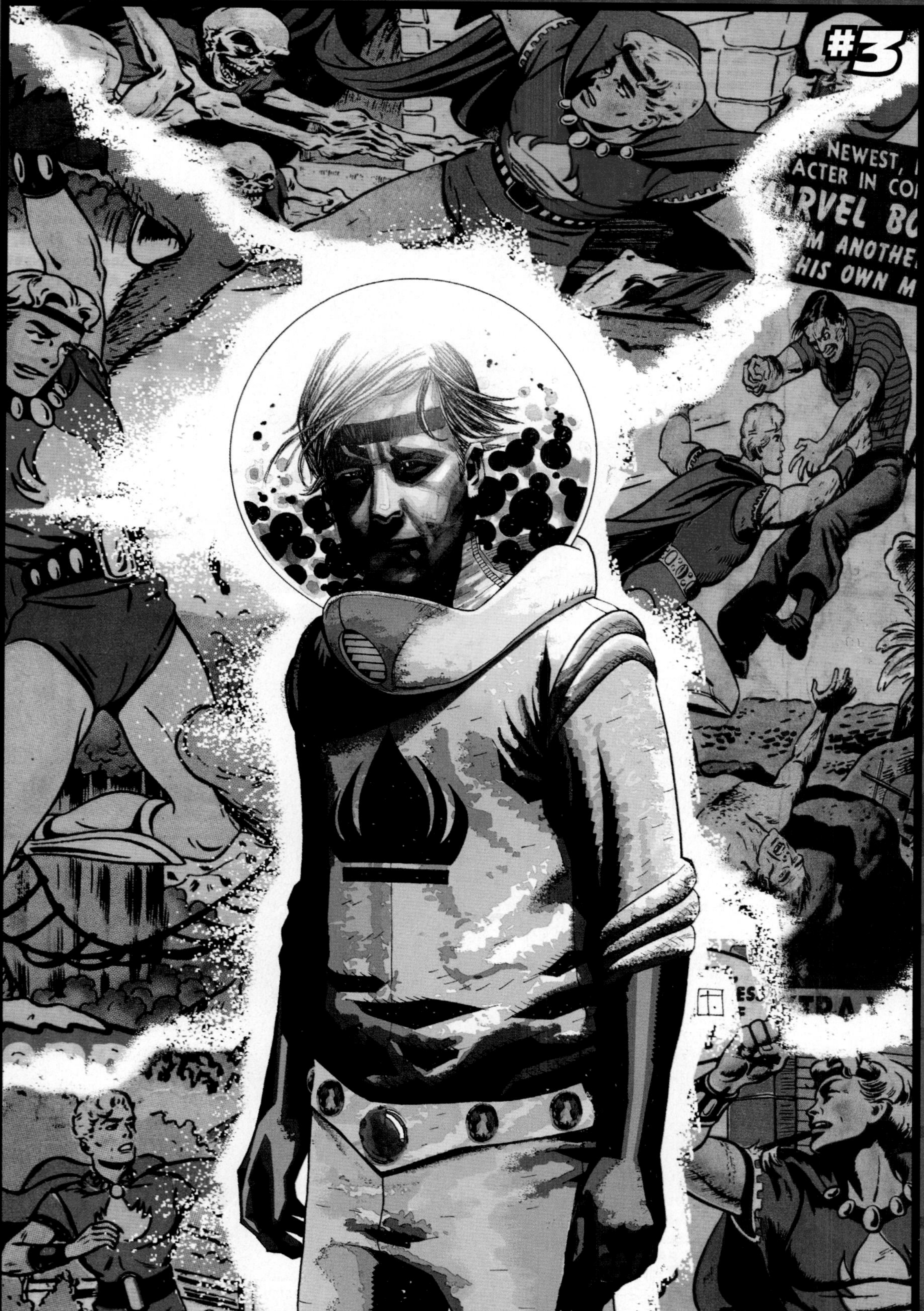
#3

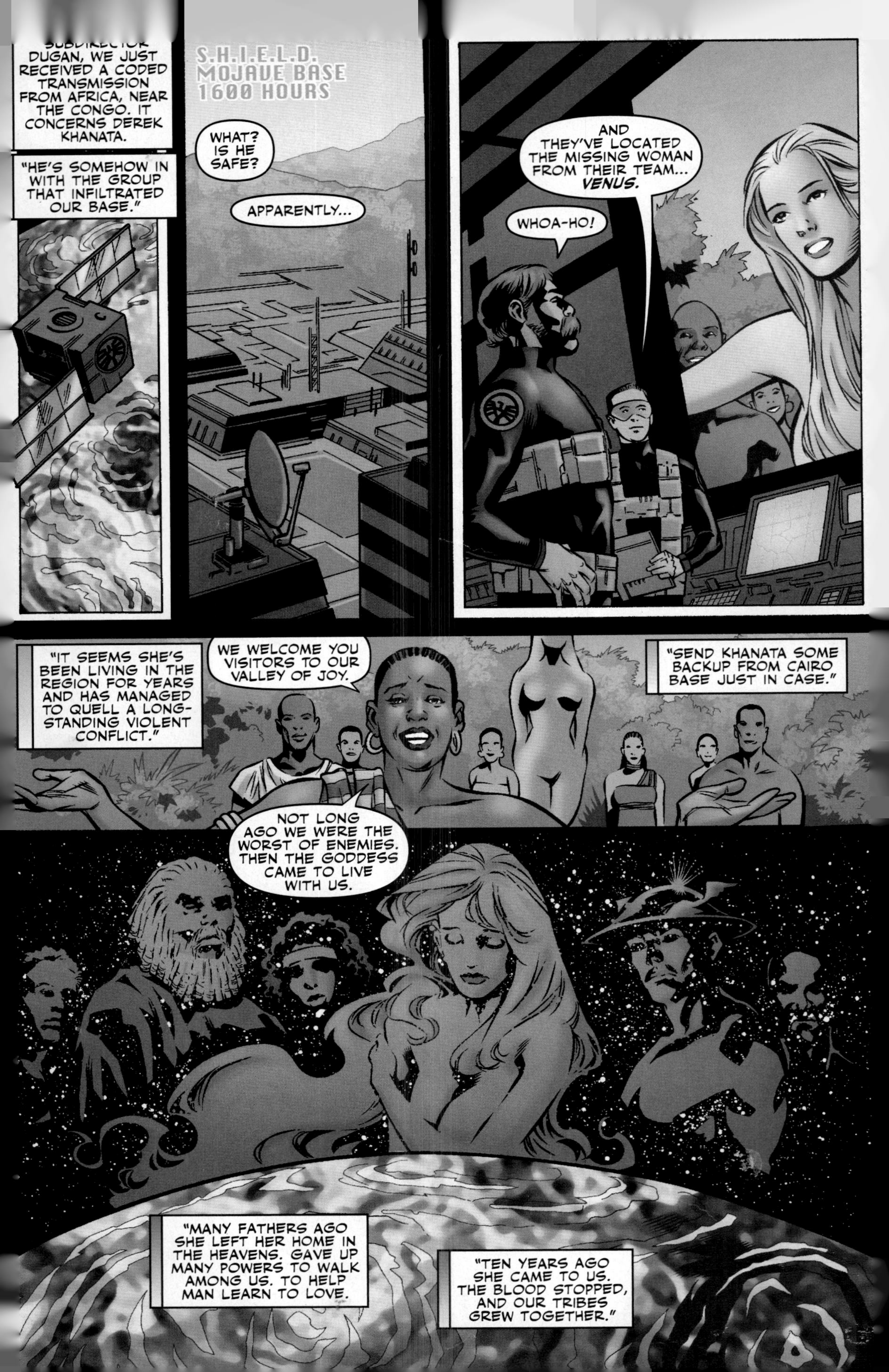
SUBDIRECTOR DUGAN, WE JUST RECEIVED A CODED TRANSMISSION FROM AFRICA, NEAR THE CONGO. IT CONCERNS DEREK KHANATA.
"HE'S SOMEHOW IN WITH THE GROUP THAT INFILTRATED OUR BASE."
S.H.I.E.L.D. MOJAVE BASE 1600 HOURS
WHAT? IS HE SAFE?
APPARENTLY...
AND THEY'VE LOCATED THE MISSING WOMAN FROM THEIR TEAM... VENUS.
WHOA-HO!
"IT SEEMS SHE'S BEEN LIVING IN THE REGION FOR YEARS AND HAS MANAGED TO QUELL A LONG-STANDING VIOLENT CONFLICT."
WE WELCOME YOU VISITORS TO OUR VALLEY OF JOY.
"SEND KHANATA SOME BACKUP FROM CAIRO BASE JUST IN CASE."
NOT LONG AGO WE WERE THE WORST OF ENEMIES. THEN THE GODDESS CAME TO LIVE WITH US.
"MANY FATHERS AGO SHE LEFT HER HOME IN THE HEAVENS. GAVE UP MANY POWERS TO WALK AMONG US. TO HELP MAN LEARN TO LOVE.
"TEN YEARS AGO SHE CAME TO US. THE BLOOD STOPPED, AND OUR TRIBES GREW TOGETHER."

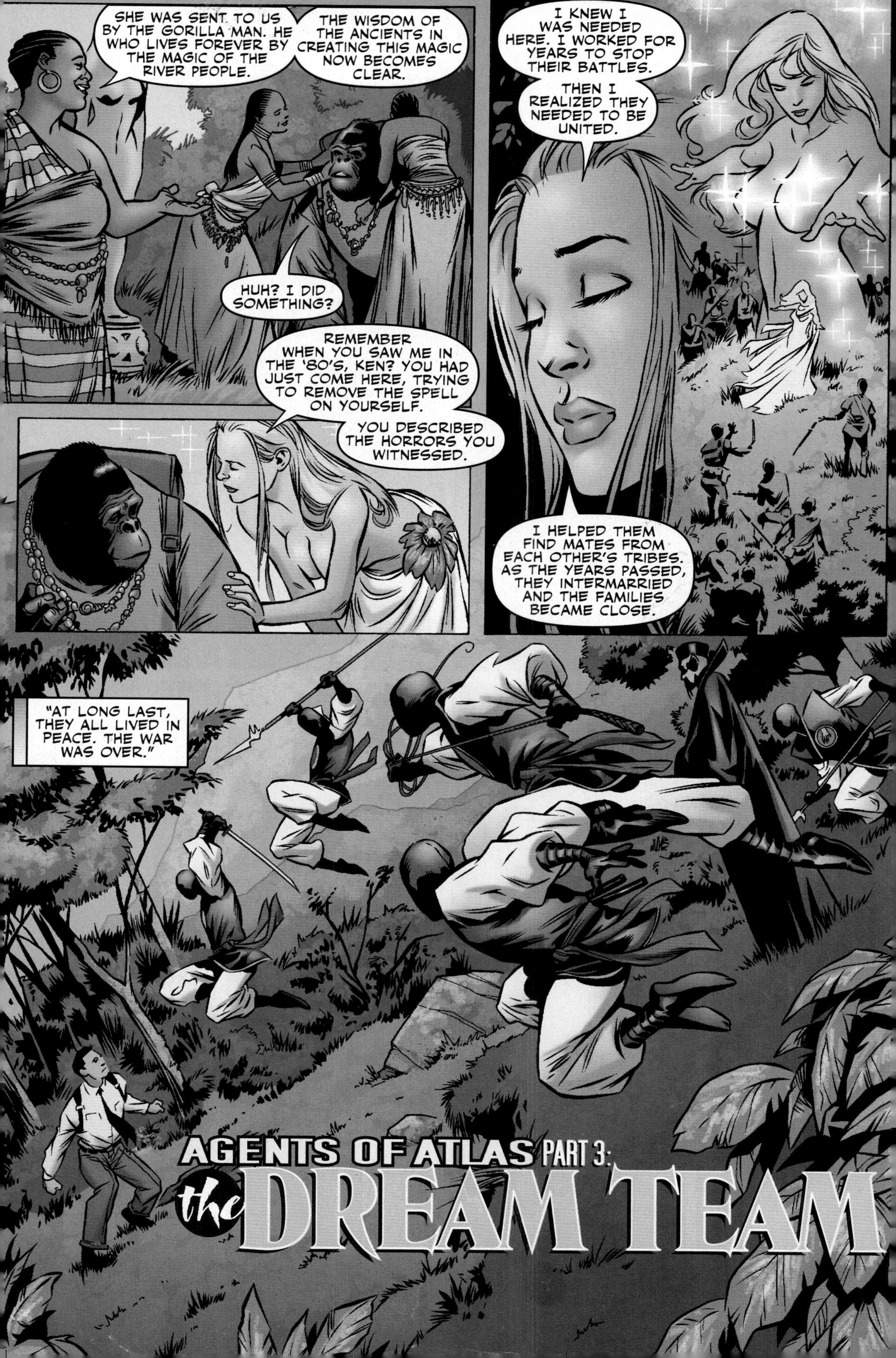
SHE WAS SENT TO US BY THE GORILLA MAN. HE WHO LIVES FOREVER BY THE MAGIC OF THE RIVER PEOPLE.
THE WISDOM OF THE ANCIENTS IN CREATING THIS MAGIC NOW BECOMES CLEAR.
HUH? I DID SOMETHING?
REMEMBER WHEN YOU SAW ME IN THE '80'S, KEN? YOU HAD JUST COME HERE, TRYING TO REMOVE THE SPELL ON YOURSELF.
YOU DESCRIBED THE HORRORS YOU WITNESSED.
I KNEW I WAS NEEDED HERE. I WORKED FOR YEARS TO STOP THEIR BATTLES.
THEN I REALIZED THEY NEEDED TO BE UNITED.
I HELPED THEM FIND MATES FROM EACH OTHER'S TRIBES. AS THE YEARS PASSED, THEY INTERMARRIED AND THE FAMILIES BECAME CLOSE.
"AT LONG LAST, THEY ALL LIVED IN PEACE. THE WAR WAS OVER."
AGENTS OF ATLAS PART 3:
the DREAM TEAM

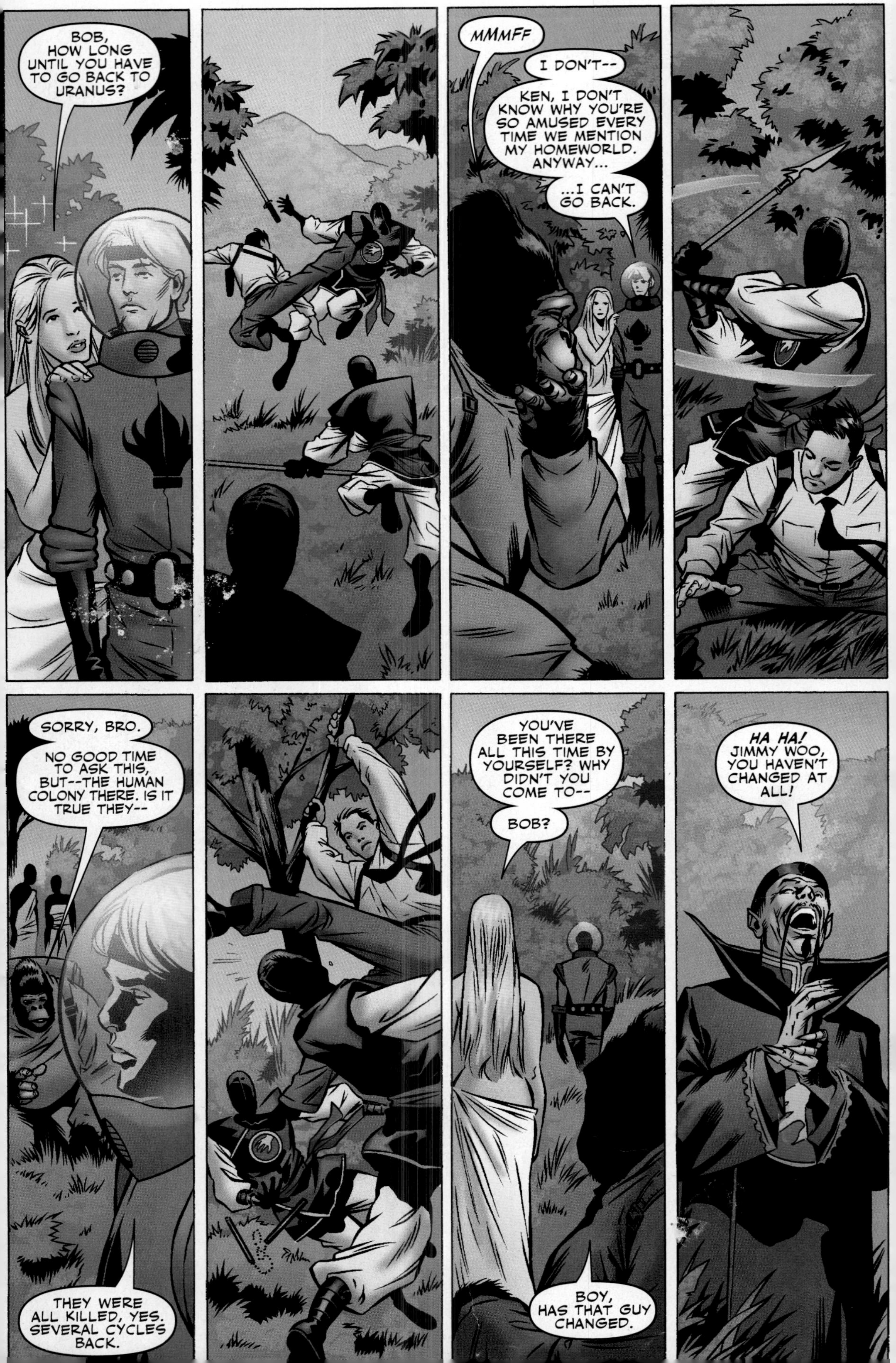
BOB, HOW LONG UNTIL YOU HAVE TO GO BACK TO URANUS?
MMMFF
I DON'T--
KEN, I DON'T KNOW WHY YOU'RE SO AMUSED EVERY TIME WE MENTION MY HOMEWORLD. ANYWAY...
...I CAN'T GO BACK.
SORRY, BRO.
NO GOOD TIME TO ASK THIS, BUT--THE HUMAN COLONY THERE. IS IT TRUE THEY--
THEY WERE ALL KILLED, YES. SEVERAL CYCLES BACK.
YOU'VE BEEN THERE ALL THIS TIME BY YOURSELF? WHY DIDN'T YOU COME TO--
BOB?
BOY, HAS THAT GUY CHANGED.
HA HA! JIMMY WOO, YOU HAVEN'T CHANGED AT ALL!

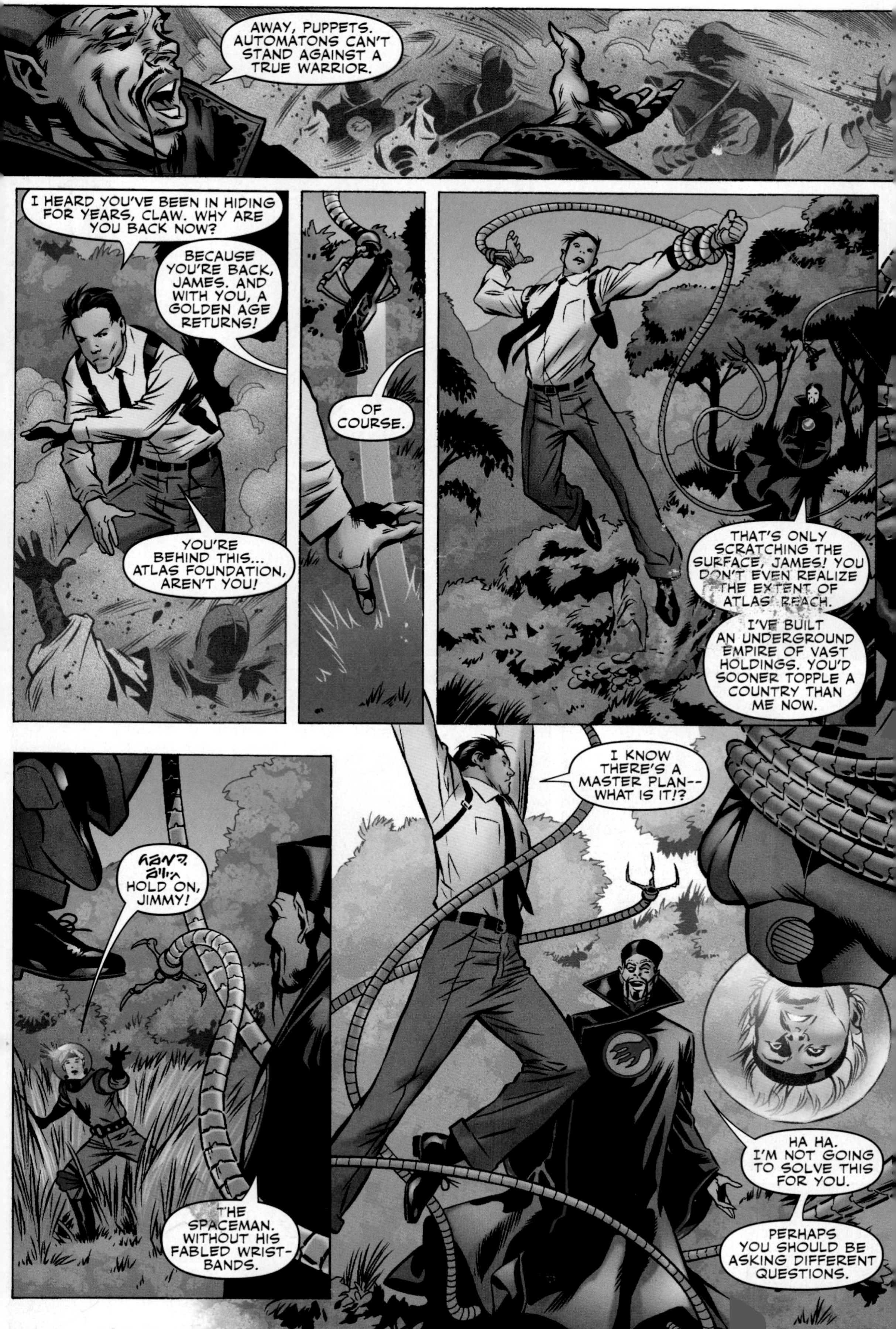
AWAY, PUPPETS. AUTOMATONS CAN'T STAND AGAINST A TRUE WARRIOR.
I HEARD YOU'VE BEEN IN HIDING FOR YEARS, CLAW. WHY ARE YOU BACK NOW?
BECAUSE YOU'RE BACK, JAMES. AND WITH YOU, A GOLDEN AGE RETURNS!
YOU'RE BEHIND THIS... ATLAS FOUNDATION, AREN'T YOU!
OF COURSE.
THAT'S ONLY SCRATCHING THE SURFACE, JAMES! YOU DON'T EVEN REALIZE THE EXTENT OF ATLAS' REACH.
I'VE BUILT AN UNDERGROUND EMPIRE OF VAST HOLDINGS. YOU'D SOONER TOPPLE A COUNTRY THAN ME NOW.
I KNOW THERE'S A MASTER PLAN-- WHAT IS IT!?
HOLD ON, JIMMY!
THE SPACEMAN. WITHOUT HIS FABLED WRIST-BANDS.
HA HA. I'M NOT GOING TO SOLVE THIS FOR YOU.
PERHAPS YOU SHOULD BE ASKING DIFFERENT QUESTIONS.

DO YOU REALIZE YOU'VE NEVER EVEN ASKED MY REAL NAME?

GOT HIM!

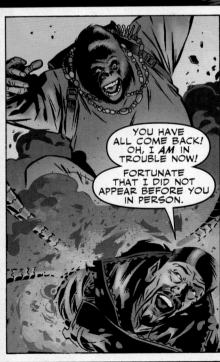

YOU HAVE ALL COME BACK! OH, I *AM* IN TROUBLE NOW!

FORTUNATE THAT I DID NOT APPEAR BEFORE YOU IN PERSON.

I MUST PREPARE FOR YOUR CERTAIN INVASION.

YOU STILL MUST FIND ME AND DESTROY ME! PREPARE WELL!

YOU CAN DO IT, JAMES-- I KNOW IT!

UH...

DID THE YELLOW CLAW JUST GIVE ME A PEP TALK?

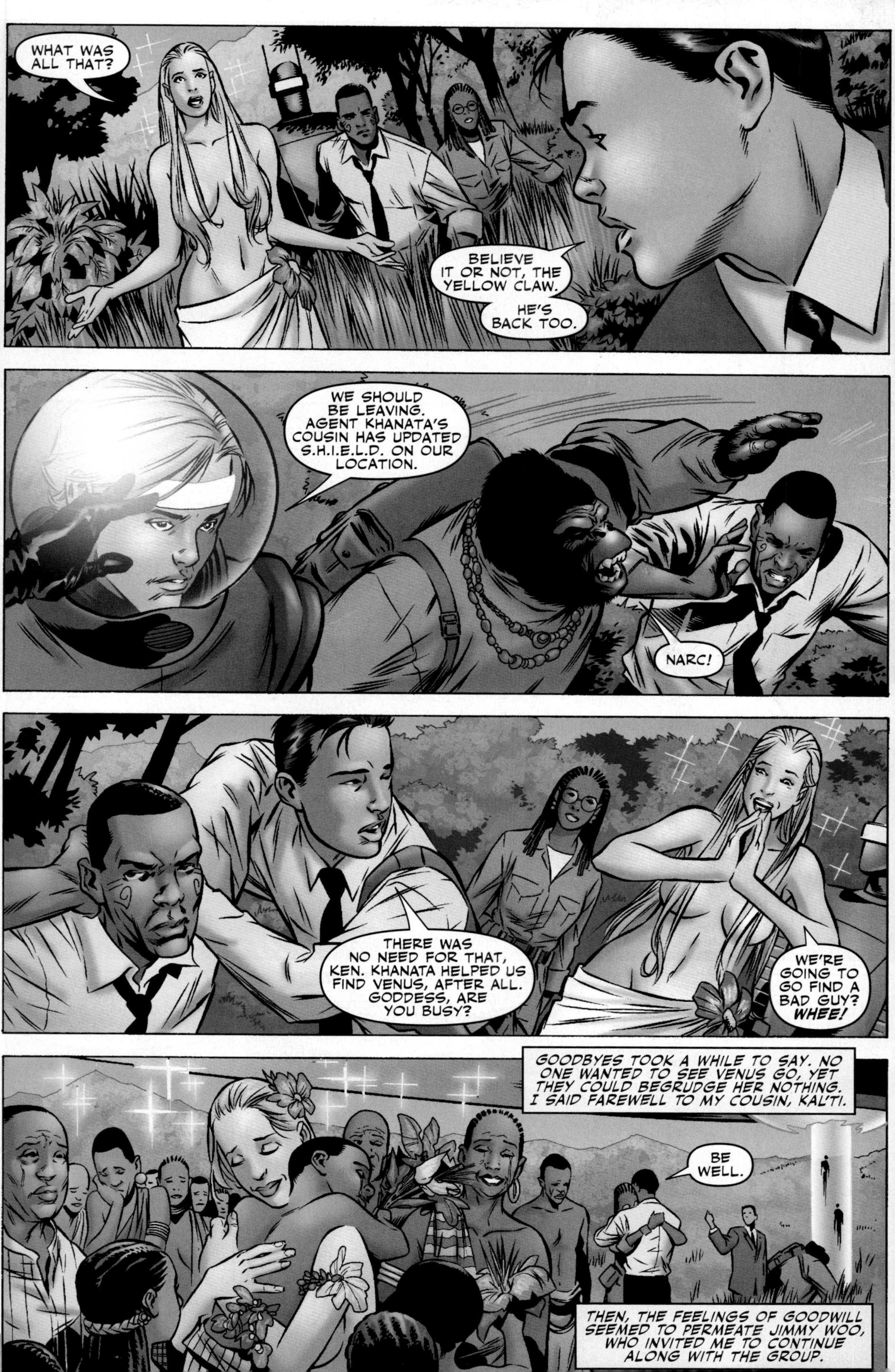
WHAT WAS ALL THAT?
BELIEVE IT OR NOT, THE YELLOW CLAW.
HE'S BACK TOO.
WE SHOULD BE LEAVING. AGENT KHANATA'S COUSIN HAS UPDATED S.H.I.E.L.D. ON OUR LOCATION.
NARC!
THERE WAS NO NEED FOR THAT, KEN. KHANATA HELPED US FIND VENUS, AFTER ALL. GODDESS, ARE YOU BUSY?
WE'RE GOING TO GO FIND A BAD GUY? *WHEE!*
GOODBYES TOOK A WHILE TO SAY. NO ONE WANTED TO SEE VENUS GO, YET THEY COULD BEGRUDGE HER NOTHING. I SAID FAREWELL TO MY COUSIN, KAL'TI.
BE WELL.
THEN, THE FEELINGS OF GOODWILL SEEMED TO PERMEATE JIMMY WOO, WHO INVITED ME TO CONTINUE ALONG WITH THE GROUP.

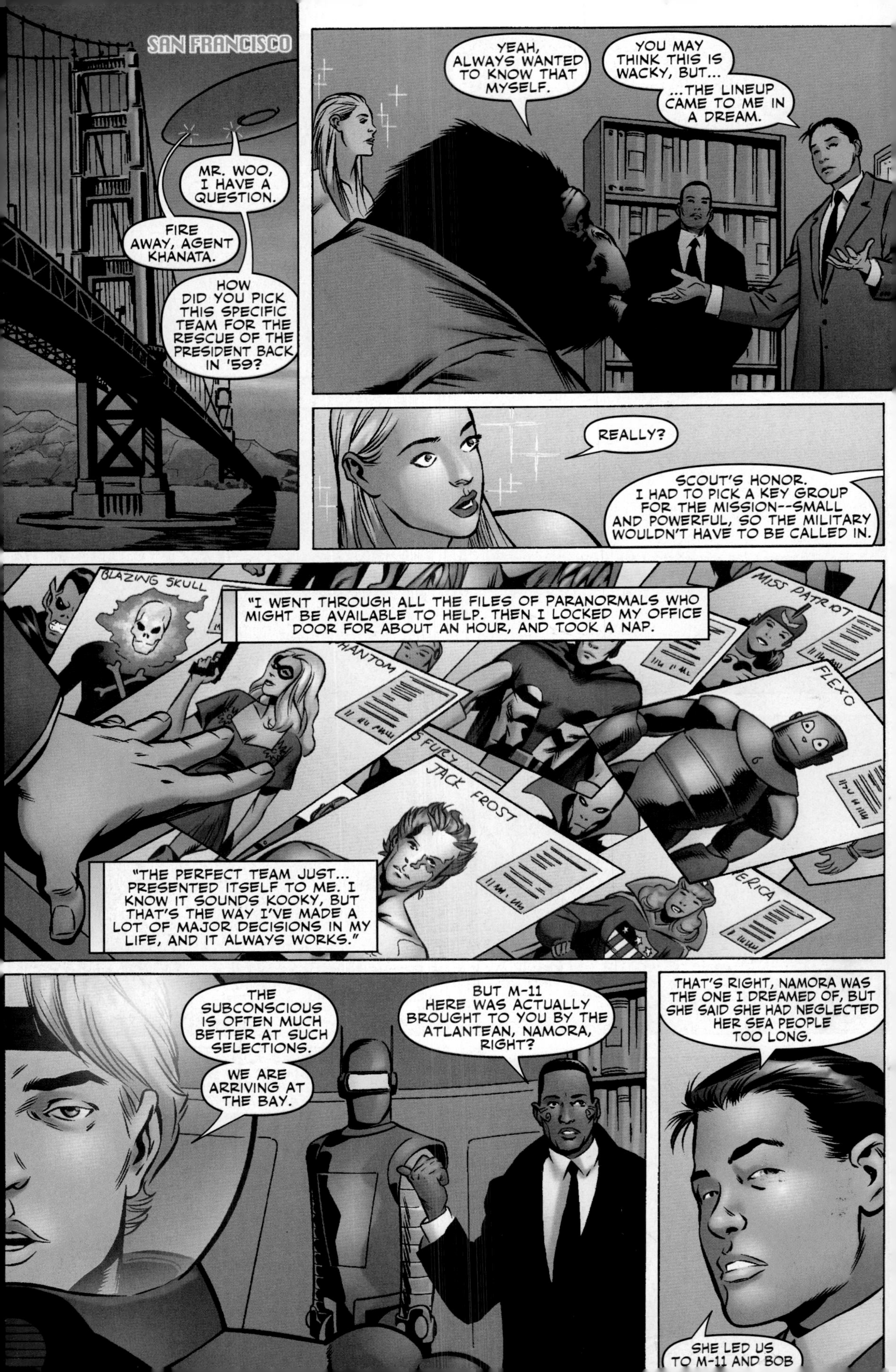
SAN FRANCISCO
MR. WOO, I HAVE A QUESTION.
FIRE AWAY, AGENT KHANATA.
HOW DID YOU PICK THIS SPECIFIC TEAM FOR THE RESCUE OF THE PRESIDENT BACK IN '59?
YEAH, ALWAYS WANTED TO KNOW THAT MYSELF.
YOU MAY THINK THIS IS WACKY, BUT...
...THE LINEUP CAME TO ME IN A DREAM.
REALLY?
SCOUT'S HONOR. I HAD TO PICK A KEY GROUP FOR THE MISSION--SMALL AND POWERFUL, SO THE MILITARY WOULDN'T HAVE TO BE CALLED IN.
"I WENT THROUGH ALL THE FILES OF PARANORMALS WHO MIGHT BE AVAILABLE TO HELP. THEN I LOCKED MY OFFICE DOOR FOR ABOUT AN HOUR, AND TOOK A NAP.
BLAZING SKULL
MISS PATRIOT
FLEXO
JACK FROST
"THE PERFECT TEAM JUST... PRESENTED ITSELF TO ME. I KNOW IT SOUNDS KOOKY, BUT THAT'S THE WAY I'VE MADE A LOT OF MAJOR DECISIONS IN MY LIFE, AND IT ALWAYS WORKS."
THE SUBCONSCIOUS IS OFTEN MUCH BETTER AT SUCH SELECTIONS.
WE ARE ARRIVING AT THE BAY.
BUT M-11 HERE WAS ACTUALLY BROUGHT TO YOU BY THE ATLANTEAN, NAMORA, RIGHT?
THAT'S RIGHT, NAMORA WAS THE ONE I DREAMED OF, BUT SHE SAID SHE HAD NEGLECTED HER SEA PEOPLE TOO LONG.
SHE LED US TO M-11 AND BOB

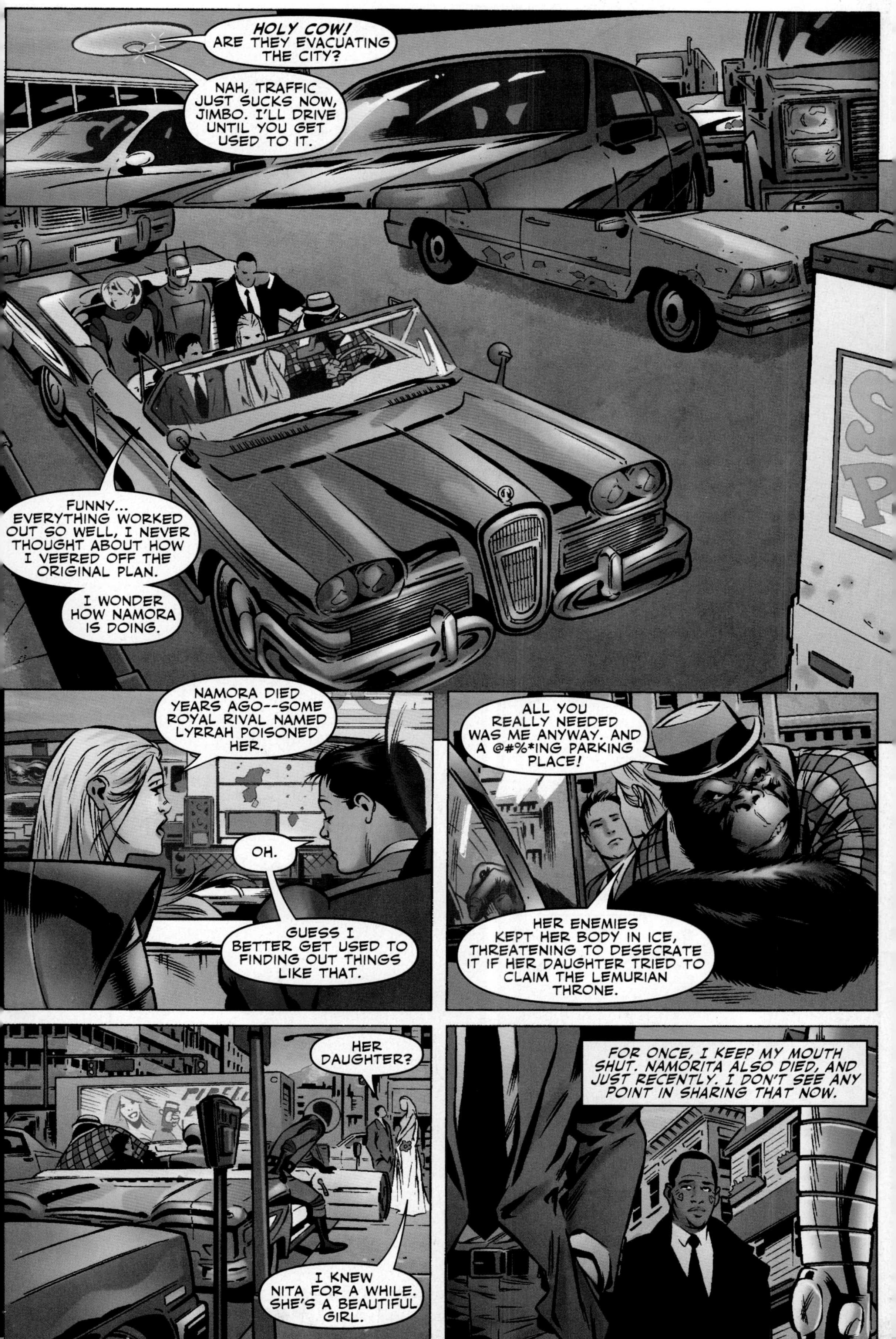
HOLY COW! ARE THEY EVACUATING THE CITY?
NAH, TRAFFIC JUST SUCKS NOW, JIMBO. I'LL DRIVE UNTIL YOU GET USED TO IT.
FUNNY... EVERYTHING WORKED OUT SO WELL, I NEVER THOUGHT ABOUT HOW I VEERED OFF THE ORIGINAL PLAN.
I WONDER HOW NAMORA IS DOING.
NAMORA DIED YEARS AGO--SOME ROYAL RIVAL NAMED LYRRAH POISONED HER.
OH.
GUESS I BETTER GET USED TO FINDING OUT THINGS LIKE THAT.
ALL YOU REALLY NEEDED WAS ME ANYWAY. AND A @#%*ING PARKING PLACE!
HER ENEMIES KEPT HER BODY IN ICE, THREATENING TO DESECRATE IT IF HER DAUGHTER TRIED TO CLAIM THE LEMURIAN THRONE.
HER DAUGHTER?
I KNEW NITA FOR A WHILE. SHE'S A BEAUTIFUL GIRL.
FOR ONCE, I KEEP MY MOUTH SHUT. NAMORITA ALSO DIED, AND JUST RECENTLY. I DON'T SEE ANY POINT IN SHARING THAT NOW.

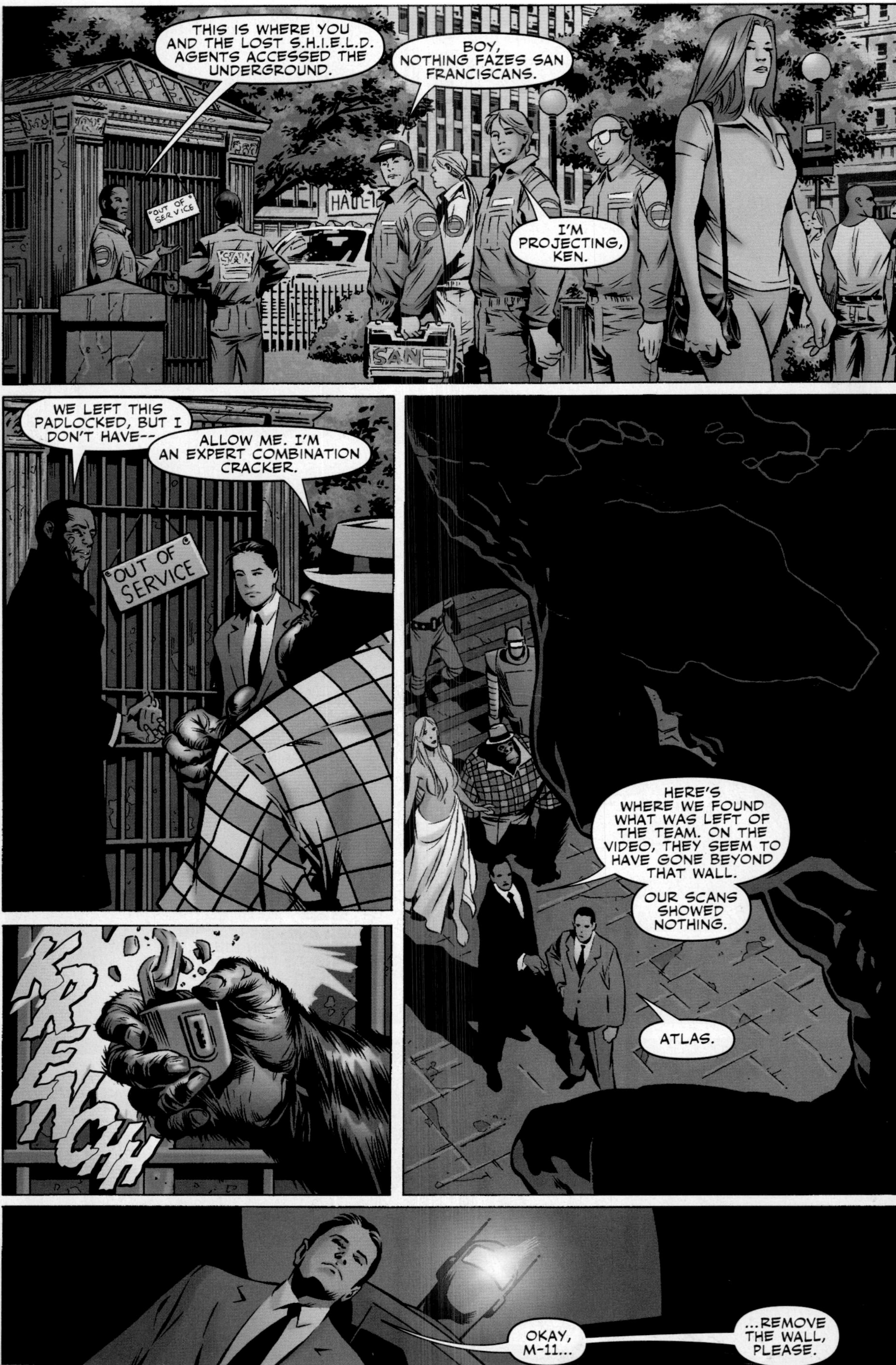
THIS IS WHERE YOU AND THE LOST S.H.I.E.L.D. AGENTS ACCESSED THE UNDERGROUND.
OUT OF SERVICE
BOY, NOTHING FAZES SAN FRANCISCANS.
I'M PROJECTING, KEN.
SAN
WE LEFT THIS PADLOCKED, BUT I DON'T HAVE--
ALLOW ME. I'M AN EXPERT COMBINATION CRACKER.
OUT OF SERVICE
KRENCHH
HERE'S WHERE WE FOUND WHAT WAS LEFT OF THE TEAM. ON THE VIDEO, THEY SEEM TO HAVE GONE BEYOND THAT WALL.
OUR SCANS SHOWED NOTHING.
ATLAS.
OKAY, M-11...
...REMOVE THE WALL, PLEASE.

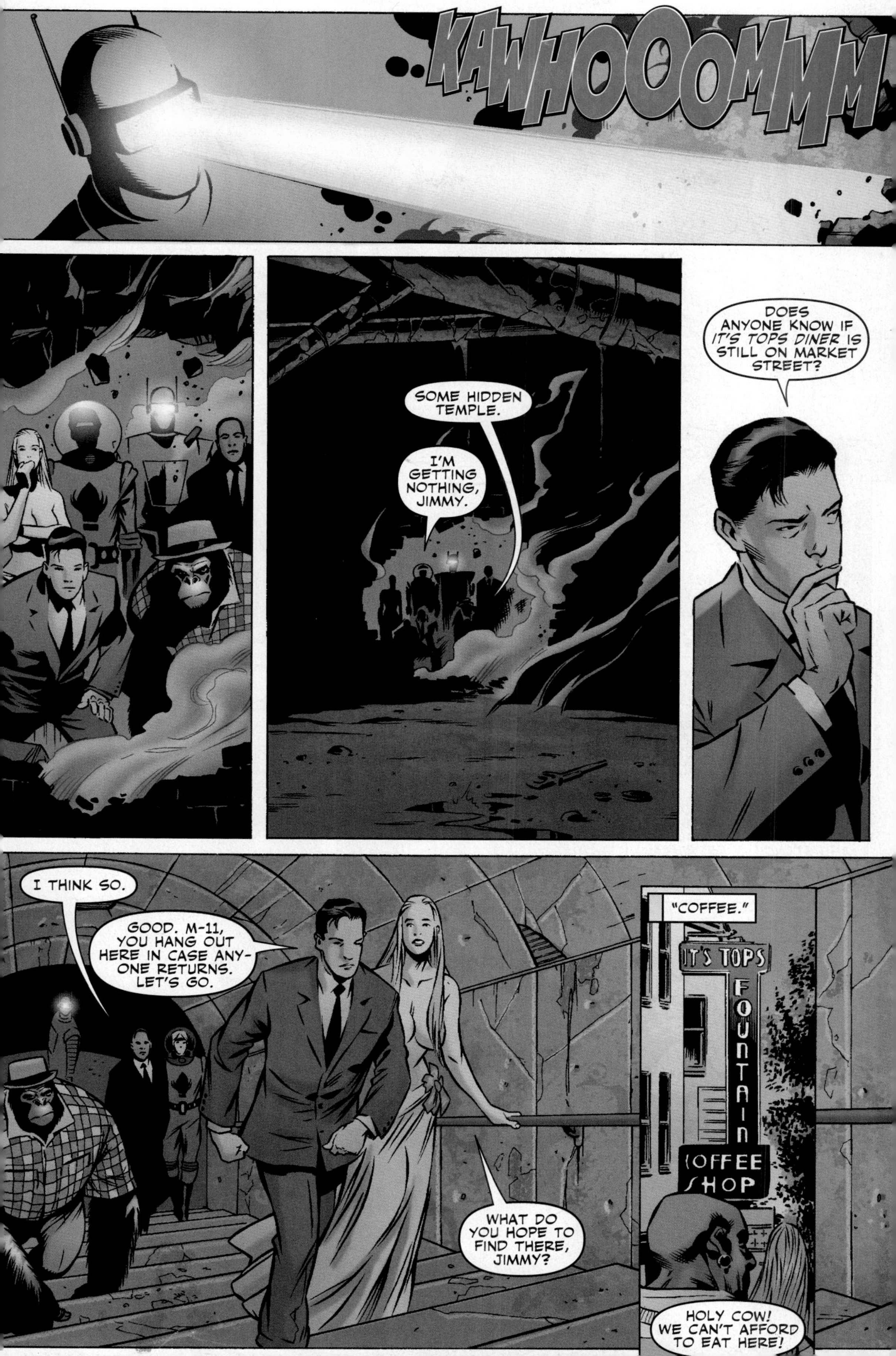
KAWHOOOOMMMM
SOME HIDDEN TEMPLE.
I'M GETTING NOTHING, JIMMY.
DOES ANYONE KNOW IF IT'S TOPS DINER IS STILL ON MARKET STREET?
I THINK SO.
GOOD. M-11, YOU HANG OUT HERE IN CASE ANY-ONE RETURNS. LET'S GO.
WHAT DO YOU HOPE TO FIND THERE, JIMMY?
"COFFEE."
IT'S TOPS
FOUNTAIN
COFFEE SHOP
HOLY COW! WE CAN'T AFFORD TO EAT HERE!

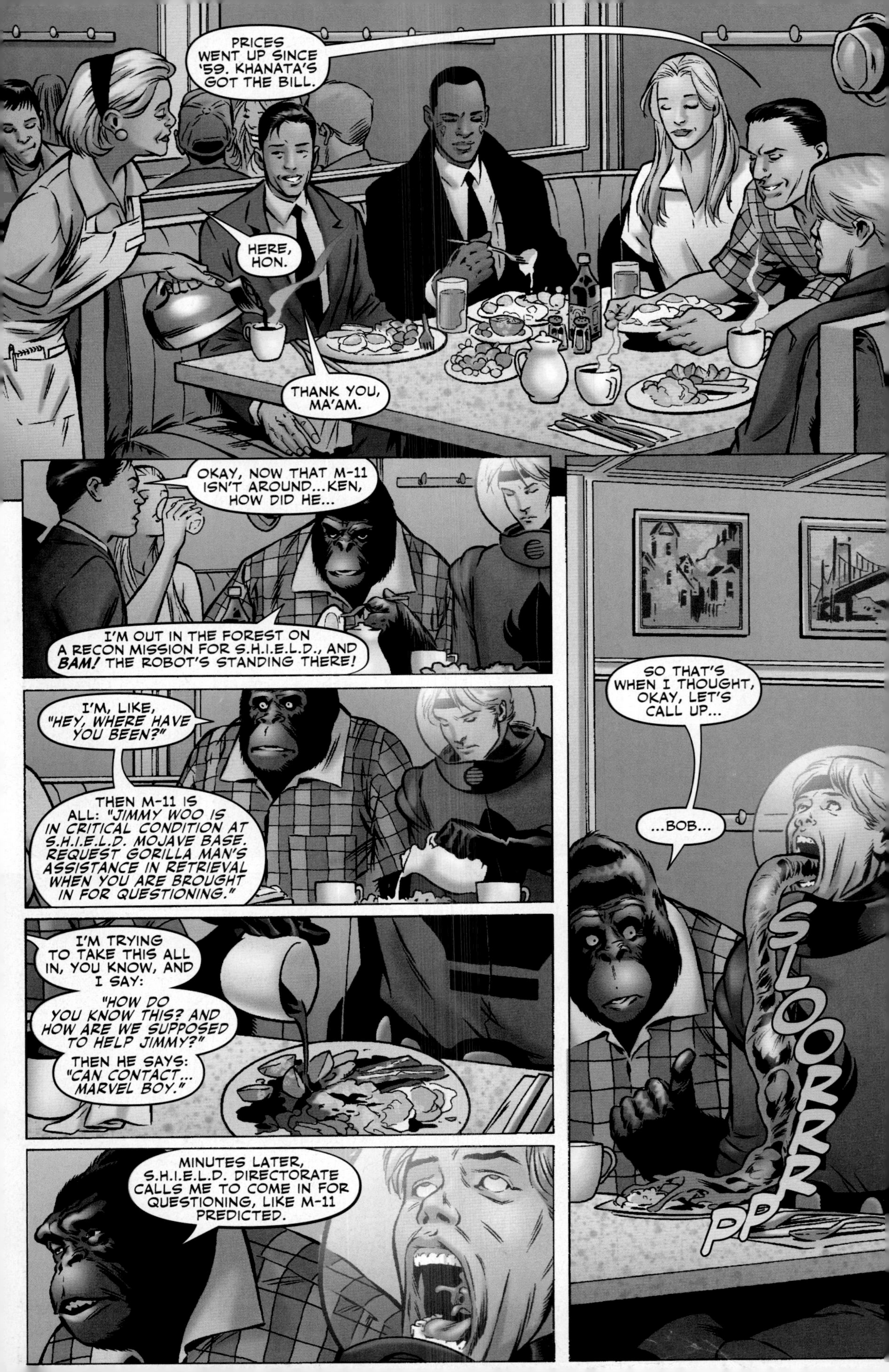
PRICES WENT UP SINCE '59. KHANATA'S GOT THE BILL.
HERE, HON.
THANK YOU, MA'AM.
OKAY, NOW THAT M-11 ISN'T AROUND...KEN, HOW DID HE...
I'M OUT IN THE FOREST ON A RECON MISSION FOR S.H.I.E.L.D., AND BAM! THE ROBOT'S STANDING THERE!
I'M, LIKE, "HEY, WHERE HAVE YOU BEEN?"
THEN M-11 IS ALL: "JIMMY WOO IS IN CRITICAL CONDITION AT S.H.I.E.L.D. MOJAVE BASE. REQUEST GORILLA MAN'S ASSISTANCE IN RETRIEVAL WHEN YOU ARE BROUGHT IN FOR QUESTIONING."
I'M TRYING TO TAKE THIS ALL IN, YOU KNOW, AND I SAY:
"HOW DO YOU KNOW THIS? AND HOW ARE WE SUPPOSED TO HELP JIMMY?"
THEN HE SAYS: "CAN CONTACT... MARVEL BOY."
MINUTES LATER, S.H.I.E.L.D. DIRECTORATE CALLS ME TO COME IN FOR QUESTIONING, LIKE M-11 PREDICTED.
SO THAT'S WHEN I THOUGHT, OKAY, LET'S CALL UP...
...BOB...
SLOORRRRPP

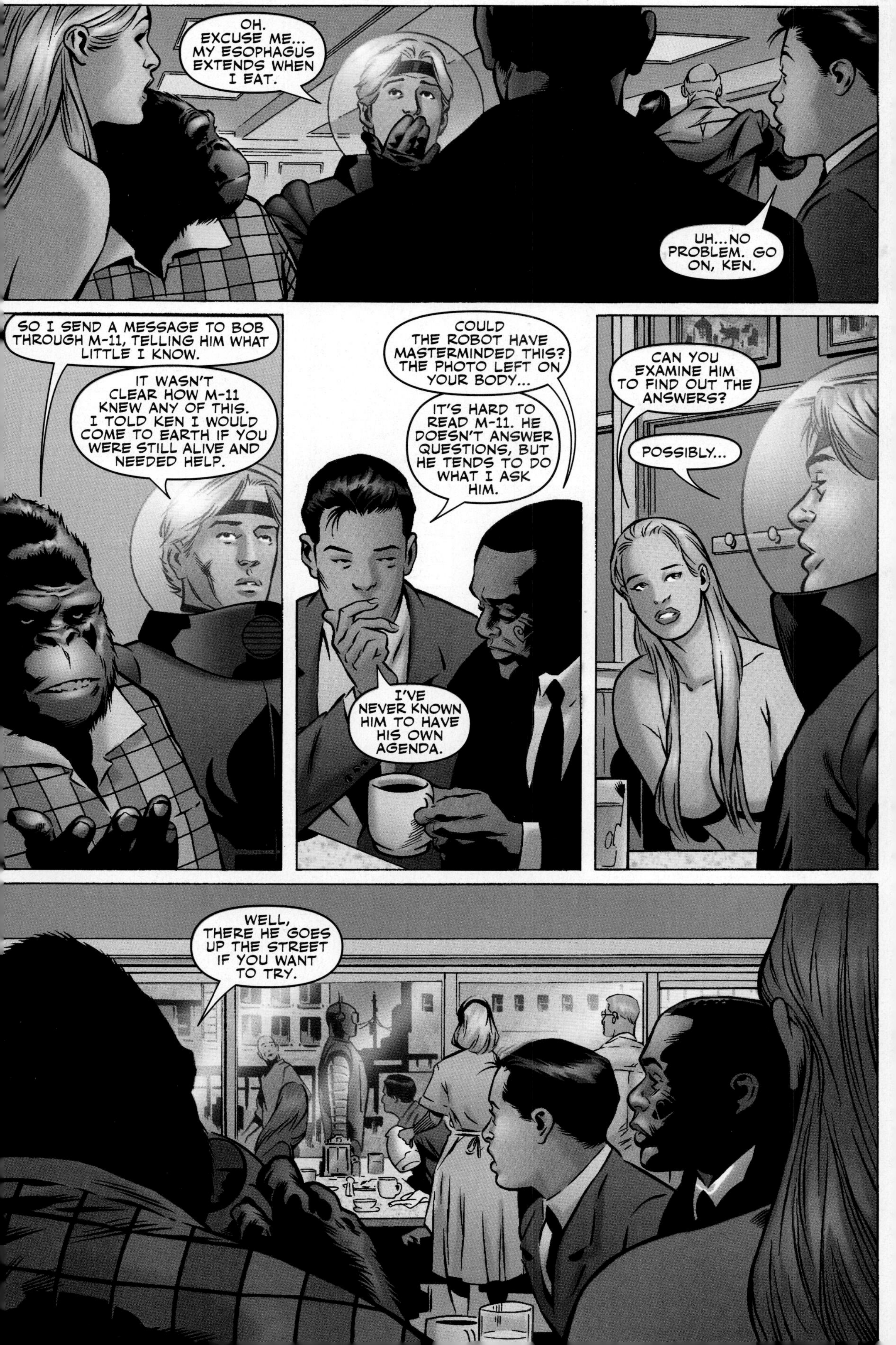
OH. EXCUSE ME... MY ESOPHAGUS EXTENDS WHEN I EAT.
UH...NO PROBLEM. GO ON, KEN.
SO I SEND A MESSAGE TO BOB THROUGH M-11, TELLING HIM WHAT LITTLE I KNOW.
IT WASN'T CLEAR HOW M-11 KNEW ANY OF THIS. I TOLD KEN I WOULD COME TO EARTH IF YOU WERE STILL ALIVE AND NEEDED HELP.
COULD THE ROBOT HAVE MASTERMINDED THIS? THE PHOTO LEFT ON YOUR BODY...
IT'S HARD TO READ M-11. HE DOESN'T ANSWER QUESTIONS, BUT HE TENDS TO DO WHAT I ASK HIM.
I'VE NEVER KNOWN HIM TO HAVE HIS OWN AGENDA.
CAN YOU EXAMINE HIM TO FIND OUT THE ANSWERS?
POSSIBLY...
WELL, THERE HE GOES UP THE STREET IF YOU WANT TO TRY.

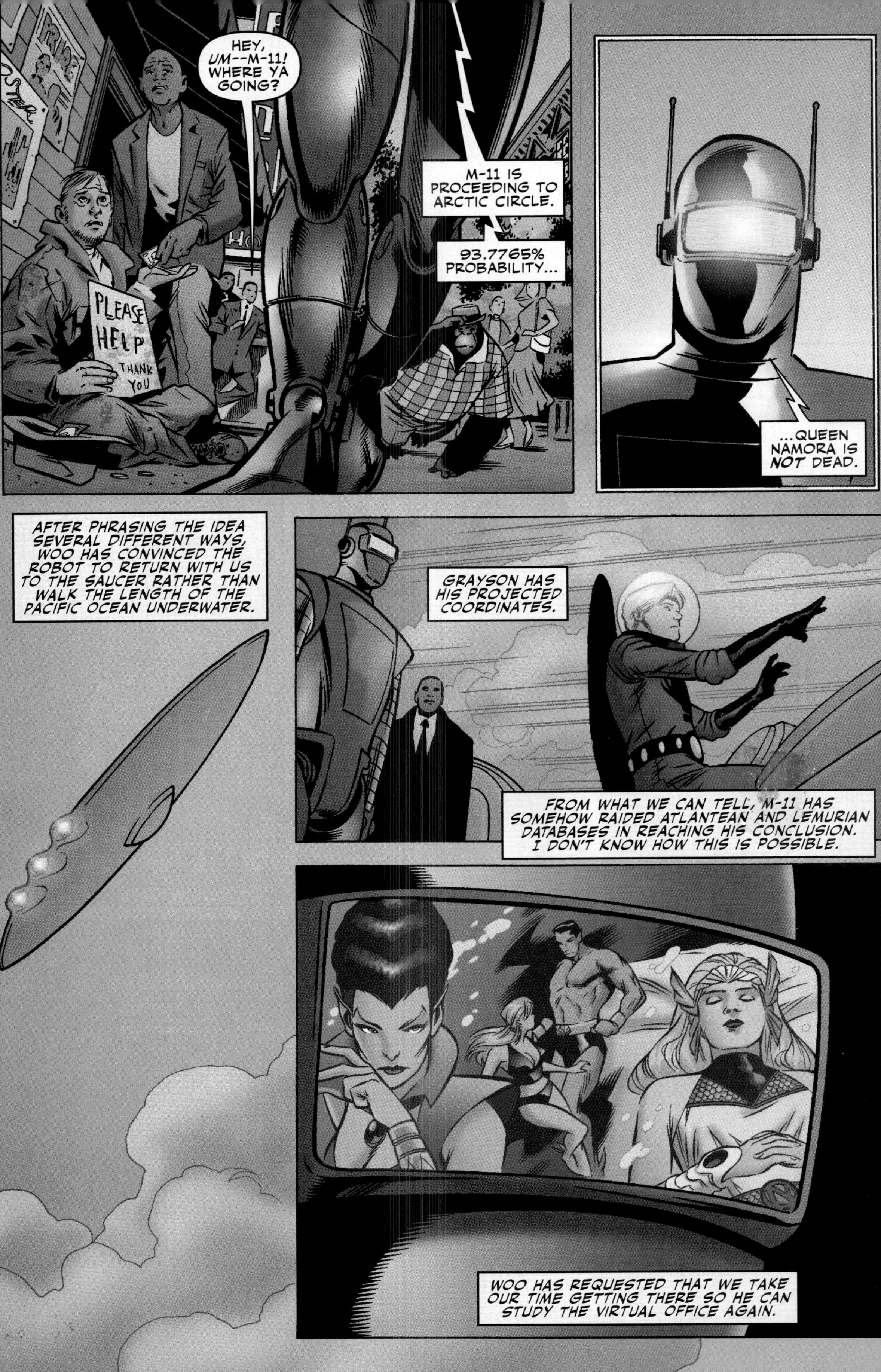
HEY, UM--M-11! WHERE YA GOING?
PLEASE HELP THANK YOU
M-11 IS PROCEEDING TO ARCTIC CIRCLE.
93.7765% PROBABILITY...
...QUEEN NAMORA IS NOT DEAD.
AFTER PHRASING THE IDEA SEVERAL DIFFERENT WAYS, WOO HAS CONVINCED THE ROBOT TO RETURN WITH US TO THE SAUCER RATHER THAN WALK THE LENGTH OF THE PACIFIC OCEAN UNDERWATER.
GRAYSON HAS HIS PROJECTED COORDINATES.
FROM WHAT WE CAN TELL, M-11 HAS SOMEHOW RAIDED ATLANTEAN AND LEMURIAN DATABASES IN REACHING HIS CONCLUSION. I DON'T KNOW HOW THIS IS POSSIBLE.
WOO HAS REQUESTED THAT WE TAKE OUR TIME GETTING THERE SO HE CAN STUDY THE VIRTUAL OFFICE AGAIN.

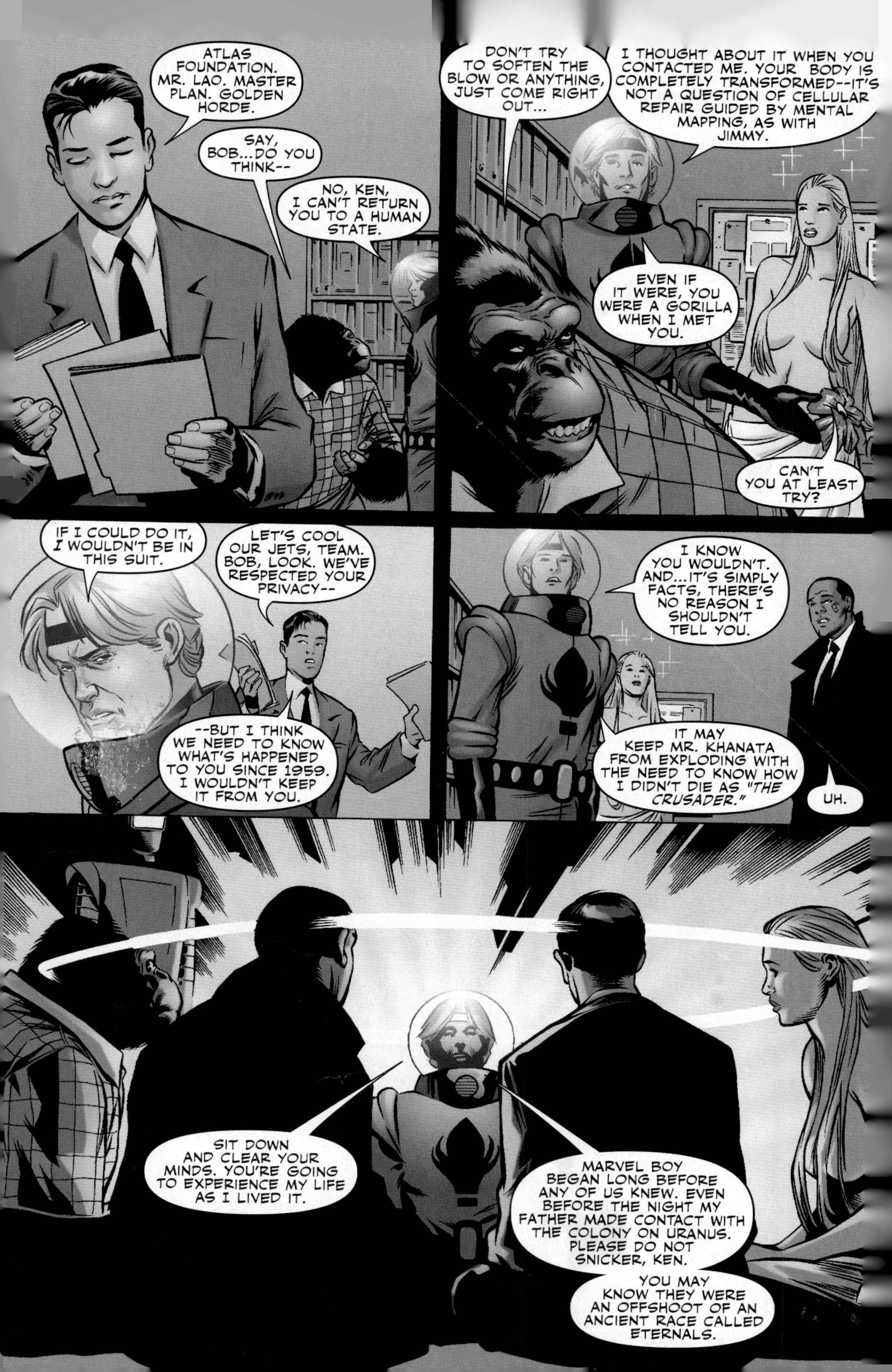
ATLAS FOUNDATION. MR. LAO. MASTER PLAN. GOLDEN HORDE.
SAY, BOB...DO YOU THINK--
NO, KEN, I CAN'T RETURN YOU TO A HUMAN STATE.
DON'T TRY TO SOFTEN THE BLOW OR ANYTHING, JUST COME RIGHT OUT...
I THOUGHT ABOUT IT WHEN YOU CONTACTED ME. YOUR BODY IS COMPLETELY TRANSFORMED--IT'S NOT A QUESTION OF CELLULAR REPAIR GUIDED BY MENTAL MAPPING, AS WITH JIMMY.
EVEN IF IT WERE, YOU WERE A GORILLA WHEN I MET YOU.
CAN'T YOU AT LEAST TRY?
IF I COULD DO IT, *I* WOULDN'T BE IN THIS SUIT.
LET'S COOL OUR JETS, TEAM. BOB, LOOK. WE'VE RESPECTED YOUR PRIVACY--
--BUT I THINK WE NEED TO KNOW WHAT'S HAPPENED TO YOU SINCE 1959. I WOULDN'T KEEP IT FROM YOU.
I KNOW YOU WOULDN'T. AND...IT'S SIMPLY FACTS, THERE'S NO REASON I SHOULDN'T TELL YOU.
IT MAY KEEP MR. KHANATA FROM EXPLODING WITH THE NEED TO KNOW HOW I DIDN'T DIE AS *"THE CRUSADER."*
UH.
SIT DOWN AND CLEAR YOUR MINDS. YOU'RE GOING TO EXPERIENCE MY LIFE AS I LIVED IT.
MARVEL BOY BEGAN LONG BEFORE ANY OF US KNEW. EVEN BEFORE THE NIGHT MY FATHER MADE CONTACT WITH THE COLONY ON URANUS. PLEASE DO NOT SNICKER, KEN.
YOU MAY KNOW THEY WERE AN OFFSHOOT OF AN ANCIENT RACE CALLED ETERNALS.

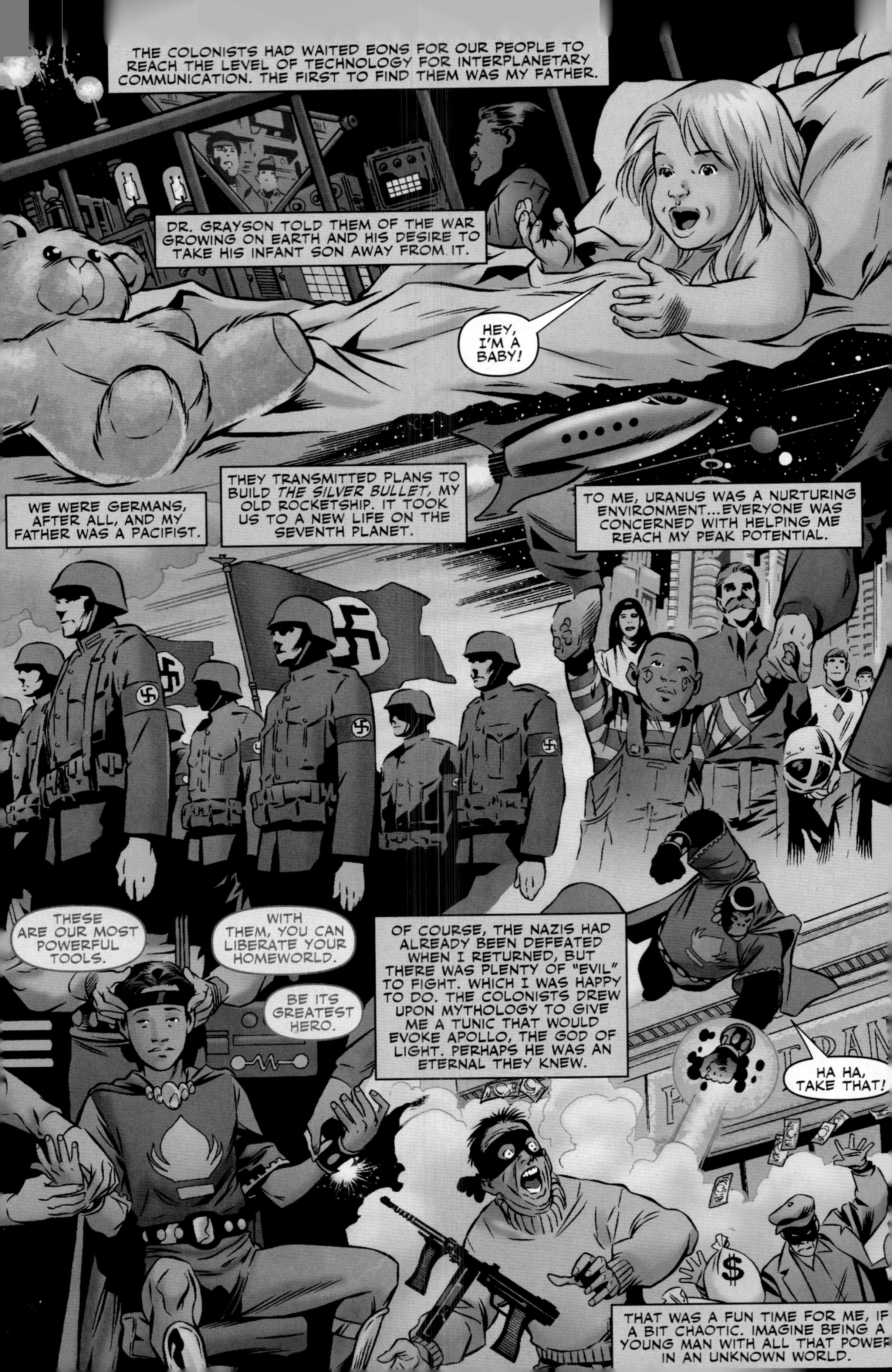
THE COLONISTS HAD WAITED EONS FOR OUR PEOPLE TO REACH THE LEVEL OF TECHNOLOGY FOR INTERPLANETARY COMMUNICATION. THE FIRST TO FIND THEM WAS MY FATHER.
DR. GRAYSON TOLD THEM OF THE WAR GROWING ON EARTH AND HIS DESIRE TO TAKE HIS INFANT SON AWAY FROM IT.
HEY, I'M A BABY!
WE WERE GERMANS, AFTER ALL, AND MY FATHER WAS A PACIFIST.
THEY TRANSMITTED PLANS TO BUILD *THE SILVER BULLET*, MY OLD ROCKETSHIP. IT TOOK US TO A NEW LIFE ON THE SEVENTH PLANET.
TO ME, URANUS WAS A NURTURING ENVIRONMENT...EVERYONE WAS CONCERNED WITH HELPING ME REACH MY PEAK POTENTIAL.
THESE ARE OUR MOST POWERFUL TOOLS.
WITH THEM, YOU CAN LIBERATE YOUR HOMEWORLD.
BE ITS GREATEST HERO.
OF COURSE, THE NAZIS HAD ALREADY BEEN DEFEATED WHEN I RETURNED, BUT THERE WAS PLENTY OF "EVIL" TO FIGHT. WHICH I WAS HAPPY TO DO. THE COLONISTS DREW UPON MYTHOLOGY TO GIVE ME A TUNIC THAT WOULD EVOKE APOLLO, THE GOD OF LIGHT. PERHAPS HE WAS AN ETERNAL THEY KNEW.
HA HA, TAKE THAT!
THAT WAS A FUN TIME FOR ME, IF A BIT CHAOTIC. IMAGINE BEING A YOUNG MAN WITH ALL THAT POWER IN AN UNKNOWN WORLD.

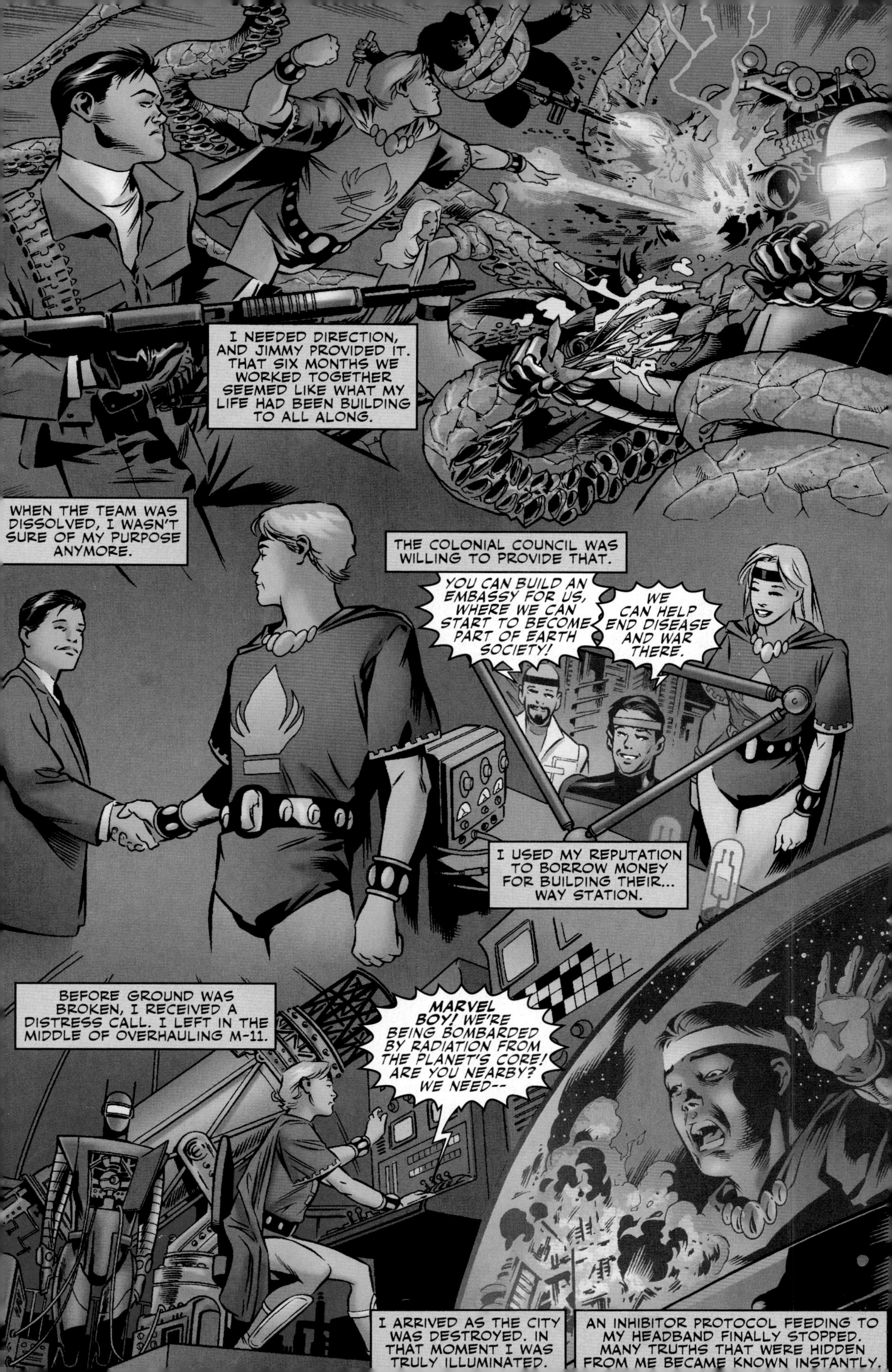

I NEEDED DIRECTION, AND JIMMY PROVIDED IT. THAT SIX MONTHS WE WORKED TOGETHER SEEMED LIKE WHAT MY LIFE HAD BEEN BUILDING TO ALL ALONG.
WHEN THE TEAM WAS DISSOLVED, I WASN'T SURE OF MY PURPOSE ANYMORE.
THE COLONIAL COUNCIL WAS WILLING TO PROVIDE THAT.
YOU CAN BUILD AN EMBASSY FOR US, WHERE WE CAN START TO BECOME PART OF EARTH SOCIETY!
WE CAN HELP END DISEASE AND WAR THERE.
I USED MY REPUTATION TO BORROW MONEY FOR BUILDING THEIR... WAY STATION.
BEFORE GROUND WAS BROKEN, I RECEIVED A DISTRESS CALL. I LEFT IN THE MIDDLE OF OVERHAULING M-11.
MARVEL BOY! WE'RE BEING BOMBARDED BY RADIATION FROM THE PLANET'S CORE! ARE YOU NEARBY? WE NEED--
I ARRIVED AS THE CITY WAS DESTROYED. IN THAT MOMENT I WAS TRULY ILLUMINATED.
AN INHIBITOR PROTOCOL FEEDING TO MY HEADBAND FINALLY STOPPED. MANY TRUTHS THAT WERE HIDDEN FROM ME BECAME KNOWN INSTANTLY.

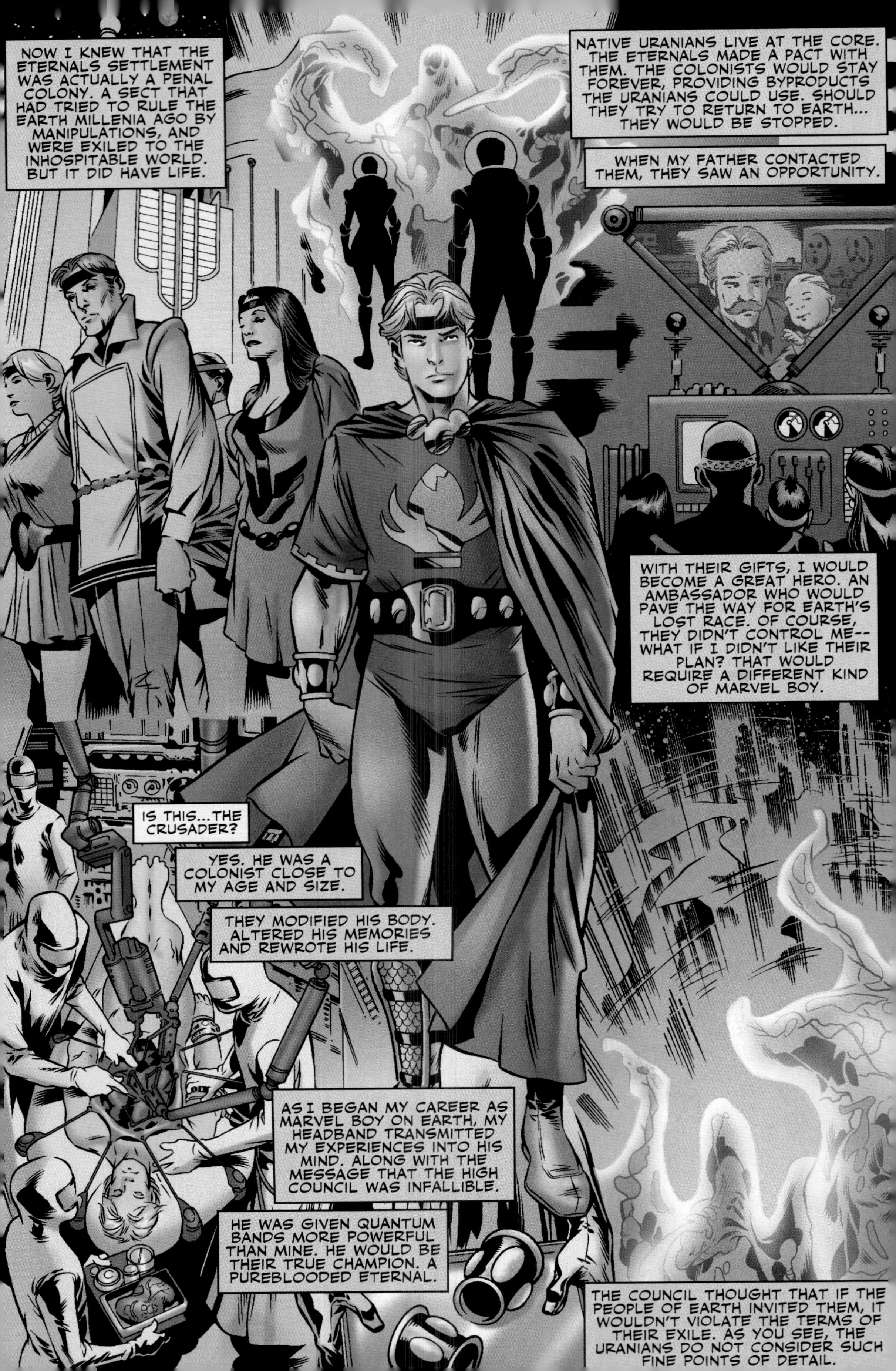
NOW I KNEW THAT THE ETERNALS SETTLEMENT WAS ACTUALLY A PENAL COLONY. A SECT THAT HAD TRIED TO RULE THE EARTH MILLENIA AGO BY MANIPULATIONS, AND WERE EXILED TO THE INHOSPITABLE WORLD. BUT IT DID HAVE LIFE.
NATIVE URANIANS LIVE AT THE CORE. THE ETERNALS MADE A PACT WITH THEM. THE COLONISTS WOULD STAY FOREVER, PROVIDING BYPRODUCTS THE URANIANS COULD USE. SHOULD THEY TRY TO RETURN TO EARTH... THEY WOULD BE STOPPED.
WHEN MY FATHER CONTACTED THEM, THEY SAW AN OPPORTUNITY.
WITH THEIR GIFTS, I WOULD BECOME A GREAT HERO. AN AMBASSADOR WHO WOULD PAVE THE WAY FOR EARTH'S LOST RACE. OF COURSE, THEY DIDN'T CONTROL ME--WHAT IF I DIDN'T LIKE THEIR PLAN? THAT WOULD REQUIRE A DIFFERENT KIND OF MARVEL BOY.
IS THIS...THE CRUSADER?
YES. HE WAS A COLONIST CLOSE TO MY AGE AND SIZE.
THEY MODIFIED HIS BODY. ALTERED HIS MEMORIES AND REWROTE HIS LIFE.
AS I BEGAN MY CAREER AS MARVEL BOY ON EARTH, MY HEADBAND TRANSMITTED MY EXPERIENCES INTO HIS MIND. ALONG WITH THE MESSAGE THAT THE HIGH COUNCIL WAS INFALLIBLE.
HE WAS GIVEN QUANTUM BANDS MORE POWERFUL THAN MINE. HE WOULD BE THEIR TRUE CHAMPION. A PUREBLOODED ETERNAL.
THE COUNCIL THOUGHT THAT IF THE PEOPLE OF EARTH INVITED THEM, IT WOULDN'T VIOLATE THE TERMS OF THEIR EXILE. AS YOU SEE, THE URANIANS DO NOT CONSIDER SUCH FINE POINTS OF DETAIL.

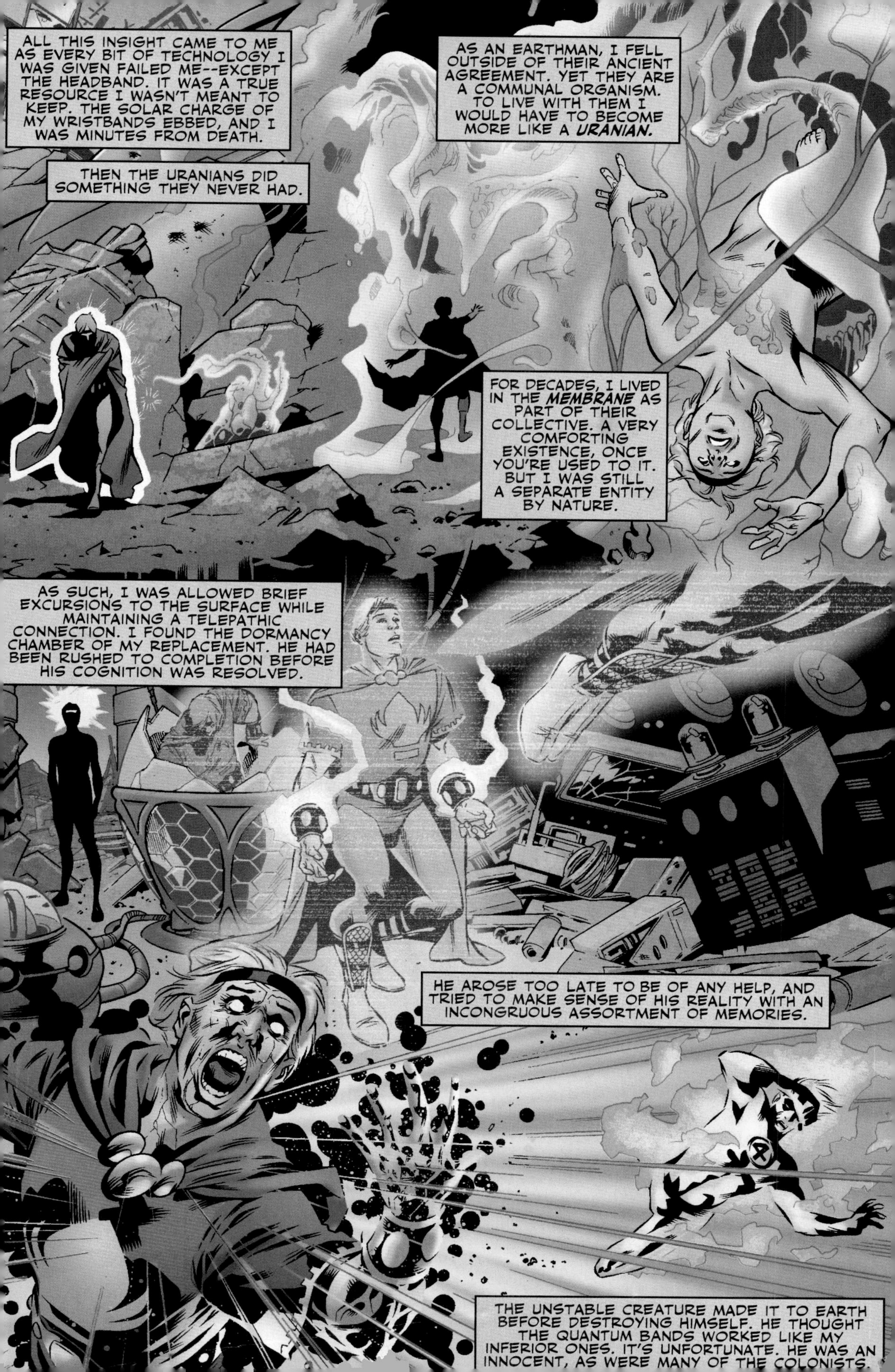
ALL THIS INSIGHT CAME TO ME AS EVERY BIT OF TECHNOLOGY I WAS GIVEN FAILED ME--EXCEPT THE HEADBAND. IT WAS A TRUE RESOURCE I WASN'T MEANT TO KEEP. THE SOLAR CHARGE OF MY WRISTBANDS EBBED, AND I WAS MINUTES FROM DEATH.
THEN THE URANIANS DID SOMETHING THEY NEVER HAD.
AS AN EARTHMAN, I FELL OUTSIDE OF THEIR ANCIENT AGREEMENT. YET THEY ARE A COMMUNAL ORGANISM. TO LIVE WITH THEM I WOULD HAVE TO BECOME MORE LIKE A URANIAN.
FOR DECADES, I LIVED IN THE MEMBRANE AS PART OF THEIR COLLECTIVE. A VERY COMFORTING EXISTENCE, ONCE YOU'RE USED TO IT. BUT I WAS STILL A SEPARATE ENTITY BY NATURE.
AS SUCH, I WAS ALLOWED BRIEF EXCURSIONS TO THE SURFACE WHILE MAINTAINING A TELEPATHIC CONNECTION. I FOUND THE DORMANCY CHAMBER OF MY REPLACEMENT. HE HAD BEEN RUSHED TO COMPLETION BEFORE HIS COGNITION WAS RESOLVED.
HE AROSE TOO LATE TO BE OF ANY HELP, AND TRIED TO MAKE SENSE OF HIS REALITY WITH AN INCONGRUOUS ASSORTMENT OF MEMORIES.
THE UNSTABLE CREATURE MADE IT TO EARTH BEFORE DESTROYING HIMSELF. HE THOUGHT THE QUANTUM BANDS WORKED LIKE MY INFERIOR ONES. IT'S UNFORTUNATE. HE WAS AN INNOCENT, AS WERE MANY OF THE COLONISTS.

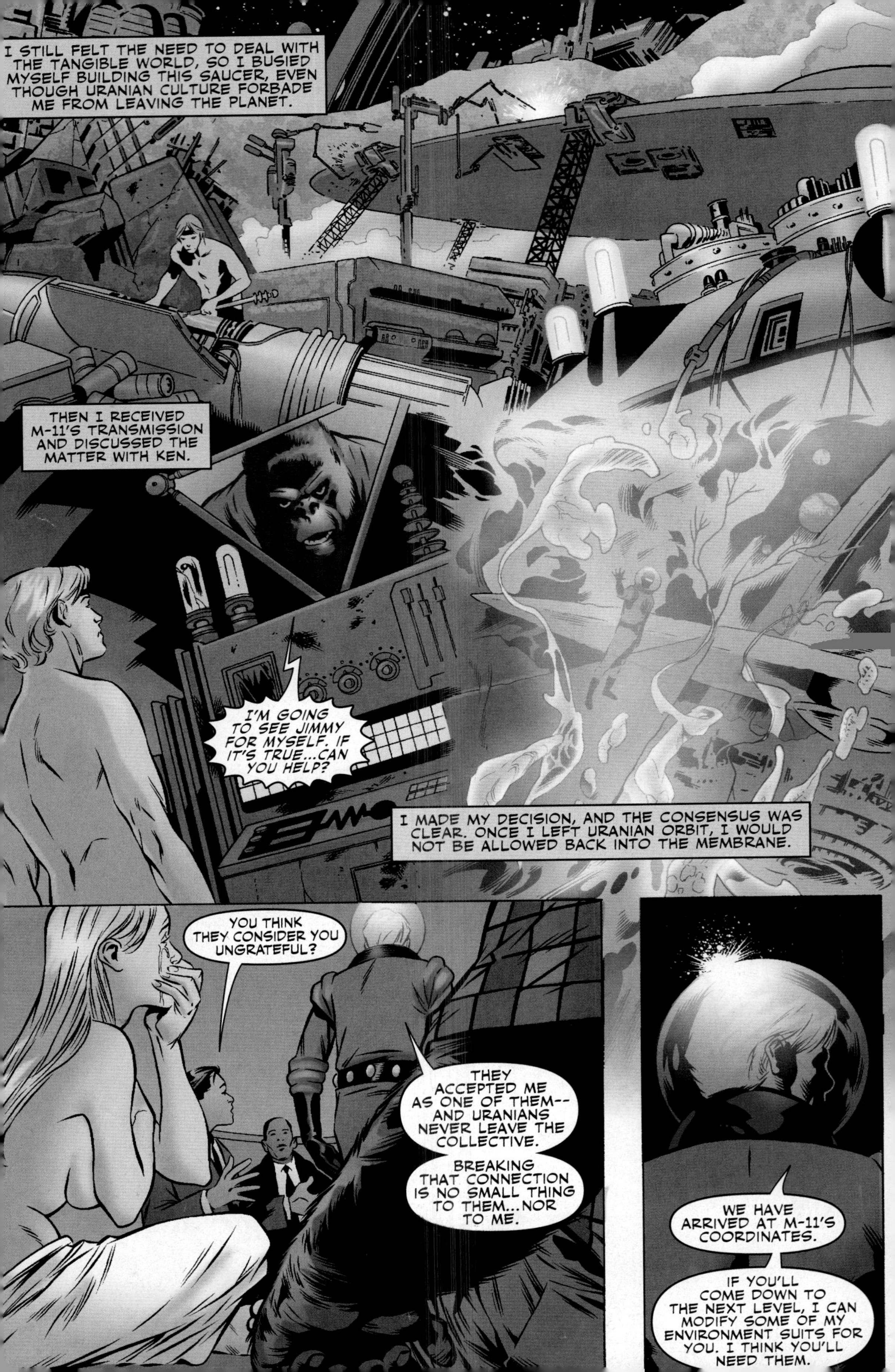
I STILL FELT THE NEED TO DEAL WITH THE TANGIBLE WORLD, SO I BUSIED MYSELF BUILDING THIS SAUCER, EVEN THOUGH URANIAN CULTURE FORBADE ME FROM LEAVING THE PLANET.
THEN I RECEIVED M-11'S TRANSMISSION AND DISCUSSED THE MATTER WITH KEN.
I'M GOING TO SEE JIMMY FOR MYSELF. IF IT'S TRUE...CAN YOU HELP?
I MADE MY DECISION, AND THE CONSENSUS WAS CLEAR. ONCE I LEFT URANIAN ORBIT, I WOULD NOT BE ALLOWED BACK INTO THE MEMBRANE.
YOU THINK THEY CONSIDER YOU UNGRATEFUL?
THEY ACCEPTED ME AS ONE OF THEM--AND URANIANS NEVER LEAVE THE COLLECTIVE.
BREAKING THAT CONNECTION IS NO SMALL THING TO THEM...NOR TO ME.
WE HAVE ARRIVED AT M-11'S COORDINATES.
IF YOU'LL COME DOWN TO THE NEXT LEVEL, I CAN MODIFY SOME OF MY ENVIRONMENT SUITS FOR YOU. I THINK YOU'LL NEED THEM.

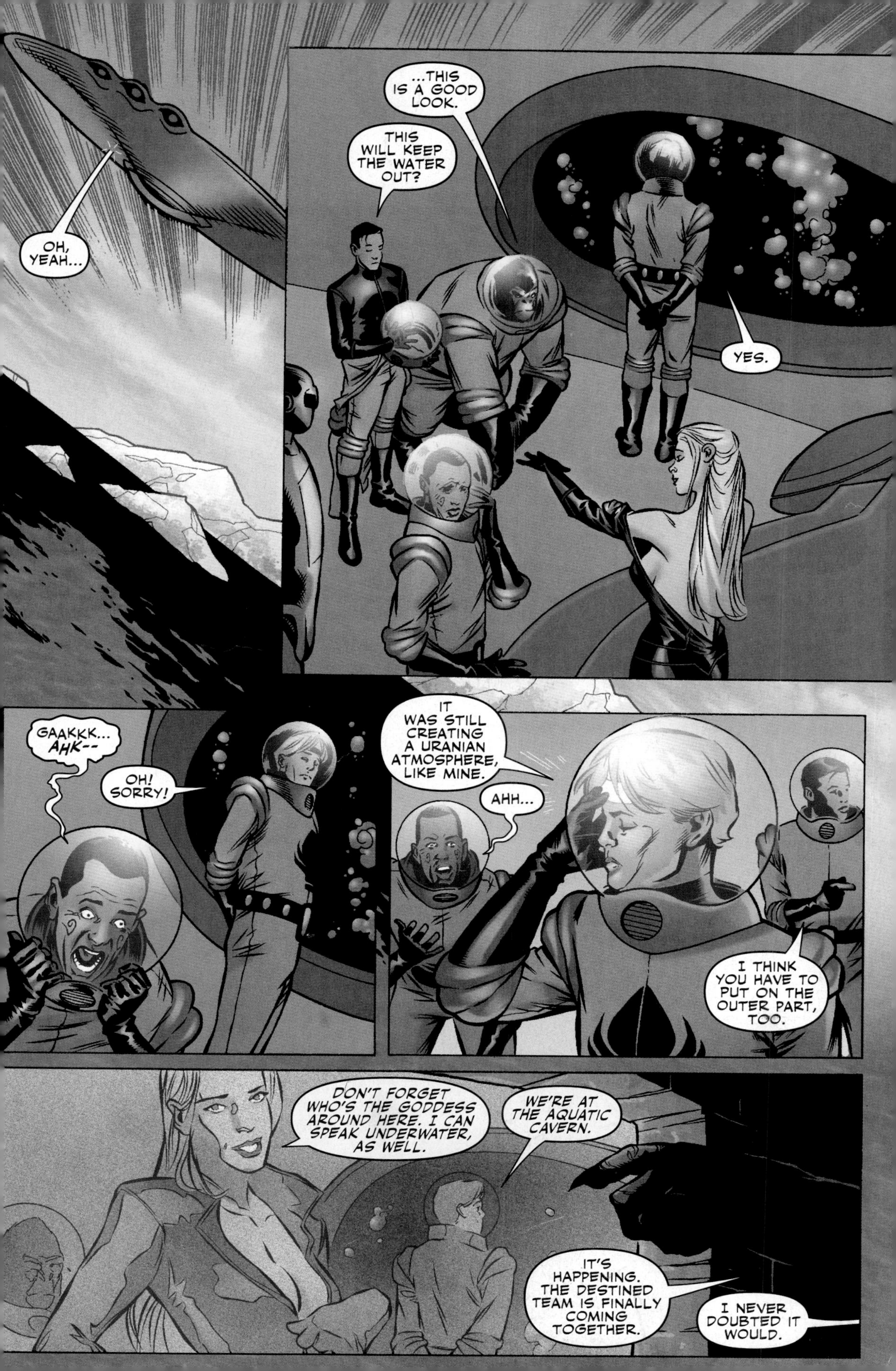
OH, YEAH...
THIS WILL KEEP THE WATER OUT?
...THIS IS A GOOD LOOK.
YES.
GAAKKK... AHK--
OH! SORRY!
IT WAS STILL CREATING A URANIAN ATMOSPHERE, LIKE MINE.
AHH...
I THINK YOU HAVE TO PUT ON THE OUTER PART, TOO.
DON'T FORGET WHO'S THE GODDESS AROUND HERE. I CAN SPEAK UNDERWATER, AS WELL.
WE'RE AT THE AQUATIC CAVERN.
IT'S HAPPENING. THE DESTINED TEAM IS FINALLY COMING TOGETHER.
I NEVER DOUBTED IT WOULD.

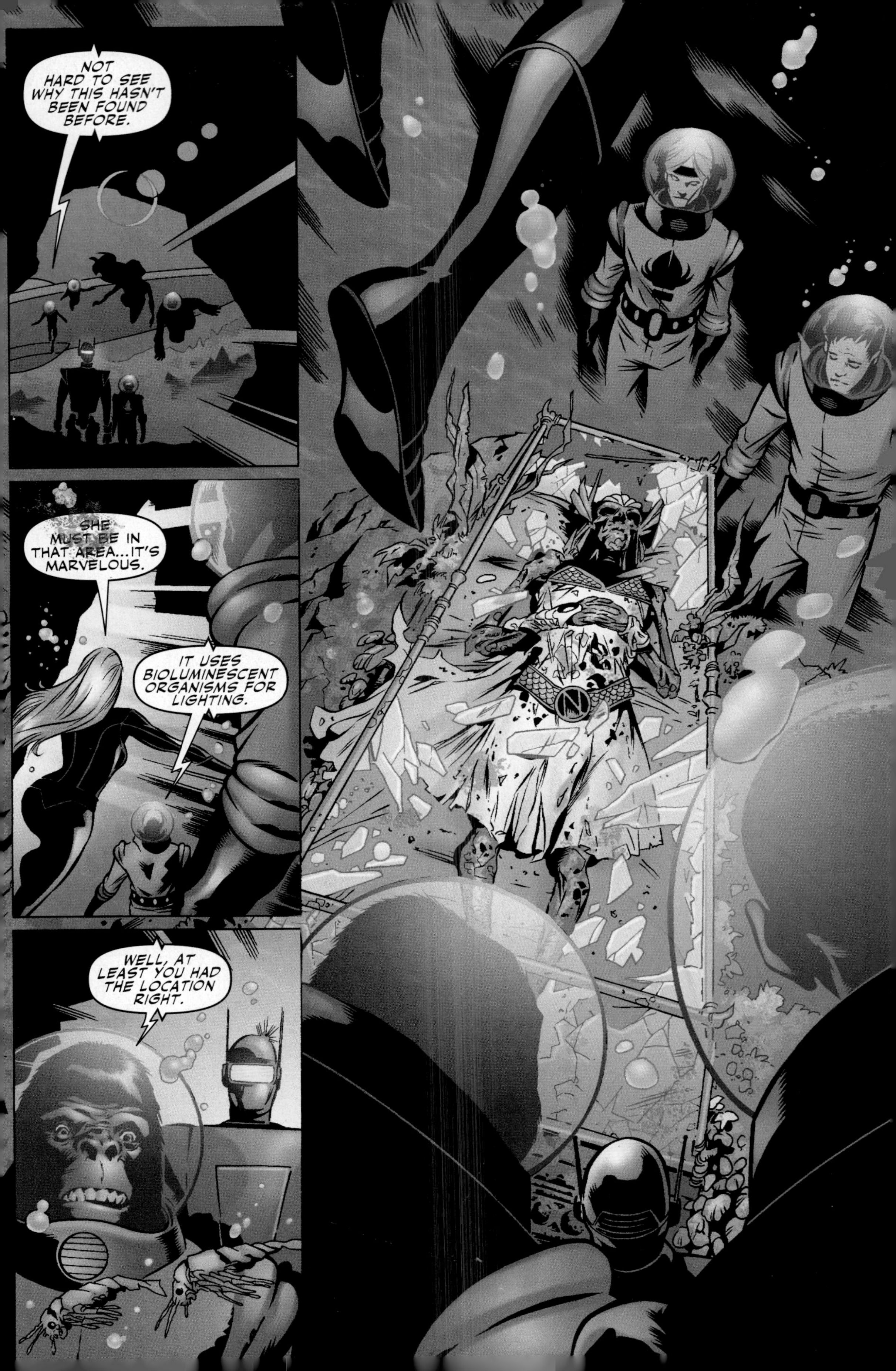
NOT HARD TO SEE WHY THIS HASN'T BEEN FOUND BEFORE.
SHE MUST BE IN THAT AREA...IT'S MARVELOUS.
IT USES BIOLUMINESCENT ORGANISMS FOR LIGHTING.
WELL, AT LEAST YOU HAD THE LOCATION RIGHT.

S.H.I.E.L.D.
OPERATIONS DATABASE

HOME | ADVANCED SEARCH | DATABASES | LOG OUT

AGENT | CRIMINAL | PROJECT | OPERATIONS ARCHIVE

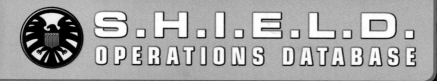

S.H.I.E.L.D. DOCUMENT 913583-29138 GRW

PROJECT DATABASE >> PROJECT: 6623279-0091 SWR >> LOGISTICS >> FIELD REPORTS & DOCS >> COMMUNICATION TRANSCRIPTS
SECRET CODE: BLUE

RECORDING DATE: 10/12/06 10:24 P.M.
OPERATOR: S.H.I.E.L.D. AGENT JENNIFER MULLINS – LEVEL 3
CALL ORIGIN: UNKNOWN
PHONE LOCATION: UNKNOWN
BROADCAST LOCKED. CODED AND SCRAMBLED USING NIC-7 CODE BLOCK.

AGENT MULLINS (OFF COMM)
...Sir, we're receiving Agent Khanata on Channel Alpha 9.
DUGAN
Put him through. Derek! What's your status?
KHANATA
Well, sir, I'm continuing my investigation with Woo and his original team. They're going to let me make short comms to keep you updated. I don't want to risk leaving the group because I don't think we'll be able to track them again.
DUGAN (OFF COMM)
Mullins! Where is this coming from?
AGENT MULLINS (OFF COMM)
We've chased the signal through 3,118 transmitters so far, sir.
DUGAN (OFF COMM)
So they know what you're saying to me.
KHANATA
Well, I'm talking to you through M-11, the robot. So, yes.
DUGAN
You gave that robot access to the Alpha 9 Channel??
KHANATA
No, it already knew about it somehow. Probably learned while it was in our Mojave Base.
DUGAN
(deleted)
KHANATA
Sorry, sir. They seem concerned with finding the facts behind the San Francisco mission as well. I think I'm in the best place to be.
DUGAN
Long as you ain't going Stockholm Syndrome on us.
KHANATA
I remember who I work for. It looks like Yellow Claw is involved.
DUGAN
Great. Doesn't anyone die anymore? Besides our agents, of course.
KHANATA
On that note, we're also going to investigate the possibility that the hybrid Merwoman Namora may still be alive.
DUGAN
The Sub-Mariner's cousin?
KHANATA
Yes, sir.
DUGAN
Don't sound like they're too worried about finding this Atlas Foundation.

SEARCH DATABASE

SEARCH

KHANATA
Actually, Jimmy Woo has been going over the clues he had been gathering over the years. Bob Grayson copied all that info from his house.
DUGAN
We're going through that, too.
KHANATA
In case you can't make out some of Jimmy's shorthand code, he's deciphered some codenames. We believe these are major Atlas online operatives:

DOOP1958 KRB NRG DPLOMBARDO MR. BLACK SLYMCYKE S. KLEEFELD KUYU001 EYECOLUMBUS JSHELMIG MARVEL LAD MSR. ORESTEUS CHRIS MCFEELY NHARTZ CALVINMARSH COMMERCIALINN

AGENT MULLINS
Now we're up to 34,212 transmitter relays, sir.
DUGAN
Thanks, we had a few of those worked out, but that'll save us some time. So--is it true he can't remember anything after '59?
KHANATA
If he's faking the memory loss, he's fooled me. While we were investigating the recovery site in San Francisco, Woo pulled a gun on someone using a cell phone--he assumed the man was a spy. Ken Hale is working to get him up to speed on the 21st century. Hale said to tell you "Wa-hoo," by the way. Whatever that means.
DUGAN
That (deleted) gorilla.
KHANATA
I believe once the Namora side trip is done, they're going to investigate some of the possible Atlas operations. Have any of our men looked into those?
DUGAN
No, almost all of our resources are tied up with this (deleted) Superhuman Registration stuff. We'll try to send you backup if you need it, but I can't promise anything.
KHANATA
I understand sir. Hale is making the "wrap-it-up" motion, I'll have to sign off for now.
DUGAN
Roger that. One last thing....
KHANATA
Sir.
DUGAN
Jimmy--so he's doing pretty good now, right?
KHANATA
He's in great shape.
DUGAN
Heh. All right, over and out.

END TRANSMISSION

DUGAN (OFF COMM TO AGENT)
What did you get?
AGENT MULLINS
We tracked the source to.... Uranus.
DUGAN
(deleted)

Transcript reviewed and edited by Maria Hill for security clearance.
195-701

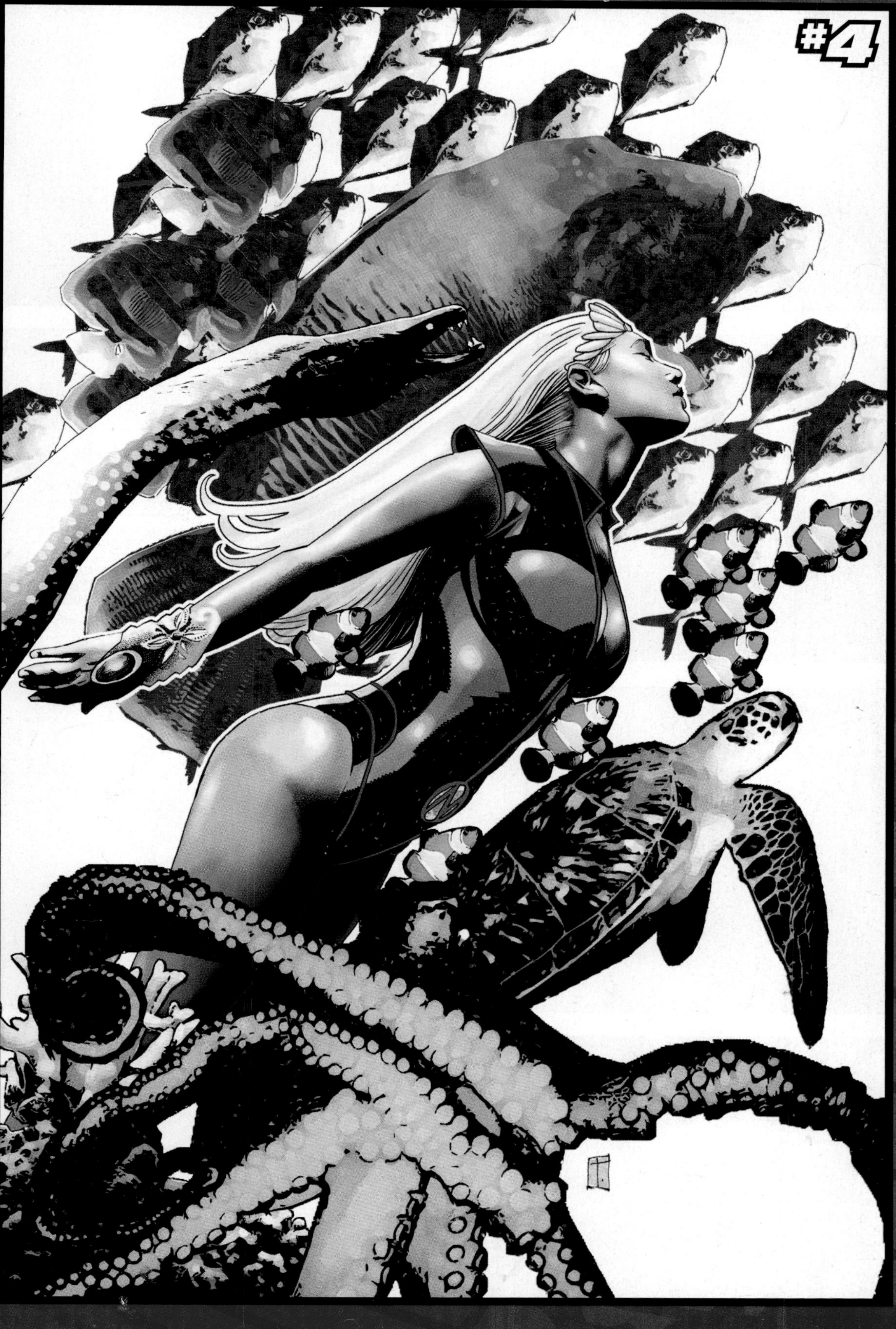
#4

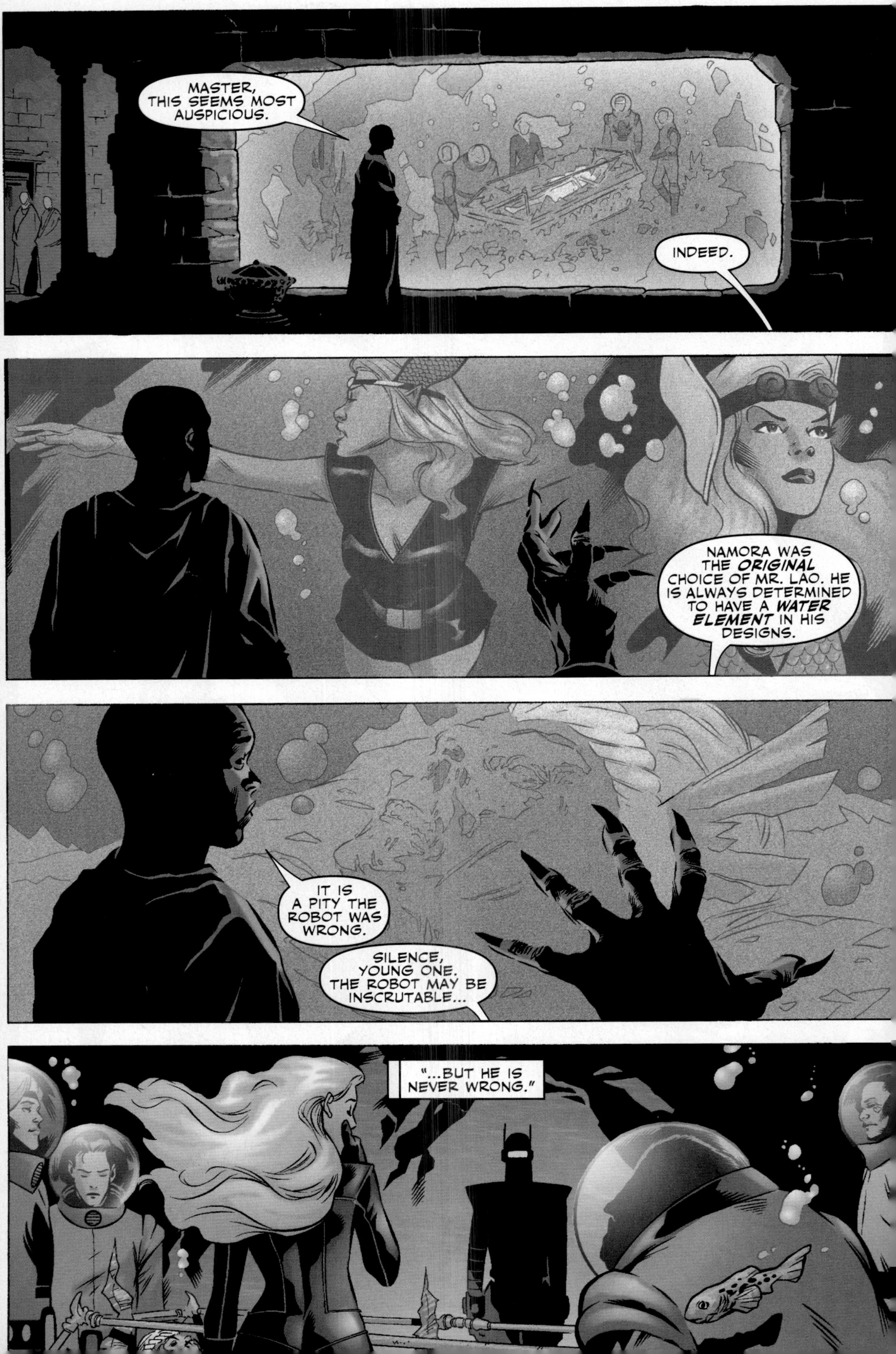
MASTER, THIS SEEMS MOST AUSPICIOUS.
INDEED.
NAMORA WAS THE ORIGINAL CHOICE OF MR. LAO. HE IS ALWAYS DETERMINED TO HAVE A WATER ELEMENT IN HIS DESIGNS.
IT IS A PITY THE ROBOT WAS WRONG.
SILENCE, YOUNG ONE. THE ROBOT MAY BE INSCRUTABLE...
"...BUT HE IS NEVER WRONG."

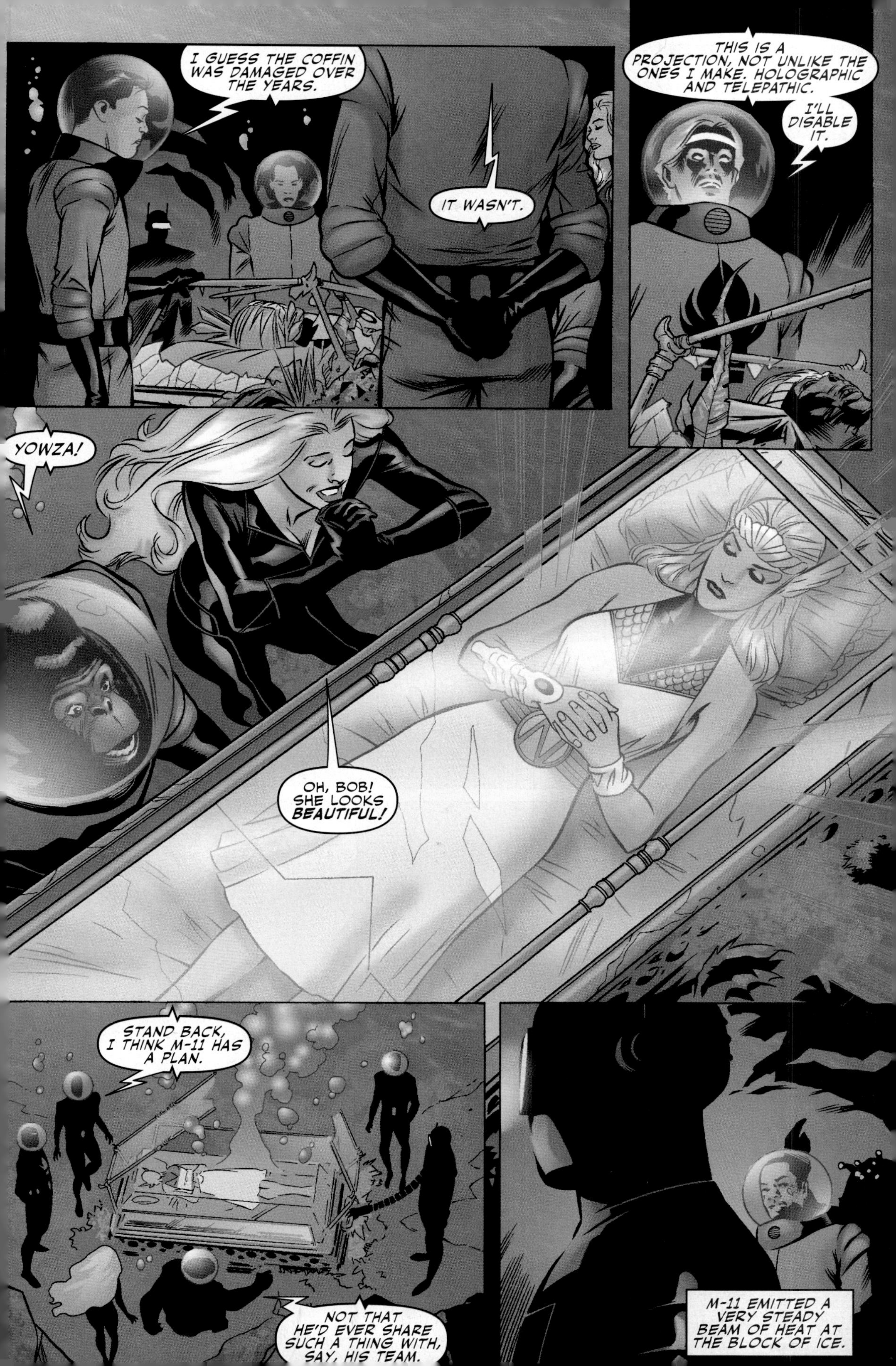
I GUESS THE COFFIN WAS DAMAGED OVER THE YEARS.
IT WASN'T.
THIS IS A PROJECTION, NOT UNLIKE THE ONES I MAKE. HOLOGRAPHIC AND TELEPATHIC.
I'LL DISABLE IT.
YOWZA!
OH, BOB! SHE LOOKS BEAUTIFUL!
STAND BACK, I THINK M-11 HAS A PLAN.
NOT THAT HE'D EVER SHARE SUCH A THING WITH, SAY, HIS TEAM.
M-11 EMITTED A VERY STEADY BEAM OF HEAT AT THE BLOCK OF ICE.

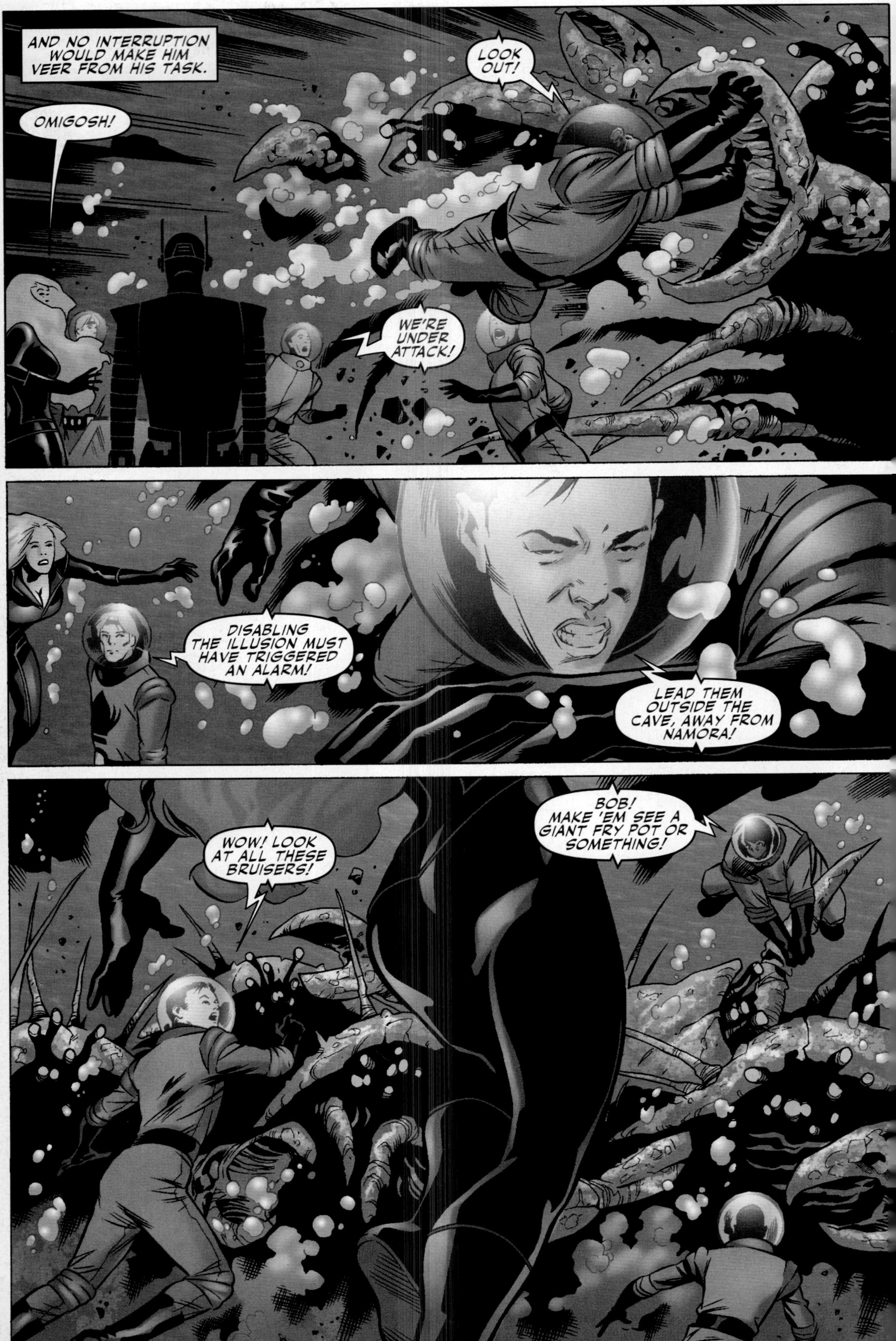
AND NO INTERRUPTION WOULD MAKE HIM VEER FROM HIS TASK.
OMIGOSH!
LOOK OUT!
WE'RE UNDER ATTACK!
DISABLING THE ILLUSION MUST HAVE TRIGGERED AN ALARM!
LEAD THEM OUTSIDE THE CAVE, AWAY FROM NAMORA!
WOW! LOOK AT ALL THESE BRUISERS!
BOB! MAKE 'EM SEE A GIANT FRY POT OR SOMETHING!

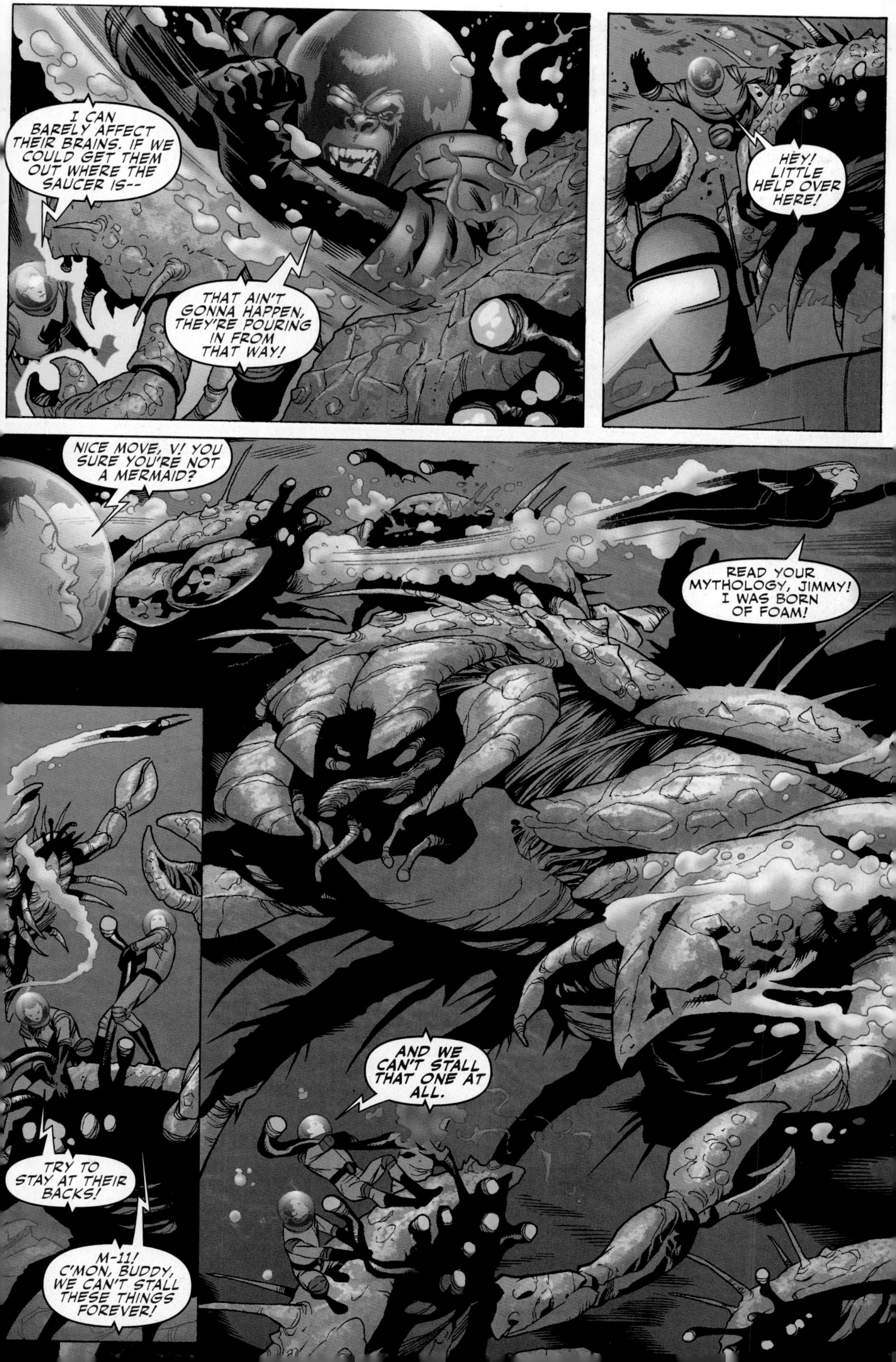
I CAN BARELY AFFECT THEIR BRAINS. IF WE COULD GET THEM OUT WHERE THE SAUCER IS--
THAT AIN'T GONNA HAPPEN, THEY'RE POURING IN FROM THAT WAY!
HEY! LITTLE HELP OVER HERE!
NICE MOVE, V! YOU SURE YOU'RE NOT A MERMAID?
READ YOUR MYTHOLOGY, JIMMY! I WAS BORN OF FOAM!
TRY TO STAY AT THEIR BACKS!
M-11! C'MON, BUDDY, WE CAN'T STALL THESE THINGS FOREVER!
AND WE CAN'T STALL THAT ONE AT ALL.

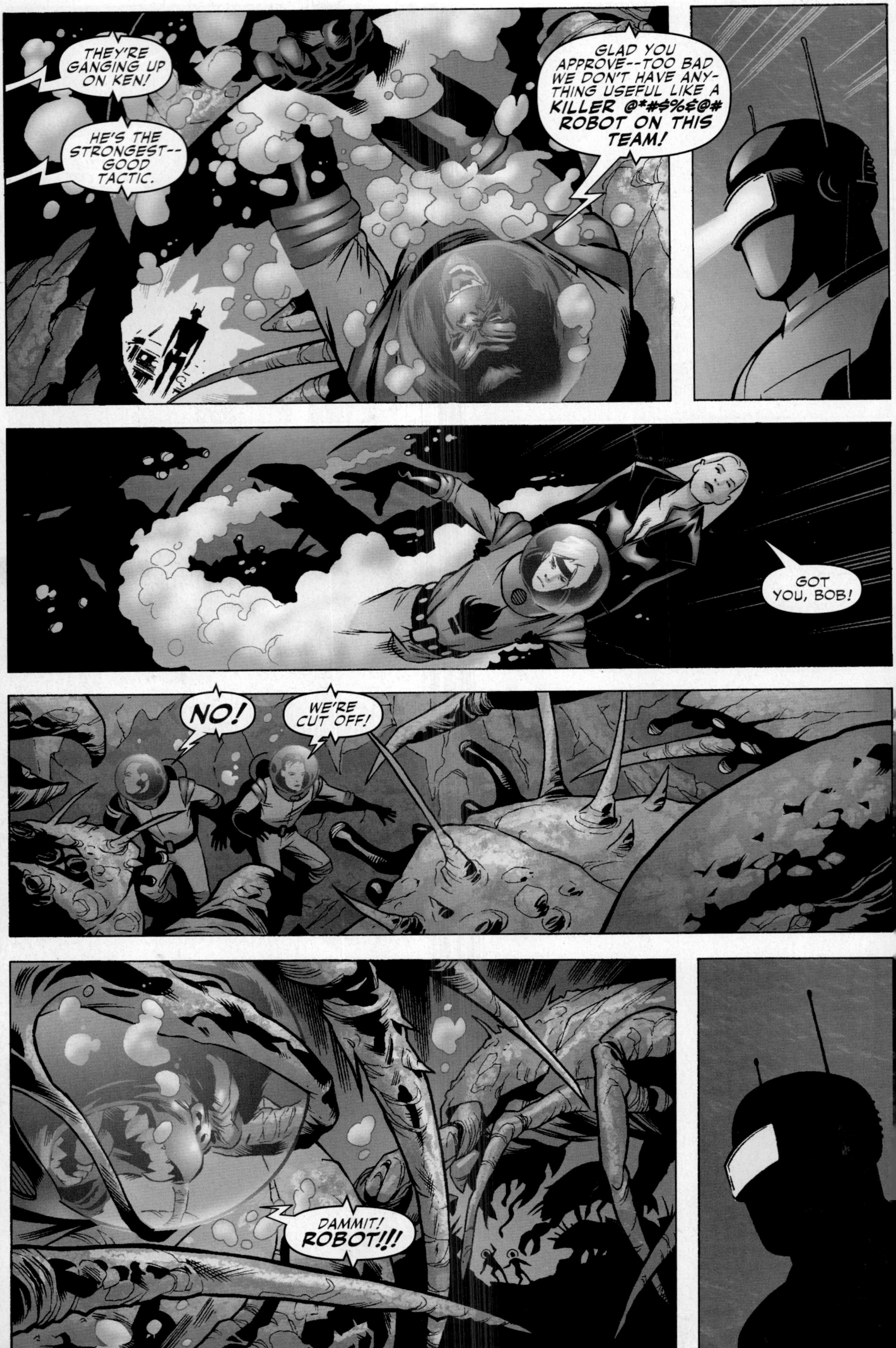
THEY'RE GANGING UP ON KEN!
HE'S THE STRONGEST--GOOD TACTIC.
GLAD YOU APPROVE--TOO BAD WE DON'T HAVE ANYTHING USEFUL LIKE A KILLER @*#$%&@# ROBOT ON THIS TEAM!
GOT YOU, BOB!
NO!
WE'RE CUT OFF!
DAMMIT! ROBOT!!!

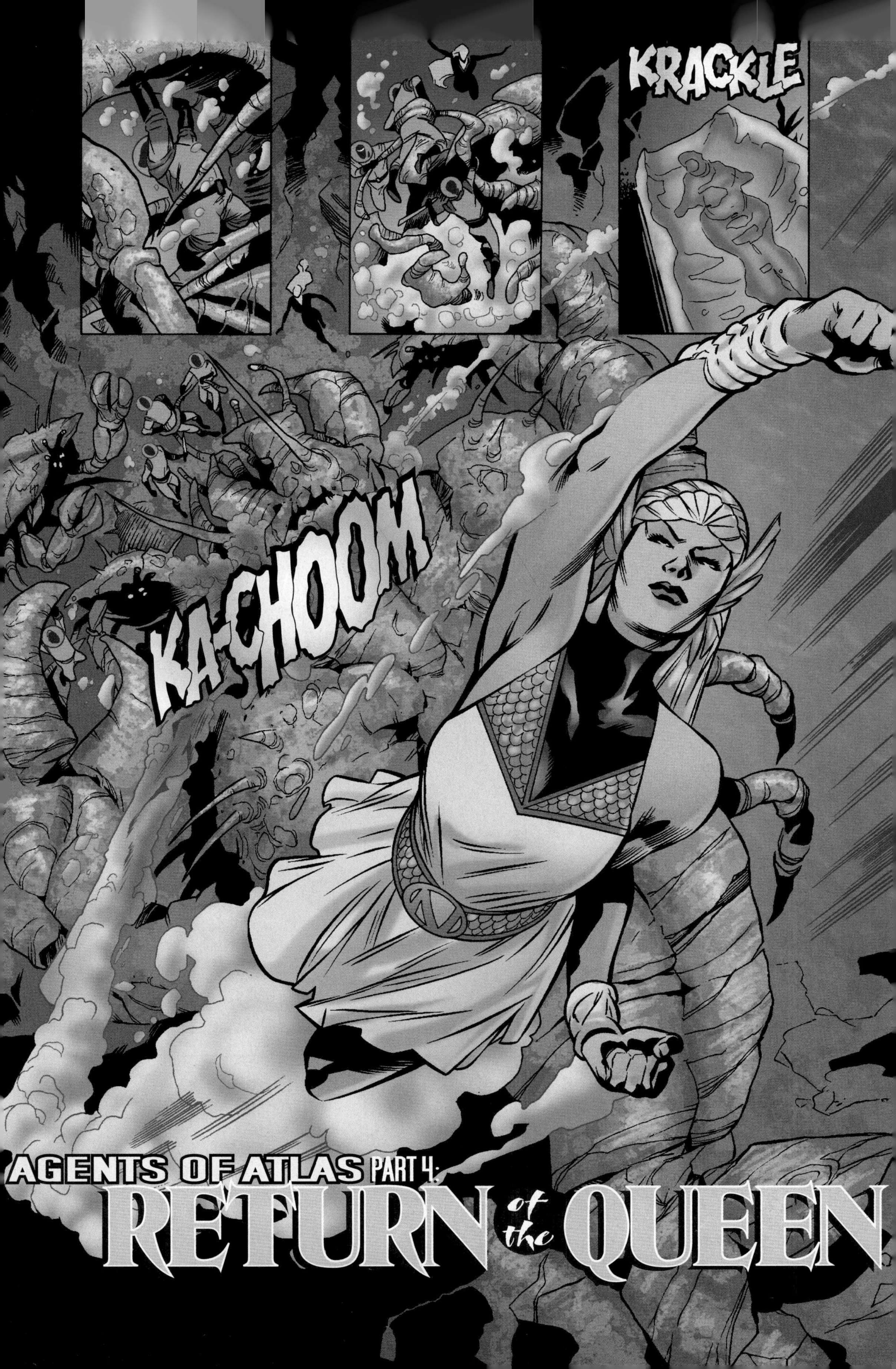
KRACKLE
KA-CHOOM
AGENTS OF ATLAS PART 4:
RETURN of the QUEEN

MY RIBS BEGAN TO GIVE WHEN I FIRST SAW HER.

I THOUGHT A TORPEDO HAD BEEN FIRED INTO THE CAVERN. THEN THE MISSILE TURNED AND CAME BACK.

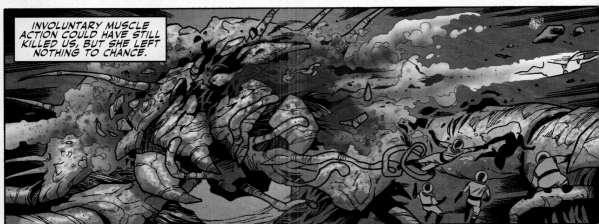

INVOLUNTARY MUSCLE ACTION COULD HAVE STILL KILLED US, BUT SHE LEFT NOTHING TO CHANCE.

THE SHEER NUMBER OF BEASTS SEEMED TOO MUCH FOR ANYONE...

...EXCEPT FOR HER.

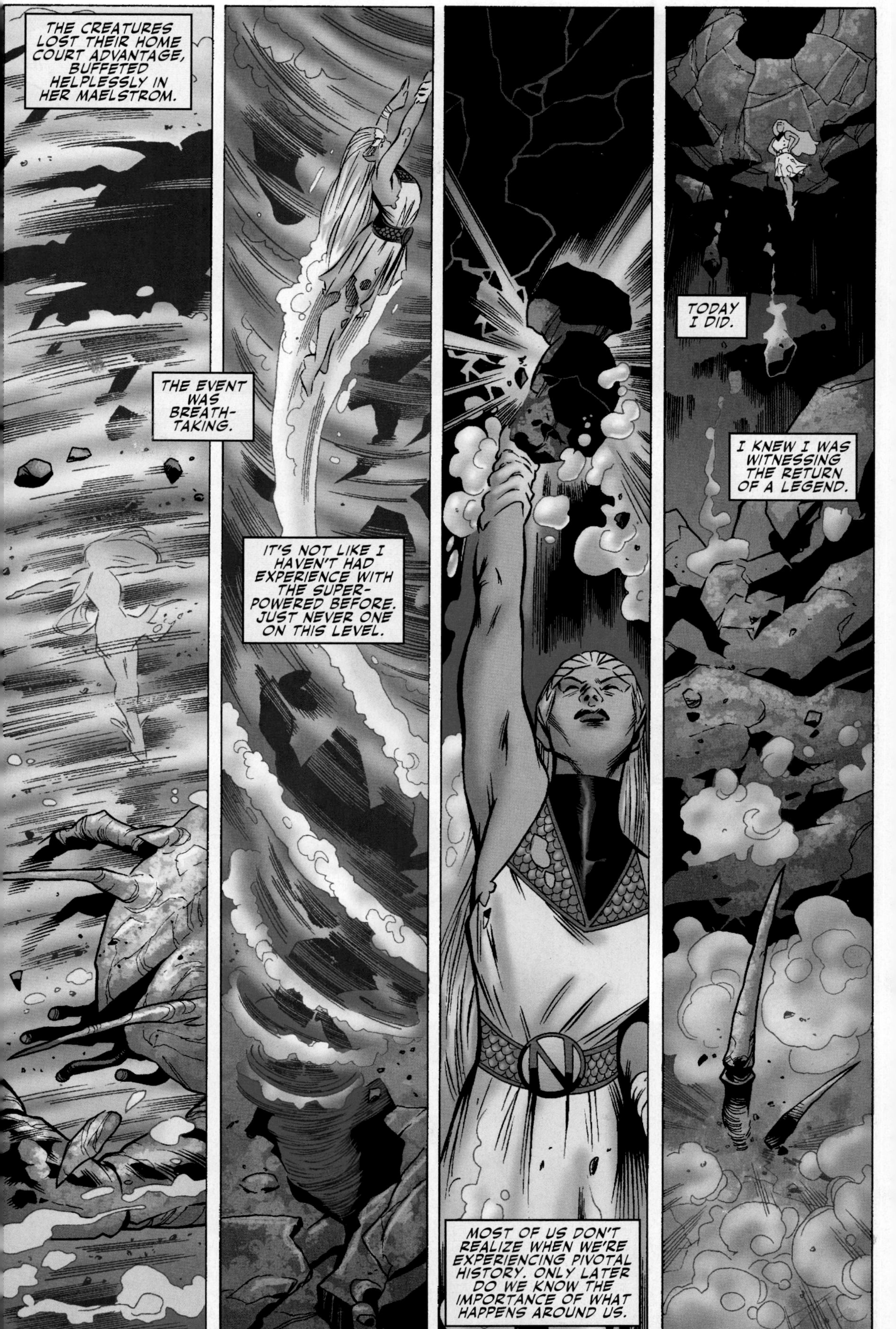
THE CREATURES LOST THEIR HOME COURT ADVANTAGE, BUFFETED HELPLESSLY IN HER MAELSTROM.
THE EVENT WAS BREATH-TAKING.
IT'S NOT LIKE I HAVEN'T HAD EXPERIENCE WITH THE SUPER-POWERED BEFORE. JUST NEVER ONE ON THIS LEVEL.
MOST OF US DON'T REALIZE WHEN WE'RE EXPERIENCING PIVOTAL HISTORY. ONLY LATER DO WE KNOW THE IMPORTANCE OF WHAT HAPPENS AROUND US.
TODAY I DID.
I KNEW I WAS WITNESSING THE RETURN OF A LEGEND.

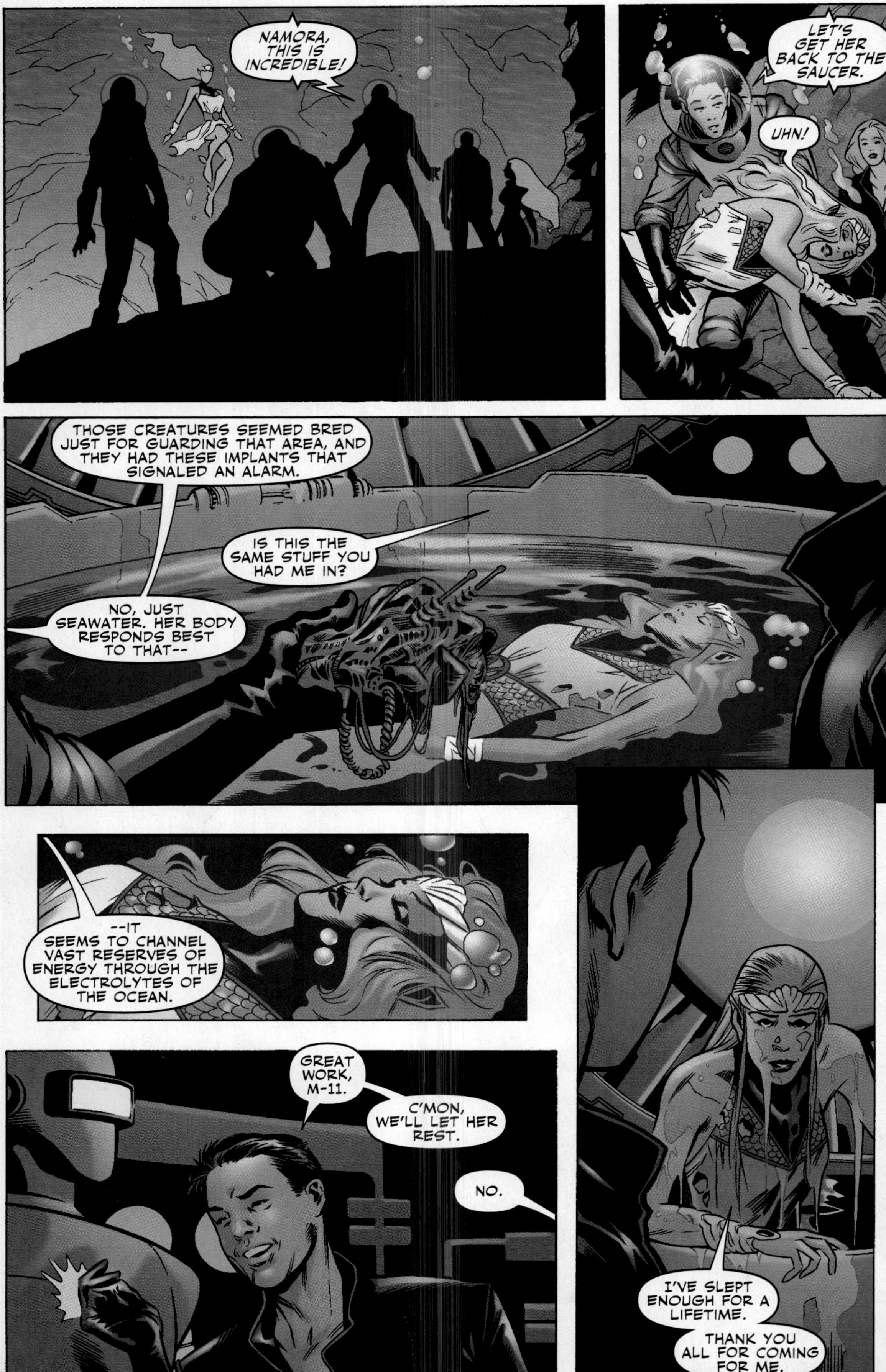
NAMORA, THIS IS INCREDIBLE!
LET'S GET HER BACK TO THE SAUCER.
UHN!
THOSE CREATURES SEEMED BRED JUST FOR GUARDING THAT AREA, AND THEY HAD THESE IMPLANTS THAT SIGNALED AN ALARM.
IS THIS THE SAME STUFF YOU HAD ME IN?
NO, JUST SEAWATER. HER BODY RESPONDS BEST TO THAT--
--IT SEEMS TO CHANNEL VAST RESERVES OF ENERGY THROUGH THE ELECTROLYTES OF THE OCEAN.
GREAT WORK, M-11.
C'MON, WE'LL LET HER REST.
NO.
I'VE SLEPT ENOUGH FOR A LIFETIME.
THANK YOU ALL FOR COMING FOR ME.

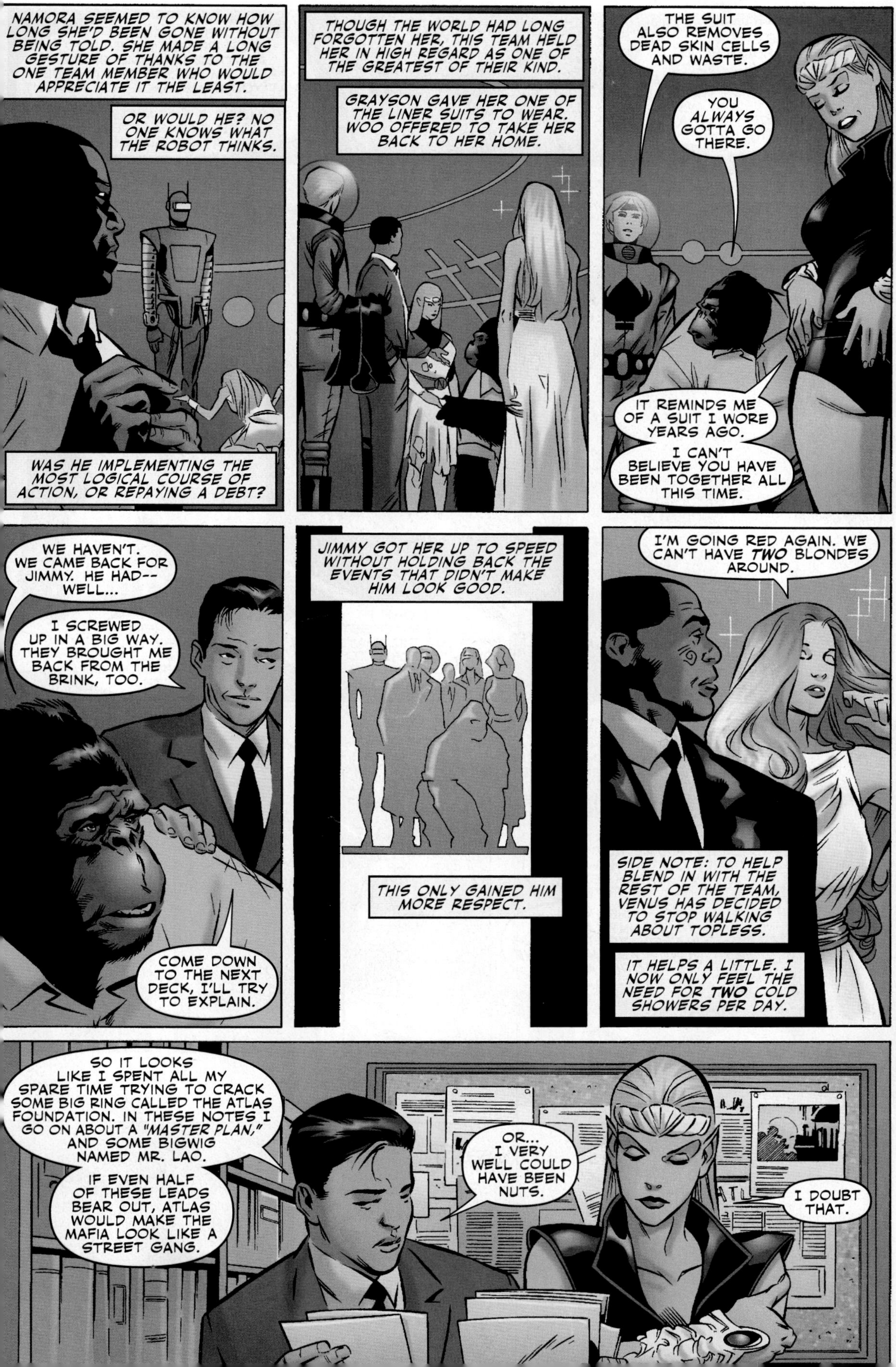

NAMORA SEEMED TO KNOW HOW LONG SHE'D BEEN GONE WITHOUT BEING TOLD. SHE MADE A LONG GESTURE OF THANKS TO THE ONE TEAM MEMBER WHO WOULD APPRECIATE IT THE LEAST.
OR WOULD HE? NO ONE KNOWS WHAT THE ROBOT THINKS.
WAS HE IMPLEMENTING THE MOST LOGICAL COURSE OF ACTION, OR REPAYING A DEBT?
THOUGH THE WORLD HAD LONG FORGOTTEN HER, THIS TEAM HELD HER IN HIGH REGARD AS ONE OF THE GREATEST OF THEIR KIND.
GRAYSON GAVE HER ONE OF THE LINER SUITS TO WEAR. WOO OFFERED TO TAKE HER BACK TO HER HOME.
THE SUIT ALSO REMOVES DEAD SKIN CELLS AND WASTE.
YOU ALWAYS GOTTA GO THERE.
IT REMINDS ME OF A SUIT I WORE YEARS AGO.
I CAN'T BELIEVE YOU HAVE BEEN TOGETHER ALL THIS TIME.
WE HAVEN'T. WE CAME BACK FOR JIMMY. HE HAD-- WELL...
I SCREWED UP IN A BIG WAY. THEY BROUGHT ME BACK FROM THE BRINK, TOO.
COME DOWN TO THE NEXT DECK, I'LL TRY TO EXPLAIN.
JIMMY GOT HER UP TO SPEED WITHOUT HOLDING BACK THE EVENTS THAT DIDN'T MAKE HIM LOOK GOOD.
THIS ONLY GAINED HIM MORE RESPECT.
I'M GOING RED AGAIN. WE CAN'T HAVE TWO BLONDES AROUND.
SIDE NOTE: TO HELP BLEND IN WITH THE REST OF THE TEAM, VENUS HAS DECIDED TO STOP WALKING ABOUT TOPLESS.
IT HELPS A LITTLE. I NOW ONLY FEEL THE NEED FOR TWO COLD SHOWERS PER DAY.
SO IT LOOKS LIKE I SPENT ALL MY SPARE TIME TRYING TO CRACK SOME BIG RING CALLED THE ATLAS FOUNDATION. IN THESE NOTES I GO ON ABOUT A "MASTER PLAN," AND SOME BIGWIG NAMED MR. LAO.
IF EVEN HALF OF THESE LEADS BEAR OUT, ATLAS WOULD MAKE THE MAFIA LOOK LIKE A STREET GANG.
OR... I VERY WELL COULD HAVE BEEN NUTS.
I DOUBT THAT.

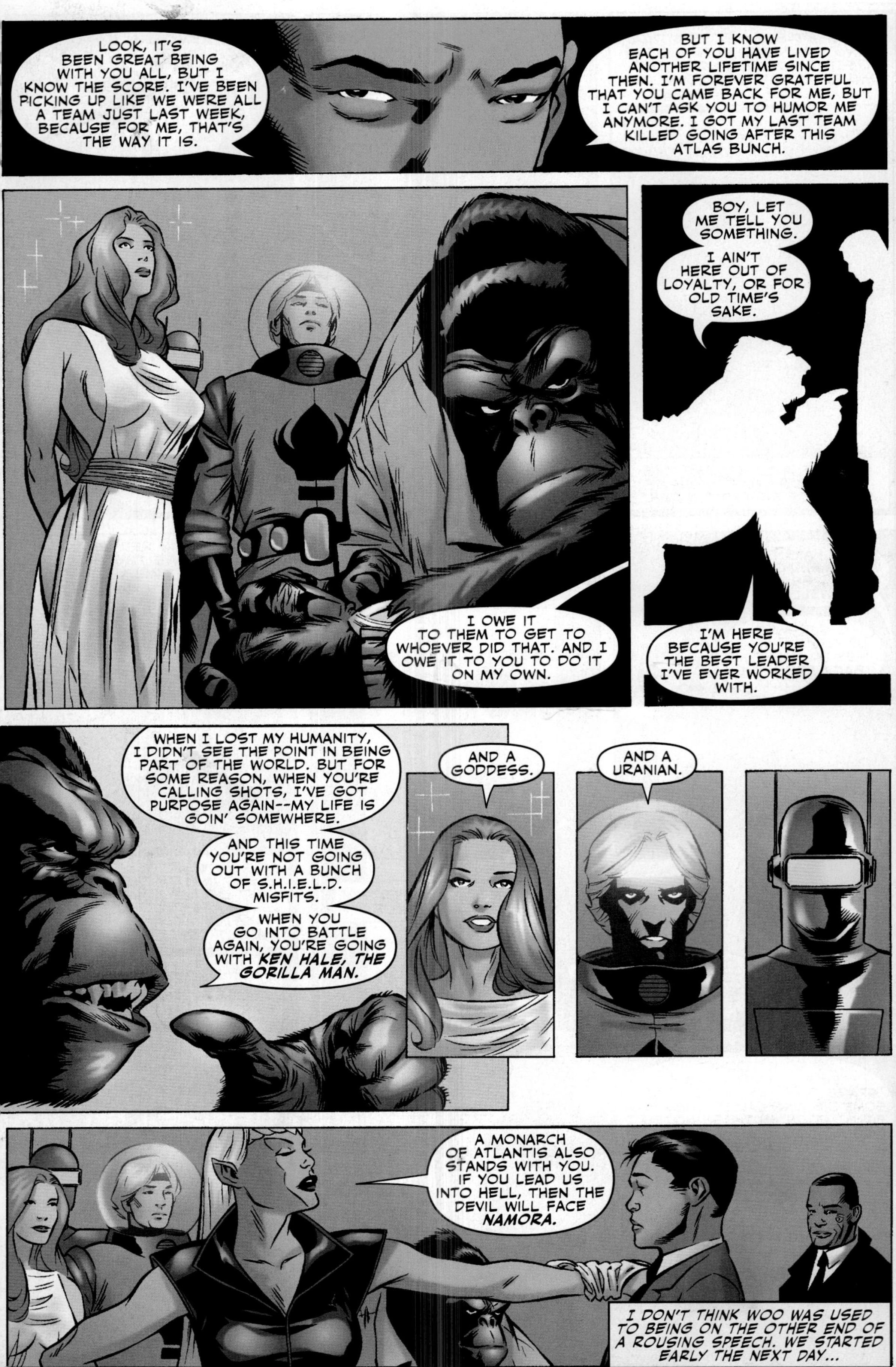
LOOK, IT'S BEEN GREAT BEING WITH YOU ALL, BUT I KNOW THE SCORE. I'VE BEEN PICKING UP LIKE WE WERE ALL A TEAM JUST LAST WEEK, BECAUSE FOR ME, THAT'S THE WAY IT IS.
BUT I KNOW EACH OF YOU HAVE LIVED ANOTHER LIFETIME SINCE THEN. I'M FOREVER GRATEFUL THAT YOU CAME BACK FOR ME, BUT I CAN'T ASK YOU TO HUMOR ME ANYMORE. I GOT MY LAST TEAM KILLED GOING AFTER THIS ATLAS BUNCH.
I OWE IT TO THEM TO GET TO WHOEVER DID THAT. AND I OWE IT TO YOU TO DO IT ON MY OWN.
BOY, LET ME TELL YOU SOMETHING.
I AIN'T HERE OUT OF LOYALTY, OR FOR OLD TIME'S SAKE.
I'M HERE BECAUSE YOU'RE THE BEST LEADER I'VE EVER WORKED WITH.
WHEN I LOST MY HUMANITY, I DIDN'T SEE THE POINT IN BEING PART OF THE WORLD. BUT FOR SOME REASON, WHEN YOU'RE CALLING SHOTS, I'VE GOT PURPOSE AGAIN--MY LIFE IS GOIN' SOMEWHERE.
AND THIS TIME YOU'RE NOT GOING OUT WITH A BUNCH OF S.H.I.E.L.D. MISFITS.
WHEN YOU GO INTO BATTLE AGAIN, YOU'RE GOING WITH ***KEN HALE, THE GORILLA MAN.***
AND A GODDESS.
AND A URANIAN.
A MONARCH OF ATLANTIS ALSO STANDS WITH YOU. IF YOU LEAD US INTO HELL, THEN THE DEVIL WILL FACE ***NAMORA.***
I DON'T THINK WOO WAS USED TO BEING ON THE OTHER END OF A ROUSING SPEECH. WE STARTED EARLY THE NEXT DAY...

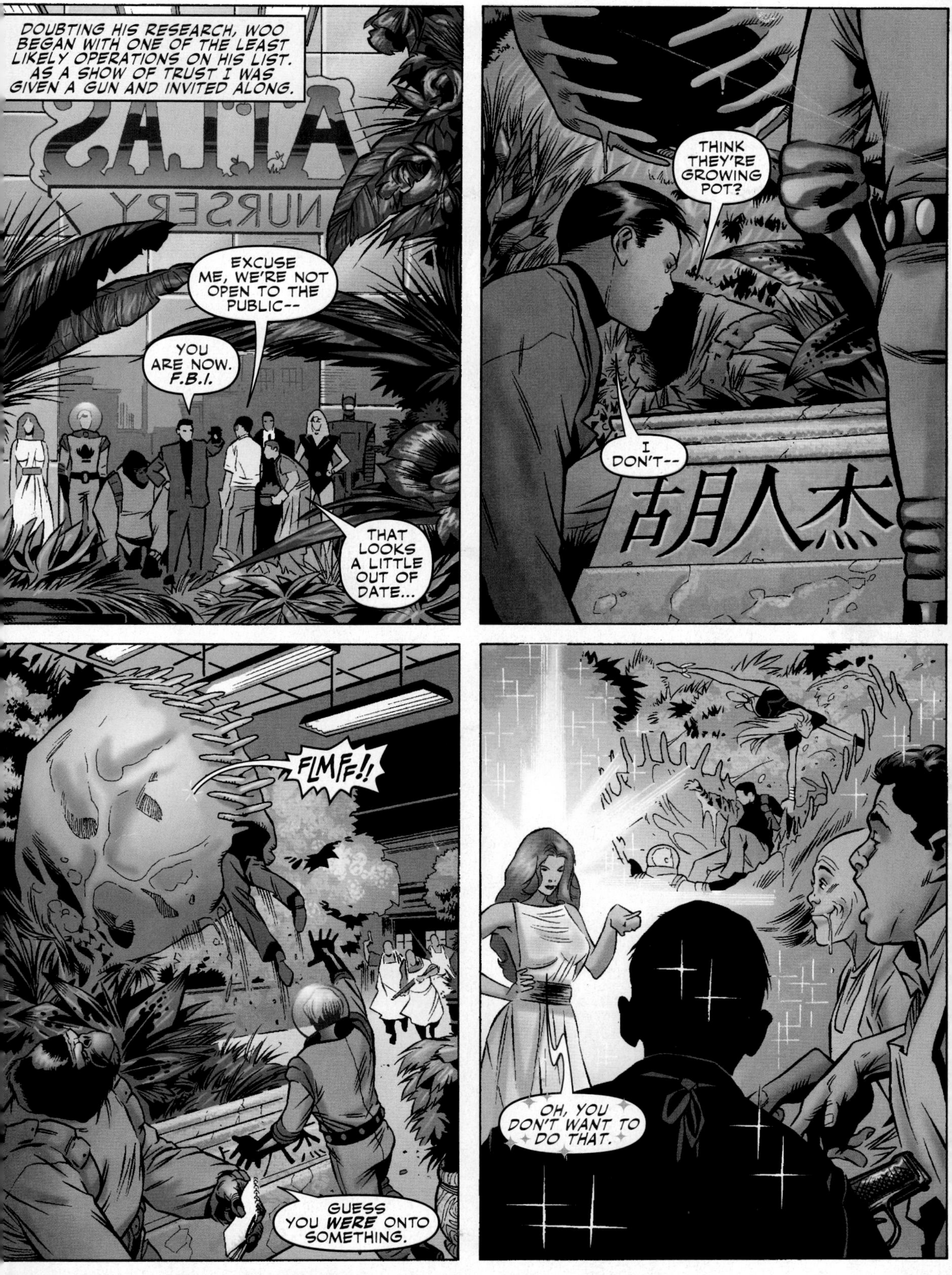
DOUBTING HIS RESEARCH, WOO BEGAN WITH ONE OF THE LEAST LIKELY OPERATIONS ON HIS LIST. AS A SHOW OF TRUST I WAS GIVEN A GUN AND INVITED ALONG.
ATLAS
NURSERY
EXCUSE ME, WE'RE NOT OPEN TO THE PUBLIC--
YOU ARE NOW. F.B.I.
THAT LOOKS A LITTLE OUT OF DATE...
THINK THEY'RE GROWING POT?
I DON'T--
胡人杰
FLMFF!!
GUESS YOU WERE ONTO SOMETHING.
OH, YOU DON'T WANT TO DO THAT.

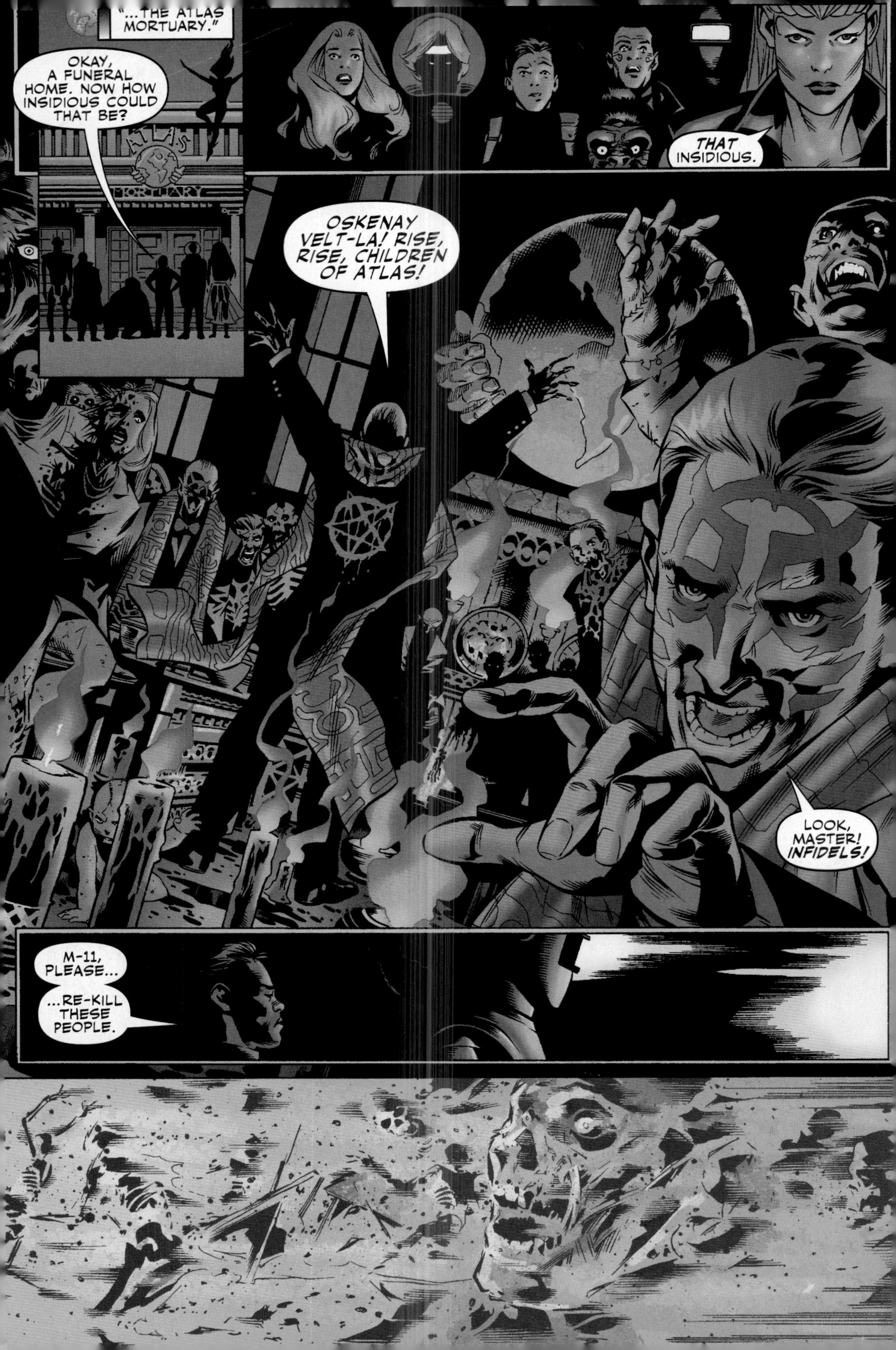

"...THE ATLAS MORTUARY."
OKAY, A FUNERAL HOME. NOW HOW INSIDIOUS COULD THAT BE?
ATLAS MORTUARY
THAT INSIDIOUS.
OSKENAY VELT-LA! RISE, RISE, CHILDREN OF ATLAS!
LOOK, MASTER! INFIDELS!
M-11, PLEASE...
...RE-KILL THESE PEOPLE.

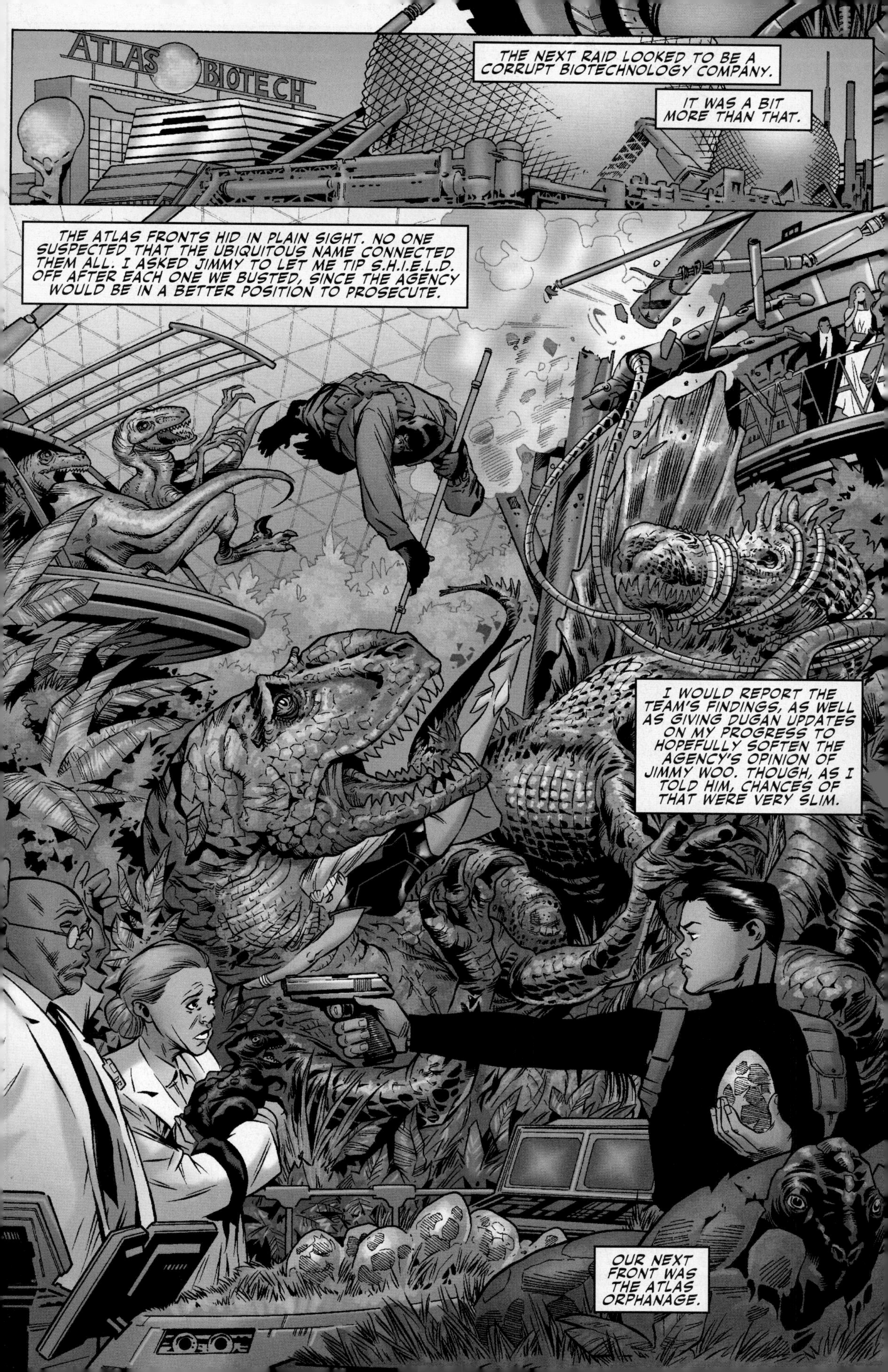
ATLAS BIOTECH
THE NEXT RAID LOOKED TO BE A CORRUPT BIOTECHNOLOGY COMPANY.
IT WAS A BIT MORE THAN THAT.
THE ATLAS FRONTS HID IN PLAIN SIGHT. NO ONE SUSPECTED THAT THE UBIQUITOUS NAME CONNECTED THEM ALL. I ASKED JIMMY TO LET ME TIP S.H.I.E.L.D. OFF AFTER EACH ONE WE BUSTED, SINCE THE AGENCY WOULD BE IN A BETTER POSITION TO PROSECUTE.
I WOULD REPORT THE TEAM'S FINDINGS, AS WELL AS GIVING DUGAN UPDATES ON MY PROGRESS TO HOPEFULLY SOFTEN THE AGENCY'S OPINION OF JIMMY WOO. THOUGH, AS I TOLD HIM, CHANCES OF THAT WERE VERY SLIM.
OUR NEXT FRONT WAS THE ATLAS ORPHANAGE.

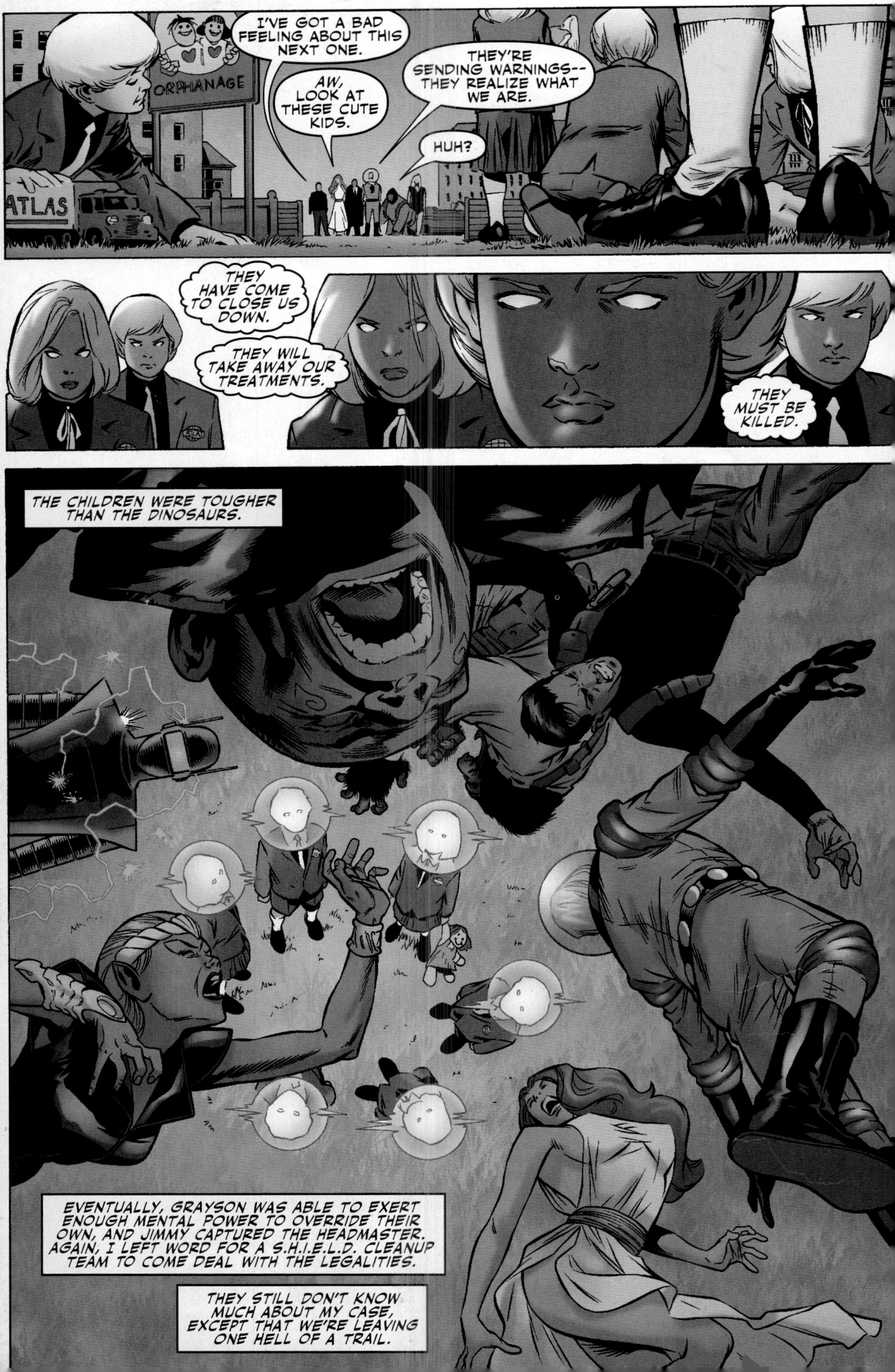
ORPHANAGE
ATLAS
I'VE GOT A BAD FEELING ABOUT THIS NEXT ONE.
AW, LOOK AT THESE CUTE KIDS.
THEY'RE SENDING WARNINGS-- THEY REALIZE WHAT WE ARE.
HUH?
THEY HAVE COME TO CLOSE US DOWN.
THEY WILL TAKE AWAY OUR TREATMENTS.
THEY MUST BE KILLED.
THE CHILDREN WERE TOUGHER THAN THE DINOSAURS.
EVENTUALLY, GRAYSON WAS ABLE TO EXERT ENOUGH MENTAL POWER TO OVERRIDE THEIR OWN, AND JIMMY CAPTURED THE HEADMASTER. AGAIN, I LEFT WORD FOR A S.H.I.E.L.D. CLEANUP TEAM TO COME DEAL WITH THE LEGALITIES.
THEY STILL DON'T KNOW MUCH ABOUT MY CASE, EXCEPT THAT WE'RE LEAVING ONE HELL OF A TRAIL.

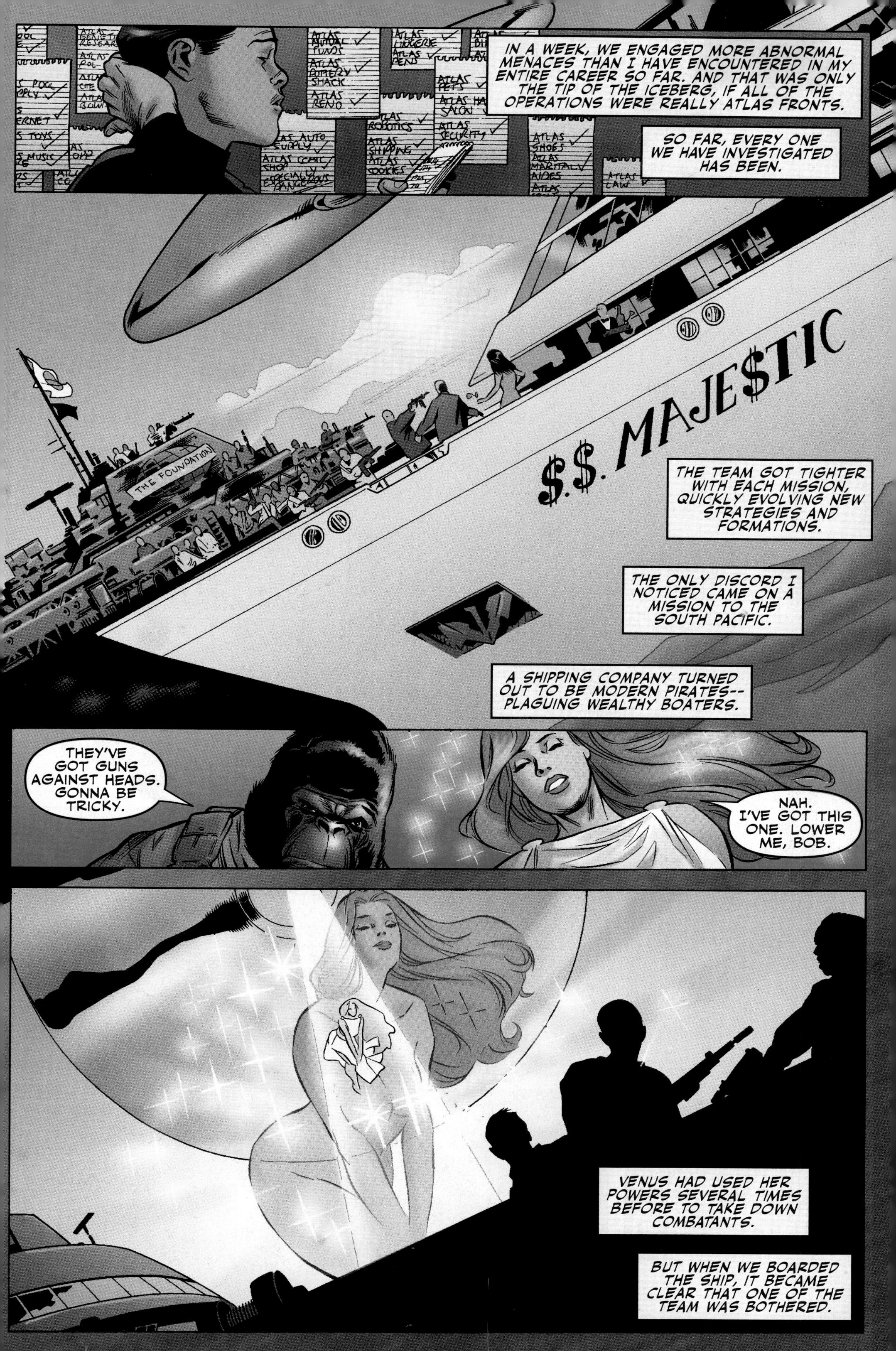
IN A WEEK, WE ENGAGED MORE ABNORMAL MENACES THAN I HAVE ENCOUNTERED IN MY ENTIRE CAREER SO FAR. AND THAT WAS ONLY THE TIP OF THE ICEBERG, IF ALL OF THE OPERATIONS WERE REALLY ATLAS FRONTS.
SO FAR, EVERY ONE WE HAVE INVESTIGATED HAS BEEN.
$.$. MAJE$TIC
THE FOUNDATION
THE TEAM GOT TIGHTER WITH EACH MISSION, QUICKLY EVOLVING NEW STRATEGIES AND FORMATIONS.
THE ONLY DISCORD I NOTICED CAME ON A MISSION TO THE SOUTH PACIFIC.
A SHIPPING COMPANY TURNED OUT TO BE MODERN PIRATES-- PLAGUING WEALTHY BOATERS.
THEY'VE GOT GUNS AGAINST HEADS. GONNA BE TRICKY.
NAH. I'VE GOT THIS ONE. LOWER ME, BOB.
VENUS HAD USED HER POWERS SEVERAL TIMES BEFORE TO TAKE DOWN COMBATANTS.
BUT WHEN WE BOARDED THE SHIP, IT BECAME CLEAR THAT ONE OF THE TEAM WAS BOTHERED.

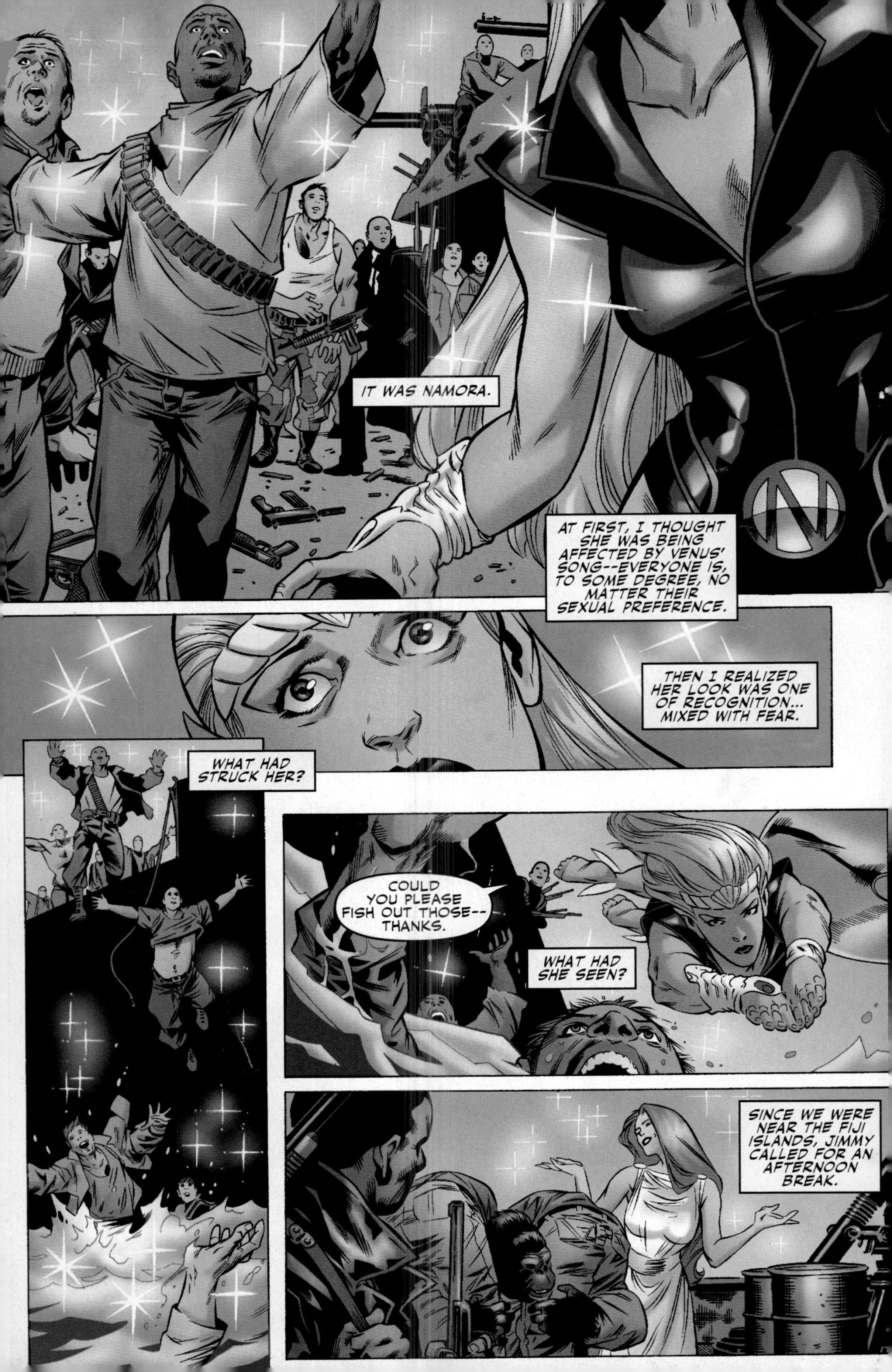
IT WAS NAMORA.
AT FIRST, I THOUGHT SHE WAS BEING AFFECTED BY VENUS' SONG--EVERYONE IS, TO SOME DEGREE, NO MATTER THEIR SEXUAL PREFERENCE.
THEN I REALIZED HER LOOK WAS ONE OF RECOGNITION... MIXED WITH FEAR.
WHAT HAD STRUCK HER?
COULD YOU PLEASE FISH OUT THOSE-- THANKS.
WHAT HAD SHE SEEN?
SINCE WE WERE NEAR THE FIJI ISLANDS, JIMMY CALLED FOR AN AFTERNOON BREAK.

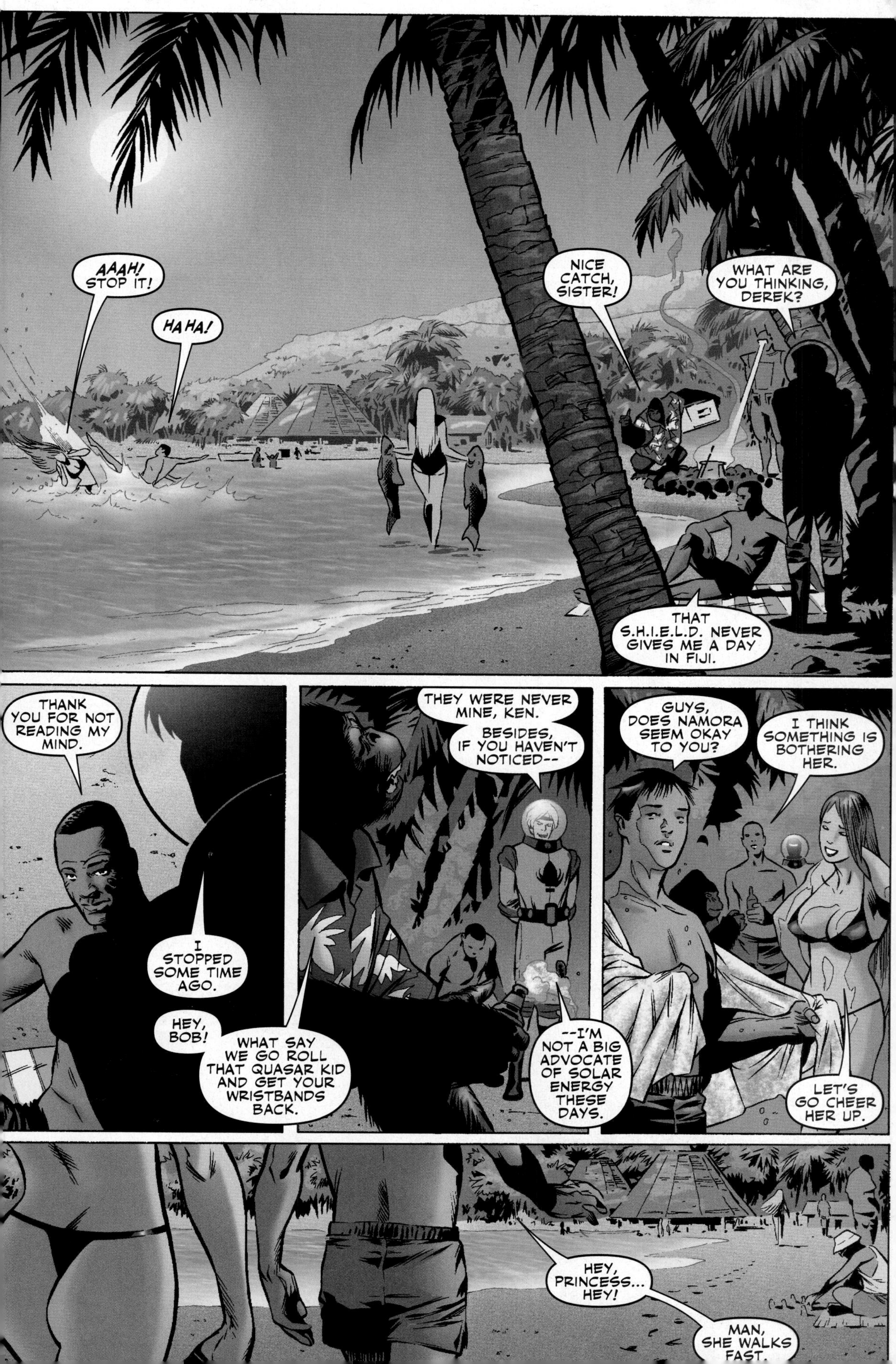
AAAH! STOP IT!
HA HA!
NICE CATCH, SISTER!
WHAT ARE YOU THINKING, DEREK?
THAT S.H.I.E.L.D. NEVER GIVES ME A DAY IN FIJI.
THANK YOU FOR NOT READING MY MIND.
I STOPPED SOME TIME AGO.
HEY, BOB!
WHAT SAY WE GO ROLL THAT QUASAR KID AND GET YOUR WRISTBANDS BACK.
THEY WERE NEVER MINE, KEN.
BESIDES, IF YOU HAVEN'T NOTICED--
--I'M NOT A BIG ADVOCATE OF SOLAR ENERGY THESE DAYS.
GUYS, DOES NAMORA SEEM OKAY TO YOU?
I THINK SOMETHING IS BOTHERING HER.
LET'S GO CHEER HER UP.
HEY, PRINCESS... HEY!
MAN, SHE WALKS FAST.

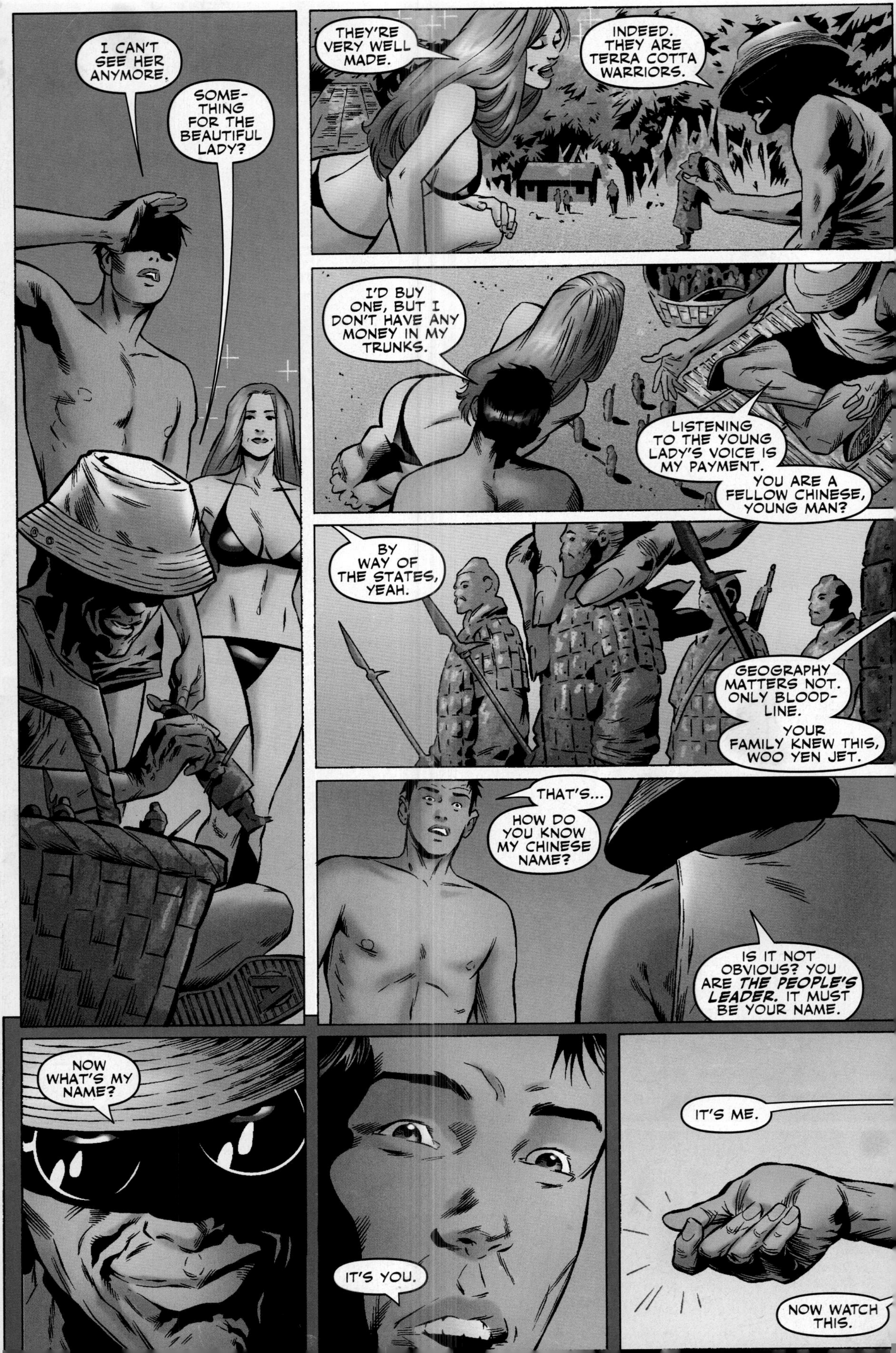

I CAN'T SEE HER ANYMORE.
SOME-THING FOR THE BEAUTIFUL LADY?
THEY'RE VERY WELL MADE.
INDEED. THEY ARE TERRA COTTA WARRIORS.
I'D BUY ONE, BUT I DON'T HAVE ANY MONEY IN MY TRUNKS.
LISTENING TO THE YOUNG LADY'S VOICE IS MY PAYMENT.
YOU ARE A FELLOW CHINESE, YOUNG MAN?
BY WAY OF THE STATES, YEAH.
GEOGRAPHY MATTERS NOT. ONLY BLOOD-LINE.
YOUR FAMILY KNEW THIS, WOO YEN JET.
THAT'S...
HOW DO YOU KNOW MY CHINESE NAME?
IS IT NOT OBVIOUS? YOU ARE *THE PEOPLE'S LEADER.* IT MUST BE YOUR NAME.
NOW WHAT'S MY NAME?
IT'S YOU.
IT'S ME.
NOW WATCH THIS.

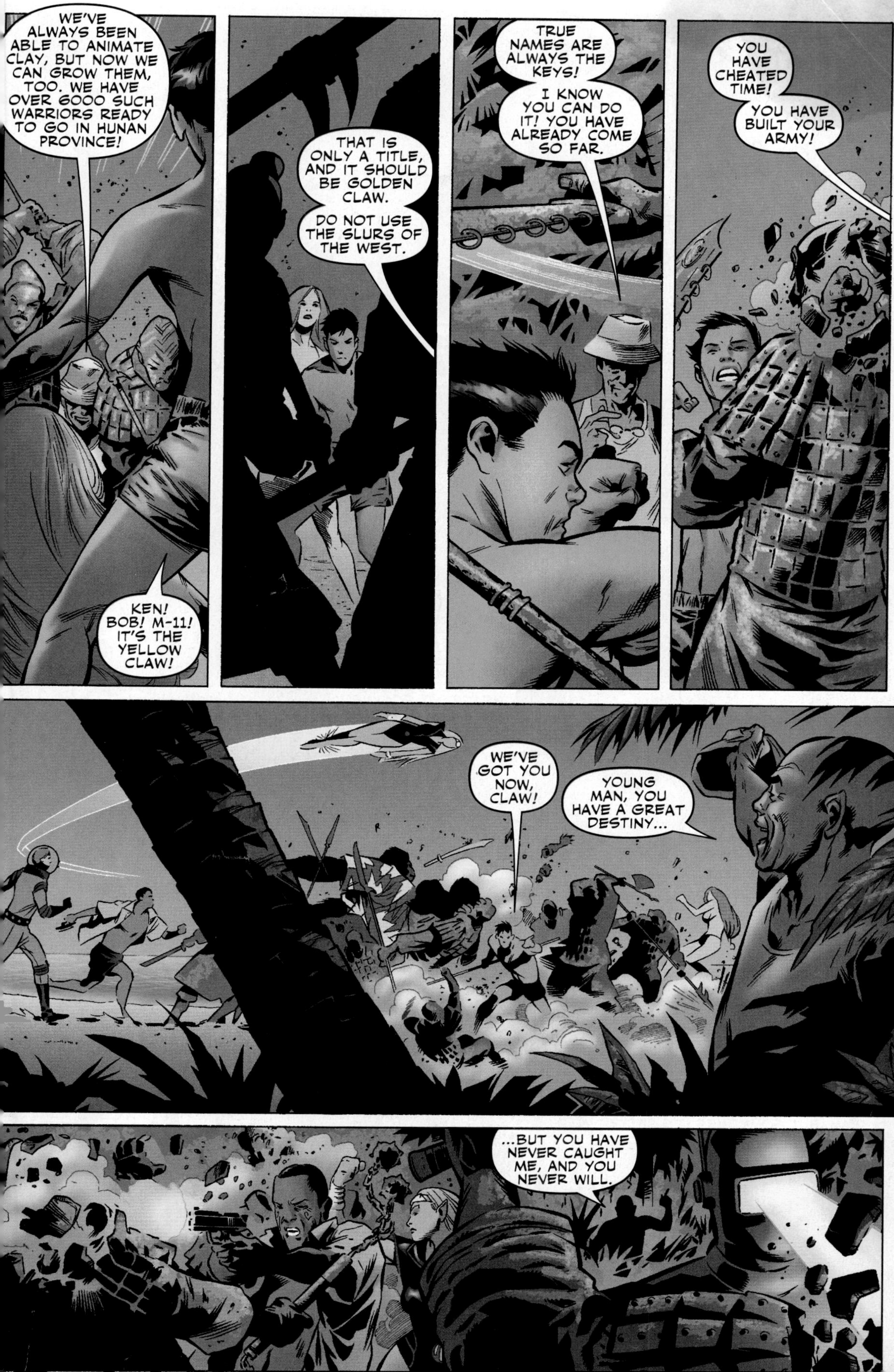

WE'VE ALWAYS BEEN ABLE TO ANIMATE CLAY, BUT NOW WE CAN GROW THEM, TOO. WE HAVE OVER 6000 SUCH WARRIORS READY TO GO IN HUNAN PROVINCE!
KEN! BOB! M-11! IT'S THE YELLOW CLAW!
THAT IS ONLY A TITLE, AND IT SHOULD BE GOLDEN CLAW.
DO NOT USE THE SLURS OF THE WEST.
TRUE NAMES ARE ALWAYS THE KEYS!
I KNOW YOU CAN DO IT! YOU HAVE ALREADY COME SO FAR.
YOU HAVE CHEATED TIME!
YOU HAVE BUILT YOUR ARMY!
WE'VE GOT YOU NOW, CLAW!
YOUNG MAN, YOU HAVE A GREAT DESTINY...
...BUT YOU HAVE NEVER CAUGHT ME, AND YOU NEVER WILL.

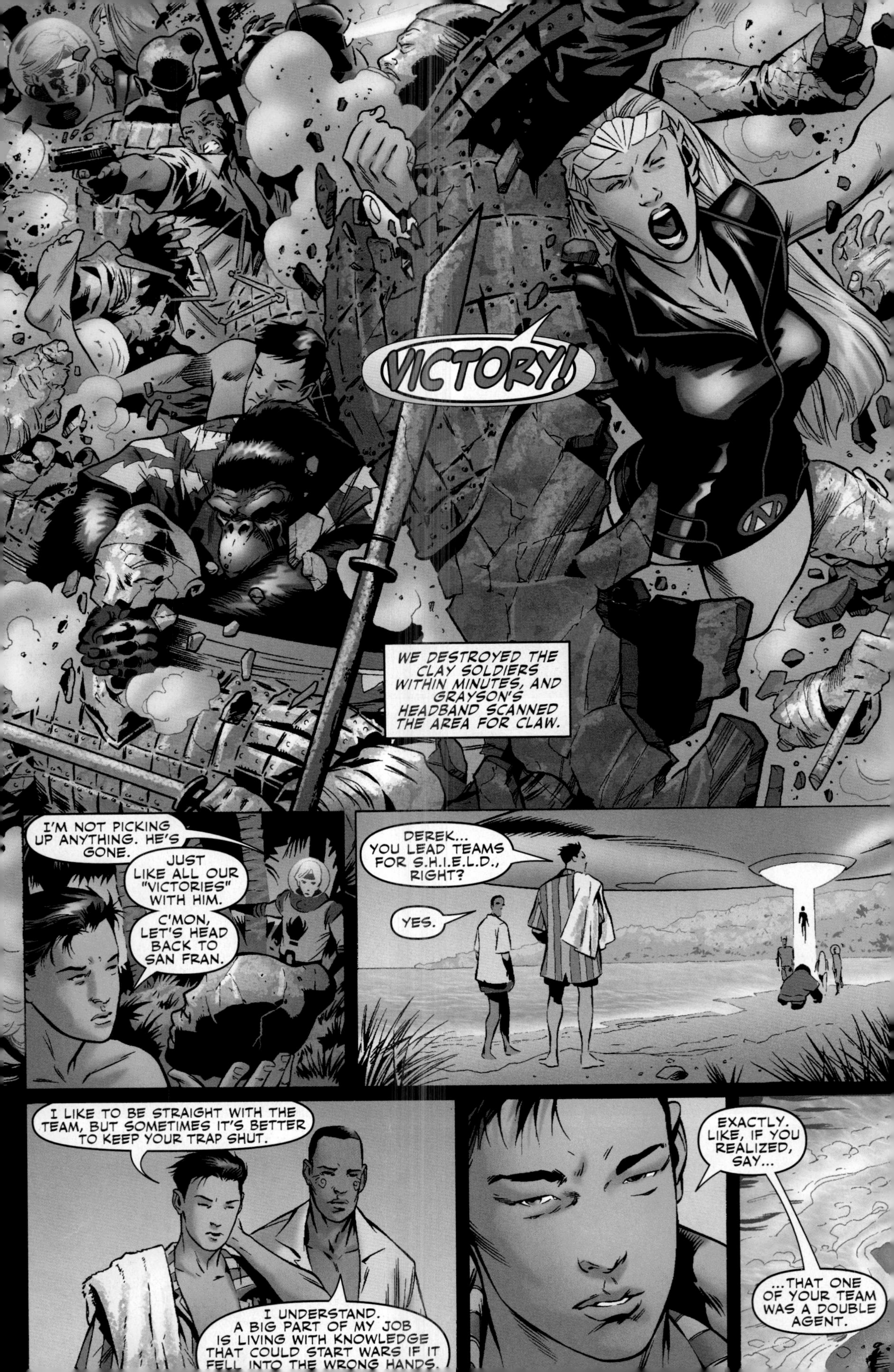
VICTORY!
WE DESTROYED THE CLAY SOLDIERS WITHIN MINUTES, AND GRAYSON'S HEADBAND SCANNED THE AREA FOR CLAW.
I'M NOT PICKING UP ANYTHING. HE'S GONE.
JUST LIKE ALL OUR "VICTORIES" WITH HIM.
C'MON, LET'S HEAD BACK TO SAN FRAN.
DEREK... YOU LEAD TEAMS FOR S.H.I.E.L.D., RIGHT?
YES.
I LIKE TO BE STRAIGHT WITH THE TEAM, BUT SOMETIMES IT'S BETTER TO KEEP YOUR TRAP SHUT.
I UNDERSTAND. A BIG PART OF MY JOB IS LIVING WITH KNOWLEDGE THAT COULD START WARS IF IT FELL INTO THE WRONG HANDS.
EXACTLY. LIKE, IF YOU REALIZED, SAY...
...THAT ONE OF YOUR TEAM WAS A DOUBLE AGENT.

FROM THE CASE FILES OF KEN HALE

Okay, I made Bob whip me up a jumbo keyboard so I can do some of these entries while Jimmy studies his research on the Atlas Foundation. We've been out, going through the list and knocking heads round the clock. Somebody has to keep track of all this stuff. I ought to let M-11 do it, that would be a hoot.

- K.H.

ATLAS RECORDS
About what you'd expect, the producers were working subliminal mind-control messages into their releases. Most of it was directed at making listeners buy more of their CD's, so they were pulling in good money. I got to punch a guy who organized boy bands, so it was a banner morning for me.

ATLAS VINEYARDS
They made truth-serum wine. We had some. Good stuff.

ATLAS MUNITIONS
Talk about heavy artillery! We non-bulletproofers hung back and let M-11 and Namora deal with those jokers. The place is a big scorched crater now.

ATLAS DAIRY
So not every business on the planet named Atlas is part of the Foundation. These people just bottle milk. We spooked a lot of cows before Bob determined that no one was up to anything. I felt bad and bought a bunch of cheese off of them to make up for it.

ATLAS COMICS
Jimmy determined this was on the up-and-up too, but I still think it's a front. They only had super hero books, and all of those had crossover stories, so you had to buy all of them to get one damn story! Gotta be a racket. And where's all the war books?

ATLAS NOVELTIES
I was sure this was going to be a bust too, then Venus opened a spring-loaded "can of peanuts" that let out real snakes--deadly adders. The manager tried to electrocute Bob with a lethal joy buzzer, but his suit rechanneled most of the current.

ATLAS ACADEMY OF MARTIAL ARTS
Now this was fun. Jimmy, Namora and I asked the others to stay outside while we got in a little hand-to-hand practice. My "pissed ape" style was too much for those hotshots and their fancy moves. Of course, Jimmy had the best form, he was flipping all over, spinning and busting heads like crazy! Every time we'd get their numbers down, a whole new team would come running out of secret doors and floorboards. Namora finally got ticked off and kicked out the wall, dropping the building on them.

FAMOUS ATLAS' COOKIES
Super-addictive cookies. We weren't sure if this was actually illegal, so we smashed their ovens and plan to get back here later for a follow-up. Everyone assumes I like coconut in sweets, but I want to make it clear that I DON'T.

ATLAS AUTO
Mostly legit--for an auto parts company, that is--but they smuggled weaponry in lots of the overseas shipments. Jimmy picked up some parts for the Edsel before we left.

ATLAS MINING
So here's where a lot of the Top 40 listeners of Atlas Records end up--digging ore out of this mountain in the San Andreas area. After we hustled the kids out of there, Bob leveled the mountain with the saucer's meteor-smasher. That was something to see.

APE ART by MIKE SHORT

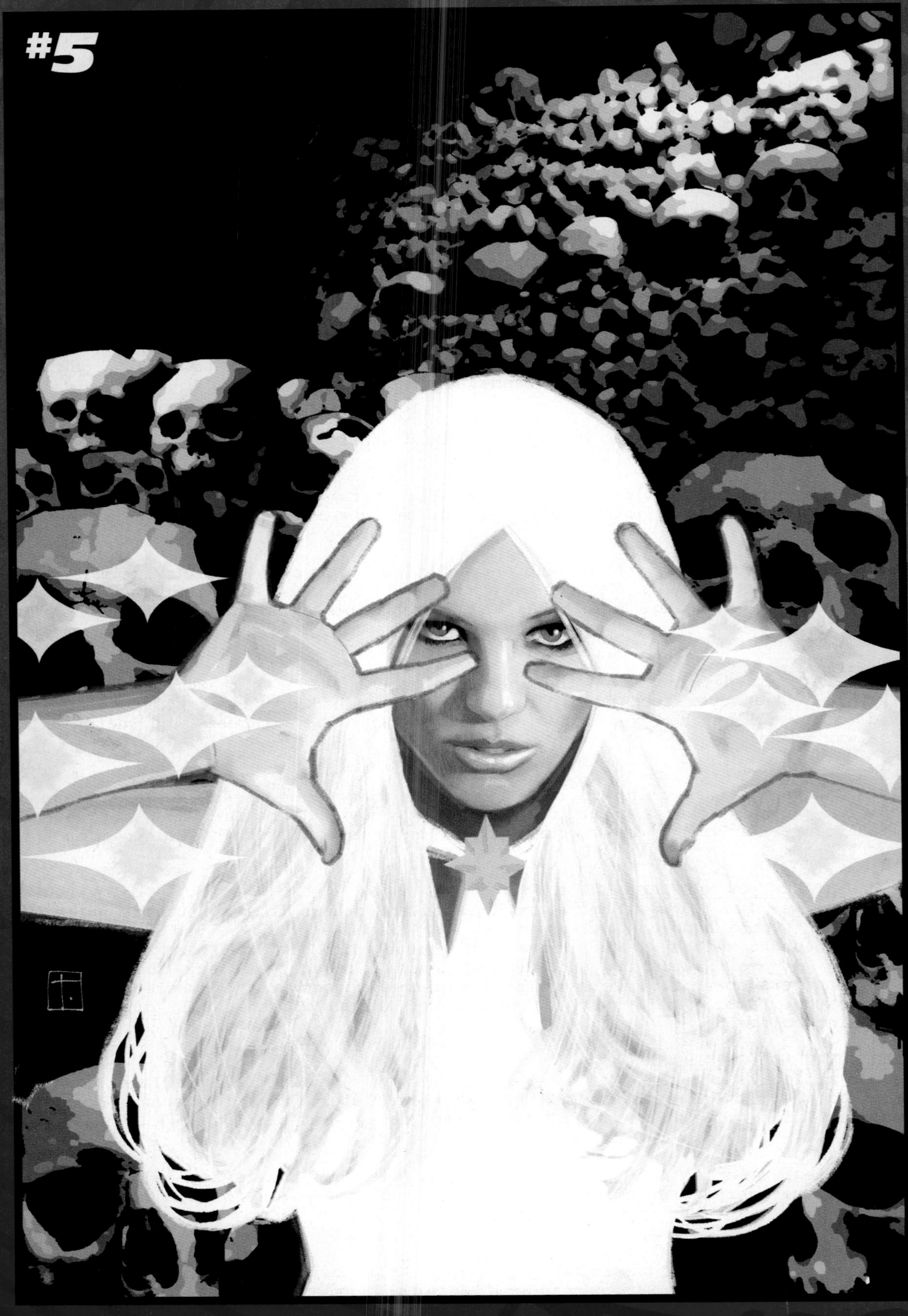
#5

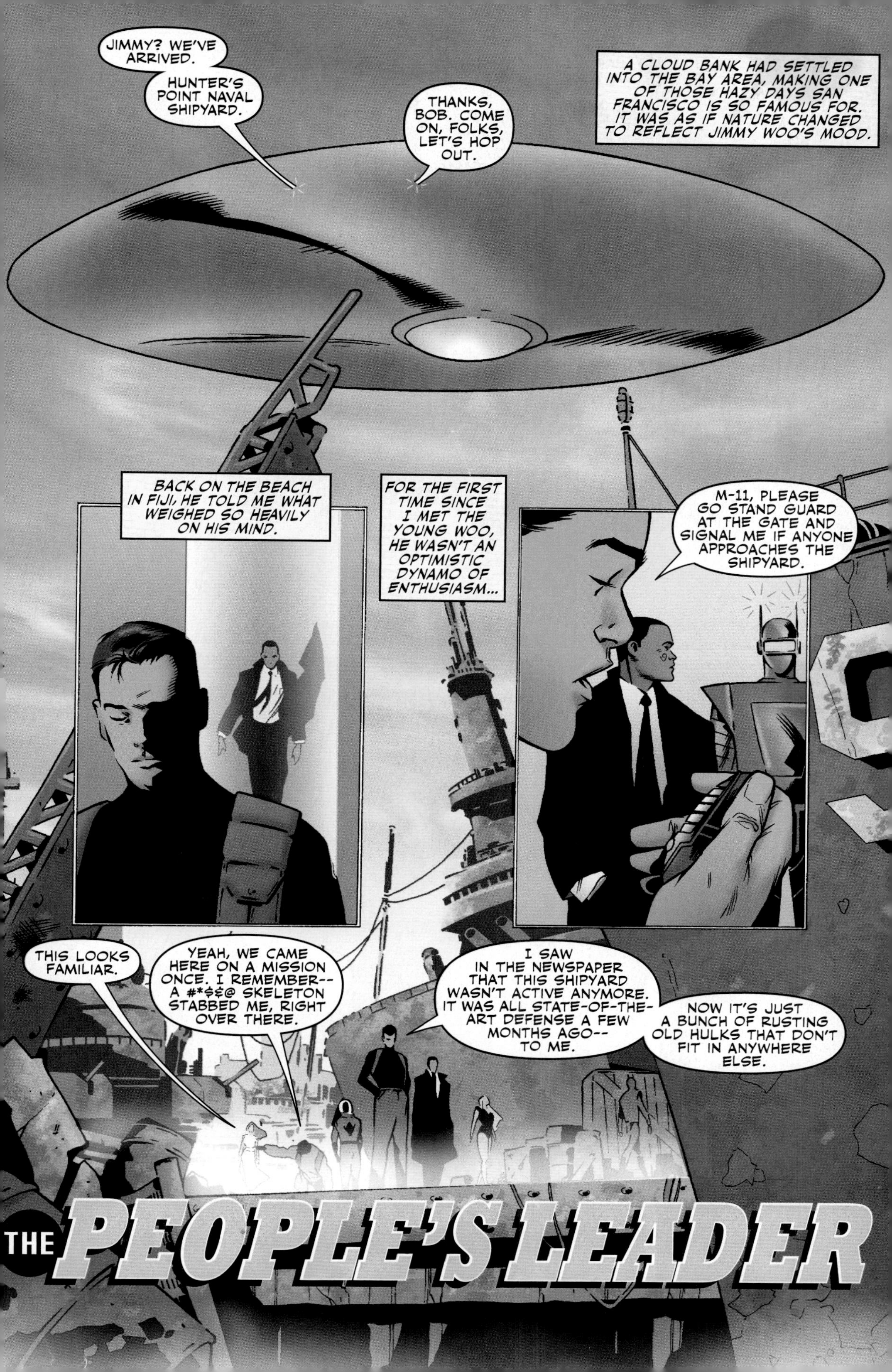
JIMMY? WE'VE ARRIVED.
HUNTER'S POINT NAVAL SHIPYARD.
THANKS, BOB. COME ON, FOLKS, LET'S HOP OUT.
A CLOUD BANK HAD SETTLED INTO THE BAY AREA, MAKING ONE OF THOSE HAZY DAYS SAN FRANCISCO IS SO FAMOUS FOR. IT WAS AS IF NATURE CHANGED TO REFLECT JIMMY WOO'S MOOD.
BACK ON THE BEACH IN FIJI, HE TOLD ME WHAT WEIGHED SO HEAVILY ON HIS MIND.
FOR THE FIRST TIME SINCE I MET THE YOUNG WOO, HE WASN'T AN OPTIMISTIC DYNAMO OF ENTHUSIASM...
M-11, PLEASE GO STAND GUARD AT THE GATE AND SIGNAL ME IF ANYONE APPROACHES THE SHIPYARD.
THIS LOOKS FAMILIAR.
YEAH, WE CAME HERE ON A MISSION ONCE. I REMEMBER-- A #*$¢@ SKELETON STABBED ME, RIGHT OVER THERE.
I SAW IN THE NEWSPAPER THAT THIS SHIPYARD WASN'T ACTIVE ANYMORE. IT WAS ALL STATE-OF-THE-ART DEFENSE A FEW MONTHS AGO-- TO ME.
NOW IT'S JUST A BUNCH OF RUSTING OLD HULKS THAT DON'T FIT IN ANYWHERE ELSE.
THE PEOPLE'S LEADER

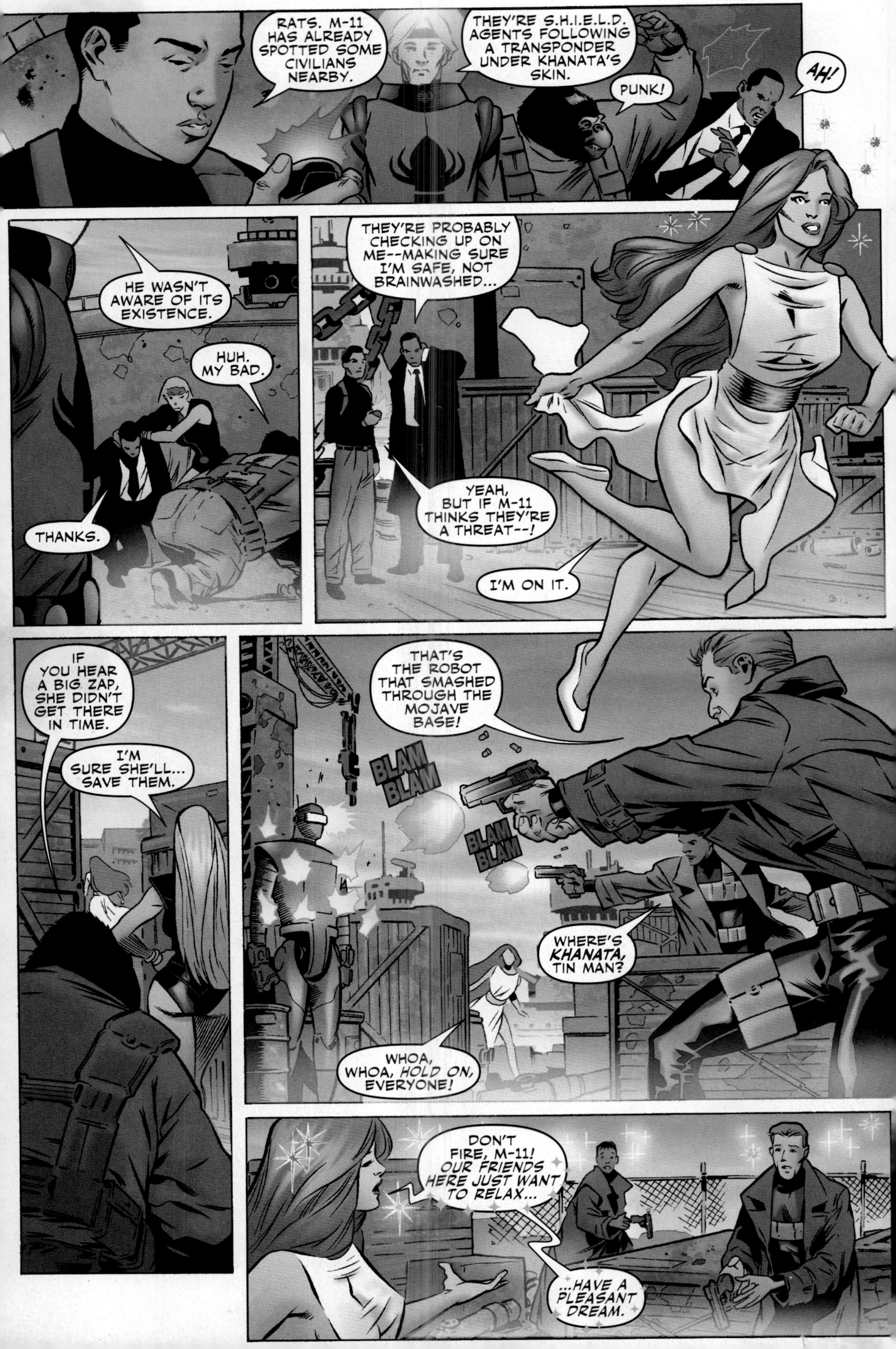
RATS. M-11 HAS ALREADY SPOTTED SOME CIVILIANS NEARBY.
THEY'RE S.H.I.E.L.D. AGENTS FOLLOWING A TRANSPONDER UNDER KHANATA'S SKIN.
PUNK!
AH!
HE WASN'T AWARE OF ITS EXISTENCE.
HUH. MY BAD.
THANKS.
THEY'RE PROBABLY CHECKING UP ON ME--MAKING SURE I'M SAFE, NOT BRAINWASHED...
YEAH, BUT IF M-11 THINKS THEY'RE A THREAT--!
I'M ON IT.
IF YOU HEAR A BIG ZAP, SHE DIDN'T GET THERE IN TIME.
I'M SURE SHE'LL... SAVE THEM.
THAT'S THE ROBOT THAT SMASHED THROUGH THE MOJAVE BASE!
BLAM BLAM
BLAM BLAM
WHERE'S KHANATA, TIN MAN?
WHOA, WHOA, HOLD ON, EVERYONE!
DON'T FIRE, M-11! OUR FRIENDS HERE JUST WANT TO RELAX...
...HAVE A PLEASANT DREAM.

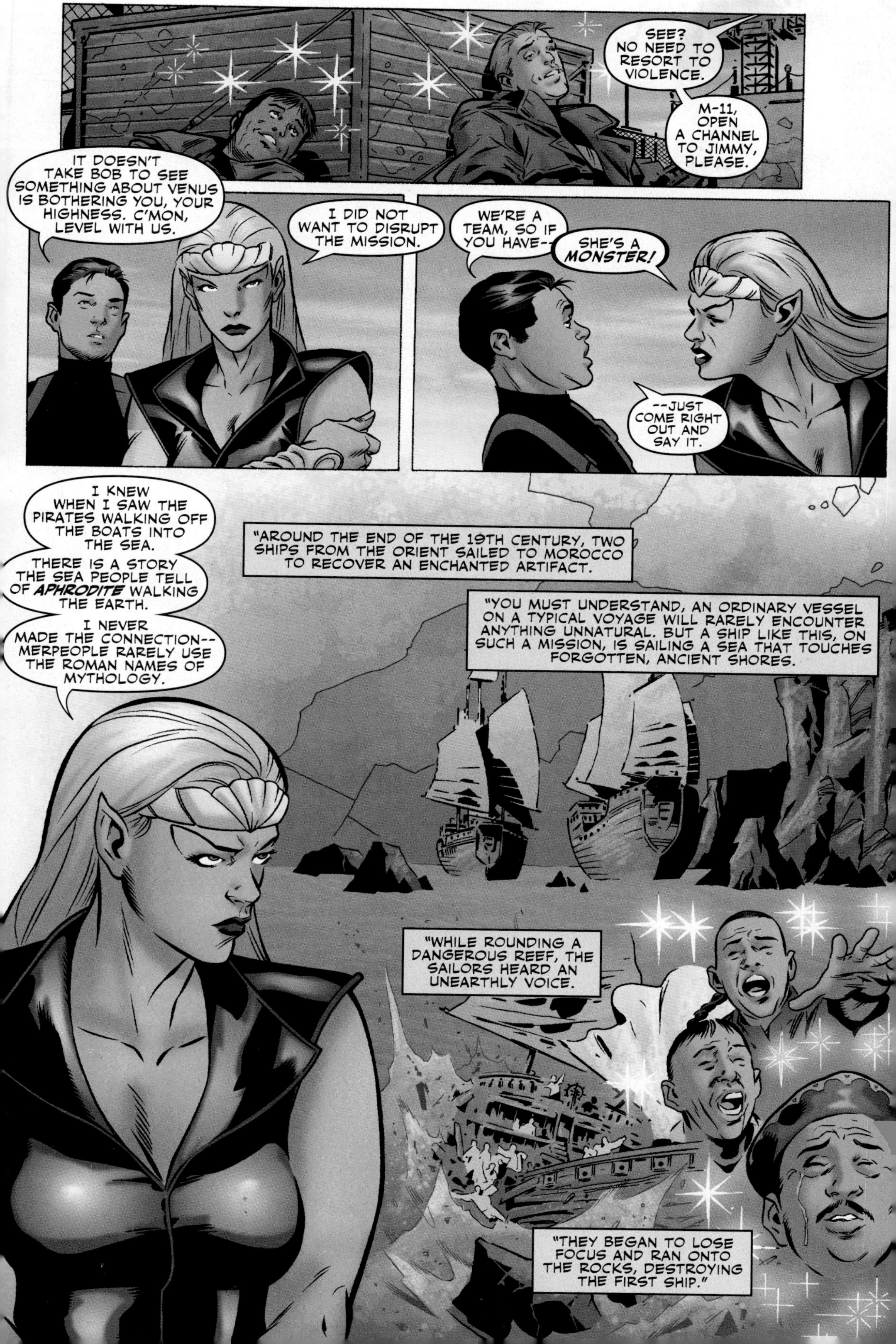

SEE? NO NEED TO RESORT TO VIOLENCE.
M-11, OPEN A CHANNEL TO JIMMY, PLEASE.
IT DOESN'T TAKE BOB TO SEE SOMETHING ABOUT VENUS IS BOTHERING YOU, YOUR HIGHNESS. C'MON, LEVEL WITH US.
I DID NOT WANT TO DISRUPT THE MISSION.
WE'RE A TEAM, SO IF YOU HAVE--
SHE'S A MONSTER!
--JUST COME RIGHT OUT AND SAY IT.
I KNEW WHEN I SAW THE PIRATES WALKING OFF THE BOATS INTO THE SEA.
THERE IS A STORY THE SEA PEOPLE TELL OF APHRODITE WALKING THE EARTH.
I NEVER MADE THE CONNECTION-- MERPEOPLE RARELY USE THE ROMAN NAMES OF MYTHOLOGY.
"AROUND THE END OF THE 19TH CENTURY, TWO SHIPS FROM THE ORIENT SAILED TO MOROCCO TO RECOVER AN ENCHANTED ARTIFACT.
"YOU MUST UNDERSTAND, AN ORDINARY VESSEL ON A TYPICAL VOYAGE WILL RARELY ENCOUNTER ANYTHING UNNATURAL. BUT A SHIP LIKE THIS, ON SUCH A MISSION, IS SAILING A SEA THAT TOUCHES FORGOTTEN, ANCIENT SHORES.
"WHILE ROUNDING A DANGEROUS REEF, THE SAILORS HEARD AN UNEARTHLY VOICE.
"THEY BEGAN TO LOSE FOCUS AND RAN ONTO THE ROCKS, DESTROYING THE FIRST SHIP."

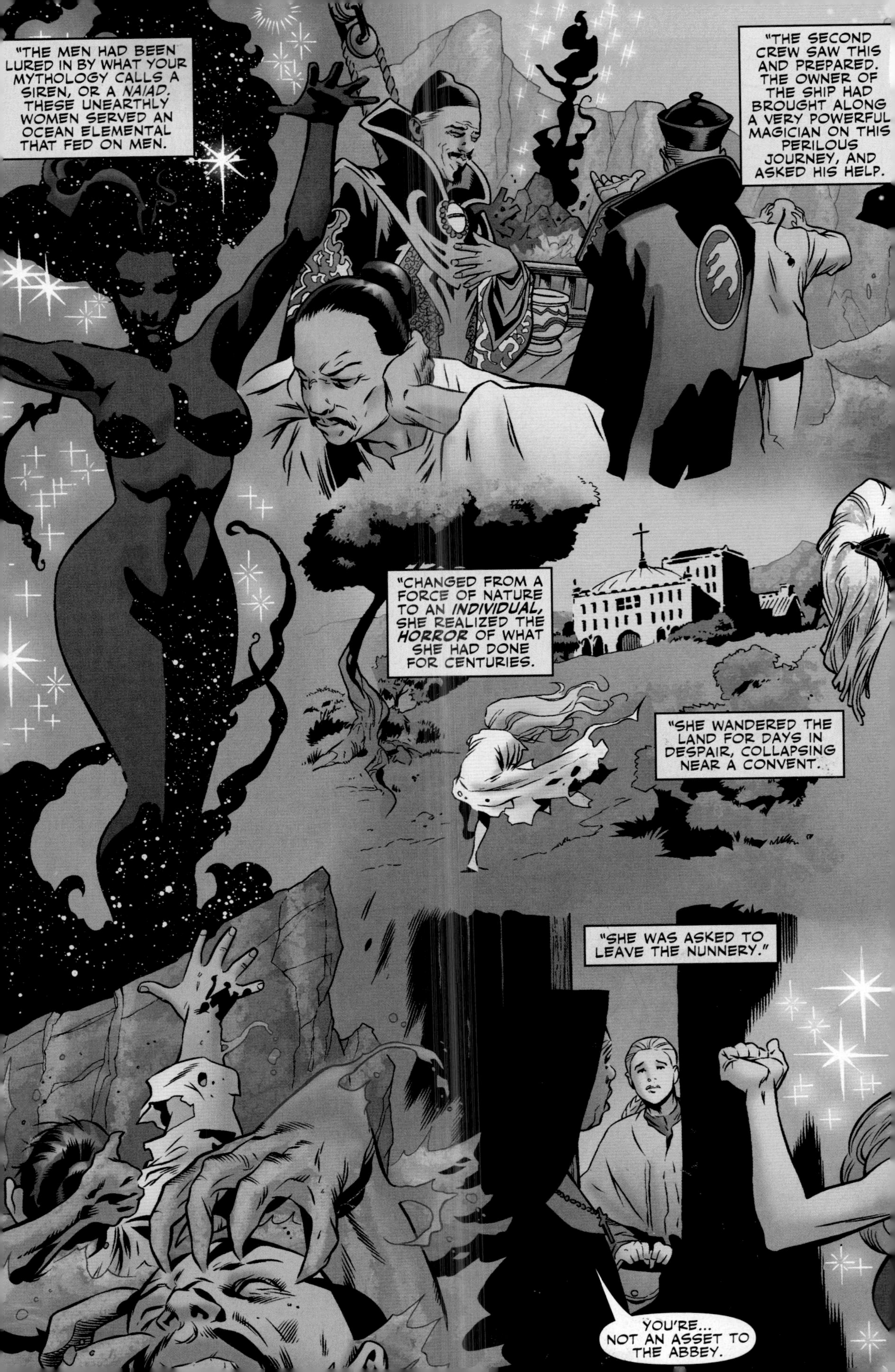
"THE MEN HAD BEEN LURED IN BY WHAT YOUR MYTHOLOGY CALLS A SIREN, OR A *NAIAD*. THESE UNEARTHLY WOMEN SERVED AN OCEAN ELEMENTAL THAT FED ON MEN.
"THE SECOND CREW SAW THIS AND PREPARED. THE OWNER OF THE SHIP HAD BROUGHT ALONG A VERY POWERFUL MAGICIAN ON THIS PERILOUS JOURNEY, AND ASKED HIS HELP.
"CHANGED FROM A FORCE OF NATURE TO AN *INDIVIDUAL*, SHE REALIZED THE ***HORROR*** OF WHAT SHE HAD DONE FOR CENTURIES.
"SHE WANDERED THE LAND FOR DAYS IN DESPAIR, COLLAPSING NEAR A CONVENT.
"SHE WAS ASKED TO LEAVE THE NUNNERY."
YOU'RE... NOT AN ASSET TO THE ABBEY.

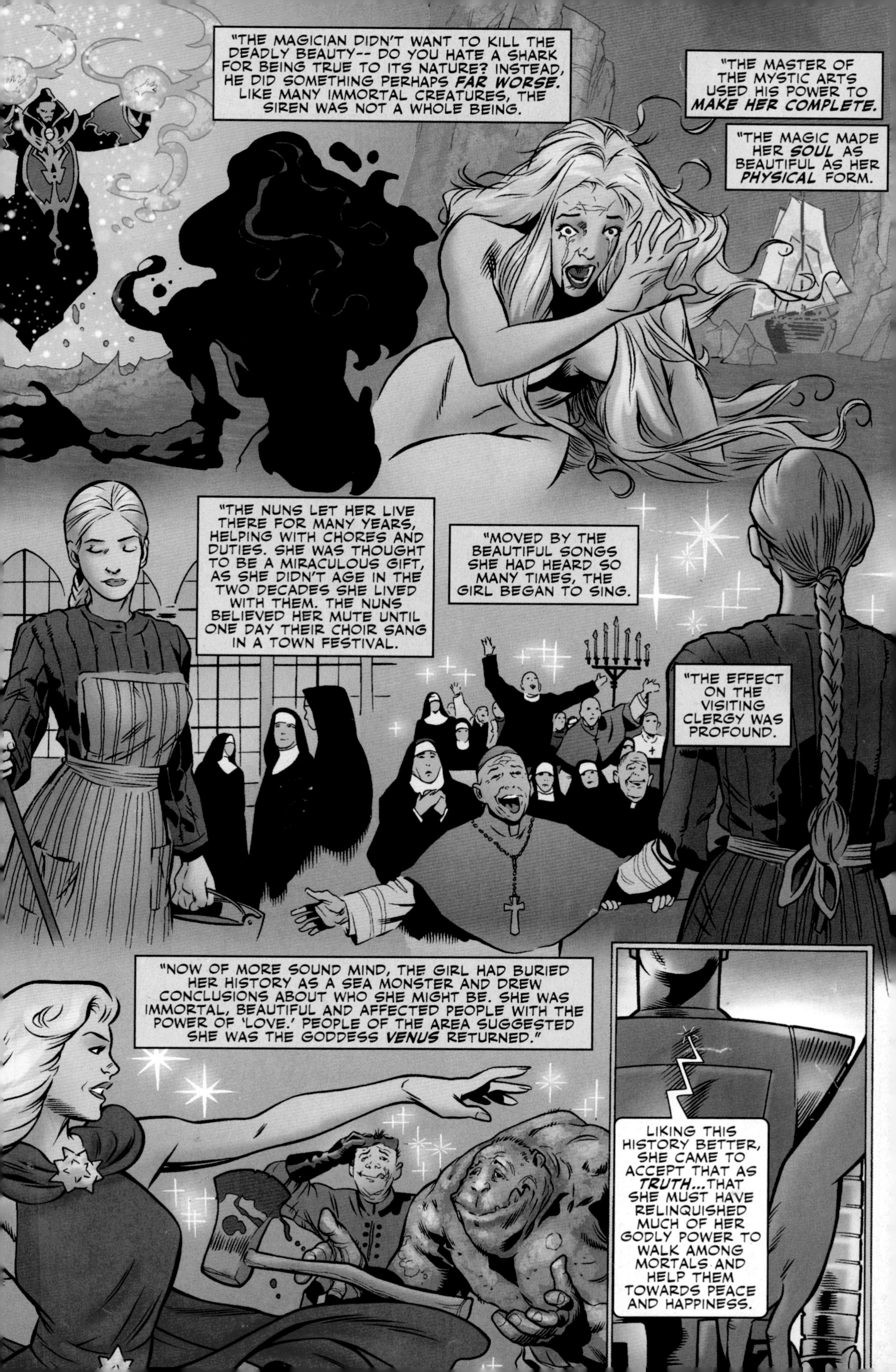
"THE MAGICIAN DIDN'T WANT TO KILL THE DEADLY BEAUTY-- DO YOU HATE A SHARK FOR BEING TRUE TO ITS NATURE? INSTEAD, HE DID SOMETHING PERHAPS FAR WORSE. LIKE MANY IMMORTAL CREATURES, THE SIREN WAS NOT A WHOLE BEING.
"THE MASTER OF THE MYSTIC ARTS USED HIS POWER TO MAKE HER COMPLETE.
"THE MAGIC MADE HER SOUL AS BEAUTIFUL AS HER PHYSICAL FORM.
"THE NUNS LET HER LIVE THERE FOR MANY YEARS, HELPING WITH CHORES AND DUTIES. SHE WAS THOUGHT TO BE A MIRACULOUS GIFT, AS SHE DIDN'T AGE IN THE TWO DECADES SHE LIVED WITH THEM. THE NUNS BELIEVED HER MUTE UNTIL ONE DAY THEIR CHOIR SANG IN A TOWN FESTIVAL.
"MOVED BY THE BEAUTIFUL SONGS SHE HAD HEARD SO MANY TIMES, THE GIRL BEGAN TO SING.
"THE EFFECT ON THE VISITING CLERGY WAS PROFOUND.
"NOW OF MORE SOUND MIND, THE GIRL HAD BURIED HER HISTORY AS A SEA MONSTER AND DREW CONCLUSIONS ABOUT WHO SHE MIGHT BE. SHE WAS IMMORTAL, BEAUTIFUL AND AFFECTED PEOPLE WITH THE POWER OF 'LOVE.' PEOPLE OF THE AREA SUGGESTED SHE WAS THE GODDESS VENUS RETURNED."
LIKING THIS HISTORY BETTER, SHE CAME TO ACCEPT THAT AS TRUTH...THAT SHE MUST HAVE RELINQUISHED MUCH OF HER GODLY POWER TO WALK AMONG MORTALS AND HELP THEM TOWARDS PEACE AND HAPPINESS.

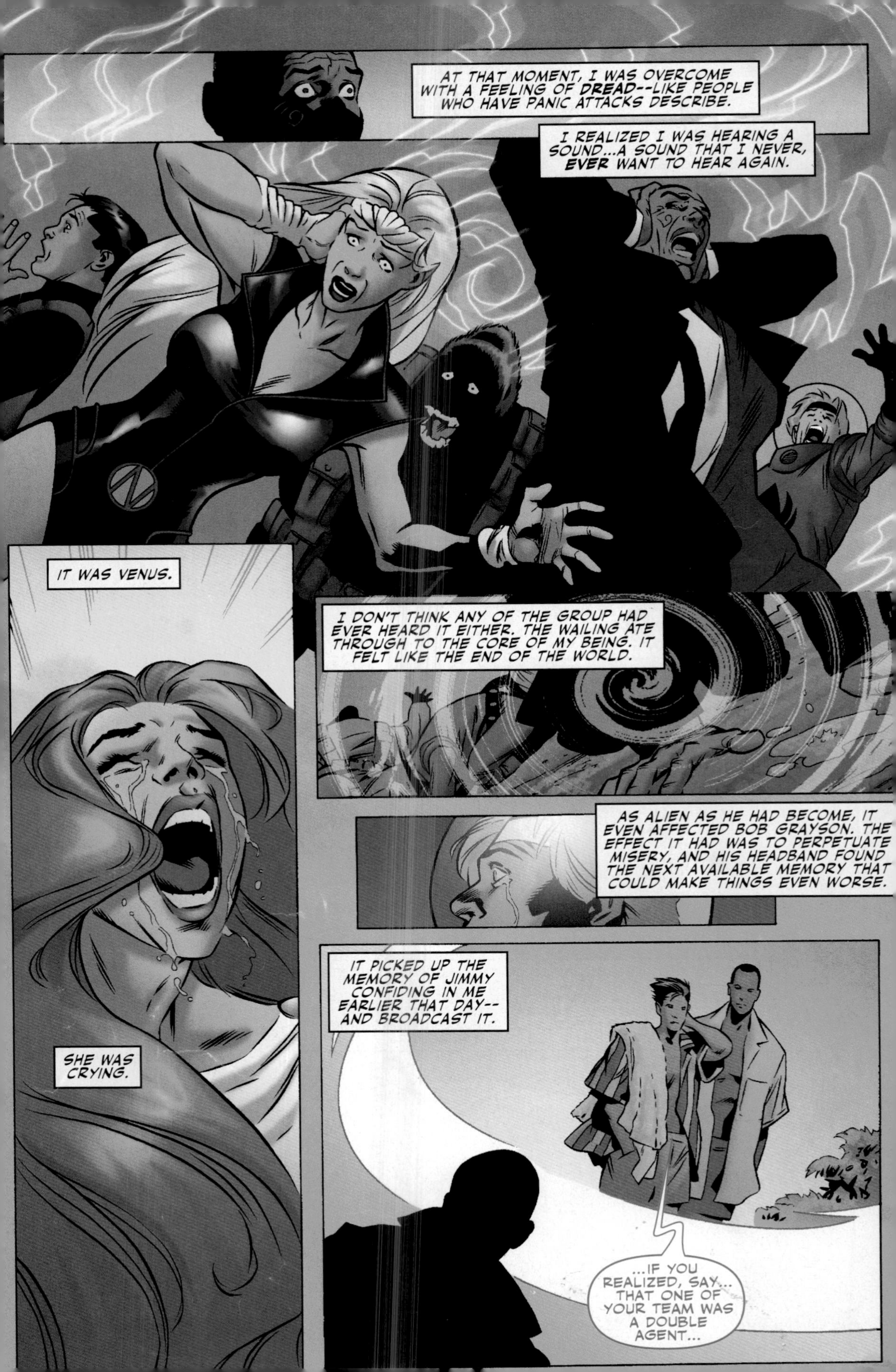
AT THAT MOMENT, I WAS OVERCOME WITH A FEELING OF DREAD--LIKE PEOPLE WHO HAVE PANIC ATTACKS DESCRIBE.
I REALIZED I WAS HEARING A SOUND...A SOUND THAT I NEVER, EVER WANT TO HEAR AGAIN.
IT WAS VENUS.
SHE WAS CRYING.
I DON'T THINK ANY OF THE GROUP HAD EVER HEARD IT EITHER. THE WAILING ATE THROUGH TO THE CORE OF MY BEING. IT FELT LIKE THE END OF THE WORLD.
AS ALIEN AS HE HAD BECOME, IT EVEN AFFECTED BOB GRAYSON. THE EFFECT IT HAD WAS TO PERPETUATE MISERY, AND HIS HEADBAND FOUND THE NEXT AVAILABLE MEMORY THAT COULD MAKE THINGS EVEN WORSE.
IT PICKED UP THE MEMORY OF JIMMY CONFIDING IN ME EARLIER THAT DAY-- AND BROADCAST IT.
...IF YOU REALIZED, SAY... THAT ONE OF YOUR TEAM WAS A DOUBLE AGENT...

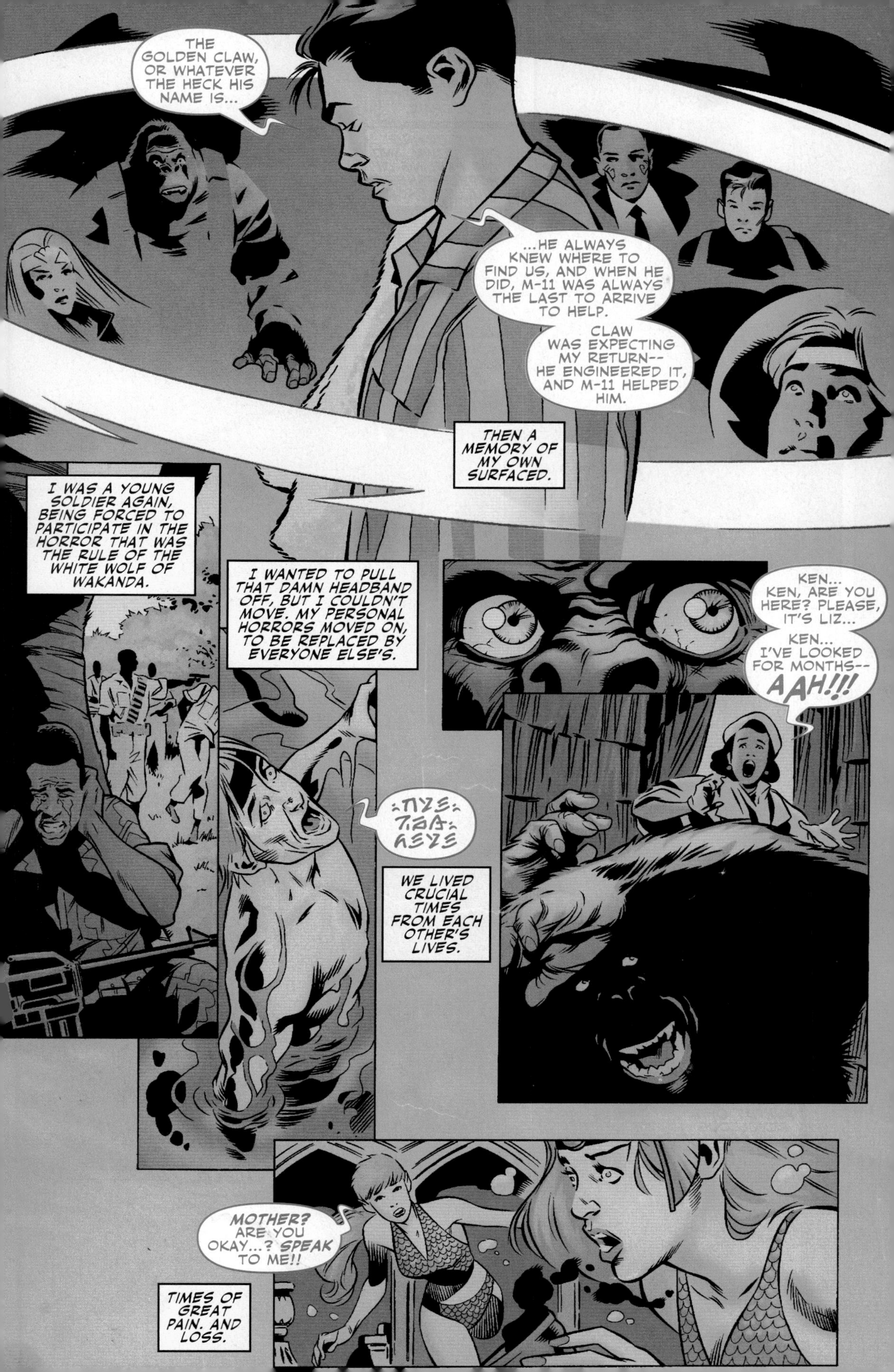
THE GOLDEN CLAW, OR WHATEVER THE HECK HIS NAME IS...
...HE ALWAYS KNEW WHERE TO FIND US, AND WHEN HE DID, M-11 WAS ALWAYS THE LAST TO ARRIVE TO HELP.
CLAW WAS EXPECTING MY RETURN-- HE ENGINEERED IT, AND M-11 HELPED HIM.
THEN A MEMORY OF MY OWN SURFACED.
I WAS A YOUNG SOLDIER AGAIN, BEING FORCED TO PARTICIPATE IN THE HORROR THAT WAS THE RULE OF THE WHITE WOLF OF WAKANDA.
I WANTED TO PULL THAT DAMN HEADBAND OFF, BUT I COULDN'T MOVE. MY PERSONAL HORRORS MOVED ON, TO BE REPLACED BY EVERYONE ELSE'S.
KEN... KEN, ARE YOU HERE? PLEASE, IT'S LIZ...
KEN... I'VE LOOKED FOR MONTHS-- AAH!!!
WE LIVED CRUCIAL TIMES FROM EACH OTHER'S LIVES.
MOTHER? ARE YOU OKAY...? SPEAK TO ME!!
TIMES OF GREAT PAIN. AND LOSS.

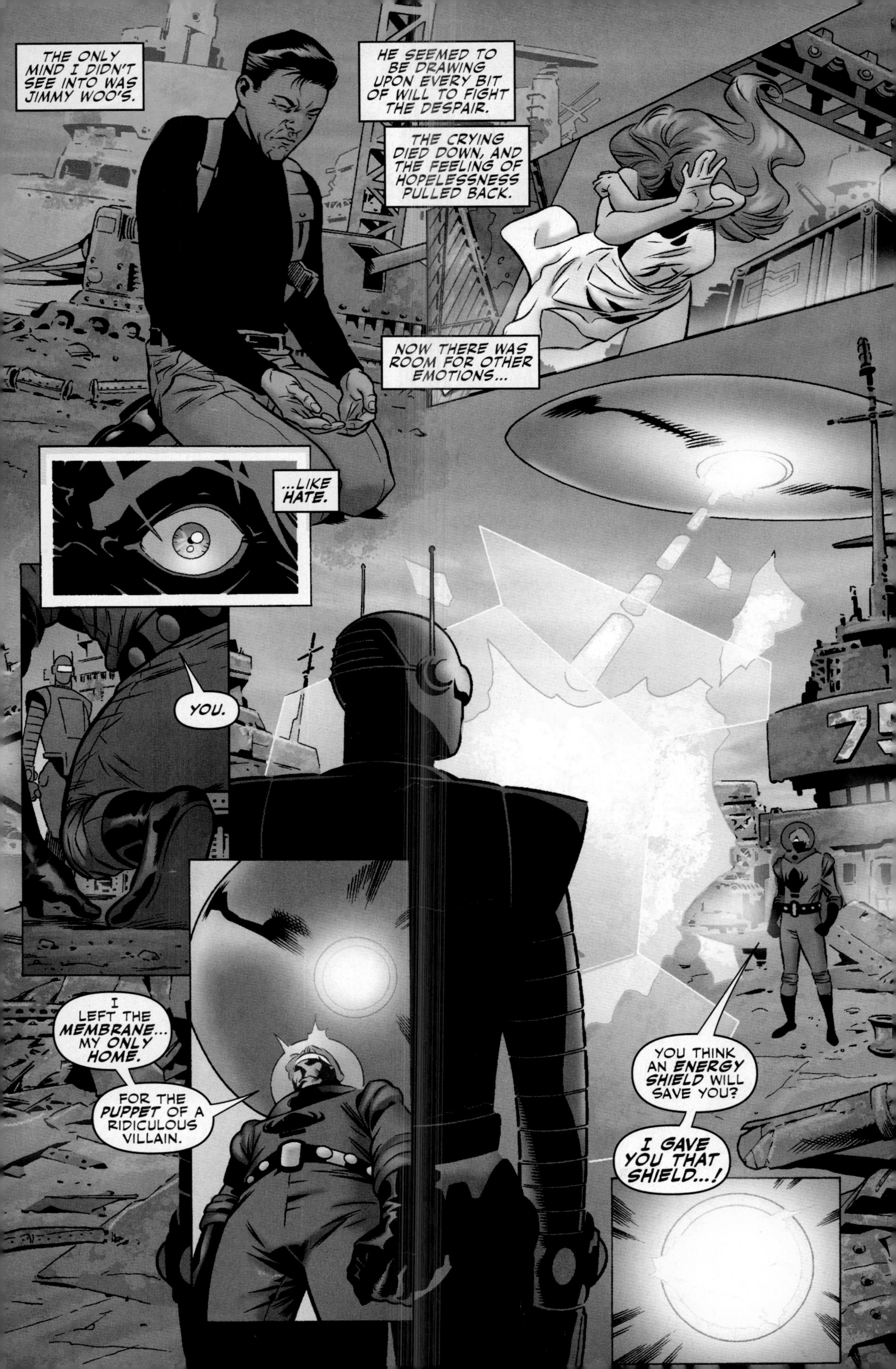
THE ONLY MIND I DIDN'T SEE INTO WAS JIMMY WOO'S.
HE SEEMED TO BE DRAWING UPON EVERY BIT OF WILL TO FIGHT THE DESPAIR.
THE CRYING DIED DOWN, AND THE FEELING OF HOPELESSNESS PULLED BACK.
NOW THERE WAS ROOM FOR OTHER EMOTIONS...
...LIKE HATE.
YOU.
75
I LEFT THE MEMBRANE... MY ONLY HOME.
FOR THE PUPPET OF A RIDICULOUS VILLAIN.
YOU THINK AN ENERGY SHIELD WILL SAVE YOU?
I GAVE YOU THAT SHIELD...!

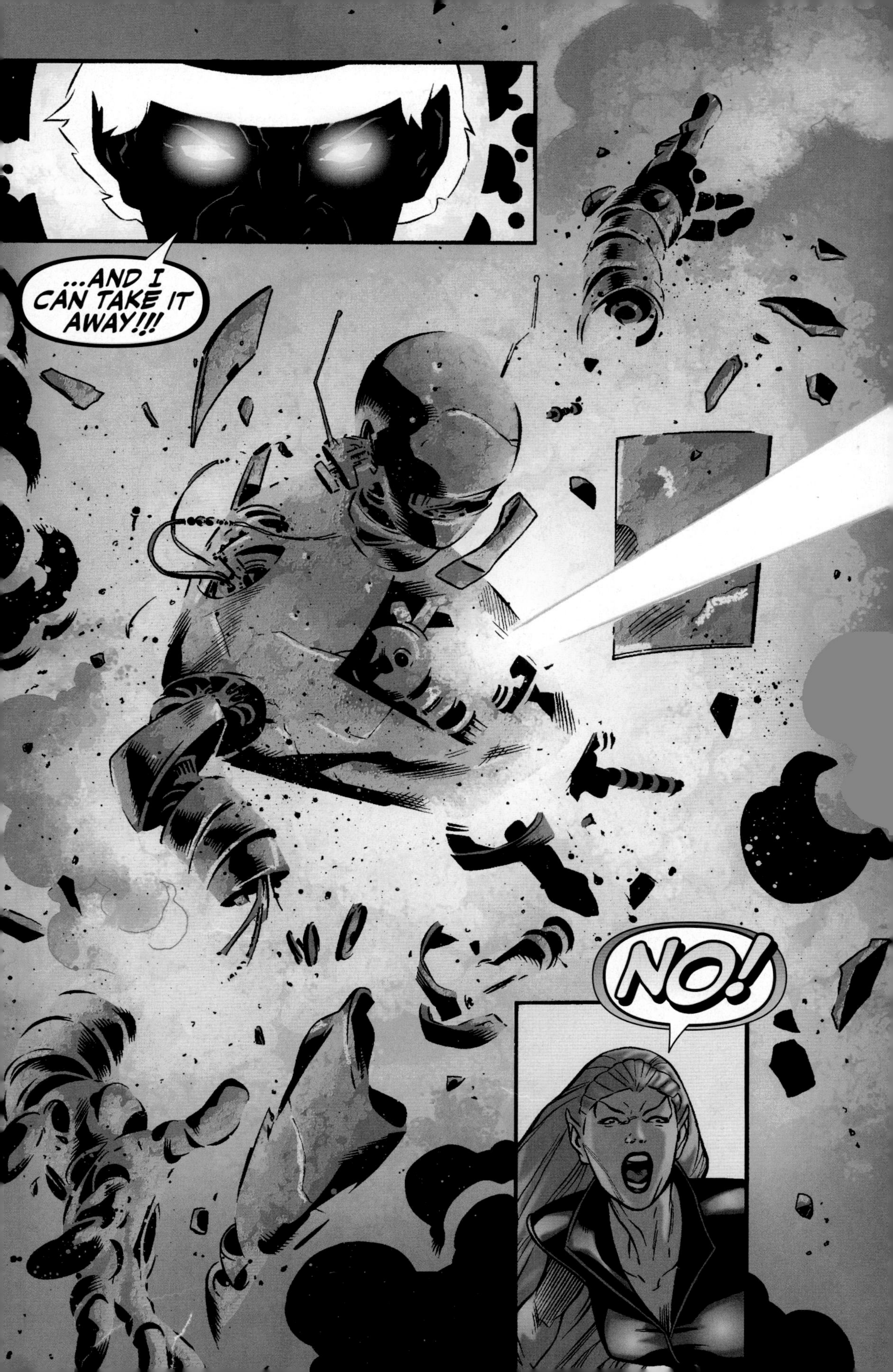
...AND I CAN TAKE IT AWAY!!!
NO!

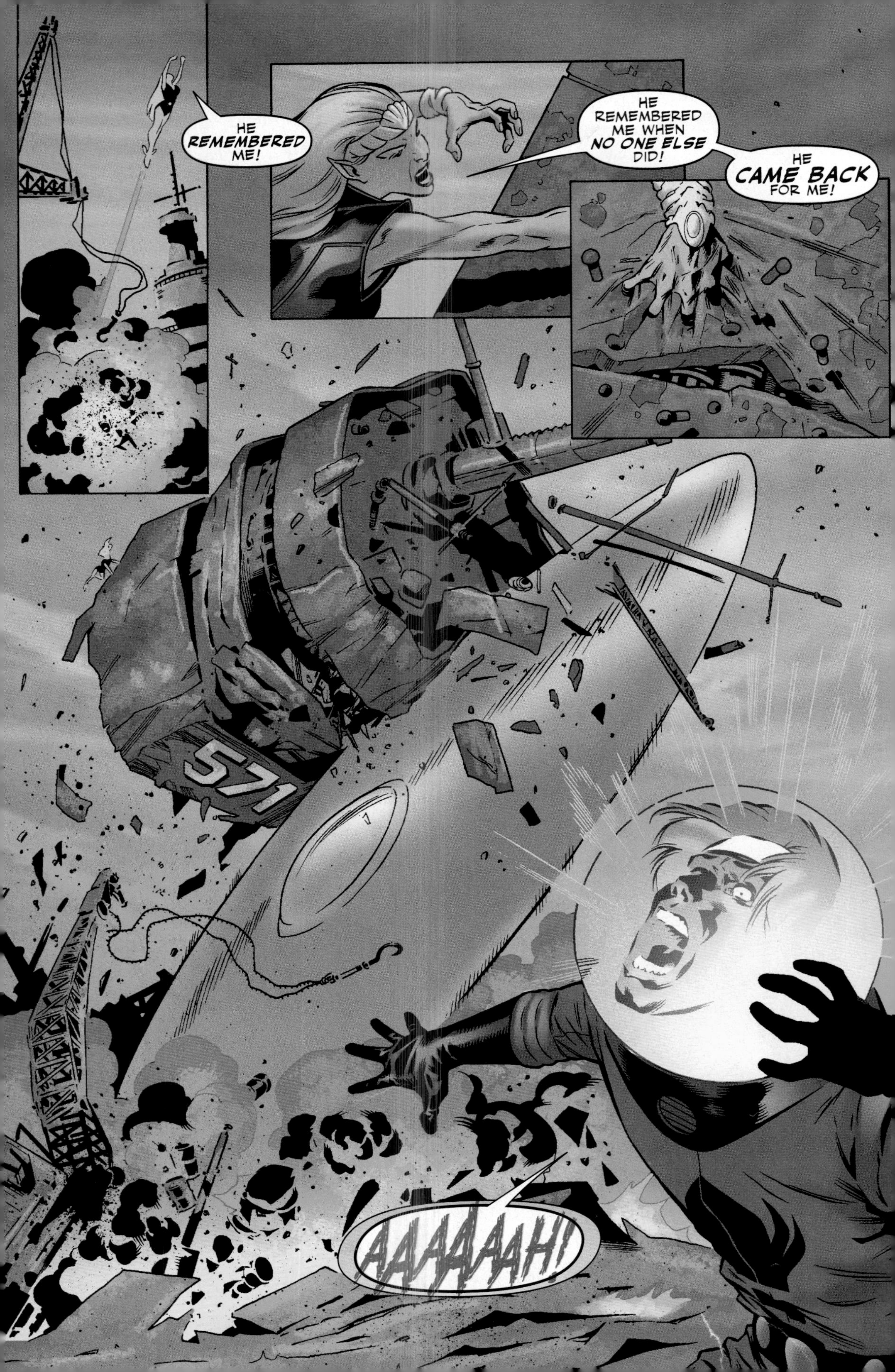
HE REMEMBERED ME!
HE REMEMBERED ME WHEN NO ONE ELSE DID!
HE CAME BACK FOR ME!
571
AAAAAAH!

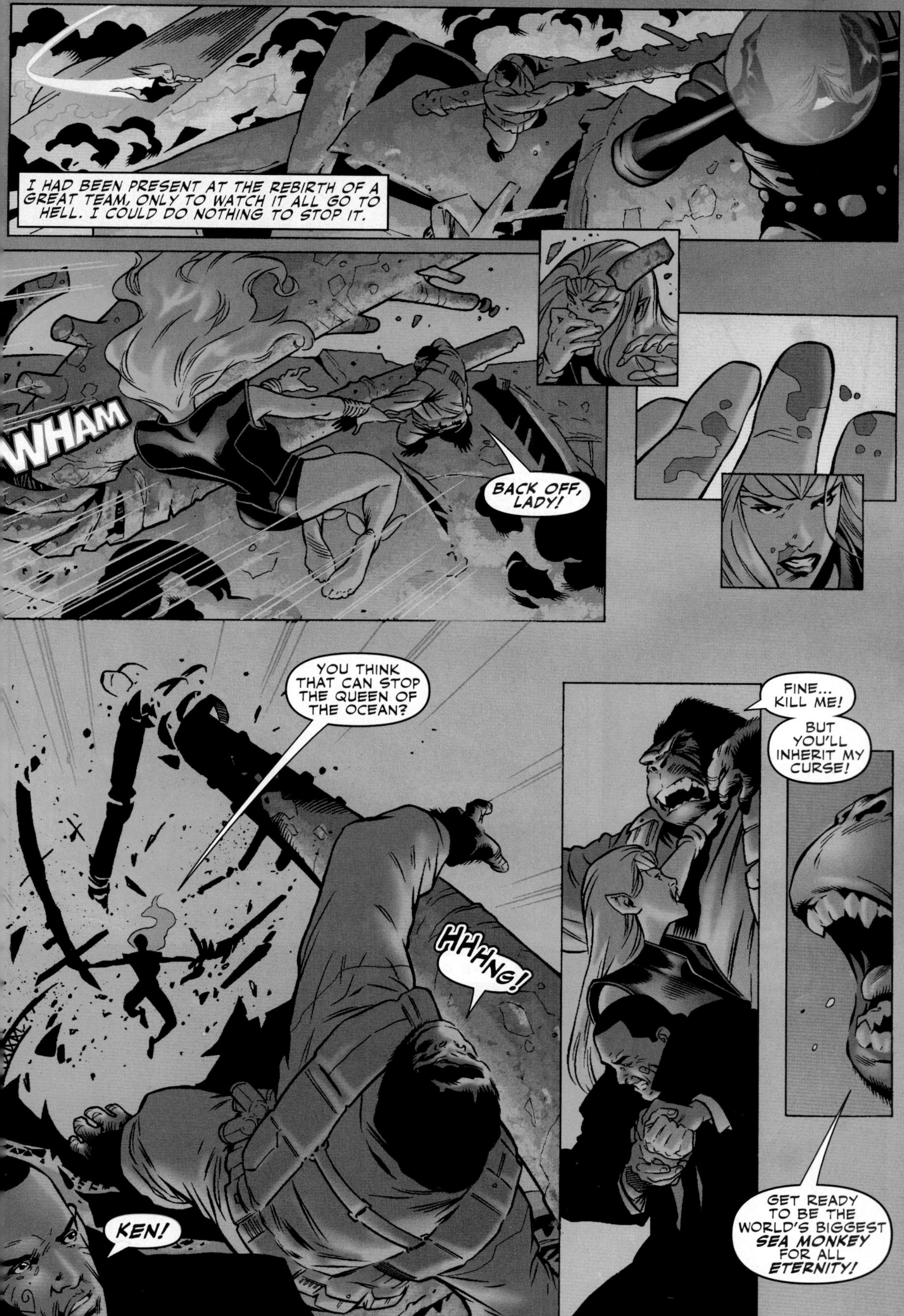
I HAD BEEN PRESENT AT THE REBIRTH OF A GREAT TEAM, ONLY TO WATCH IT ALL GO TO HELL. I COULD DO NOTHING TO STOP IT.
WHAM
BACK OFF, LADY!
YOU THINK THAT CAN STOP THE QUEEN OF THE OCEAN?
HHHNG!
KEN!
FINE... KILL ME!
BUT YOU'LL INHERIT MY CURSE!
GET READY TO BE THE WORLD'S BIGGEST SEA MONKEY FOR ALL ETERNITY!

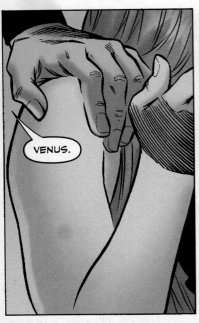

VENUS.

DON'T *CALL* ME THAT! WHAT A *SICK* JOKE!

IT'S ALL TRUE...I'M NO GODDESS OF LOVE. I'M A *MONSTER!*

LISTEN TO ME. THIS IS JIMMY, AND I'VE NEVER LIED TO YOU.

AND I NEVER WILL.

YOU CAN'T HELP WHAT YOU *WERE.* AS SOON AS YOU HAD CONTROL OF YOURSELF, YOU DID THE RIGHT THING.

YOU'VE SAVED A LOT OF LIVES JUST IN THE TIME I'VE KNOWN YOU.

HECK, YOU STOPPED A WHOLE WAR IN THAT REGION OF AFRICA. AS FAR AS THEY'RE CONCERNED, AND THIS STILL GOES FOR ME...

...YOU *ARE* A GODDESS.

YOU'RE THE ONLY ONE WHO CAN SAVE THIS TEAM NOW.

PLEASE. PULL IT TOGETHER...

"SAVE US."

GET OUT OF MY HEAD, URANIAN!!

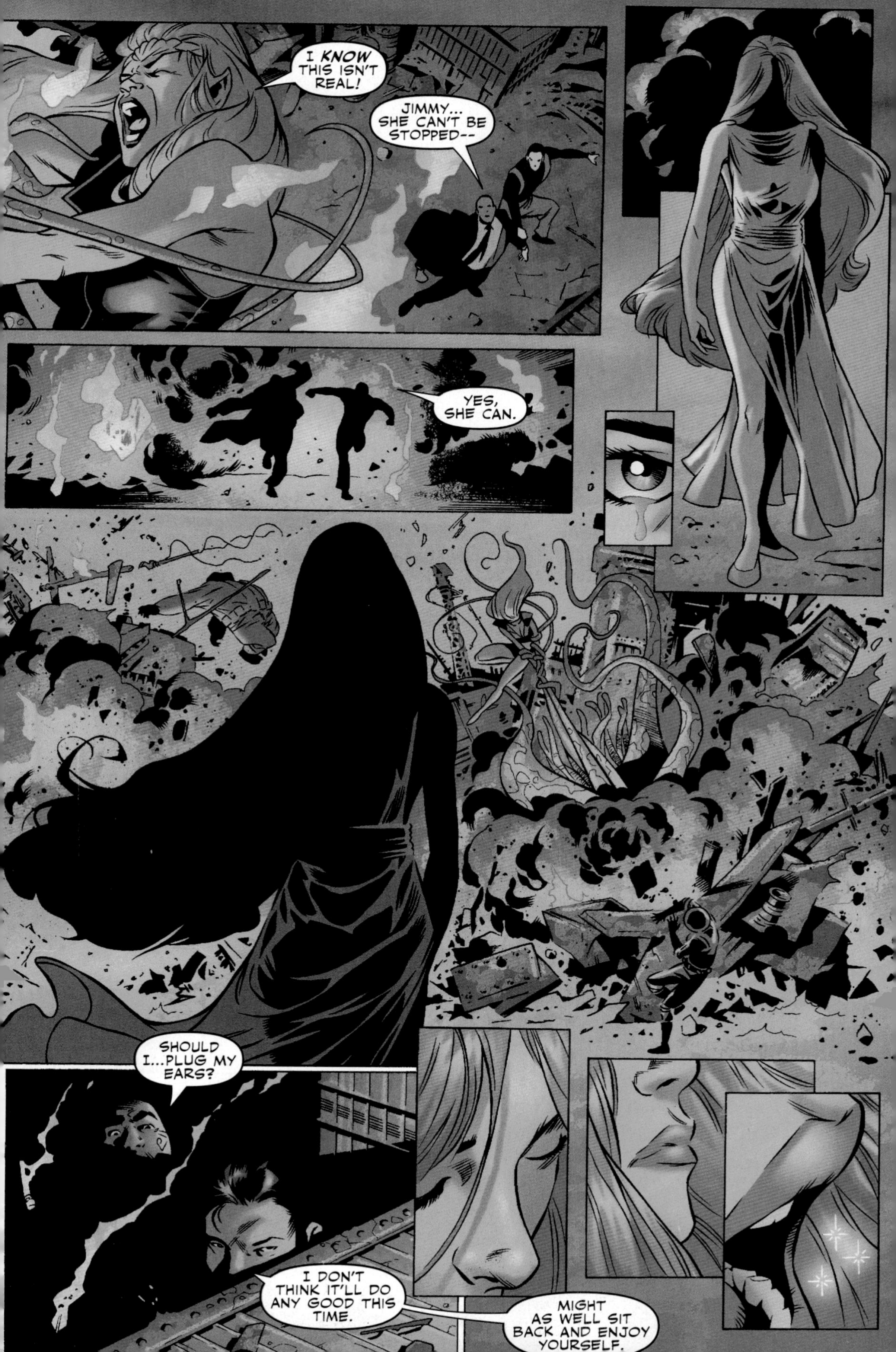
I KNOW THIS ISN'T REAL!
JIMMY... SHE CAN'T BE STOPPED--
YES, SHE CAN.
SHOULD I...PLUG MY EARS?
I DON'T THINK IT'LL DO ANY GOOD THIS TIME.
MIGHT AS WELL SIT BACK AND ENJOY YOURSELF.

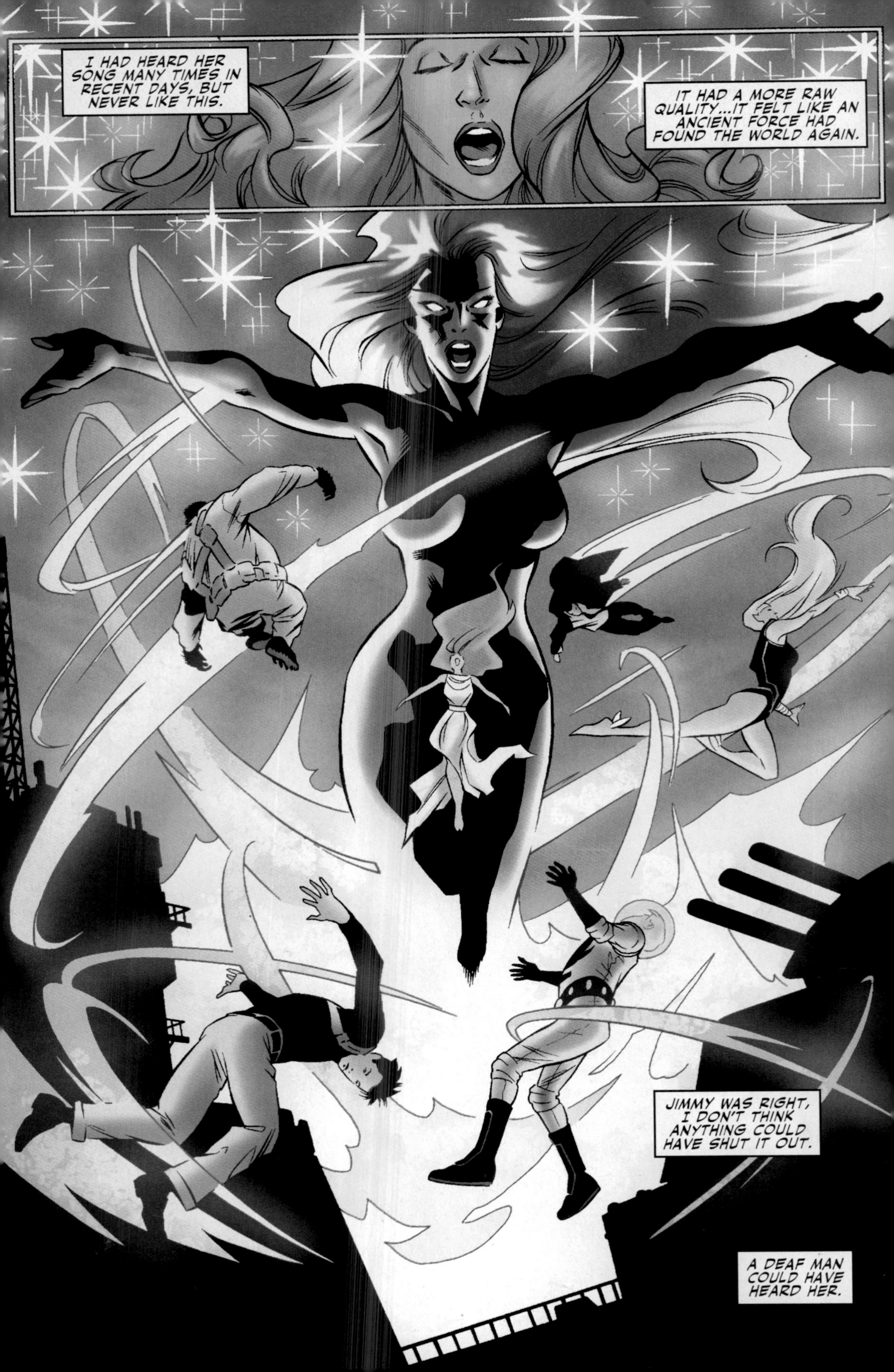
I HAD HEARD HER SONG MANY TIMES IN RECENT DAYS, BUT NEVER LIKE THIS.
IT HAD A MORE RAW QUALITY...IT FELT LIKE AN ANCIENT FORCE HAD FOUND THE WORLD AGAIN.
JIMMY WAS RIGHT, I DON'T THINK ANYTHING COULD HAVE SHUT IT OUT.
A DEAF MAN COULD HAVE HEARD HER.

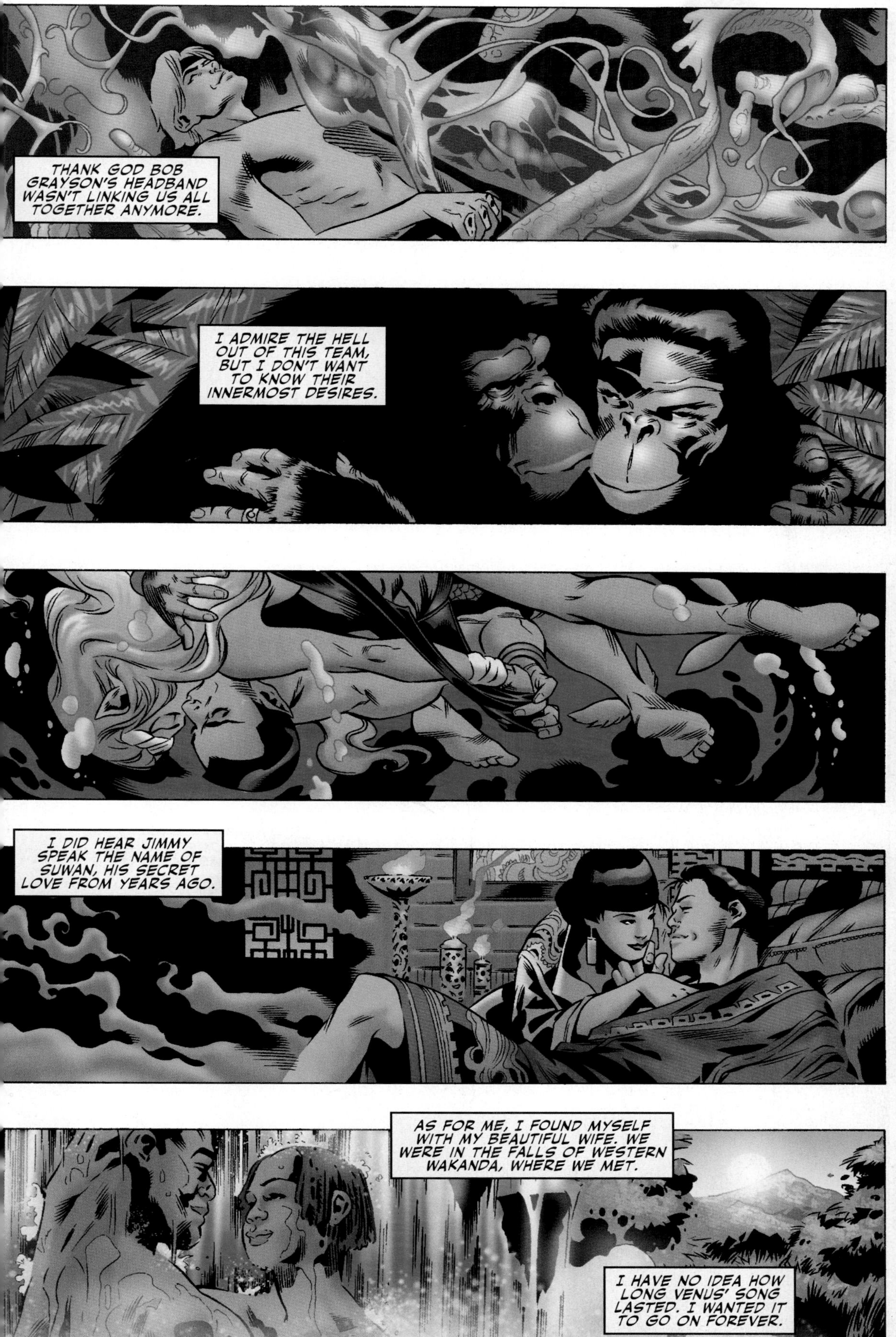
THANK GOD BOB GRAYSON'S HEADBAND WASN'T LINKING US ALL TOGETHER ANYMORE.
I ADMIRE THE HELL OUT OF THIS TEAM, BUT I DON'T WANT TO KNOW THEIR INNERMOST DESIRES.
I DID HEAR JIMMY SPEAK THE NAME OF SUWAN, HIS SECRET LOVE FROM YEARS AGO.
AS FOR ME, I FOUND MYSELF WITH MY BEAUTIFUL WIFE. WE WERE IN THE FALLS OF WESTERN WAKANDA, WHERE WE MET.
I HAVE NO IDEA HOW LONG VENUS' SONG LASTED. I WANTED IT TO GO ON FOREVER.

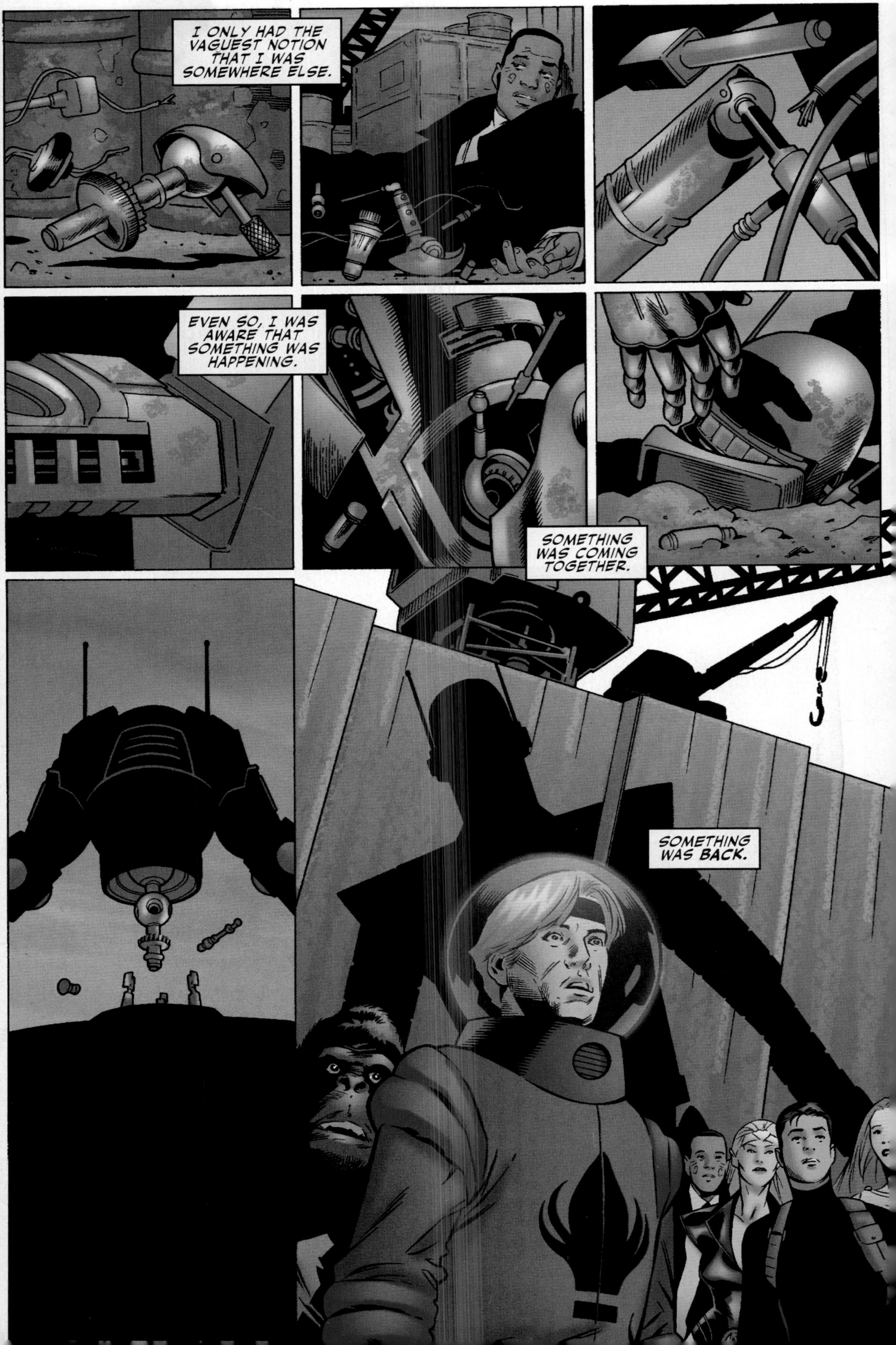
I ONLY HAD THE VAGUEST NOTION THAT I WAS SOMEWHERE ELSE.
EVEN SO, I WAS AWARE THAT SOMETHING WAS HAPPENING.
SOMETHING WAS COMING TOGETHER.
SOMETHING WAS BACK.

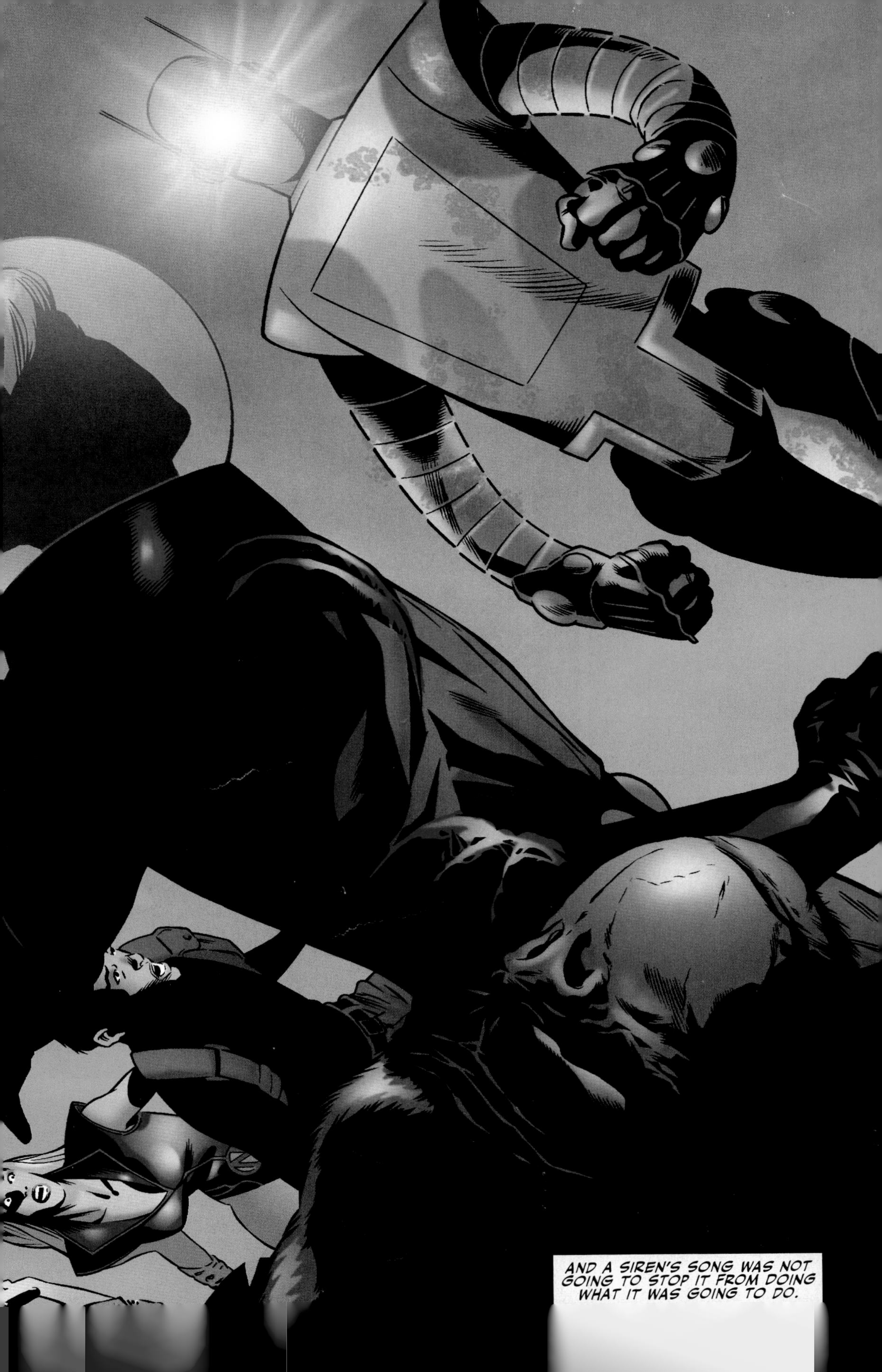
AND A SIREN'S SONG WAS NOT GOING TO STOP IT FROM DOING WHAT IT WAS GOING TO DO.

STAND DOWN, M-11.

IF YOU WANT TO DISINTEGRATE BOB, YOU'RE GOING TO HAVE TO SHOOT THROUGH ME.

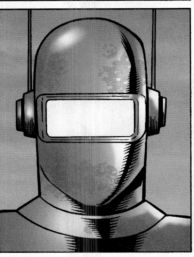

THANKS, BUDDY. NOW I'VE GOT ANOTHER REQUEST.

I KNOW I CAN'T MAKE YOU DO IT. BUT... AS A MEMBER OF THIS TEAM...

...WILL YOU PLEASE SEVER YOUR CONNECTION TO YELLOW CLAW?

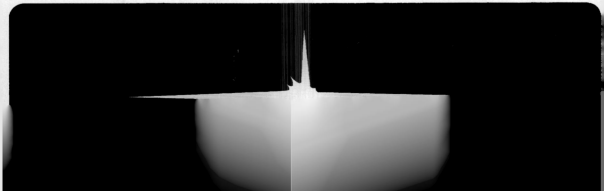

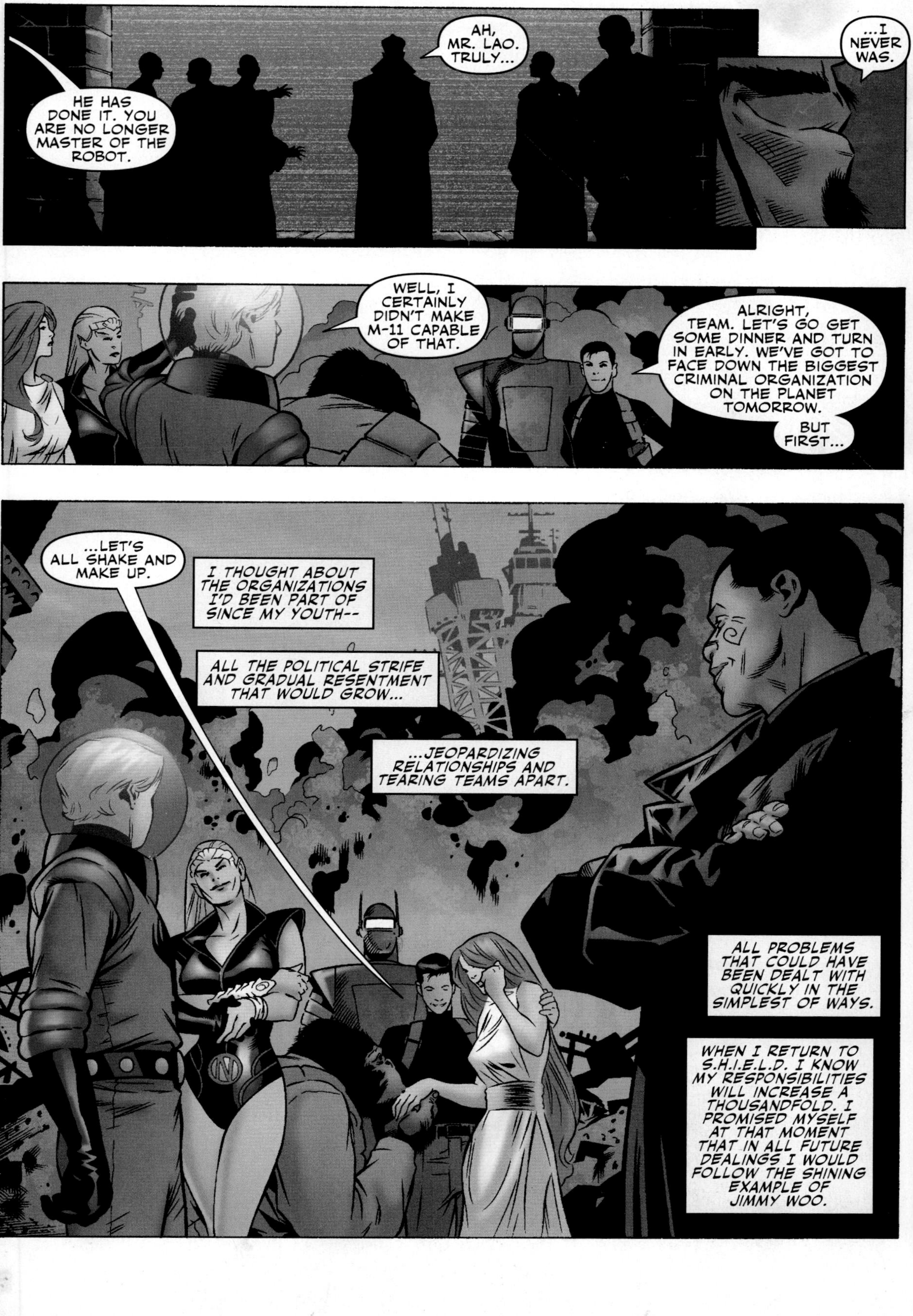
HE HAS DONE IT. YOU ARE NO LONGER MASTER OF THE ROBOT.
AH, MR. LAO. TRULY...
...I NEVER WAS.
WELL, I CERTAINLY DIDN'T MAKE M-11 CAPABLE OF THAT.
ALRIGHT, TEAM. LET'S GO GET SOME DINNER AND TURN IN EARLY. WE'VE GOT TO FACE DOWN THE BIGGEST CRIMINAL ORGANIZATION ON THE PLANET TOMORROW.
BUT FIRST...
...LET'S ALL SHAKE AND MAKE UP.
I THOUGHT ABOUT THE ORGANIZATIONS I'D BEEN PART OF SINCE MY YOUTH--
ALL THE POLITICAL STRIFE AND GRADUAL RESENTMENT THAT WOULD GROW...
...JEOPARDIZING RELATIONSHIPS AND TEARING TEAMS APART.
ALL PROBLEMS THAT COULD HAVE BEEN DEALT WITH QUICKLY IN THE SIMPLEST OF WAYS.
WHEN I RETURN TO S.H.I.E.L.D. I KNOW MY RESPONSIBILITIES WILL INCREASE A THOUSANDFOLD. I PROMISED MYSELF AT THAT MOMENT THAT IN ALL FUTURE DEALINGS I WOULD FOLLOW THE SHINING EXAMPLE OF JIMMY WOO.

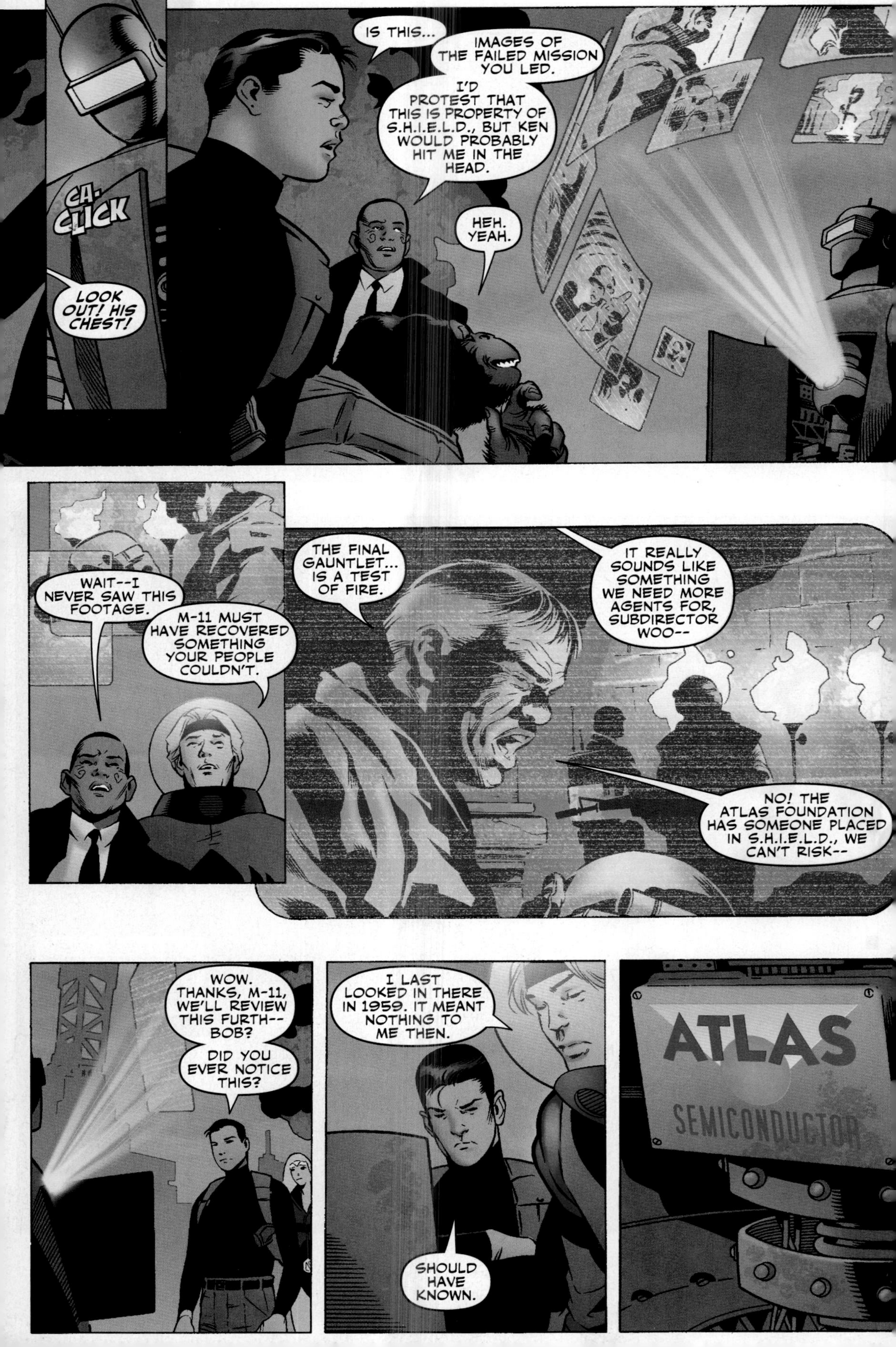
CA-CLICK
LOOK OUT! HIS CHEST!
IS THIS...
IMAGES OF THE FAILED MISSION YOU LED.
I'D PROTEST THAT THIS IS PROPERTY OF S.H.I.E.L.D., BUT KEN WOULD PROBABLY HIT ME IN THE HEAD.
HEH. YEAH.
WAIT--I NEVER SAW THIS FOOTAGE.
M-11 MUST HAVE RECOVERED SOMETHING YOUR PEOPLE COULDN'T.
THE FINAL GAUNTLET... IS A TEST OF FIRE.
IT REALLY SOUNDS LIKE SOMETHING WE NEED MORE AGENTS FOR, SUBDIRECTOR WOO--
NO! THE ATLAS FOUNDATION HAS SOMEONE PLACED IN S.H.I.E.L.D., WE CAN'T RISK--
WOW. THANKS, M-11, WE'LL REVIEW THIS FURTH-- BOB?
DID YOU EVER NOTICE THIS?
I LAST LOOKED IN THERE IN 1959. IT MEANT NOTHING TO ME THEN.
SHOULD HAVE KNOWN.
ATLAS
SEMICONDUCTOR

SHORE TO SHORE AM

WITH YOUR HOST WEBB TERRY
The Radio Call-In Show of The Unexplained

BROADCAST TRANSCRIPT: SHOW 5765-"GODS WALK AMONG US"

Webb Terry: Welcome back to hour two of tonight's show with our guest author Professor Derek Schiller, who has a new book out, "The Gods Walk Among Us." Dr. Schiller's book focuses mainly on one mythical figure in particular, though--the goddess, Venus.

Derek Schiller: That's right, Webb. I do touch upon other earthbound deities that we hear of in the news, though, like Hercules, Thor, Ares. Most people assume these are superhumans merely using the names of legends, but I'm finding more support for the idea that many are the figures from myth.

WT: But you say the woman who calls herself Venus is a bit more elusive than that?

DS: Yes. The woman I met in the late 50's and whom I've documented the most has a very sweet personality. This contradicts a lot of what Greco-Roman myths say about Venus or Aphrodite. Ancient writings give us a very temperamental figure that could be quite malicious when she wanted to. It seems night and day with the woman I write about.

WT: Guess someone could change in a few thousand years! (laughter)

DS: (laughter) Well, sure. Or we have more than one entity going by that name. A Venus interacted with the West Coast group called The Champions a few years ago. Now...Hercules was purported to have recognized this woman...

WT: Assuming he's real, that would support her existence.

DS: Yes, but no one there had interacted with the woman in these other cases I've documented. No, what I think is that maybe MY Venus is someone or something else altogether. And the Champions' woman may have been the actual Aphrodite, come to Earth, looking for who had been using her name.

WT: I would NOT want a possibly vengeful goddess on my case. (laughter)

DS: Nor I. (laughter)

WT: Let's go to the phones--east of the Rockies, we have Rich.

RICH: Hi, Webb, Dr. Schiller. I've read excerpts of your book already, and I'm wondering if this woman you describe might not be what we consider a "Nordic."

WT: Extraterrestrial with Scandinavian features, usually benevolent.

DS: That's...not where my studies go, but I've been made aware of this idea by UFOlogists, and I do find it interesting that these aliens often claim to be from the planet Venus!

WT: Hmmm.

RICH: But don't you think there's a cold war being waged by the Nordics and the Grays, using our planet as--

WT: We've lost Rich. West of the Rockies, we have Dylan.

DYLAN: Hi, Webb! Now, haven't there been really frequent sightings of flying saucers in the past month? Could that connect to this Venus girl?

DS: I don't....

WT: That's more a question for Jonas Casey, tomorrow night's guest. ETs are on the rise, and Mr. Casey will explain why. Ken in San Francisco, you're on Shore to Shore!

KEN: Hi, Webb, longtime listener, first-time caller. Hey, you mentioned earlier that you saw this gal at Hunter's Point in the 50's riding in a car with a gorilla and a robot.

DS: Yes.

KEN: What. The talkin' gorilla and the robot didn't make an impression? Where's their books?

DS: Well, I describe it some more in detail, it was very--

KEN: Then they all fought a skeleton flying a Mustang a few minutes later--didja get that in there?

WT: Okay, Ken, you know our pranks rule, we're going--

DS: Wait! How do you know about the skeleton fight!? Do you know this group--have you seen her??

KEN: Aw, calm down, you'll see her again. Ooh--hey, *Iron Chef*'s on. Gotta go!

DS: Wait! Sir! Ken, wait!

KEN: Oh, one more thing, Webb--the Patterson footage? That's me walking by the woods. Alright, later, guys!

(hangs up)

DS: NO!!! Please, call back!

WT: We're going to take a station break, you're listening to Shore to Shore AM!

END OF TRANSCRIPT

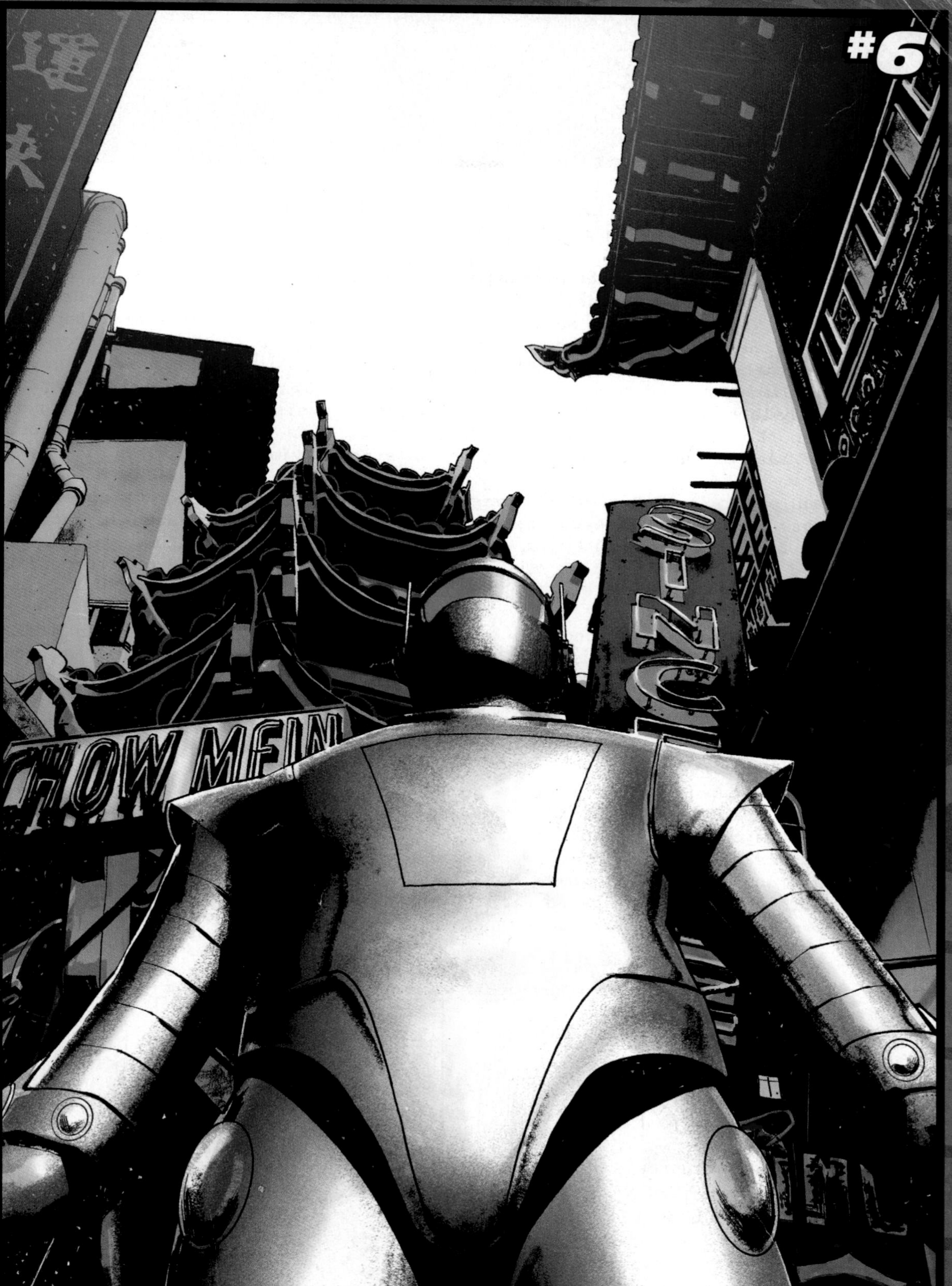
#6
CHOW MEIN

It's all going down tomorrow, baby! Can't believe the turns my life has taken in the last few weeks. Well, they're not "turning-into-a-gorilla" big, but still.

The last couple of years I've been working in this Special Ops section of S.H.I.E.L.D., kicking monster ass, when one day M-11, "The Human Robot," tracks me down. He and I used to work for Jimmy Woo on a secret FBI team in '58--I didn't know what happened with him after that. So M-11 tells me Jimmy's in S.H.I.E.L.D.'s Mojave Base on life support, and that our old bud Bob "Marvel Boy" Grayson can save him if we get in touch. Seems Jimmy had led some crazy secret mission against a group called "Atlas" and got his whole team killed. I couldn't stand the thought of my old boss going out like that, so the robot and I call up Uranus (heh). Ends up with me and the robot trashing the base and snatching Jimmy with Bob's new flying saucer.

Bob's gotten pretty weird over the years--he doesn't fly around in underpants shining lights in everyone's eyes anymore, and you DO NOT want to see him eat. But his headband is really powerful now, and he was able to restore Jimmy to the way he remembered him in the Fifties. That's as far as his memories go now, too. (Fun fact: Jimmy's Chinese name is Woo Yen Jet.)

Next thing I know, we're putting the band back together, finding Venus in Africa and even going to the bottom of the ocean and breaking Namora out of ice! All the while Yellow Claw...excuse me, GOLDEN Claw keeps popping up like he knows our every move. And he did, 'cause the damn robot kept TELLING him our every move! I'd bust his tin head, but apparently he can just rebuild himself from obliteration, so whatcha gonna do?

Anyway, Jimmy thinks we just need to go back to that underground room and say Open Sesame or something. Hell, the kid hasn't been wrong yet. We're heading down tomorrow. Now maybe I'll get to find out:
1. What that Eisenhower kidnapping was all about
2. Where the robot was for 50 years
3. And why Jimmy's life was spared when he attacked the Atlas Foundation
Or I'll get killed. One way or another, it's gonna be a big day.

the spy	the spaceman	the goddess	the mermaid	the robot	the gorilla

JIMMY WOO	BOB GRAYSON MARVEL BOY	VENUS	NAMORA	M-11 HUMAN ROBOT	KEN HALE GORILLA MAN

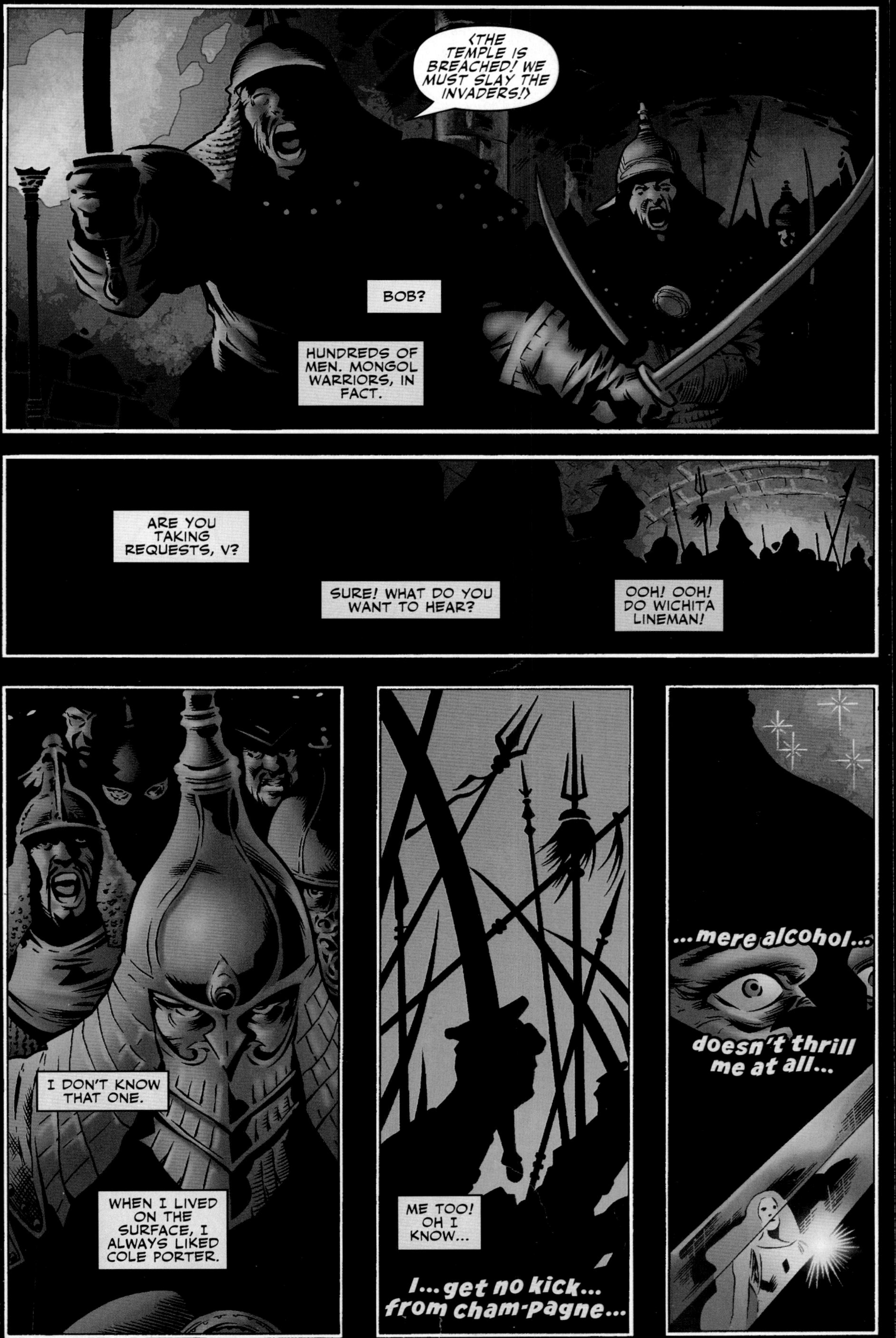
‹THE TEMPLE IS BREACHED! WE MUST SLAY THE INVADERS!›
BOB?
HUNDREDS OF MEN. MONGOL WARRIORS, IN FACT.
ARE YOU TAKING REQUESTS, V?
SURE! WHAT DO YOU WANT TO HEAR?
OOH! OOH! DO WICHITA LINEMAN!
I DON'T KNOW THAT ONE.
WHEN I LIVED ON THE SURFACE, I ALWAYS LIKED COLE PORTER.
ME TOO! OH I KNOW...
I... get no kick... from cham-pagne...
...mere alcohol...
doesn't thrill me at all...

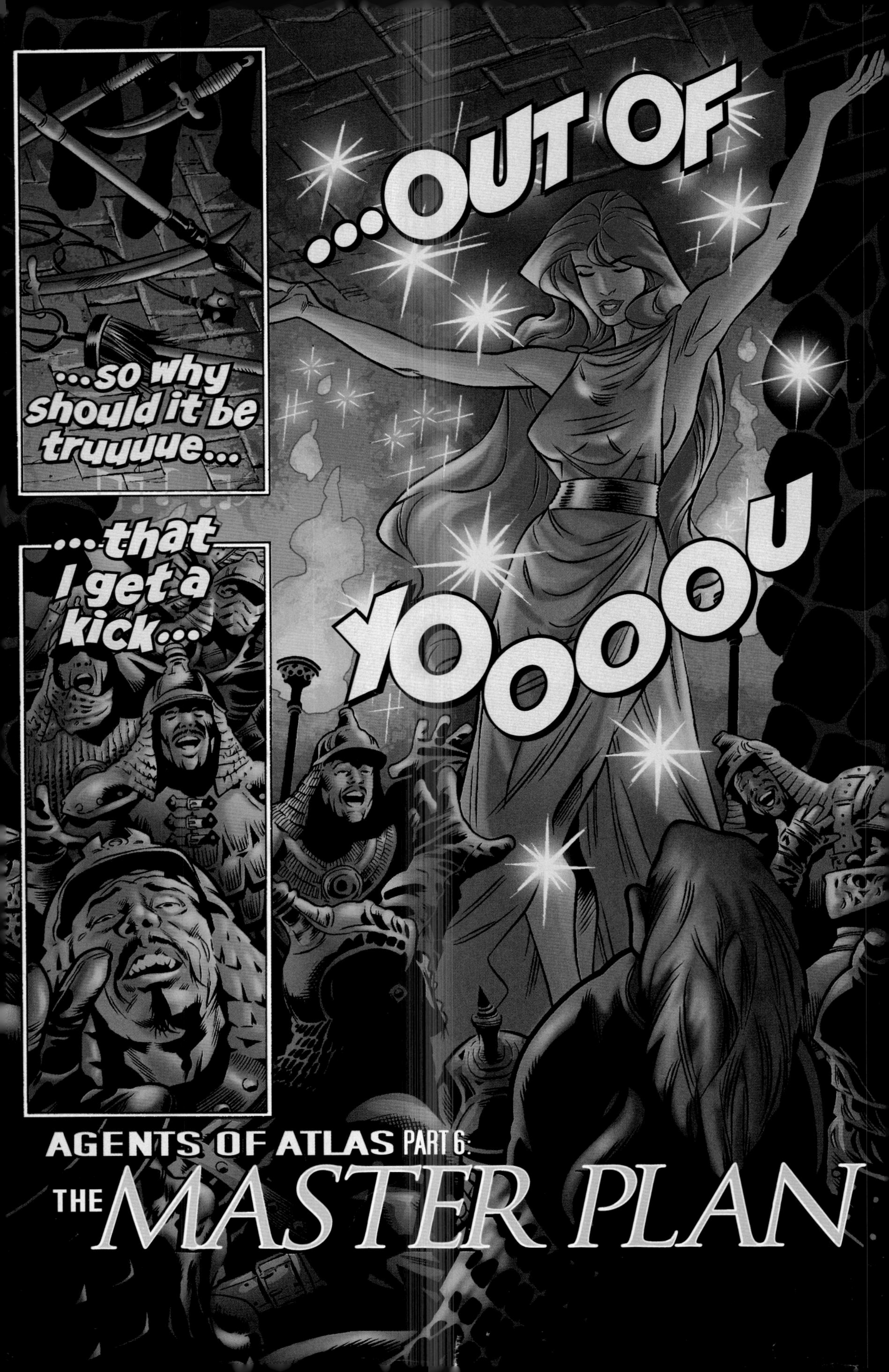
...so why should it be truuuue...
...that I get a kick...
...OUT OF YOOOOOU
AGENTS OF ATLAS PART 6:
THE MASTER PLAN

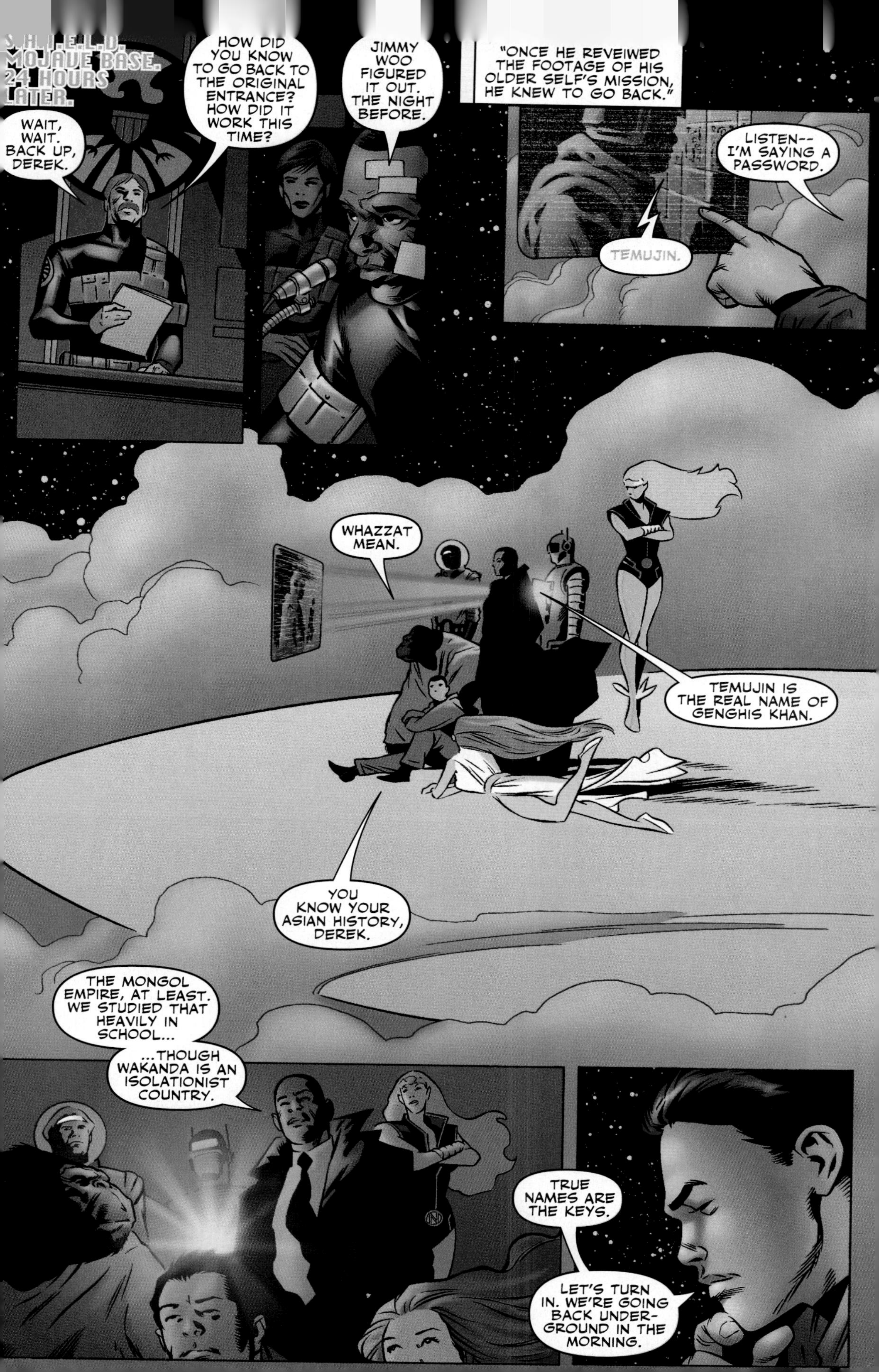
S.H.I.E.L.D. MOJAVE BASE. 24 HOURS LATER.
WAIT, WAIT. BACK UP, DEREK.
HOW DID YOU KNOW TO GO BACK TO THE ORIGINAL ENTRANCE? HOW DID IT WORK THIS TIME?
JIMMY WOO FIGURED IT OUT. THE NIGHT BEFORE.
"ONCE HE REVEIWED THE FOOTAGE OF HIS OLDER SELF'S MISSION, HE KNEW TO GO BACK."
LISTEN-- I'M SAYING A PASSWORD.
TEMUJIN.
WHAZZAT MEAN.
TEMUJIN IS THE REAL NAME OF GENGHIS KHAN.
YOU KNOW YOUR ASIAN HISTORY, DEREK.
THE MONGOL EMPIRE, AT LEAST. WE STUDIED THAT HEAVILY IN SCHOOL...
...THOUGH WAKANDA IS AN ISOLATIONIST COUNTRY.
TRUE NAMES ARE THE KEYS.
LET'S TURN IN. WE'RE GOING BACK UNDER-GROUND IN THE MORNING.

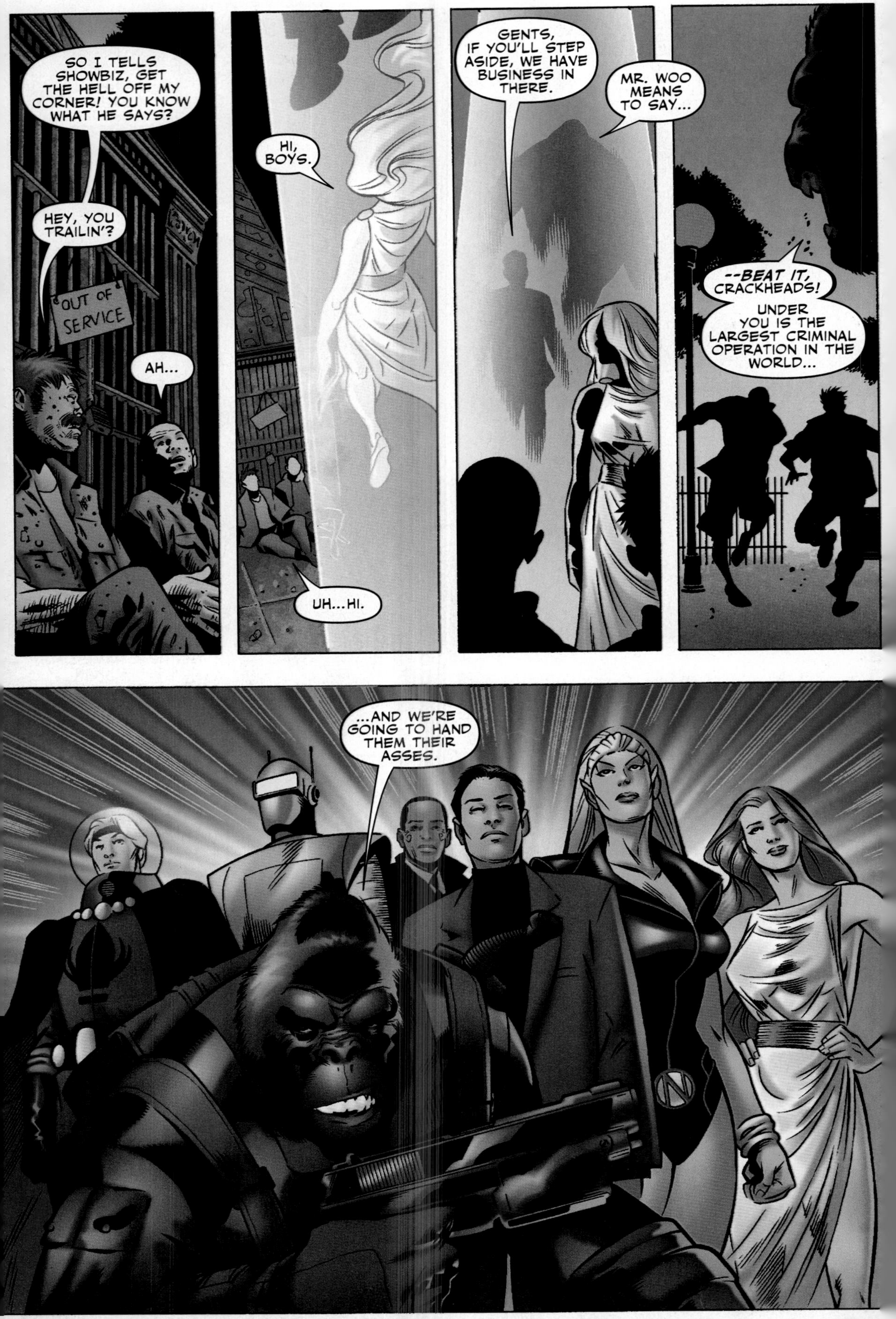
SO I TELLS SHOWBIZ, GET THE HELL OFF MY CORNER! YOU KNOW WHAT HE SAYS?
HEY, YOU TRAILIN'?
OUT OF SERVICE
AH...
HI, BOYS.
UH...HI.
GENTS, IF YOU'LL STEP ASIDE, WE HAVE BUSINESS IN THERE.
MR. WOO MEANS TO SAY...
--BEAT IT, CRACKHEADS!
UNDER YOU IS THE LARGEST CRIMINAL OPERATION IN THE WORLD...
...AND WE'RE GOING TO HAND THEM THEIR ASSES.

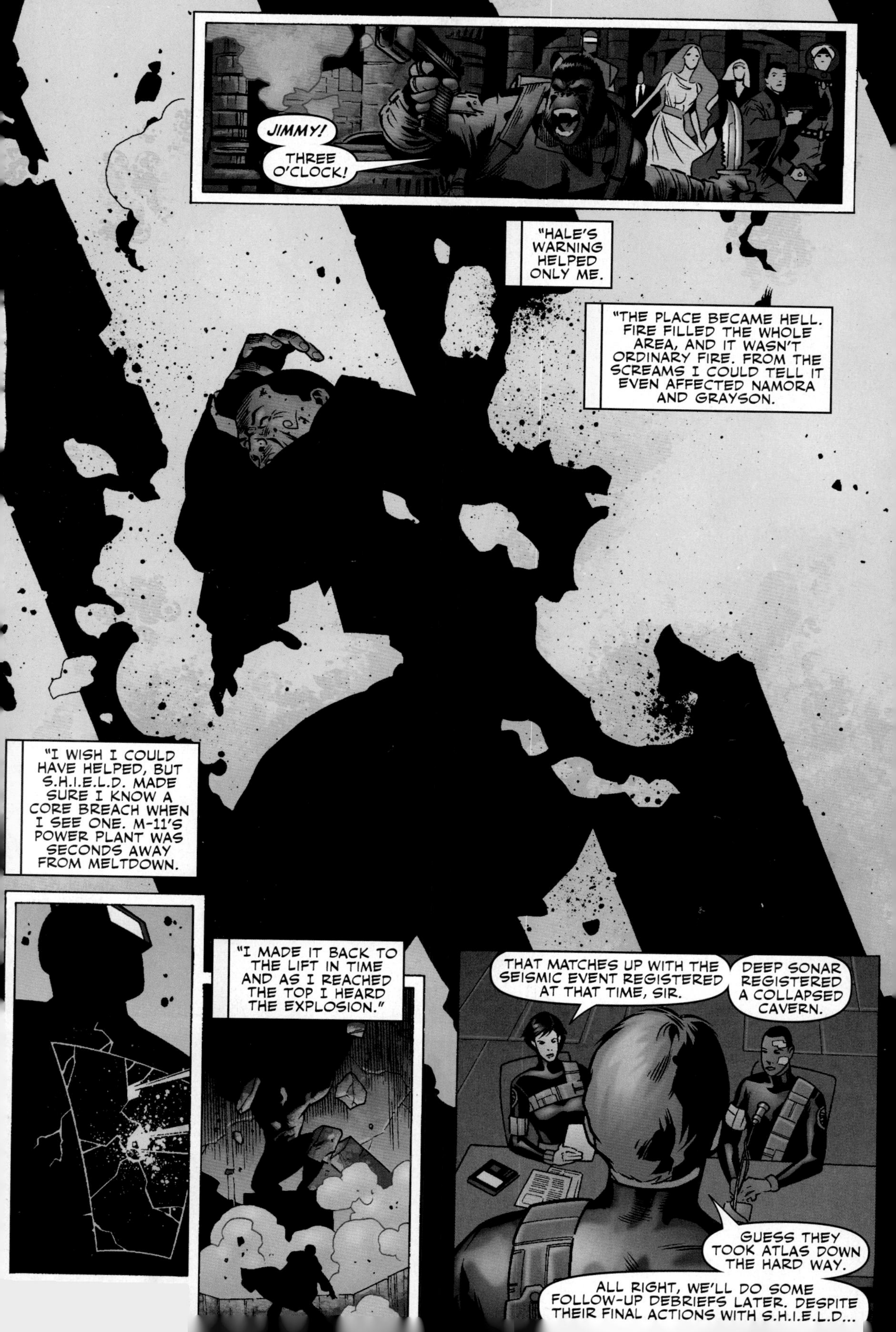
JIMMY!
THREE O'CLOCK!
"HALE'S WARNING HELPED ONLY ME.
"THE PLACE BECAME HELL. FIRE FILLED THE WHOLE AREA, AND IT WASN'T ORDINARY FIRE. FROM THE SCREAMS I COULD TELL IT EVEN AFFECTED NAMORA AND GRAYSON.
"I WISH I COULD HAVE HELPED, BUT S.H.I.E.L.D. MADE SURE I KNOW A CORE BREACH WHEN I SEE ONE. M-11'S POWER PLANT WAS SECONDS AWAY FROM MELTDOWN.
"I MADE IT BACK TO THE LIFT IN TIME AND AS I REACHED THE TOP I HEARD THE EXPLOSION."
THAT MATCHES UP WITH THE SEISMIC EVENT REGISTERED AT THAT TIME, SIR.
DEEP SONAR REGISTERED A COLLAPSED CAVERN.
GUESS THEY TOOK ATLAS DOWN THE HARD WAY.
ALL RIGHT, WE'LL DO SOME FOLLOW-UP DEBRIEFS LATER. DESPITE THEIR FINAL ACTIONS WITH S.H.I.E.L.D...

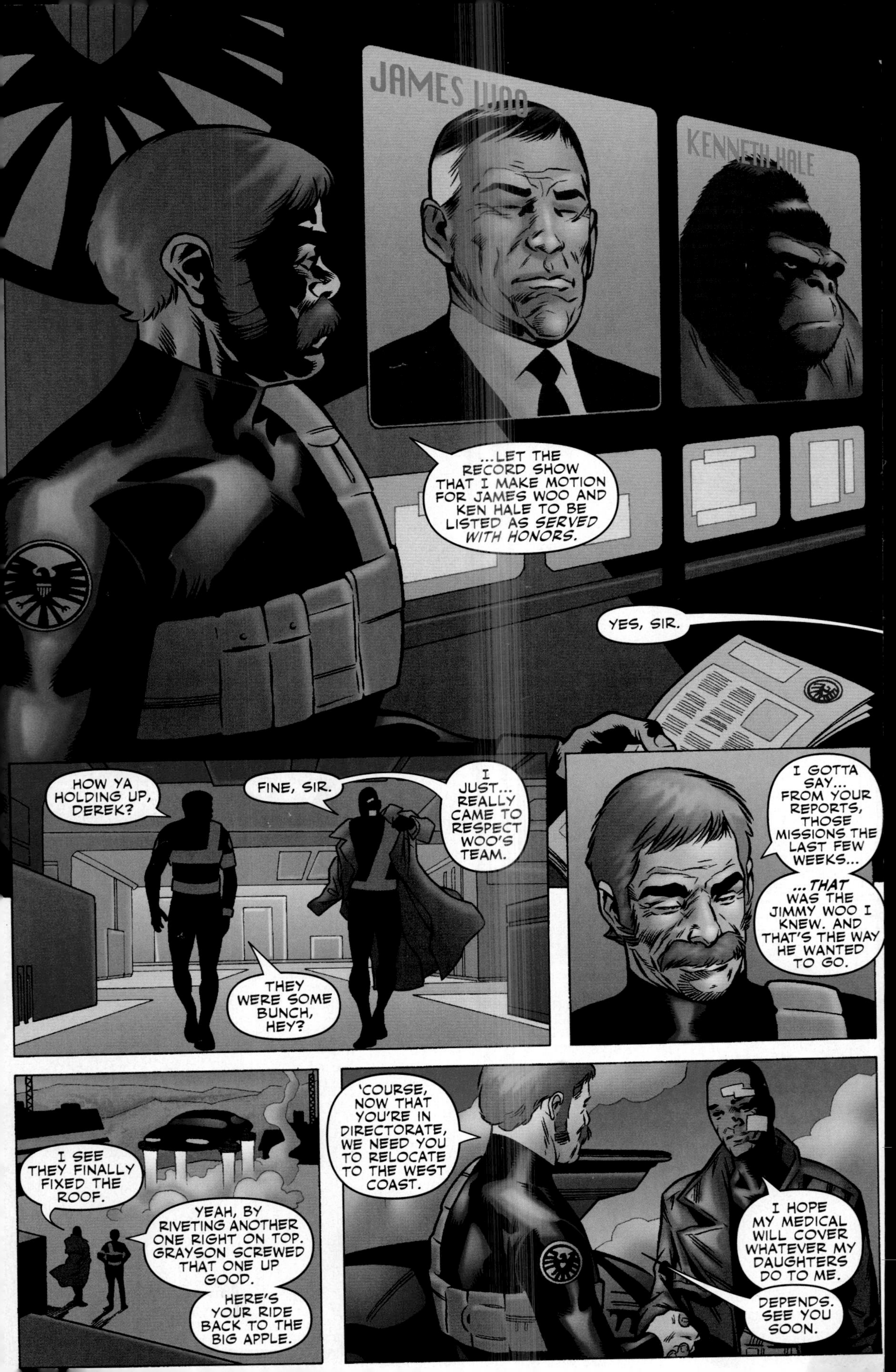

JAMES WOO
KENNETH HALE
...LET THE RECORD SHOW THAT I MAKE MOTION FOR JAMES WOO AND KEN HALE TO BE LISTED AS *SERVED WITH HONORS.*
YES, SIR.
HOW YA HOLDING UP, DEREK?
FINE, SIR.
I JUST... REALLY CAME TO RESPECT WOO'S TEAM.
THEY WERE SOME BUNCH, HEY?
I GOTTA SAY... FROM YOUR REPORTS, THOSE MISSIONS THE LAST FEW WEEKS...
...THAT WAS THE JIMMY WOO I KNEW. AND THAT'S THE WAY HE WANTED TO GO.
I SEE THEY FINALLY FIXED THE ROOF.
YEAH, BY RIVETING ANOTHER ONE RIGHT ON TOP. GRAYSON SCREWED THAT ONE UP GOOD.
HERE'S YOUR RIDE BACK TO THE BIG APPLE.
'COURSE, NOW THAT YOU'RE IN DIRECTORATE, WE NEED YOU TO RELOCATE TO THE WEST COAST.
I HOPE MY MEDICAL WILL COVER WHATEVER MY DAUGHTERS DO TO ME.
DEPENDS. SEE YOU SOON.

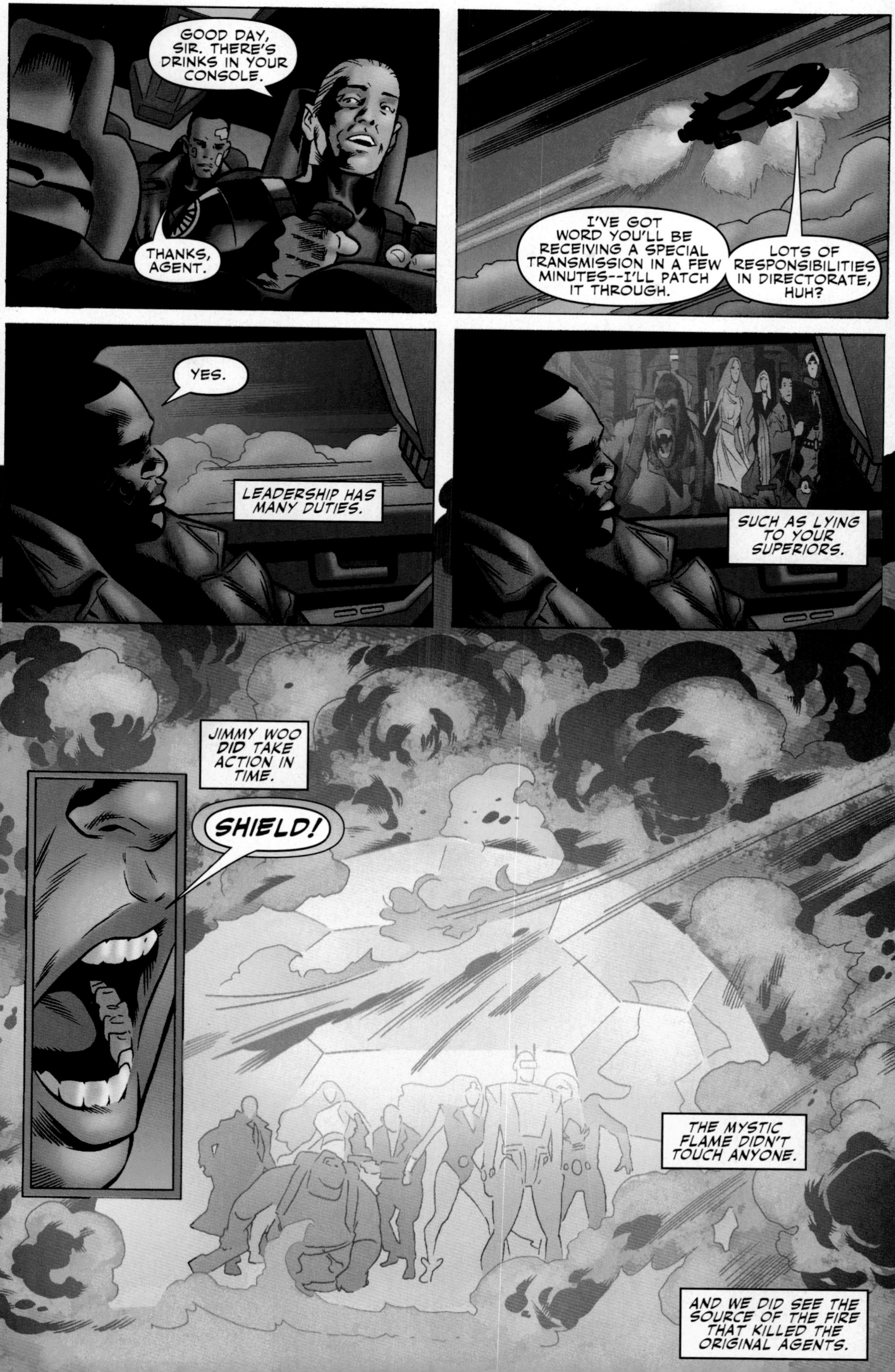
GOOD DAY, SIR. THERE'S DRINKS IN YOUR CONSOLE.
THANKS, AGENT.
I'VE GOT WORD YOU'LL BE RECEIVING A SPECIAL TRANSMISSION IN A FEW MINUTES--I'LL PATCH IT THROUGH.
LOTS OF RESPONSIBILITIES IN DIRECTORATE, HUH?
YES.
LEADERSHIP HAS MANY DUTIES.
SUCH AS LYING TO YOUR SUPERIORS.
JIMMY WOO DID TAKE ACTION IN TIME.
SHIELD!
THE MYSTIC FLAME DIDN'T TOUCH ANYONE.
AND WE DID SEE THE SOURCE OF THE FIRE THAT KILLED THE ORIGINAL AGENTS.

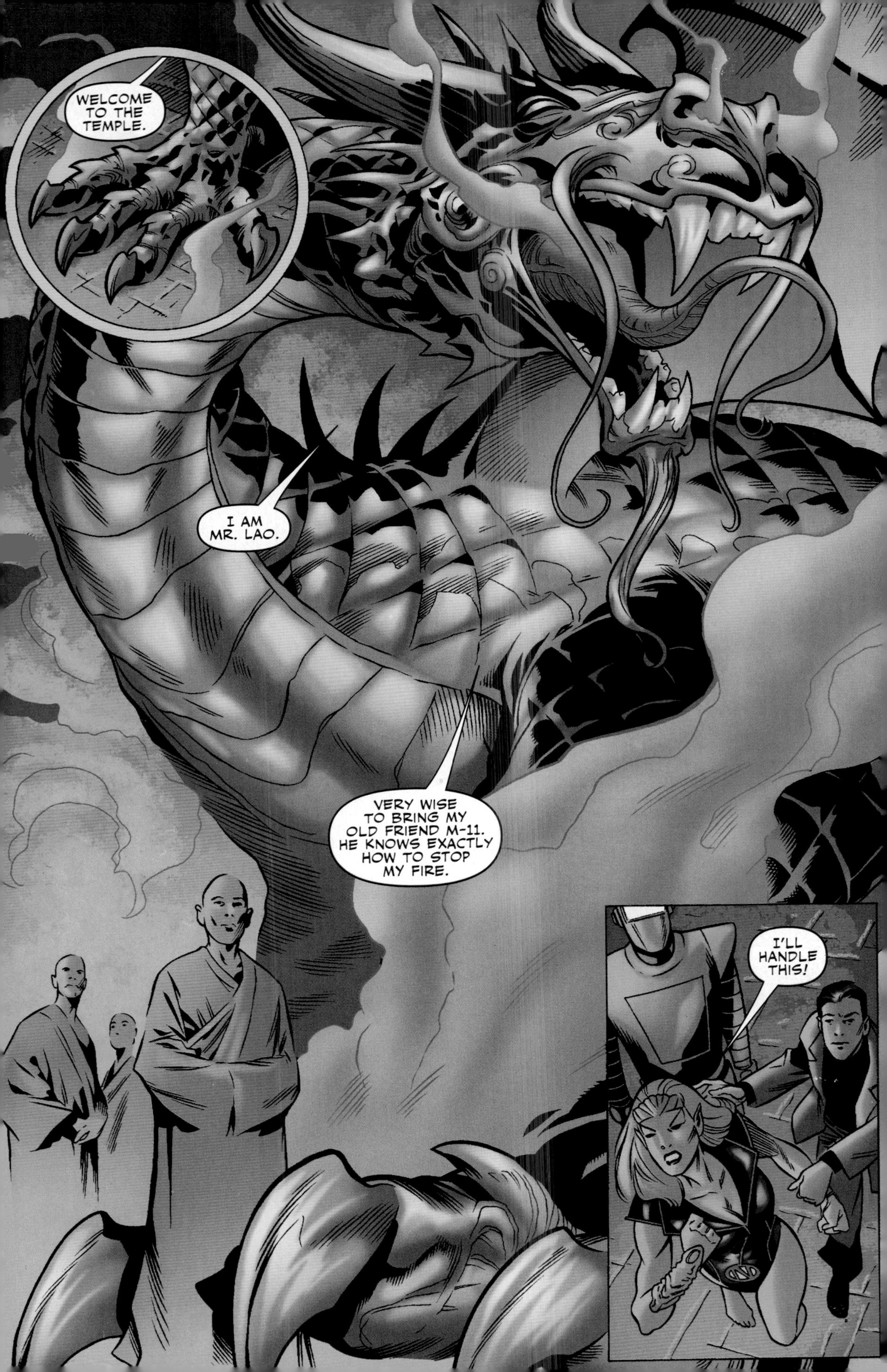
WELCOME TO THE TEMPLE.
I AM MR. LAO.
VERY WISE TO BRING MY OLD FRIEND M-11. HE KNOWS EXACTLY HOW TO STOP MY FIRE.
I'LL HANDLE THIS!

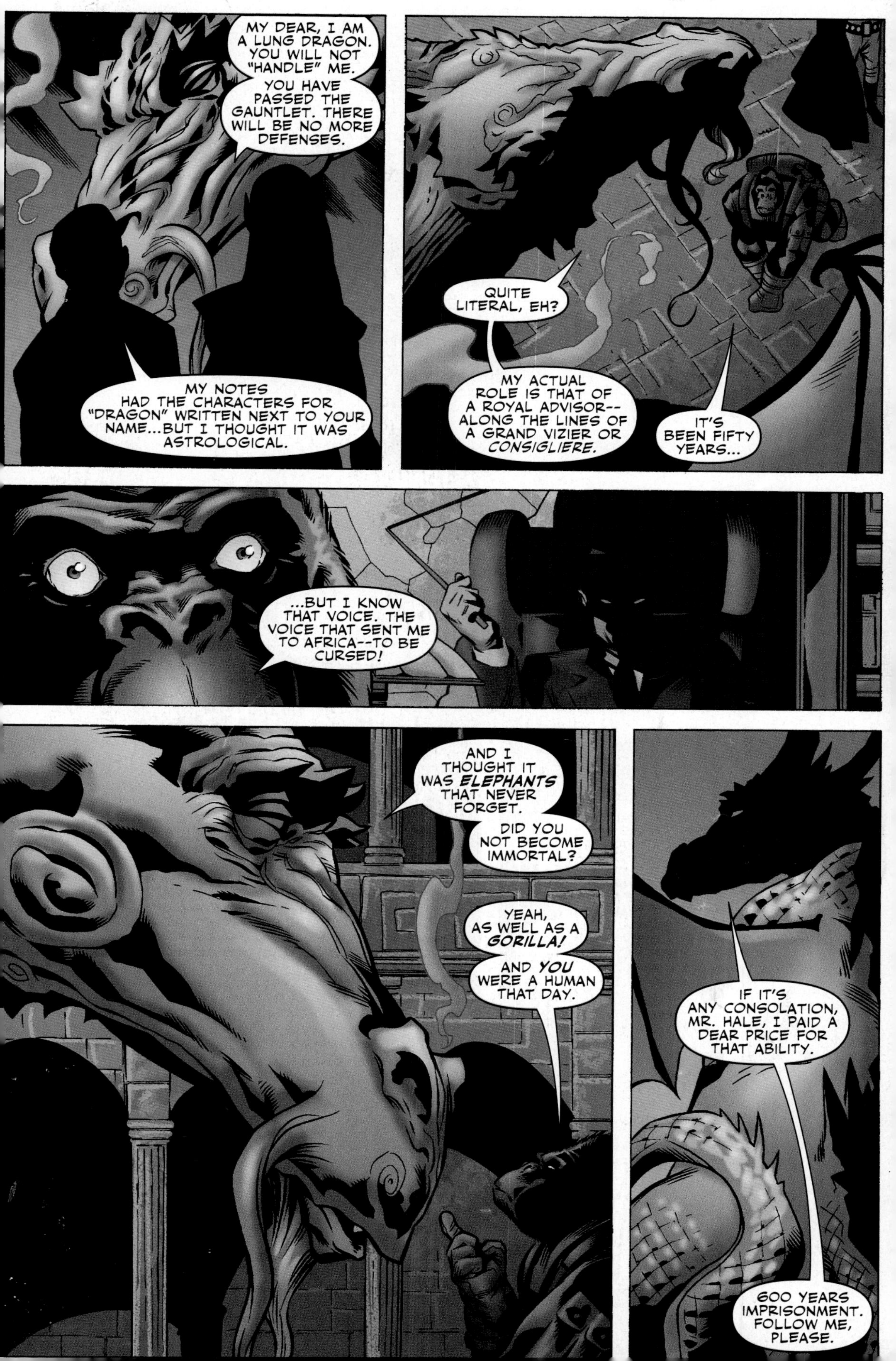
MY DEAR, I AM A LUNG DRAGON. YOU WILL NOT "HANDLE" ME.
YOU HAVE PASSED THE GAUNTLET. THERE WILL BE NO MORE DEFENSES.
MY NOTES HAD THE CHARACTERS FOR "DRAGON" WRITTEN NEXT TO YOUR NAME...BUT I THOUGHT IT WAS ASTROLOGICAL.
QUITE LITERAL, EH?
MY ACTUAL ROLE IS THAT OF A ROYAL ADVISOR--ALONG THE LINES OF A GRAND VIZIER OR *CONSIGLIERE.*
IT'S BEEN FIFTY YEARS...
...BUT I KNOW THAT VOICE. THE VOICE THAT SENT ME TO AFRICA--TO BE *CURSED!*
AND I THOUGHT IT WAS ***ELEPHANTS*** THAT NEVER FORGET.
DID YOU NOT BECOME IMMORTAL?
YEAH, AS WELL AS A ***GORILLA!***
AND ***YOU*** WERE A HUMAN THAT DAY.
IF IT'S ANY CONSOLATION, MR. HALE, I PAID A DEAR PRICE FOR THAT ABILITY.
600 YEARS IMPRISONMENT. FOLLOW ME, PLEASE.

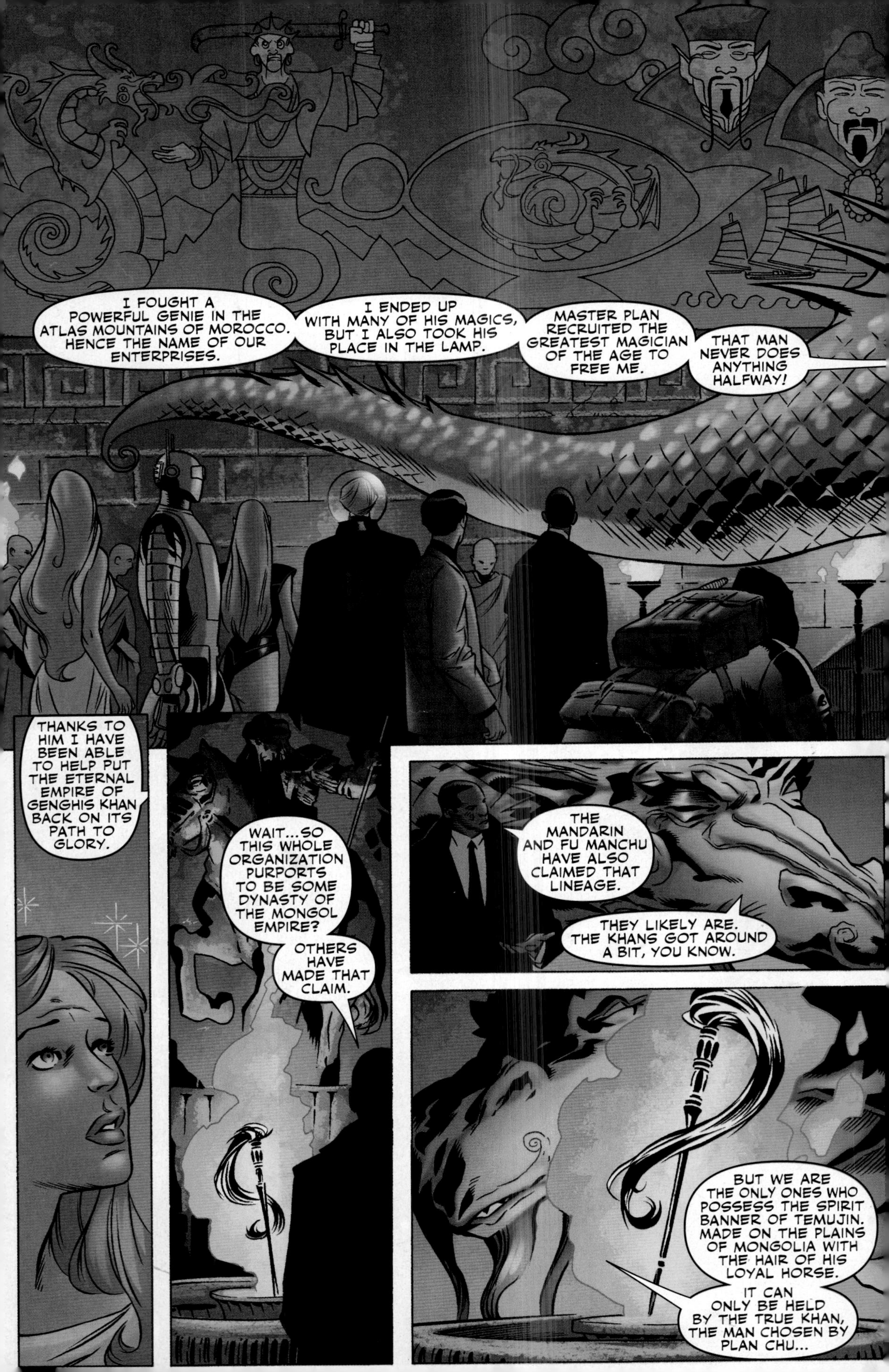
I FOUGHT A POWERFUL GENIE IN THE ATLAS MOUNTAINS OF MOROCCO. HENCE THE NAME OF OUR ENTERPRISES.
I ENDED UP WITH MANY OF HIS MAGICS, BUT I ALSO TOOK HIS PLACE IN THE LAMP.
MASTER PLAN RECRUITED THE GREATEST MAGICIAN OF THE AGE TO FREE ME.
THAT MAN NEVER DOES ANYTHING HALFWAY!
THANKS TO HIM I HAVE BEEN ABLE TO HELP PUT THE ETERNAL EMPIRE OF GENGHIS KHAN BACK ON ITS PATH TO GLORY.
WAIT...SO THIS WHOLE ORGANIZATION PURPORTS TO BE SOME DYNASTY OF THE MONGOL EMPIRE?
OTHERS HAVE MADE THAT CLAIM.
THE MANDARIN AND FU MANCHU HAVE ALSO CLAIMED THAT LINEAGE.
THEY LIKELY ARE. THE KHANS GOT AROUND A BIT, YOU KNOW.
BUT WE ARE THE ONLY ONES WHO POSSESS THE SPIRIT BANNER OF TEMUJIN. MADE ON THE PLAINS OF MONGOLIA WITH THE HAIR OF HIS LOYAL HORSE.
IT CAN ONLY BE HELD BY THE TRUE KHAN, THE MAN CHOSEN BY PLAN CHU...

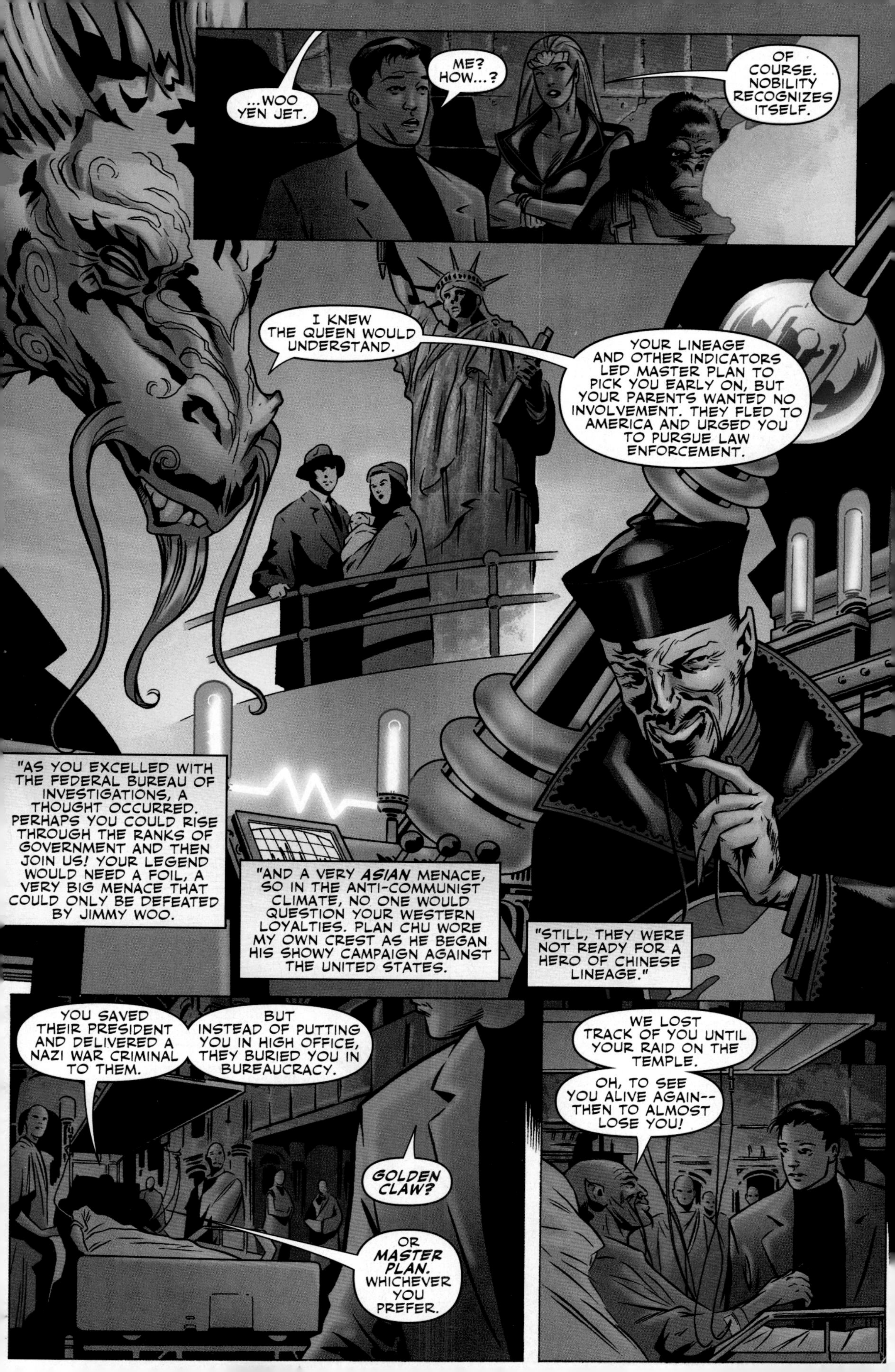
...WOO YEN JET.
ME? HOW...?
OF COURSE. NOBILITY RECOGNIZES ITSELF.
I KNEW THE QUEEN WOULD UNDERSTAND.
YOUR LINEAGE AND OTHER INDICATORS LED MASTER PLAN TO PICK YOU EARLY ON, BUT YOUR PARENTS WANTED NO INVOLVEMENT. THEY FLED TO AMERICA AND URGED YOU TO PURSUE LAW ENFORCEMENT.
"AS YOU EXCELLED WITH THE FEDERAL BUREAU OF INVESTIGATIONS, A THOUGHT OCCURRED. PERHAPS YOU COULD RISE THROUGH THE RANKS OF GOVERNMENT AND THEN JOIN US! YOUR LEGEND WOULD NEED A FOIL, A VERY BIG MENACE THAT COULD ONLY BE DEFEATED BY JIMMY WOO.
"AND A VERY *ASIAN* MENACE, SO IN THE ANTI-COMMUNIST CLIMATE, NO ONE WOULD QUESTION YOUR WESTERN LOYALTIES. PLAN CHU WORE MY OWN CREST AS HE BEGAN HIS SHOWY CAMPAIGN AGAINST THE UNITED STATES.
"STILL, THEY WERE NOT READY FOR A HERO OF CHINESE LINEAGE."
YOU SAVED THEIR PRESIDENT AND DELIVERED A NAZI WAR CRIMINAL TO THEM.
BUT INSTEAD OF PUTTING YOU IN HIGH OFFICE, THEY BURIED YOU IN BUREAUCRACY.
GOLDEN CLAW?
OR *MASTER PLAN.* WHICHEVER YOU PREFER.
WE LOST TRACK OF YOU UNTIL YOUR RAID ON THE TEMPLE.
OH, TO SEE YOU ALIVE AGAIN-- THEN TO ALMOST LOSE YOU!

HELP ME UP, PLEASE. THAT EXCURSION TO FIJI TOOK MUCH OUT OF ME.

AH... YES, SIR.

I SUSPECTED SOMETHING WHEN I SAW MY NAME REFERRED TO AT THE ATLAS FRONTS.

DID WE ACHIEVE *ANYTHING* ON OUR OWN?

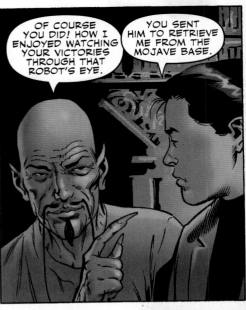

OF COURSE YOU DID! HOW I ENJOYED WATCHING YOUR VICTORIES THROUGH THAT ROBOT'S EYE.

YOU SENT HIM TO RETRIEVE ME FROM THE MOJAVE BASE.

"OH NO. I HAVE NO REAL CONTROL OVER M-11. I PRESENTED MY PLAN TO HIM."

THE URANIAN CAN RESTORE HIM. THE APE MAN CAN GET YOU INTO THEIR BASE.

"YOUR FATE WAS IN HIS HANDS, THEN."

THOUGH WE COMMISSIONED HIM, M-11 IS STILL A MYSTERY. WE CAME FOR HIM AFTER GRAYSON RETURNED TO SPACE.

HE STAYED WITH US EVER SINCE AND LET US MAKE MORE IMPROVEMENTS.

DID YOU KNOW HE CAN ACCESS ANY COMPUTER NETWORK ON THE PLANET?

I THINK THE RESTORATION ENCHANTMENT I ADDED WAS THE GREATER ADD-ON.

INTERESTING.

THIS IS *NOT* HOW I IMAGINED ALL THIS GOING DOWN.

COME, JAMES. WE HAVE USED ALL GOOD FORTUNE.

NOW IT IS TIME TO PASS ON THE MANTLE OF THE KHAN.

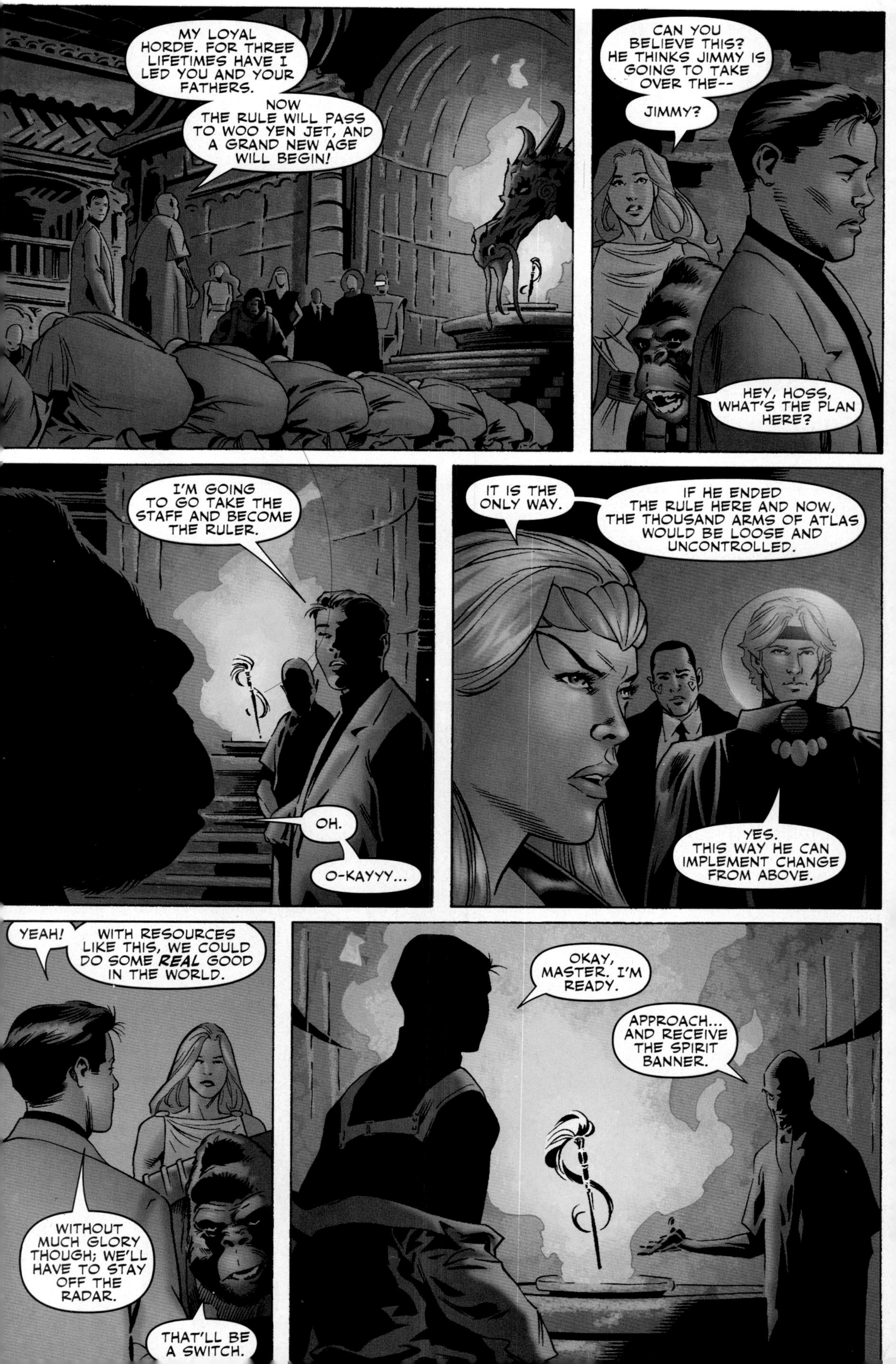
MY LOYAL HORDE. FOR THREE LIFETIMES HAVE I LED YOU AND YOUR FATHERS.
NOW THE RULE WILL PASS TO WOO YEN JET, AND A GRAND NEW AGE WILL BEGIN!
CAN YOU BELIEVE THIS? HE THINKS JIMMY IS GOING TO TAKE OVER THE--
JIMMY?
HEY, HOSS, WHAT'S THE PLAN HERE?
I'M GOING TO GO TAKE THE STAFF AND BECOME THE RULER.
OH.
O-KAYYY...
IT IS THE ONLY WAY.
IF HE ENDED THE RULE HERE AND NOW, THE THOUSAND ARMS OF ATLAS WOULD BE LOOSE AND UNCONTROLLED.
YES. THIS WAY HE CAN IMPLEMENT CHANGE FROM ABOVE.
YEAH!
WITH RESOURCES LIKE THIS, WE COULD DO SOME *REAL* GOOD IN THE WORLD.
WITHOUT MUCH GLORY THOUGH; WE'LL HAVE TO STAY OFF THE RADAR.
THAT'LL BE A SWITCH.
OKAY, MASTER. I'M READY.
APPROACH... AND RECEIVE THE SPIRIT BANNER.

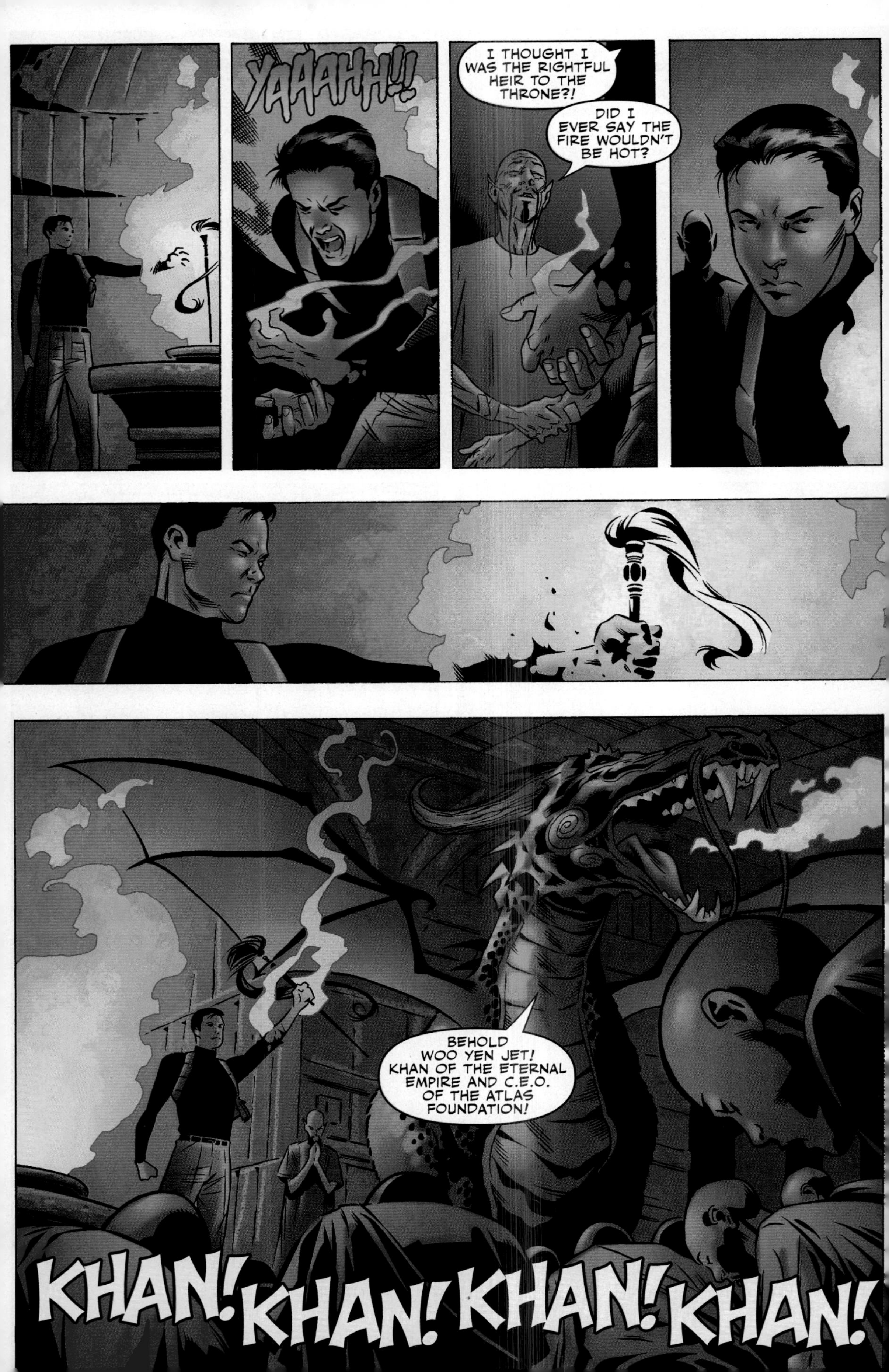
YAAAHH!!
I THOUGHT I WAS THE RIGHTFUL HEIR TO THE THRONE?!
DID I EVER SAY THE FIRE WOULDN'T BE HOT?
BEHOLD WOO YEN JET! KHAN OF THE ETERNAL EMPIRE AND C.E.O. OF THE ATLAS FOUNDATION!
KHAN! KHAN! KHAN! KHAN!

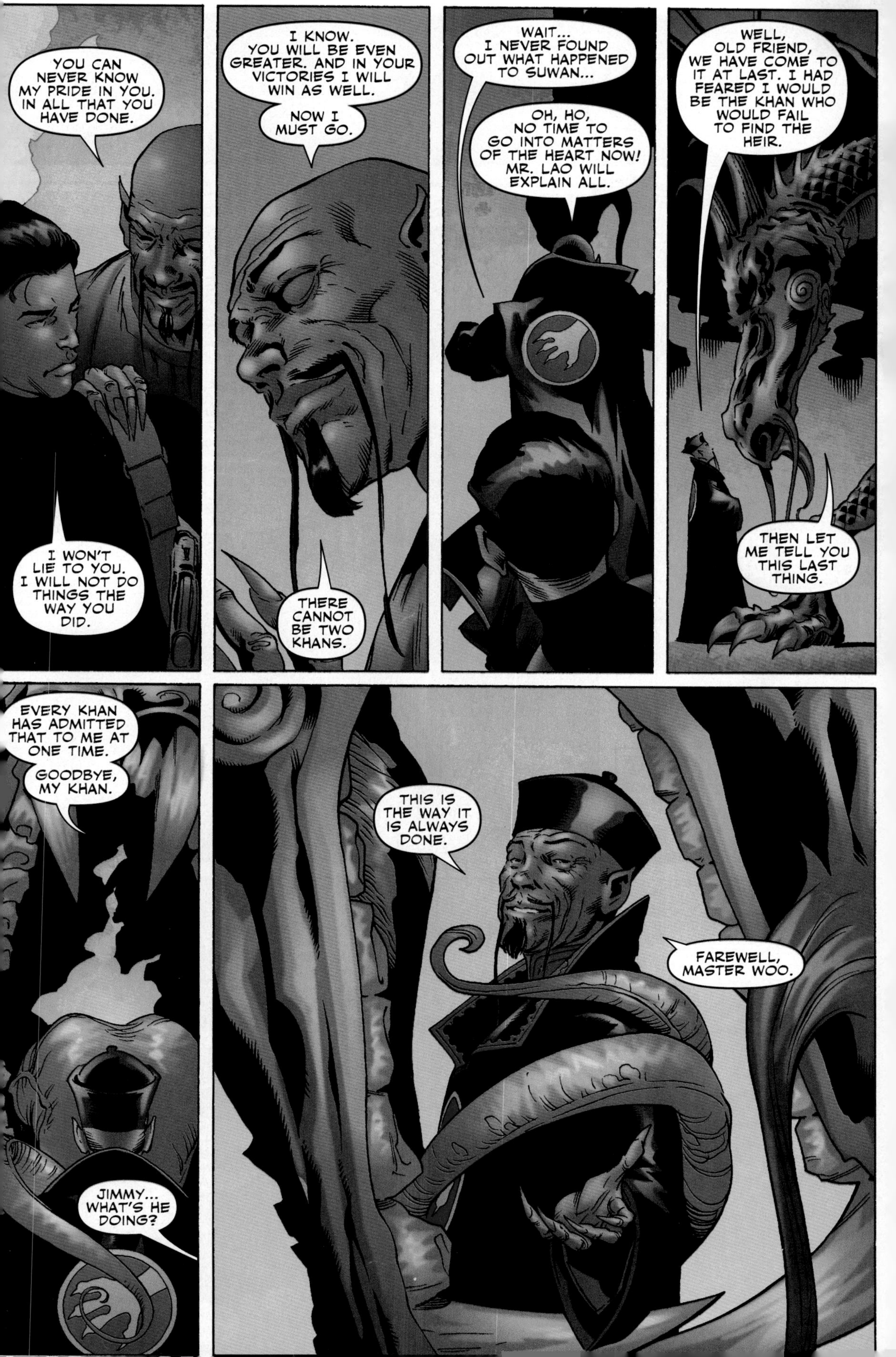
YOU CAN NEVER KNOW MY PRIDE IN YOU. IN ALL THAT YOU HAVE DONE.
I WON'T LIE TO YOU. I WILL NOT DO THINGS THE WAY YOU DID.
I KNOW. YOU WILL BE EVEN GREATER. AND IN YOUR VICTORIES I WILL WIN AS WELL.
NOW I MUST GO.
THERE CANNOT BE TWO KHANS.
WAIT... I NEVER FOUND OUT WHAT HAPPENED TO SUWAN...
OH, HO, NO TIME TO GO INTO MATTERS OF THE HEART NOW! MR. LAO WILL EXPLAIN ALL.
WELL, OLD FRIEND, WE HAVE COME TO IT AT LAST. I HAD FEARED I WOULD BE THE KHAN WHO WOULD FAIL TO FIND THE HEIR.
THEN LET ME TELL YOU THIS LAST THING.
EVERY KHAN HAS ADMITTED THAT TO ME AT ONE TIME.
GOODBYE, MY KHAN.
JIMMY... WHAT'S HE DOING?
THIS IS THE WAY IT IS ALWAYS DONE.
FAREWELL, MASTER WOO.

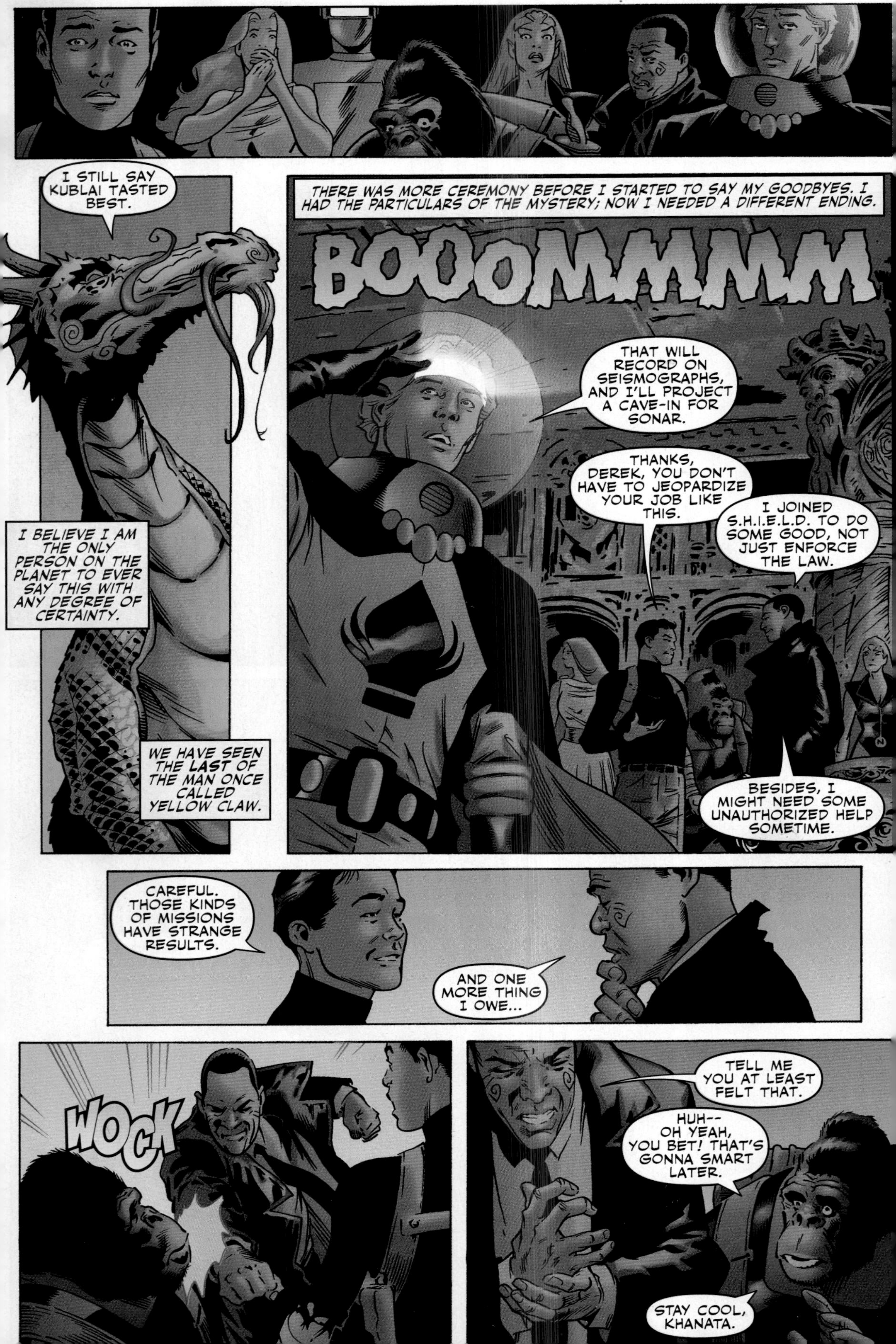

I STILL SAY KUBLAI TASTED BEST.
I BELIEVE I AM THE ONLY PERSON ON THE PLANET TO EVER SAY THIS WITH ANY DEGREE OF CERTAINTY.
WE HAVE SEEN THE LAST OF THE MAN ONCE CALLED YELLOW CLAW.
THERE WAS MORE CEREMONY BEFORE I STARTED TO SAY MY GOODBYES. I HAD THE PARTICULARS OF THE MYSTERY; NOW I NEEDED A DIFFERENT ENDING.
BOOOMMMM
THAT WILL RECORD ON SEISMOGRAPHS, AND I'LL PROJECT A CAVE-IN FOR SONAR.
THANKS, DEREK, YOU DON'T HAVE TO JEOPARDIZE YOUR JOB LIKE THIS.
I JOINED S.H.I.E.L.D. TO DO SOME GOOD, NOT JUST ENFORCE THE LAW.
BESIDES, I MIGHT NEED SOME UNAUTHORIZED HELP SOMETIME.
CAREFUL. THOSE KINDS OF MISSIONS HAVE STRANGE RESULTS.
AND ONE MORE THING I OWE...
WOCK
TELL ME YOU AT LEAST FELT THAT.
HUH-- OH YEAH, YOU BET! THAT'S GONNA SMART LATER.
STAY COOL, KHANATA.

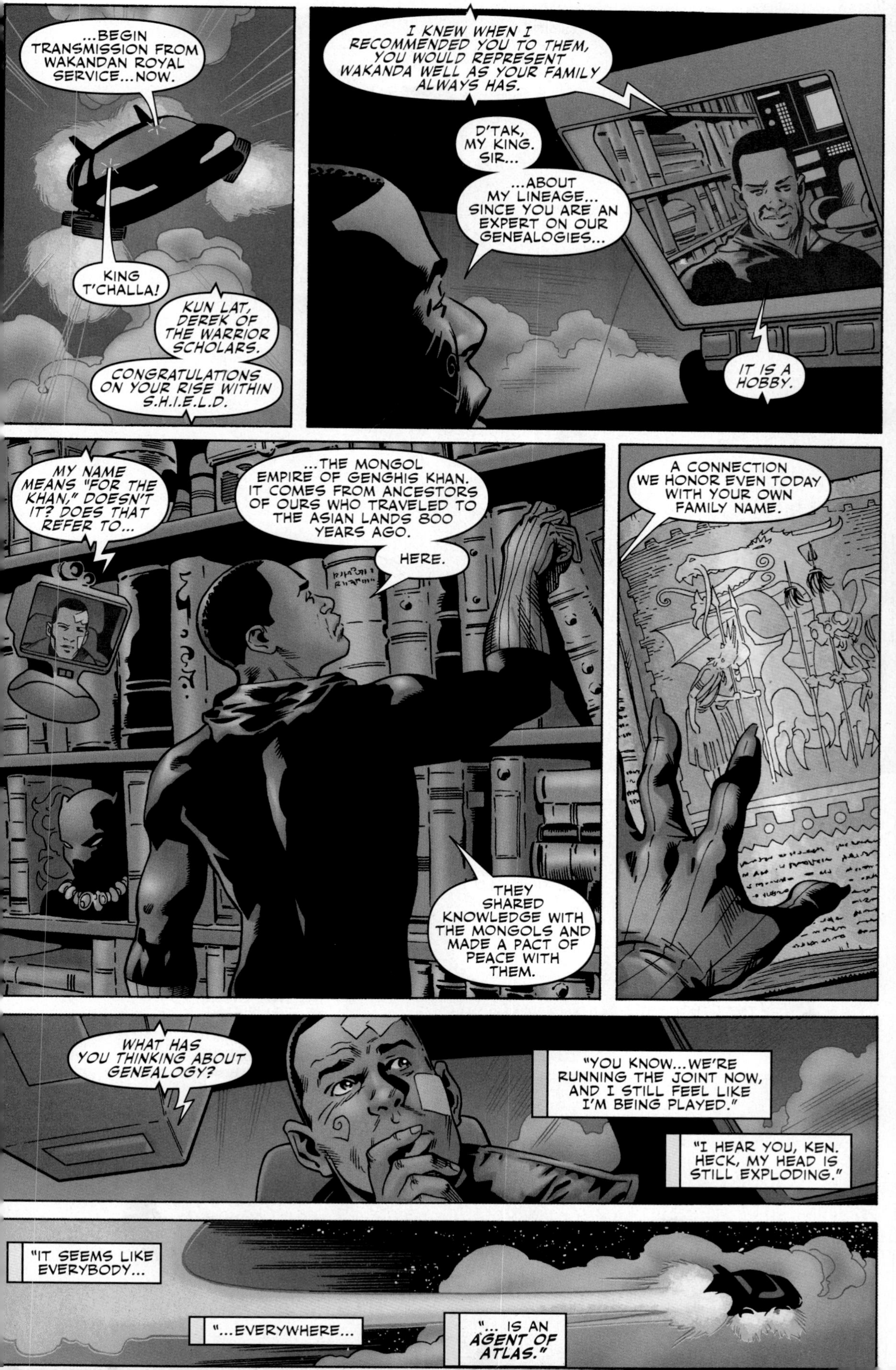
...BEGIN TRANSMISSION FROM WAKANDAN ROYAL SERVICE...NOW.
KING T'CHALLA!
KUN LAT, DEREK OF THE WARRIOR SCHOLARS.
CONGRATULATIONS ON YOUR RISE WITHIN S.H.I.E.L.D.
I KNEW WHEN I RECOMMENDED YOU TO THEM, YOU WOULD REPRESENT WAKANDA WELL AS YOUR FAMILY ALWAYS HAS.
D'TAK, MY KING. SIR...
...ABOUT MY LINEAGE... SINCE YOU ARE AN EXPERT ON OUR GENEALOGIES...
IT IS A HOBBY.
MY NAME MEANS "FOR THE KHAN," DOESN'T IT? DOES THAT REFER TO...
...THE MONGOL EMPIRE OF GENGHIS KHAN. IT COMES FROM ANCESTORS OF OURS WHO TRAVELED TO THE ASIAN LANDS 800 YEARS AGO.
HERE.
THEY SHARED KNOWLEDGE WITH THE MONGOLS AND MADE A PACT OF PEACE WITH THEM.
A CONNECTION WE HONOR EVEN TODAY WITH YOUR OWN FAMILY NAME.
WHAT HAS YOU THINKING ABOUT GENEALOGY?
"YOU KNOW...WE'RE RUNNING THE JOINT NOW, AND I STILL FEEL LIKE I'M BEING PLAYED."
"I HEAR YOU, KEN. HECK, MY HEAD IS STILL EXPLODING."
"IT SEEMS LIKE EVERYBODY...
"...EVERYWHERE...
"... IS AN AGENT OF ATLAS."

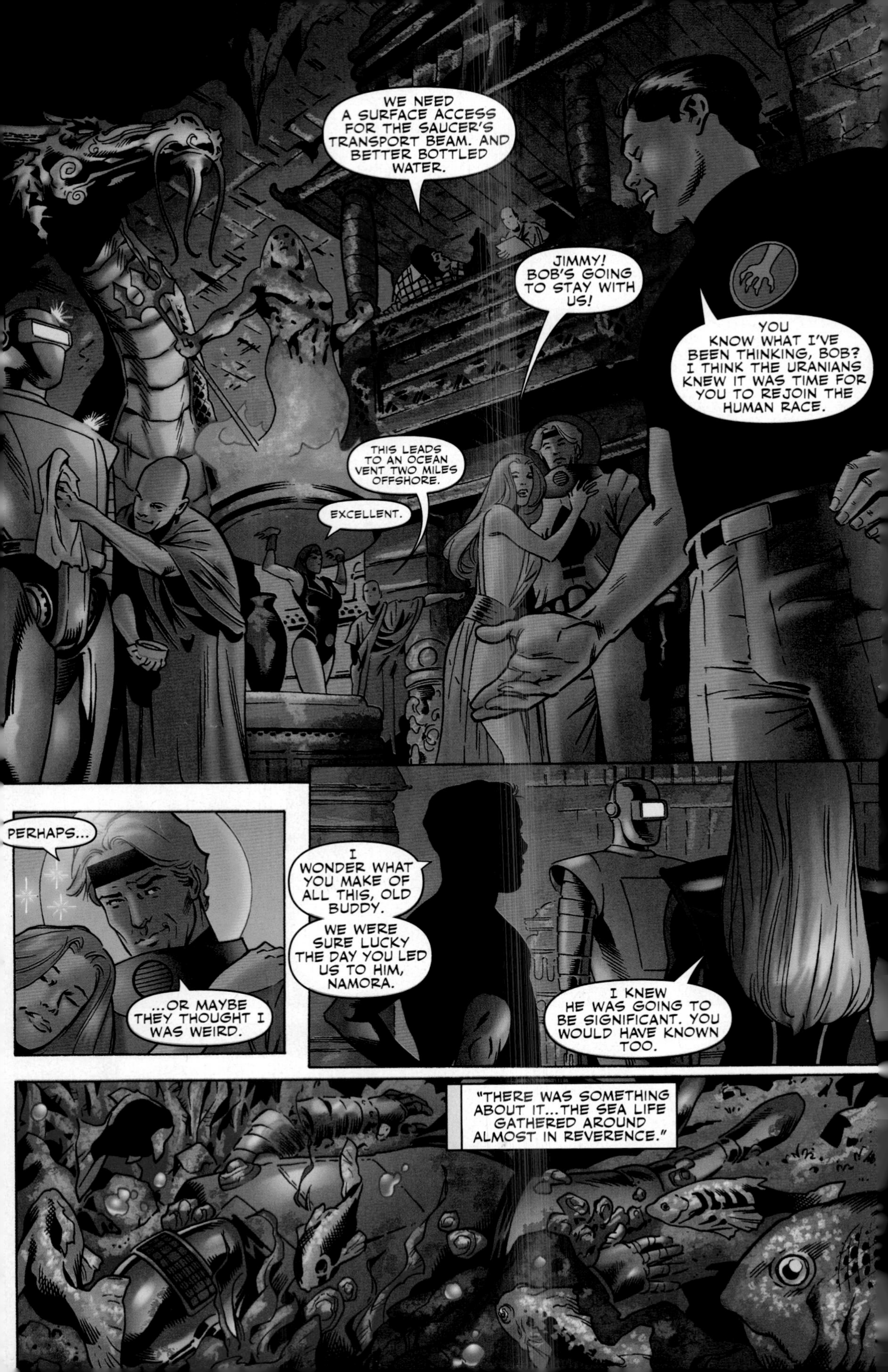
WE NEED A SURFACE ACCESS FOR THE SAUCER'S TRANSPORT BEAM. AND BETTER BOTTLED WATER.
JIMMY! BOB'S GOING TO STAY WITH US!
YOU KNOW WHAT I'VE BEEN THINKING, BOB? I THINK THE URANIANS KNEW IT WAS TIME FOR YOU TO REJOIN THE HUMAN RACE.
THIS LEADS TO AN OCEAN VENT TWO MILES OFFSHORE.
EXCELLENT.
PERHAPS...
...OR MAYBE THEY THOUGHT I WAS WEIRD.
I WONDER WHAT YOU MAKE OF ALL THIS, OLD BUDDY.
WE WERE SURE LUCKY THE DAY YOU LED US TO HIM, NAMORA.
I KNEW HE WAS GOING TO BE SIGNIFICANT. YOU WOULD HAVE KNOWN TOO.
"THERE WAS SOMETHING ABOUT IT...THE SEA LIFE GATHERED AROUND ALMOST IN REVERENCE."

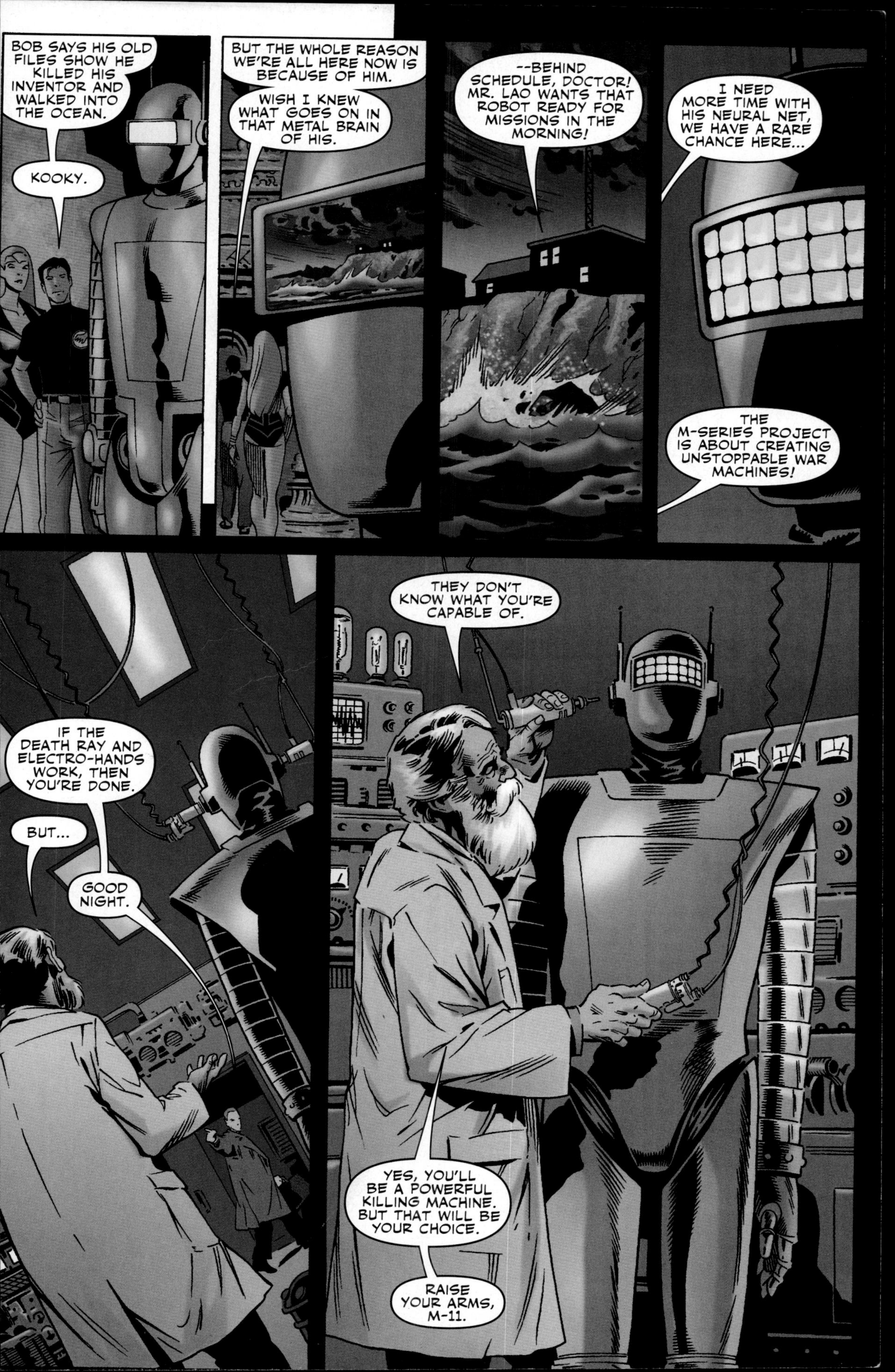
BOB SAYS HIS OLD FILES SHOW HE KILLED HIS INVENTOR AND WALKED INTO THE OCEAN.
KOOKY.
BUT THE WHOLE REASON WE'RE ALL HERE NOW IS BECAUSE OF HIM.
WISH I KNEW WHAT GOES ON IN THAT METAL BRAIN OF HIS.
--BEHIND SCHEDULE, DOCTOR! MR. LAO WANTS THAT ROBOT READY FOR MISSIONS IN THE MORNING!
I NEED MORE TIME WITH HIS NEURAL NET, WE HAVE A RARE CHANCE HERE...
THE M-SERIES PROJECT IS ABOUT CREATING UNSTOPPABLE WAR MACHINES!
IF THE DEATH RAY AND ELECTRO-HANDS WORK, THEN YOU'RE DONE.
BUT...
GOOD NIGHT.
THEY DON'T KNOW WHAT YOU'RE CAPABLE OF.
YES, YOU'LL BE A POWERFUL KILLING MACHINE. BUT THAT WILL BE YOUR CHOICE.
RAISE YOUR ARMS, M-11.

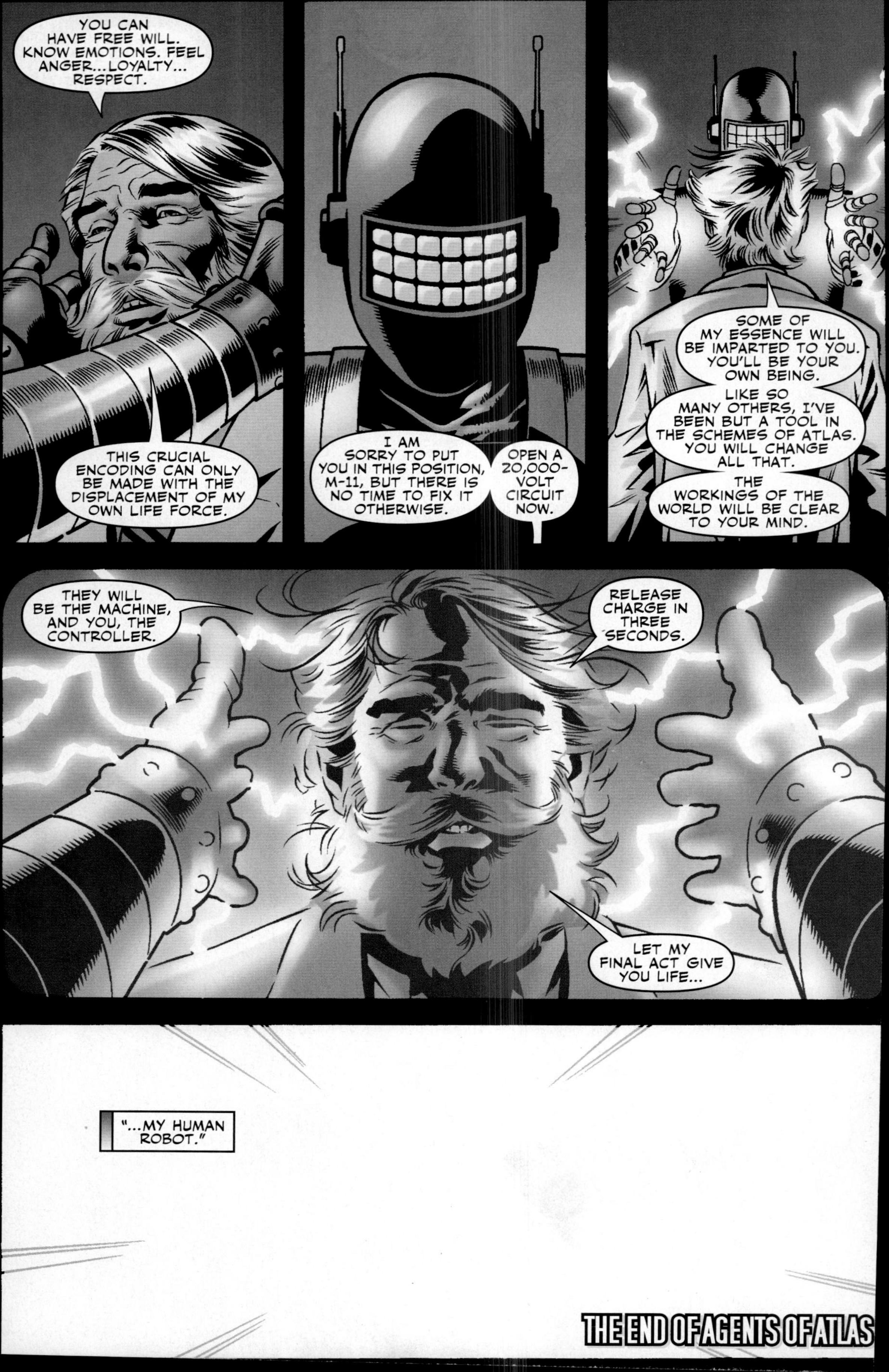
YOU CAN HAVE FREE WILL. KNOW EMOTIONS. FEEL ANGER...LOYALTY... RESPECT.
THIS CRUCIAL ENCODING CAN ONLY BE MADE WITH THE DISPLACEMENT OF MY OWN LIFE FORCE.
I AM SORRY TO PUT YOU IN THIS POSITION, M-11, BUT THERE IS NO TIME TO FIX IT OTHERWISE.
OPEN A 20,000-VOLT CIRCUIT NOW.
SOME OF MY ESSENCE WILL BE IMPARTED TO YOU. YOU'LL BE YOUR OWN BEING.
LIKE SO MANY OTHERS, I'VE BEEN BUT A TOOL IN THE SCHEMES OF ATLAS. YOU WILL CHANGE ALL THAT.
THE WORKINGS OF THE WORLD WILL BE CLEAR TO YOUR MIND.
THEY WILL BE THE MACHINE, AND YOU, THE CONTROLLER.
RELEASE CHARGE IN THREE SECONDS.
LET MY FINAL ACT GIVE YOU LIFE...
"...MY HUMAN ROBOT."
THE END OF AGENTS OF ATLAS

A Congratulations To My Successor, To Be Presented After My Death

James,

You are reading this, so the greatest undertaking of my career must have succeeded. Once I saw you on my very doorstep, even in such condition, it was clear the Fates were finally acknowledging my will. At last I can end the transfusions and consumption of elixirs that have granted me the lifetimes of three men, and go to my rest. You cannot imagine my relief.

Once you accept the mantle of Khan of the Eternal Empire, I will step into the jaws of the Dragon. Death will be abrupt, but it is always done thus, so the Horde Elite will see and know the passage of power. I also fear that you may change your mind, as you are less concerned with acquisition of power than previous rulers. No, you are ever in pursuit of adventure, and of that you shall have plenty. There are many paths to conquering the world, and if anyone can find a new way, it will be you and your Agents.

It has pained me to be so deceitful with you, but adversarial mentoring is a tradition within the empire. Just as the new Khan must break through the Royal Chamber defenses (how I look forward to seeing how you will achieve that with your mighty team!) to take the Spirit Banner. However, it could never equal my surprise as to how you assailed our Mongolian fortress in 1958. We had suspected you would recruit Marvel Boy, but had little influence there. Of course, our goal of one of the few successful Human/Merman hybrids was thwarted. Yet when you arrived with one of our very own M-series warbots—! Then I knew I had chosen a man of destiny. The siege began none too soon, thanks to my own legendary hospitality. Your Mr. Eisenhower was becoming relentless in trying to persuade me to create the world's largest golfing resort in Outer Mongolia. Americans and their sport...

When we lost track of you, I suspected you might be involved with S.H.I.E.L.D., but Mr. Lao believed you dead. You no doubt notice my own public activities ended at that time. In grief, I did as Lao had advised for years and began to concentrate on our influence in the world of commerce. I had always pictured myself as a conqueror in the classic mold; bold victories in the field and commanding respect with an iron will. Quietly acquiring large tracts of the economy is certainly the modern method, but I find it too easy and unrewarding.

You've likely guessed by now that I always wanted you to wed my niece (actually great-great-grand-niece), Suwan. I made much show of keeping you apart, the time-tested surest route to kindling your passions. No doubt you will want to know what became of her, and Mr. Lao will have to apprise you of that situation. It is ever the prerogative of rulers to pass down the greatest dilemmas to the next administration, and I am no different in that regard. I can say with certainty that it will be one of your greatest challenges.

Regarding our esteemed advisor, I should give you this advice of my own—do not trust that dragon! True, I love him as much as I could any human, and his return to the court has been the greatest boon towards putting a wayward campaign back on track. His presence is intoxicating, and his knowledge so deep that to be around him is like having the ear of God. But all dragons have their own agendas that they never disclose. Most of the time you will find him invaluable, but never forget that you are the Master of this Empire and he answers to you. It is to this end that I "urged" you to pick Venus for your team. Your experience in

resisting her voice will serve you well against the persuasions of Mr. Lao. I couldn't have dreamed she would prove so formidable in her own right! I also suspect Mr. Hale will have a healthy disrespect for the dragon to further temper the balance. Ah, if only I had had such a general as that gorilla serving under me...

Yes, this inner circle of yours exceeds all expectations. Never has a Khan combined the cerebral prowess of the Uranian and the sheer raw power of the Sea Queen. As to the inscrutable Robot, we have yet to see the end of his capabilities, and he never fails to surprise. Still, you have the drive and purpose that they all need. It is those attributes above all that move this world and determine history. There are also many, many hours of writings and recordings by me on all matters concerning the Empire that I hope will be of help. If it seems a bit like string-pulling from the grave, well, what can I say? I am who I am.

You will likely, as did I, feel some remorse upon the realization that your lifelong enemy was in truth a guiding member of your extended family. I assure you this gives the Khan greater drive in his duties. Only in taking my place will you know who I truly was. Shed no tears for me, Woo Yen Jet. For now I am on a celestial steed riding across the steppes with Temujin and his Golden Horde. We will feast under the stars and share tales of our victories by the fire. And we will await the distant day when you join our number, bringing the new legends that only you can tell. Until that time, know that you have made an old Chinese the happiest he has ever been.

Your Exalted Master and Humble Servant,

Plan Chu
The Golden Claw

AGENTS OF ATLAS:
THE ONLINE STORY

Mark Paniccia wanted Nate Cosby and I to brainstorm ideas to promote *Agents* on a budget of...nothing. So while I was visiting the offices in New York we went around the corner to get pizza for lunch and discuss a mad scheme. I had recently worked with my studio mates on a section of an Alternate Reality Game that Sean Stewart (sci-fi writer and a pioneer of ARGs) directed, *Last Call Poker*. My thought was to introduce an enigmatic character who would make cryptic statements and leave trails on the internet, and players would have to solve these puzzles to release sections of an online story. The story premise would be that this was an appropriated FBI file documenting a secret mission of Jimmy Woo's team in 1958. Artist Steve Lieber suggested that we make some of the answers available at participating local comics shops, so there would be a "real-world" element to the gameplay. Marvel VP David Gabriel briefed retailers that they would be receiving passwords to give to customers, and John Dokes and Peter Olson set up the *Temple of Atlas* weblog where the story would run. Jim McCann got the word out to the online comics community that we needed co-conspirators to plant fake news stories and hide clues, and for most of the summer of 2006 we brought the "Menace From Space" story to the world.

Running the game story was exhilarating, fun and a lot of work. Dozens of people volunteered their time and web space, and many comics-shop owners lent their names to "news" stories that often implicated them in a vast conspiracy that mirrored the workings of the Atlas Foundation in our story. The game didn't virally spread as wide as I'd hoped, but I'm not sure I could have handled the workload if it had. Clever players were already devoting lots of energy and time to problem solving and searching for clues. I had to make clues harder and more obscure just to buy myself enough time to write the story each week. For instance, one week they had to follow clues embedded in the chapter to the *About* page of Newsarama.com and find text hidden in a black field at the bottom of the page, written in Greek. Then they had to translate that to get a password to take to a participating comics shop and return to the blog with the keyword the store gave them. Some played purely by armchair and handed off "field work" duties to others, and it evolved into a neat active community.

Ultimately, the game shaped the series profoundly. The dragon that attacks Woo's first strike force was originally going to be only a guard beast — but once I started planning out Mr. Lao's appearances, I realized he and the dragon should be one. As "Menace From Space" came together, I kept finding ways to refer to it in the series, and then a key scene near the end took place at the Naval shipyard from the online story. The serialized story is too long to reprint here, but can be found in total at Marvel.com. I'd like to revisit the ARG-style promotion again on a larger scale at some point, with a crew of writers and webmasters. I love problem-solving exercises, and the idea of following difficult and cryptic trails that actually lead to answers, so the entire time I was envious of the players. They were having fun!

Your Humble Servant,

Parker

THE TEMPLE OF ATLAS

2006-06-16 14:16:32

Welcome. As you have found this site, you are clearly one of those rare people who realize there's more to the world than what you see on the surface. You may qualify for membership in an organization of which I am involved. My name, at least one that you can pronounce, is Mr. Lao.

Some of you were promised a "decoder ring", yet you will receive something of more worth than a mere plastic decrypting toy. No, the Decoder Ring of which I speak is all of YOU- working together as a whole. If you are the first to reach the Temple, do sign in now.

What you'll receive are classified FBI documents, on a weekly schedule. (Needless to say, anyone who feels they should reveal this to the Bureau, will find themselves in a very wet climate lacking in oxygen) These records we've retrieved for you concern a mission from 1959, headed by a young firebrand named James "Jimmy" Woo. With special powers given him by your government, Special Agent Woo assembled a very unusual team that worked together for just more than six months. It is of relevance because this team has recently reunited. This is a team with which my organization is quite concerned. Our destinies are intertwined, and I believe will be coming to a resolution in the near future.

The story is broken up in separate entries, transcribed years ago by Federal Agent Angela Wellington, a young woman who clearly had a fondness for the old pulp magazines, as you'll see by her writing style. She left the agency in 1960 and became a full time science fiction writer. While she did take liberties in detailing the facts at hand, it does make the file a bit less dry than most government documents. Much of the information is reliable as it was taken from recordings made regularly by one of Woo's agents.

Now I shall leave you to the lost art of reading for a few minutes. After you've reviewed the excerpt, more direction will be offered. Enjoy.

Glowing embers pulsed and hoarded their heat in the large fireplace. The metal hand telescoped in to turn the logs over, then the other placed two more large chunks of pine on top. With a casual squeeze the hands split open the new timbers

so that they might catch aflame faster. Within minutes a sizable conflagration roared steady like an engine, warming the old Federal drawing room and all the agents inside. The tender of the fire stepped to the side of the mantle and resumed a vigilant position. A brandy snifter smashed suddenly against the crackling wood fueling a bright flare, and the unmoving figure spun its head around to rest a cyclopic gaze on the gorilla, who winced.

"Watch where you're pointing that death ray, Howdy Doody! Throwing the glass in the fire is an old custom. Hey, when's Golden Boy showing up? I'm ready for dinner." Ken Hale loped over to the chair next to Jimmy Woo's desk to pore through a stack of betting forms.

The reclining figure on the couch stretched and pushed back a thick drape of shining hair to let more of the fire's heat warm her perfect face. She didn't open her eyes, but smiled as she answered her teammate.

"I believe Bob is in Huntsville, Alabama consulting Dr. Von Braun and the new space agency on stellar travel. He should be back soon. He gets so frustrated when Earth scientists can't follow his directions."

Though the young woman's response was brief and factual, her speech had a profound effect on the visiting government agents in the room. Both went into a slight stupor as the ethereal locution wound through the men, like a ghostly serpent coursing through their bodies. The man seated at the large oaken desk kept his fingers against his temples, calm and unaffected. Some have supposed that his ability to retain his wits at these instances was the result of having mastered ancient Chinese disciplines of meditation and concentration. In fact, a careful observer would notice that the fingers against his temples was not a gesture of focus, but a convenient way to put his thumbs in his ears whenever the woman began to speak.

The taller man, Oglethorpe, shook his head quickly as if to revive. "Ahem... so, ah, those are the ships that disappeared last week. None of the cargo has been reported turning up yet, at least not at the ports we can rely on to admit it."

"If this is all part of the same operation, it's one heck of an operation, I'll say. So why are you guys coming to us in particular with this? Because one of the ships was docked out here at Hunter's Point?"

"Actually, Mr. Woo," the shorter man volunteered,"because it does look to be so large an effort, Washington suggested that it's probably the work of someone you know best. The eastern mastermind known as-"

"YELLOW CLAW?!?" roared Gorilla-Man. The visiting agents both crouched a bit, bracing themselves against Jimmy Woo's desk. The pencil he held with his toes snapped in two. Jimmy Woo held up his hand to indicate that calm and order was called for. Disturbed from her firewatching, Venus sat up and rested her head and arms on the plush back of the leather couch.

"I seriously doubt The Yellow Claw is behind this,"said Jimmy Woo."My team and I delivered a major setback to his organization just over a month ago."

"There's a great big hole in Outer Mongolia where a fortress used to be." Gorilla-Man added smugly.

"Well sure," Agent Dirsken rejoined,"there's no arguing your outfit is top dog since that big rescue mission. Don't think the rest of back in D.C aren't green all over- I mean, the fact that you can run a team like this out of San Francisco proves you don't really answer to J. Edgar!"

"We completely respect the Director's wishes," Jimmy assured the man.

"Well sure. I didn't mean to- anyway, what I'm getting at is that--Yellow Claw or no- whoever's behind this thing has a major network behind him." Gorilla Man lost interest in the visiting agent and picked up the newspaper.

"Or her." Venus added. Normally a reminder to consider female prowess rubbed Agent Dirsken the wrong way, as it usually came from his wife or her sister. Instead of offering his glare in such cases, Dirsken made a grateful smile to let Venus know that he would never think her as intruding, and in fact her help was very, very welcome.

A flash reflected on the glass of the grandfather clock near Woo's desk, catching the eye of Agent Oglethorpe. He looked out the large french windows for the source. Over the buildings in the distance hung layers of cloud banks trapping a citywide cache of fog that kept the sky gray and visibility to a minimum. As the cumulonimbus lit up, the agent thought he was seeing a lightning storm. Then he remembered that the west coast rarely gets such electrical activity, and the flashes were coming closer. They seemed to be forming a trail. Agents Oglethorpe and Dirsken quickly stepped away from the window while Jimmy Woo simply raised his hand to shield his eyes. An aurous glow flooded the opening and bathed half of the room in shimmering warm light that looked to have the consistency of water. The lithe figure of a young man gracefully described an arc through the window and glided to a stop before the office door. Rather than switch off when the man stopped, the light seemed to retreat into the thick bands around his wrists.

That is all for now. You may respond in the Comments section of this web log, which will be at this website unless matters of urgency force us to relocate. Pick a code name and keep using it that I may track your progress. Please observe some decorum with name selection. We may be murderers, smugglers, dictators and charlatans, but we frown on vulgarity and will ignore such missives. You may be asked to solve a small problem and report back, and I will need your code name to distinguish your actions. A list of exceptional agents will likely be printed in the AGENTS OF ATLAS "comic book" later. We often pass on coded information through these fantastic periodicals, so I suggest you purchase them if you wish to stay abreast of our current machinations.

Our first exercise this week is ridiculously simple (though that will change). You need only locate a key phrase that I have placed in cyberspace. Once you've found it, share the link here. The path can be found in the first part of the classified mission!

--Mr. Lao

UPDATE: New arrivals- please continue to check in, though you do not need to mention the key phrase. There is, however, a successive post after this you may notice to your right (Timely's weblog archives immediately!) where you might wish to hazard a guess on the addition to Jimmy Woo's team of agents. As no one has guessed correctly, I fear we may not have psychic ability amongst our new recruits. There is also a piece of iconography in the next post you may wish to keep.

WHO...OR WHAT...IS HE??!
YELLOW CLAW
APPROVED BY THE COMICS CODE AUTHORITY
YELLOW CLAW
OCT.
10¢
ALL-NEW THRILLS WITH THE MOST DANGEROUS MAN OF ALL TIME!
AT LAST IT CAN BE TOLD!

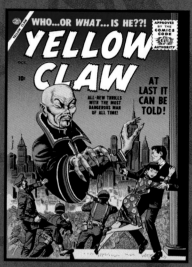

Agent's Response

It appears that I am the first to have reached the Temple of Atlas and, as commanded, I have signed in.
I believe the code Mr. Lao refers to is the scrambled words from the press release: helpmate, falsetto and bowleg. (The other words were comic book titles previously published by Timely.) Unscrambling the letters reveals where we are now: The Temple of Atlas Blog.

CBR SPOTLIGHT ON AGENTS OF ATLAS

Posted: May 12 - June 16, 2006

BY DAVE RICHARDS, STAFF WRITER, COMICBOOKRESOURCES.COM

WEEK 1: EDITOR MARK PANICCIA
AGENT PROFILE: *GORILLA MAN*

Posted: May 12, 2006

SECRET AVENGERS REASSEMBLED? PANICCIA TALKS "AGENTS OF ATLAS"

In the 1940's during one of the Marvel Universe's darkest hours, a legion of super powered heroes came forward. These heroes stood up to the menace of the Axis Powers and then seemingly disappeared until many like Captain America reappeared when the second age of Marvels began years later. What happened during those intervening years? Who protected the Marvel Universe from otherworldly threats? "Agents of Atlas," a new five issue mini-series by writer Jeff Parker and artist Leonard Kirk, will answer these questions and many more. The mini-series follows the modern day adventures of a reunited team of heroes who defended the Marvel Universe before The Avengers ever assembled. In part one of our spotlight on Agents of Atlas CBR News spoke with Editor Mark Paniccia about the series.

"Agents of Atlas" was born when Paniccia stumbled across an old 1978 issue of Marvel's "What If?" The issue #9, was "What If the Avengers Fought Evil During the 1950s?" and the cover depicted a number of characters from Marvel's past charging forward, while the present day members of The Avengers looked on. "That cover was intriguing," Paniccia told CBR News. "It instantly tickles the nostalgia bone."

The nostalgic characters that composed the 1950s Avengers: Marvel Boy, Gorilla-Man, Venus, 3-D Man, and the Human Robot, all first appeared during the Golden Age of Comics and were unlike any of the later Marvel Comics characters. "They are most definitely a product of a different era," Paniccia explained. "When you look at the original versions of these characters, they're like something out of an Ed Wood movie. That surface impression is what helps them stand out from the 'modern' Marvel hero, but there's more to all of them than meets the eye."

To help show off the hidden qualities of these characters, Paniccia enlisted Jeff Parker to chronicle their modern day adventures in "Agents of Atlas." "Jeff is cool," Paniccia said. "But besides that, he not only gets the appeal of bizarre characters like this, he understands how to apply them in contemporary terms without losing that nostalgic charm that they have. When I first saw these guys, I called him right away. We were both looking at the cover online and he started giving me this 'Doom Patrol' meets 'JSA' take — which was spot on."

And to bring Parker's take on the characters to life, Paniccia recruited the artistic talents of Leonard Kirk, "Leonard is a superb draftsman," Paniccia stated. "He can draw anything from a 1950s-style rocket to a lavish jungle scene to an alien cityscape. I ask, what makes him not perfect for this book?"

One thing Kirk won't be drawing in "Agents of Atlas" is 3-D Man. Paniccia told CBR News that there were no plans for 3-D Man or his modern day counterpart the former Avengers member

Triathlon to appear in "Agents of Atlas." The team, which was originally assembled by former FBI agent and current SHIELD agent Jimmy Woo, will include Gorilla Man, Marvel Boy, Venus, The Human Robot, and a fifth member whose identity Marvel wants to remain a mystery for the time being.

Readers looking for a good mystery set in the Marvel Universe will want to pick up "Agents of Atlas." "There are super powered beings in it, but there's a grand mystery involved here," Paniccia explained. "Part of the fun is going to be watching that mystery unravel - and see how it ties into the Marvel Universe."

The team members of Agents of Atlas all have ties to the early days of the Marvel Universe, but readers who may be unfamiliar with the characters' histories will have no problem understanding and enjoying the series. Paniccia said, "I think this is a good series for anyone who is looking for something a little different to jump into."

CBR's "Agents of Atlas" coverage continues next week with an in-depth interview with series writer Jeff Parker. Also, each week we'll bring you another Agent Profile, where Jeff Parker gives CBR News the inside info on the team members that compose the Agents of Atlas. Find below the first of those profiles as Jeff Parker tells us more about Gorilla-Man. In the weeks ahead, look for the identity of the mysterious fifth team member to be revealed exclusively here at CBR.

AGENTS OF ATLAS
KEN HALE
"PRE-GORILLA"

AGENT PROFILE: *GORILLA MAN*

When the Agents of Atlas reunite this August in the pages of their self titled mini-series, many readers will be meeting this bizarre and eclectic troop of heroes for the first time, even though they've been around for over fifty years. Many of the characters debuted in titles published by Atlas Comics, the company that would eventually become Marvel Comics. In order to better acquaint readers with the cast of "Agents of Atlas" and offer some insight into their roles in the mini-series, CBR News has compiled a

NOBODY CALLS ME MAGILLA!

AGENTS OF ATLAS

GORILLA MAN

number of "Agent Profiles" by speaking with "Agents" writer Jeff Parker. The first Agent profiled is the team's expert on Guerilla warfare, Gorilla-Man.

There have actually been a number of Atlas/Marvel characters with the moniker of Gorilla-Man. "One was a mad scientist who was sure that taking the form of a gorilla would help him enslave the world," Parker told CBR News. "Ours is Ken Hale, the Gorilla Man who appeared in Men's Adventure #26. That version is credited to Stan Lee and Robert Q. Sale."

Like any good primate, Ken Hale has evolved since his debut appearance. "I think that what happens with a lot of good characters is that they slowly create themselves," Parker said. "What readers enjoy sticks, and what they don't falls by the wayside. At least that's the way it should work. It's interesting how even just looking at pictures of the

characters, readers gravitate to Gorilla Man. Smart talking gorillas are a beloved staple of comic books, and people don't think of Marvel as having any. But we've got Gorilla Man, and that's better than a barrel full of monkeys."

To help distinguish Ken Hale from the band of other four color Gorilla characters, Parker has further defined Gorilla-Man's background and made him a simian super solider. "We've added more to his origin to help the logic of why he was brought into the group originally, and this is one of those cases where the character has become more of what people want him to be," Parker stated. "People like him being a big-action weapons expert, and now that's part of his back-story. We find out Ken was a Soldier of Fortune who was a force to reckon with even as a human. You curse him with the immortal body of a gorilla, and you have a major @$$-kicker.

"He's very strong, agile and proficient with all manner of weaponry. Actually, he's a bit bigger than a mountain gorilla. He also doesn't age, as you'll read more about in the story. His most valuable function in the group now is actually as the touchstone to the present day. Everyone else has been largely cut off from the modern world except for him."

Gorilla-Man was last seen interacting with the modern world in the pages of "Nick Fury's Howling Commandos" "The Howling Commandos unit has had him busy in secret operations so he doesn't know much about what's going on with specific things like say, the events of 'Civil War,'" Parker said.

When "Agents of Atlas" begins, Gorilla-Man is still serving as an agent of SHIELD, which will put him in an emotionally difficult spot. "He's got a really tough decision to make about his allegiances (not unlike 'Civil War', I guess!)," Parker explained." He's one of SHIELD's go-to guys, but being part of Jimmy Woo's team was a key time in his life. What you have to know about Ken is that loyalty is very important to him; he's pretty old-fashioned when it comes to values like that. Not the type to leave a man behind, definitely someone you want to have your back."

WEEK 2: WRITER JEFF PARKER
AGENT PROFILE: *VENUS*

Posted: May 19, 2006

THE MARVEL UNIVERSE NOW WITH EXTRA PULP: PARKER TALKS "AGENTS OF ATLAS."

AGENTS OF ATLAS
VENUS COSTUME

- NOT COMPLETELY TRANSPARENT BUT PRETTY DARN CLOSE.

9/7/06

In part one of our spotlight on "Agents of Atlas," CBR News got inside info on the background of the five issue mini-series from Editor Mark Paniccia. For part two of our in-depth look at Marvel's "Agents of Atlas," CBR News spoke with writer Jeff Parker for the scoop on the series, which reunites a group of heroes that defended the Marvel Universe of the 1950s for a modern day adventure.

As we revealed last time, "Agents of Atlas" was born out of a phone conversation between Parker and Paniccia after the editor rediscovered "What If?" issue number #9, which asked the question "What if the Avengers Fought Evil During the 1950s?" What impressed Parker and Paniccia the most about the issue was the unique characters. "He had a gut feeling about those characters," Parker told CBR News. "It's easy to see why — they're not simply older superheroes, they're pulp adventure icons.

"I'm a sucker more for what they represent — gorillas, spacemen, robots, etc.," Parker continued. "They're going to be a clean slate to lots of readers, so we'll be referencing their past adventures when we can. Okay, I'll admit I found Venus a little bit hot."

The name "Agents of Atlas" is a reference to the characters' past, but it also has plot significance. "The original name for the group of course was essentially The Secret Avengers," Parker said. "But since then Marvel has determined that no prior group called themselves that, so we couldn't use it. We were a bit bummed at first, and then when we realized we could mark out historical territory by using the Atlas name, we cheered up pretty fast! There's no need to ride the coattails of another team, 'AOA' should show that they deserve a book on their own strengths."

One man saw the strengths of the "Agents of Atlas" and brought them together as a group. "The glue is Jimmy Woo!" Parker stated. "They're from before the generations of bickering infighting teams. It's all about loyalty and honoring a connection they had together years ago. That said, they will run into a pretty huge intrateam conflict that there's no way of avoiding. That's when we'll see what Jimmy is really made of."

Jimmy is going to have to be made of some stern stuff to survive the perils he and his team will face in "Agents of Atlas." "Jimmy is in... pretty horrible shape at the beginning of the series," Parker explained. "His life has gone way off course from where it was in the 1950s. He's way up in SHIELD, in Directorate, but it's an ugly job and he hasn't seen field work in years. Unknown to the rest of SHIELD, he's been investigating a personal mystery for the past few years, and though he's in his twilight years, he heads an unauthorized mission that ends as bad as it possibly could.

"No one at SHIELD really knew Jimmy in his heyday; A young slang- talking firebrand who would routinely run into danger with impossible odds," Parker continued. "Had James Dean known about Woo at the time, he would have abandoned Hollywood to join the FBI and emulate Jimmy! Jimmy had such a strong sense of direction and self-assurance that he radiated leadership. People respond to that in a big way. It's almost like a superpower itself — better in some ways. Jimmy's short-lived team felt a sense of belonging and purpose in that few months together that none of them

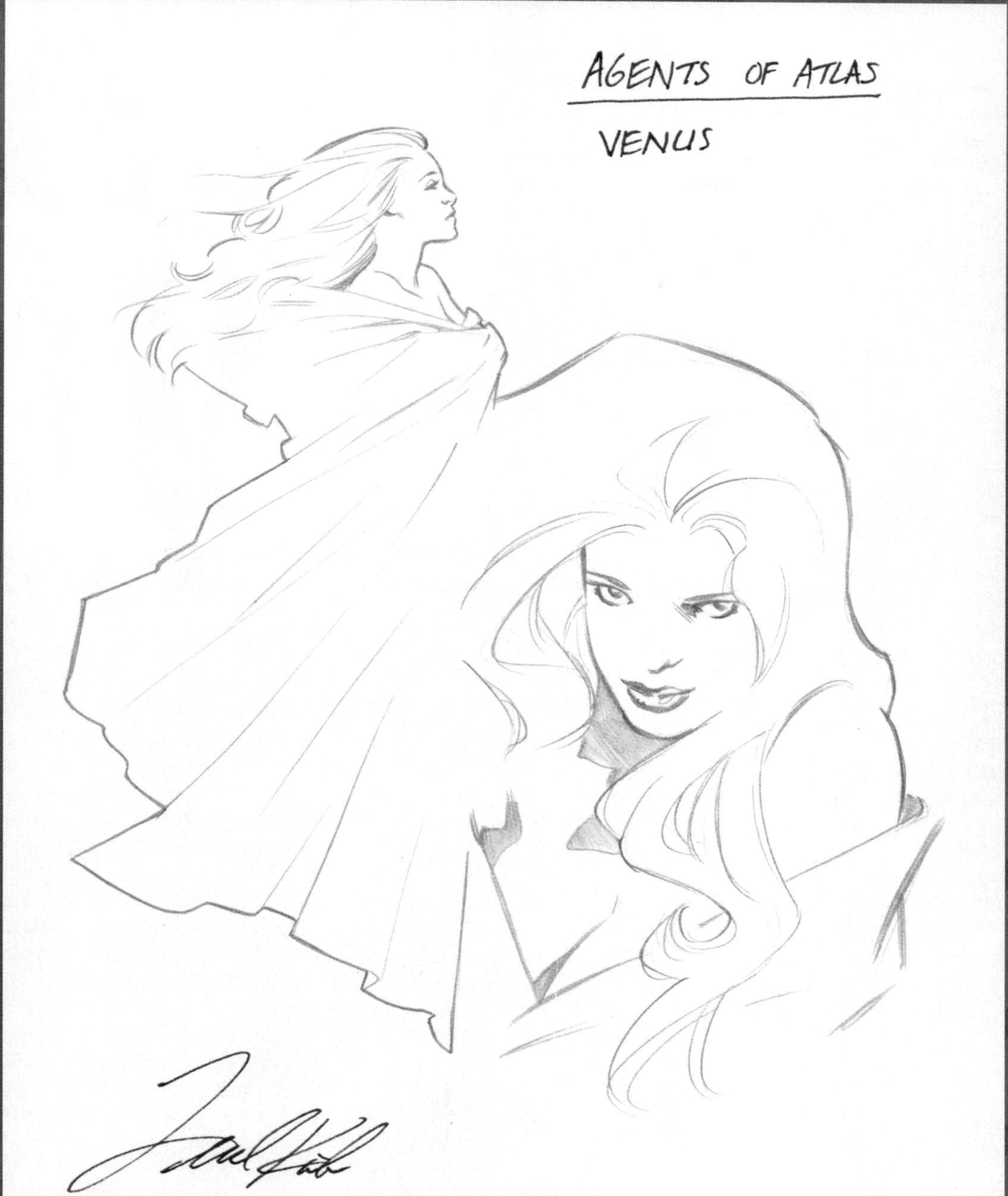
AGENTS OF ATLAS
VENUS

ever did afterward. And that's why even after almost fifty years, when word gets out that Jimmy's in trouble, the team comes back for him."

The team's quest to save Jimmy will have them traversing the globe. "This bounces around the world a bit, from the Mojave Desert, to Africa, and colder regions," Parker said. "That's another Golden Age difference — whereas '60s Marvel stories hang around Manhattan mostly, the '50s ones hopped the planet a lot. Our main American city is going to be San Francisco."

As the Agents trek around the world to save their friend, readers will learn more about them in a series of flashbacks to the Agents' original adventures. "Though the initial 'What If?' story said that the team was disbanded after their one successful rescue mission, we're establishing that they were together for about six months after that," Parker stated. "Remember, Iron Man and even The Watcher said the events being seen on the Avengers computer might not be the exact events from our (616) history! It could pick up things that happened in alternate realities. So this will determine how it all went down in our timeline."

When Jimmy Woo wasn't working with the Agents of Atlas in the 1950s, he was most likely serving as an agent of the FBI and working hard to foil the latest nefarious scheme of his arch-foe, the Yellow Claw. "If you want to dig up some of his bouts with the Yellow Claw affordably, they ran them later as back ups in 'Giant Size Master of Kung Fu.'" Parker said. "Someone re-lettered the parts that said 'FBI Agent Jimmy Woo' to 'S.H.I.E.L.D. Agent Jimmy Woo!' You couldn't really say there was a cohesive

Marvel Universe then, but it's pretty interesting. The creators were trying all kinds of genres to see what would stick, and indulging their interests. When you look at the range of genres, you see the groundwork, the foundation of what the '60s books would be built upon. Look at the Fantastic Four as the best example of taking what came before. Reed and Sue are straight out of the Romance books with the science-fantasy added, Ben is a carryover from the Monster comics, and of course Johnny is an update of an earlier superhero. Bring them all together and you've got a quirky and exciting team that redefines what a superhero comic book is. This is why I think it's important to not dismiss those pre-Marvel years. Much of the success of the Silver Age grew out of the experimenting that happened then."

When Jimmy's old team reunites in the present day to rescue him, they'll find to save their friend they must confront his chief foe from the Pre-Marvel Years. "You're going to see the Yellow Claw, and just as there's more to each of our heroes, there's a lot more to him, too," Parker explained. "I mean, you know his name probably isn't really 'Yellow Claw,' right? And why would a diabolical mastermind even refer to himself with some stereotypical racist 'yellow peril'-style name anyway? In other words, there's a good chance everyone who fought him was being played in a major way! And as if he wasn't manipulative enough, we're going to be introduced to a mysterious advisor of his, essentially the consigliere to the mastermind."

The "Agents of Atlas" will also have advisors of their own; some of the agents of SHIELD that are part of the series supporting cast. "Besides our main heroes, we'll be seeing a stalwart of SHIELD, Dum Dum Dugan," Parker said. "Much of the investigation from their perspective will be handled by agent Derek Khanata, who appeared in 'Amazing Fantasy.' His Wakandan origins figure in very well with some aspects of our story. In a way, he sort of steps into the position Jimmy Woo had in the original 'Secret Avengers' story, where now Jimmy takes a much more active role with the team."

SHIELD might be able to offer some assistance, but the "Agents of Atlas" shouldn't count on any of the Marvel Universe's costumed champions to be of much help. "The other heroes have their hands full with 'Civil War,' but there'll be some brief communications with Reed Richards and King T'Challa," Parker explained.

The Agents of Atlas might not be directly involved in the epic conflict that is "Civil War," but the events of the mega story will affect the series. " 'Civil War' doesn't impact directly on our group; they're all very separated from current society- at least at first," Parker said. "Something that happens in 'Civil War' will affect one of them later, though. It's not something we were anticipating either, it just worked out that way."

Parker hopes things work out with "Agents of Atlas" because he has plenty more tales of the team that he'd love to tell. "As you'll see at the end of the series, if we continue their adventures, the dynamic will be pretty different than other hero-team books. We're counting on readers being ready for something different, because if we made the Agents of Atlas work in similar fashion to other superheroes, there really wouldn't be any point to bringing them back. What I'd like is for a threat to present itself, and readers to say 'Sure, the Avengers or the X-Men could deal with this menace... but I'd really like to see how these guys handle it.'"

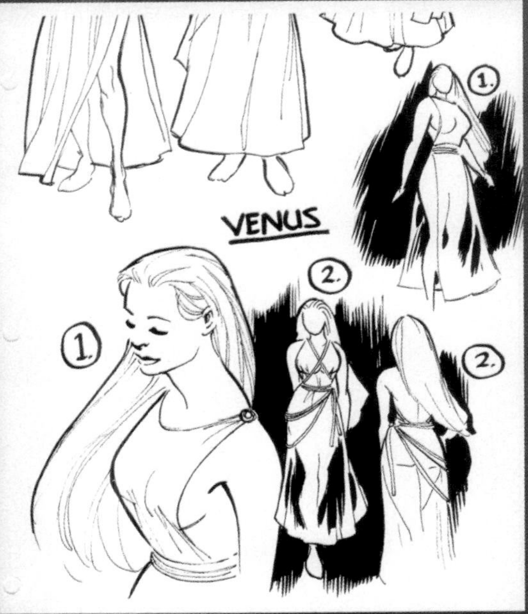
VENUS
1.
2.
1.
2.

AGENT PROFILE: *VENUS*

Last week things got a little hairy around these parts as Jeff Parker brought us an Agent Profile on the "Agents of Atlas" member Gorilla-Man. This week love is in the air as Parker brings us the latest Agent Profile: Venus.

Venus made her debut in issue #1 of her self titled series in 1948. "I don't know who wrote the first story, but the first artist was Ken Bald, who Timely often went to for drawing heroines," Parker told CBR News. "She started out in stories that were more about cheesecake and humor. What's interesting is how that gradually started bending to the supernatural and horror, so more often than not Venus is having run-ins with living skeletons, monsters, and the undead, and so on. Our arc for her character is very much a tribute to that development. It's interesting to me that in today's adventure and superhero comics, most characters showing up on the scene are likely to cause some friction with other characters. By her very nature though, Venus doesn't do that. When she's around, people tend to forget why they were angry or fighting. What we want to show with her is that such an effect can be even more potent than destructive power."

Venus's potent powers allow her to influence even the most confident and self assured individuals. "On a small, human scale, you've probably experienced women like her," Parker explained. "An attractive woman with such presence that when she says the briefest of things to men-and looks them in the eye- they just lose it. They can't focus, they feel like they're underwater and even the most James Bond of the bunch can't keep his composure. It's generally pretty hard to say what's affecting the guys the most. Sure she's gorgeous, but so are other girls and they don't all make you walk into walls because you're trying to keep track of where she is in the room. Is it something in her eyes, or the unearthly quality of her voice?

"If you've encountered one of these mind-wiping women, then you have some limited idea of the effect Venus has on people she wants to influence," Parker continued. "Or even those whom she doesn't. She tries to rein in her effect when

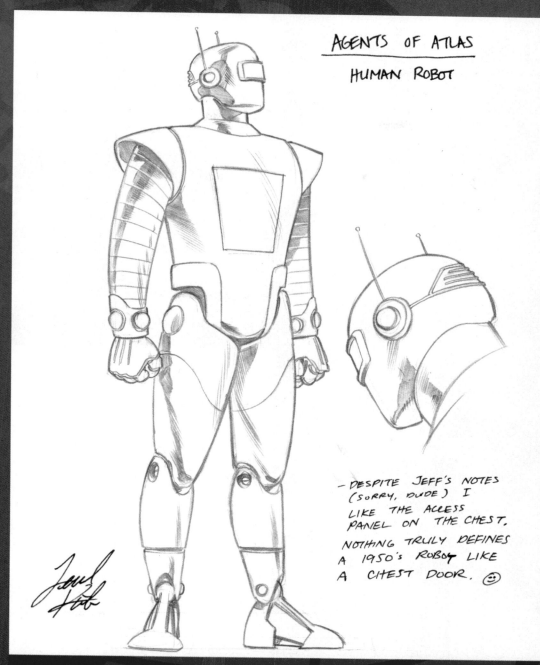

AGENTS OF ATLAS

HUMAN ROBOT

— DESPITE JEFF'S NOTES (SORRY, DUDE) I LIKE THE ACCESS PANEL ON THE CHEST. NOTHING TRULY DEFINES A 1950's ROBOT LIKE A CHEST DOOR. ☺

it's not needed, but it's so much a part of her nature that it's not possible to muffle completely. Her own team has come up with various solutions to stay on course. Jimmy Woo often sticks his fingers in his ears when she's talking to dampen the vocal effect."

When "Agents of Atlas" begins, Venus isn't looking to dampen the effects of her powers, she's quite happy using them to spread joy. "She is still living among humans and using her abilities for good," Parker said. "But she's not bothering with the secret identity when we meet her again. That's not to say she won't use it in the future."

Vicki Starr is the secret identity Venus often employed in the past and she still maintains to actually be the goddess of love. When asked about Venus's claim of godhood Parker cryptically hinted, "As we've said, there's more to all of these characters than we may have thought."

WEEK 3: PENCILER LEONARD KIRK - AGENT PROFILE: *THE HUMAN ROBOT*

Posted: May 26, 2006

THE WEIGHT OF THE WORLD ON HIS PENCIL: KIRK TALKS "AGENTS OF ATLAS"

In part one of CBR News's focus on Marvel Comics' "Agents of Atlas" mini-series, Editor Mark Paniccia gave us the background and basics on the series. Last week, writer Jeff Parker gave us an in-depth look at the series. Today, in part three of our coverage, CBR News chats with the man responsible for bringing Parker's action packed scripts to life, artist Leonard Kirk.

"Agents of Atlas" is the first in a number of projects at Marvel for Kirk, who CBR News has learned recently signed an exclusive contract with the company. "In all honesty, this is the first time anyone has offered me an exclusive," Kirk told CBR News. "As for going with Marvel, I just felt it was time. DC has been great for me over the years and I'd love to work with them again someday but there are still some characters and projects that I'd like to work with that are only available through Marvel.

"After being offered the exclusive, I was already working on one project with Marvel when I got a call from Mark Paniccia about 'Agents of Atlas,'" Kirk continued, "That's about it. He described the project, sent me the outline and I jumped aboard."

It was the chance to illustrate an eclectic group of bizarre characters that drew Kirk to "Agents of Atlas." "The appeal for me was the histories of the characters themselves," Kirk said. "I'm not very familiar with them, but what I did learn from my research was what clinched the deal for me. How the hell do you say no to a project featuring characters named the Human Robot, Marvel Boy, Venus and Gorilla Man? Being a fan of 'Planet of the Apes,' I certainly wasn't going to pass up the chance at drawing a talking gorilla."

For Kirk, the chance to illustrate a talking gorilla and other offbeat and obscure characters was the most fun and rewarding aspect of "Agents of Atlas." "The term 'obscure' might bother some fans but, really, many of the gang you'll see in this series have made only sporadic appearances since their Atlas days. Some of them haven¹t shown up in comics for years," Kirk explained. "I like working with characters like this because I have a little more freedom with how they can be depicted. There aren't the kinds of restrictions in place that you might encounter when working with characters like Spider-Man or the X-Men."

The lack of restrictions has made "Agents of Atlas" an almost difficulty free assignment for Kirk. "I don't know that I'd call this a difficulty but Marvel has insisted that I turn in layouts of the pages before doing the finished pencils," Kirk stated. "I generally prefer to go straight to drawing on the board, but that's OK. The process adds a little time to my work week, but not much. Also, there are advantages to fleshing things out ahead of time. Aside from that, and digging up a bundle of reference, I can't really think of any difficulties I've had with this project so far."

For Kirk, collaborating with Jeff Parker was another difficulty free and fun part of "Agents of Atlas." "Working with Jeff has been great," Kirk said. "He's good to talk with, really open to suggestions and I can honestly say that he has given me fewer wedgies during the typical work week than any other writer (Peter David included). Also, he's so personable over e-mail that you'd never guess he had those huge Borg-like cybernetic implants imbedded in his skull unless you saw him in person. However, if you ever do see Jeff in person, I strongly suggest you stay on your side of the Plexiglas barrier. If you want an autograph, just pass your comic through the sliding panel to the right."

Kirk was greatly impressed by Parker's script and wanted to capture all the major elements, with the characters being the most important element. "Gorilla Man is probably the one character I most wanted to properly flesh out," Kirk said. "However, I really enjoy working with the rest of the cast as well."

Fans of Kirk's other work on titles like "Freshmen" will be happy to hear that he's bringing the cast and action of "Agents of Atlas" to life with his usual artistic style. "I don't think my style is going to be all that different than what you've seen from me before," Kirk explained. "In my opinion, this isn't the kind of project that's really suited to something too radical. However, as far as backgrounds are concerned, especially when we find ourselves inside Marvel Boy's flying saucer, I will definitely be pulling some inspiration from Wally Wood and some of the great sci-fi backgrounds he did in the '50s and '60s."

Kirk already has another project lined up after "Agents of Atlas" which he had to remain mum about. "All I can say is that it stars some of my favorite Marvel characters," Kirk said. "I got started on it before 'Agents of Atlas' was dropped in my lap and one issue has already been finished."

Kirk hopes that when "Agents of Atlas" finishes with issue five that readers will want more because he'd love to depict the team's future exploits. "I hope that everyone enjoys 'Agents of Atlas' and that they go out and buy lots of copies. Lots and lots of copies," he joked. "Seriously, break the frickin' bank, people. Poppa needs a new car."

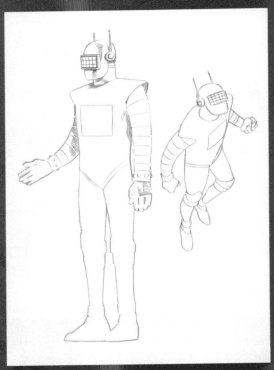

AGENT PROFILE: *THE HUMAN ROBOT*

Last week CBR Readers felt the love as they learned about the Agents of Atlas member, Venus. This week readers will be saying, "Domo Arigato, Mr. Roboto," as CBR News again chats with "AOA" writer Jeff Parker for the latest Agent Profile: The Human Robot.

The Human Robot sprang to life for the first time in 1954 in the pages of "Menace" #11. "He was created by the team that would later make regular comics history, Stan Lee and John Romita!" Parker told CBR News. "It's a very brief horror story that's simply about a killer robot following instructions a bit too literally after it was rushed into

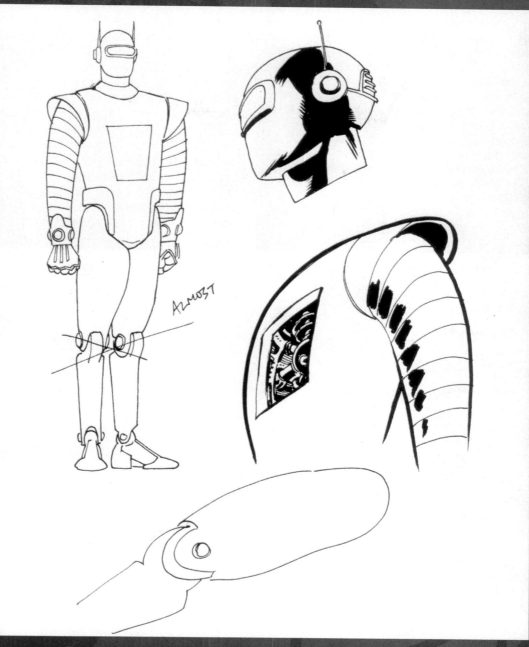

ALMOST

development. According to the letter column in 'What If' #9, when Roy Thomas was concocting the idea of a 1950s super team, it was writer Don Glut who remembered the 'Menace' story and suggested that the robot ended up sinking into the harbor. The choice of that robot in the 'Secret Avengers' story is the most interesting one they made, I think. I like the fact that Namora is the one who found it and put Jimmy Woo onto the robot, and that Marvel Boy restored it.

"Since the original story left out a lot of detail — it doesn't give you the name of the scientist who builds the robot, the company he works for, or why he's built what is apparently a killing machine — it gives us a nice blank slate to fill in," Parker continued. "You rarely get an opportunity like this! So we're going to find out a bit more about the organization responsible for building this machine in the first place. I'll give you a hint — it starts with an A!"

The organization responsible for the Robot's creation didn't build your garden variety automaton, as the character's name suggests, they built a Human Robot. "We're going to address exactly why he's called that, beyond being a bipedal construct," Parker explained. "Still, it's a bit ungainly when the group talks for everyone to say, 'Hey, The Human Robot, come here,' and simply referring to him as robot seemed too demeaning. So we've given him a designation as his builder would no doubt have done. His proper name is M-11, the reference of which will now be obvious to CBR readers, at least."

M-11 is equipped with a variety of awesome and mysterious capabilities which make him an asset to the Agents of Atlas. "He's clearly very strong," Parker stated. "In the preview you saw him throw a tank through the door of the fortress they stormed. It's also revealing about his nature that he has a Death Ray that fires from his eye at various levels of intensity. We know it's a Death Ray because if you look on the inside of his chest plate there's a diagram that says 'Death Ray!' When Marvel Boy repaired M-11 originally, he changed the structure of the robot's metal to an alloy that will be near impossible to affect with earthly weapons. As the story goes on, we find some more modifications that weren't made by Marvel Boy, which begs the question: who made them? M-11 now seems to be able to infiltrate any computer system he wants. In fact, he's constantly accessing datastreams from the internet as well as many other normally secured systems around the world. What's he doing with all this information? Suddenly what everyone thought of as a relatively primitive killing machine seems to be a lot more sophisticated and versatile. Appropriately for the most cryptic member of the team though, his secrets are going to be revealed last."

In addition to being a walking arsenal shrouded in secrecy, Parker feels that the Human Robot will strike a chord with readers because of his retro style appearance. "Visually, the robot is cool because he embodies the robot menace of the pulp adventures," Parker said. "With that cyclopean eye, no mouth, the antennae — he's got a classic look that conjures up everything from Gort in 'The Day the Earth Stood Still' to the giant robots in 'Sky Captain.' His body is a bit more detailed than in the 'Menace' story — we kind of approach that as 'what would the artist have likely done had he more time than a weekend to design this guy' and so he gets a little more definition and a nice solid eyepiece instead of one that looks like a lightboard. I was originally suggesting that we leave off his chest door or move it to the back, but Leonard Kirk was adamant that he needed it up front to really convey 'classic robot.' He's right of course."

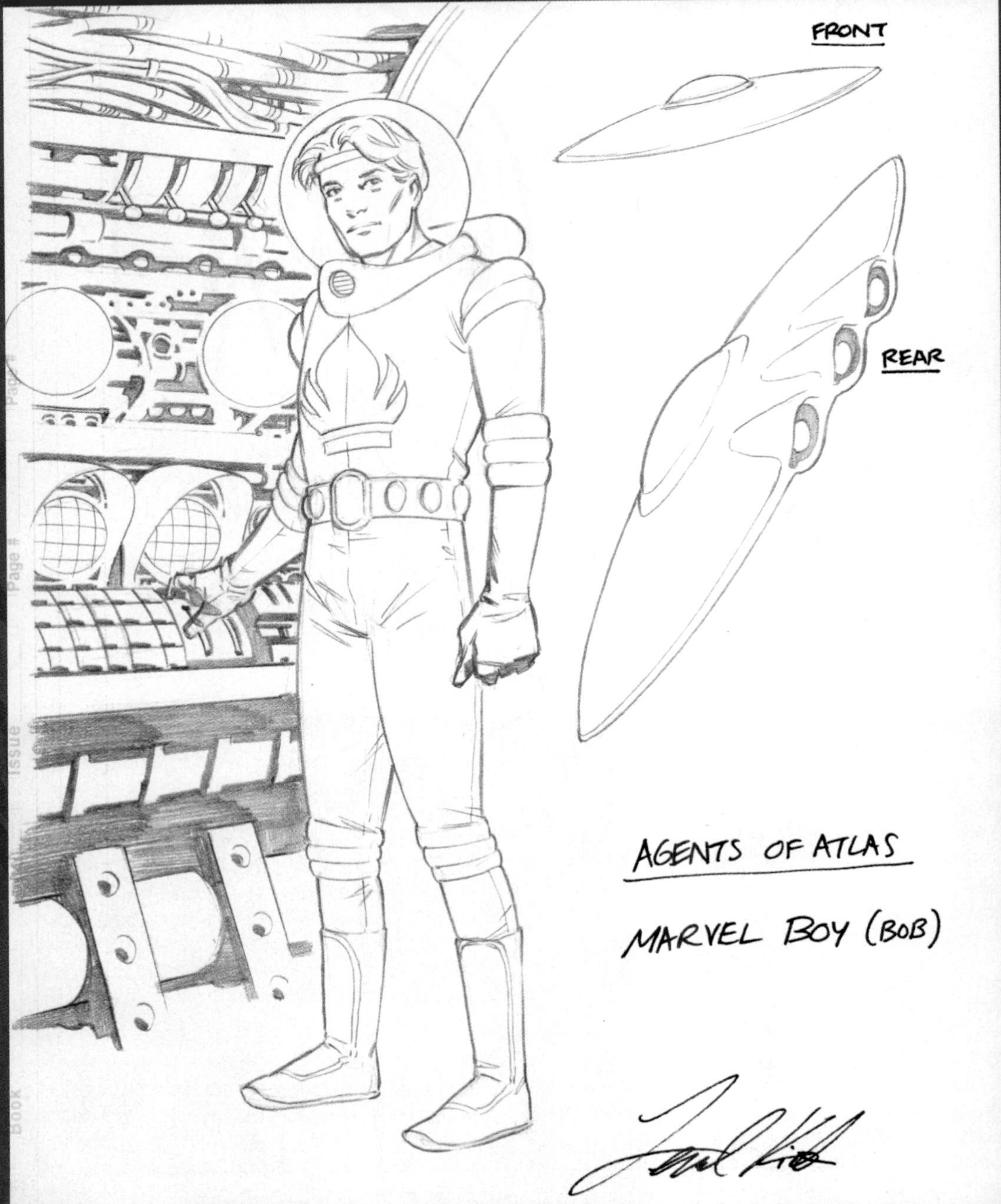
FRONT
REAR
AGENTS OF ATLAS
MARVEL BOY (BOB)

That classic robot has been MIA for decades when "Agents of Atlas" begins. "No one has seen M-11 since the late 50's," Parker explained. "He was hanging out with Marvel Boy, but we're going to find out that Bob Grayson had to leave Earth in a hurry and didn't take the robot with him. So, where's he been all this time? He's a really tough nut to crack, because he doesn't say much. But he seems to respond to Jimmy Woo. He turns out to be very important in bringing the team back together, but it's going to very puzzling for a while. What's his agenda? Does he even have agendas? Should we even refer to him as 'he?'"

WEEK 4: AGENT PROFILE: MARVEL BOY & A CRYPTIC INVITATION

Posted: June 3, 2006

Last week CBR News was doing the robot as "Agents of Atlas" writer Jeff Parker acquainted us with M-11 AKA the Human Robot. This week Parker plays Ground Control to our Major Tom as he checks back in with the latest Agent Profile for Marvel Boy. Also CBR News feature on "AoA" has caught the eye of a mysterious stranger and we share with our readers the cryptic invitation that he sent us.

Marvel Boy made his debut in the 1950s in issues #3-6 of the Timely-Atlas title "Astonishing" and went on to star in his own self-titled series. It was the character's last known appearance that has many fans puzzled at Marvel Boy's inclusion in the modern day line up of the "Agents of Atlas." "He's probably the character that the most talk has been about since this project was announced," Parker told CBR News. "Didn't he die in 'Fantastic Four' #165? Doesn't the hero Quasar have his bands now- the Quantum Bands? How many Marvel Boys are there? Wasn't one a New Warrior? Wasn't one a Kree Warrior?

"Let's go back to the beginning," Parker continued. "Our Marvel Boy is Bob Grayson, who was born in Germany as the Nazi party was coming into power. His father Matthew was a scientist who built a rocketship so he and his son could flee the Earth for another more peaceful planet without dictators. And that planet turned out to be the 7th one in our solar system, Uranus. Not habitable you say? In fact there was a paradise full of other humans that existed in the life-supporting Omnidome, and they took the Graysons in."

The Graysons' benefactors turned out to be an offshoot of the immortal, earth born, aliens, The Eternals. "They were very advanced, and as Bob grew up they bestowed many of their technological gifts upon him," Parker explained. "As a teenager, he returned to Earth with strength enhanced by pills they gave him, and he could fly and manipulate light in powerful ways thanks to these armbands he wore. He also had a headband that allowed him extra mental abilities such as telepathy."

Bob Grayson returned to Earth and attempted to be a hero, but ultimately his return to his birth planet proved to be his downfall. "The last time we saw Bob he was giving the Fantastic Four a hard time, frothing at the mouth and calling himself The Crusader," Parker stated. "Apparently, the Uranian colonists were in need of medical supplies, so Grayson tried to borrow money from a bank to raise what he needed to help the colonists. It was for nothing, because a vaguely described cataclysm destroyed them. Here's a good webpage that fills in some of that info. Anyway, the wristbands themselves destroyed the Crusader, and that's the last we've seen of him."

The reason behind Bob's strange reappearance among the living in "Agents of Atlas" can be found by probing the mysteries of his past. "Rather than also vaporize continuity that doesn't work for our purposes, 'Agents of Atlas' takes into account all of these major points in Marvel Boy's history and treats it as a mystery story," Parker explained. "So many things don't add up. Why could Marvel Boy never make the bands work to the extent that Quasar could? Since when do ultra-advanced civilizations need our medical help? Weren't those colonists exiles, after all? Heck, how did Dr. Grayson manage to build a spaceship and find them in the first place? To get to the bottom of the mystery, we address practically everything!"

Whatever it was that caused Bob's return, he did not emerge from the process unscathed. "When we meet Bob in the present day, he's a little different," Parker stated. "It takes him a while to get the hang of English again. He's not flying around, he's no stronger than anyone else, and he sure doesn't have those wristbands. He has to wear a suit that keeps him in an environment he can live in — breathing a mixture of hydrogen, methane and helium — and a temperature a couple hundred degrees below what we can stand. That looks like a glass bubble helmet, but it's actually a field generated by the suit to hold in the cold and gases. He can reach through it to say, eat dinner. But trust us... you do not want to see Bob eat.

"Nonetheless, Jimmy Woo and the gang are very glad to have their interplanetary pal back even if he has changed," Parker continued. "And there do seem to be some pros to his new condition. His mental ability is much broader than what it was- he has lots of abilities you would associate with 'Grey' aliens. And he hasn't aged nearly as much as we would have expected him to by now. Is he still human? That will be determined by the end of the series."

It will also be determined by the end of the series whether or not Marvel Boy is still a fitting heroic moniker for the seemingly resurrected Bob Grayson. "Just as the team always refers to Gorilla Man as Ken, everyone calls him Bob," Parker said. "The title Marvel Boy seems a little young for him now (and of course, there are others as we mentioned), but we'll leave it to readers to ultimately decide how to refer to him. I like the term one of our yet-to-be-introduced characters uses to refer to him: The Uranian."

Speaking of mysterious characters, this reporter received an interesting bit of mail yesterday. Which is strange, because Comic Book Resources only lists my email address. I suppose since this person is that resourceful, I should share the message!

Mr. Richards.

It has not escaped my notice that you are documenting information relating to The Atlas Foundation. The thoroughness of this feature persuades me to extend an invitation to you and your readers. Stay alert next week. There will be an announcement made by one very loyal to my Order. Exceptional minds shall be led to an offering of what you might call a "decoder ring." I believe you are schooled enough in our methods that you will recognize the announcement when you see it.

Your Humble Servant

That was it. There was no name. The invitation arrived in an odd crimson envelope with a wax seal on the back. Now, I wish I hadn't opened it that way because the seal appeared to be some kind of symbol, but you can't make it out now.

WEEK 5: AGENT PROFILE: *JIMMY WOO*

Posted: June 12, 2006

For weeks now readers have been following CBR News's coverage of Marvel Comics "Agents of Atlas" mini-series and wondering who the mysterious fifth member of the team was. This week Jeff Parker declassifies the identity of the fifth team member, with the agent profile of former FBI and current SHIELD agent Jimmy Woo. Some readers might be thinking that that's not such a big revelation and they would be right. CBR News is proud to announce that its "Agents of Atlas" coverage will be expanded to one more part - this Friday we'll reveal for the first time anywhere the identity of the mysterious sixth team member of the Agents of Atlas.

Parker briefly discussed Jimmy with CBR News in his in-depth interview weeks ago, but since Jimmy is a core, active member of the Agents, he felt that Woo merited an expanded Agent Profile.

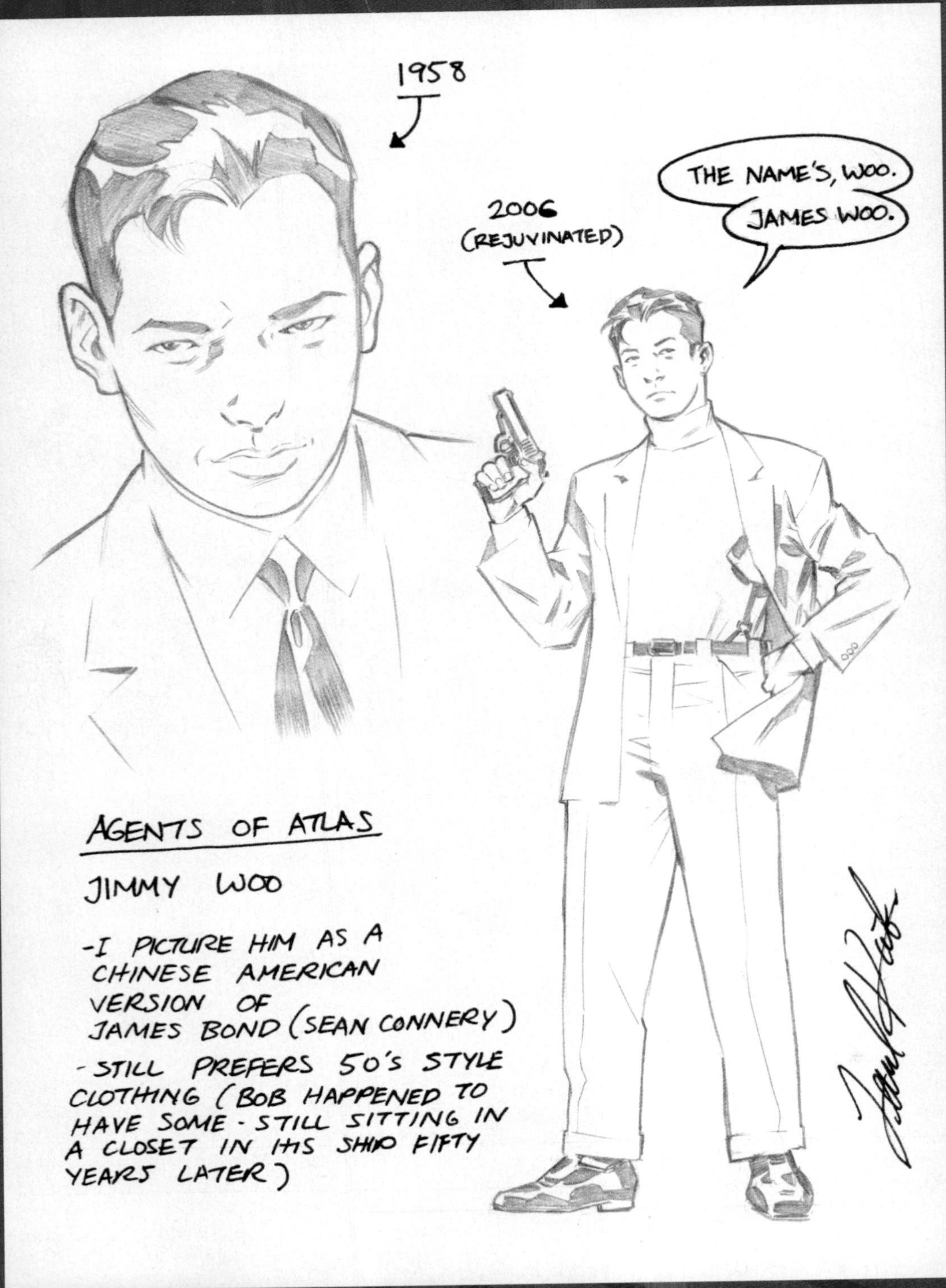
1958
THE NAME'S, WOO. JAMES WOO.
2006 (REJUVINATED)
AGENTS OF ATLAS
JIMMY WOO
-I PICTURE HIM AS A CHINESE AMERICAN VERSION OF JAMES BOND (SEAN CONNERY)
-STILL PREFERS 50'S STYLE CLOTHING (BOB HAPPENED TO HAVE SOME - STILL SITTING IN A CLOSET IN HIS SHIP FIFTY YEARS LATER)

- TRIED HIM WITH PUPILS
- HATED IT!

VERY DARK, SLICK & SHINY

ALMOST SMOOTH NOT SO "SCALY"

MR. LAO SKETCH #1

"He's worked a lot in interrogation, and that's obviously not a pretty job. While he likely knew about the more questionable activities his own people were involved with, he wouldn't have much room to judge. He was hip deep in questionable activities of his own."

As "Agents of Atlas" begins, the chickens of Jimmy's questionable activities are coming home to roost. "At this point we're seeing a Woo near retirement, higher up in SHIELD hierarchy," Parker explained. "As we discussed before, at the beginning of' 'Agents' we find out Jimmy was running an investigation no one in SHIELD Directorate knew about, and an unauthorized mission he was in no condition for went horribly wrong. Had he been working on this secret for all those years, and what is this secret so big he didn't trust his own agency? But one of the themes of this whole storyline is the Second Chance. Life passes people by and windows of opportunity close. Maybe, just maybe, if you stick to your guns and never give up on your goal, even in the final inning a window will open again. And though you've been tainted by a grey world, that doesn't outweigh your time as a young optimistic idealist who could inspire some of the strangest people on Earth to charge into the demon pit with you. Somewhere in Jimmy Woo is that young, natural-born leader who some old buddies think is worth betraying allegiances and traveling 1.6 billion miles!"

Jimmy Woo will definitely need the help of his friends to survive his ordeal in the demon pit, but readers shouldn't think he's totally defenseless or dependant on them. "I'm sure some readers are wondering how Jimmy is supposed to hang with teammates who can control minds, fire death rays and the like. I don't think there'll be much doubt once he's back in action, and especially when his very grand destiny is revealed.

"And that's the team," Parker said. "Oh wait; we're forgetting someone, aren't we?"

Be sure to check back here on Friday when Parker remembers who we forgot and brings us the final agent profile, where we reveal his identity exclusively here on CBR!

Unlike the rest of his compatriots, many Marvel readers might be aware of Jimmy as a character, but not really know it. "Jimmy Woo is like one of those lovable character actors whose name you can't ever get," Parker told CBR News. "He's been backing up bigger names in the Marvel Universe for years, and he's one of the characters they allowed to age. Though that wasn't always played up — just a few years ago he appeared looking pretty young, but if you read his recent SHIELD profile, he's pretty advanced in years. No one gave him a formula to drink or dropped him in suspended animation, he just kept working. You've got to choose what's canon. For example, I'm fine with saying he was flying around with Dum Dum Dugan in the Helicarrier chasing Godzilla, but I'm thinking Marvel proper isn't!"

Like his other team mates, Jimmy was introduced to readers before there was a proper Marvel Universe. "Jimmy came from the 'Yellow Claw' comic book of the '50s, tirelessly on the case of the criminal mastermind," Parker stated. "I don't know if there was simply a mandate to put out a Fu Manchu-clone book, but what I find interesting is that they at least let the hero be of Chinese roots, in a time that being balanced towards minorities just wasn't a priority. That has to be due to Al Feldstein beginning the writing of the book. He was a forward thinker and dealt with a broad range of social issues in his work, especially at EC Comics. The first art by Joe Maneely is lush and evocative, using Asian imagery as a design element throughout. It's too bad they didn't keep doing it, because the book really had its own feel. Not that anyone can complain about who took over next — Jack Kirby! — but his stories were much more influenced by Doc Savage novels, a different thing altogether. Jim Steranko brought Jimmy into SHIELD a few years later because, hey, the Yellow Claw turned up. That turned out to be a robot, but it gave Jimmy another chance to shine, so it's worth it."

Since he was brought into SHIELD, Jimmy has had many scandalous experiences. "Jimmy Woo has been in SHIELD for years, and close to some ugly secrets," Parker said.

MR. LAO SKETCH #2.

YOU REALLY SHOULD CUT DOWN ON THE JALEPENOS

MR. AVERAGE © 2006 FOR SCALE

NAMORA

"DEATH GOWN" COLOR SCHEME

WEEK 6: AGENT PROFILE: *NAMORA*

Posted: June 16, 2006

For weeks now writer Jeff Parker has been reintroducing CBR readers to a group of golden age Marvel Comics characters who will be reassembling in the present day to continue the fight against injustice in the pages of "Agents of Atlas," a six issue mini-series debuting in August. Readers have also been eagerly awaiting the revelation of the identity of the final mysterious member of the "Agents." Well the wait is over! But before we begin, this reporter must apologize for the accidental use of the pronoun "he" in last week's feature, which proved misleading to some readers trying to guess the identity of the final member. So, without further ado . . . Everybody out of the pool! Jeff Parker checks in again one last time with the final Agent Profile: Namora.

Readers not familiar with Namora might assume she has a connection with the Avenging Son of Atlantis, Prince Namor, and they would be right. "Namora is credited to Ken Bald, who we mentioned in talking about Venus, and I'm not sure if the writer was ever named," Parker told CBR News. "And of course, she was presented quite a bit by Bill Everett [creator of Namor]. She's Prince Namor's cousin, which makes her royalty as well. Namora was a name she gave herself to note her dedication to stomping evil — her original name is Aquaria Nautica Neptuna — quite possibly the most sea-related name a character could have!"

In the original "What If the Avengers Fought Evil in the 1950s" story that inspired "Agents of Atlas," Namora makes a brief appearance and assists the group in the salvaging of an important find from the sea. "In the 'What If' story, Namora helps out the Secret Avengers by bringing them an interesting find — the Human Robot," Parker explained. "We mention in some of the preview pages that Jimmy asked her to join the team, but she declined. Though her excuse is the need to deal with her undersea affairs, it's worth noting the year always given for the birth of her daughter — 1958!

"When I reread the 'What If' story, I think I had the same reaction as a lot of readers. They bring Namora into the story for a minute and I immediately thought, 'Hey, why isn't she on the team? Then you'd have a lot of extra power, and a heroine with actual history!' The obvious reason is they were more concerned with making this team a counterpart of the current Avengers," Parker continued. "But if you have Namora on board, besides the fact that she was an actual character from the time, then you have a team of archetypes, pulp icons. I quickly went digging for her last appearance to see what became of her and lo and behold I found the issue of 'Sub-Mariner.' There she is, frozen in a block of ice. I don't know about you, but when I see a Golden Age Marvel hero in a block of ice . . ."

In her last appearance Namora was confined to a frozen prison, but much of the world believes her dead. "As Bill Everett later wrote, Namora was poisoned by her rival Llyra. Then all the info we have is from Namorita, who believes her mother is dead," Parker said. "So a 14 year old is convinced, but for some reason Submariner's enemy Byrrah kept her on ice. The popular complaint with this is that poison wouldn't take out Namor, so it's unlikely it would her either. I mean, she can survive a direct hit from a torpedo!

"It seemed clear to me that Everett wasn't just keeping her body around for decoration," Parker continued. "Then I found out, thanks to the posters over at the Invaders Message Board at Comicboards.com, that Roy Thomas even wrote that Bill Everett planned to bring her back — but of course Everett's health was deteriorating then. He died soon after, and Marvel had a rare full page tribute to him, which coincidentally Tom Spurgeon ran on the Comics Reporter site recently."

Unfortunately for Namora her resurfacing coincides with a tragic event for her. "I have to say this, since people will immediately wonder. When I told my editor (and subsequently other editors and executives) my intent to bring Namora back, I had no idea what was going to happen in 'Civil War.' By which I refer to her daughter Namorita being killed along with most of the New Warriors. I think some readers are going to assume it was planned, but when I found out that was happening, it was pretty bizarre — it felt like some cosmic trade-off was happening. It's a little strange because, as you'll see, our story is very much about grand manipulations, where destinies are being decided in secret, and though I'm still fairly sure bringing Namora back was my idea, it doesn't feel like it!"

Parker concluded the agent profile with a dedication. He said, "Bill, this one's for you."

That wraps up CBR News' spotlight on "Agents of Atlas." We would like to thank Jeff Parker, Leonard Kirk, Mark Paniccia, and Jim McCann for all their contributions to our multi part feature.

AGENTS OF ATLAS

NAMORA

← SEEING AS
SHE'S BEEN
RESSURECTED,
I THINK SHE
CAN GET AWAY
WITH THE
PUPIL-LESS LOOK. ☺

- THE CHANGE IN
COSTUME CAN
BE EXPLAINED
AWAY AS THIS
BEING MORE
REGAL ATTIRE
SHE WAS
ENTOMBED WITH.

HOWEVER, THERE
ARE STILL SOME
BASIC ELEMENTS
FROM HER
ORIGINAL OUTFIT
THAT I KEPT

← "WINGS" REPLACED
WITH FLIPPERS (LIKE
THE TRANSPARENT ONES
FOUND ON "FLYING FISH")

NAMORA- NEW COSTUME SKETCHES

NAMORA- NEW COSTUME SKETCHES

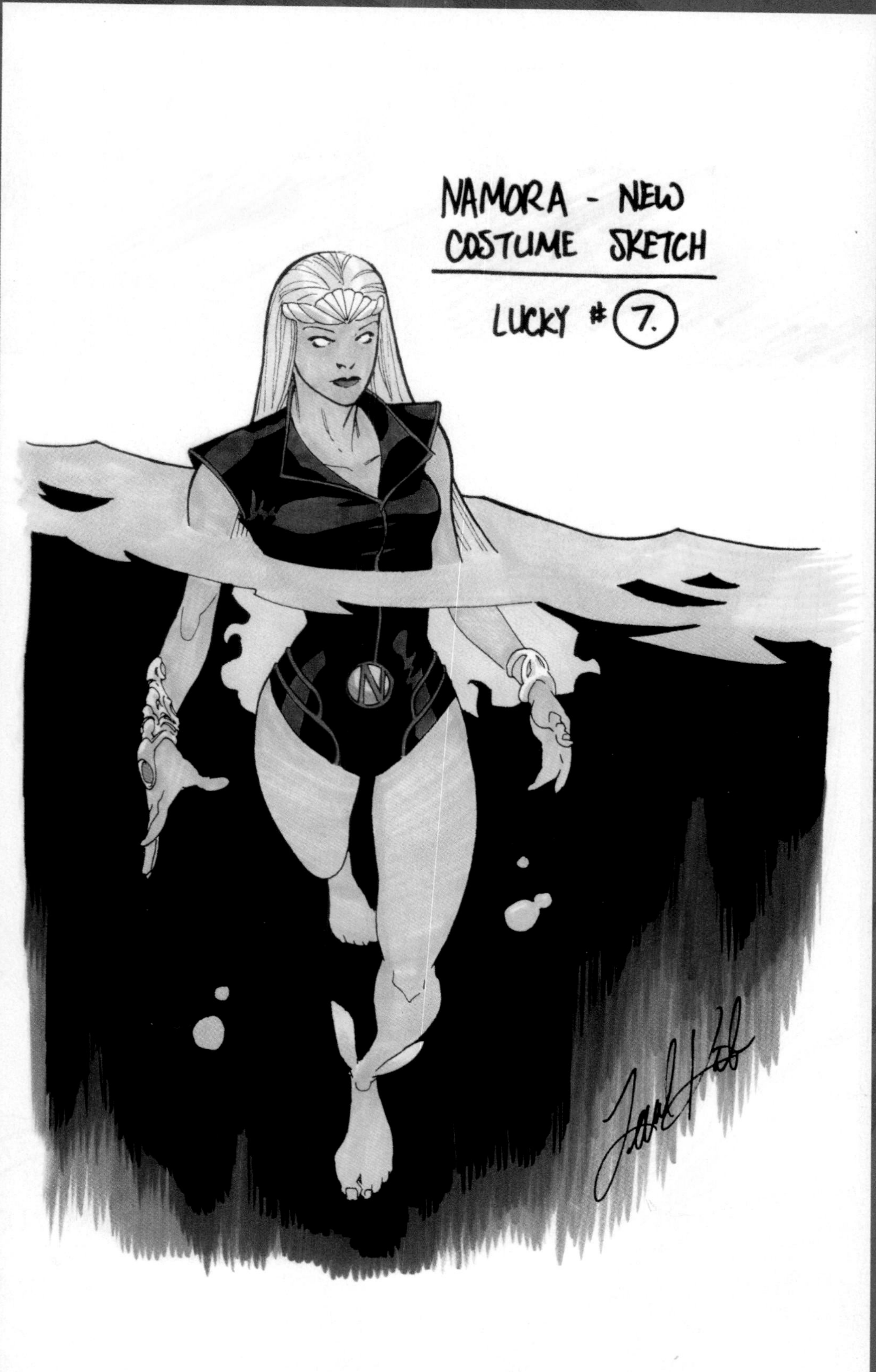
NAMORA - NEW
COSTUME SKETCH
LUCKY # 7.

MARVEL MYSTERY COMICS #82 (MAY 1947) THE FIRST APPEARANCE OF NAMORA

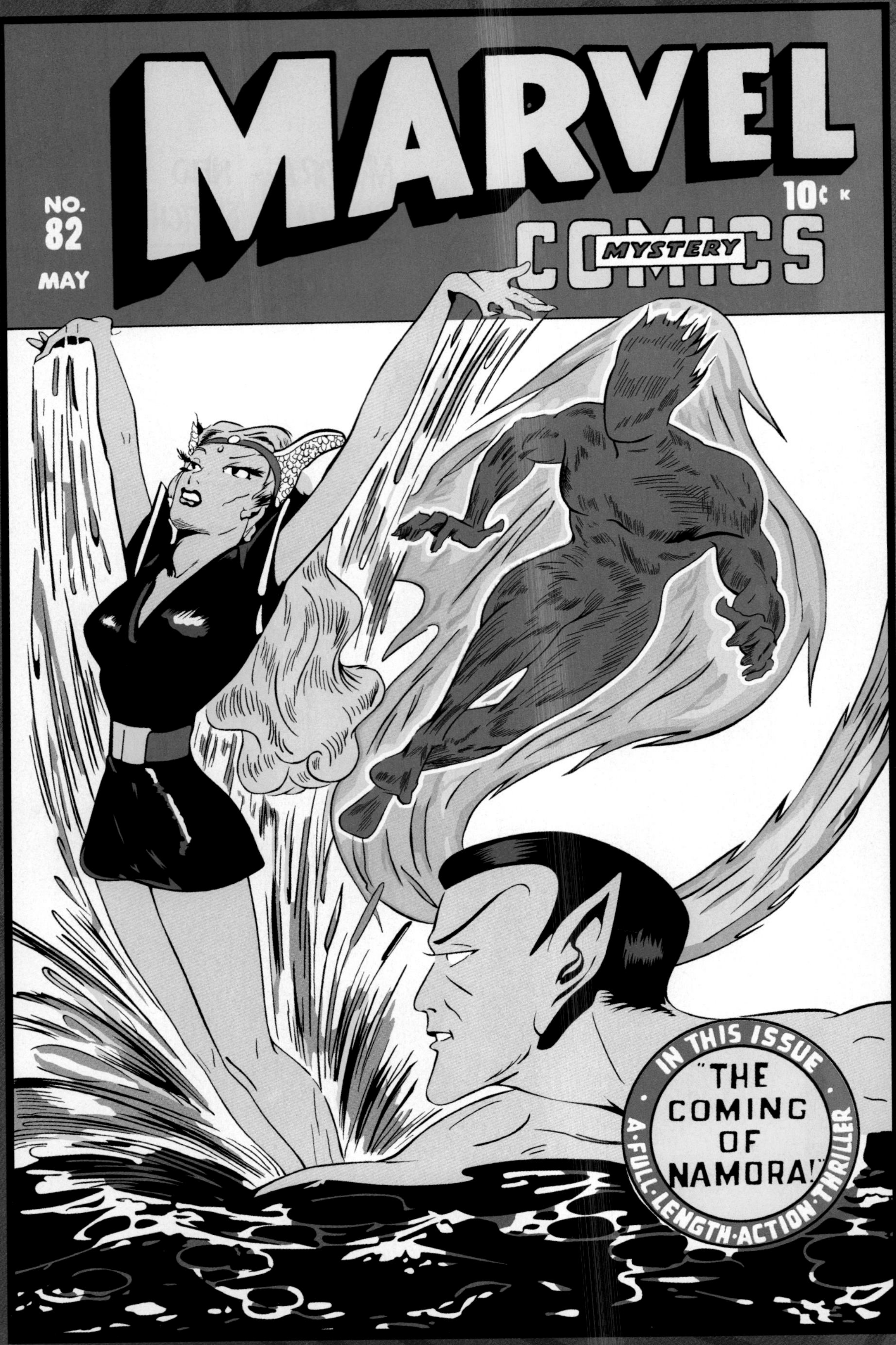
MARVEL
NO. 82
MAY
10¢
MYSTERY
COMICS
IN THIS ISSUE
"THE COMING OF NAMORA!"
A·FULL·LENGTH·ACTION·THRILLER

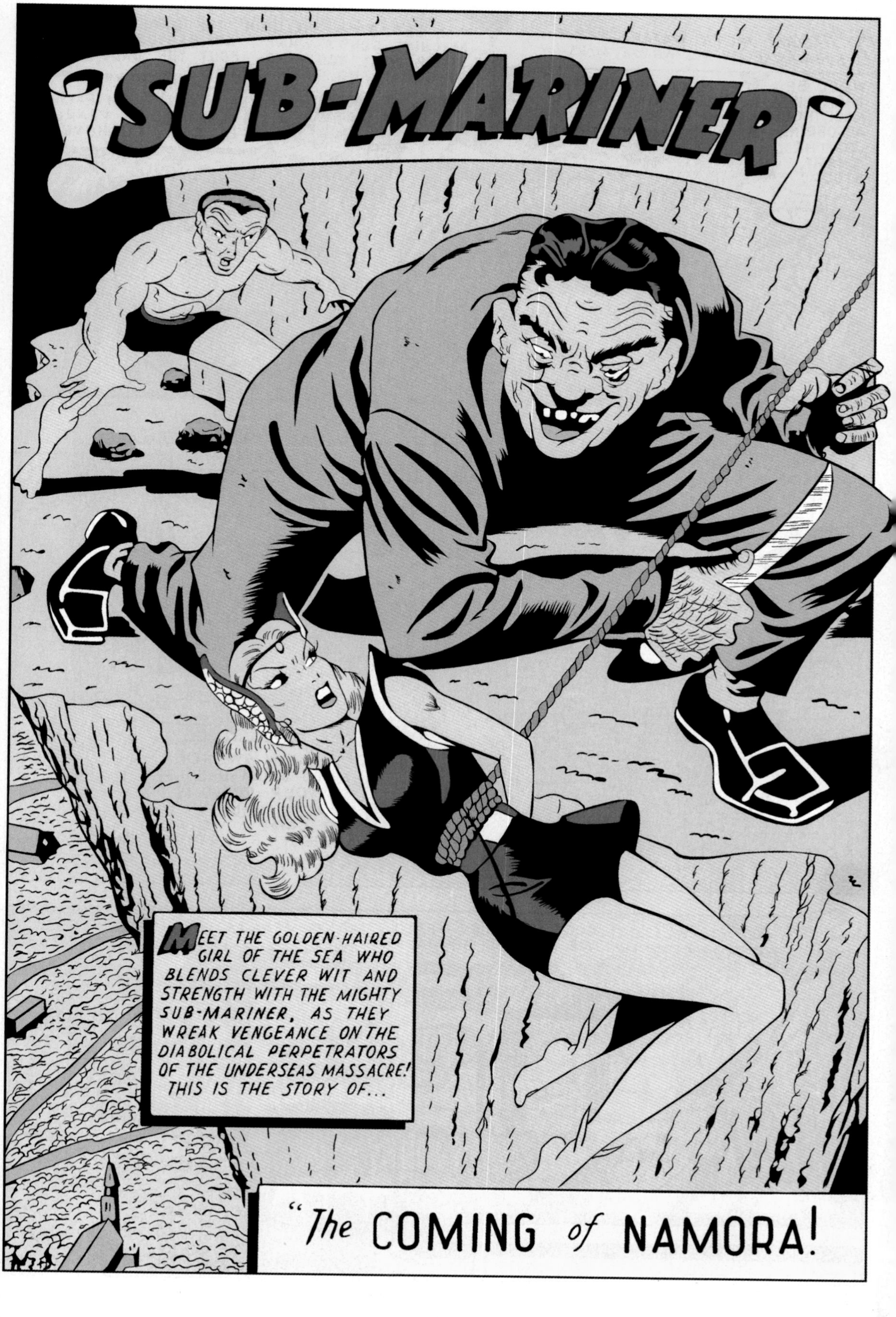
SUB-MARINER
MEET THE GOLDEN-HAIRED GIRL OF THE SEA WHO BLENDS CLEVER WIT AND STRENGTH WITH THE MIGHTY SUB-MARINER, AS THEY WREAK VENGEANCE ON THE DIABOLICAL PERPETRATORS OF THE UNDERSEAS MASSACRE! THIS IS THE STORY OF...
"The COMING of NAMORA!

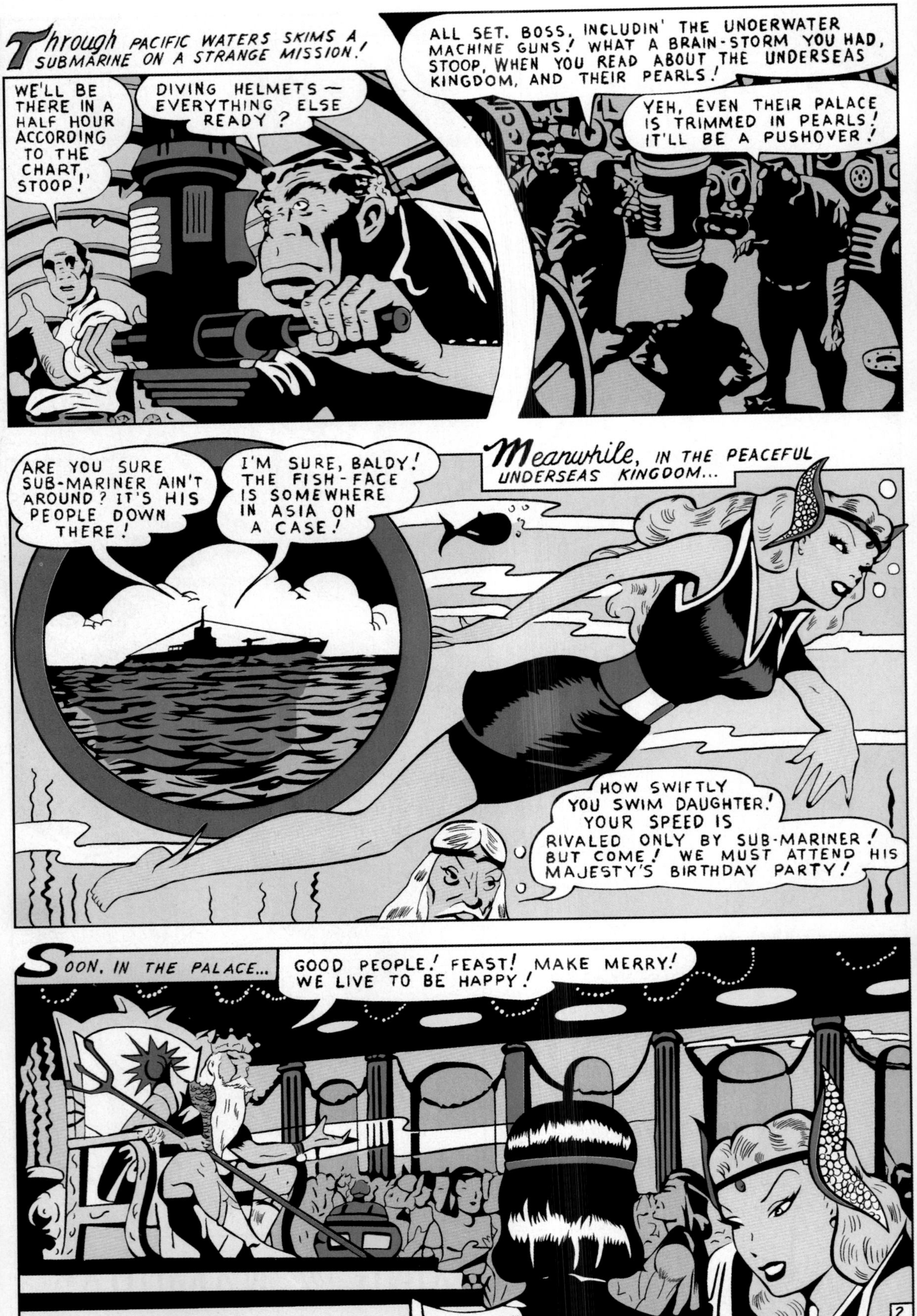

THROUGH PACIFIC WATERS SKIMS A SUBMARINE ON A STRANGE MISSION!
WE'LL BE THERE IN A HALF HOUR ACCORDING TO THE CHART, STOOP!
DIVING HELMETS — EVERYTHING ELSE READY?
ALL SET. BOSS, INCLUDIN' THE UNDERWATER MACHINE GUNS! WHAT A BRAIN-STORM YOU HAD, STOOP, WHEN YOU READ ABOUT THE UNDERSEAS KINGDOM, AND THEIR PEARLS!
YEH, EVEN THEIR PALACE IS TRIMMED IN PEARLS! IT'LL BE A PUSHOVER!
ARE YOU SURE SUB-MARINER AIN'T AROUND? IT'S HIS PEOPLE DOWN THERE!
I'M SURE, BALDY! THE FISH-FACE IS SOMEWHERE IN ASIA ON A CASE!
MEANWHILE, IN THE PEACEFUL UNDERSEAS KINGDOM...
HOW SWIFTLY YOU SWIM DAUGHTER! YOUR SPEED IS RIVALED ONLY BY SUB-MARINER! BUT COME! WE MUST ATTEND HIS MAJESTY'S BIRTHDAY PARTY!
SOON, IN THE PALACE...
GOOD PEOPLE! FEAST! MAKE MERRY! WE LIVE TO BE HAPPY!
2

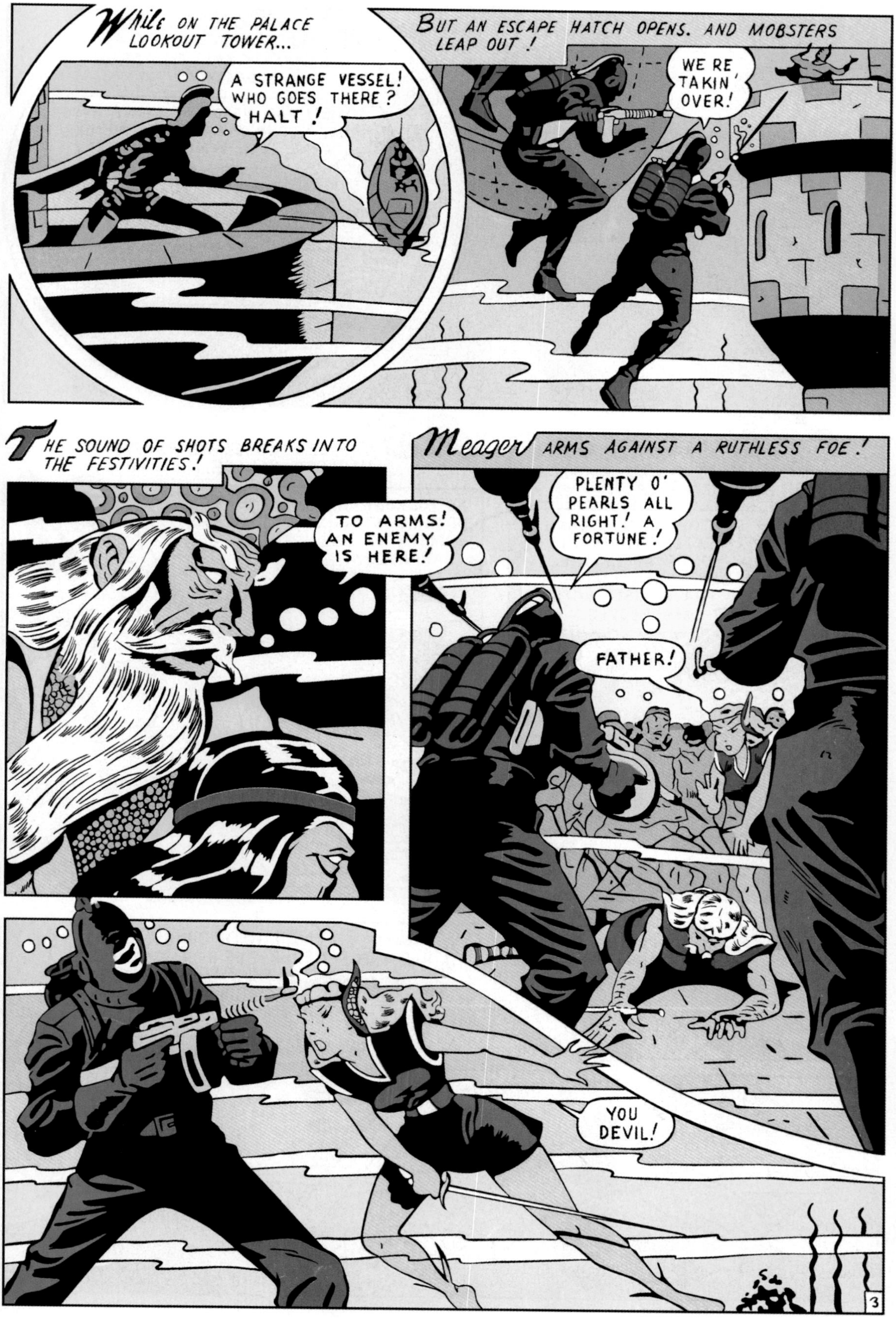

WHILE ON THE PALACE LOOKOUT TOWER...
A STRANGE VESSEL! WHO GOES THERE? HALT!
BUT AN ESCAPE HATCH OPENS. AND MOBSTERS LEAP OUT!
WE'RE TAKIN' OVER!
THE SOUND OF SHOTS BREAKS INTO THE FESTIVITIES!
TO ARMS! AN ENEMY IS HERE!
MEAGER ARMS AGAINST A RUTHLESS FOE!
PLENTY O' PEARLS ALL RIGHT! A FORTUNE!
FATHER!
YOU DEVIL!
3

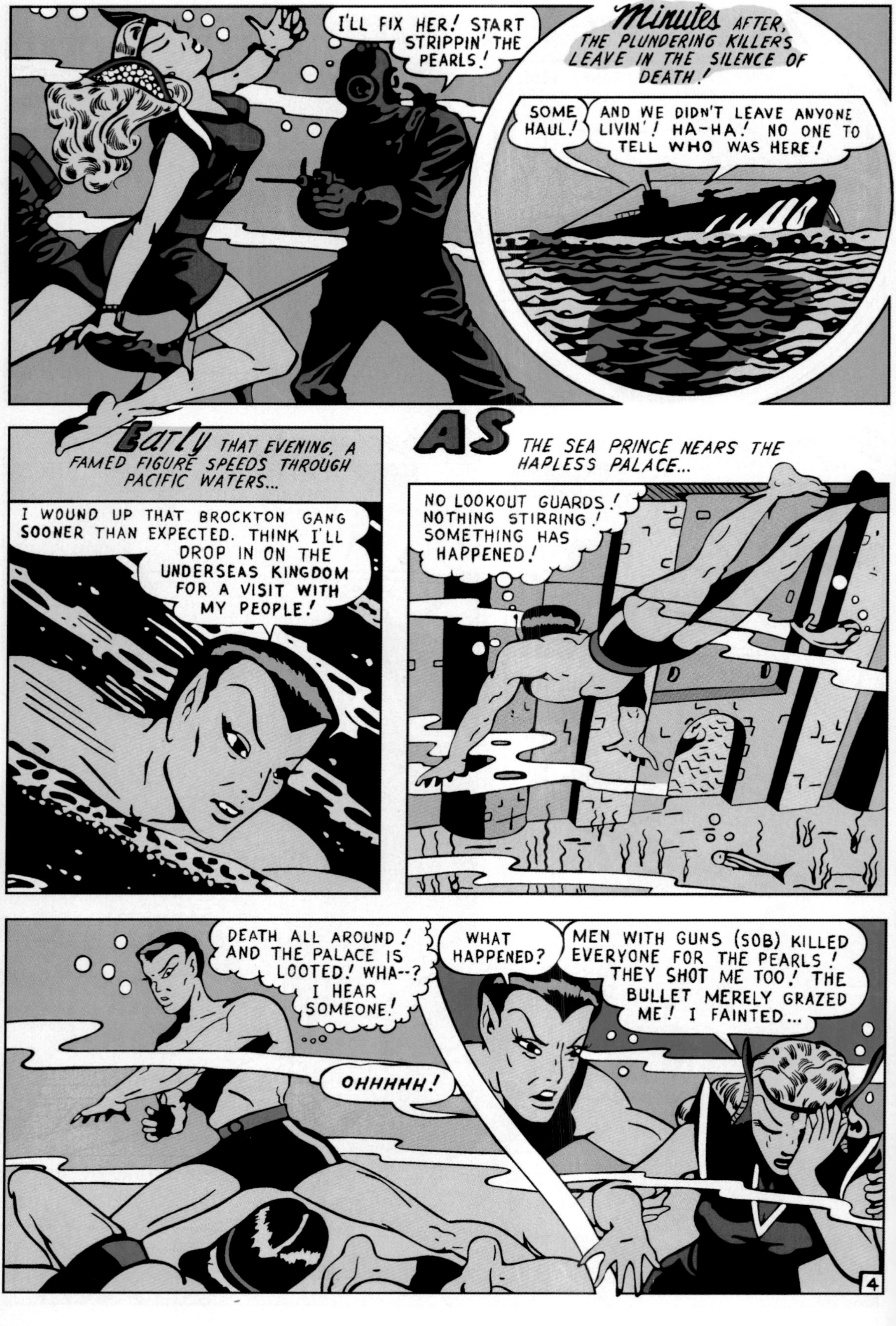
I'LL FIX HER! START STRIPPIN' THE PEARLS!
MINUTES AFTER, THE PLUNDERING KILLERS LEAVE IN THE SILENCE OF DEATH!
SOME HAUL!
AND WE DIDN'T LEAVE ANYONE LIVIN'! HA-HA! NO ONE TO TELL WHO WAS HERE!
EARLY THAT EVENING, A FAMED FIGURE SPEEDS THROUGH PACIFIC WATERS...
I WOUND UP THAT BROCKTON GANG SOONER THAN EXPECTED. THINK I'LL DROP IN ON THE UNDERSEAS KINGDOM FOR A VISIT WITH MY PEOPLE!
AS THE SEA PRINCE NEARS THE HAPLESS PALACE...
NO LOOKOUT GUARDS! NOTHING STIRRING! SOMETHING HAS HAPPENED!
DEATH ALL AROUND! AND THE PALACE IS LOOTED! WHA--? I HEAR SOMEONE!
OHHHHH!
WHAT HAPPENED?
MEN WITH GUNS (SOB) KILLED EVERYONE FOR THE PEARLS! THEY SHOT ME TOO! THE BULLET MERELY GRAZED ME! I FAINTED...
4

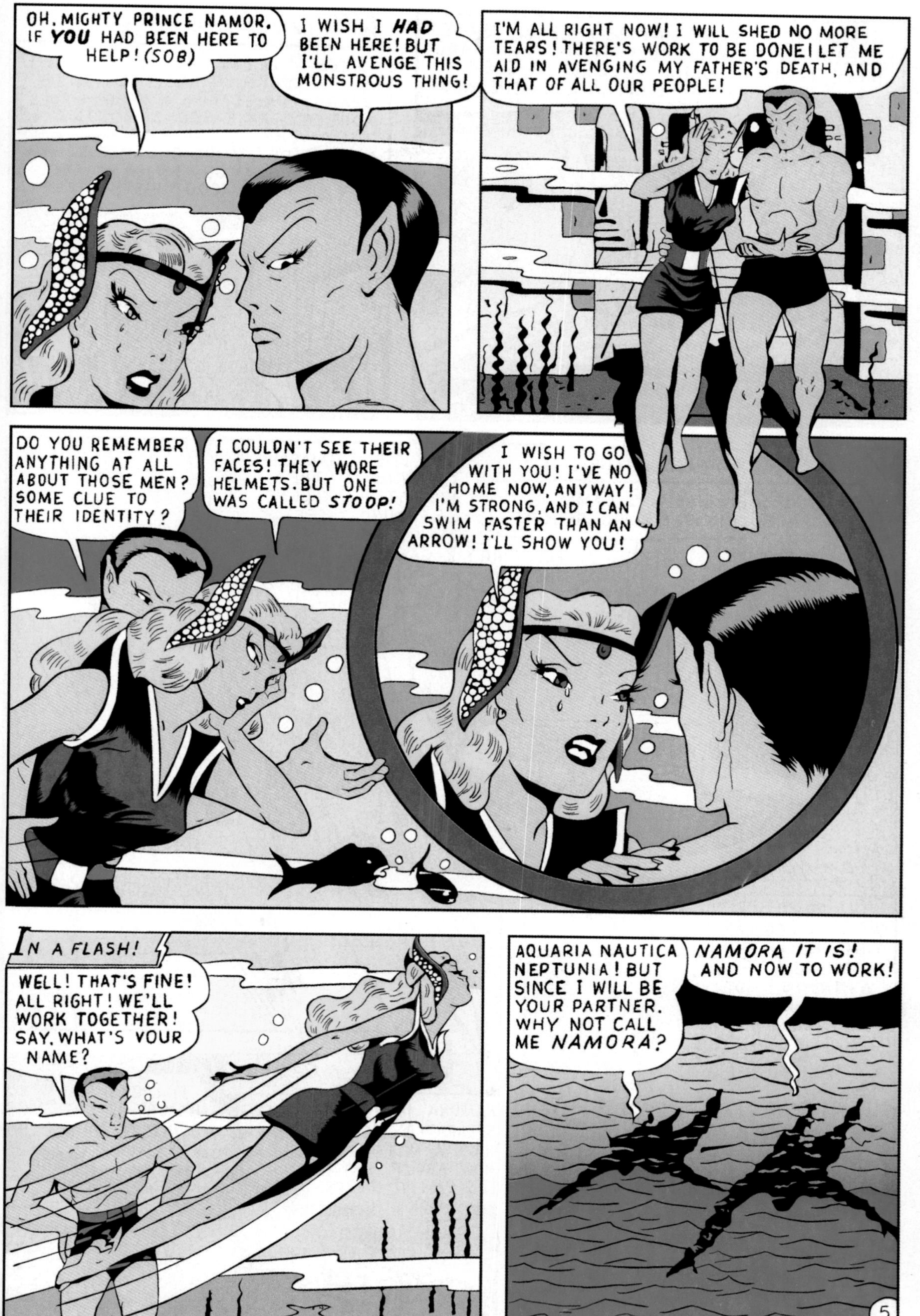

OH, MIGHTY PRINCE NAMOR, IF YOU HAD BEEN HERE TO HELP! (SOB)
I WISH I HAD BEEN HERE! BUT I'LL AVENGE THIS MONSTROUS THING!
I'M ALL RIGHT NOW! I WILL SHED NO MORE TEARS! THERE'S WORK TO BE DONE! LET ME AID IN AVENGING MY FATHER'S DEATH, AND THAT OF ALL OUR PEOPLE!
DO YOU REMEMBER ANYTHING AT ALL ABOUT THOSE MEN? SOME CLUE TO THEIR IDENTITY?
I COULDN'T SEE THEIR FACES! THEY WORE HELMETS. BUT ONE WAS CALLED STOOP!
I WISH TO GO WITH YOU! I'VE NO HOME NOW, ANYWAY! I'M STRONG, AND I CAN SWIM FASTER THAN AN ARROW! I'LL SHOW YOU!
IN A FLASH!
WELL! THAT'S FINE! ALL RIGHT! WE'LL WORK TOGETHER! SAY, WHAT'S YOUR NAME?
AQUARIA NAUTICA NEPTUNIA! BUT SINCE I WILL BE YOUR PARTNER, WHY NOT CALL ME NAMORA?
NAMORA IT IS! AND NOW TO WORK!

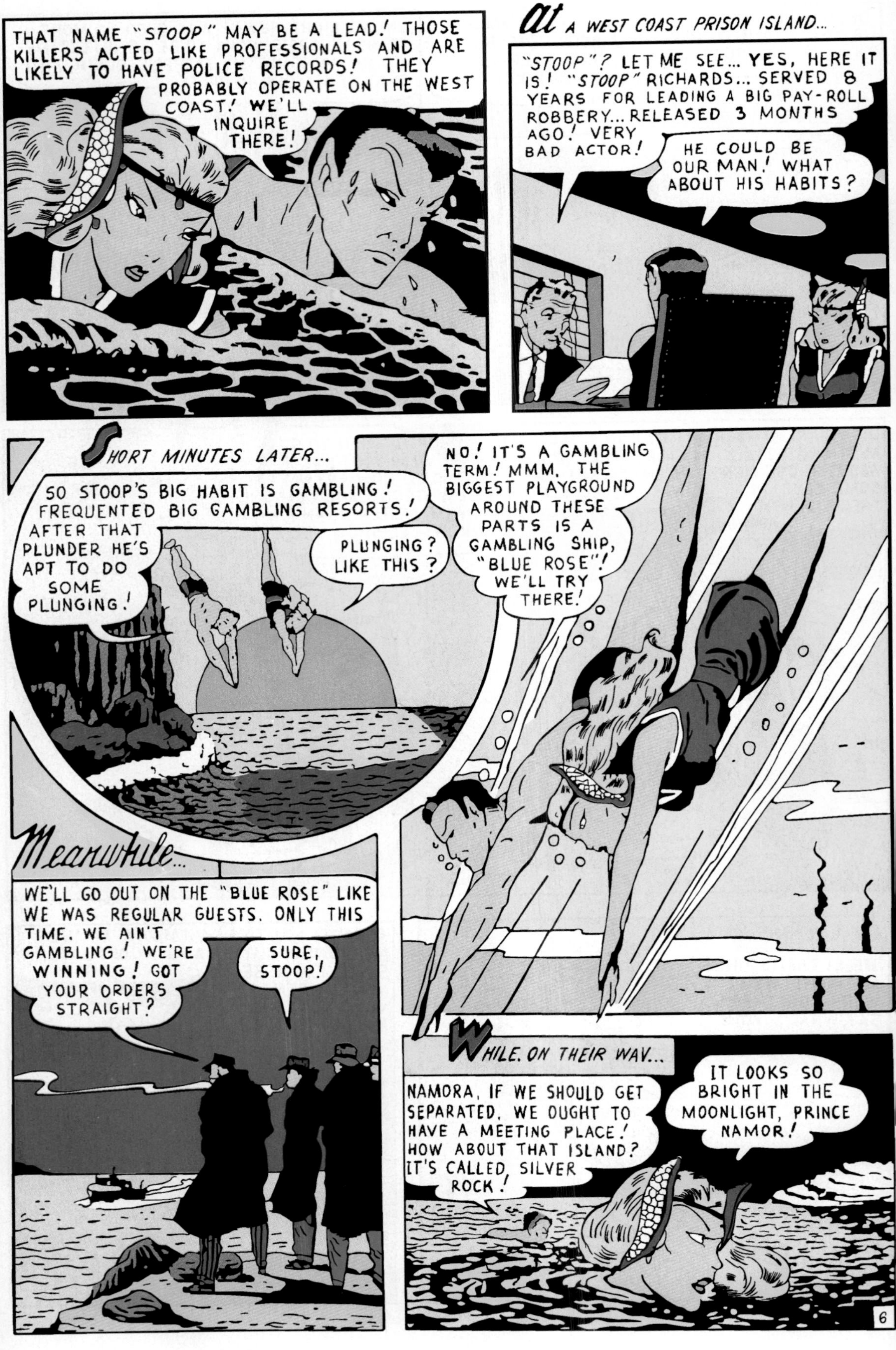
THAT NAME "STOOP" MAY BE A LEAD! THOSE KILLERS ACTED LIKE PROFESSIONALS AND ARE LIKELY TO HAVE POLICE RECORDS! THEY PROBABLY OPERATE ON THE WEST COAST! WE'LL INQUIRE THERE!
At A WEST COAST PRISON ISLAND...
"STOOP"? LET ME SEE... YES, HERE IT IS! "STOOP" RICHARDS... SERVED 8 YEARS FOR LEADING A BIG PAY-ROLL ROBBERY... RELEASED 3 MONTHS AGO! VERY BAD ACTOR!
HE COULD BE OUR MAN! WHAT ABOUT HIS HABITS?
SHORT MINUTES LATER...
SO STOOP'S BIG HABIT IS GAMBLING! FREQUENTED BIG GAMBLING RESORTS! AFTER THAT PLUNDER HE'S APT TO DO SOME PLUNGING!
PLUNGING? LIKE THIS?
NO! IT'S A GAMBLING TERM! MMM, THE BIGGEST PLAYGROUND AROUND THESE PARTS IS A GAMBLING SHIP, "BLUE ROSE"! WE'LL TRY THERE!
Meanwhile...
WE'LL GO OUT ON THE "BLUE ROSE" LIKE WE WAS REGULAR GUESTS. ONLY THIS TIME, WE AIN'T GAMBLING! WE'RE WINNING! GOT YOUR ORDERS STRAIGHT?
SURE, STOOP!
WHILE ON THEIR WAY...
NAMORA, IF WE SHOULD GET SEPARATED, WE OUGHT TO HAVE A MEETING PLACE! HOW ABOUT THAT ISLAND? IT'S CALLED, SILVER ROCK!
IT LOOKS SO BRIGHT IN THE MOONLIGHT, PRINCE NAMOR!

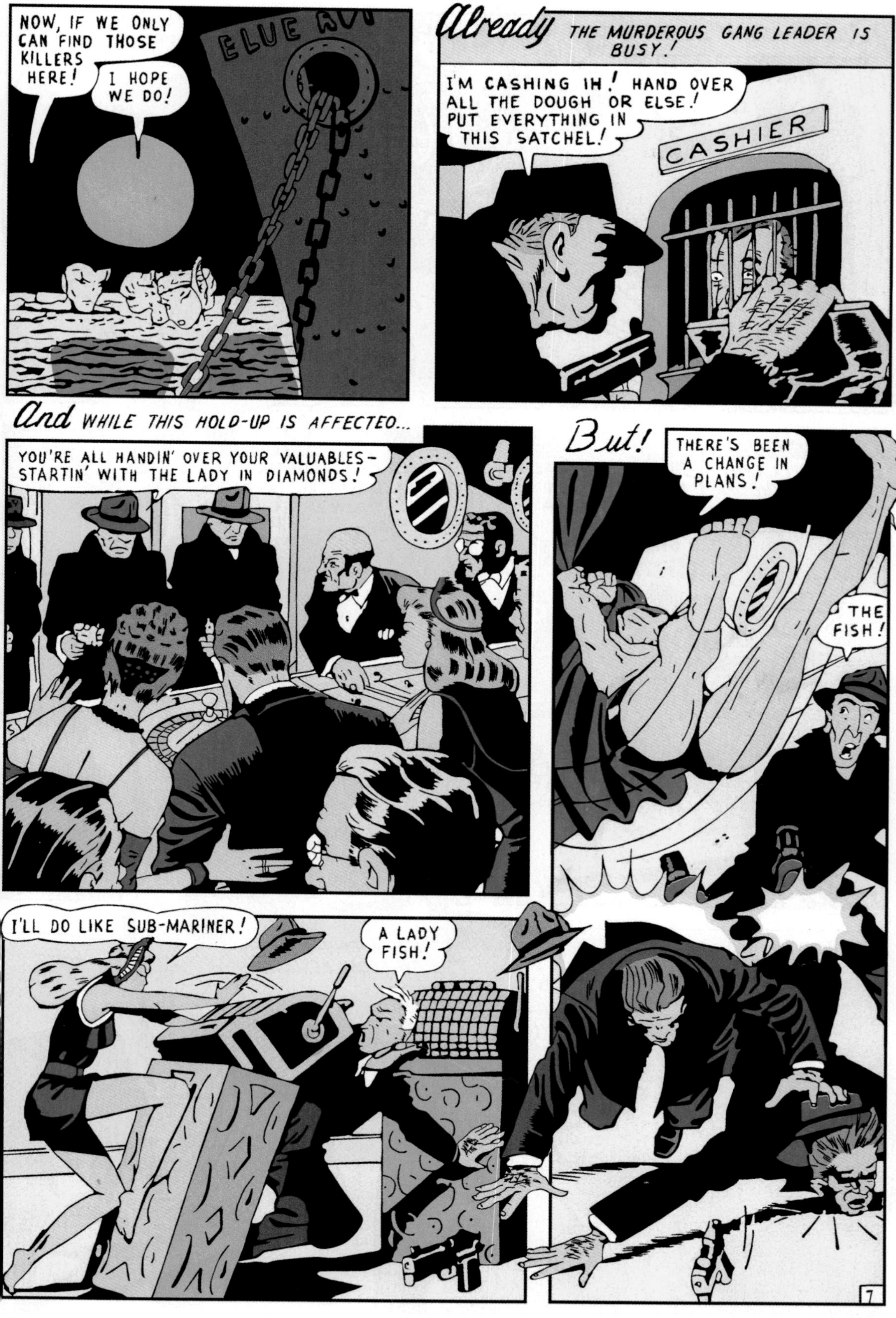
NOW, IF WE ONLY CAN FIND THOSE KILLERS HERE!
I HOPE WE DO!
Already THE MURDEROUS GANG LEADER IS BUSY!
I'M CASHING IN! HAND OVER ALL THE DOUGH OR ELSE! PUT EVERYTHING IN THIS SATCHEL!
CASHIER
And WHILE THIS HOLD-UP IS AFFECTED...
YOU'RE ALL HANDIN' OVER YOUR VALUABLES—STARTIN' WITH THE LADY IN DIAMONDS!
But!
THERE'S BEEN A CHANGE IN PLANS!
THE FISH!
I'LL DO LIKE SUB-MARINER!
A LADY FISH!

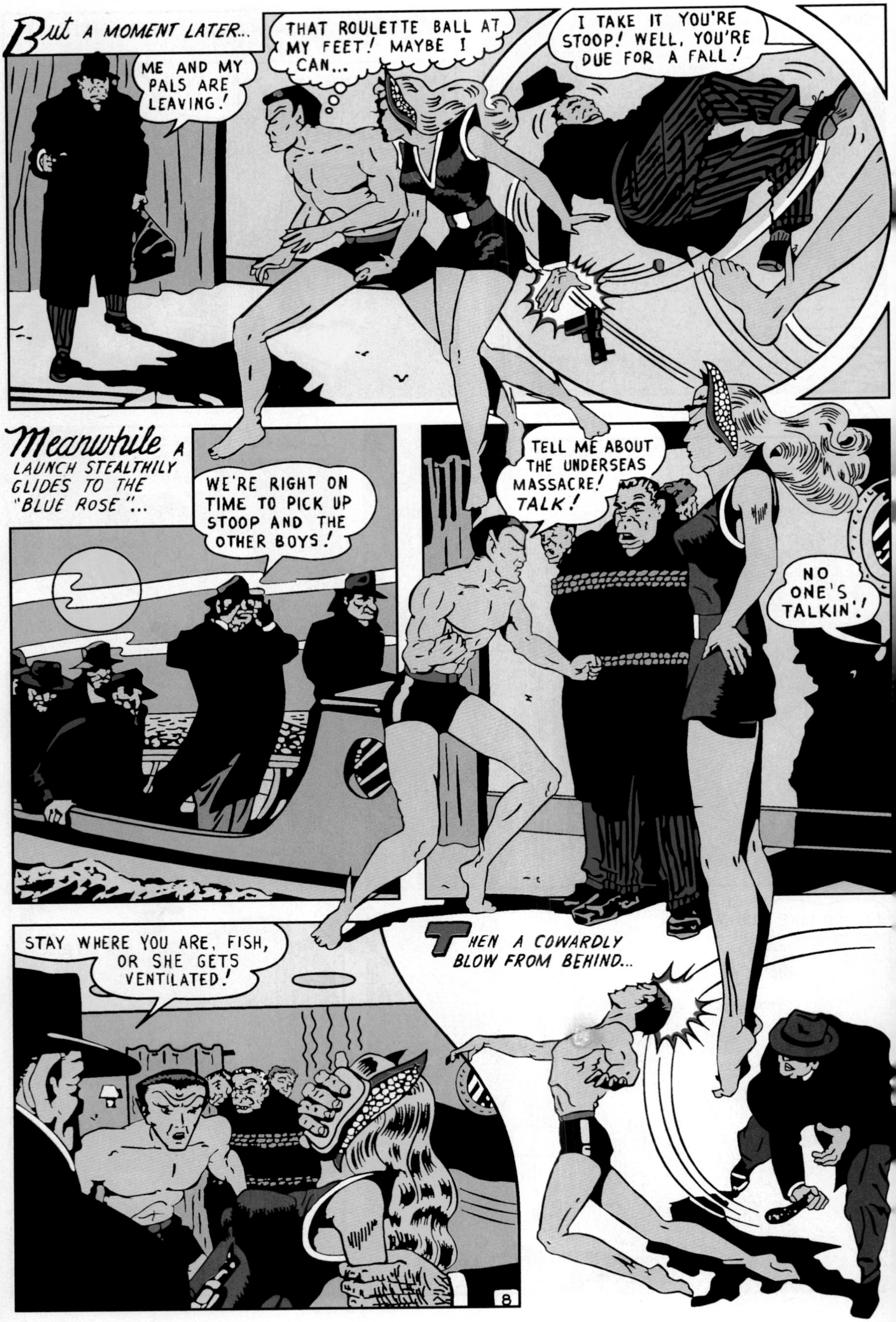
But a moment later...
ME AND MY PALS ARE LEAVING!
THAT ROULETTE BALL AT MY FEET! MAYBE I CAN...
I TAKE IT YOU'RE STOOP! WELL, YOU'RE DUE FOR A FALL!
Meanwhile a launch stealthily glides to the "Blue Rose"...
WE'RE RIGHT ON TIME TO PICK UP STOOP AND THE OTHER BOYS!
TELL ME ABOUT THE UNDERSEAS MASSACRE! TALK!
NO ONE'S TALKIN'!
STAY WHERE YOU ARE, FISH, OR SHE GETS VENTILATED!
Then a cowardly blow from behind...
8

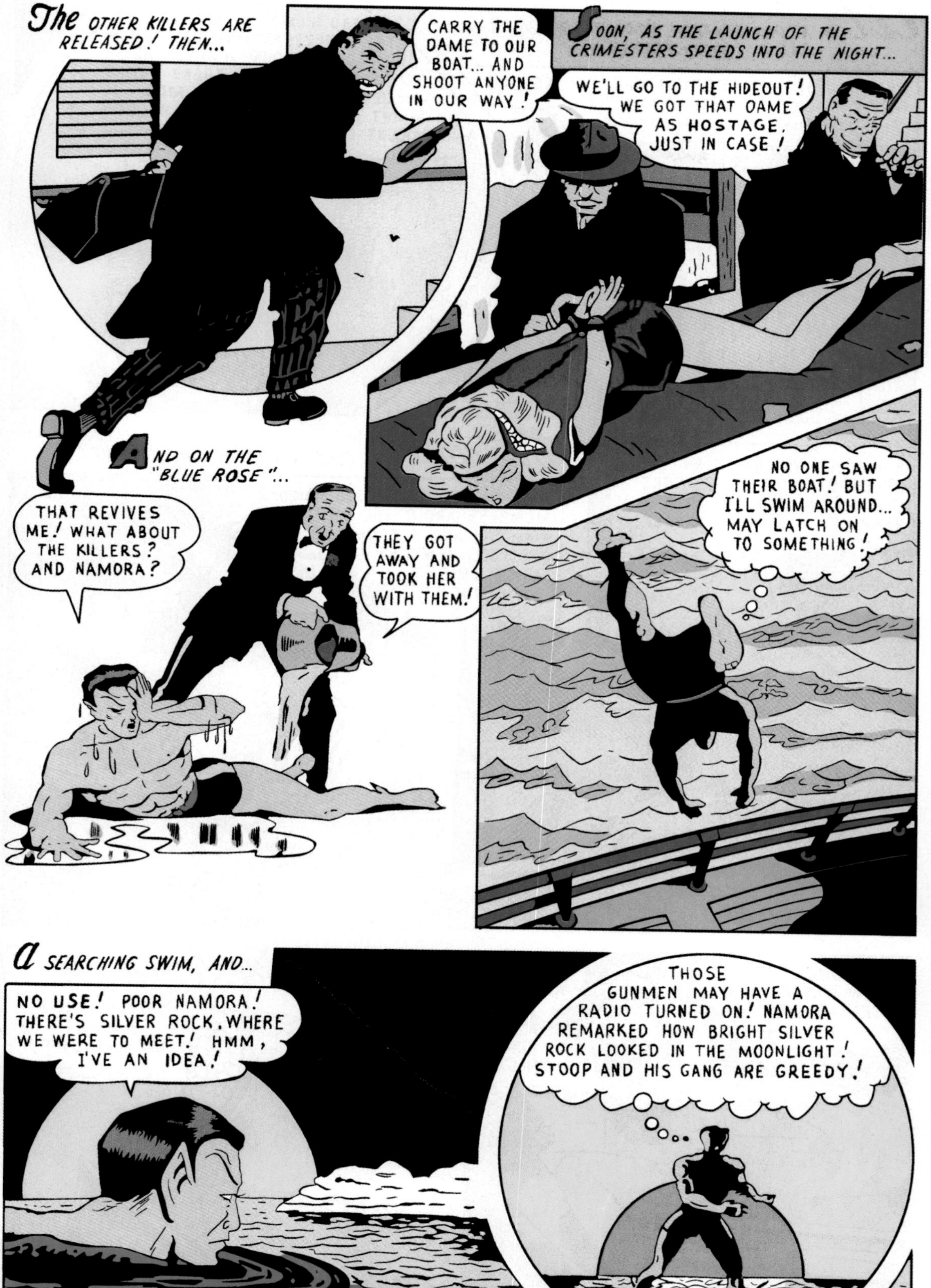
The other killers are released! Then...
CARRY THE DAME TO OUR BOAT... AND SHOOT ANYONE IN OUR WAY!
Soon, as the launch of the crimesters speeds into the night...
WE'LL GO TO THE HIDEOUT! WE GOT THAT DAME AS HOSTAGE, JUST IN CASE!
And on the "Blue Rose"...
THAT REVIVES ME! WHAT ABOUT THE KILLERS? AND NAMORA?
THEY GOT AWAY AND TOOK HER WITH THEM!
NO ONE SAW THEIR BOAT! BUT I'LL SWIM AROUND... MAY LATCH ON TO SOMETHING!
A searching swim, and...
NO USE! POOR NAMORA! THERE'S SILVER ROCK, WHERE WE WERE TO MEET! HMM, I'VE AN IDEA!
THOSE GUNMEN MAY HAVE A RADIO TURNED ON! NAMORA REMARKED HOW BRIGHT SILVER ROCK LOOKED IN THE MOONLIGHT! STOOP AND HIS GANG ARE GREEDY!
9

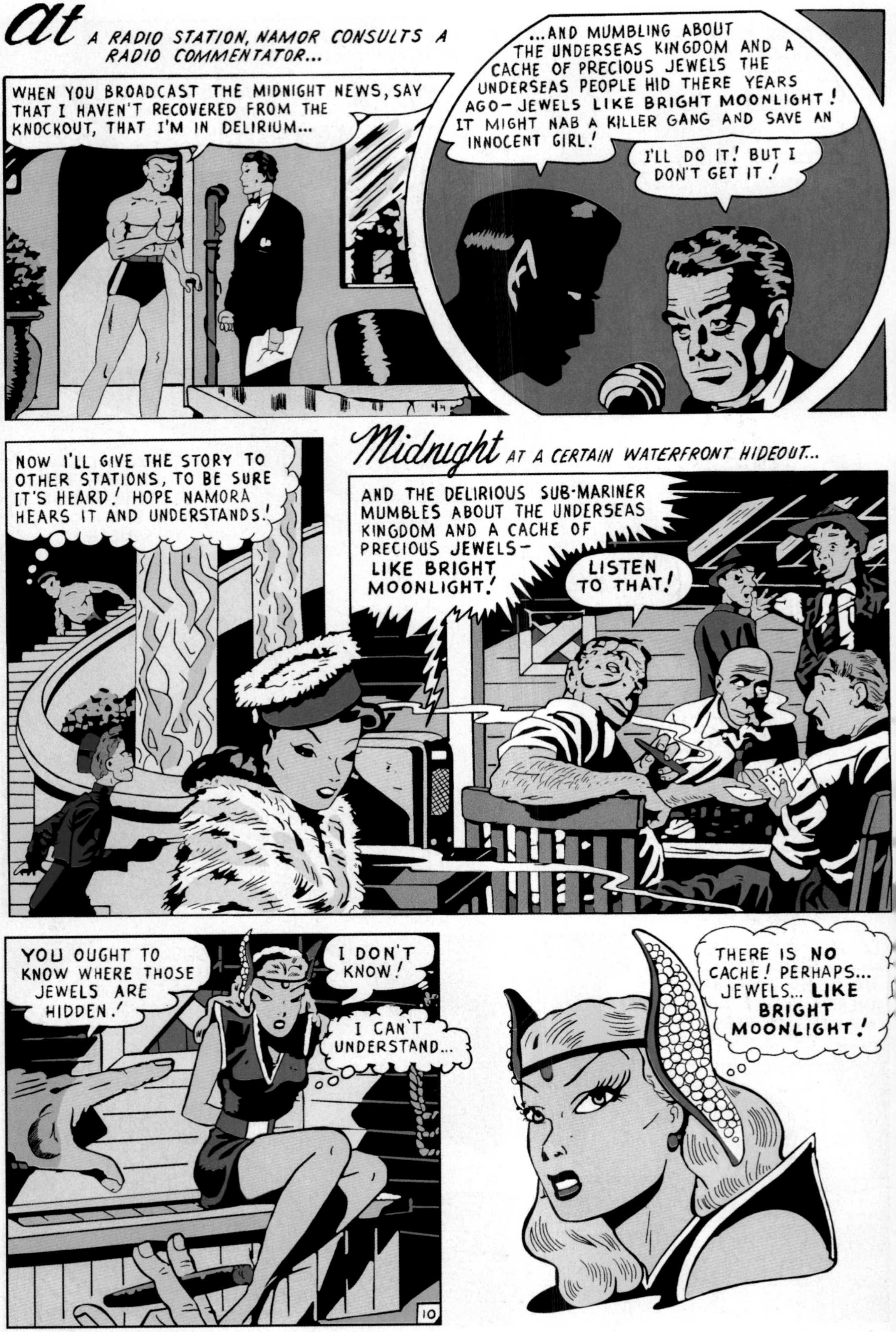
At A RADIO STATION, NAMOR CONSULTS A RADIO COMMENTATOR...
WHEN YOU BROADCAST THE MIDNIGHT NEWS, SAY THAT I HAVEN'T RECOVERED FROM THE KNOCKOUT, THAT I'M IN DELIRIUM...
...AND MUMBLING ABOUT THE UNDERSEAS KINGDOM AND A CACHE OF PRECIOUS JEWELS THE UNDERSEAS PEOPLE HID THERE YEARS AGO- JEWELS LIKE BRIGHT MOONLIGHT! IT MIGHT NAB A KILLER GANG AND SAVE AN INNOCENT GIRL!
I'LL DO IT! BUT I DON'T GET IT!
NOW I'LL GIVE THE STORY TO OTHER STATIONS, TO BE SURE IT'S HEARD! HOPE NAMORA HEARS IT AND UNDERSTANDS!
Midnight AT A CERTAIN WATERFRONT HIDEOUT...
AND THE DELIRIOUS SUB-MARINER MUMBLES ABOUT THE UNDERSEAS KINGDOM AND A CACHE OF PRECIOUS JEWELS- LIKE BRIGHT MOONLIGHT!
LISTEN TO THAT!
YOU OUGHT TO KNOW WHERE THOSE JEWELS ARE HIDDEN!
I DON'T KNOW!
I CAN'T UNDERSTAND...
THERE IS NO CACHE! PERHAPS... JEWELS... LIKE BRIGHT MOONLIGHT!
10

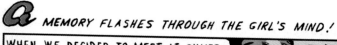
MEMORY FLASHES THROUGH THE GIRL'S MIND!

WHEN WE DECIDED TO MEET AT SILVER ROCK, I SAID, "IT LOOKS SO BRIGHT IN THE MOONLIGHT!" COULD THIS BE A MESSAGE?

TALK!

NO! DON'T KILL ME! THE JEWELS ARE HIDDEN ON SILVER ROCK!

Soon...

WHERE ARE THE JEWELS HIDDEN? AND NO TRICKS!

WHAT SHALL I DO NOW?

SPLIT SECOND LATER!

NAMOR!

SMART WORK, NAMORA, TO CATCH MY CUE!

A TRAP! GET HIM!

11

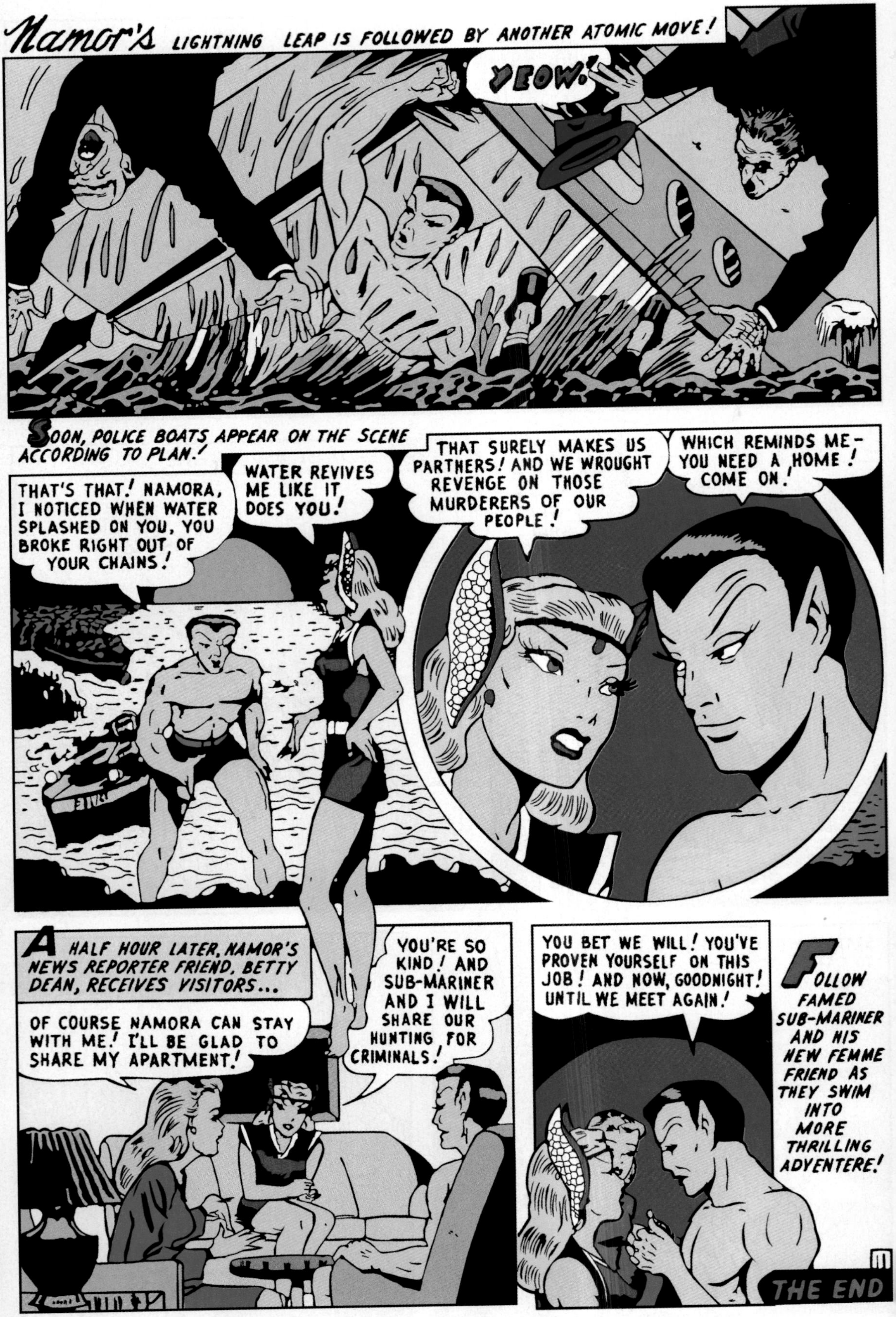
Namor's LIGHTNING LEAP IS FOLLOWED BY ANOTHER ATOMIC MOVE!
YEOW!
SOON, POLICE BOATS APPEAR ON THE SCENE ACCORDING TO PLAN!
THAT'S THAT! NAMORA, I NOTICED WHEN WATER SPLASHED ON YOU, YOU BROKE RIGHT OUT OF YOUR CHAINS!
WATER REVIVES ME LIKE IT DOES YOU!
THAT SURELY MAKES US PARTHERS! AND WE WROUGHT REVENGE ON THOSE MURDERERS OF OUR PEOPLE!
WHICH REMINDS ME- YOU NEED A HOME! COME ON!
A HALF HOUR LATER, NAMOR'S NEWS REPORTER FRIEND, BETTY DEAN, RECEIVES VISITORS...
OF COURSE NAMORA CAN STAY WITH ME! I'LL BE GLAD TO SHARE MY APARTMENT!
YOU'RE SO KIND! AND SUB-MARINER AND I WILL SHARE OUR HUNTING FOR CRIMINALS!
YOU BET WE WILL! YOU'VE PROVEN YOURSELF ON THIS JOB! AND NOW, GOODNIGHT! UNTIL WE MEET AGAIN!
FOLLOW FAMED SUB-MARINER AND HIS NEW FEMME FRIEND AS THEY SWIM INTO MORE THRILLING ADVENTERE!
THE END

VENUS #1 **(AUGUST 1948) THE FIRST APPEARANCE OF VENUS**

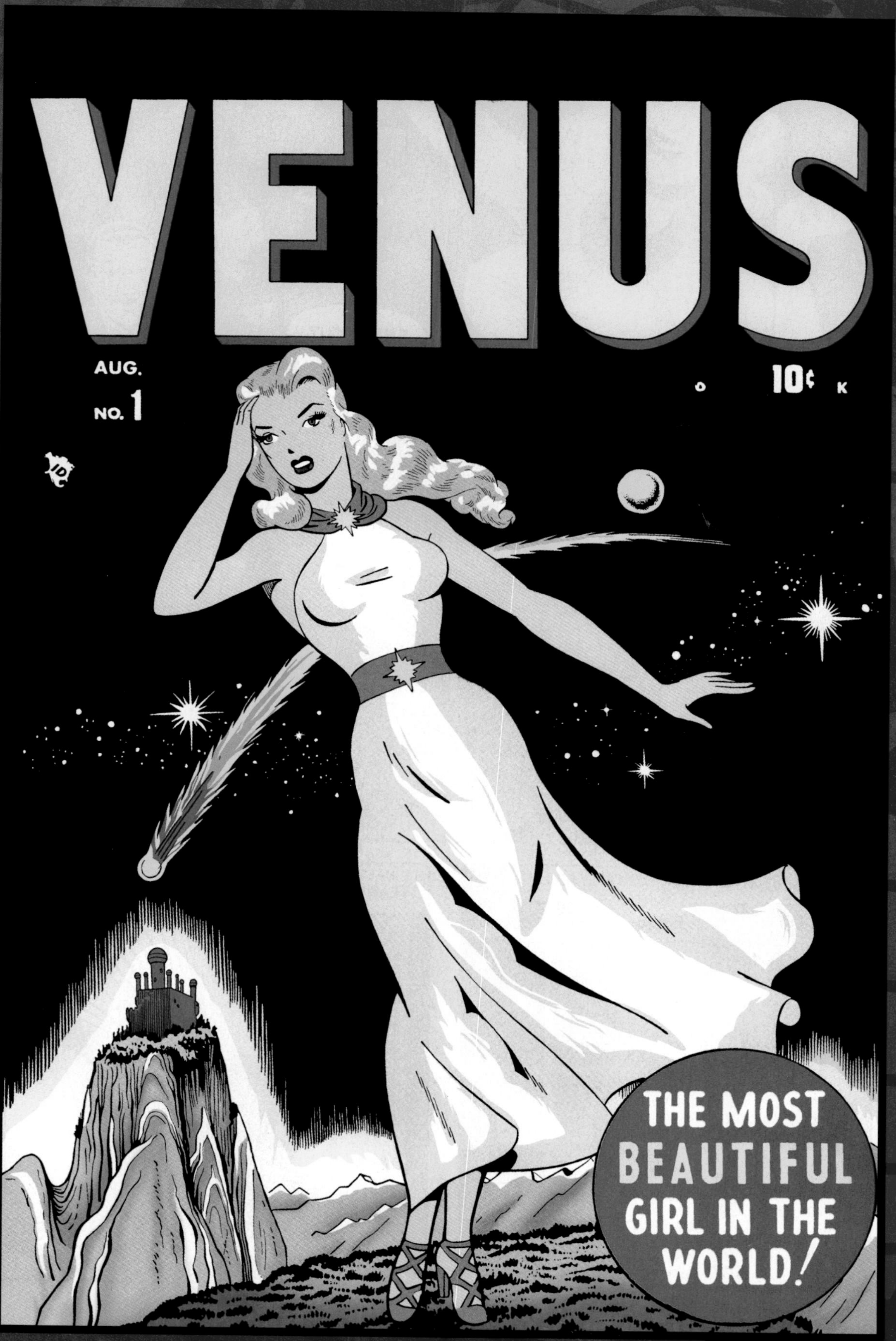

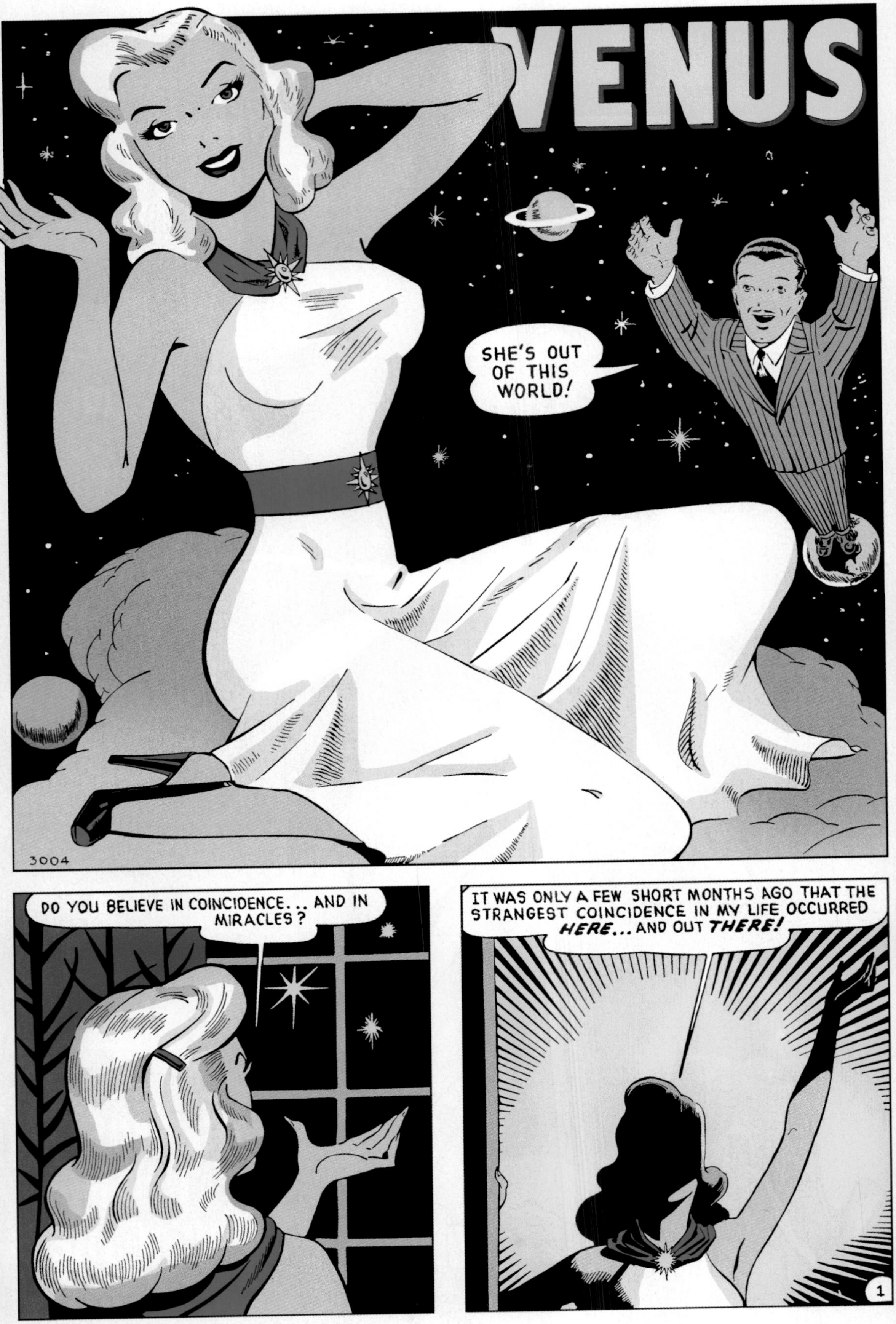
VENUS
SHE'S OUT OF THIS WORLD!
3004
DO YOU BELIEVE IN COINCIDENCE... AND IN MIRACLES?
IT WAS ONLY A FEW SHORT MONTHS AGO THAT THE STRANGEST COINCIDENCE IN MY LIFE OCCURRED HERE... AND OUT THERE!
1

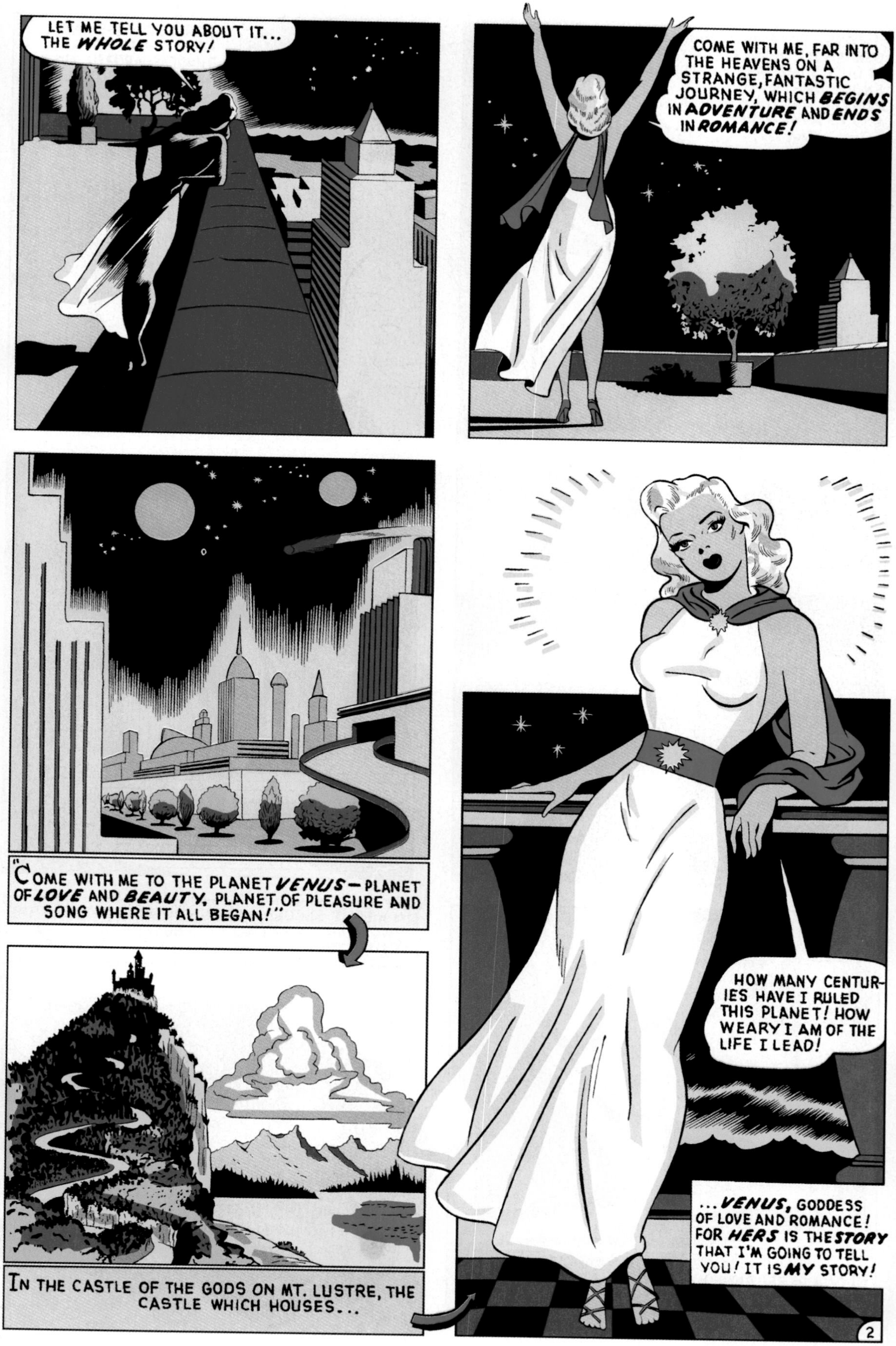
LET ME TELL YOU ABOUT IT... THE WHOLE STORY!
COME WITH ME, FAR INTO THE HEAVENS ON A STRANGE, FANTASTIC JOURNEY, WHICH BEGINS IN ADVENTURE AND ENDS IN ROMANCE!
"COME WITH ME TO THE PLANET VENUS — PLANET OF LOVE AND BEAUTY, PLANET OF PLEASURE AND SONG WHERE IT ALL BEGAN!"
IN THE CASTLE OF THE GODS ON MT. LUSTRE, THE CASTLE WHICH HOUSES...
HOW MANY CENTURIES HAVE I RULED THIS PLANET! HOW WEARY I AM OF THE LIFE I LEAD!
...VENUS, GODDESS OF LOVE AND ROMANCE! FOR HERS IS THE STORY THAT I'M GOING TO TELL YOU! IT IS MY STORY!
2

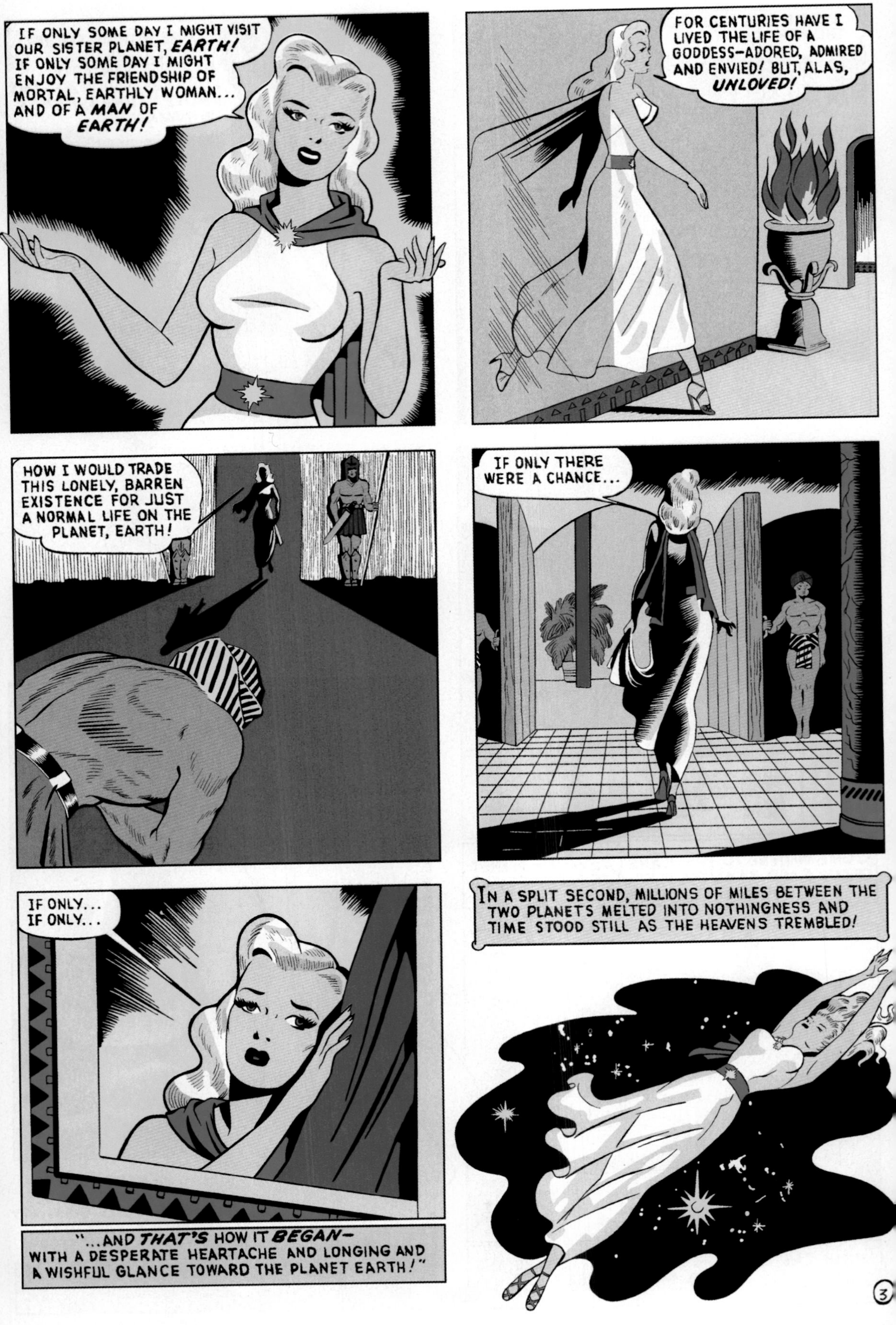
IF ONLY SOME DAY I MIGHT VISIT OUR SISTER PLANET, EARTH! IF ONLY SOME DAY I MIGHT ENJOY THE FRIENDSHIP OF MORTAL, EARTHLY WOMAN... AND OF A MAN OF EARTH!
FOR CENTURIES HAVE I LIVED THE LIFE OF A GODDESS–ADORED, ADMIRED AND ENVIED! BUT, ALAS, UNLOVED!
HOW I WOULD TRADE THIS LONELY, BARREN EXISTENCE FOR JUST A NORMAL LIFE ON THE PLANET, EARTH!
IF ONLY THERE WERE A CHANCE...
IF ONLY... IF ONLY...
"...AND THAT'S HOW IT BEGAN– WITH A DESPERATE HEARTACHE AND LONGING AND A WISHFUL GLANCE TOWARD THE PLANET EARTH!"
IN A SPLIT SECOND, MILLIONS OF MILES BETWEEN THE TWO PLANETS MELTED INTO NOTHINGNESS AND TIME STOOD STILL AS THE HEAVENS TREMBLED!

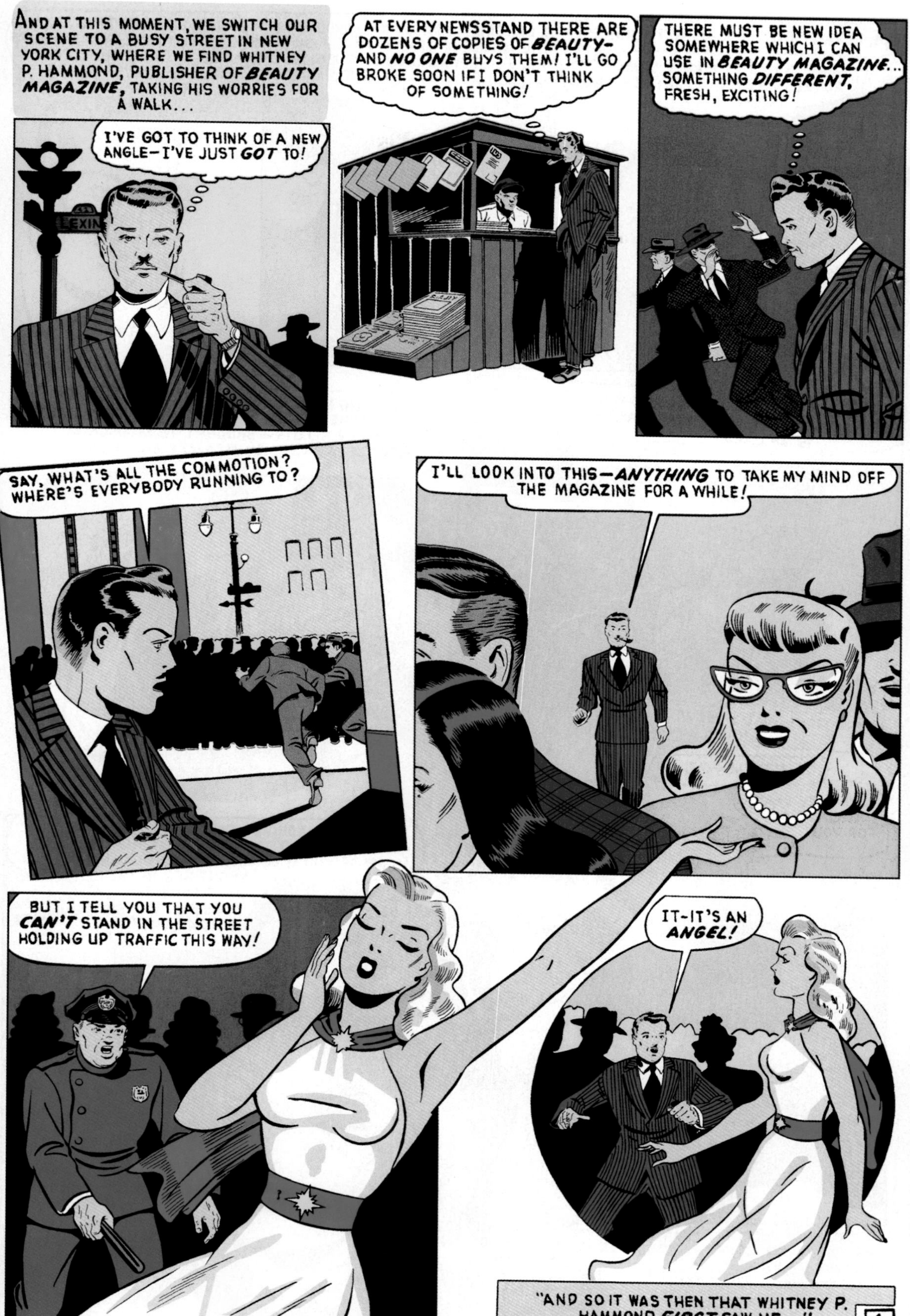

AND AT THIS MOMENT, WE SWITCH OUR SCENE TO A BUSY STREET IN NEW YORK CITY, WHERE WE FIND WHITNEY P. HAMMOND, PUBLISHER OF *BEAUTY MAGAZINE*, TAKING HIS WORRIES FOR A WALK...
I'VE GOT TO THINK OF A NEW ANGLE—I'VE JUST *GOT* TO!
AT EVERY NEWSSTAND THERE ARE DOZENS OF COPIES OF *BEAUTY*—AND *NO ONE* BUYS THEM! I'LL GO BROKE SOON IF I DON'T THINK OF SOMETHING!
THERE MUST BE NEW IDEA SOMEWHERE WHICH I CAN USE IN *BEAUTY MAGAZINE*... SOMETHING *DIFFERENT*, FRESH, EXCITING!
SAY, WHAT'S ALL THE COMMOTION? WHERE'S EVERYBODY RUNNING TO?
I'LL LOOK INTO THIS—*ANYTHING* TO TAKE MY MIND OFF THE MAGAZINE FOR A WHILE!
BUT I TELL YOU THAT YOU *CAN'T* STAND IN THE STREET HOLDING UP TRAFFIC THIS WAY!
IT-IT'S AN *ANGEL*!
"AND SO IT WAS THEN THAT WHITNEY P. HAMMOND *FIRST* SAW ME..."

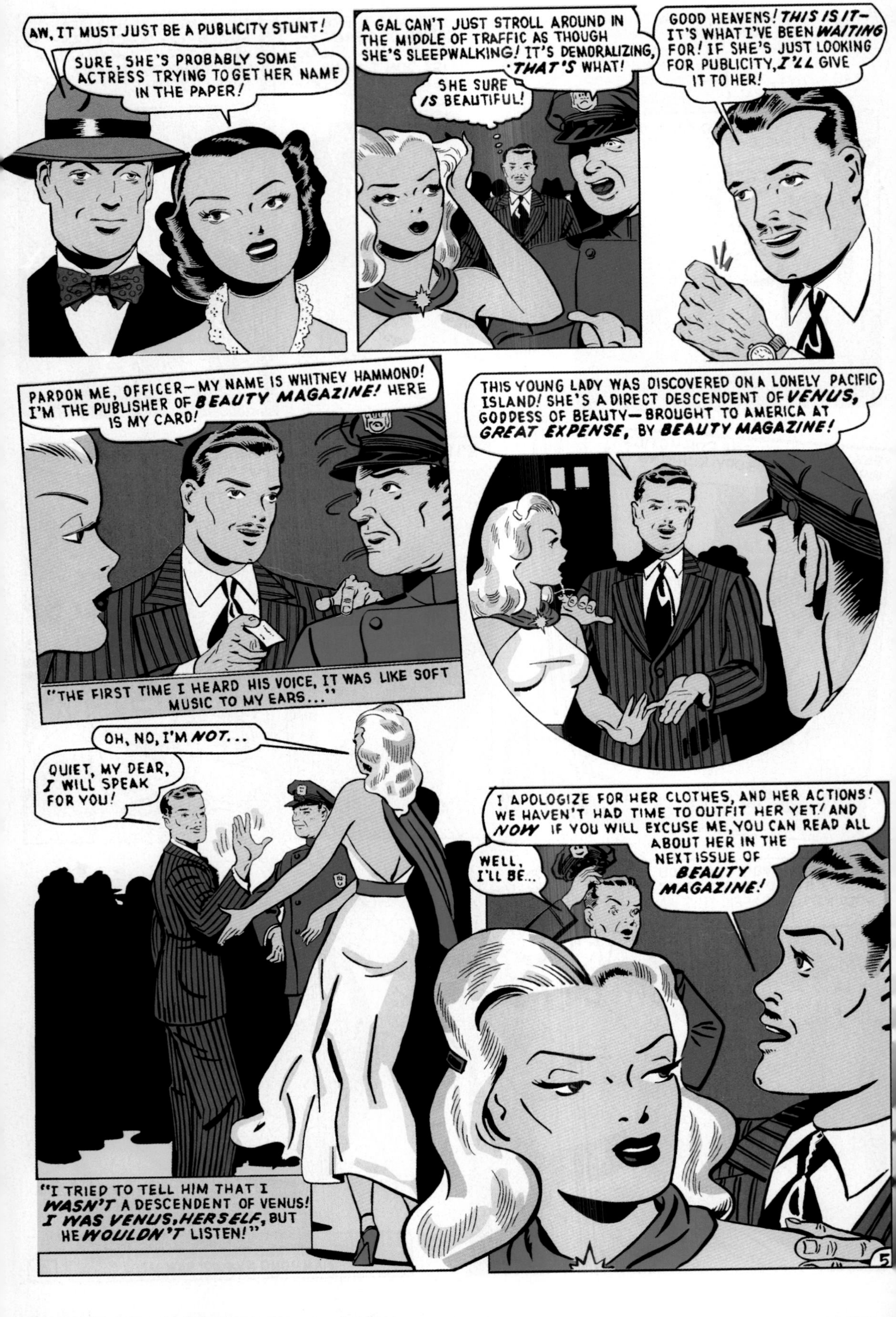
AW, IT MUST JUST BE A PUBLICITY STUNT!
SURE, SHE'S PROBABLY SOME ACTRESS TRYING TO GET HER NAME IN THE PAPER!
A GAL CAN'T JUST STROLL AROUND IN THE MIDDLE OF TRAFFIC AS THOUGH SHE'S SLEEPWALKING! IT'S DEMORALIZING, THAT'S WHAT!
SHE SURE IS BEAUTIFUL!
GOOD HEAVENS! THIS IS IT— IT'S WHAT I'VE BEEN WAITING FOR! IF SHE'S JUST LOOKING FOR PUBLICITY, I'LL GIVE IT TO HER!
PARDON ME, OFFICER— MY NAME IS WHITNEY HAMMOND! I'M THE PUBLISHER OF BEAUTY MAGAZINE! HERE IS MY CARD!
"THE FIRST TIME I HEARD HIS VOICE, IT WAS LIKE SOFT MUSIC TO MY EARS..."
THIS YOUNG LADY WAS DISCOVERED ON A LONELY PACIFIC ISLAND! SHE'S A DIRECT DESCENDENT OF VENUS, GODDESS OF BEAUTY— BROUGHT TO AMERICA AT GREAT EXPENSE, BY BEAUTY MAGAZINE!
OH, NO, I'M NOT...
QUIET, MY DEAR, I WILL SPEAK FOR YOU!
"I TRIED TO TELL HIM THAT I WASN'T A DESCENDENT OF VENUS! I WAS VENUS, HERSELF, BUT HE WOULDN'T LISTEN!"
I APOLOGIZE FOR HER CLOTHES, AND HER ACTIONS! WE HAVEN'T HAD TIME TO OUTFIT HER YET! AND NOW IF YOU WILL EXCUSE ME, YOU CAN READ ALL ABOUT HER IN THE NEXT ISSUE OF BEAUTY MAGAZINE!
WELL, I'LL BE...
5

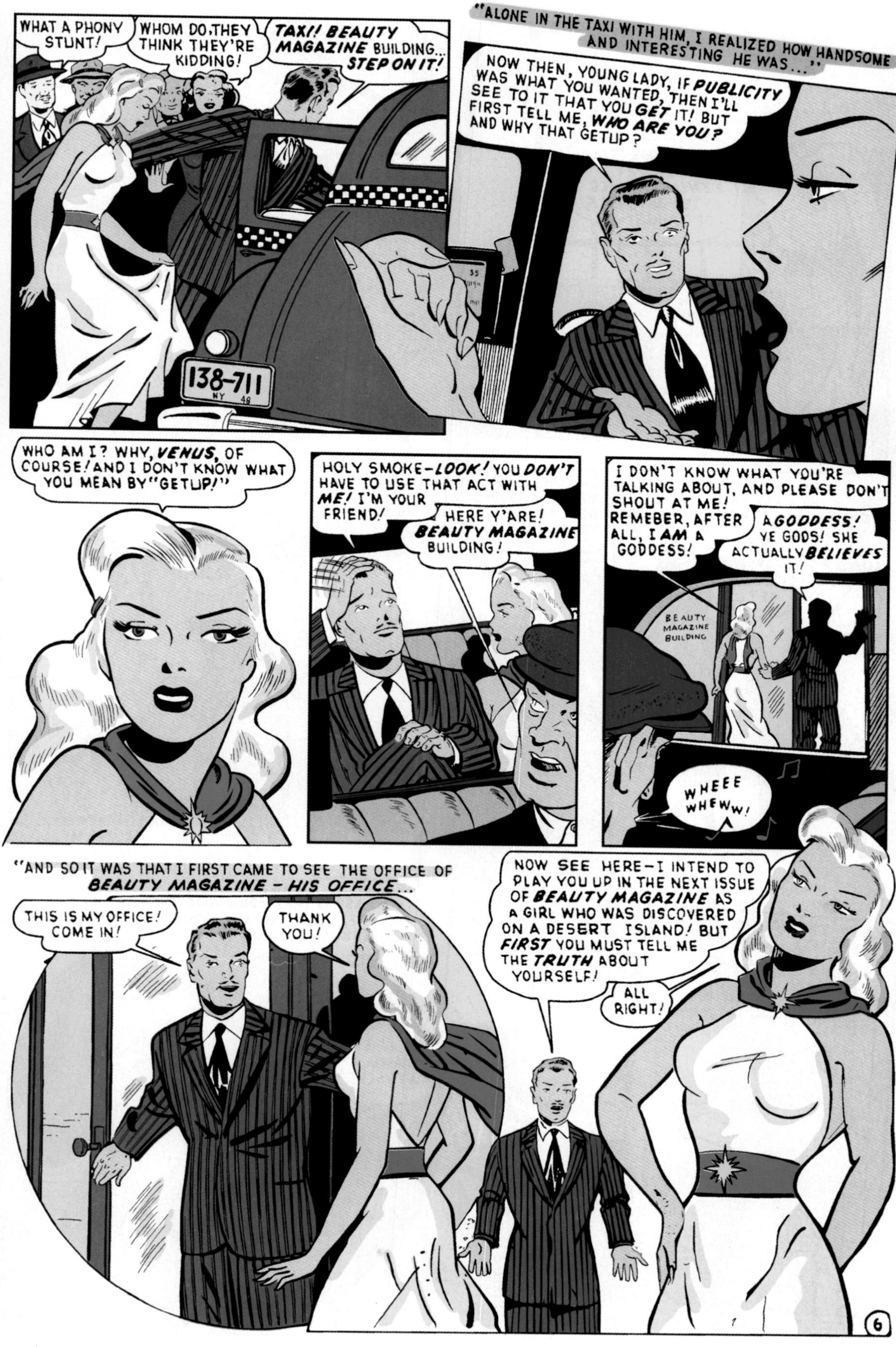
WHAT A PHONY STUNT!
WHOM DO THEY THINK THEY'RE KIDDING!
TAXI! BEAUTY MAGAZINE BUILDING... STEP ON IT!
"ALONE IN THE TAXI WITH HIM, I REALIZED HOW HANDSOME AND INTERESTING HE WAS..."
NOW THEN, YOUNG LADY, IF PUBLICITY WAS WHAT YOU WANTED, THEN I'LL SEE TO IT THAT YOU GET IT! BUT FIRST TELL ME, WHO ARE YOU? AND WHY THAT GETUP?
138-711
NY 48
WHO AM I? WHY, VENUS, OF COURSE! AND I DON'T KNOW WHAT YOU MEAN BY "GETUP!"
HOLY SMOKE-LOOK! YOU DON'T HAVE TO USE THAT ACT WITH ME! I'M YOUR FRIEND!
HERE Y'ARE! BEAUTY MAGAZINE BUILDING!
I DON'T KNOW WHAT YOU'RE TALKING ABOUT, AND PLEASE DON'T SHOUT AT ME! REMEBER, AFTER ALL, I AM A GODDESS!
A GODDESS! YE GODS! SHE ACTUALLY BELIEVES IT!
BEAUTY MAGAZINE BUILDING
WHEEE WHEWW!
"AND SO IT WAS THAT I FIRST CAME TO SEE THE OFFICE OF BEAUTY MAGAZINE - HIS OFFICE...
THIS IS MY OFFICE! COME IN!
THANK YOU!
NOW SEE HERE-I INTEND TO PLAY YOU UP IN THE NEXT ISSUE OF BEAUTY MAGAZINE AS A GIRL WHO WAS DISCOVERED ON A DESERT ISLAND! BUT FIRST YOU MUST TELL ME THE TRUTH ABOUT YOURSELF!
ALL RIGHT!

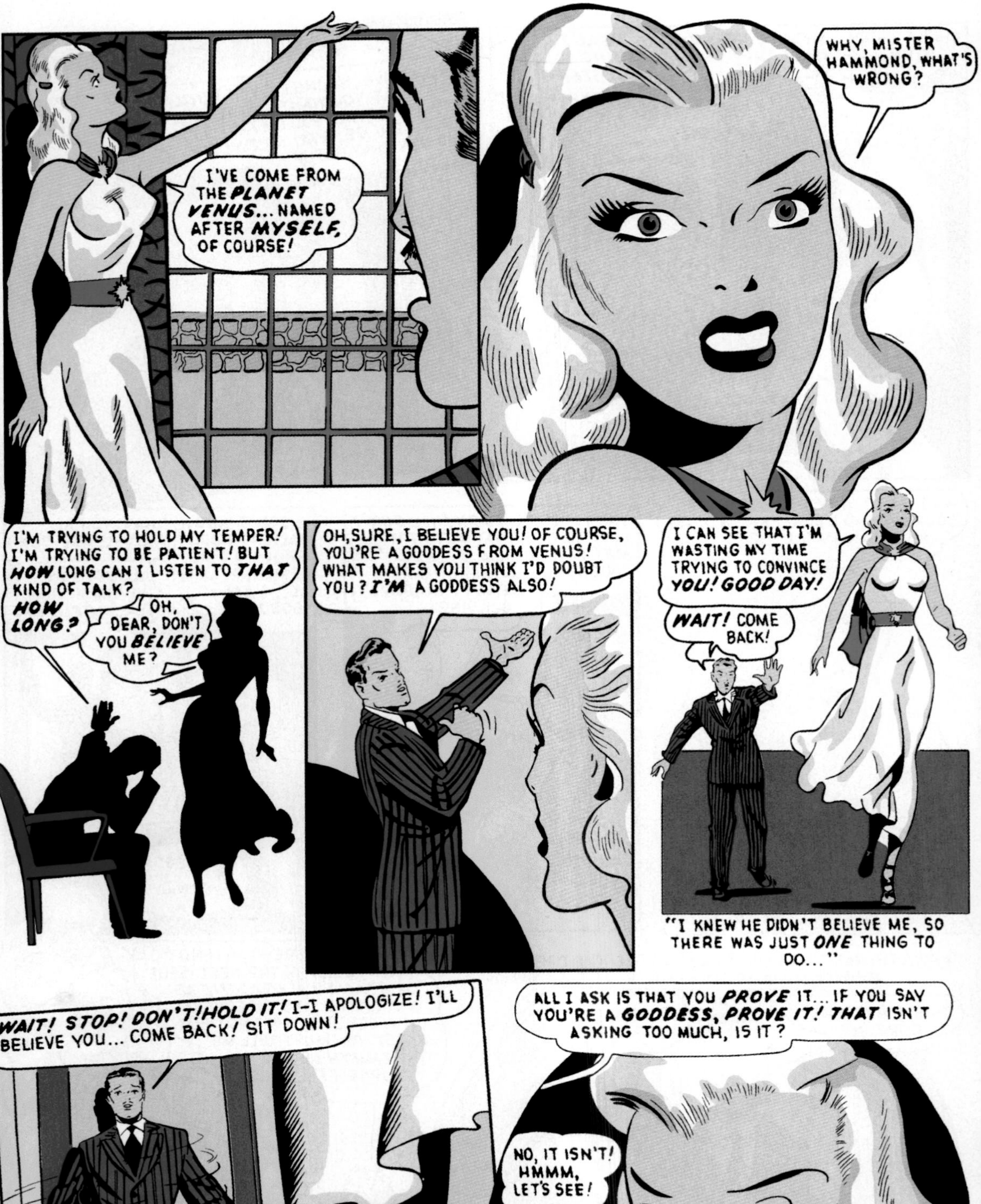
I'VE COME FROM THE PLANET VENUS... NAMED AFTER MYSELF, OF COURSE!
WHY, MISTER HAMMOND, WHAT'S WRONG?
I'M TRYING TO HOLD MY TEMPER! I'M TRYING TO BE PATIENT! BUT HOW LONG CAN I LISTEN TO THAT KIND OF TALK? HOW LONG?
OH, DEAR, DON'T YOU BELIEVE ME?
OH, SURE, I BELIEVE YOU! OF COURSE, YOU'RE A GODDESS FROM VENUS! WHAT MAKES YOU THINK I'D DOUBT YOU? I'M A GODDESS ALSO!
I CAN SEE THAT I'M WASTING MY TIME TRYING TO CONVINCE YOU! GOOD DAY!
WAIT! COME BACK!
"I KNEW HE DIDN'T BELIEVE ME, SO THERE WAS JUST ONE THING TO DO..."
WAIT! STOP! DON'T! HOLD IT! I-I APOLOGIZE! I'LL BELIEVE YOU... COME BACK! SIT DOWN!
"BUT HE INSISTED THAT I RETURN AND LISTEN TO HIM!"
ALL I ASK IS THAT YOU PROVE IT... IF YOU SAY YOU'RE A GODDESS, PROVE IT! THAT ISN'T ASKING TOO MUCH, IS IT?
NO, IT ISN'T! HMMM, LET'S SEE!

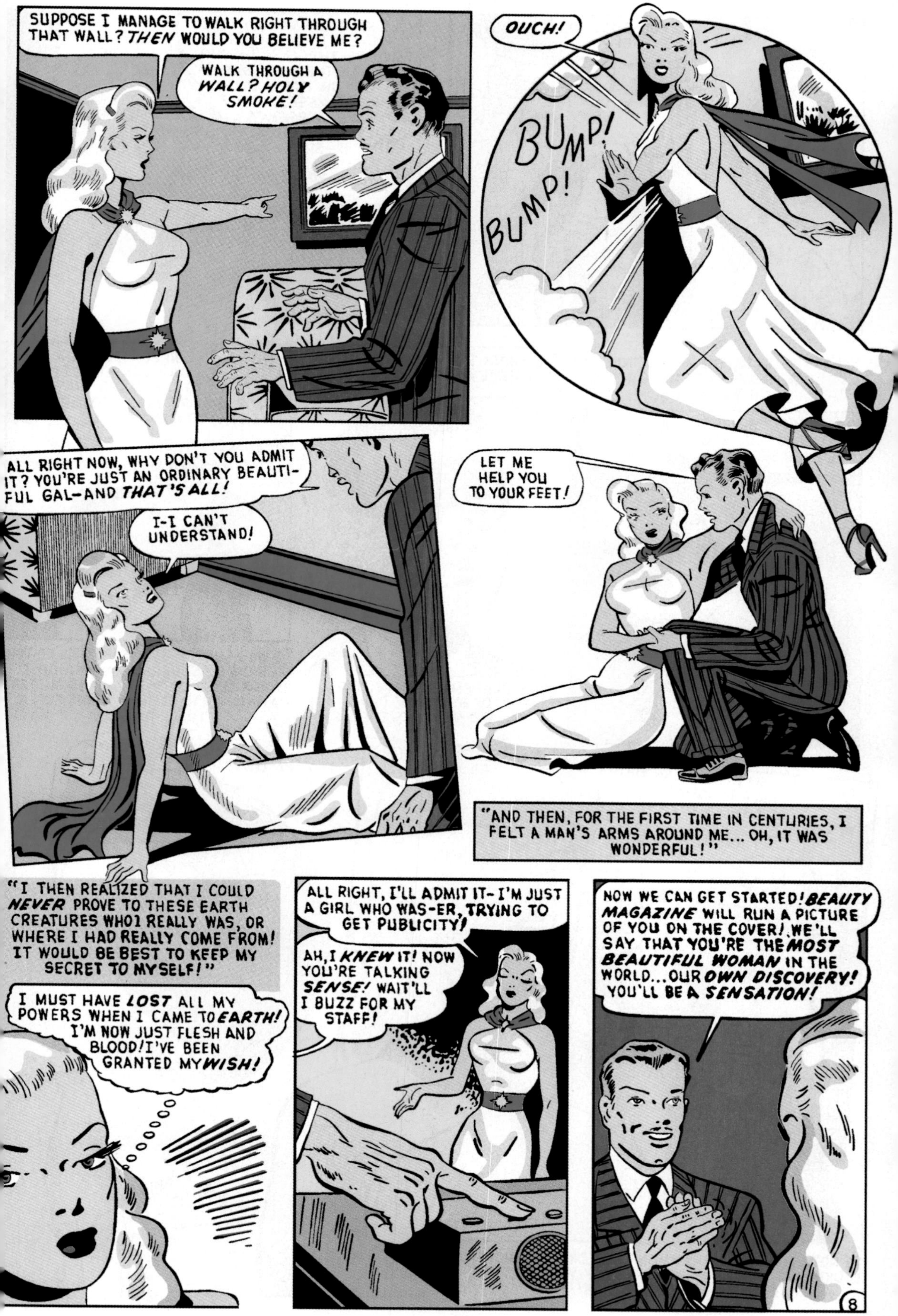
SUPPOSE I MANAGE TO WALK RIGHT THROUGH THAT WALL? THEN WOULD YOU BELIEVE ME?
WALK THROUGH A WALL? HOLY SMOKE!
OUCH!
BUMP!
BUMP!
ALL RIGHT NOW, WHY DON'T YOU ADMIT IT? YOU'RE JUST AN ORDINARY BEAUTIFUL GAL—AND THAT'S ALL!
I-I CAN'T UNDERSTAND!
LET ME HELP YOU TO YOUR FEET!
"AND THEN, FOR THE FIRST TIME IN CENTURIES, I FELT A MAN'S ARMS AROUND ME... OH, IT WAS WONDERFUL!"
"I THEN REALIZED THAT I COULD NEVER PROVE TO THESE EARTH CREATURES WHO I REALLY WAS, OR WHERE I HAD REALLY COME FROM! IT WOULD BE BEST TO KEEP MY SECRET TO MYSELF!"
I MUST HAVE LOST ALL MY POWERS WHEN I CAME TO EARTH! I'M NOW JUST FLESH AND BLOOD! I'VE BEEN GRANTED MY WISH!
ALL RIGHT, I'LL ADMIT IT— I'M JUST A GIRL WHO WAS-ER, TRYING TO GET PUBLICITY!
AH, I KNEW IT! NOW YOU'RE TALKING SENSE! WAIT'LL I BUZZ FOR MY STAFF!
NOW WE CAN GET STARTED! BEAUTY MAGAZINE WILL RUN A PICTURE OF YOU ON THE COVER! WE'LL SAY THAT YOU'RE THE MOST BEAUTIFUL WOMAN IN THE WORLD... OUR OWN DISCOVERY! YOU'LL BE A SENSATION!

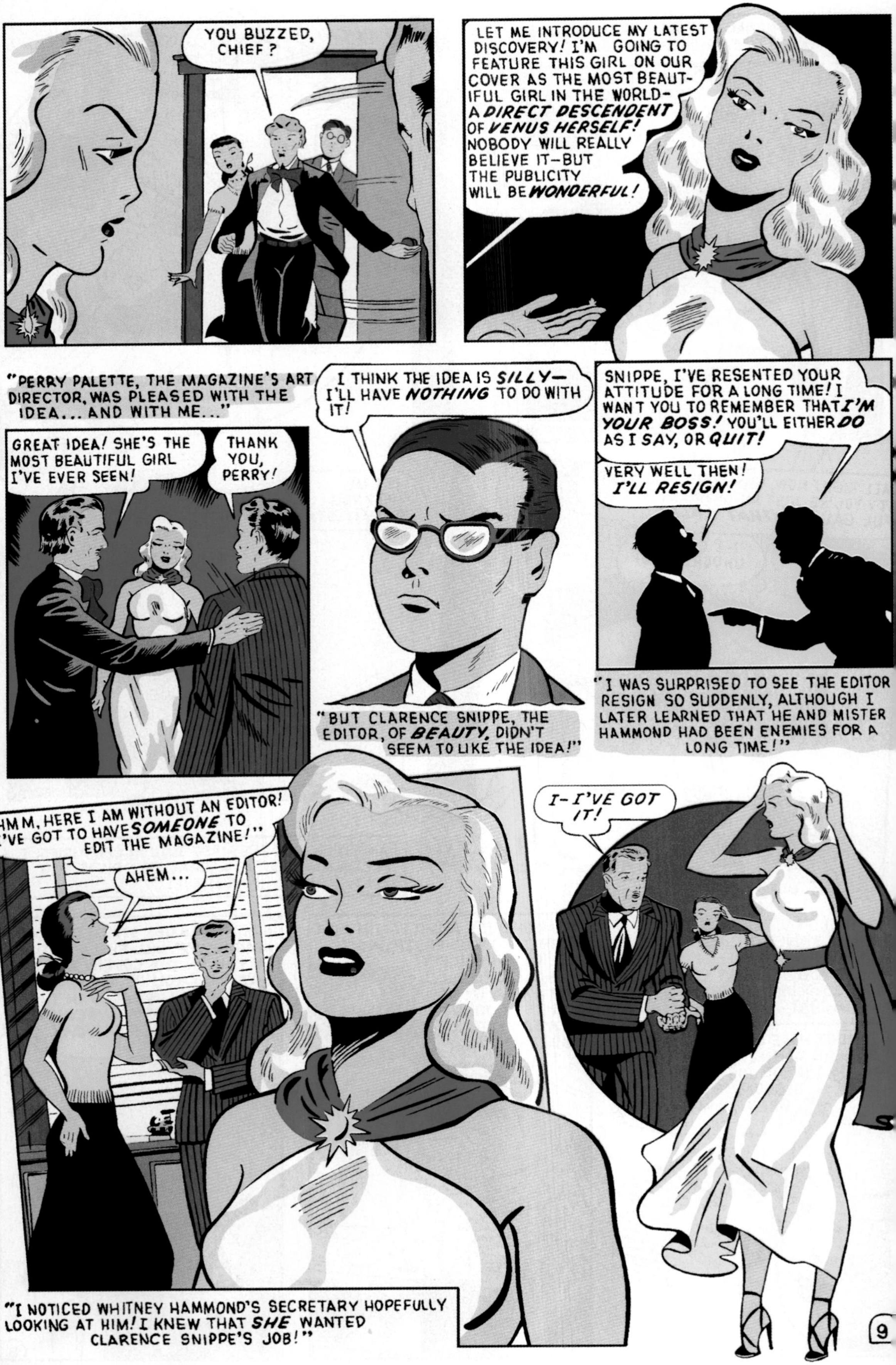
YOU BUZZED, CHIEF?
LET ME INTRODUCE MY LATEST DISCOVERY! I'M GOING TO FEATURE THIS GIRL ON OUR COVER AS THE MOST BEAUTIFUL GIRL IN THE WORLD-A DIRECT DESCENDENT OF VENUS HERSELF! NOBODY WILL REALLY BELIEVE IT-BUT THE PUBLICITY WILL BE WONDERFUL!
"PERRY PALETTE, THE MAGAZINE'S ART DIRECTOR, WAS PLEASED WITH THE IDEA... AND WITH ME..."
GREAT IDEA! SHE'S THE MOST BEAUTIFUL GIRL I'VE EVER SEEN!
THANK YOU, PERRY!
I THINK THE IDEA IS SILLY—I'LL HAVE NOTHING TO DO WITH IT!
"BUT CLARENCE SNIPPE, THE EDITOR, OF BEAUTY, DIDN'T SEEM TO LIKE THE IDEA!"
SNIPPE, I'VE RESENTED YOUR ATTITUDE FOR A LONG TIME! I WANT YOU TO REMEMBER THAT I'M YOUR BOSS! YOU'LL EITHER DO AS I SAY, OR QUIT!
VERY WELL THEN! I'LL RESIGN!
"I WAS SURPRISED TO SEE THE EDITOR RESIGN SO SUDDENLY, ALTHOUGH I LATER LEARNED THAT HE AND MISTER HAMMOND HAD BEEN ENEMIES FOR A LONG TIME!"
HMM, HERE I AM WITHOUT AN EDITOR! I'VE GOT TO HAVE SOMEONE TO EDIT THE MAGAZINE!"
AHEM...
"I NOTICED WHITNEY HAMMOND'S SECRETARY HOPEFULLY LOOKING AT HIM! I KNEW THAT SHE WANTED CLARENCE SNIPPE'S JOB!"
I-I'VE GOT IT!

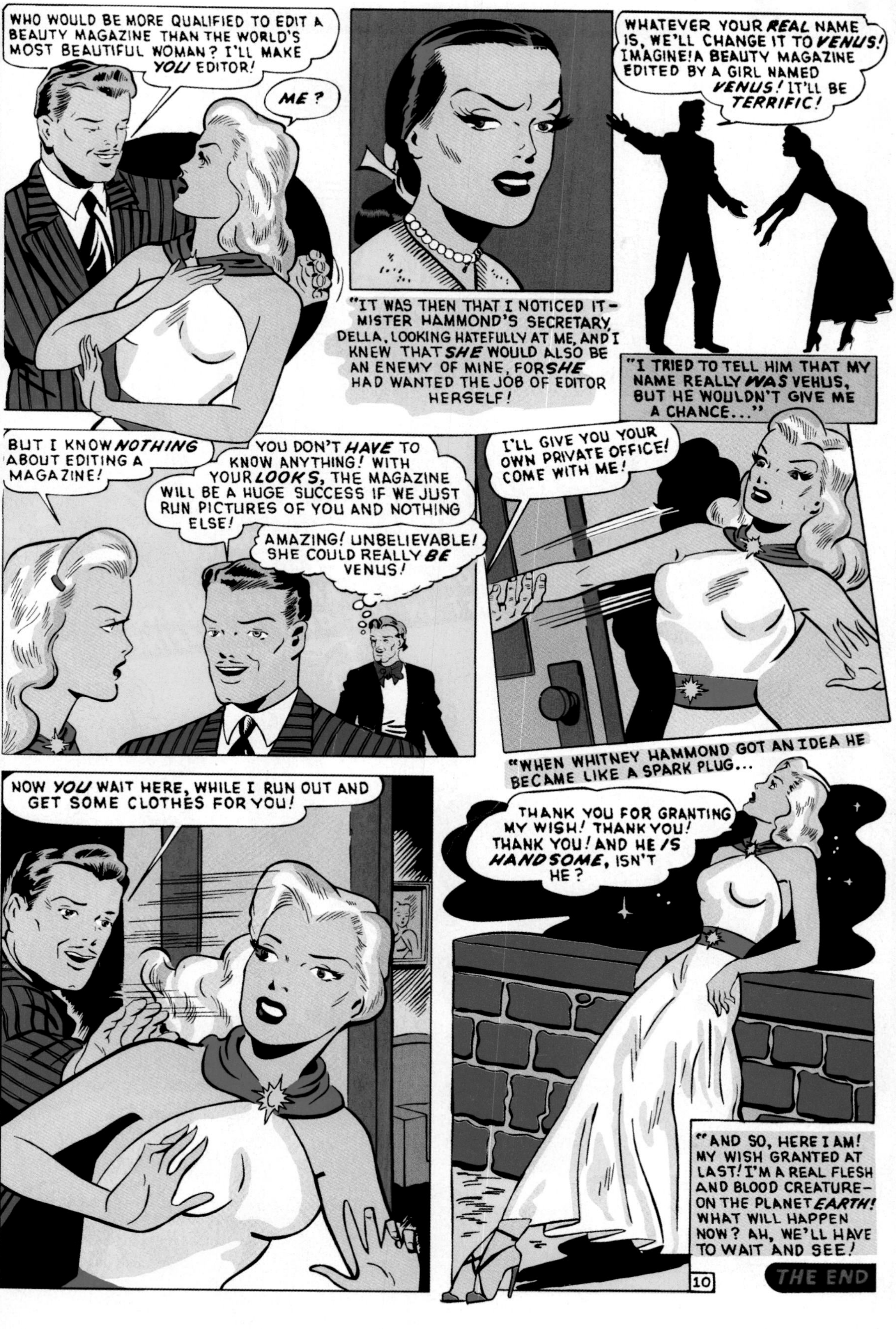

WHO WOULD BE MORE QUALIFIED TO EDIT A BEAUTY MAGAZINE THAN THE WORLD'S MOST BEAUTIFUL WOMAN? I'LL MAKE YOU EDITOR!
ME?
"IT WAS THEN THAT I NOTICED IT — MISTER HAMMOND'S SECRETARY, DELLA, LOOKING HATEFULLY AT ME, AND I KNEW THAT SHE WOULD ALSO BE AN ENEMY OF MINE, FOR SHE HAD WANTED THE JOB OF EDITOR HERSELF!
WHATEVER YOUR REAL NAME IS, WE'LL CHANGE IT TO VENUS! IMAGINE! A BEAUTY MAGAZINE EDITED BY A GIRL NAMED VENUS! IT'LL BE TERRIFIC!
"I TRIED TO TELL HIM THAT MY NAME REALLY WAS VENUS, BUT HE WOULDN'T GIVE ME A CHANCE..."
BUT I KNOW NOTHING ABOUT EDITING A MAGAZINE!
YOU DON'T HAVE TO KNOW ANYTHING! WITH YOUR LOOKS, THE MAGAZINE WILL BE A HUGE SUCCESS IF WE JUST RUN PICTURES OF YOU AND NOTHING ELSE!
AMAZING! UNBELIEVABLE! SHE COULD REALLY BE VENUS!
I'LL GIVE YOU YOUR OWN PRIVATE OFFICE! COME WITH ME!
NOW YOU WAIT HERE, WHILE I RUN OUT AND GET SOME CLOTHES FOR YOU!
"WHEN WHITNEY HAMMOND GOT AN IDEA HE BECAME LIKE A SPARK PLUG...
THANK YOU FOR GRANTING MY WISH! THANK YOU! THANK YOU! AND HE IS HANDSOME, ISN'T HE?
"AND SO, HERE I AM! MY WISH GRANTED AT LAST! I'M A REAL FLESH AND BLOOD CREATURE — ON THE PLANET EARTH! WHAT WILL HAPPEN NOW? AH, WE'LL HAVE TO WAIT AND SEE!
10
THE END

MARVEL BOY #1 (DECEMBER 1950) THE FIRST APPEARANCE OF MARVEL BOY

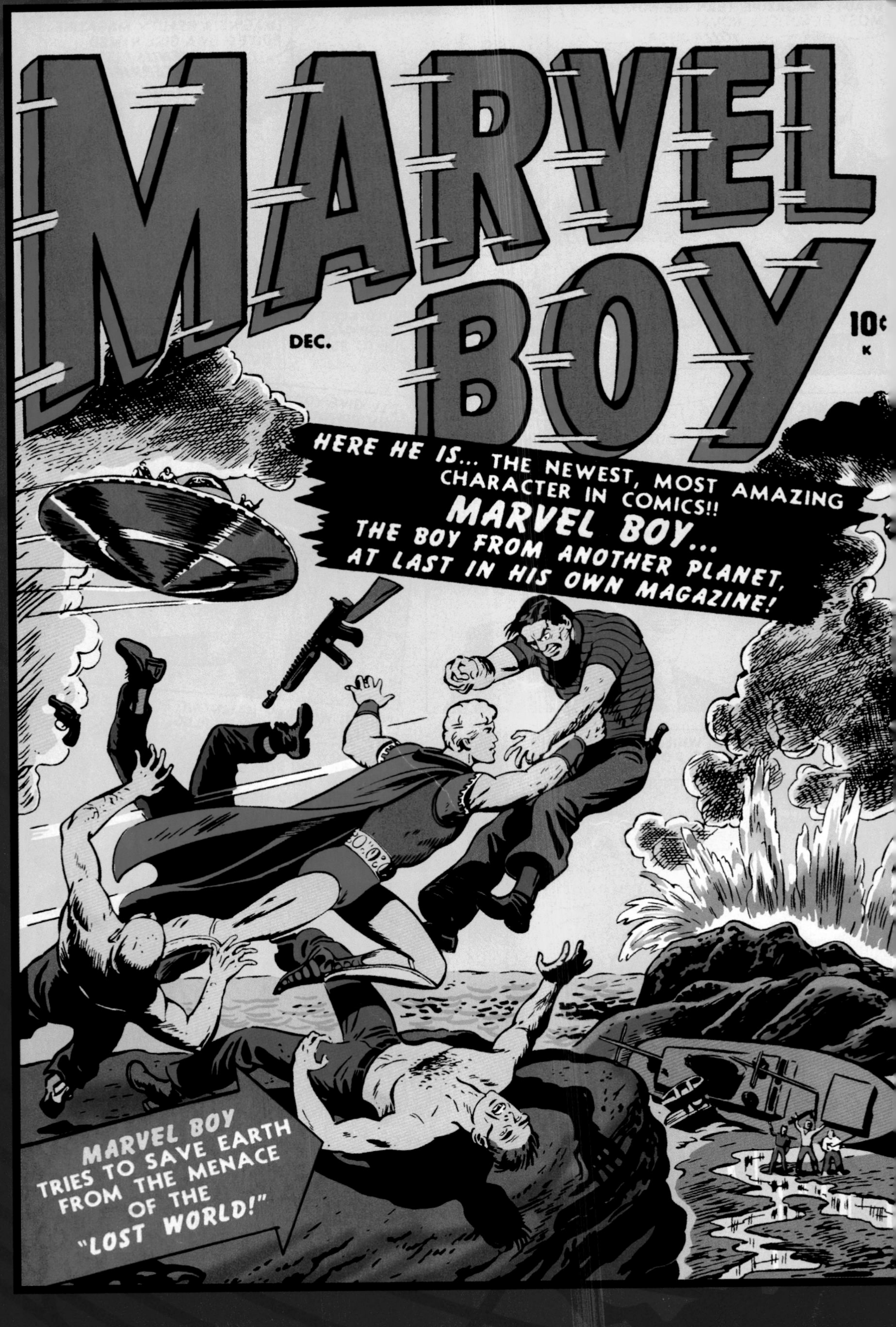

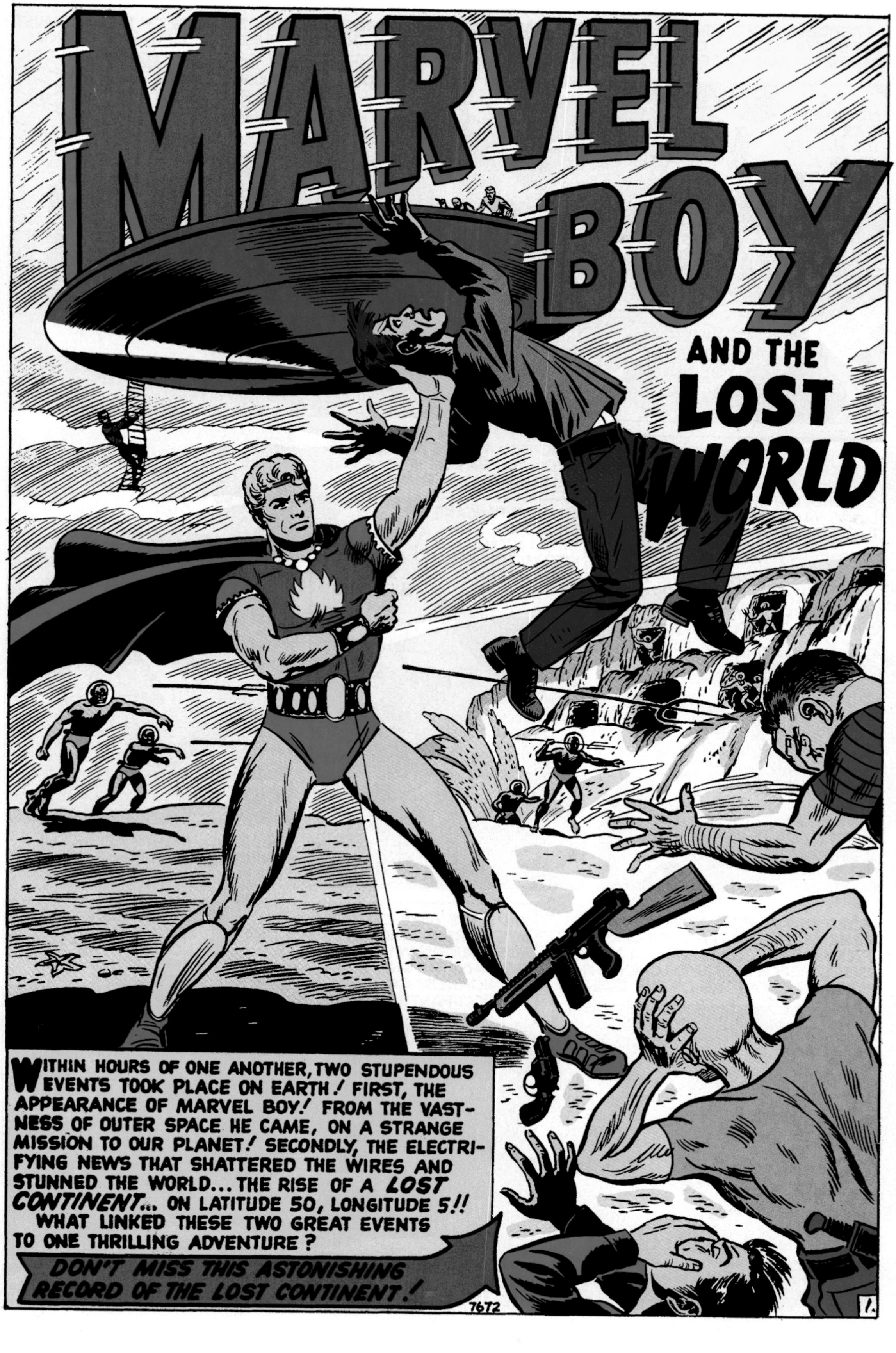
MARVEL BOY
AND THE LOST WORLD
WITHIN HOURS OF ONE ANOTHER, TWO STUPENDOUS EVENTS TOOK PLACE ON EARTH! FIRST, THE APPEARANCE OF MARVEL BOY! FROM THE VASTNESS OF OUTER SPACE HE CAME, ON A STRANGE MISSION TO OUR PLANET! SECONDLY, THE ELECTRIFYING NEWS THAT SHATTERED THE WIRES AND STUNNED THE WORLD... THE RISE OF A *LOST CONTINENT*... ON LATITUDE 50, LONGITUDE 5!! WHAT LINKED THESE TWO GREAT EVENTS TO ONE THRILLING ADVENTURE?
DON'T MISS THIS ASTONISHING RECORD OF THE LOST CONTINENT!
7672
1.

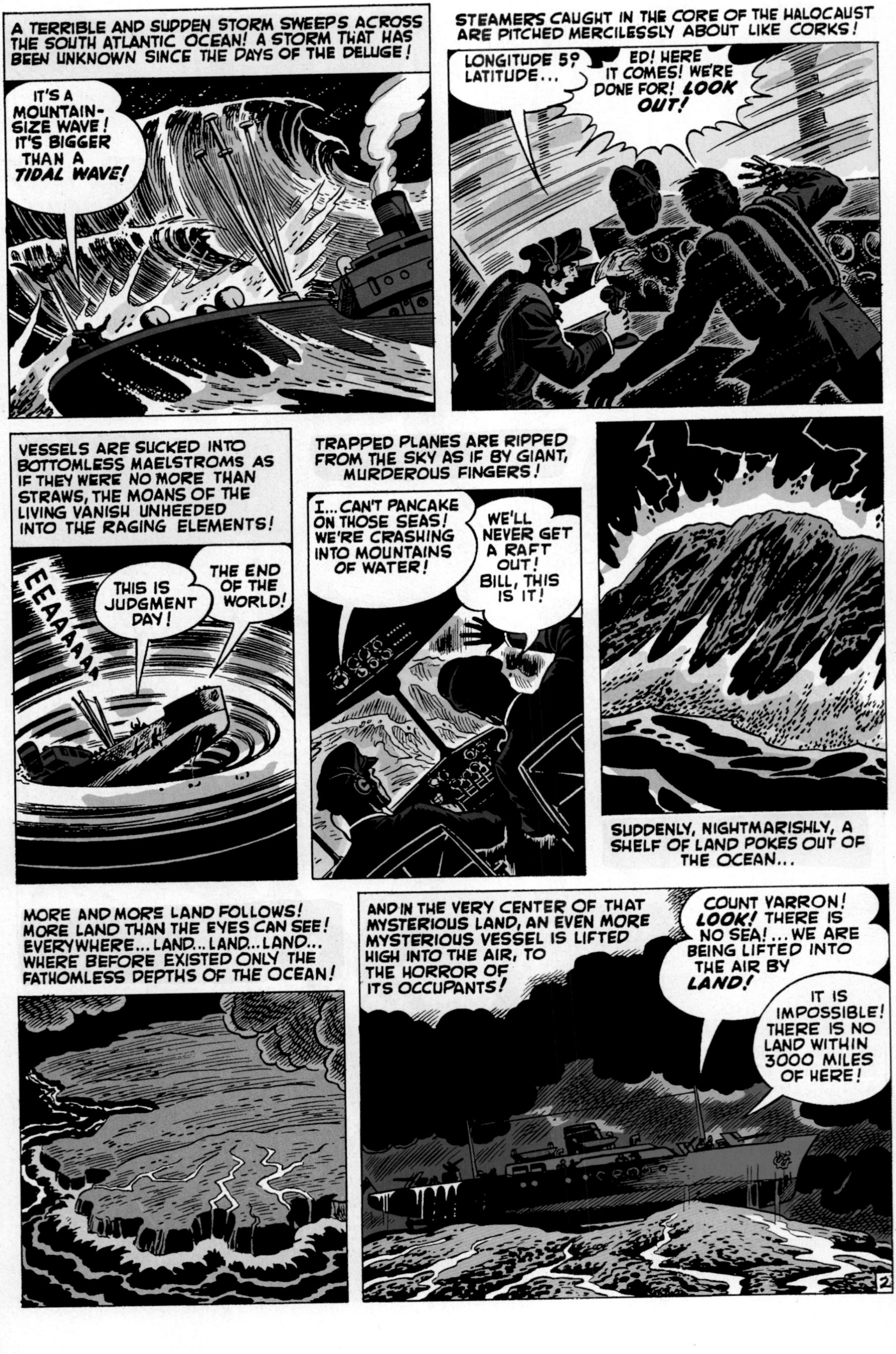
A TERRIBLE AND SUDDEN STORM SWEEPS ACROSS THE SOUTH ATLANTIC OCEAN! A STORM THAT HAS BEEN UNKNOWN SINCE THE DAYS OF THE DELUGE!
IT'S A MOUNTAIN-SIZE WAVE! IT'S BIGGER THAN A TIDAL WAVE!
STEAMERS CAUGHT IN THE CORE OF THE HALOCAUST ARE PITCHED MERCILESSLY ABOUT LIKE CORKS!
LONGITUDE 59, LATITUDE...
ED! HERE IT COMES! WE'RE DONE FOR! LOOK OUT!
VESSELS ARE SUCKED INTO BOTTOMLESS MAELSTROMS AS IF THEY WERE NO MORE THAN STRAWS, THE MOANS OF THE LIVING VANISH UNHEEDED INTO THE RAGING ELEMENTS!
EEAAAAAA
THIS IS JUDGMENT DAY!
THE END OF THE WORLD!
TRAPPED PLANES ARE RIPPED FROM THE SKY AS IF BY GIANT, MURDEROUS FINGERS!
I... CAN'T PANCAKE ON THOSE SEAS! WE'RE CRASHING INTO MOUNTAINS OF WATER!
WE'LL NEVER GET A RAFT OUT! BILL, THIS IS IT!
SUDDENLY, NIGHTMARISHLY, A SHELF OF LAND POKES OUT OF THE OCEAN...
MORE AND MORE LAND FOLLOWS! MORE LAND THAN THE EYES CAN SEE! EVERYWHERE... LAND... LAND... LAND... WHERE BEFORE EXISTED ONLY THE FATHOMLESS DEPTHS OF THE OCEAN!
AND IN THE VERY CENTER OF THAT MYSTERIOUS LAND, AN EVEN MORE MYSTERIOUS VESSEL IS LIFTED HIGH INTO THE AIR, TO THE HORROR OF ITS OCCUPANTS!
COUNT VARRON! LOOK! THERE IS NO SEA! ... WE ARE BEING LIFTED INTO THE AIR BY LAND!
IT IS IMPOSSIBLE! THERE IS NO LAND WITHIN 3000 MILES OF HERE!
2

BUT IT IS LAND! WE'RE *AGROUND!* AGROUND ON *WHAT?* GREAT SCOTT! WHAT COULD HAVE *HAPPENED* HERE?

ALL OVER THE WORLD THE SAME QUESTION IS RAISED IN SHRIEKS OF HORROR—IN WHISPERS OF AWE—WHAT IS HAPPENING? WHERE ARE THE TIDAL WAVES COMING FROM?

WHAT ARE THESE EARTH TREMORS AND EARTHQUAKES? WHAT IS MOVING THE CRUST OF THE EARTH?—SMASHING BUILDINGS? SNATCHING LIVES?

THE ANSWER IS PLAINLY REVEALED IN THE WILDLY-- JERKING INDICATORS OF A THOUSAND SEISMOGRAPHS!

LONGITUDE 5, LATITUDE 50! A NEW CONTINENT HAS ARISEN!

A NEW CONTINENT?? A SEVENTH ONE?!!

MORE STARTLING STILL ARE THE IMPLICATIONS OF THE PHENOMENON! ALL OVER THE WORLD, THE RACE IS ON TO BE THE FIRST TO REACH THE NEW LAND! THE LAND BELONGS TO THE COUNTRY THAT DISCOVERS IT FIRST! INTERNATIONAL LAW STATES THAT THE COUNTRY THAT DISCOVERS IT FIRST SHALL HAVE THE RIGHTS OF EXPLORATION... AND WAITING THERE, WITHOUT...

...A SIGN OF LIFE ON ITS BROAD EXPANSE, LIES THE SEVENTH CONTINENT! WHAT RICHES LIE IN ITS BOWELS? WHAT OIL? WHAT ORE? WHAT POSSIBILITIES FOR COLONIZATION? OF WHAT USE AS A MILITARY AIR BASE?

AS THOUGH SYMBOLIZING THE GREED AND POWER-LUST OF THIS MAD EARTH, ONE MAN ALONE SEES THE PICTURE IN ALL ITS FACETS...COUNT VARRON, KING OF CRIME, LORD OF ROGUES, AND NOW, SUDDENLY, *MAN WITHOUT A COUNTRY!*

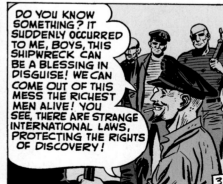

DO YOU KNOW SOMETHING? IT SUDDENLY OCCURRED TO ME, BOYS, THIS SHIPWRECK CAN BE A BLESSING IN DISGUISE! WE CAN COME OUT OF THIS MESS THE RICHEST MEN ALIVE! YOU SEE, THERE ARE STRANGE INTERNATIONAL LAWS, PROTECTING THE RIGHTS OF DISCOVERY!

3

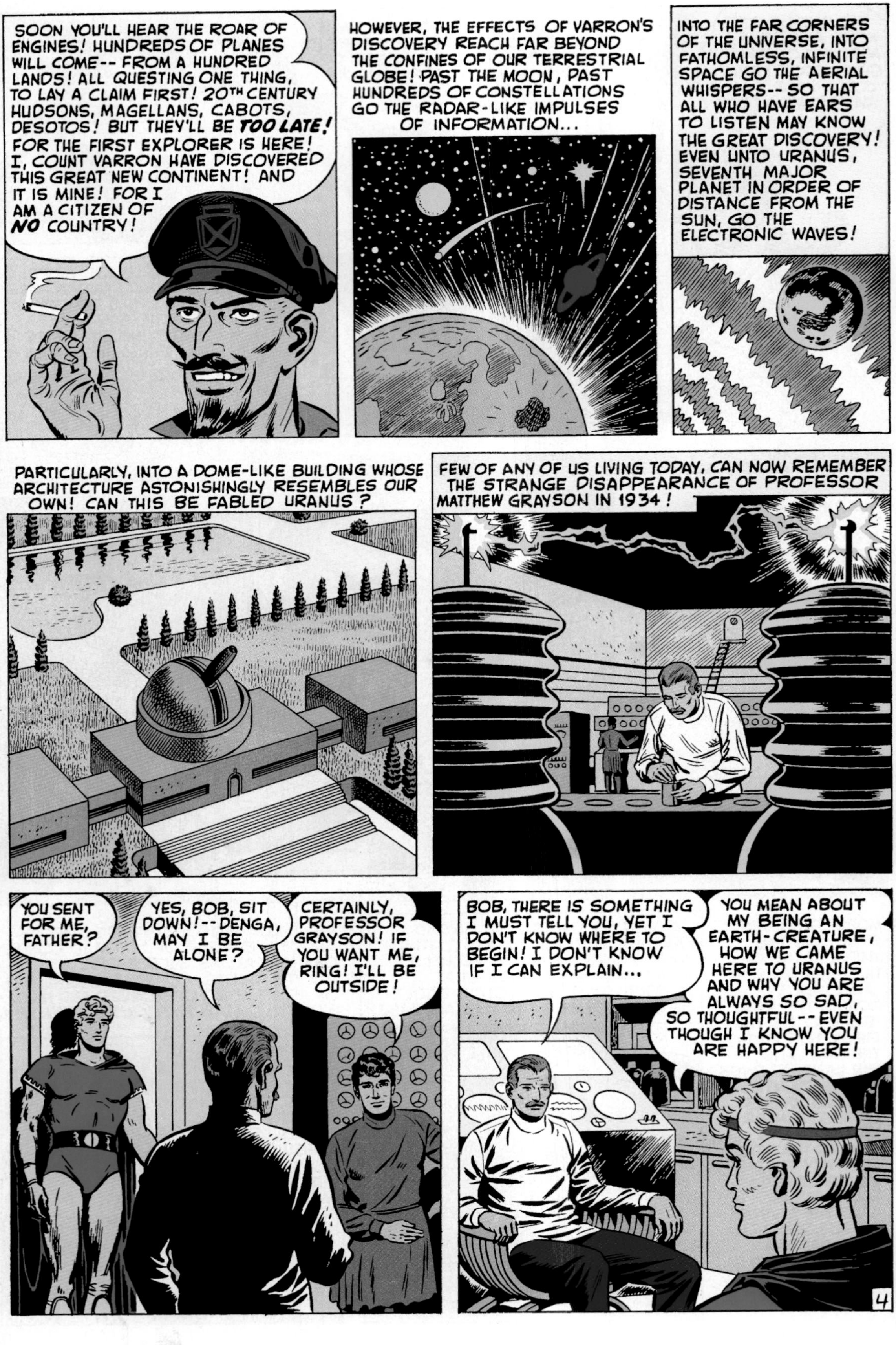
SOON YOU'LL HEAR THE ROAR OF ENGINES! HUNDREDS OF PLANES WILL COME-- FROM A HUNDRED LANDS! ALL QUESTING ONE THING, TO LAY A CLAIM FIRST! 20TH CENTURY HUDSONS, MAGELLANS, CABOTS, DESOTOS! BUT THEY'LL BE TOO LATE! FOR THE FIRST EXPLORER IS HERE! I, COUNT VARRON HAVE DISCOVERED THIS GREAT NEW CONTINENT! AND IT IS MINE! FOR I AM A CITIZEN OF NO COUNTRY!
HOWEVER, THE EFFECTS OF VARRON'S DISCOVERY REACH FAR BEYOND THE CONFINES OF OUR TERRESTRIAL GLOBE! PAST THE MOON, PAST HUNDREDS OF CONSTELLATIONS GO THE RADAR-LIKE IMPULSES OF INFORMATION...
INTO THE FAR CORNERS OF THE UNIVERSE, INTO FATHOMLESS, INFINITE SPACE GO THE AERIAL WHISPERS-- SO THAT ALL WHO HAVE EARS TO LISTEN MAY KNOW THE GREAT DISCOVERY! EVEN UNTO URANUS, SEVENTH MAJOR PLANET IN ORDER OF DISTANCE FROM THE SUN, GO THE ELECTRONIC WAVES!
PARTICULARLY, INTO A DOME-LIKE BUILDING WHOSE ARCHITECTURE ASTONISHINGLY RESEMBLES OUR OWN! CAN THIS BE FABLED URANUS?
FEW OF ANY OF US LIVING TODAY, CAN NOW REMEMBER THE STRANGE DISAPPEARANCE OF PROFESSOR MATTHEW GRAYSON IN 1934!
YOU SENT FOR ME, FATHER?
YES, BOB, SIT DOWN!--DENGA, MAY I BE ALONE?
CERTAINLY, PROFESSOR GRAYSON! IF YOU WANT ME, RING! I'LL BE OUTSIDE!
BOB, THERE IS SOMETHING I MUST TELL YOU, YET I DON'T KNOW WHERE TO BEGIN! I DON'T KNOW IF I CAN EXPLAIN...
YOU MEAN ABOUT MY BEING AN EARTH-CREATURE, HOW WE CAME HERE TO URANUS AND WHY YOU ARE ALWAYS SO SAD, SO THOUGHTFUL-- EVEN THOUGH I KNOW YOU ARE HAPPY HERE!
4

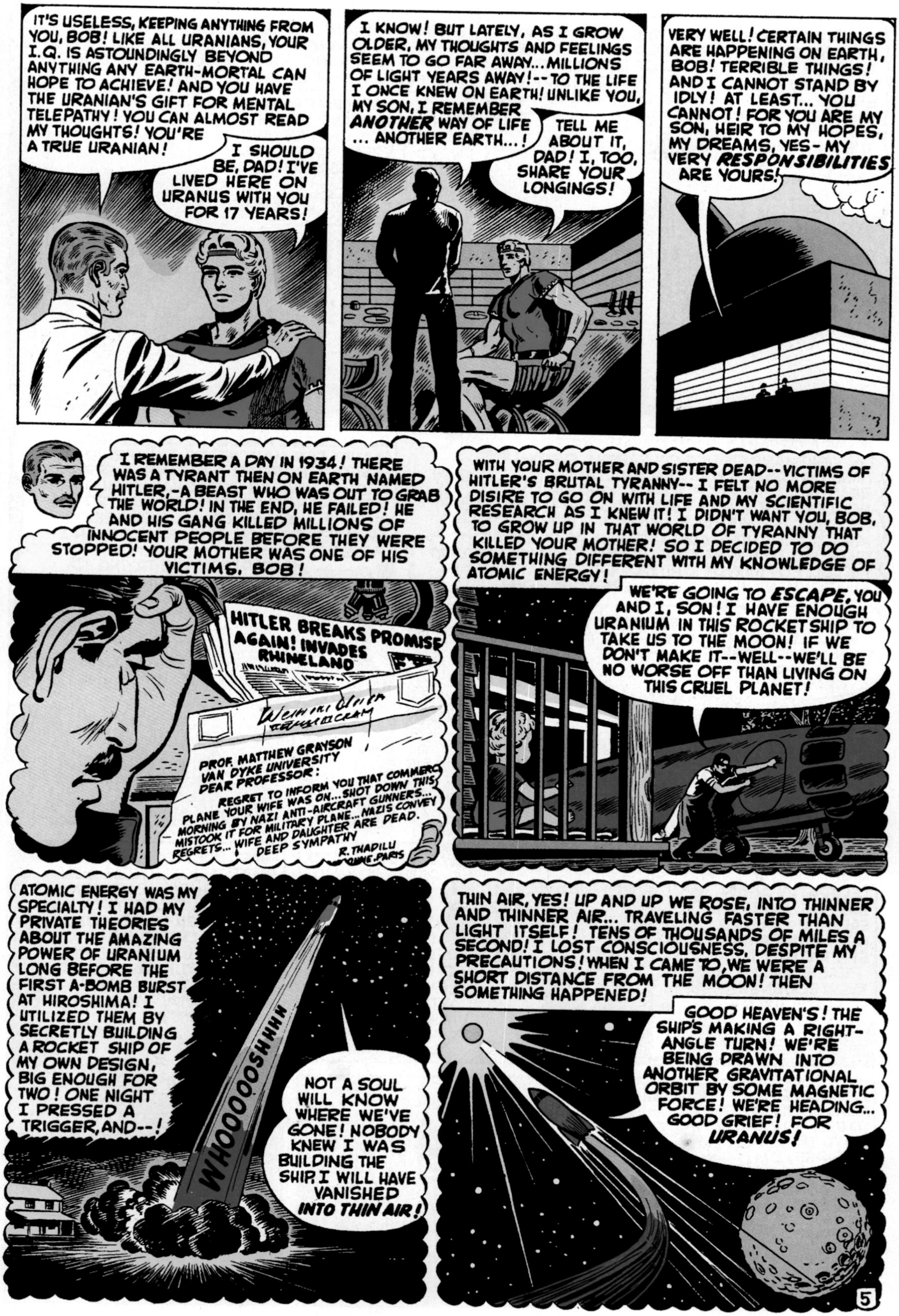
IT'S USELESS, KEEPING ANYTHING FROM YOU, BOB! LIKE ALL URANIANS, YOUR I.Q. IS ASTOUNDINGLY BEYOND ANYTHING ANY EARTH-MORTAL CAN HOPE TO ACHIEVE! AND YOU HAVE THE URANIAN'S GIFT FOR MENTAL TELEPATHY! YOU CAN ALMOST READ MY THOUGHTS! YOU'RE A TRUE URANIAN!
I SHOULD BE, DAD! I'VE LIVED HERE ON URANUS WITH YOU FOR 17 YEARS!
I KNOW! BUT LATELY, AS I GROW OLDER, MY THOUGHTS AND FEELINGS SEEM TO GO FAR AWAY... MILLIONS OF LIGHT YEARS AWAY!--TO THE LIFE I ONCE KNEW ON EARTH! UNLIKE YOU, MY SON, I REMEMBER ANOTHER WAY OF LIFE ... ANOTHER EARTH...!
TELL ME ABOUT IT, DAD! I, TOO, SHARE YOUR LONGINGS!
VERY WELL! CERTAIN THINGS ARE HAPPENING ON EARTH, BOB! TERRIBLE THINGS! AND I CANNOT STAND BY IDLY! AT LEAST... YOU CANNOT! FOR YOU ARE MY SON, HEIR TO MY HOPES, MY DREAMS, YES- MY VERY RESPONSIBILITIES ARE YOURS!
I REMEMBER A DAY IN 1934! THERE WAS A TYRANT THEN ON EARTH NAMED HITLER,-A BEAST WHO WAS OUT TO GRAB THE WORLD! IN THE END, HE FAILED! HE AND HIS GANG KILLED MILLIONS OF INNOCENT PEOPLE BEFORE THEY WERE STOPPED! YOUR MOTHER WAS ONE OF HIS VICTIMS, BOB!
HITLER BREAKS PROMISE AGAIN! INVADES RHINELAND
PROF. MATTHEW GRAYSON VAN DYKE UNIVERSITY DEAR PROFESSOR:
REGRET TO INFORM YOU THAT COMMERC PLANE YOUR WIFE WAS ON...SHOT DOWN THIS MORNING BY NAZI ANTI-AIRCRAFT GUNNERS... MISTOOK IT FOR MILITARY PLANE...NAZIS CONVEY REGRETS... WIFE AND DAUGHTER ARE DEAD. DEEP SYMPATHY
R. THADILU
WITH YOUR MOTHER AND SISTER DEAD--VICTIMS OF HITLER'S BRUTAL TYRANNY-- I FELT NO MORE DISIRE TO GO ON WITH LIFE AND MY SCIENTIFIC RESEARCH AS I KNEW IT! I DIDN'T WANT YOU, BOB, TO GROW UP IN THAT WORLD OF TYRANNY THAT KILLED YOUR MOTHER! SO I DECIDED TO DO SOMETHING DIFFERENT WITH MY KNOWLEDGE OF ATOMIC ENERGY!
WE'RE GOING TO ESCAPE, YOU AND I, SON! I HAVE ENOUGH URANIUM IN THIS ROCKET SHIP TO TAKE US TO THE MOON! IF WE DON'T MAKE IT--WELL--WE'LL BE NO WORSE OFF THAN LIVING ON THIS CRUEL PLANET!
ATOMIC ENERGY WAS MY SPECIALTY! I HAD MY PRIVATE THEORIES ABOUT THE AMAZING POWER OF URANIUM LONG BEFORE THE FIRST A-BOMB BURST AT HIROSHIMA! I UTILIZED THEM BY SECRETLY BUILDING A ROCKET SHIP OF MY OWN DESIGN, BIG ENOUGH FOR TWO! ONE NIGHT I PRESSED A TRIGGER, AND--!
WHOOOOOSHHHH
NOT A SOUL WILL KNOW WHERE WE'VE GONE! NOBODY KNEW I WAS BUILDING THE SHIP. I WILL HAVE VANISHED INTO THIN AIR!
THIN AIR, YES! UP AND UP WE ROSE, INTO THINNER AND THINNER AIR... TRAVELING FASTER THAN LIGHT ITSELF! TENS OF THOUSANDS OF MILES A SECOND! I LOST CONSCIOUSNESS, DESPITE MY PRECAUTIONS! WHEN I CAME TO, WE WERE A SHORT DISTANCE FROM THE MOON! THEN SOMETHING HAPPENED!
GOOD HEAVEN'S! THE SHIP'S MAKING A RIGHT-ANGLE TURN! WE'RE BEING DRAWN INTO ANOTHER GRAVITATIONAL ORBIT BY SOME MAGNETIC FORCE! WE'RE HEADING... GOOD GRIEF! FOR URANUS!
5

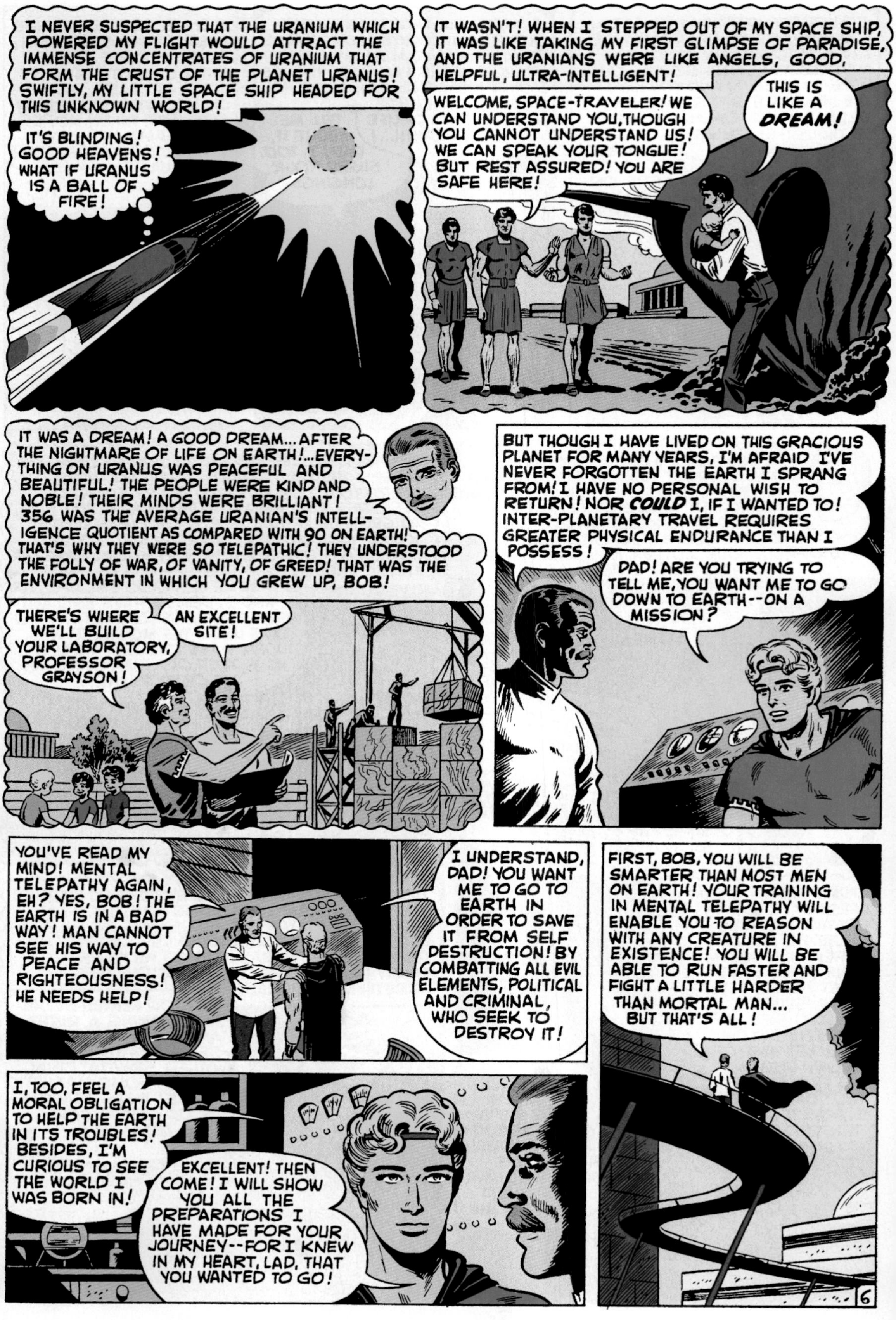
I NEVER SUSPECTED THAT THE URANIUM WHICH POWERED MY FLIGHT WOULD ATTRACT THE IMMENSE CONCENTRATES OF URANIUM THAT FORM THE CRUST OF THE PLANET URANUS! SWIFTLY, MY LITTLE SPACE SHIP HEADED FOR THIS UNKNOWN WORLD!
IT'S BLINDING! GOOD HEAVENS! WHAT IF URANUS IS A BALL OF FIRE!
IT WASN'T! WHEN I STEPPED OUT OF MY SPACE SHIP, IT WAS LIKE TAKING MY FIRST GLIMPSE OF PARADISE, AND THE URANIANS WERE LIKE ANGELS, GOOD, HELPFUL, ULTRA-INTELLIGENT!
WELCOME, SPACE-TRAVELER! WE CAN UNDERSTAND YOU, THOUGH YOU CANNOT UNDERSTAND US! WE CAN SPEAK YOUR TONGUE! BUT REST ASSURED! YOU ARE SAFE HERE!
THIS IS LIKE A DREAM!
IT WAS A DREAM! A GOOD DREAM... AFTER THE NIGHTMARE OF LIFE ON EARTH!...EVERYTHING ON URANUS WAS PEACEFUL AND BEAUTIFUL! THE PEOPLE WERE KIND AND NOBLE! THEIR MINDS WERE BRILLIANT! 356 WAS THE AVERAGE URANIAN'S INTELLIGENCE QUOTIENT AS COMPARED WITH 90 ON EARTH! THAT'S WHY THEY WERE SO TELEPATHIC! THEY UNDERSTOOD THE FOLLY OF WAR, OF VANITY, OF GREED! THAT WAS THE ENVIRONMENT IN WHICH YOU GREW UP, BOB!
THERE'S WHERE WE'LL BUILD YOUR LABORATORY, PROFESSOR GRAYSON!
AN EXCELLENT SITE!
BUT THOUGH I HAVE LIVED ON THIS GRACIOUS PLANET FOR MANY YEARS, I'M AFRAID I'VE NEVER FORGOTTEN THE EARTH I SPRANG FROM! I HAVE NO PERSONAL WISH TO RETURN! NOR COULD I, IF I WANTED TO! INTER-PLANETARY TRAVEL REQUIRES GREATER PHYSICAL ENDURANCE THAN I POSSESS!
DAD! ARE YOU TRYING TO TELL ME, YOU WANT ME TO GO DOWN TO EARTH--ON A MISSION?
YOU'VE READ MY MIND! MENTAL TELEPATHY AGAIN, EH? YES, BOB! THE EARTH IS IN A BAD WAY! MAN CANNOT SEE HIS WAY TO PEACE AND RIGHTEOUSNESS! HE NEEDS HELP!
I UNDERSTAND, DAD! YOU WANT ME TO GO TO EARTH IN ORDER TO SAVE IT FROM SELF DESTRUCTION! BY COMBATTING ALL EVIL ELEMENTS, POLITICAL AND CRIMINAL, WHO SEEK TO DESTROY IT!
FIRST, BOB, YOU WILL BE SMARTER THAN MOST MEN ON EARTH! YOUR TRAINING IN MENTAL TELEPATHY WILL ENABLE YOU TO REASON WITH ANY CREATURE IN EXISTENCE! YOU WILL BE ABLE TO RUN FASTER AND FIGHT A LITTLE HARDER THAN MORTAL MAN... BUT THAT'S ALL!
I, TOO, FEEL A MORAL OBLIGATION TO HELP THE EARTH IN ITS TROUBLES! BESIDES, I'M CURIOUS TO SEE THE WORLD I WAS BORN IN!
EXCELLENT! THEN COME! I WILL SHOW YOU ALL THE PREPARATIONS I HAVE MADE FOR YOUR JOURNEY--FOR I KNEW IN MY HEART, LAD, THAT YOU WANTED TO GO!
6

WHEN YOU GET TO EARTH, THE DIFFERENCE IN ATMOSPHERE WILL LEAVE YOU *WEAKER* THAN ANY MORTAL MAN! TO PREVENT THE LOSS OF YOUR POWERS, YOU MUST TAKE ONE OF THESE PILLS EVERY 24 HOURS! WITHOUT THESE PILLS YOU MAY EVEN DIE!

I'LL ATTACH THEM TO MY BELT, WHERE I WON'T LOSE THEM!

THIS LARGE JEWEL WILL FIRE A BEAM OF LIGHT THAT WILL TEMPORARILY BLIND YOUR ENEMY! IT CAN'T KILL! YOU MUST NOT KILL, BOB, EXCEPT IN DEFENCE OF INNOCENT LIFE!

I UNDERSTAND, FATHER! WHAT A DAZZLING LIGHT! I WOULDN'T WANT TO FACE IT!

AND HERE'S YOUR UNIFORM, BOB! PUT IT ON INSIDE!

YOU LOOK MARVELOUS, BOB! NOW TO YOUR SPACE SHIP! THIS WAY!

THIS FLYING SAUCER SPACE SHIP WILL TAKE YOU ACROSS THE INTER-PLANETARY VOID IN A MATTER OF HOURS! ACROSS EARTH IN A FEW SECONDS! IT'S POWERED BY A SPECIALLY DEVELOPED, HYDROGEN-URANIUM COMPOUND THAT'S INEXHAUSTIBLE!

I'M SPEECHLESS, DAD! IT'S WONDERFUL!

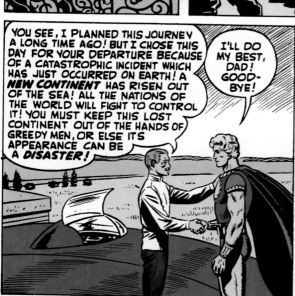

YOU SEE, I PLANNED THIS JOURNEY A LONG TIME AGO! BUT I CHOSE THIS DAY FOR YOUR DEPARTURE BECAUSE OF A CATASTROPHIC INCIDENT WHICH HAS JUST OCCURRED ON EARTH! A *NEW CONTINENT* HAS RISEN OUT OF THE SEA! ALL THE NATIONS OF THE WORLD WILL FIGHT TO CONTROL IT! YOU MUST KEEP THIS LOST CONTINENT OUT OF THE HANDS OF GREEDY MEN, OR ELSE ITS APPEARANCE CAN BE A *DISASTER!*

I'LL DO MY BEST, DAD! GOOD-BYE!

WITH A SOUND NO LOUDER THAN THE RUSTLE OF SILK, THE SPACE SHIP WHIRLS FURIOUSLY INTO THE AIR!

DON'T WORRY, PROFESSOR, HE'LL SUCCEED!

YES, DENGA, FOR HE IS A BORN HELPER OF HUMANITY! ....A *MARVEL BOY.*

7

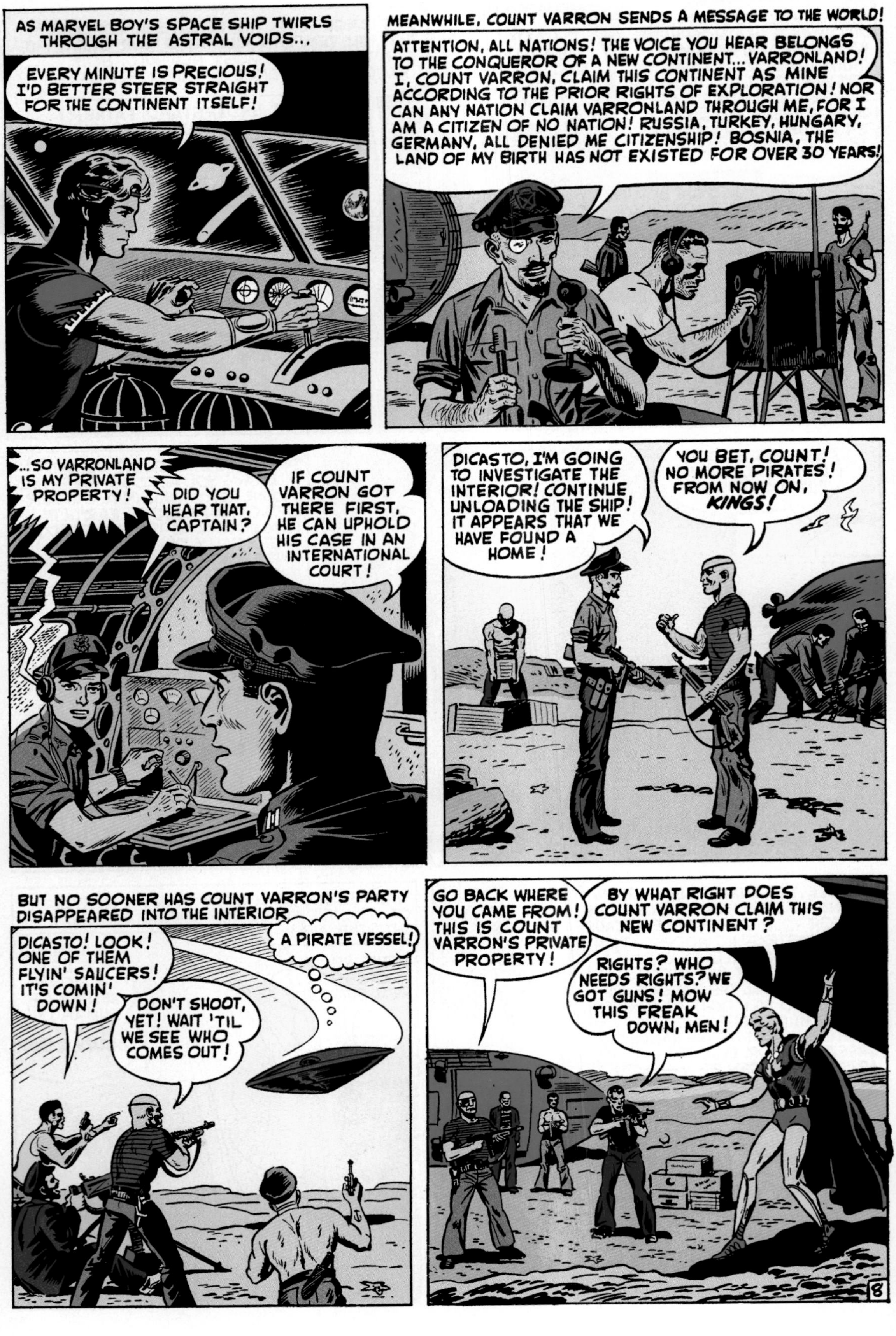

AS MARVEL BOY'S SPACE SHIP TWIRLS THROUGH THE ASTRAL VOIDS...
EVERY MINUTE IS PRECIOUS! I'D BETTER STEER STRAIGHT FOR THE CONTINENT ITSELF!
MEANWHILE, COUNT VARRON SENDS A MESSAGE TO THE WORLD!
ATTENTION, ALL NATIONS! THE VOICE YOU HEAR BELONGS TO THE CONQUEROR OF A NEW CONTINENT... VARRONLAND! I, COUNT VARRON, CLAIM THIS CONTINENT AS MINE ACCORDING TO THE PRIOR RIGHTS OF EXPLORATION! NOR CAN ANY NATION CLAIM VARRONLAND THROUGH ME, FOR I AM A CITIZEN OF NO NATION! RUSSIA, TURKEY, HUNGARY, GERMANY, ALL DENIED ME CITIZENSHIP! BOSNIA, THE LAND OF MY BIRTH HAS NOT EXISTED FOR OVER 30 YEARS!
...SO VARRONLAND IS MY PRIVATE PROPERTY!
DID YOU HEAR THAT, CAPTAIN?
IF COUNT VARRON GOT THERE FIRST, HE CAN UPHOLD HIS CASE IN AN INTERNATIONAL COURT!
DICASTO, I'M GOING TO INVESTIGATE THE INTERIOR! CONTINUE UNLOADING THE SHIP! IT APPEARS THAT WE HAVE FOUND A HOME!
YOU BET, COUNT! NO MORE PIRATES! FROM NOW ON, KINGS!
BUT NO SOONER HAS COUNT VARRON'S PARTY DISAPPEARED INTO THE INTERIOR
A PIRATE VESSEL!
DICASTO! LOOK! ONE OF THEM FLYIN' SAUCERS! IT'S COMIN' DOWN!
DON'T SHOOT, YET! WAIT 'TIL WE SEE WHO COMES OUT!
GO BACK WHERE YOU CAME FROM! THIS IS COUNT VARRON'S PRIVATE PROPERTY!
BY WHAT RIGHT DOES COUNT VARRON CLAIM THIS NEW CONTINENT?
RIGHTS? WHO NEEDS RIGHTS? WE GOT GUNS! MOW THIS FREAK DOWN, MEN!
8

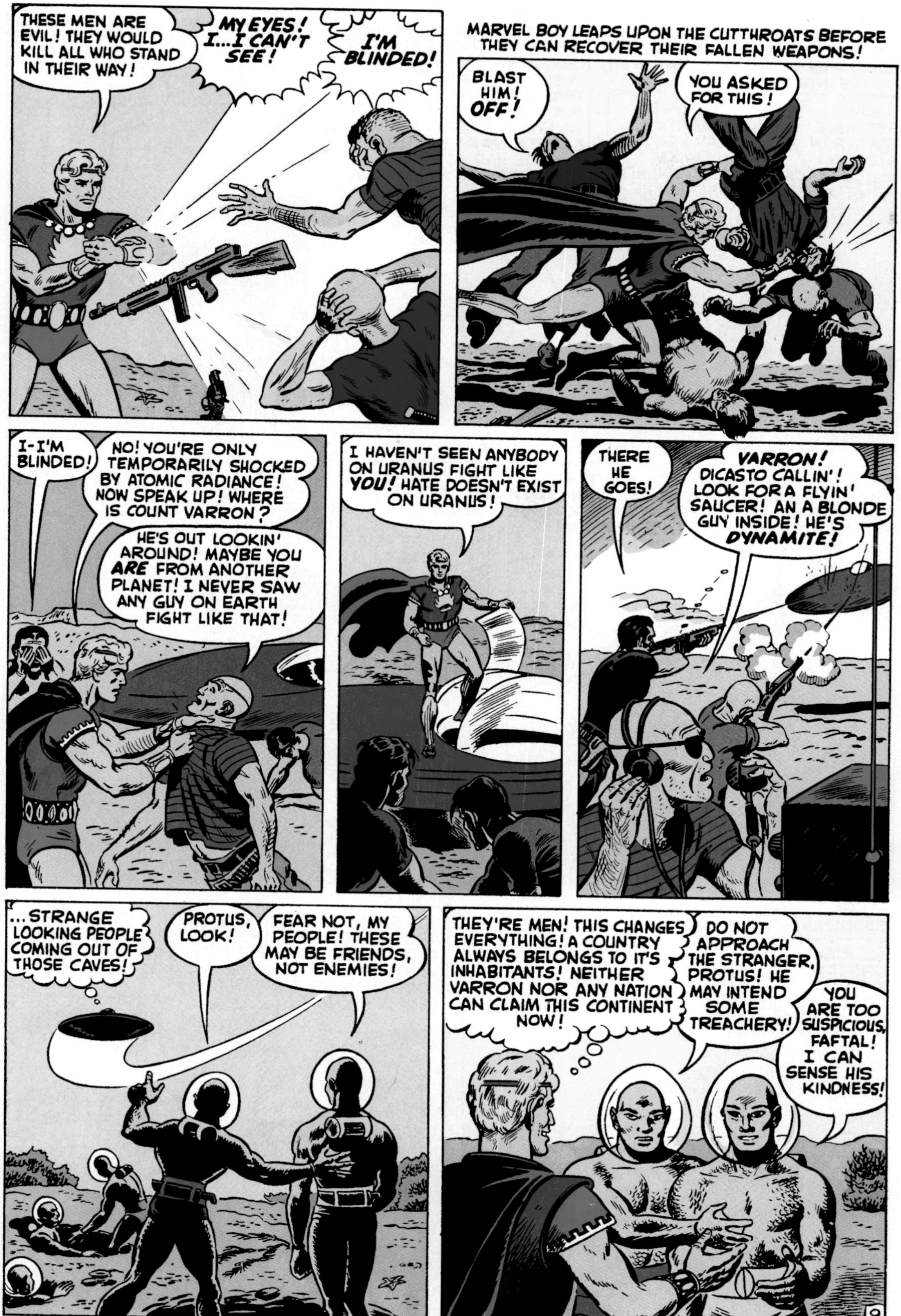
THESE MEN ARE EVIL! THEY WOULD KILL ALL WHO STAND IN THEIR WAY!
MY EYES! I...I CAN'T SEE!
I'M BLINDED!
MARVEL BOY LEAPS UPON THE CUTTHROATS BEFORE THEY CAN RECOVER THEIR FALLEN WEAPONS!
BLAST HIM! OFF!
YOU ASKED FOR THIS!
I-I'M BLINDED!
NO! YOU'RE ONLY TEMPORARILY SHOCKED BY ATOMIC RADIANCE! NOW SPEAK UP! WHERE IS COUNT VARRON?
HE'S OUT LOOKIN' AROUND! MAYBE YOU ARE FROM ANOTHER PLANET! I NEVER SAW ANY GUY ON EARTH FIGHT LIKE THAT!
I HAVEN'T SEEN ANYBODY ON URANUS FIGHT LIKE YOU! HATE DOESN'T EXIST ON URANUS!
THERE HE GOES!
VARRON! DICASTO CALLIN'! LOOK FOR A FLYIN' SAUCER! AN A BLONDE GUY INSIDE! HE'S DYNAMITE!
...STRANGE LOOKING PEOPLE COMING OUT OF THOSE CAVES!
PROTUS, LOOK!
FEAR NOT, MY PEOPLE! THESE MAY BE FRIENDS, NOT ENEMIES!
THEY'RE MEN! THIS CHANGES EVERYTHING! A COUNTRY ALWAYS BELONGS TO IT'S INHABITANTS! NEITHER VARRON NOR ANY NATION CAN CLAIM THIS CONTINENT NOW!
DO NOT APPROACH THE STRANGER, PROTUS! HE MAY INTEND SOME TREACHERY!
YOU ARE TOO SUSPICIOUS, FAFTAL! I CAN SENSE HIS KINDNESS!
9

ONCE AGAIN, MARVEL BOY'S STRONG TELEPATHIC POWERS ALLOW HIM TO CONVERSE FLUENTLY WITH THE STRANGERS...

YOU RESEMBLE EARTH MEN CLOSELY!

WE SHOULD! WE LIVED ON EARTH TILL 1200 YEARS AGO, AN EARTHQUAKE CAUSED OUR CONTINENT TO SINK BENEATH THE SEA! MILLIONS OF OUR PEOPLE DIED! WE ARE THE DESENDENTS OF A FEW SURVIVORS...

...THEY WERE TRAPPED IN AN UNDERWATER CAVE AND FOR CENTURIES BREATHED THRU A 300 FOOT FUNNEL THAT PROTRUDED ABOVE THE OCEAN! 500 YEARS AGO, A GREAT STORM TORE OFF THAT SOURCE OF AIR! BUT BY THAT TIME WE HAD ADAPTED OURSELVES TO SEA LIFE, AS YOU SEE!

LOOK, VARRON! DICASTO WASN'T CRAZY! THERE'S THE FLYIN' SAUCER!

GET DOWN! DON'T LET THEM SEE YOU! WHO THE DEVIL ARE THOSE GOOKS HE'S TALKING TO?

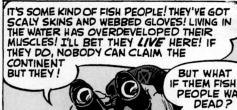

IT'S SOME KIND OF FISH PEOPLE! THEY'VE GOT SCALY SKINS AND WEBBED GLOVES! LIVING IN THE WATER HAS OVERDEVELOPED THEIR MUSCLES! I'LL BET THEY LIVE HERE! IF THEY DO, NOBODY CAN CLAIM THE CONTINENT BUT THEY!

BUT WHAT IF THEM FISH PEOPLE WAS DEAD?

MY CLAIM WOULD STILL HOLD GOOD! CLEVER, NICK! OF COURSE! THE BUMP-OFF'S THE ONLY WAY! WE'LL SURROUND THEM! WE MUSTN'T FAIL AS DICASTO DID!

THEY WON'T KNOW WHAT HIT 'EM!

SUDDENLY, WITHOUT WARNING!

ALL RIGHT! GIVE IT TO THEM! KILL 'EM ALL!

YEAAAAAA

YOU SEE HOW OUR PEOPLE DIE AROUND US! THIS COMES OF TRUSTING STRANGERS! THEY WANT NOT ONLY YOUR LAND, FOOLISH PROTUS, BUT OUR PEOPLE'S LIVES!

I CANNOT UNDERSTAND IT! RETREAT! BACK TO THE CAVES!

IT MUST BE VARRON!

10

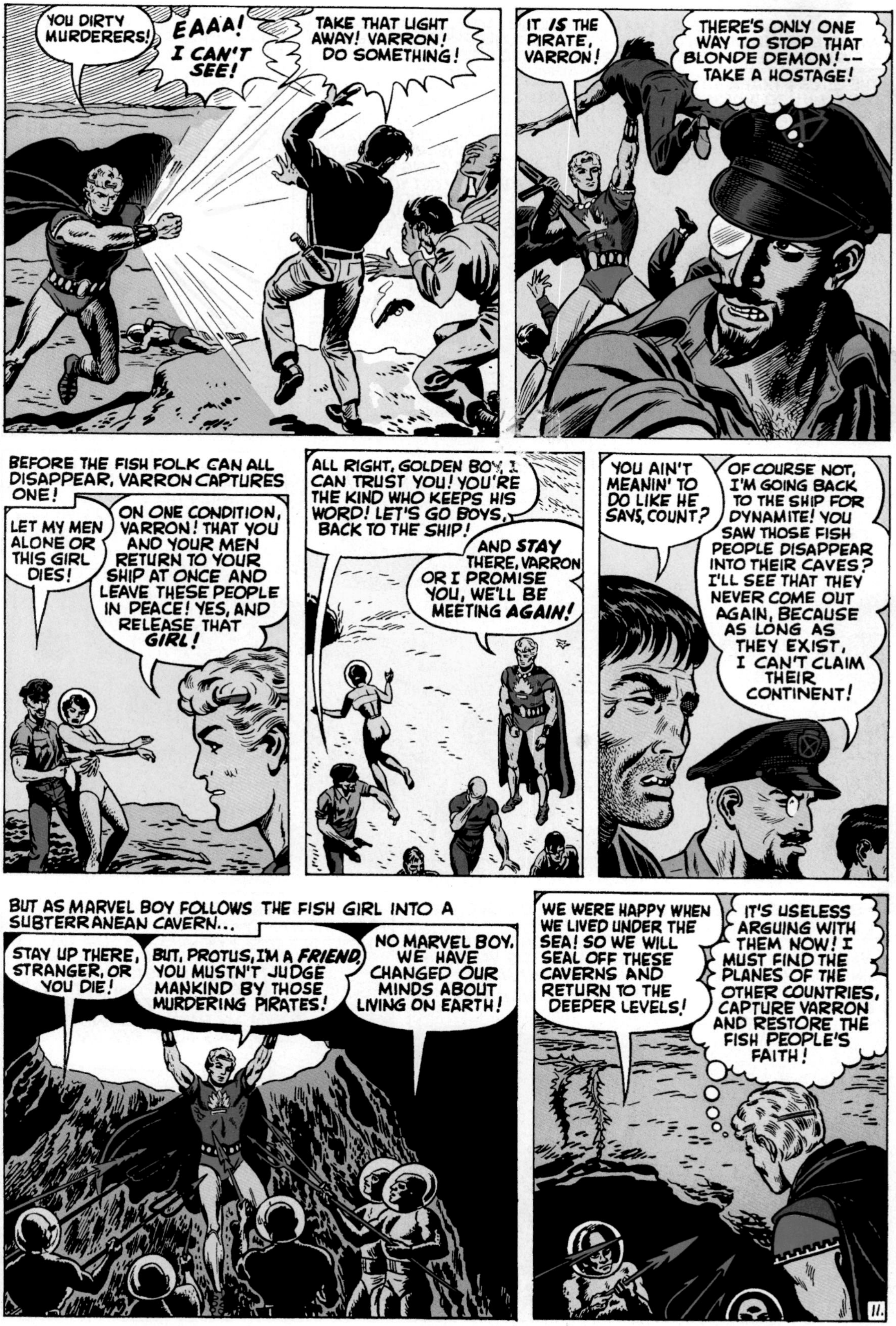

YOU DIRTY MURDERERS!
EAAA! I CAN'T SEE!
TAKE THAT LIGHT AWAY! VARRON! DO SOMETHING!
IT IS THE PIRATE, VARRON!
THERE'S ONLY ONE WAY TO STOP THAT BLONDE DEMON! -- TAKE A HOSTAGE!
BEFORE THE FISH FOLK CAN ALL DISAPPEAR, VARRON CAPTURES ONE!
LET MY MEN ALONE OR THIS GIRL DIES!
ON ONE CONDITION, VARRON! THAT YOU AND YOUR MEN RETURN TO YOUR SHIP AT ONCE AND LEAVE THESE PEOPLE IN PEACE! YES, AND RELEASE THAT GIRL!
ALL RIGHT, GOLDEN BOY, I CAN TRUST YOU! YOU'RE THE KIND WHO KEEPS HIS WORD! LET'S GO BOYS, BACK TO THE SHIP!
AND STAY THERE, VARRON OR I PROMISE YOU, WE'LL BE MEETING AGAIN!
YOU AIN'T MEANIN' TO DO LIKE HE SAYS, COUNT?
OF COURSE NOT, I'M GOING BACK TO THE SHIP FOR DYNAMITE! YOU SAW THOSE FISH PEOPLE DISAPPEAR INTO THEIR CAVES? I'LL SEE THAT THEY NEVER COME OUT AGAIN, BECAUSE AS LONG AS THEY EXIST, I CAN'T CLAIM THEIR CONTINENT!
BUT AS MARVEL BOY FOLLOWS THE FISH GIRL INTO A SUBTERRANEAN CAVERN...
STAY UP THERE, STRANGER, OR YOU DIE!
BUT, PROTUS, I'M A FRIEND, YOU MUSTN'T JUDGE MANKIND BY THOSE MURDERING PIRATES!
NO MARVEL BOY. WE HAVE CHANGED OUR MINDS ABOUT LIVING ON EARTH!
WE WERE HAPPY WHEN WE LIVED UNDER THE SEA! SO WE WILL SEAL OFF THESE CAVERNS AND RETURN TO THE DEEPER LEVELS!
IT'S USELESS ARGUING WITH THEM NOW! I MUST FIND THE PLANES OF THE OTHER COUNTRIES, CAPTURE VARRON AND RESTORE THE FISH PEOPLE'S FAITH!
11.

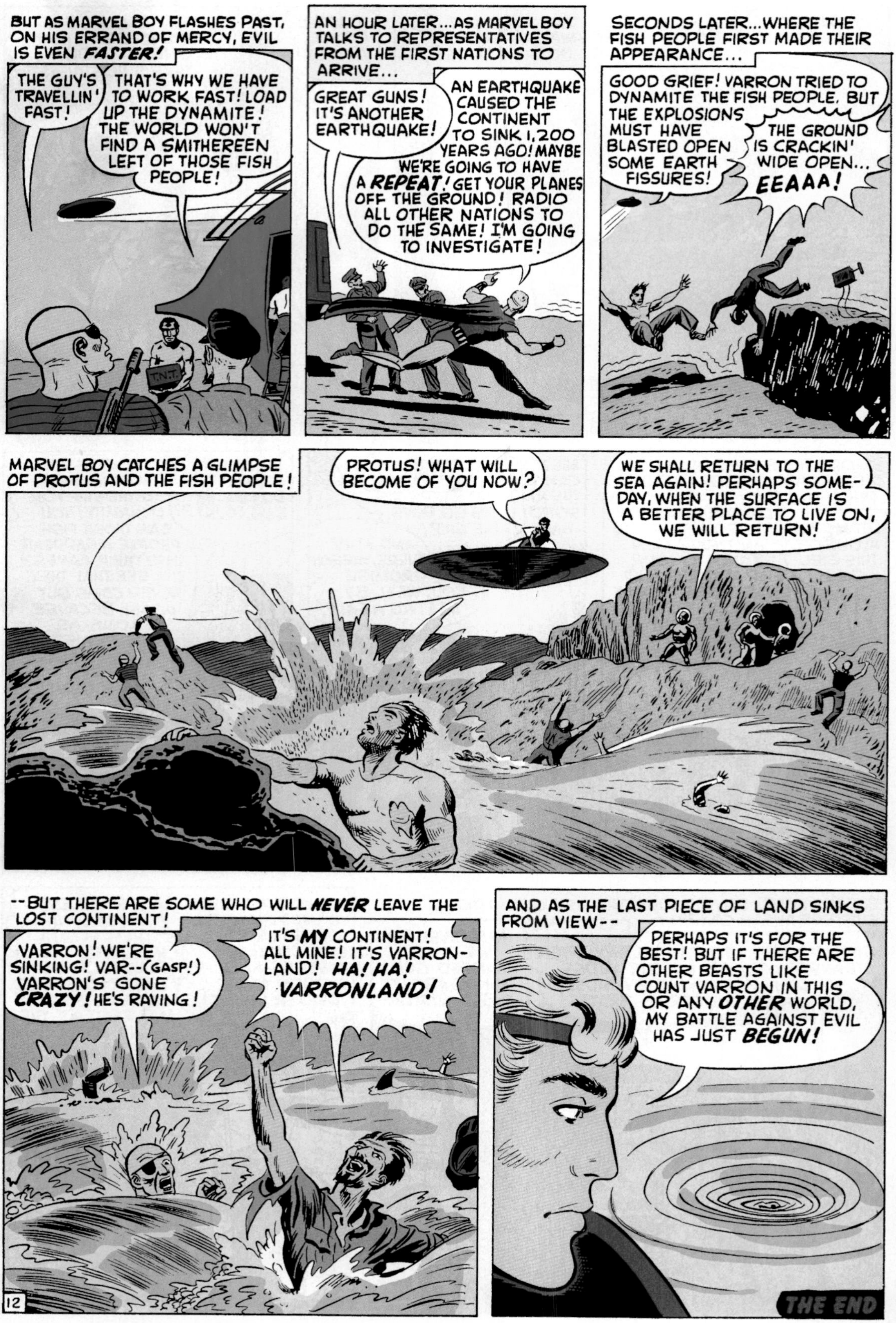
BUT AS MARVEL BOY FLASHES PAST, ON HIS ERRAND OF MERCY, EVIL IS EVEN FASTER!
THE GUY'S TRAVELLIN' FAST!
THAT'S WHY WE HAVE TO WORK FAST! LOAD UP THE DYNAMITE! THE WORLD WON'T FIND A SMITHEREEN LEFT OF THOSE FISH PEOPLE!
T.N.T.
AN HOUR LATER...AS MARVEL BOY TALKS TO REPRESENTATIVES FROM THE FIRST NATIONS TO ARRIVE...
GREAT GUNS! IT'S ANOTHER EARTHQUAKE!
AN EARTHQUAKE CAUSED THE CONTINENT TO SINK 1,200 YEARS AGO! MAYBE WE'RE GOING TO HAVE A REPEAT! GET YOUR PLANES OFF THE GROUND! RADIO ALL OTHER NATIONS TO DO THE SAME! I'M GOING TO INVESTIGATE!
SECONDS LATER...WHERE THE FISH PEOPLE FIRST MADE THEIR APPEARANCE...
GOOD GRIEF! VARRON TRIED TO DYNAMITE THE FISH PEOPLE, BUT THE EXPLOSIONS MUST HAVE BLASTED OPEN SOME EARTH FISSURES!
THE GROUND IS CRACKIN' WIDE OPEN... EEAAA!
MARVEL BOY CATCHES A GLIMPSE OF PROTUS AND THE FISH PEOPLE!
PROTUS! WHAT WILL BECOME OF YOU NOW?
WE SHALL RETURN TO THE SEA AGAIN! PERHAPS SOMEDAY, WHEN THE SURFACE IS A BETTER PLACE TO LIVE ON, WE WILL RETURN!
--BUT THERE ARE SOME WHO WILL NEVER LEAVE THE LOST CONTINENT!
VARRON! WE'RE SINKING! VAR--(GASP!) VARRON'S GONE CRAZY! HE'S RAVING!
IT'S MY CONTINENT! ALL MINE! IT'S VARRONLAND! HA! HA! VARRONLAND!
12
AND AS THE LAST PIECE OF LAND SINKS FROM VIEW--
PERHAPS IT'S FOR THE BEST! BUT IF THERE ARE OTHER BEASTS LIKE COUNT VARRON IN THIS OR ANY OTHER WORLD, MY BATTLE AGAINST EVIL HAS JUST BEGUN!
THE END

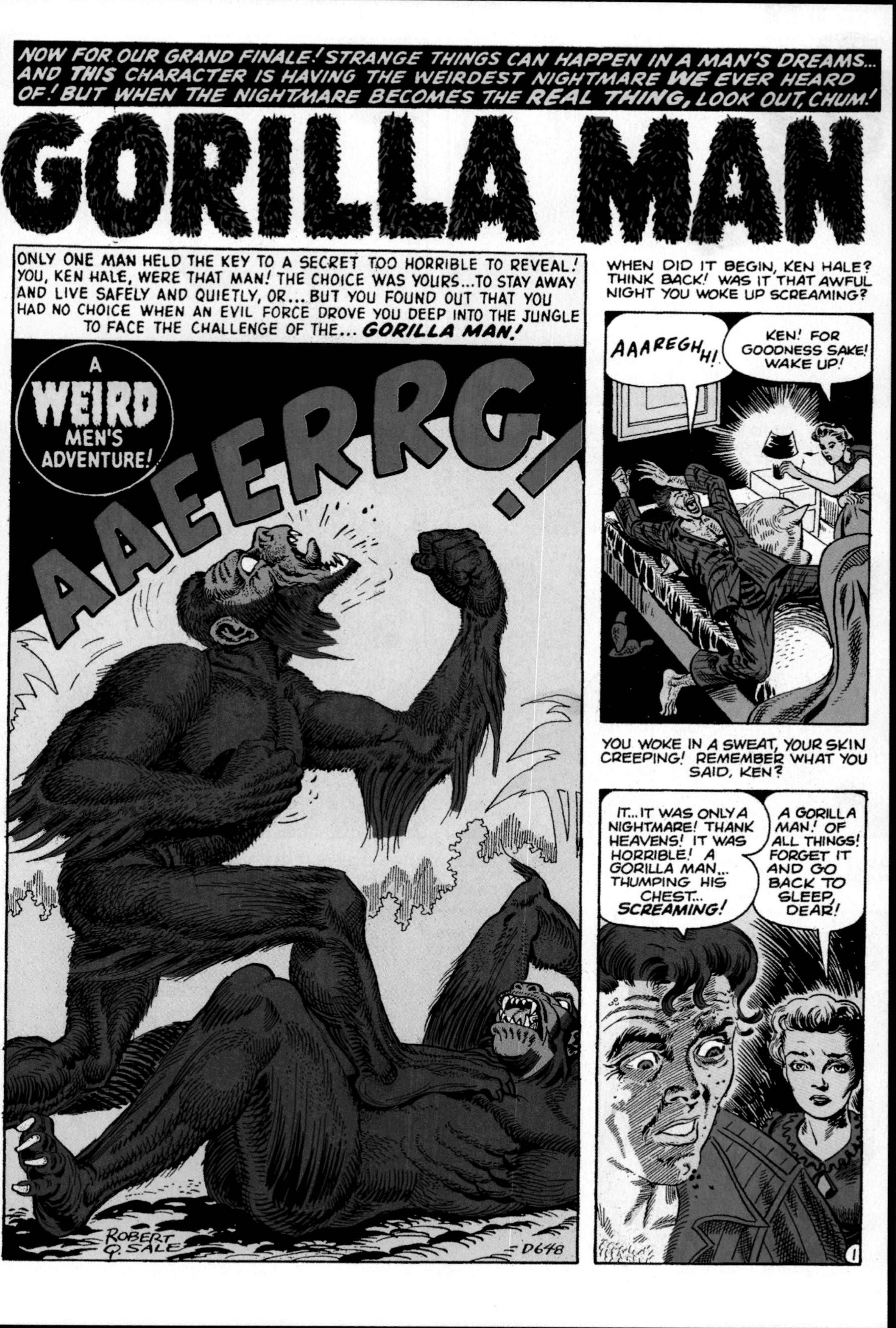
NOW FOR OUR GRAND FINALE! STRANGE THINGS CAN HAPPEN IN A MAN'S DREAMS... AND THIS CHARACTER IS HAVING THE WEIRDEST NIGHTMARE WE EVER HEARD OF! BUT WHEN THE NIGHTMARE BECOMES THE REAL THING, LOOK OUT, CHUM!
GORILLA MAN
ONLY ONE MAN HELD THE KEY TO A SECRET TOO HORRIBLE TO REVEAL! YOU, KEN HALE, WERE THAT MAN! THE CHOICE WAS YOURS...TO STAY AWAY AND LIVE SAFELY AND QUIETLY, OR... BUT YOU FOUND OUT THAT YOU HAD NO CHOICE WHEN AN EVIL FORCE DROVE YOU DEEP INTO THE JUNGLE TO FACE THE CHALLENGE OF THE... GORILLA MAN!
A WEIRD MEN'S ADVENTURE!
AAEERRG!
ROBERT Q. SALE
D648
WHEN DID IT BEGIN, KEN HALE? THINK BACK! WAS IT THAT AWFUL NIGHT YOU WOKE UP SCREAMING?
AAAREGHHH!
KEN! FOR GOODNESS SAKE! WAKE UP!
YOU WOKE IN A SWEAT, YOUR SKIN CREEPING! REMEMBER WHAT YOU SAID, KEN?
IT... IT WAS ONLY A NIGHTMARE! THANK HEAVENS! IT WAS HORRIBLE! A GORILLA MAN... THUMPING HIS CHEST... SCREAMING!
A GORILLA MAN! OF ALL THINGS! FORGET IT AND GO BACK TO SLEEP, DEAR!
1

IT WAS EASY FOR *HER* TO SAY, BUT LET *HER* TRY TO SLEEP WITH THAT AWFUL MEMORY OF THE NIGHTMARE IN HER MIND... REMEMBERING AS YOU DO THE TWO GIGANTIC, SAVAGE BODIES LOCKED TOGETHER IN A RELENTLESS DEATH STRUGGLE!

YOU COULDN'T FORGET IT BY THE NEXT DAY! YOU KEPT HEARING THAT UNEARTHLY SCREAM AND YOU KEPT THINKING *GORILLA MAN! GORILLA MAN!*

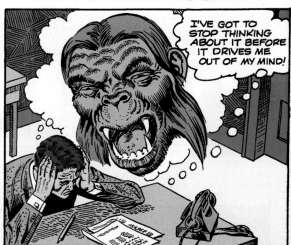

I'VE GOT TO STOP THINKING ABOUT IT BEFORE IT DRIVES ME OUT OF MY MIND!

EASY FOR YOU TO SAY, EH? BUT IT WAS ALWAYS WITH YOU... THE SIGHT AND THE SCREAM...

AAAAEEERAUGHHHH

THERE IT IS! DON'T YOU HEAR IT?

I DON'T HEAR A THING!

THAT AWFUL SCREAM!

OH, GO TO SLEEP!

WHY? WHY? WHY DID THIS CALL HAUNT YOU? YOU CHECKED WITH YOUR DOCTOR...

YOU'RE STRONG AS AN OX, KEN! MAYBE YOU'RE EATING TOO MUCH BEFORE YOU GO TO BED...

YEAH... MAYBE!

A RELENTLESS IMPULSE DROVE YOU TO THE LIBRARY! YOU *HAD* TO FIND OUT ABOUT...

GORILLA MEN? THEY EXIST ONLY IN THE MINDS OF FICTION WRITERS!

I'VE GOT TO FIND OUT... GOT TO!

THEN YOUR FRANTIC URGE DROVE YOU TO A LAST RESORT... YOUR OLD FRIEND BENSON AT THE EXPLORERS' CLUB...

GORILLA MEN? WHAT DO YOU KNOW ABOUT THEM?

NOTHING! THAT'S WHY I CAME TO *YOU!*

2

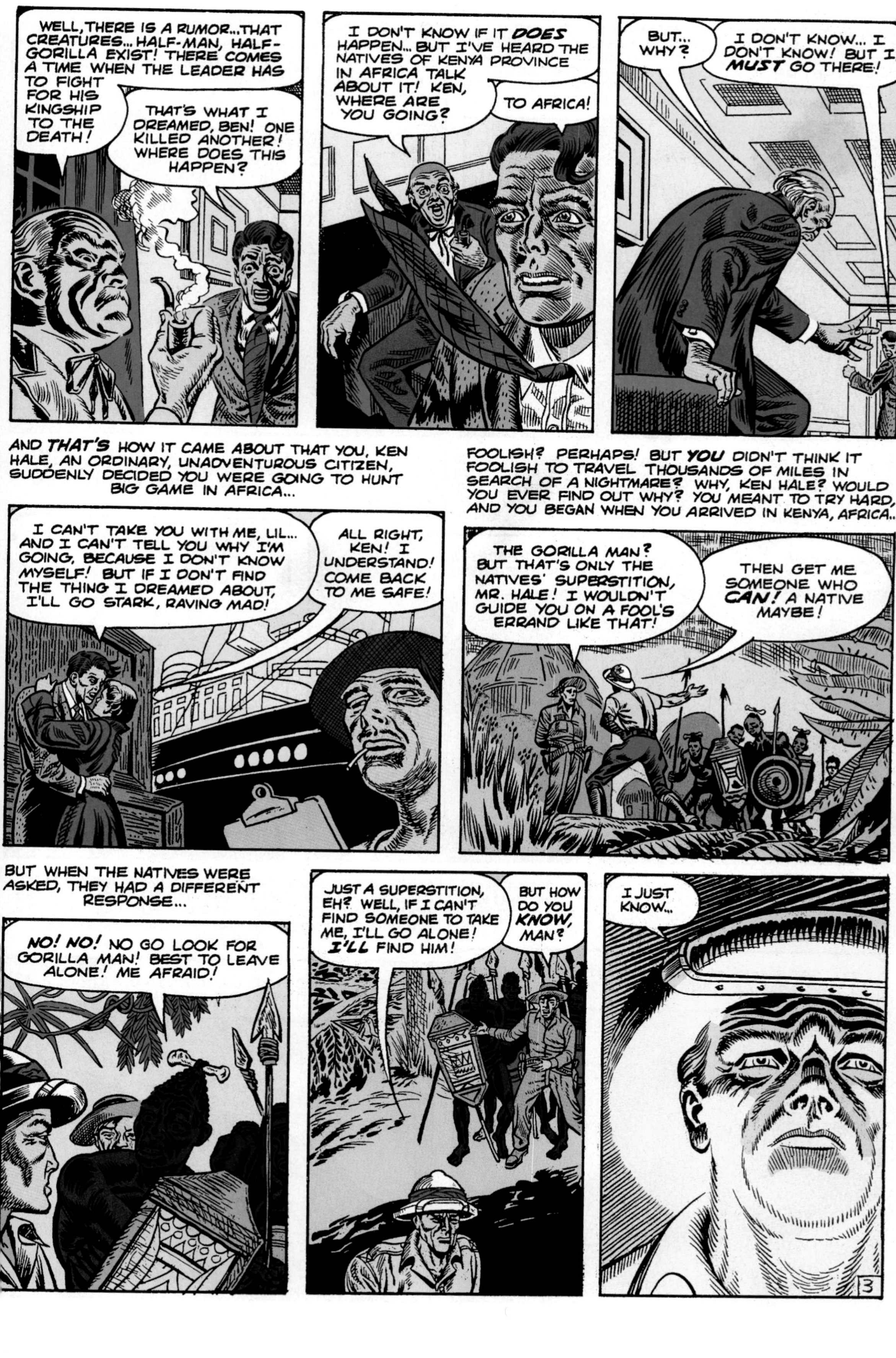
WELL, THERE IS A RUMOR...THAT CREATURES... HALF-MAN, HALF-GORILLA EXIST! THERE COMES A TIME WHEN THE LEADER HAS TO FIGHT FOR HIS KINGSHIP TO THE DEATH!
THAT'S WHAT I DREAMED, BEN! ONE KILLED ANOTHER! WHERE DOES THIS HAPPEN?
I DON'T KNOW IF IT DOES HAPPEN... BUT I'VE HEARD THE NATIVES OF KENYA PROVINCE IN AFRICA TALK ABOUT IT! KEN, WHERE ARE YOU GOING?
TO AFRICA!
BUT... WHY?
I DON'T KNOW... I DON'T KNOW! BUT I MUST GO THERE!
AND THAT'S HOW IT CAME ABOUT THAT YOU, KEN HALE, AN ORDINARY, UNADVENTUROUS CITIZEN, SUDDENLY DECIDED YOU WERE GOING TO HUNT BIG GAME IN AFRICA...
I CAN'T TAKE YOU WITH ME, LIL... AND I CAN'T TELL YOU WHY I'M GOING, BECAUSE I DON'T KNOW MYSELF! BUT IF I DON'T FIND THE THING I DREAMED ABOUT, I'LL GO STARK, RAVING MAD!
ALL RIGHT, KEN! I UNDERSTAND! COME BACK TO ME SAFE!
FOOLISH? PERHAPS! BUT YOU DIDN'T THINK IT FOOLISH TO TRAVEL THOUSANDS OF MILES IN SEARCH OF A NIGHTMARE? WHY, KEN HALE? WOULD YOU EVER FIND OUT WHY? YOU MEANT TO TRY HARD, AND YOU BEGAN WHEN YOU ARRIVED IN KENYA, AFRICA...
THE GORILLA MAN? BUT THAT'S ONLY THE NATIVES' SUPERSTITION, MR. HALE! I WOULDN'T GUIDE YOU ON A FOOL'S ERRAND LIKE THAT!
THEN GET ME SOMEONE WHO CAN! A NATIVE MAYBE!
BUT WHEN THE NATIVES WERE ASKED, THEY HAD A DIFFERENT RESPONSE...
NO! NO! NO GO LOOK FOR GORILLA MAN! BEST TO LEAVE ALONE! ME AFRAID!
JUST A SUPERSTITION, EH? WELL, IF I CAN'T FIND SOMEONE TO TAKE ME, I'LL GO ALONE! I'LL FIND HIM!
BUT HOW DO YOU KNOW, MAN?
I JUST KNOW...
3

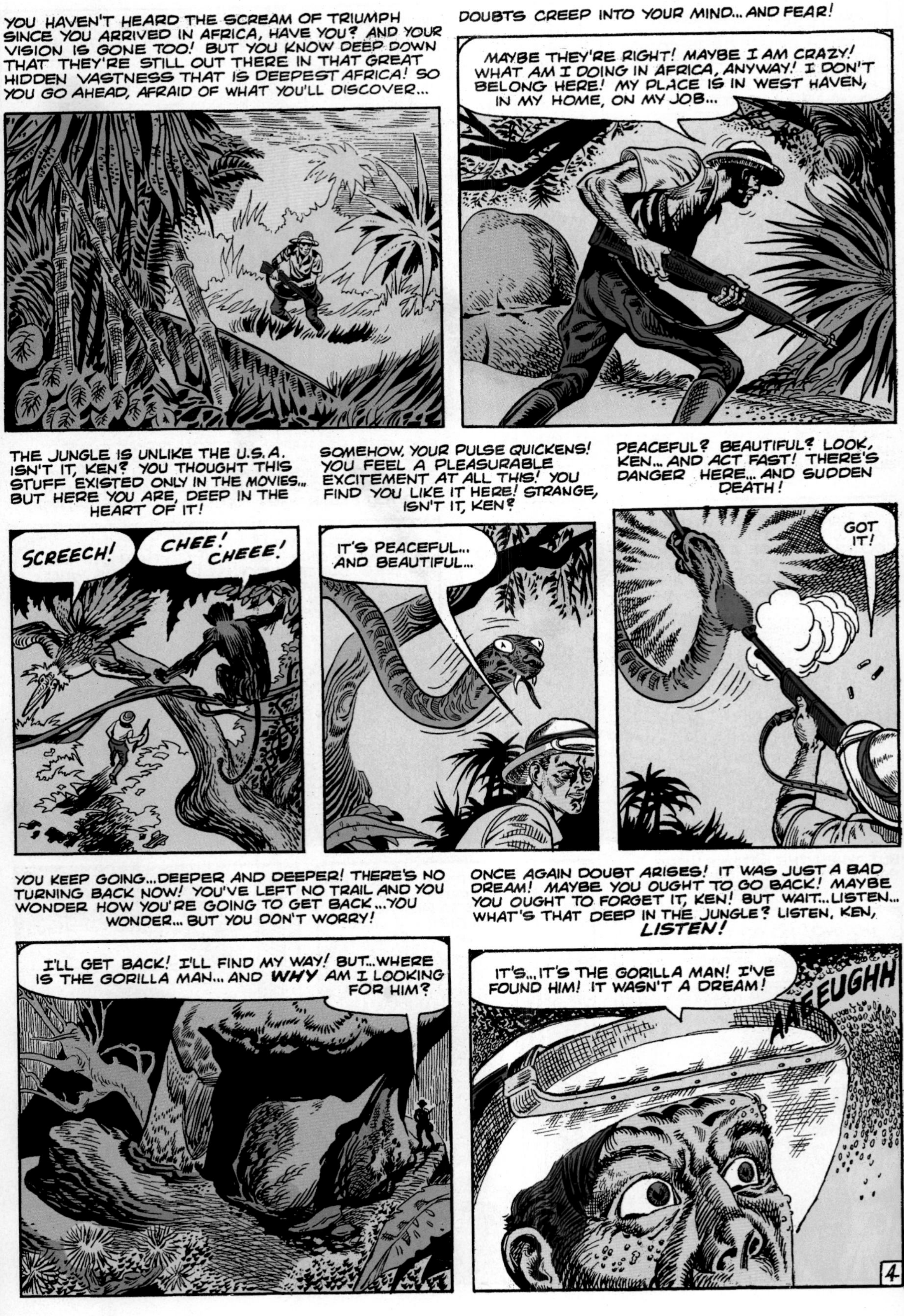
YOU HAVEN'T HEARD THE SCREAM OF TRIUMPH SINCE YOU ARRIVED IN AFRICA, HAVE YOU? AND YOUR VISION IS GONE TOO! BUT YOU KNOW DEEP DOWN THAT THEY'RE STILL OUT THERE IN THAT GREAT HIDDEN VASTNESS THAT IS DEEPEST AFRICA! SO YOU GO AHEAD, AFRAID OF WHAT YOU'LL DISCOVER...
DOUBTS CREEP INTO YOUR MIND... AND FEAR!
MAYBE THEY'RE RIGHT! MAYBE I AM CRAZY! WHAT AM I DOING IN AFRICA, ANYWAY! I DON'T BELONG HERE! MY PLACE IS IN WEST HAVEN, IN MY HOME, ON MY JOB...
THE JUNGLE IS UNLIKE THE U.S.A. ISN'T IT, KEN? YOU THOUGHT THIS STUFF EXISTED ONLY IN THE MOVIES... BUT HERE YOU ARE, DEEP IN THE HEART OF IT!
SCREECH!
CHEE! CHEEE!
SOMEHOW, YOUR PULSE QUICKENS! YOU FEEL A PLEASURABLE EXCITEMENT AT ALL THIS! YOU FIND YOU LIKE IT HERE! STRANGE, ISN'T IT, KEN?
IT'S PEACEFUL... AND BEAUTIFUL...
PEACEFUL? BEAUTIFUL? LOOK, KEN... AND ACT FAST! THERE'S DANGER HERE... AND SUDDEN DEATH!
GOT IT!
YOU KEEP GOING... DEEPER AND DEEPER! THERE'S NO TURNING BACK NOW! YOU'VE LEFT NO TRAIL AND YOU WONDER HOW YOU'RE GOING TO GET BACK... YOU WONDER... BUT YOU DON'T WORRY!
I'LL GET BACK! I'LL FIND MY WAY! BUT... WHERE IS THE GORILLA MAN... AND WHY AM I LOOKING FOR HIM?
ONCE AGAIN DOUBT ARISES! IT WAS JUST A BAD DREAM! MAYBE YOU OUGHT TO GO BACK! MAYBE YOU OUGHT TO FORGET IT, KEN! BUT WAIT... LISTEN... WHAT'S THAT DEEP IN THE JUNGLE? LISTEN, KEN, LISTEN!
IT'S... IT'S THE GORILLA MAN! I'VE FOUND HIM! IT WASN'T A DREAM!
AAEEUGHH

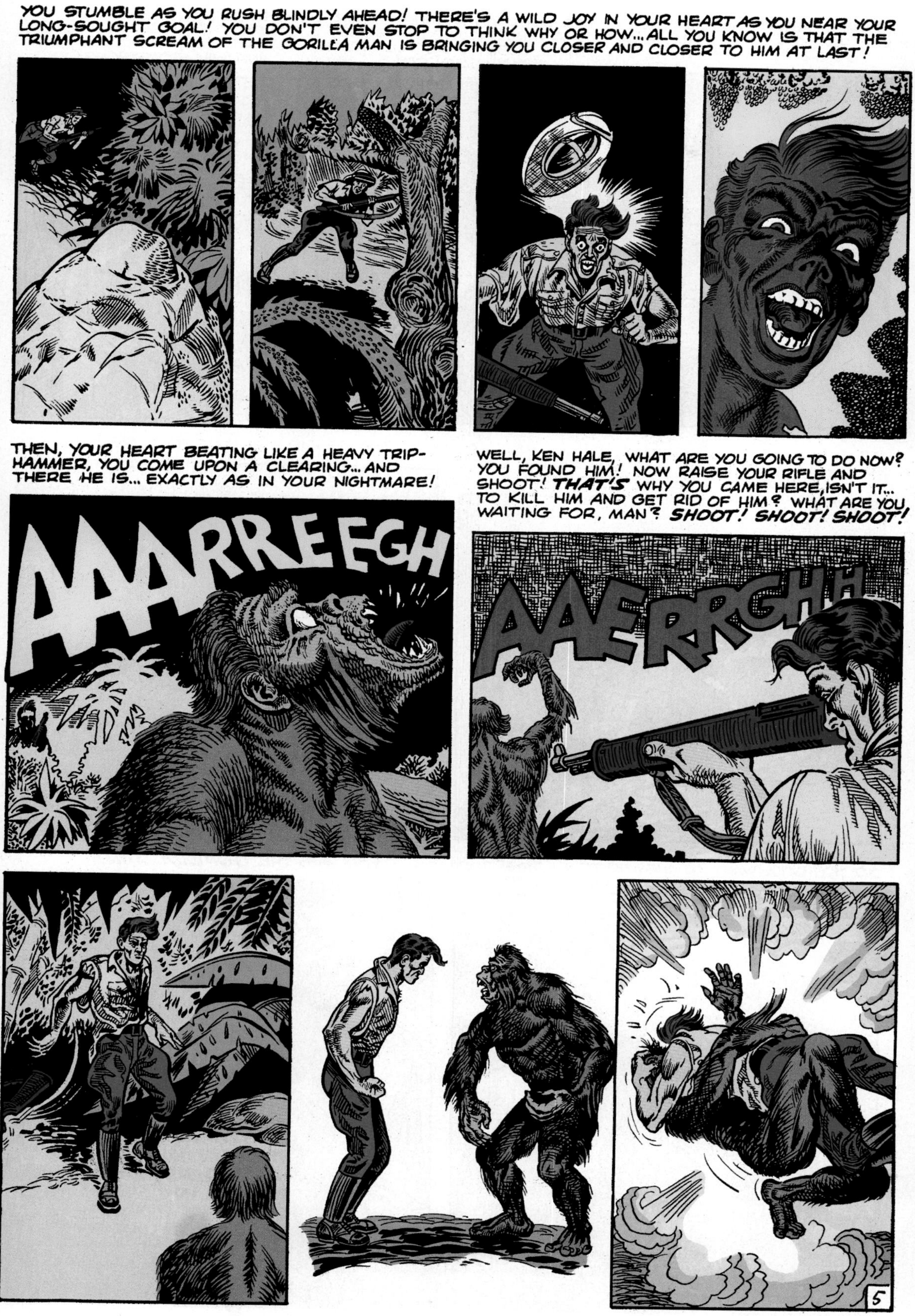

YOU STUMBLE AS YOU RUSH BLINDLY AHEAD! THERE'S A WILD JOY IN YOUR HEART AS YOU NEAR YOUR LONG-SOUGHT GOAL! YOU DON'T EVEN STOP TO THINK WHY OR HOW... ALL YOU KNOW IS THAT THE TRIUMPHANT SCREAM OF THE GORILLA MAN IS BRINGING YOU CLOSER AND CLOSER TO HIM AT LAST!
THEN, YOUR HEART BEATING LIKE A HEAVY TRIP-HAMMER, YOU COME UPON A CLEARING... AND THERE HE IS... EXACTLY AS IN YOUR NIGHTMARE!
AAARREEGH
WELL, KEN HALE, WHAT ARE YOU GOING TO DO NOW? YOU FOUND HIM! NOW RAISE YOUR RIFLE AND SHOOT! THAT'S WHY YOU CAME HERE, ISN'T IT... TO KILL HIM AND GET RID OF HIM? WHAT ARE YOU WAITING FOR, MAN? SHOOT! SHOOT! SHOOT!
AAERRGHH

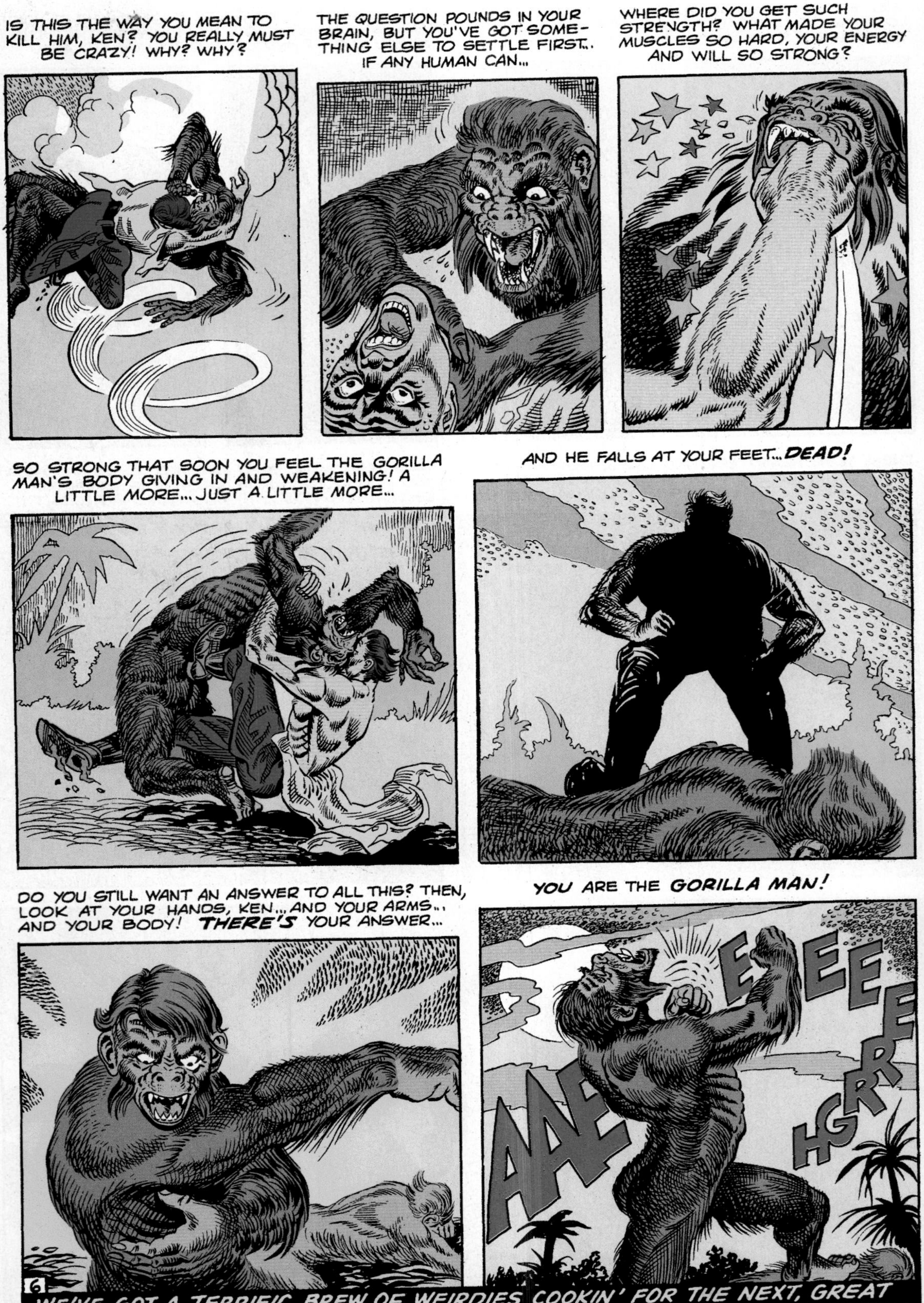
IS THIS THE WAY YOU MEAN TO KILL HIM, KEN? YOU REALLY MUST BE CRAZY! WHY? WHY?
THE QUESTION POUNDS IN YOUR BRAIN, BUT YOU'VE GOT SOMETHING ELSE TO SETTLE FIRST... IF ANY HUMAN CAN...
WHERE DID YOU GET SUCH STRENGTH? WHAT MADE YOUR MUSCLES SO HARD, YOUR ENERGY AND WILL SO STRONG?
SO STRONG THAT SOON YOU FEEL THE GORILLA MAN'S BODY GIVING IN AND WEAKENING! A LITTLE MORE... JUST A LITTLE MORE...
AND HE FALLS AT YOUR FEET... DEAD!
DO YOU STILL WANT AN ANSWER TO ALL THIS? THEN, LOOK AT YOUR HANDS, KEN... AND YOUR ARMS... AND YOUR BODY! THERE'S YOUR ANSWER...
YOU ARE THE GORILLA MAN!
AAAEEEEEEE RRRGH
6
WE'VE GOT A TERRIFIC BREW OF WEIRDIES COOKIN' FOR THE NEXT, GREAT ISSUE OF MEN'S ADVENTURES! DON'T MISS IT! WE'LL BE EXPECTING YA!

I, THE ROBOT

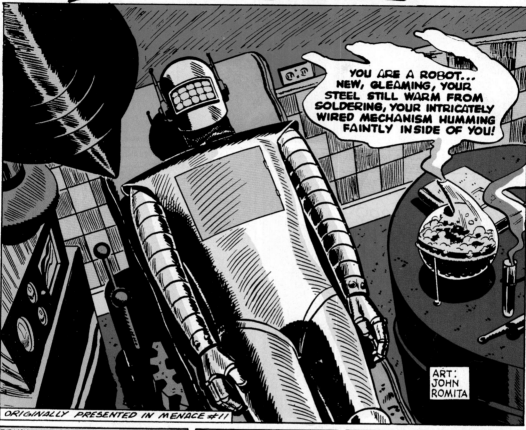

ORIGINALLY PRESENTED IN MENACE #11

ART: JOHN ROMITA

YOU ARE A ROBOT... NEW, GLEAMING, YOUR STEEL STILL WARM FROM SOLDERING, YOUR INTRICATELY WIRED MECHANISM HUMMING FAINTLY INSIDE OF YOU!

THE MAN WITH THE BEARD IS YOUR CREATOR! THE HUM OF HIS VOICE MAKES YOUR SENSITIVE AUDIOPHONES VIBRATE! BUT NO GEARS SHIFT INSIDE YOU, YOU RESPOND TO AUDIOIMPULSES ONLY WHEN ADDRESSED ON A *SECRET FREQUENCY!*

HE'S NOT FINISHED, I TELL YOU! CREATING A ROBOT WHICH OBEYS ORDERS ISN'T EASY! THE ROBOT HAS TO BE TAUGHT HOW TO OBEY!

I'M YOUR BUSINESS MANAGER, PROFESSOR...YOU GOTTA LISTEN TO ME! THEY'LL GIVE US FIVE MILLION BUCKS IF YOU RELEASE IT BEFORE THE END OF THE MONTH!

I'M NOT RELEASING ANY DATA TILL MY ROBOT IS *PERFECT!* NOW LEAVE ME ALONE... I HAVE TO CONDUCT ANOTHER TEST!

NOW YOUR CREATOR IS STANDING OVER YOU... YOU REMAIN MOTIONLESS ON YOUR SLAB! YOU ARE A ROBOT, FASHIONED INTO THE SHAPE OF A MAN, BUT WITHOUT WILL, POWERLESS TO MOVE UNLESS COMMANDED ON YOUR *SECRET FREQUENCY!*

1

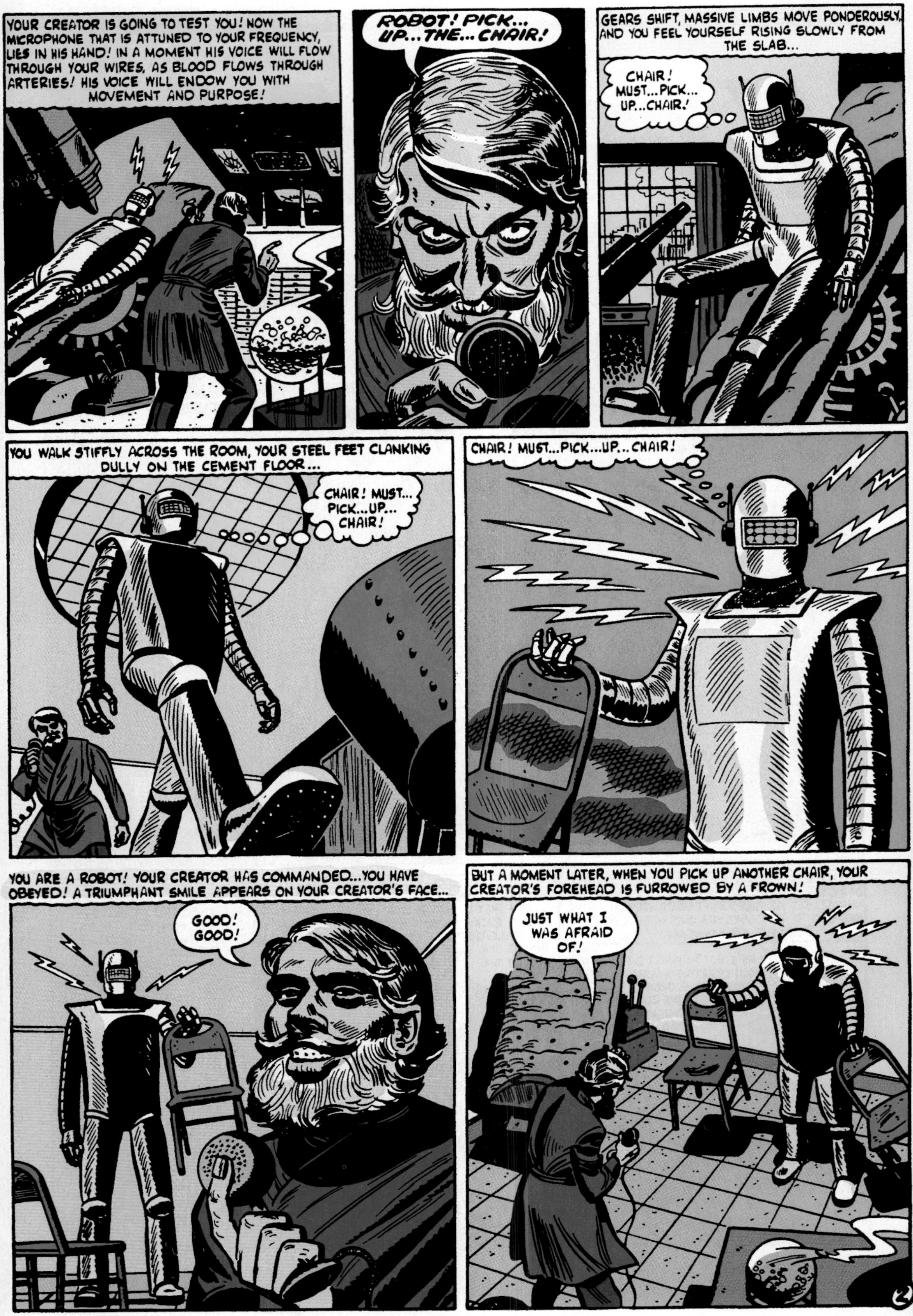
YOUR CREATOR IS GOING TO TEST YOU! NOW THE MICROPHONE THAT IS ATTUNED TO YOUR FREQUENCY, LIES IN HIS HAND! IN A MOMENT HIS VOICE WILL FLOW THROUGH YOUR WIRES, AS BLOOD FLOWS THROUGH ARTERIES! HIS VOICE WILL ENDOW YOU WITH MOVEMENT AND PURPOSE!
ROBOT! PICK... UP... THE... CHAIR!
GEARS SHIFT, MASSIVE LIMBS MOVE PONDEROUSLY, AND YOU FEEL YOURSELF RISING SLOWLY FROM THE SLAB...
CHAIR! MUST...PICK... UP...CHAIR!
YOU WALK STIFFLY ACROSS THE ROOM, YOUR STEEL FEET CLANKING DULLY ON THE CEMENT FLOOR...
CHAIR! MUST... PICK...UP... CHAIR!
CHAIR! MUST...PICK...UP...CHAIR!
YOU ARE A ROBOT! YOUR CREATOR HAS COMMANDED...YOU HAVE OBEYED! A TRIUMPHANT SMILE APPEARS ON YOUR CREATOR'S FACE...
GOOD! GOOD!
BUT A MOMENT LATER, WHEN YOU PICK UP ANOTHER CHAIR, YOUR CREATOR'S FOREHEAD IS FURROWED BY A FROWN!
JUST WHAT I WAS AFRAID OF!
2

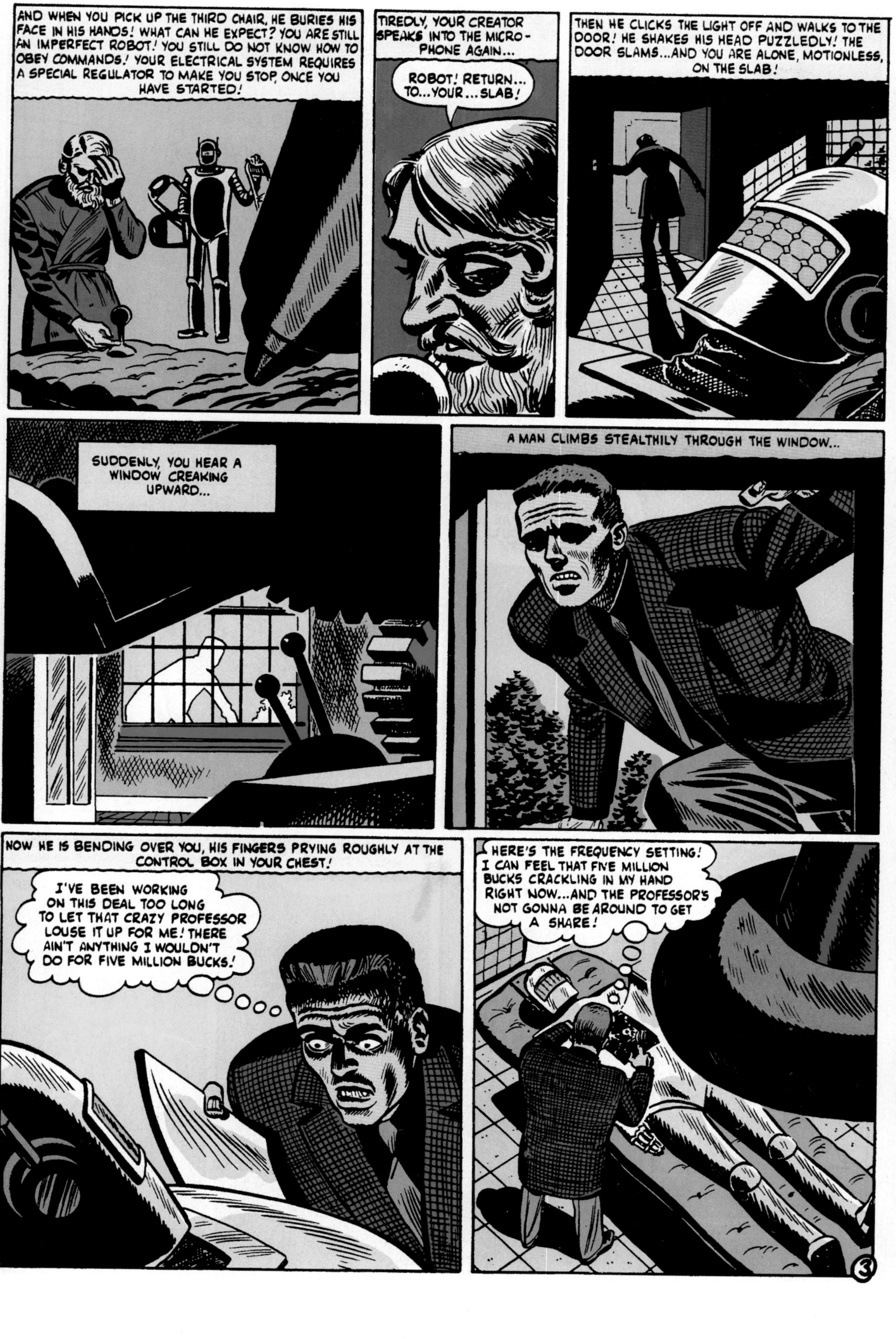
AND WHEN YOU PICK UP THE THIRD CHAIR, HE BURIES HIS FACE IN HIS HANDS! WHAT CAN HE EXPECT? YOU ARE STILL AN IMPERFECT ROBOT! YOU STILL DO NOT KNOW HOW TO OBEY COMMANDS! YOUR ELECTRICAL SYSTEM REQUIRES A SPECIAL REGULATOR TO MAKE YOU STOP, ONCE YOU HAVE STARTED!
TIREDLY, YOUR CREATOR SPEAKS INTO THE MICRO-PHONE AGAIN...
ROBOT! RETURN... TO... YOUR... SLAB!
THEN HE CLICKS THE LIGHT OFF AND WALKS TO THE DOOR! HE SHAKES HIS HEAD PUZZLEDLY! THE DOOR SLAMS... AND YOU ARE ALONE, MOTIONLESS, ON THE SLAB!
SUDDENLY, YOU HEAR A WINDOW CREAKING UPWARD...
A MAN CLIMBS STEALTHILY THROUGH THE WINDOW...
NOW HE IS BENDING OVER YOU, HIS FINGERS PRYING ROUGHLY AT THE CONTROL BOX IN YOUR CHEST!
I'VE BEEN WORKING ON THIS DEAL TOO LONG TO LET THAT CRAZY PROFESSOR LOUSE IT UP FOR ME! THERE AIN'T ANYTHING I WOULDN'T DO FOR FIVE MILLION BUCKS!
HERE'S THE FREQUENCY SETTING! I CAN FEEL THAT FIVE MILLION BUCKS CRACKLING IN MY HAND RIGHT NOW... AND THE PROFESSOR'S NOT GONNA BE AROUND TO GET A SHARE!
3

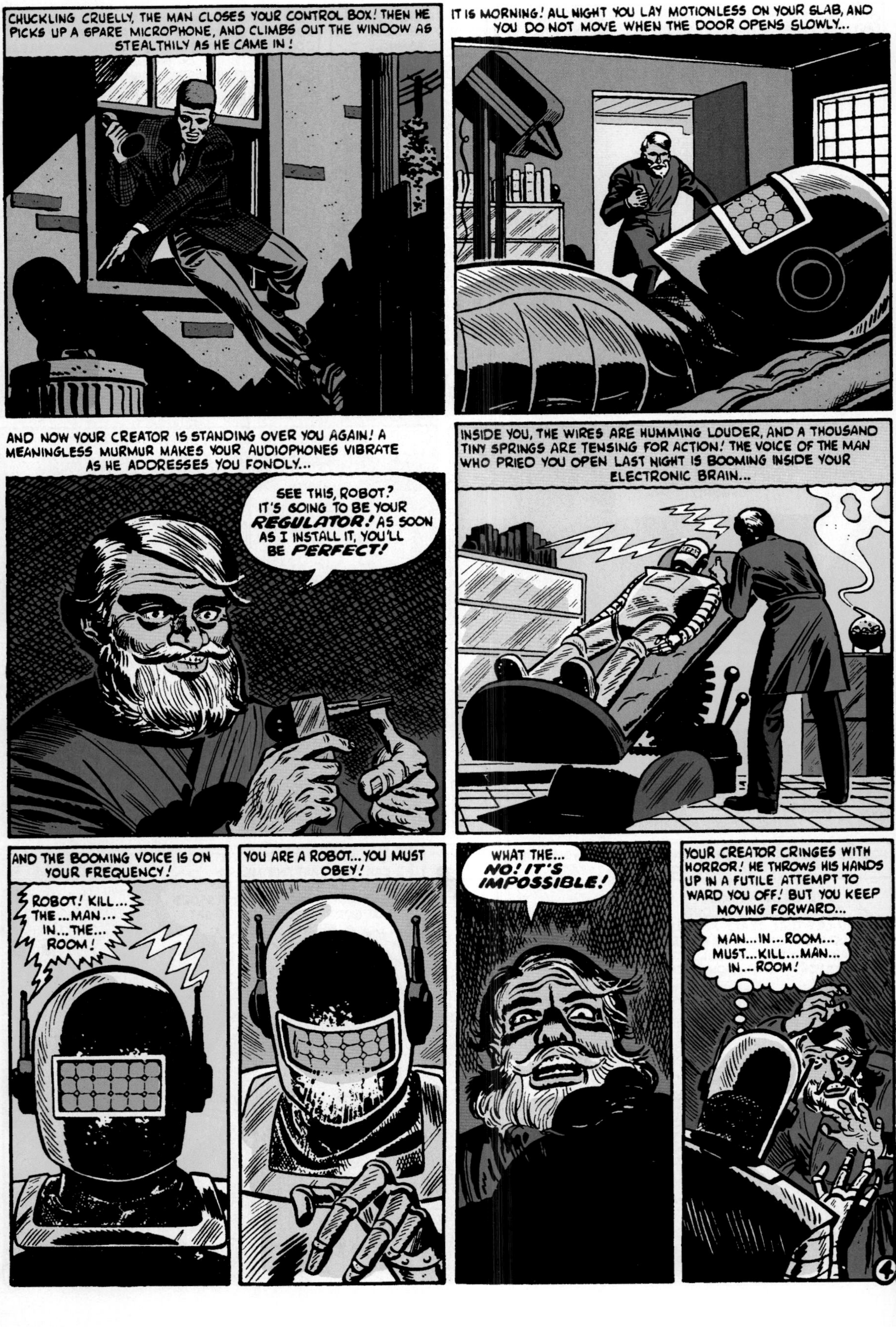
CHUCKLING CRUELLY, THE MAN CLOSES YOUR CONTROL BOX! THEN HE PICKS UP A SPARE MICROPHONE, AND CLIMBS OUT THE WINDOW AS STEALTHILY AS HE CAME IN!
IT IS MORNING! ALL NIGHT YOU LAY MOTIONLESS ON YOUR SLAB, AND YOU DO NOT MOVE WHEN THE DOOR OPENS SLOWLY...
AND NOW YOUR CREATOR IS STANDING OVER YOU AGAIN! A MEANINGLESS MURMUR MAKES YOUR AUDIOPHONES VIBRATE AS HE ADDRESSES YOU FONDLY...
SEE THIS, ROBOT? IT'S GOING TO BE YOUR REGULATOR! AS SOON AS I INSTALL IT, YOU'LL BE PERFECT!
INSIDE YOU, THE WIRES ARE HUMMING LOUDER, AND A THOUSAND TINY SPRINGS ARE TENSING FOR ACTION! THE VOICE OF THE MAN WHO PRIED YOU OPEN LAST NIGHT IS BOOMING INSIDE YOUR ELECTRONIC BRAIN...
AND THE BOOMING VOICE IS ON YOUR FREQUENCY!
ROBOT! KILL... THE... MAN... IN... THE... ROOM!
YOU ARE A ROBOT... YOU MUST OBEY!
WHAT THE... NO! IT'S IMPOSSIBLE!
YOUR CREATOR CRINGES WITH HORROR! HE THROWS HIS HANDS UP IN A FUTILE ATTEMPT TO WARD YOU OFF! BUT YOU KEEP MOVING FORWARD...
MAN... IN... ROOM... MUST... KILL... MAN... IN... ROOM!
4

AAARRGGHHH!

YOU STAND SWAYING OVER THE CRUMPLED BODY OF YOUR CREATOR! THE WIRES INSIDE OF YOU ARE STILL HUMMING SHRILLY! YOUR STEEL HANDS ARE STILL CURVED AND TAUT! YOUR ELECTRIC EYES KEEP DARTING AROUND THE ROOM...

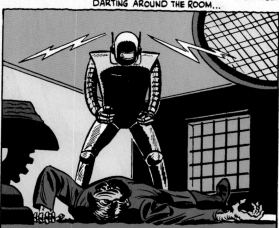

THE DOOR OPENS! ANOTHER MAN IN THE ROOM...

IT WORKED! THE PROFESSOR'S DEAD... NOW ALL I GOTTA DO IS MARCH THIS HUNK OF TIN DOWN TO THE SUCKERS WHO WANNA PAY FIVE MILLION BUCKS FOR IT!

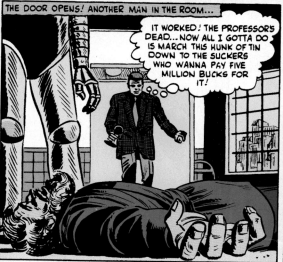

BUT *YOU* ARE A *ROBOT*... BRAND-NEW, IMPERFECT, IN NEED OF A *REGULATOR!*

HEY!

MAN...IN...ROOM...MUST ...KILL...MAN...IN... ROOM!

THE VOICE ON YOUR FREQUENCY HAS COMMANDED... *YOU MUST OBEY!*

AND YOU WILL KEEP OBEYING THE COMMAND!

YOUR STEEL FEET MAKE HOLLOW, CLANKING SOUNDS THAT ECHO RASPINGLY IN THE NARROW CORRIDOR! YOU ARE ON YOUR WAY! *YOU WILL KILL MEN IN ROOMS WHER-EVER YOU FIND THEM! YOU ARE A ROBOT! YOU MUST OBEY!*

THE END

***YELLOW CLAW #1* (OCTOBER 1956) THE FIRST APPEARANCE OF YELLOW CLAW AND JIMMY WOO**

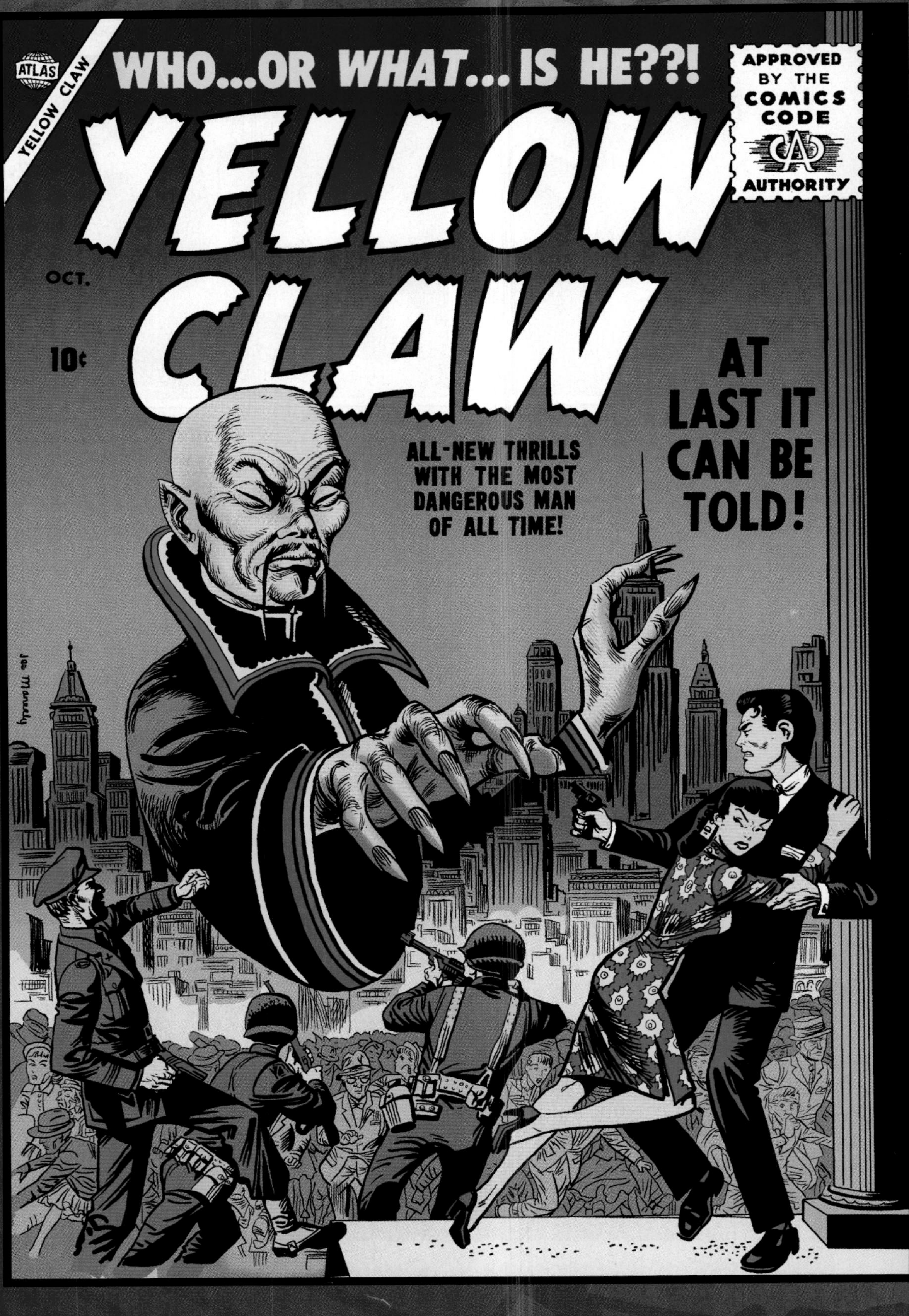
ATLAS
YELLOW CLAW
WHO...OR WHAT...IS HE??!
APPROVED BY THE COMICS CODE AUTHORITY
YELLOW CLAW
OCT.
10¢
ALL-NEW THRILLS WITH THE MOST DANGEROUS MAN OF ALL TIME!
AT LAST IT CAN BE TOLD!

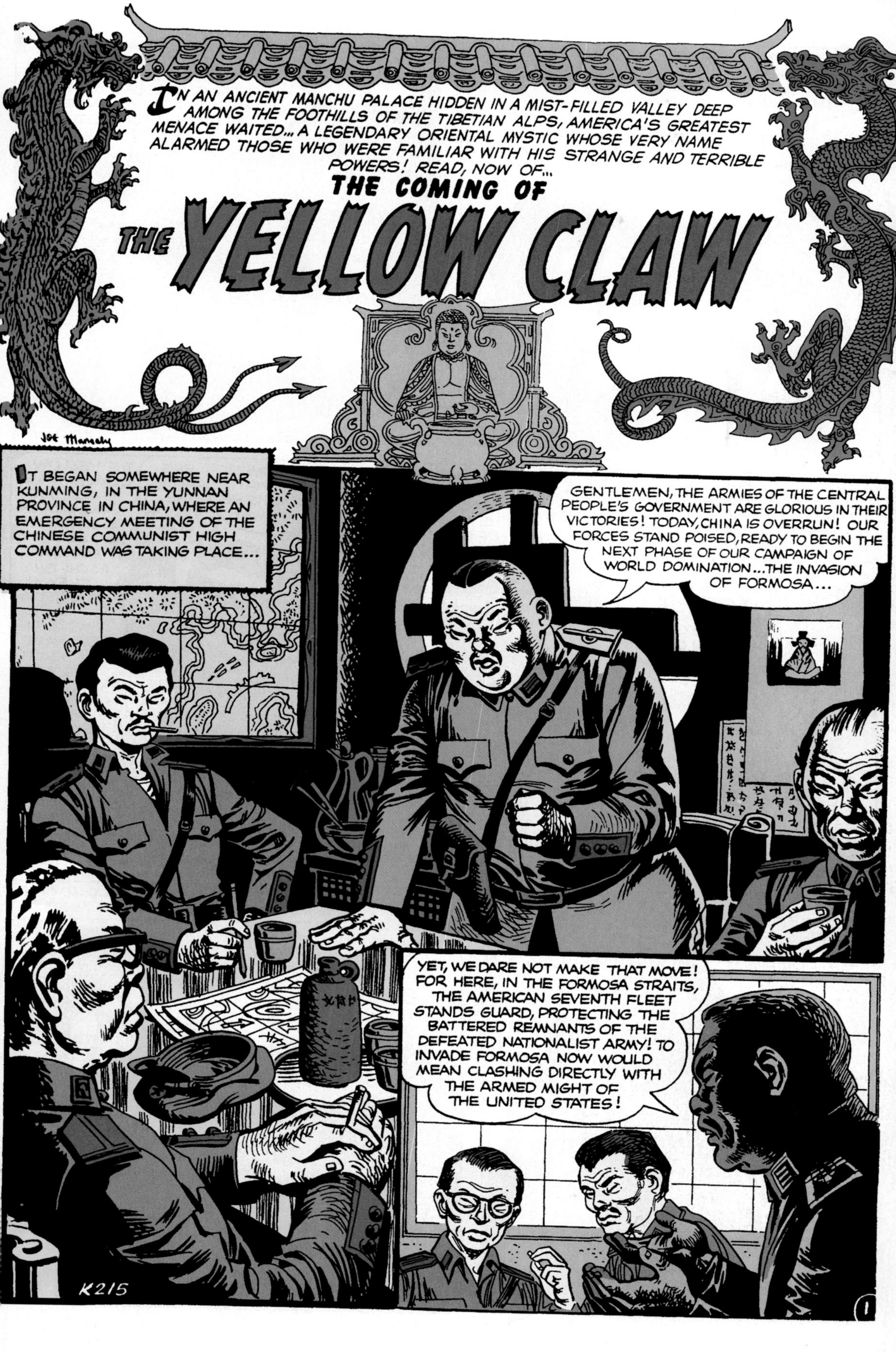
IN AN ANCIENT MANCHU PALACE HIDDEN IN A MIST-FILLED VALLEY DEEP AMONG THE FOOTHILLS OF THE TIBETIAN ALPS, AMERICA'S GREATEST MENACE WAITED... A LEGENDARY ORIENTAL MYSTIC WHOSE VERY NAME ALARMED THOSE WHO WERE FAMILIAR WITH HIS STRANGE AND TERRIBLE POWERS! READ, NOW OF...
THE COMING OF
THE YELLOW CLAW
JOE MANEELY
IT BEGAN SOMEWHERE NEAR KUNMING, IN THE YUNNAN PROVINCE IN CHINA, WHERE AN EMERGENCY MEETING OF THE CHINESE COMMUNIST HIGH COMMAND WAS TAKING PLACE...
GENTLEMEN, THE ARMIES OF THE CENTRAL PEOPLE'S GOVERNMENT ARE GLORIOUS IN THEIR VICTORIES! TODAY, CHINA IS OVERRUN! OUR FORCES STAND POISED, READY TO BEGIN THE NEXT PHASE OF OUR CAMPAIGN OF WORLD DOMINATION...THE INVASION OF FORMOSA...
YET, WE DARE NOT MAKE THAT MOVE! FOR HERE, IN THE FORMOSA STRAITS, THE AMERICAN SEVENTH FLEET STANDS GUARD, PROTECTING THE BATTERED REMNANTS OF THE DEFEATED NATIONALIST ARMY! TO INVADE FORMOSA NOW WOULD MEAN CLASHING DIRECTLY WITH THE ARMED MIGHT OF THE UNITED STATES!
K215
1

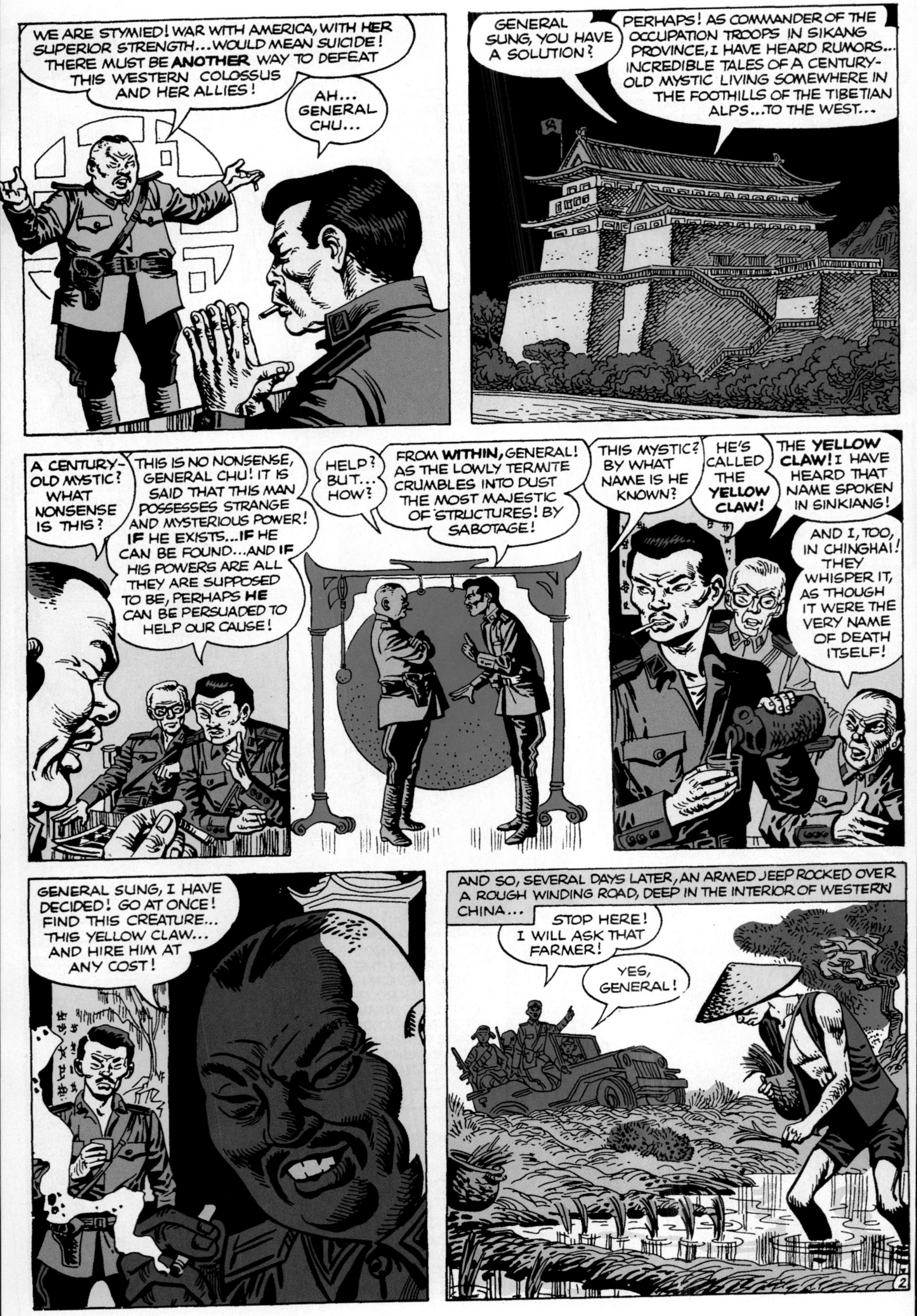

WE ARE STYMIED! WAR WITH AMERICA, WITH HER SUPERIOR STRENGTH... WOULD MEAN SUICIDE! THERE MUST BE ANOTHER WAY TO DEFEAT THIS WESTERN COLOSSUS AND HER ALLIES!
AH... GENERAL CHU...
GENERAL SUNG, YOU HAVE A SOLUTION?
PERHAPS! AS COMMANDER OF THE OCCUPATION TROOPS IN SIKANG PROVINCE, I HAVE HEARD RUMORS... INCREDIBLE TALES OF A CENTURY-OLD MYSTIC LIVING SOMEWHERE IN THE FOOTHILLS OF THE TIBETIAN ALPS...TO THE WEST...
A CENTURY-OLD MYSTIC? WHAT NONSENSE IS THIS?
THIS IS NO NONSENSE, GENERAL CHU! IT IS SAID THAT THIS MAN POSSESSES STRANGE AND MYSTERIOUS POWER! IF HE EXISTS... IF HE CAN BE FOUND... AND IF HIS POWERS ARE ALL THEY ARE SUPPOSED TO BE, PERHAPS HE CAN BE PERSUADED TO HELP OUR CAUSE!
HELP? BUT... HOW?
FROM WITHIN, GENERAL! AS THE LOWLY TERMITE CRUMBLES INTO DUST THE MOST MAJESTIC OF STRUCTURES! BY SABOTAGE!
THIS MYSTIC? BY WHAT NAME IS HE KNOWN?
HE'S CALLED THE YELLOW CLAW!
THE YELLOW CLAW! I HAVE HEARD THAT NAME SPOKEN IN SINKIANG!
AND I, TOO, IN CHINGHAI! THEY WHISPER IT, AS THOUGH IT WERE THE VERY NAME OF DEATH ITSELF!
GENERAL SUNG, I HAVE DECIDED! GO AT ONCE! FIND THIS CREATURE... THIS YELLOW CLAW... AND HIRE HIM AT ANY COST!
AND SO, SEVERAL DAYS LATER, AN ARMED JEEP ROCKED OVER A ROUGH WINDING ROAD, DEEP IN THE INTERIOR OF WESTERN CHINA...
STOP HERE! I WILL ASK THAT FARMER!
YES, GENERAL!
2

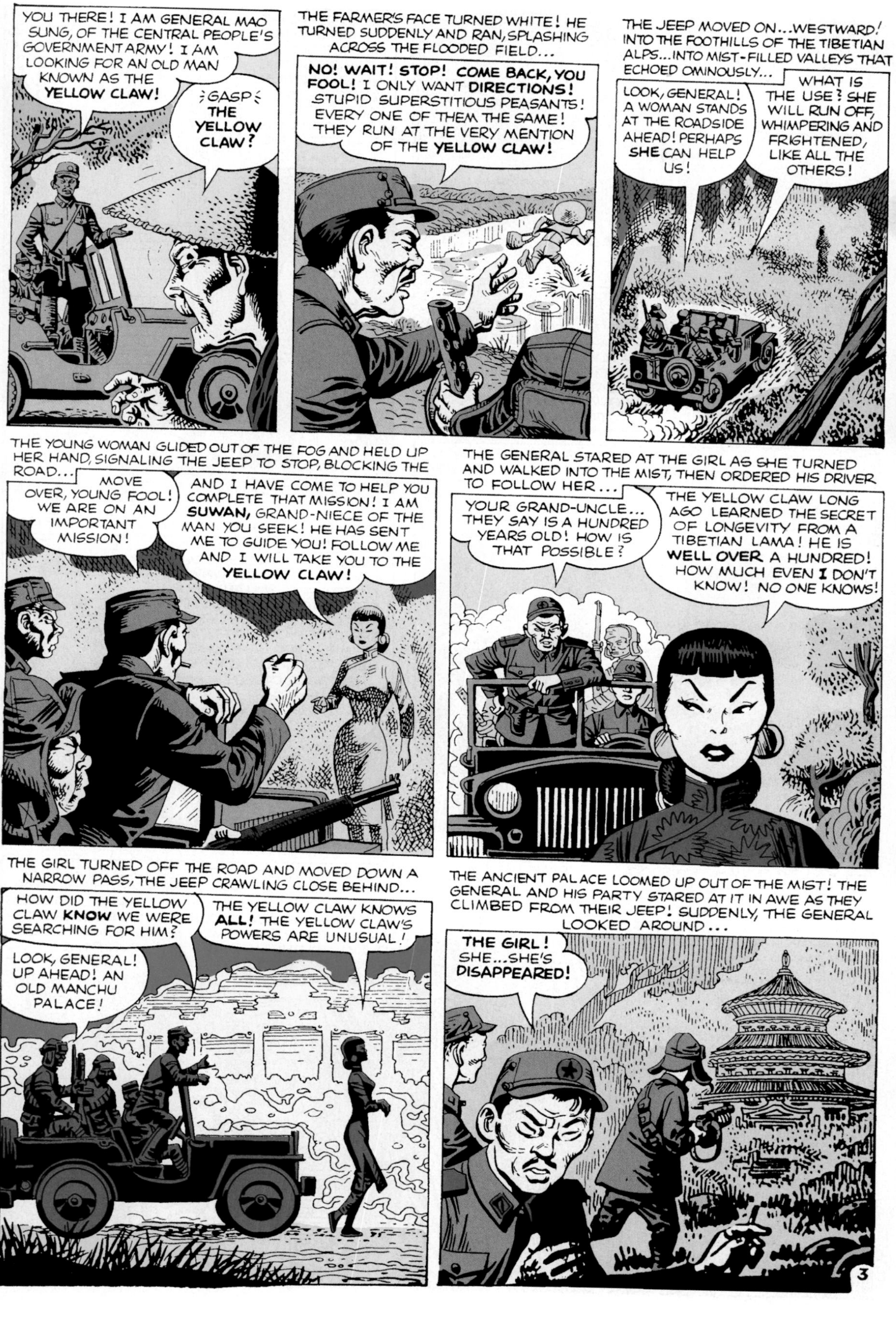
YOU THERE! I AM GENERAL MAO SUNG, OF THE CENTRAL PEOPLE'S GOVERNMENT ARMY! I AM LOOKING FOR AN OLD MAN KNOWN AS THE YELLOW CLAW!
GASP THE YELLOW CLAW?
THE FARMER'S FACE TURNED WHITE! HE TURNED SUDDENLY AND RAN, SPLASHING ACROSS THE FLOODED FIELD...
NO! WAIT! STOP! COME BACK, YOU FOOL! I ONLY WANT DIRECTIONS! STUPID SUPERSTITIOUS PEASANTS! EVERY ONE OF THEM THE SAME! THEY RUN AT THE VERY MENTION OF THE YELLOW CLAW!
THE JEEP MOVED ON...WESTWARD! INTO THE FOOTHILLS OF THE TIBETIAN ALPS...INTO MIST-FILLED VALLEYS THAT ECHOED OMINOUSLY...
LOOK, GENERAL! A WOMAN STANDS AT THE ROADSIDE AHEAD! PERHAPS SHE CAN HELP US!
WHAT IS THE USE? SHE WILL RUN OFF, WHIMPERING AND FRIGHTENED, LIKE ALL THE OTHERS!
THE YOUNG WOMAN GLIDED OUT OF THE FOG AND HELD UP HER HAND, SIGNALING THE JEEP TO STOP, BLOCKING THE ROAD...
MOVE OVER, YOUNG FOOL! WE ARE ON AN IMPORTANT MISSION!
AND I HAVE COME TO HELP YOU COMPLETE THAT MISSION! I AM SUWAN, GRAND-NIECE OF THE MAN YOU SEEK! HE HAS SENT ME TO GUIDE YOU! FOLLOW ME AND I WILL TAKE YOU TO THE YELLOW CLAW!
THE GENERAL STARED AT THE GIRL AS SHE TURNED AND WALKED INTO THE MIST, THEN ORDERED HIS DRIVER TO FOLLOW HER...
YOUR GRAND-UNCLE... THEY SAY IS A HUNDRED YEARS OLD! HOW IS THAT POSSIBLE?
THE YELLOW CLAW LONG AGO LEARNED THE SECRET OF LONGEVITY FROM A TIBETIAN LAMA! HE IS WELL OVER A HUNDRED! HOW MUCH EVEN I DON'T KNOW! NO ONE KNOWS!
THE GIRL TURNED OFF THE ROAD AND MOVED DOWN A NARROW PASS, THE JEEP CRAWLING CLOSE BEHIND...
HOW DID THE YELLOW CLAW KNOW WE WERE SEARCHING FOR HIM?
THE YELLOW CLAW KNOWS ALL! THE YELLOW CLAW'S POWERS ARE UNUSUAL!
LOOK, GENERAL! UP AHEAD! AN OLD MANCHU PALACE!
THE ANCIENT PALACE LOOMED UP OUT OF THE MIST! THE GENERAL AND HIS PARTY STARED AT IT IN AWE AS THEY CLIMBED FROM THEIR JEEP! SUDDENLY, THE GENERAL LOOKED AROUND...
THE GIRL! SHE...SHE'S DISAPPEARED!
3

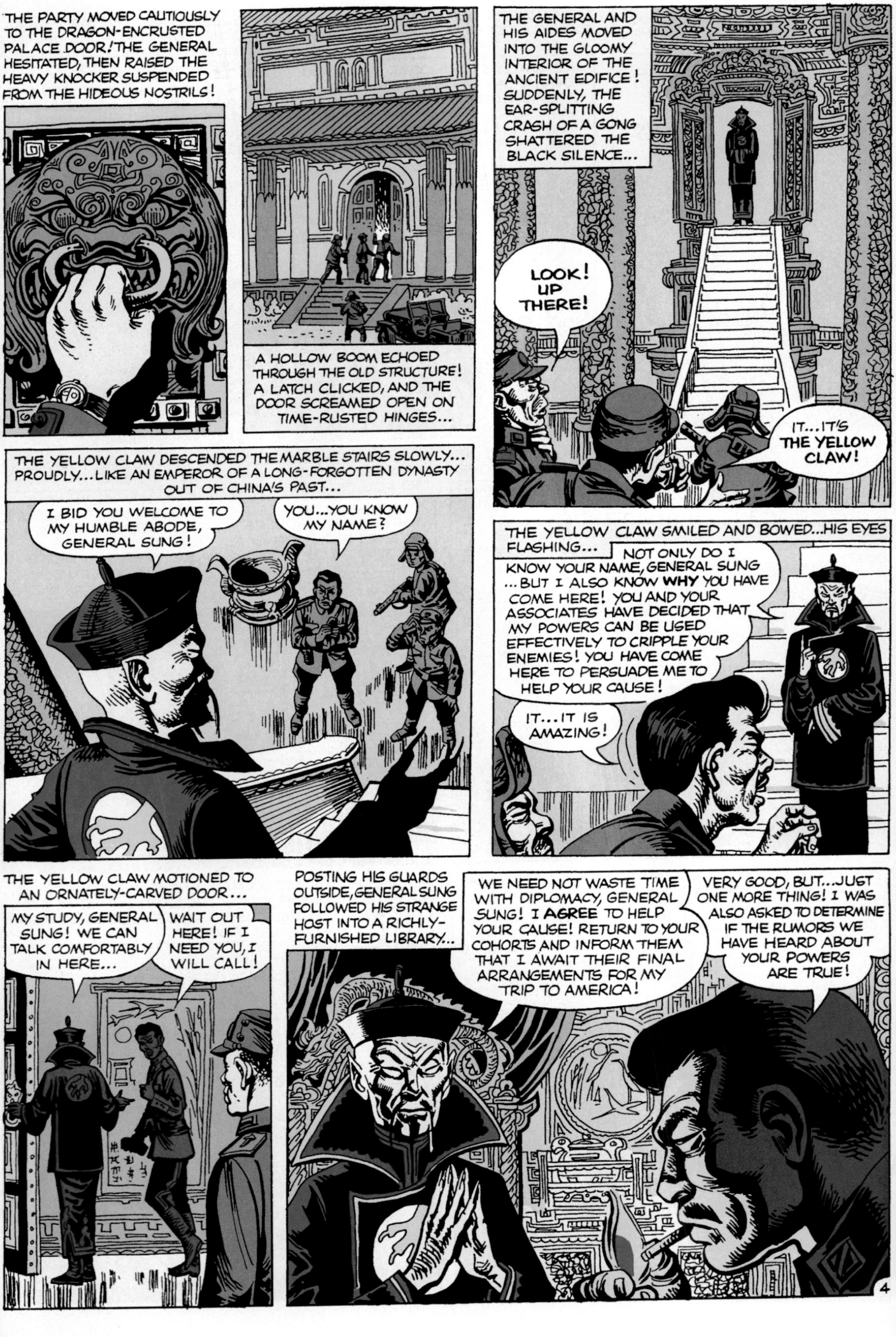

THE PARTY MOVED CAUTIOUSLY TO THE DRAGON-ENCRUSTED PALACE DOOR! THE GENERAL HESITATED, THEN RAISED THE HEAVY KNOCKER SUSPENDED FROM THE HIDEOUS NOSTRILS!
A HOLLOW BOOM ECHOED THROUGH THE OLD STRUCTURE! A LATCH CLICKED, AND THE DOOR SCREAMED OPEN ON TIME-RUSTED HINGES...
THE GENERAL AND HIS AIDES MOVED INTO THE GLOOMY INTERIOR OF THE ANCIENT EDIFICE! SUDDENLY, THE EAR-SPLITTING CRASH OF A GONG SHATTERED THE BLACK SILENCE...
LOOK! UP THERE!
IT...IT'S THE YELLOW CLAW!
THE YELLOW CLAW DESCENDED THE MARBLE STAIRS SLOWLY... PROUDLY...LIKE AN EMPEROR OF A LONG-FORGOTTEN DYNASTY OUT OF CHINA'S PAST...
I BID YOU WELCOME TO MY HUMBLE ABODE, GENERAL SUNG!
YOU...YOU KNOW MY NAME?
THE YELLOW CLAW SMILED AND BOWED...HIS EYES FLASHING...
NOT ONLY DO I KNOW YOUR NAME, GENERAL SUNG ...BUT I ALSO KNOW WHY YOU HAVE COME HERE! YOU AND YOUR ASSOCIATES HAVE DECIDED THAT MY POWERS CAN BE USED EFFECTIVELY TO CRIPPLE YOUR ENEMIES! YOU HAVE COME HERE TO PERSUADE ME TO HELP YOUR CAUSE!
IT...IT IS AMAZING!
THE YELLOW CLAW MOTIONED TO AN ORNATELY-CARVED DOOR...
MY STUDY, GENERAL SUNG! WE CAN TALK COMFORTABLY IN HERE...
WAIT OUT HERE! IF I NEED YOU, I WILL CALL!
POSTING HIS GUARDS OUTSIDE, GENERAL SUNG FOLLOWED HIS STRANGE HOST INTO A RICHLY-FURNISHED LIBRARY...
WE NEED NOT WASTE TIME WITH DIPLOMACY, GENERAL SUNG! I AGREE TO HELP YOUR CAUSE! RETURN TO YOUR COHORTS AND INFORM THEM THAT I AWAIT THEIR FINAL ARRANGEMENTS FOR MY TRIP TO AMERICA!
VERY GOOD, BUT...JUST ONE MORE THING! I WAS ALSO ASKED TO DETERMINE IF THE RUMORS WE HAVE HEARD ABOUT YOUR POWERS ARE TRUE!

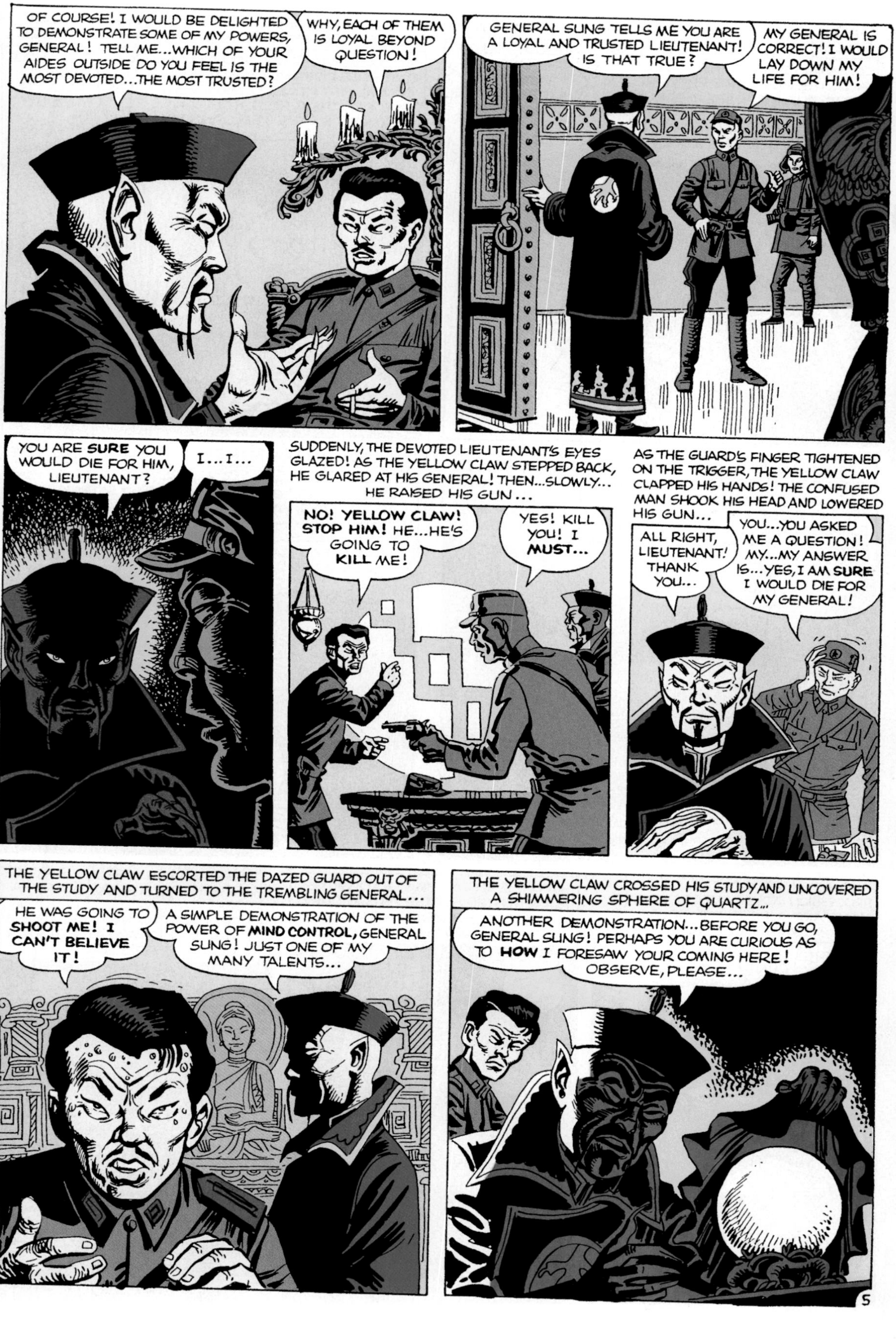
OF COURSE! I WOULD BE DELIGHTED TO DEMONSTRATE SOME OF MY POWERS, GENERAL! TELL ME...WHICH OF YOUR AIDES OUTSIDE DO YOU FEEL IS THE MOST DEVOTED...THE MOST TRUSTED?
WHY, EACH OF THEM IS LOYAL BEYOND QUESTION!
GENERAL SUNG TELLS ME YOU ARE A LOYAL AND TRUSTED LIEUTENANT! IS THAT TRUE?
MY GENERAL IS CORRECT! I WOULD LAY DOWN MY LIFE FOR HIM!
YOU ARE **SURE** YOU WOULD DIE FOR HIM, LIEUTENANT?
I...I...
SUDDENLY, THE DEVOTED LIEUTENANT'S EYES GLAZED! AS THE YELLOW CLAW STEPPED BACK, HE GLARED AT HIS GENERAL! THEN...SLOWLY... HE RAISED HIS GUN...
NO! YELLOW CLAW! STOP HIM! HE...HE'S GOING TO **KILL** ME!
YES! KILL YOU! I **MUST...**
AS THE GUARD'S FINGER TIGHTENED ON THE TRIGGER, THE YELLOW CLAW CLAPPED HIS HANDS! THE CONFUSED MAN SHOOK HIS HEAD AND LOWERED HIS GUN...
ALL RIGHT, LIEUTENANT! THANK YOU...
YOU...YOU ASKED ME A QUESTION! MY...MY ANSWER IS...YES, I AM **SURE** I WOULD DIE FOR MY GENERAL!
THE YELLOW CLAW ESCORTED THE DAZED GUARD OUT OF THE STUDY AND TURNED TO THE TREMBLING GENERAL...
HE WAS GOING TO **SHOOT ME! I CAN'T BELIEVE IT!**
A SIMPLE DEMONSTRATION OF THE POWER OF **MIND CONTROL**, GENERAL SUNG! JUST ONE OF MY MANY TALENTS...
THE YELLOW CLAW CROSSED HIS STUDY AND UNCOVERED A SHIMMERING SPHERE OF QUARTZ...
ANOTHER DEMONSTRATION...BEFORE YOU GO, GENERAL SUNG! PERHAPS YOU ARE CURIOUS AS TO **HOW** I FORESAW YOUR COMING HERE! OBSERVE, PLEASE...

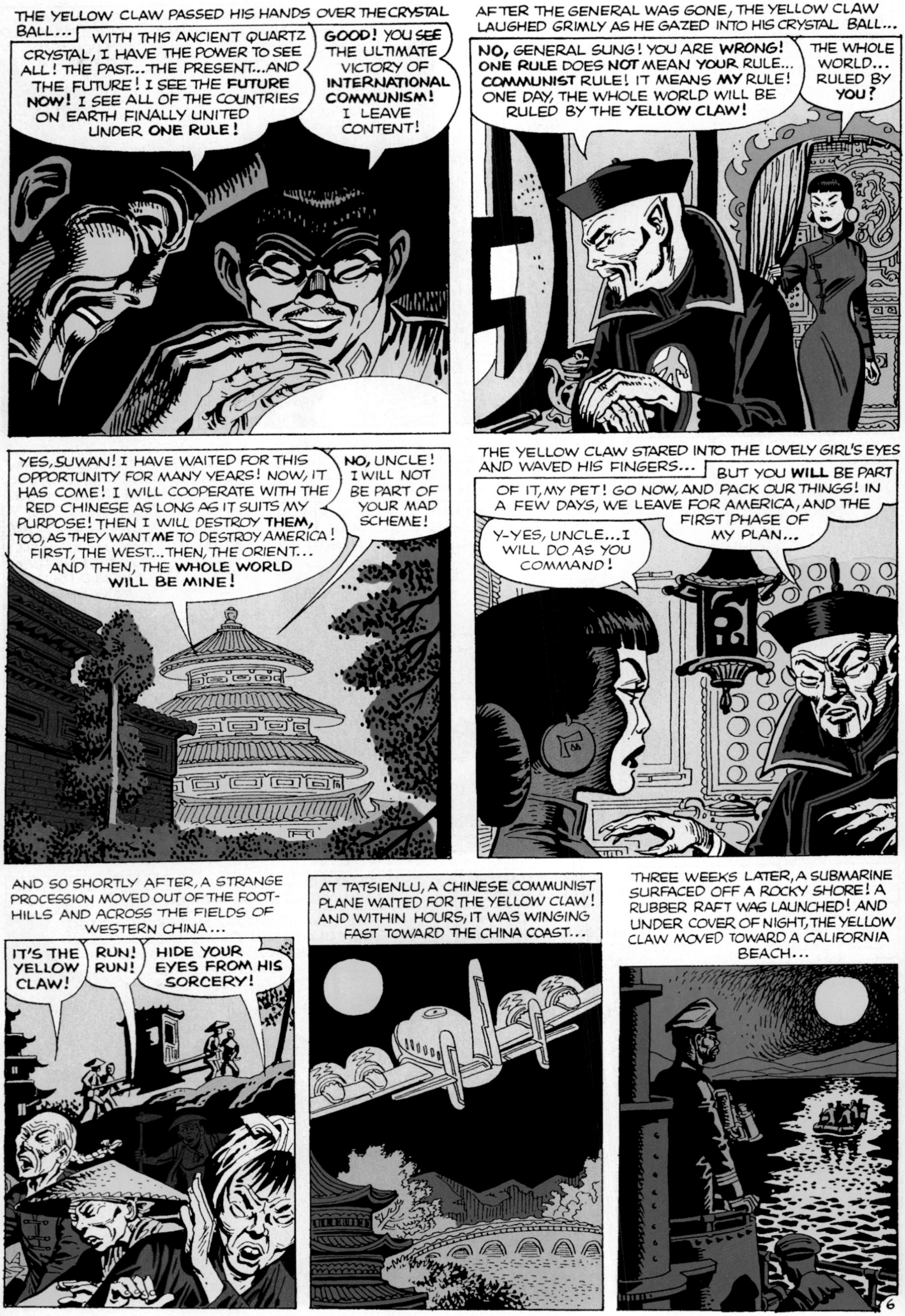

THE YELLOW CLAW PASSED HIS HANDS OVER THE CRYSTAL BALL...
WITH THIS ANCIENT QUARTZ CRYSTAL, I HAVE THE POWER TO SEE ALL! THE PAST...THE PRESENT...AND THE FUTURE! I SEE THE FUTURE NOW! I SEE ALL OF THE COUNTRIES ON EARTH FINALLY UNITED UNDER ONE RULE!
GOOD! YOU SEE THE ULTIMATE VICTORY OF INTERNATIONAL COMMUNISM! I LEAVE CONTENT!
AFTER THE GENERAL WAS GONE, THE YELLOW CLAW LAUGHED GRIMLY AS HE GAZED INTO HIS CRYSTAL BALL...
NO, GENERAL SUNG! YOU ARE WRONG! ONE RULE DOES NOT MEAN YOUR RULE... COMMUNIST RULE! IT MEANS MY RULE! ONE DAY, THE WHOLE WORLD WILL BE RULED BY THE YELLOW CLAW!
THE WHOLE WORLD... RULED BY YOU?
YES, SUWAN! I HAVE WAITED FOR THIS OPPORTUNITY FOR MANY YEARS! NOW, IT HAS COME! I WILL COOPERATE WITH THE RED CHINESE AS LONG AS IT SUITS MY PURPOSE! THEN I WILL DESTROY THEM, TOO, AS THEY WANT ME TO DESTROY AMERICA! FIRST, THE WEST...THEN, THE ORIENT... AND THEN, THE WHOLE WORLD WILL BE MINE!
NO, UNCLE! I WILL NOT BE PART OF YOUR MAD SCHEME!
THE YELLOW CLAW STARED INTO THE LOVELY GIRL'S EYES AND WAVED HIS FINGERS...
BUT YOU WILL BE PART OF IT, MY PET! GO NOW, AND PACK OUR THINGS! IN A FEW DAYS, WE LEAVE FOR AMERICA, AND THE FIRST PHASE OF MY PLAN...
Y-YES, UNCLE...I WILL DO AS YOU COMMAND!
AND SO SHORTLY AFTER, A STRANGE PROCESSION MOVED OUT OF THE FOOT-HILLS AND ACROSS THE FIELDS OF WESTERN CHINA...
IT'S THE YELLOW CLAW!
RUN! RUN!
HIDE YOUR EYES FROM HIS SORCERY!
AT TATSIENLU, A CHINESE COMMUNIST PLANE WAITED FOR THE YELLOW CLAW! AND WITHIN HOURS, IT WAS WINGING FAST TOWARD THE CHINA COAST...
THREE WEEKS LATER, A SUBMARINE SURFACED OFF A ROCKY SHORE! A RUBBER RAFT WAS LAUNCHED! AND UNDER COVER OF NIGHT, THE YELLOW CLAW MOVED TOWARD A CALIFORNIA BEACH...
6

AND SO IT WAS THAT THE YELLOW CLAW CAME TO AMERICA! IN AN OLD CURIO SHOP IN THE CHINESE SECTION OF SAN FRANCISCO, HE SET UP HIS HEADQUARTERS...

ACH! YOU ARE MAD, YELLOW CLAW! I VOULD NEFFER VORK FOR YOU...

BUT, YOU **WILL** WORK FOR ME, HERR VOLTZMANN... AND **GLADLY**!

...BECAUSE, IF YOU **REFUSE**, THE AMERICAN AUTHORITIES WILL LEARN WHERE THEY CAN FIND KARL VON HORSTBADEN... ALIAS FRITZ VOLTZMANN...THE MISSING EX-COMMANDANT OF AUSCHWITZ CONCENTRATION CAMP...AND ONE OF THE WORLD'S MOST WANTED NAZI WAR CRIMINALS!

IN WASHINGTON, D.C., A YOUNG F.B.I. AGENT WAITED TO CONFER WITH HIS SUPERIOR...

MR. JAMES WOO TO SEE YOU, SIR...

GOOD... SHOW HIM RIGHT IN!

JIMMY, WE'VE GOT A TOUGH CASE ON OUR HANDS! I THINK **YOU'RE** THE MAN TO HANDLE IT! OUR INFORMANT IN THE RED CHINESE HIGH COMMAND REPORTS THAT THE COMMUNISTS HAVE SENT A SPECIAL AGENT TO WRECK THE U.S. DEFENSE EFFORT!

WHAT THIS AGENT LOOKS LIKE...OR HOW HE OPERATES, WE DON'T KNOW! THE ONLY INFO WE HAVE IS THAT THE GUY IS SOME SORT OF LEGENDARY FIGURE ...A CHINESE MYSTIC CALLED THE YELLOW CLAW!

THE **YELLOW CLAW**? I'VE HEARD OF HIM! WHEN I WAS A KID, MY PARENTS SPOKE OF HIM! BUT I NEVER BELIEVED HE EXISTED!

HE EXISTS, ALL RIGHT! IN FACT, WE BELIEVE HE'S IN THIS COUNTRY RIGHT NOW...SOMEWHERE IN SAN FRANCISCO! JIMMY, YOU'VE GOT TO TRACK HIM DOWN...**BEFORE** HE DOES ANY DAMAGE!

I'LL DO MY BEST, CHIEF! I'LL LEAVE FOR THE COAST ON THE NEXT PLANE...

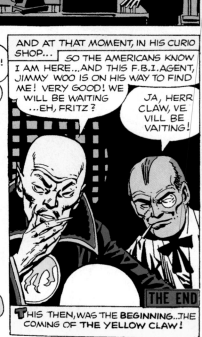

AND AT THAT MOMENT, IN HIS CURIO SHOP...

SO THE AMERICANS KNOW I AM HERE...AND THIS F.B.I. AGENT, JIMMY WOO IS ON HIS WAY TO FIND ME! VERY GOOD! WE WILL BE WAITING ...EH, FRITZ?

JA, HERR CLAW, VE VILL BE VAITING!

THE END

THIS THEN, WAS THE **BEGINNING**...THE COMING OF **THE YELLOW CLAW**!

WHAT IF? #9 (JUNE 1978) THE FIRST APPEARANCE OF THE 1950S AVENGERS

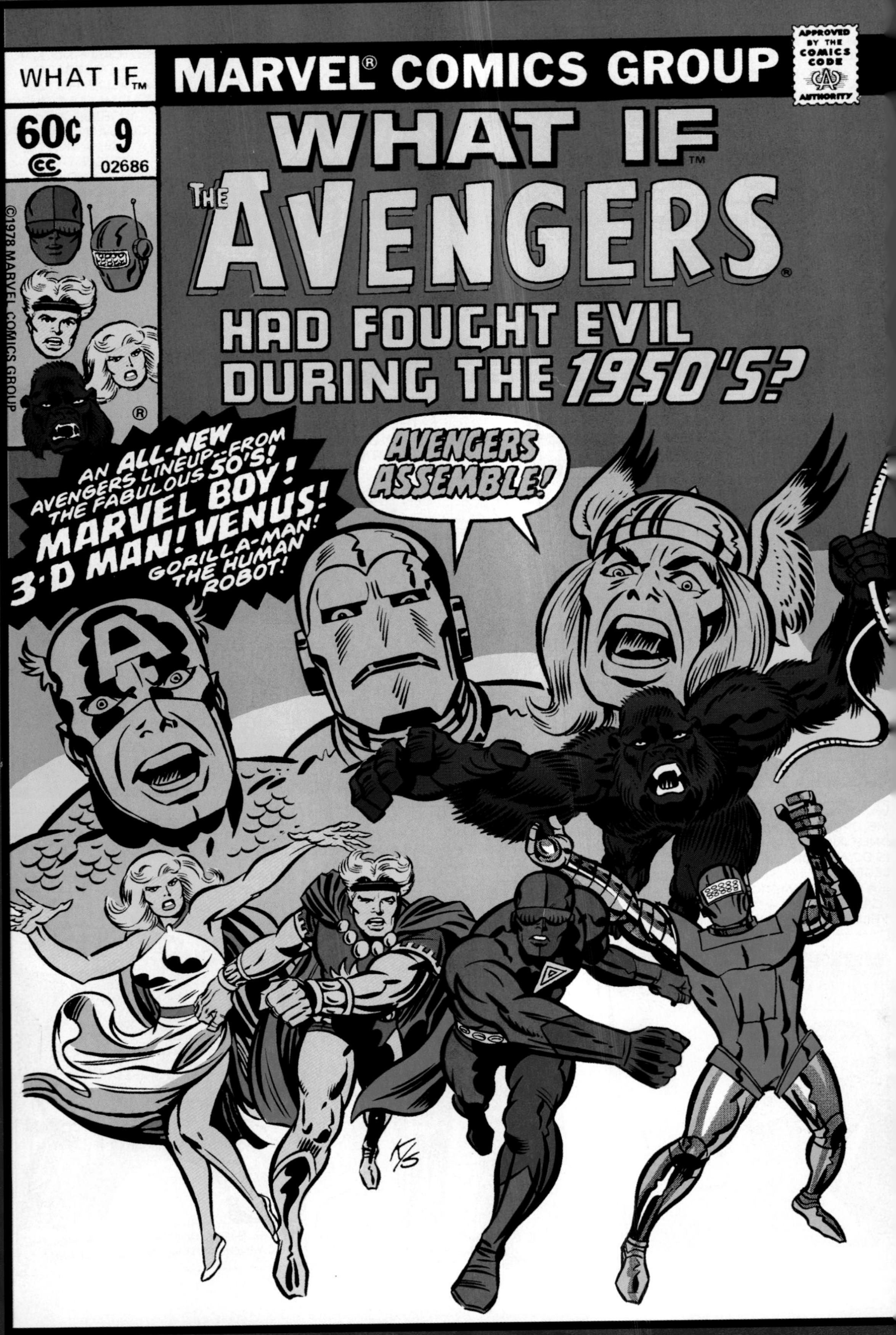

WHAT IF™
MARVEL® COMICS GROUP
APPROVED BY THE COMICS CODE AUTHORITY
60¢
9
02686
WHAT IF™
THE AVENGERS®
HAD FOUGHT EVIL DURING THE 1950'S?
©1978 MARVEL COMICS GROUP
AN ALL-NEW AVENGERS LINEUP--FROM THE FABULOUS 50'S! MARVEL BOY! 3-D MAN! VENUS! GORILLA-MAN! THE HUMAN ROBOT!
AVENGERS ASSEMBLE!

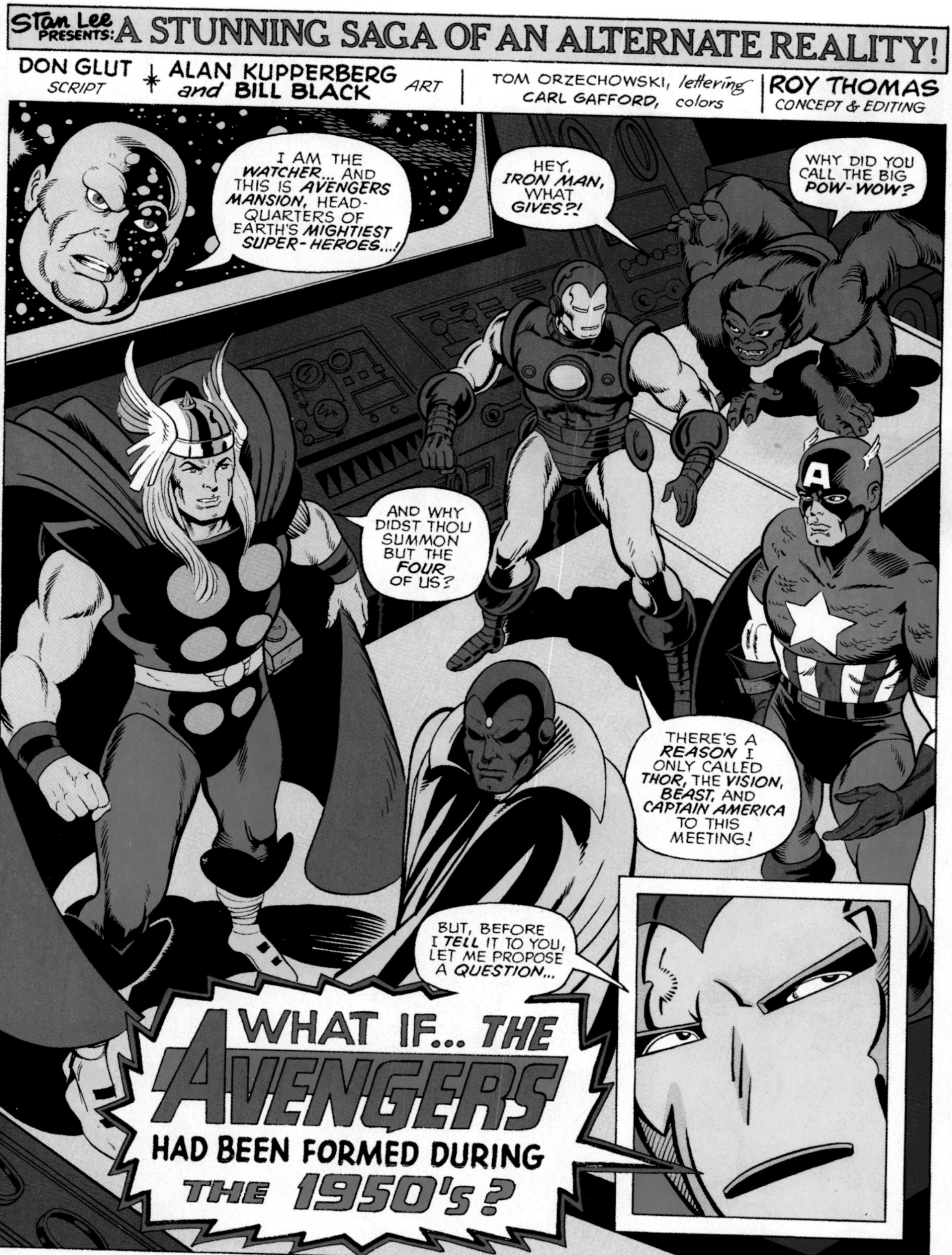
Stan Lee PRESENTS: A STUNNING SAGA OF AN ALTERNATE REALITY!
DON GLUT SCRIPT
ALAN KUPPERBERG and BILL BLACK ART
TOM ORZECHOWSKI, lettering
CARL GAFFORD, colors
ROY THOMAS CONCEPT & EDITING
I AM THE WATCHER... AND THIS IS AVENGERS MANSION, HEADQUARTERS OF EARTH'S MIGHTIEST SUPER-HEROES...!
HEY, IRON MAN, WHAT GIVES?!
WHY DID YOU CALL THE BIG POW-WOW?
AND WHY DIDST THOU SUMMON BUT THE FOUR OF US?
THERE'S A REASON I ONLY CALLED THOR, THE VISION, BEAST, AND CAPTAIN AMERICA TO THIS MEETING!
BUT, BEFORE I TELL IT TO YOU, LET ME PROPOSE A QUESTION...
WHAT IF... THE AVENGERS HAD BEEN FORMED DURING THE 1950's?

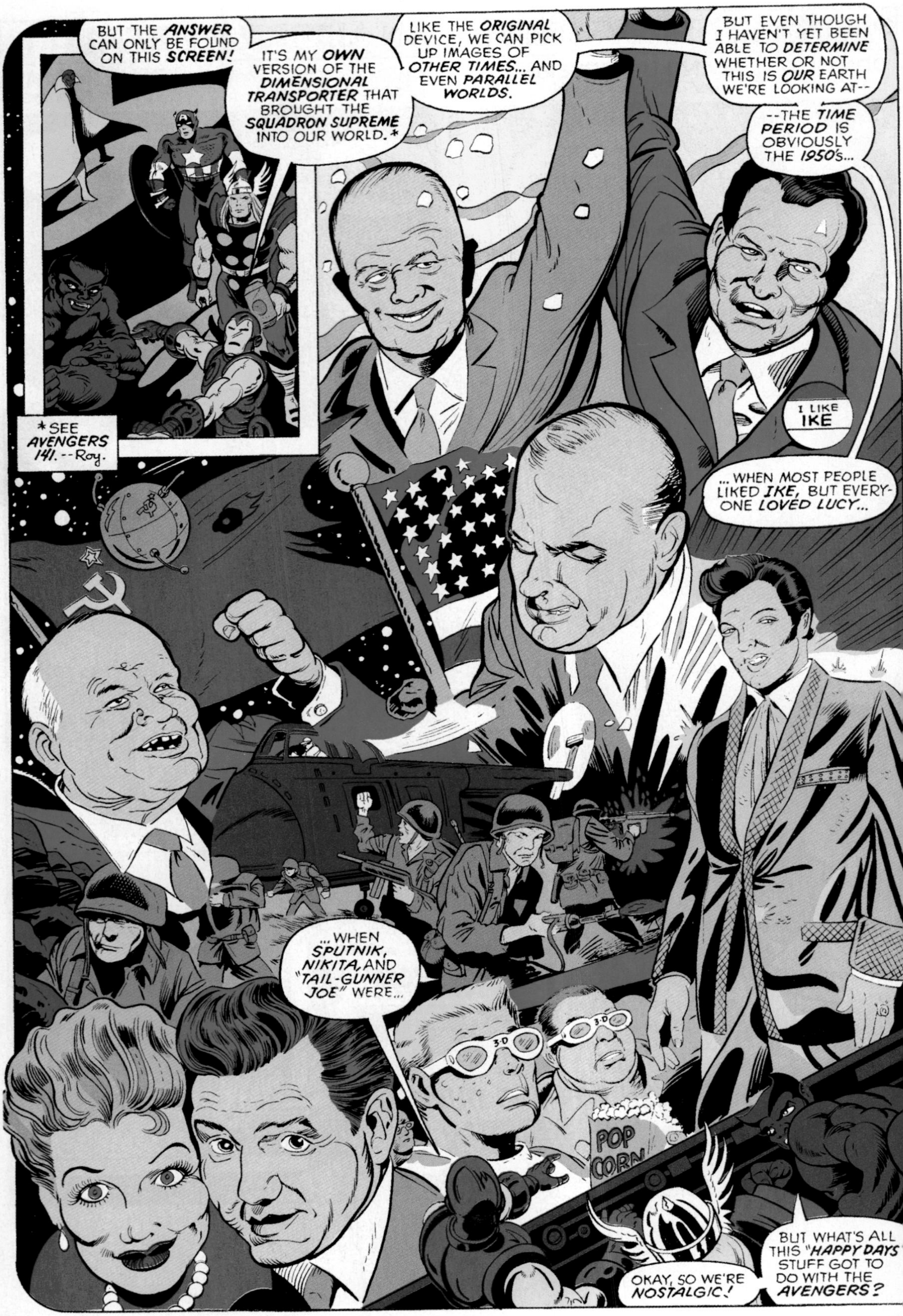
BUT THE ANSWER CAN ONLY BE FOUND ON THIS SCREEN!
IT'S MY OWN VERSION OF THE DIMENSIONAL TRANSPORTER THAT BROUGHT THE SQUADRON SUPREME INTO OUR WORLD.*
LIKE THE ORIGINAL DEVICE, WE CAN PICK UP IMAGES OF OTHER TIMES... AND EVEN PARALLEL WORLDS.
BUT EVEN THOUGH I HAVEN'T YET BEEN ABLE TO DETERMINE WHETHER OR NOT THIS IS OUR EARTH WE'RE LOOKING AT--
--THE TIME PERIOD IS OBVIOUSLY THE 1950's...
*SEE AVENGERS 141. --Roy.
I LIKE IKE
...WHEN MOST PEOPLE LIKED IKE, BUT EVERY-ONE LOVED LUCY...
...WHEN SPUTNIK, NIKITA, AND "TAIL-GUNNER JOE" WERE...
3-D
3-D
POP CORN
OKAY, SO WE'RE NOSTALGIC!
BUT WHAT'S ALL THIS "HAPPY DAYS" STUFF GOT TO DO WITH THE AVENGERS?

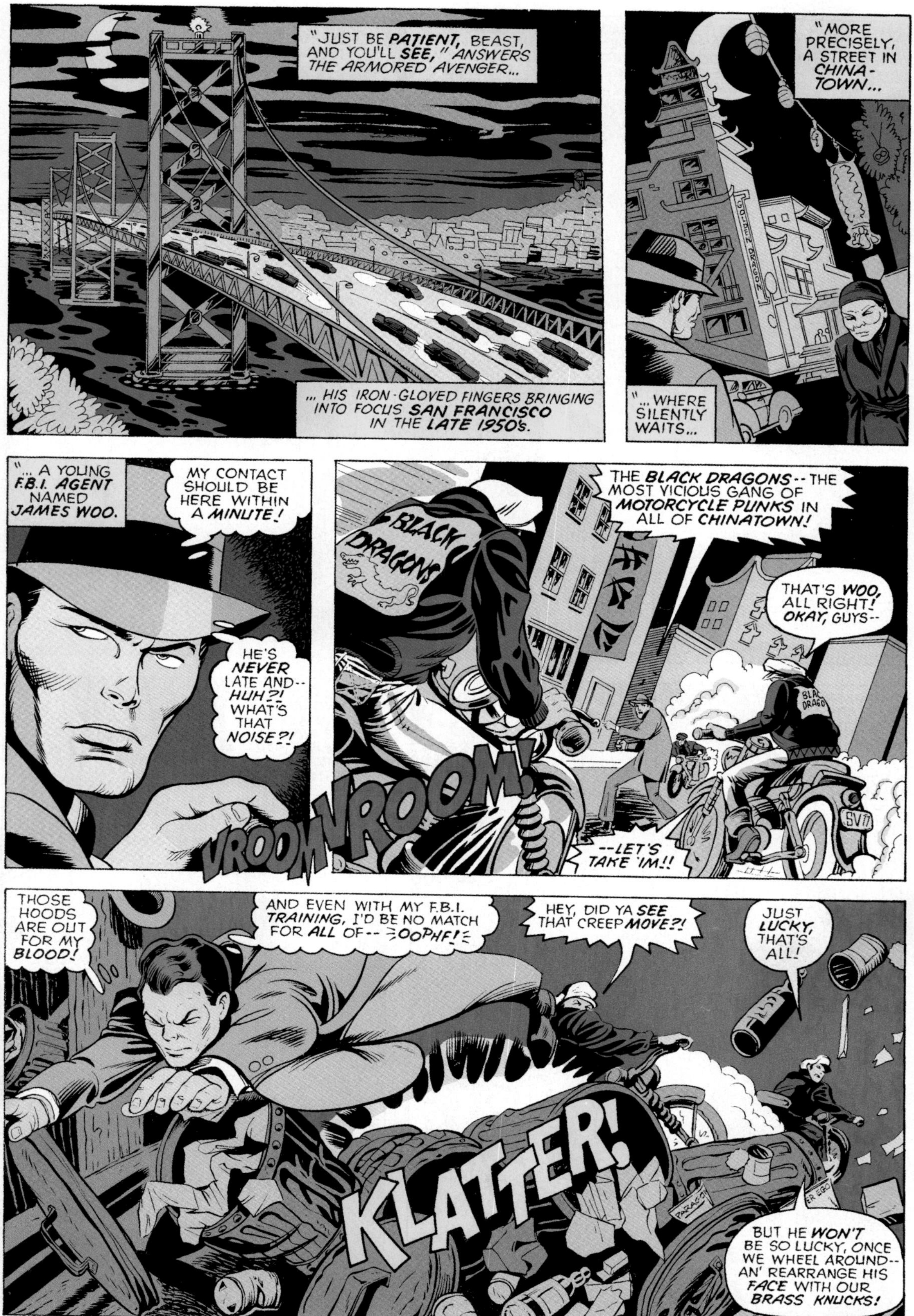

"JUST BE PATIENT, BEAST, AND YOU'LL SEE," ANSWERS THE ARMORED AVENGER...
... HIS IRON-GLOVED FINGERS BRINGING INTO FOCUS SAN FRANCISCO IN THE LATE 1950's.
"MORE PRECISELY, A STREET IN CHINA-TOWN...
GOLDEN DRAGON
"... WHERE SILENTLY WAITS...
"... A YOUNG F.B.I. AGENT NAMED JAMES WOO.
MY CONTACT SHOULD BE HERE WITHIN A MINUTE!
HE'S NEVER LATE AND-- HUH?! WHAT'S THAT NOISE?!
VROOM VROOM!
BLACK DRAGONS
THE BLACK DRAGONS -- THE MOST VICIOUS GANG OF MOTORCYCLE PUNKS IN ALL OF CHINATOWN!
THAT'S WOO, ALL RIGHT! OKAY, GUYS--
SV17
--LET'S TAKE 'IM!!
THOSE HOODS ARE OUT FOR MY BLOOD!
AND EVEN WITH MY F.B.I. TRAINING, I'D BE NO MATCH FOR ALL OF-- OOPHF!
HEY, DID YA SEE THAT CREEP MOVE?!
JUST LUCKY, THAT'S ALL!
KLATTER!
BUT HE WON'T BE SO LUCKY, ONCE WE WHEEL AROUND-- AN' REARRANGE HIS FACE WITH OUR BRASS KNUCKS!

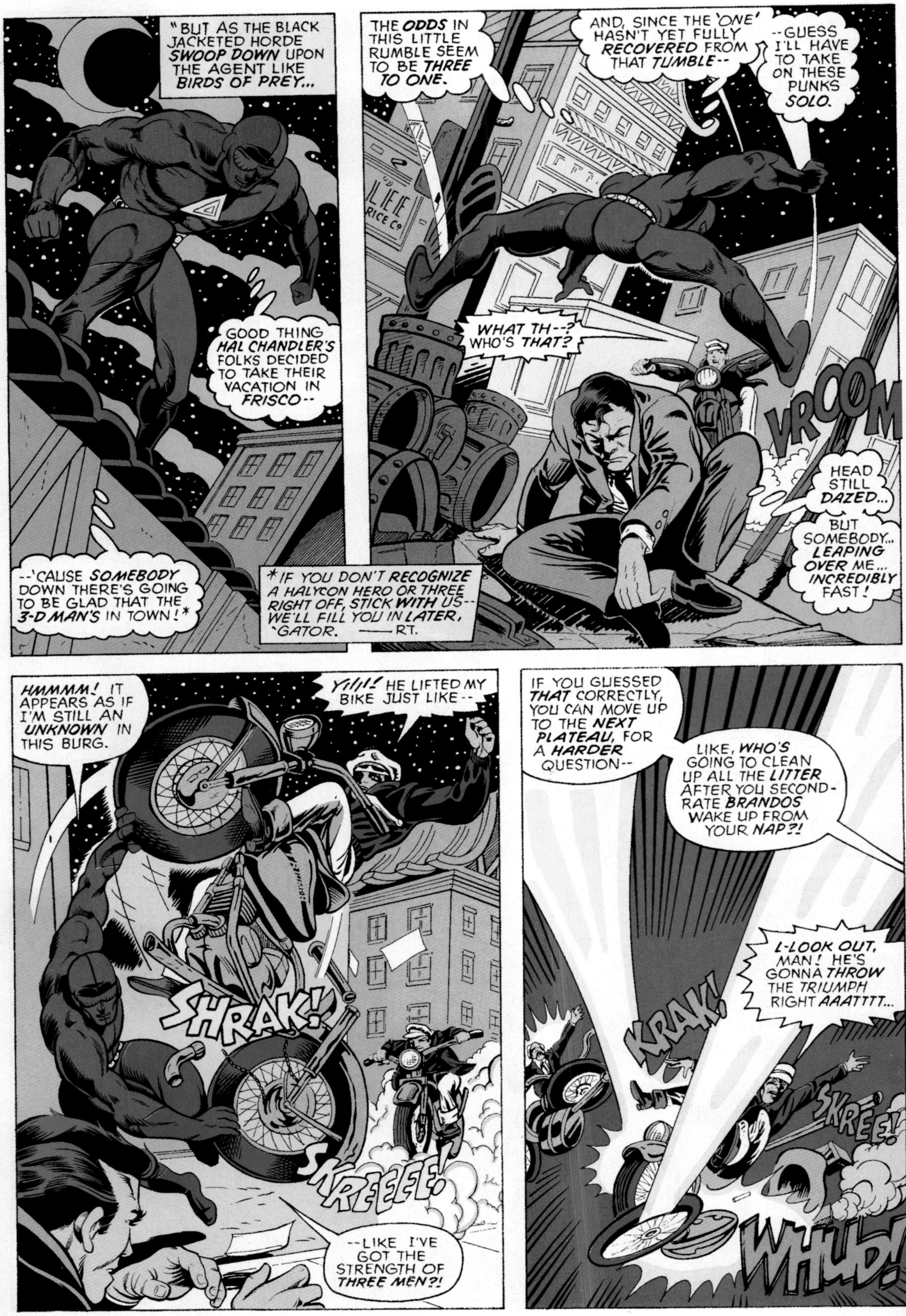
"BUT AS THE BLACK JACKETED HORDE SWOOP DOWN UPON THE AGENT LIKE BIRDS OF PREY...
GOOD THING HAL CHANDLER'S FOLKS DECIDED TO TAKE THEIR VACATION IN FRISCO--
--'CAUSE SOMEBODY DOWN THERE'S GOING TO BE GLAD THAT THE 3-D MAN'S IN TOWN!*
*IF YOU DON'T RECOGNIZE A HALYCON HERO OR THREE RIGHT OFF, STICK WITH US--WE'LL FILL YOU IN LATER, 'GATOR. ——RT.
THE ODDS IN THIS LITTLE RUMBLE SEEM TO BE THREE TO ONE.
AND, SINCE THE 'ONE' HASN'T YET FULLY RECOVERED FROM THAT TUMBLE--
--GUESS I'LL HAVE TO TAKE ON THESE PUNKS SOLO.
WHAT TH--? WHO'S THAT?
VROOOM
HEAD STILL DAZED... BUT SOMEBODY... LEAPING OVER ME... INCREDIBLY FAST!
HMMMM! IT APPEARS AS IF I'M STILL AN UNKNOWN IN THIS BURG.
YIIII! HE LIFTED MY BIKE JUST LIKE--
SHRAK!
SKREEEEE!
--LIKE I'VE GOT THE STRENGTH OF THREE MEN?!
IF YOU GUESSED THAT CORRECTLY, YOU CAN MOVE UP TO THE NEXT PLATEAU, FOR A HARDER QUESTION--
LIKE, WHO'S GOING TO CLEAN UP ALL THE LITTER AFTER YOU SECOND-RATE BRANDOS WAKE UP FROM YOUR NAP?!
L-LOOK OUT, MAN! HE'S GONNA THROW THE TRIUMPH RIGHT AAATTTT...
KRAK!
SKREE!
WHUD!

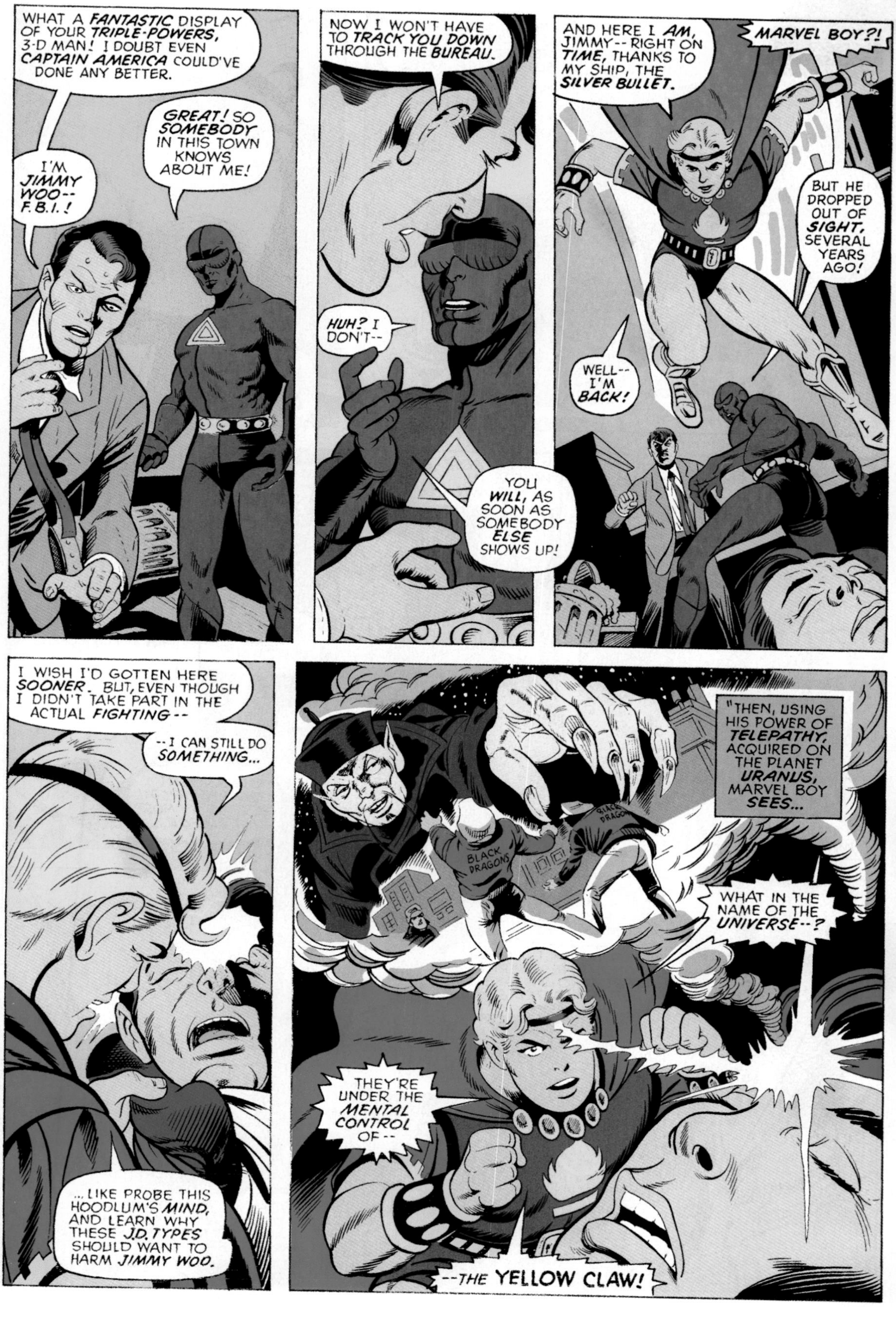

WHAT A FANTASTIC DISPLAY OF YOUR TRIPLE-POWERS, 3-D MAN! I DOUBT EVEN CAPTAIN AMERICA COULD'VE DONE ANY BETTER.
I'M JIMMY WOO-- F.B.I.!
GREAT! SO SOMEBODY IN THIS TOWN KNOWS ABOUT ME!
NOW I WON'T HAVE TO TRACK YOU DOWN THROUGH THE BUREAU.
HUH? I DON'T--
YOU WILL, AS SOON AS SOMEBODY ELSE SHOWS UP!
AND HERE I AM, JIMMY-- RIGHT ON TIME, THANKS TO MY SHIP, THE SILVER BULLET.
MARVEL BOY?!
BUT HE DROPPED OUT OF SIGHT, SEVERAL YEARS AGO!
WELL-- I'M BACK!
I WISH I'D GOTTEN HERE SOONER. BUT, EVEN THOUGH I DIDN'T TAKE PART IN THE ACTUAL FIGHTING--
--I CAN STILL DO SOMETHING...
...LIKE PROBE THIS HOODLUM'S MIND, AND LEARN WHY THESE J.D. TYPES SHOULD WANT TO HARM JIMMY WOO.
"THEN, USING HIS POWER OF TELEPATHY, ACQUIRED ON THE PLANET URANUS, MARVEL BOY SEES...
BLACK DRAGONS
BLACK DRAGON
WHAT IN THE NAME OF THE UNIVERSE--?
THEY'RE UNDER THE MENTAL CONTROL OF--
--THE YELLOW CLAW!

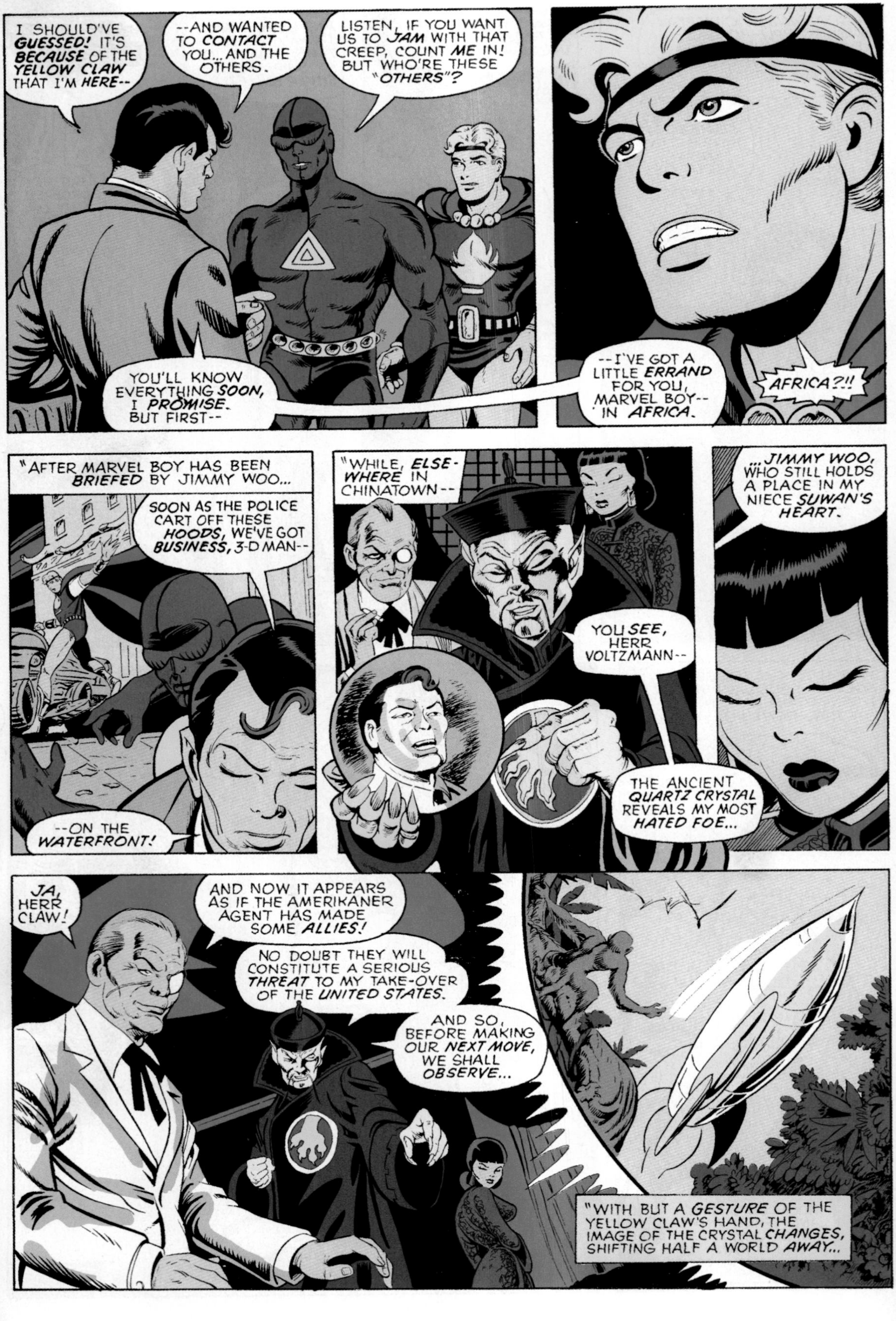
I SHOULD'VE GUESSED! IT'S BECAUSE OF THE YELLOW CLAW THAT I'M HERE--
--AND WANTED TO CONTACT YOU... AND THE OTHERS.
LISTEN, IF YOU WANT US TO JAM WITH THAT CREEP, COUNT ME IN! BUT WHO'RE THESE "OTHERS"?
YOU'LL KNOW EVERYTHING SOON, I PROMISE. BUT FIRST--
--I'VE GOT A LITTLE ERRAND FOR YOU, MARVEL BOY-- IN AFRICA.
AFRICA?!!
"AFTER MARVEL BOY HAS BEEN BRIEFED BY JIMMY WOO...
SOON AS THE POLICE CART OFF THESE HOODS, WE'VE GOT BUSINESS, 3-D MAN--
--ON THE WATERFRONT!
"WHILE, ELSEWHERE IN CHINATOWN--
YOU SEE, HERR VOLTZMANN--
THE ANCIENT QUARTZ CRYSTAL REVEALS MY MOST HATED FOE...
...JIMMY WOO, WHO STILL HOLDS A PLACE IN MY NIECE SUWAN'S HEART.
JA, HERR CLAW!
AND NOW IT APPEARS AS IF THE AMERIKANER AGENT HAS MADE SOME ALLIES!
NO DOUBT THEY WILL CONSTITUTE A SERIOUS THREAT TO MY TAKE-OVER OF THE UNITED STATES.
AND SO, BEFORE MAKING OUR NEXT MOVE, WE SHALL OBSERVE...
"WITH BUT A GESTURE OF THE YELLOW CLAW'S HAND, THE IMAGE OF THE CRYSTAL CHANGES, SHIFTING HALF A WORLD AWAY...

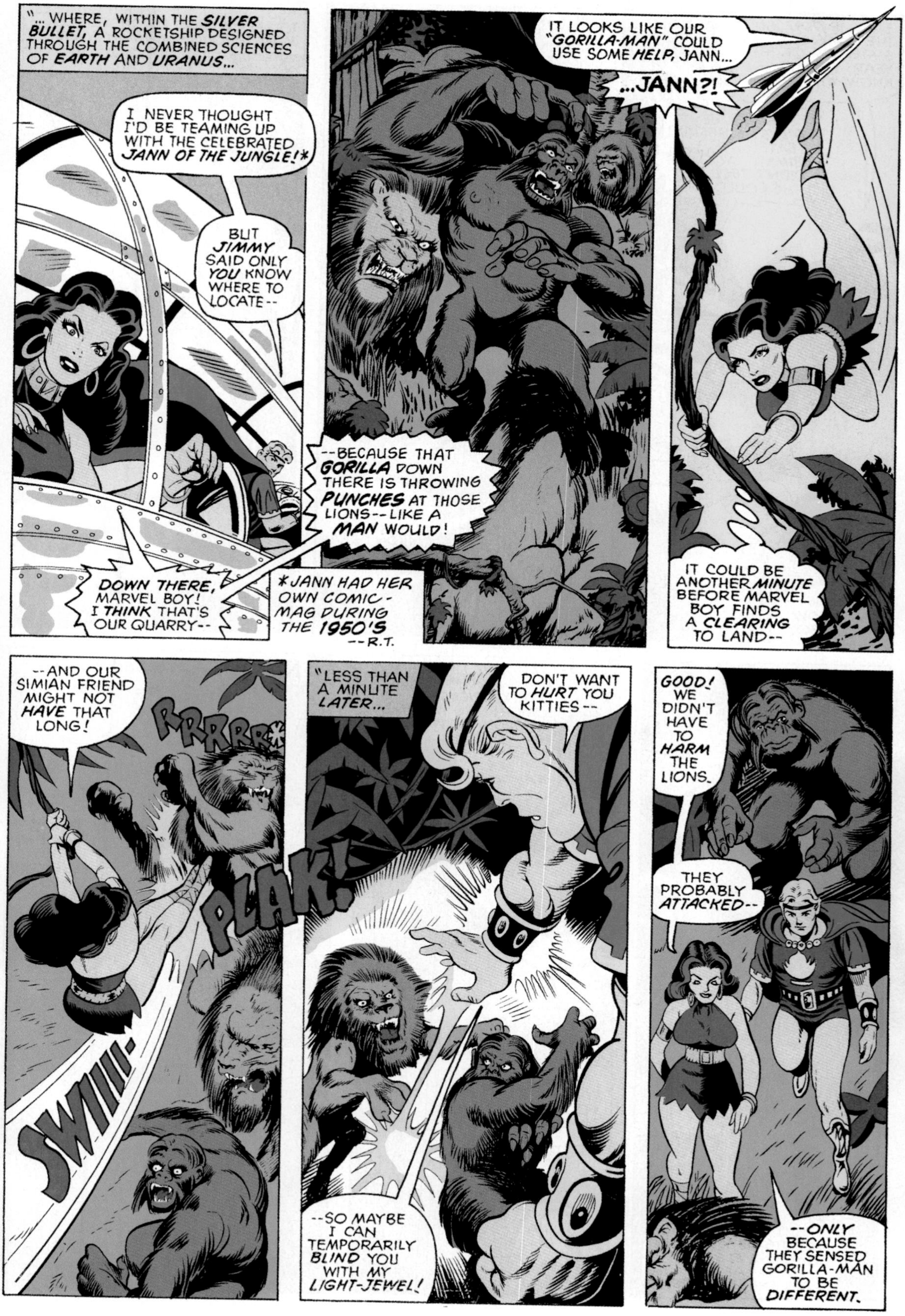
"... WHERE, WITHIN THE SILVER BULLET, A ROCKETSHIP DESIGNED THROUGH THE COMBINED SCIENCES OF EARTH AND URANUS...
I NEVER THOUGHT I'D BE TEAMING UP WITH THE CELEBRATED JANN OF THE JUNGLE!*
BUT JIMMY SAID ONLY YOU KNOW WHERE TO LOCATE--
DOWN THERE, MARVEL BOY! I THINK THAT'S OUR QUARRY--
*JANN HAD HER OWN COMIC-MAG DURING THE 1950'S --R.T.
--BECAUSE THAT GORILLA DOWN THERE IS THROWING PUNCHES AT THOSE LIONS--LIKE A MAN WOULD!
IT LOOKS LIKE OUR "GORILLA-MAN" COULD USE SOME HELP, JANN...
...JANN?!
IT COULD BE ANOTHER MINUTE BEFORE MARVEL BOY FINDS A CLEARING TO LAND--
--AND OUR SIMIAN FRIEND MIGHT NOT HAVE THAT LONG!
RRRRR
PLAK!
SWIIII-
"LESS THAN A MINUTE LATER...
DON'T WANT TO HURT YOU KITTIES--
--SO MAYBE I CAN TEMPORARILY BLIND YOU WITH MY LIGHT-JEWEL!
GOOD! WE DIDN'T HAVE TO HARM THE LIONS.
THEY PROBABLY ATTACKED--
--ONLY BECAUSE THEY SENSED GORILLA-MAN TO BE DIFFERENT.

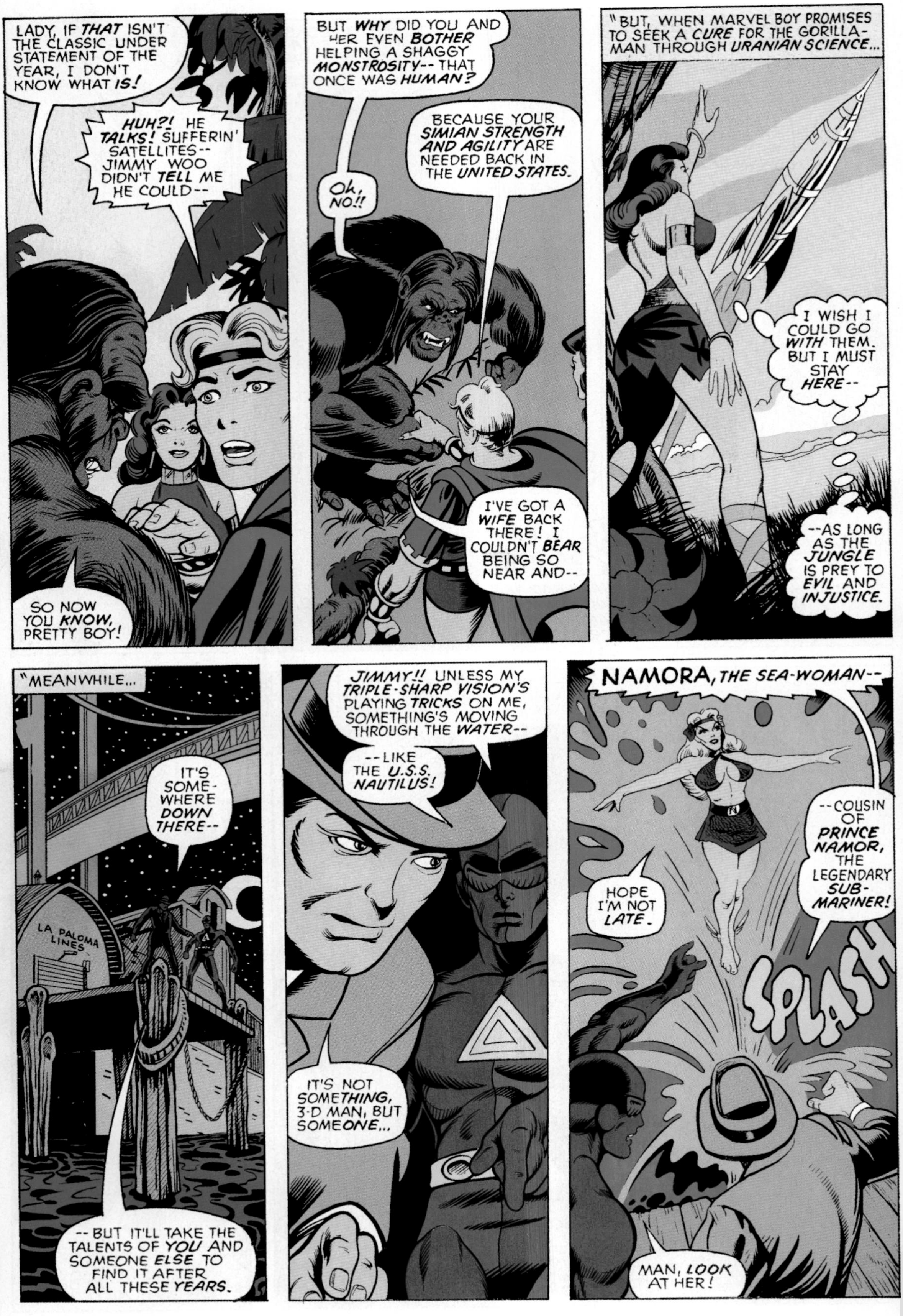

LADY, IF THAT ISN'T THE CLASSIC UNDER STATEMENT OF THE YEAR, I DON'T KNOW WHAT IS!
HUH?! HE TALKS! SUFFERIN' SATELLITES-- JIMMY WOO DIDN'T TELL ME HE COULD--
SO NOW YOU KNOW, PRETTY BOY!
BUT WHY DID YOU AND HER EVEN BOTHER HELPING A SHAGGY MONSTROSITY-- THAT ONCE WAS HUMAN?
BECAUSE YOUR SIMIAN STRENGTH AND AGILITY ARE NEEDED BACK IN THE UNITED STATES.
Oh, NO!!
I'VE GOT A WIFE BACK THERE! I COULDN'T BEAR BEING SO NEAR AND--
"BUT, WHEN MARVEL BOY PROMISES TO SEEK A CURE FOR THE GORILLA-MAN THROUGH URANIAN SCIENCE...
I WISH I COULD GO WITH THEM. BUT I MUST STAY HERE--
--AS LONG AS THE JUNGLE IS PREY TO EVIL AND INJUSTICE.
"MEANWHILE...
LA PALOMA LINES
IT'S SOMEWHERE DOWN THERE--
-- BUT IT'LL TAKE THE TALENTS OF YOU AND SOMEONE ELSE TO FIND IT AFTER ALL THESE YEARS.
JIMMY!! UNLESS MY TRIPLE-SHARP VISION'S PLAYING TRICKS ON ME, SOMETHING'S MOVING THROUGH THE WATER--
--LIKE THE U.S.S. NAUTILUS!
IT'S NOT SOMETHING, 3-D MAN, BUT SOMEONE...
NAMORA, THE SEA-WOMAN--
--COUSIN OF PRINCE NAMOR, THE LEGENDARY SUB-MARINER!
HOPE I'M NOT LATE.
SPLASH
MAN, LOOK AT HER!

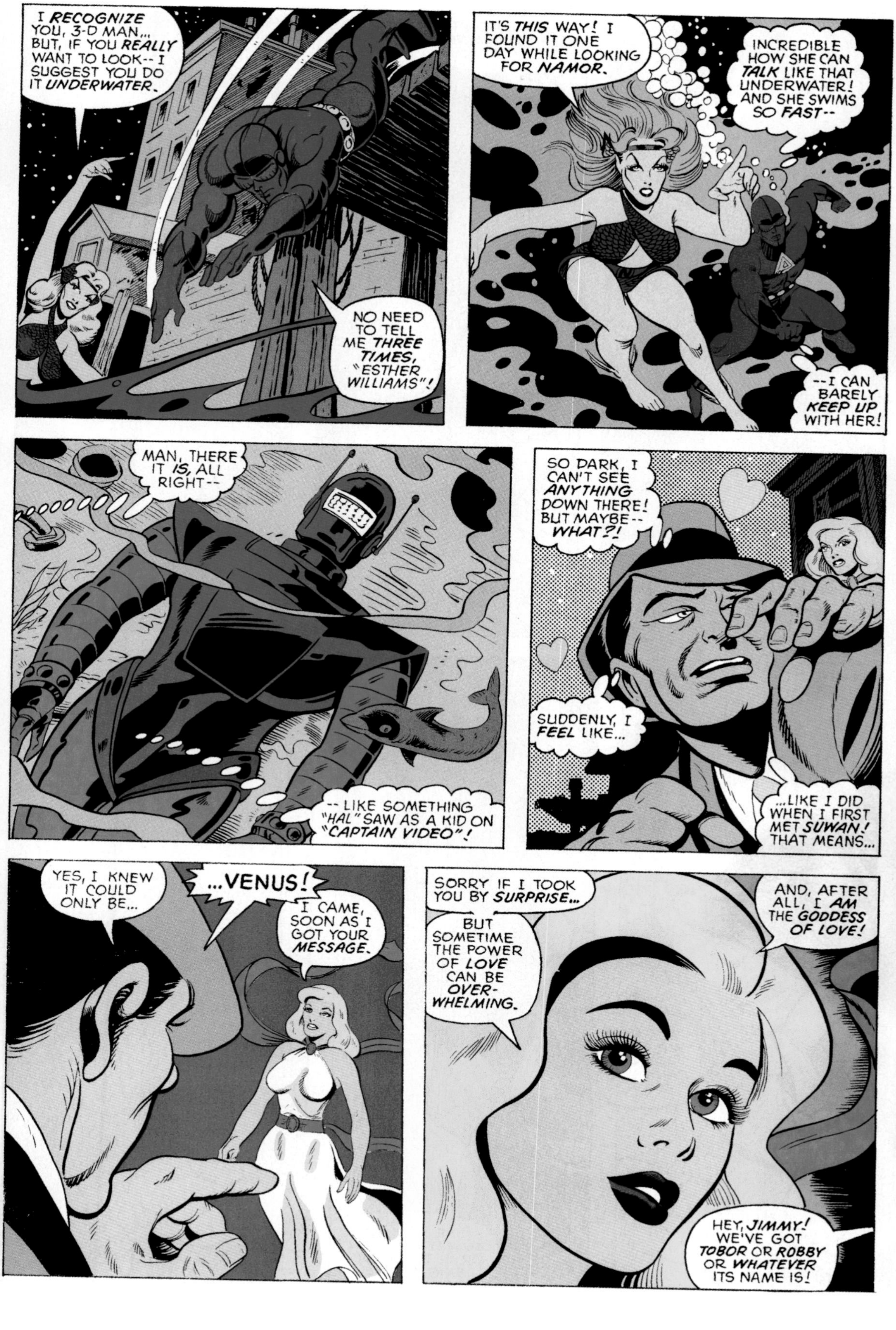
I RECOGNIZE YOU, 3-D MAN... BUT, IF YOU REALLY WANT TO LOOK-- I SUGGEST YOU DO IT UNDERWATER.
NO NEED TO TELL ME THREE TIMES, "ESTHER WILLIAMS"!
IT'S THIS WAY! I FOUND IT ONE DAY WHILE LOOKING FOR NAMOR.
INCREDIBLE HOW SHE CAN TALK LIKE THAT UNDERWATER! AND SHE SWIMS SO FAST--
--I CAN BARELY KEEP UP WITH HER!
MAN, THERE IT IS, ALL RIGHT--
--LIKE SOMETHING "HAL" SAW AS A KID ON "CAPTAIN VIDEO"!
SO DARK, I CAN'T SEE ANYTHING DOWN THERE! BUT MAYBE-- WHAT?!
SUDDENLY, I FEEL LIKE...
...LIKE I DID WHEN I FIRST MET SUWAN! THAT MEANS...
YES, I KNEW IT COULD ONLY BE...
...VENUS!
I CAME, SOON AS I GOT YOUR MESSAGE.
SORRY IF I TOOK YOU BY SURPRISE...
BUT SOMETIME THE POWER OF LOVE CAN BE OVER-WHELMING.
AND, AFTER ALL, I AM THE GODDESS OF LOVE!
HEY, JIMMY! WE'VE GOT TOBOR OR ROBBY OR WHATEVER ITS NAME IS!

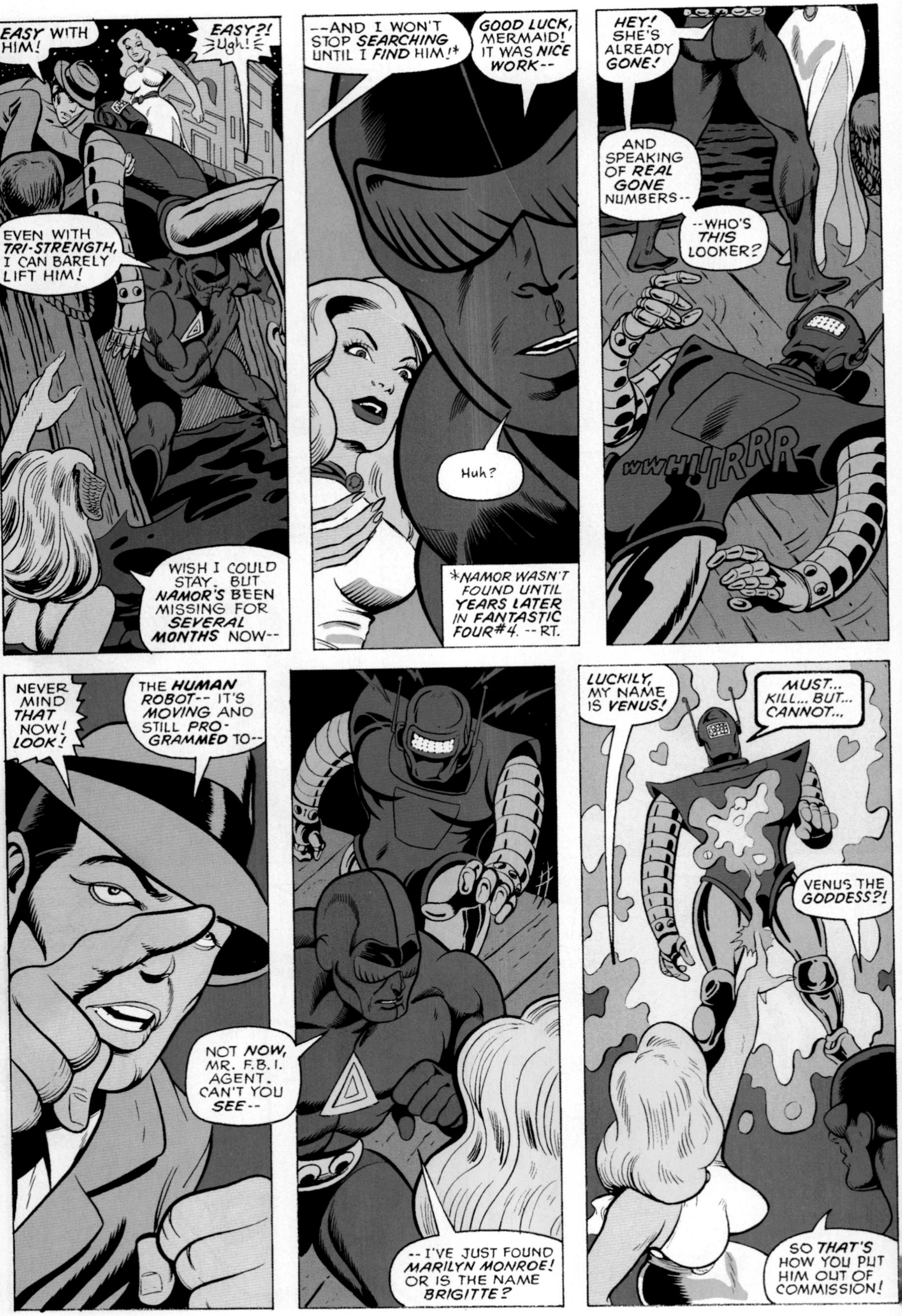
EASY WITH HIM!
EASY?! Ugh!
EVEN WITH TRI-STRENGTH, I CAN BARELY LIFT HIM!
WISH I COULD STAY. BUT NAMOR'S BEEN MISSING FOR SEVERAL MONTHS NOW--
--AND I WON'T STOP SEARCHING UNTIL I FIND HIM!*
GOOD LUCK, MERMAID! IT WAS NICE WORK--
Huh?
*NAMOR WASN'T FOUND UNTIL YEARS LATER IN FANTASTIC FOUR #4. --RT.
HEY! SHE'S ALREADY GONE!
AND SPEAKING OF REAL GONE NUMBERS--
--WHO'S THIS LOOKER?
WWHIIIRRR
NEVER MIND THAT NOW! LOOK!
THE HUMAN ROBOT-- IT'S MOVING AND STILL PRO-GRAMMED TO--
NOT NOW, MR. F.B.I. AGENT. CAN'T YOU SEE--
--I'VE JUST FOUND MARILYN MONROE! OR IS THE NAME BRIGITTE?
LUCKILY, MY NAME IS VENUS!
MUST... KILL... BUT... CANNOT...
VENUS THE GODDESS?!
SO THAT'S HOW YOU PUT HIM OUT OF COMMISSION!

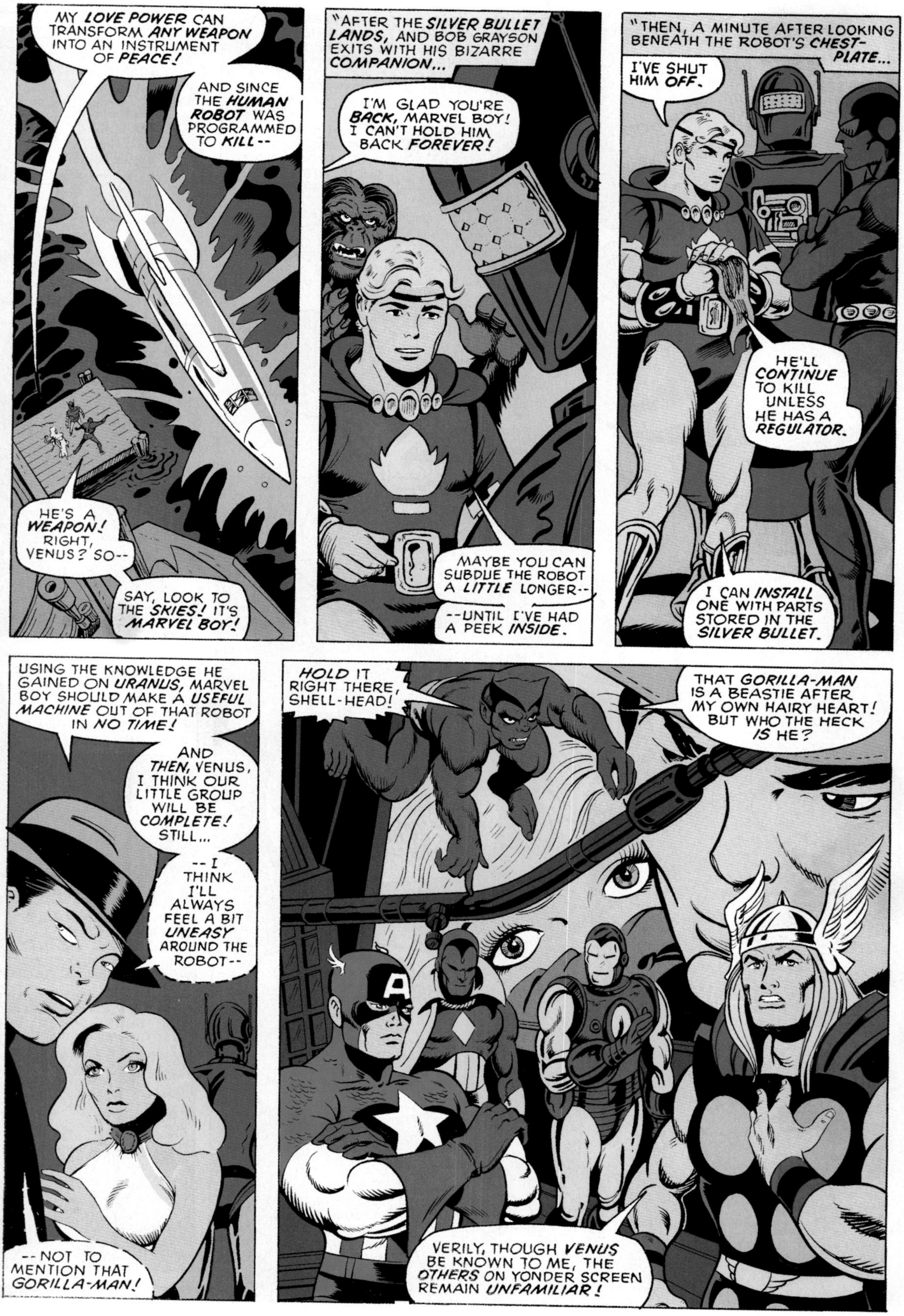
MY *LOVE POWER* CAN TRANSFORM *ANY WEAPON* INTO AN INSTRUMENT OF *PEACE!*
AND SINCE THE *HUMAN ROBOT* WAS PROGRAMMED TO *KILL*--
HE'S A *WEAPON!* RIGHT, VENUS? SO--
SAY, LOOK TO THE *SKIES!* IT'S *MARVEL BOY!*
"AFTER THE *SILVER BULLET LANDS,* AND BOB GRAYSON EXITS WITH HIS BIZARRE *COMPANION...*
I'M GLAD YOU'RE *BACK,* MARVEL BOY! I CAN'T HOLD HIM BACK *FOREVER!*
MAYBE YOU CAN SUBDUE THE ROBOT A *LITTLE* LONGER--
--UNTIL I'VE HAD A PEEK *INSIDE.*
"THEN, A MINUTE AFTER LOOKING BENEATH THE ROBOT'S *CHEST-PLATE...*
I'VE SHUT HIM *OFF.*
HE'LL *CONTINUE* TO KILL UNLESS HE HAS A *REGULATOR.*
I CAN *INSTALL* ONE WITH PARTS STORED IN THE *SILVER BULLET.*
USING THE KNOWLEDGE HE GAINED ON *URANUS,* MARVEL BOY SHOULD MAKE A *USEFUL MACHINE* OUT OF THAT ROBOT IN *NO TIME!*
AND *THEN,* VENUS, I THINK OUR LITTLE GROUP WILL BE *COMPLETE!* STILL...
-- I THINK I'LL ALWAYS FEEL A BIT *UNEASY* AROUND THE ROBOT--
--NOT TO MENTION THAT *GORILLA-MAN!*
HOLD IT RIGHT THERE, SHELL-HEAD!
THAT *GORILLA-MAN* IS A BEASTIE AFTER MY OWN HAIRY HEART! BUT WHO THE HECK *IS* HE?
VERILY, THOUGH *VENUS* BE KNOWN TO ME, THE *OTHERS* ON YONDER SCREEN REMAIN *UNFAMILIAR!*

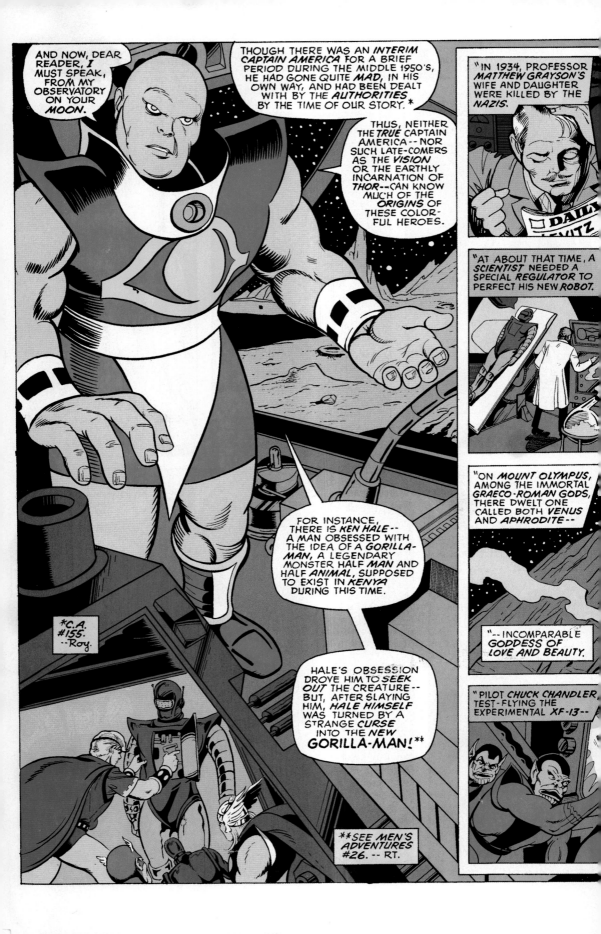

AND NOW, DEAR READER, I MUST SPEAK, FROM MY OBSERVATORY ON YOUR MOON.

THOUGH THERE WAS AN *INTERIM CAPTAIN AMERICA* FOR A BRIEF PERIOD DURING THE MIDDLE 1950'S, HE HAD GONE QUITE *MAD*, IN HIS OWN WAY, AND HAD BEEN DEALT WITH BY THE *AUTHORITIES* BY THE TIME OF OUR STORY. *

THUS, NEITHER THE *TRUE* CAPTAIN AMERICA -- NOR SUCH LATE-COMERS AS THE *VISION* OR THE EARTHLY INCARNATION OF *THOR* -- CAN KNOW MUCH OF THE *ORIGINS* OF THESE COLOR-FUL HEROES.

FOR INSTANCE, THERE IS *KEN HALE* -- A MAN OBSESSED WITH THE IDEA OF A *GORILLA-MAN*, A LEGENDARY MONSTER HALF MAN AND HALF *ANIMAL*, SUPPOSED TO EXIST IN *KENYA* DURING THIS TIME.

*C.A. #155. --Roy.

HALE'S OBSESSION DROVE HIM TO *SEEK OUT* THE CREATURE -- BUT, AFTER SLAYING HIM, *HALE* HIMSELF WAS TURNED BY A STRANGE *CURSE* INTO THE *NEW GORILLA-MAN!* **

**SEE MEN'S ADVENTURES #26. -- RT.

"IN 1934, PROFESSOR *MATTHEW GRAYSON'S* WIFE AND DAUGHTER WERE KILLED BY THE *NAZIS.*

"AT ABOUT THAT TIME, A *SCIENTIST* NEEDED A SPECIAL *REGULATOR* TO PERFECT HIS NEW *ROBOT.*

"ON *MOUNT OLYMPUS,* AMONG THE IMMORTAL *GRAECO-ROMAN* GODS, THERE DWELT ONE CALLED BOTH *VENUS* AND *APHRODITE* --

"-- INCOMPARABLE *GODDESS OF LOVE AND BEAUTY.*

"PILOT *CHUCK CHANDLER,* TEST-FLYING THE EXPERIMENTAL *XF-13* --

"WITH HIS INFANT SON *BOB,* GRAYSON FLED HITLER'S TYRANNY IN AN EARLY *ATOMIC-POWERED* CRAFT.

"BUT, HIS MOON-BOUND SHIP WENT INEXPLICABLY *OFF-COURSE...*

...REACHING THE PLANET *URANUS,* WHERE HIS GROWING SON ACQUIRED THE NAME AND ABILITIES OF... *MARVEL BOY.* *

*SEE MARVEL BOY #1, 1951. --R.

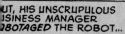

UT, HIS UNSCRUPULOUS USINESS MANAGER ABOTAGED THE ROBOT...

PROGRAMMING IT TO ILL ITS CREATOR...

"...WHICH IT *DID!*

"BUT, *WITHOUT* THE REGULATOR...

"...THE '*KILL*' ORDER *REMAINED!*

"AFTER KILLING BOTH MEN, THE *HUMAN ROBOT* SOUGHT OUT *MORE* VICTIMS.

"SHORT-CIRCUITED BY WATER, IT DID NOT GET *FAR.* *

*MENACE #11. --Roy.

"SHE IS THE DAUGHTER OF *ZEUS* -- AND COUSIN OF *HERCULES,* PRINCE OF POWER.

"YET, SHE *RENOUNCED* ALL HER GODLY ATTRIBUTES SAVE THE POWER OF *LOVE* ITSELF --

"--TO DWELL AMONG THE *MORTALS* WHO SEEMED SO MUCH TO *NEED* WHAT SHE ALONE COULD *BESTOW.* *

*SEE VENUS' OWN MAGAZINE, DURING THE 1950'S. -- GUESS WHO.

WAS NOT PREPARED OR HIS *CAPTURE* BY R ALIEN *SKRULLS* --

"--OR FOR THE *EXPLOSION* OF THEIR *FLYING SAUCER* --

"--WHICH CREATED AN EERIE *RELATIONSHIP* BETWEEN HIMSELF AND HIS YOUNGER BROTHER *HAL.*

" MERGING INTO *ONE BEING* WHENEVER HAL DONNED CERTAIN *GLASSES* --

"--THEY COULD BECOME-- THE *3-D MAN!* *

*MARVEL PREMIERE #35.-- Roy.

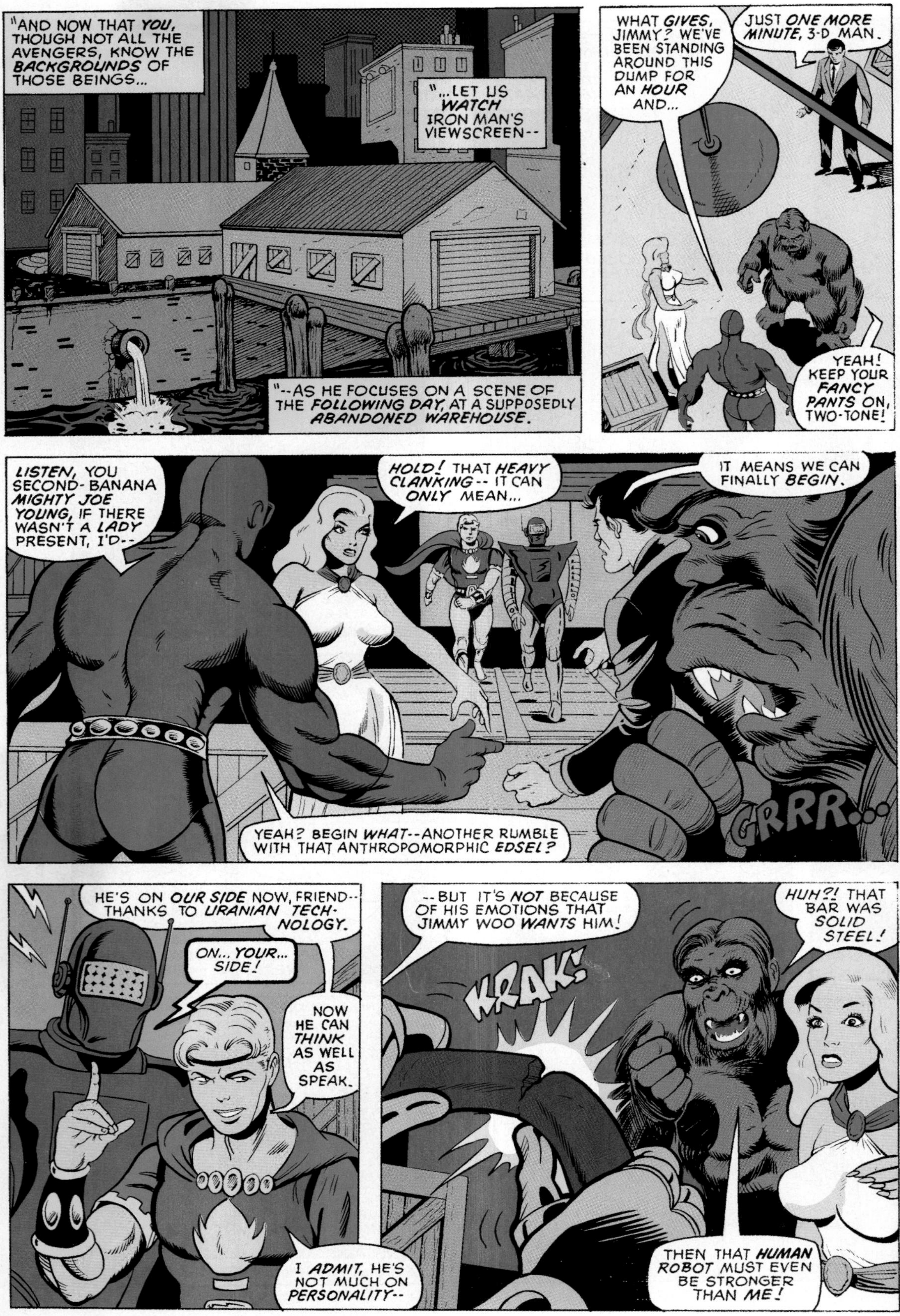

"AND NOW THAT YOU, THOUGH NOT ALL THE AVENGERS, KNOW THE BACKGROUNDS OF THOSE BEINGS...
"...LET US WATCH IRON MAN'S VIEWSCREEN--
"--AS HE FOCUSES ON A SCENE OF THE FOLLOWING DAY, AT A SUPPOSEDLY ABANDONED WAREHOUSE.
WHAT GIVES, JIMMY? WE'VE BEEN STANDING AROUND THIS DUMP FOR AN HOUR AND...
JUST ONE MORE MINUTE, 3-D MAN.
YEAH! KEEP YOUR FANCY PANTS ON, TWO-TONE!
LISTEN, YOU SECOND-BANANA MIGHTY JOE YOUNG, IF THERE WASN'T A LADY PRESENT, I'D--
HOLD! THAT HEAVY CLANKING-- IT CAN ONLY MEAN...
IT MEANS WE CAN FINALLY BEGIN.
GRRR...
YEAH? BEGIN WHAT--ANOTHER RUMBLE WITH THAT ANTHROPOMORPHIC EDSEL?
HE'S ON OUR SIDE NOW, FRIEND-- THANKS TO URANIAN TECHNOLOGY.
ON... YOUR... SIDE!
NOW HE CAN THINK AS WELL AS SPEAK.
I ADMIT, HE'S NOT MUCH ON PERSONALITY--
--BUT IT'S NOT BECAUSE OF HIS EMOTIONS THAT JIMMY WOO WANTS HIM!
KRAK!
HUH?! THAT BAR WAS SOLID STEEL!
THEN THAT HUMAN ROBOT MUST EVEN BE STRONGER THAN ME!

I NEED HIS STRENGTH-- AS I NEED ALL OF YOUR SPECIAL POWERS, MR. HALE.

RECENTLY, I'VE BEEN ASSIGNED AS A PERSONAL BODYGUARD TO PRESIDENT EISENHOWER.

IN THE PAST MONTH, THERE HAVE BEEN THREE ATTEMPTS ON THE PRESIDENT'S LIFE, ALL LINKED--

--TO THE YELLOW CLAW, THAT CENTURY-OLD MYSTIC FROM THE FOOTHILLS OF THE TIBETAN ALPS...

...WHO FIRST WANTS TO RULE THE UNITED STATES, AND THEN THE WORLD! *

*SEE YELLOW CLAW #1. -- R.

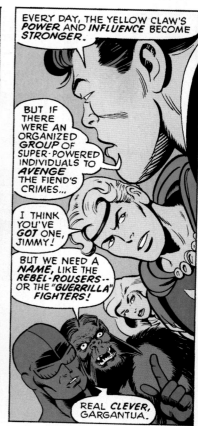

EVERY DAY, THE YELLOW CLAW'S POWER AND INFLUENCE BECOME STRONGER.

BUT IF THERE WERE AN ORGANIZED GROUP OF SUPER-POWERED INDIVIDUALS TO AVENGE THE FIEND'S CRIMES...

I THINK YOU'VE GOT ONE, JIMMY!

BUT WE NEED A NAME, LIKE THE REBEL-ROUSERS-- OR THE "GUERRILLA" FIGHTERS!

REAL CLEVER, GARGANTUA.

BUT... WOO... ALREADY... GAVE... US... NAME.

THE ROBOT'S RIGHT! IF WE'RE GOING TO AVENGE THE CRIMES OF THE YELLOW CLAW...

GRRRR

WHAT BETTER NAME CAN THERE BE FOR THIS WAY-OUT COMBO THAN...

"The AVENGERS!"

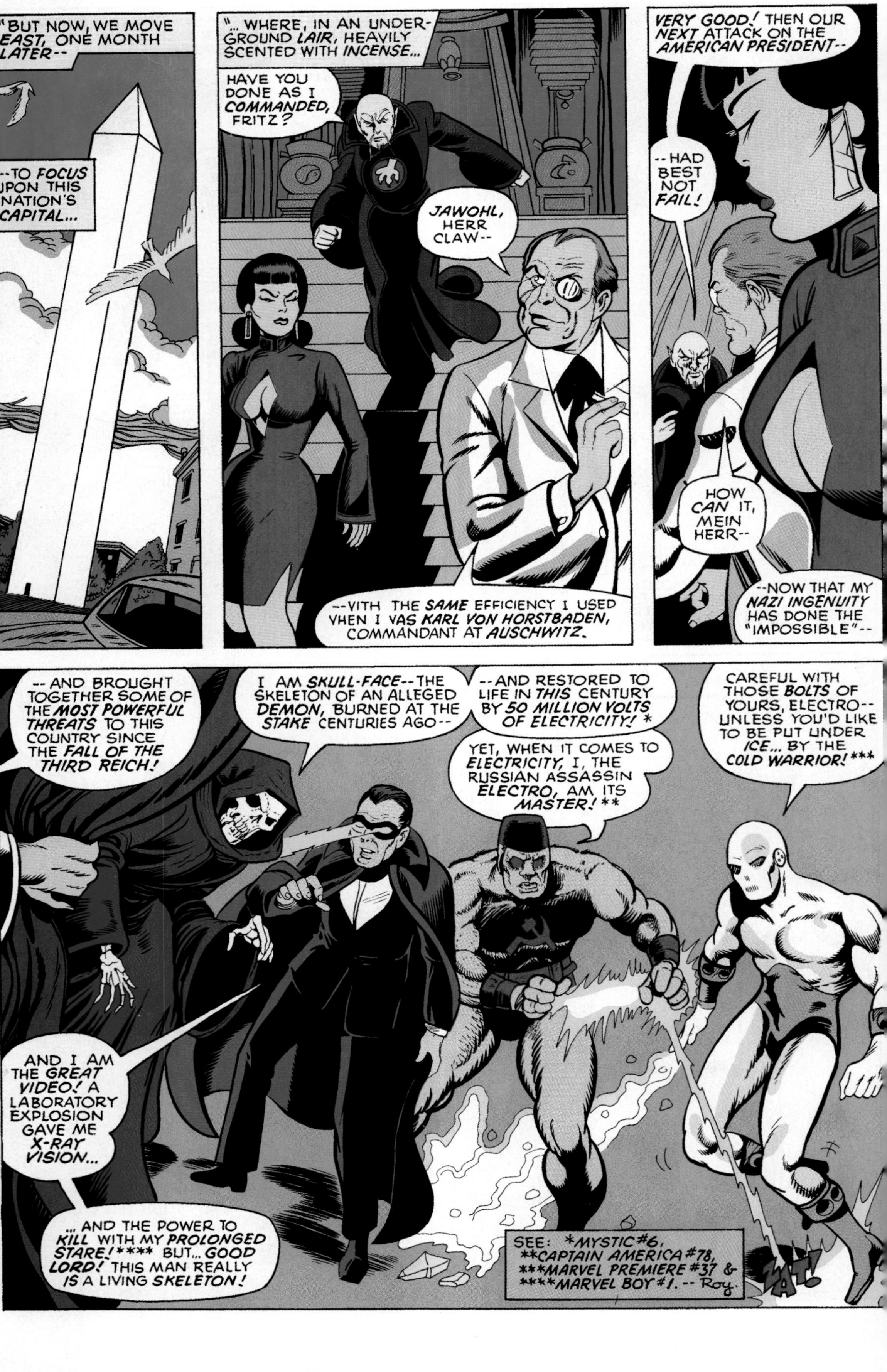
"BUT NOW, WE MOVE EAST, ONE MONTH LATER--
"--TO FOCUS UPON THIS NATION'S CAPITAL...
"... WHERE, IN AN UNDER-GROUND LAIR, HEAVILY SCENTED WITH INCENSE...
HAVE YOU DONE AS I COMMANDED, FRITZ?
JAWOHL, HERR CLAW--
--VITH THE SAME EFFICIENCY I USED VHEN I VAS KARL VON HORSTBADEN, COMMANDANT AT AUSCHWITZ.
VERY GOOD! THEN OUR NEXT ATTACK ON THE AMERICAN PRESIDENT--
--HAD BEST NOT FAIL!
HOW CAN IT, MEIN HERR--
--NOW THAT MY NAZI INGENUITY HAS DONE THE "IMPOSSIBLE"--
-- AND BROUGHT TOGETHER SOME OF THE MOST POWERFUL THREATS TO THIS COUNTRY SINCE THE FALL OF THE THIRD REICH!
I AM SKULL-FACE--THE SKELETON OF AN ALLEGED DEMON, BURNED AT THE STAKE CENTURIES AGO--
--AND RESTORED TO LIFE IN THIS CENTURY BY 50 MILLION VOLTS OF ELECTRICITY! *
YET, WHEN IT COMES TO ELECTRICITY, I, THE RUSSIAN ASSASSIN ELECTRO, AM ITS MASTER! **
CAREFUL WITH THOSE BOLTS OF YOURS, ELECTRO--UNLESS YOU'D LIKE TO BE PUT UNDER ICE... BY THE COLD WARRIOR! ***
AND I AM THE GREAT VIDEO! A LABORATORY EXPLOSION GAVE ME X-RAY VISION...
... AND THE POWER TO KILL WITH MY PROLONGED STARE! **** BUT... GOOD LORD! THIS MAN REALLY IS A LIVING SKELETON!
SEE: *MYSTIC #6, **CAPTAIN AMERICA #78, ***MARVEL PREMIERE #37 & ****MARVEL BOY #1. -- Roy.

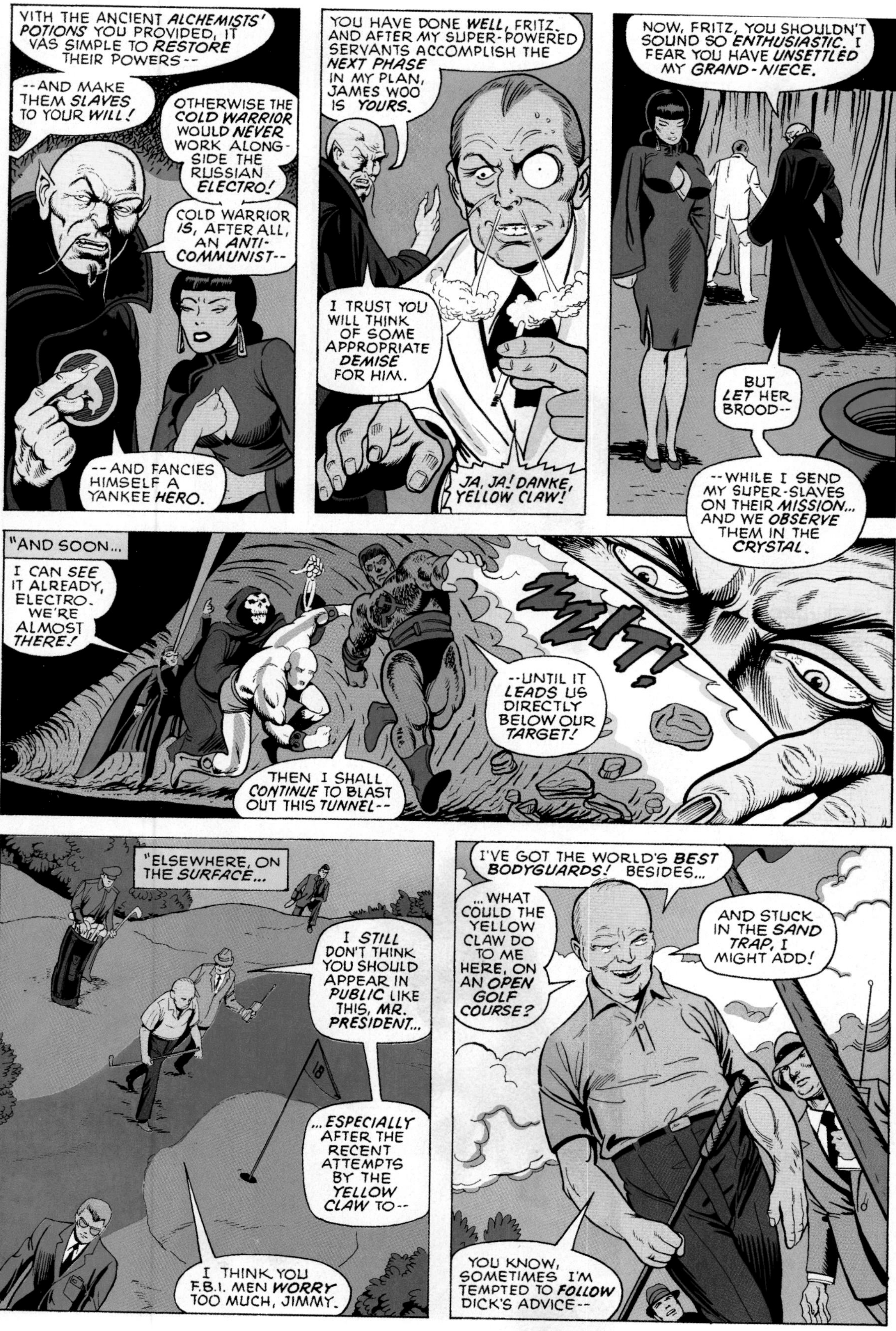
VITH THE ANCIENT ALCHEMISTS' POTIONS YOU PROVIDED, IT VAS SIMPLE TO RESTORE THEIR POWERS--
--AND MAKE THEM SLAVES TO YOUR WILL!
OTHERWISE THE COLD WARRIOR WOULD NEVER WORK ALONGSIDE THE RUSSIAN ELECTRO!
COLD WARRIOR IS, AFTER ALL, AN ANTI-COMMUNIST--
--AND FANCIES HIMSELF A YANKEE HERO.
YOU HAVE DONE WELL, FRITZ. AND AFTER MY SUPER-POWERED SERVANTS ACCOMPLISH THE NEXT PHASE IN MY PLAN, JAMES WOO IS YOURS.
I TRUST YOU WILL THINK OF SOME APPROPRIATE DEMISE FOR HIM.
JA, JA! DANKE, YELLOW CLAW!
NOW, FRITZ, YOU SHOULDN'T SOUND SO ENTHUSIASTIC. I FEAR YOU HAVE UNSETTLED MY GRAND-NIECE.
BUT LET HER BROOD--
--WHILE I SEND MY SUPER-SLAVES ON THEIR MISSION... AND WE OBSERVE THEM IN THE CRYSTAL.
"AND SOON...
I CAN SEE IT ALREADY, ELECTRO. WE'RE ALMOST THERE!
ZZZIT!
THEN I SHALL CONTINUE TO BLAST OUT THIS TUNNEL--
--UNTIL IT LEADS US DIRECTLY BELOW OUR TARGET!
"ELSEWHERE, ON THE SURFACE...
I STILL DON'T THINK YOU SHOULD APPEAR IN PUBLIC LIKE THIS, MR. PRESIDENT...
...ESPECIALLY AFTER THE RECENT ATTEMPTS BY THE YELLOW CLAW TO--
I THINK YOU F.B.I. MEN WORRY TOO MUCH, JIMMY.
18
I'VE GOT THE WORLD'S BEST BODYGUARDS! BESIDES...
...WHAT COULD THE YELLOW CLAW DO TO ME HERE, ON AN OPEN GOLF COURSE?
AND STUCK IN THE SAND TRAP, I MIGHT ADD!
YOU KNOW, SOMETIMES I'M TEMPTED TO FOLLOW DICK'S ADVICE--

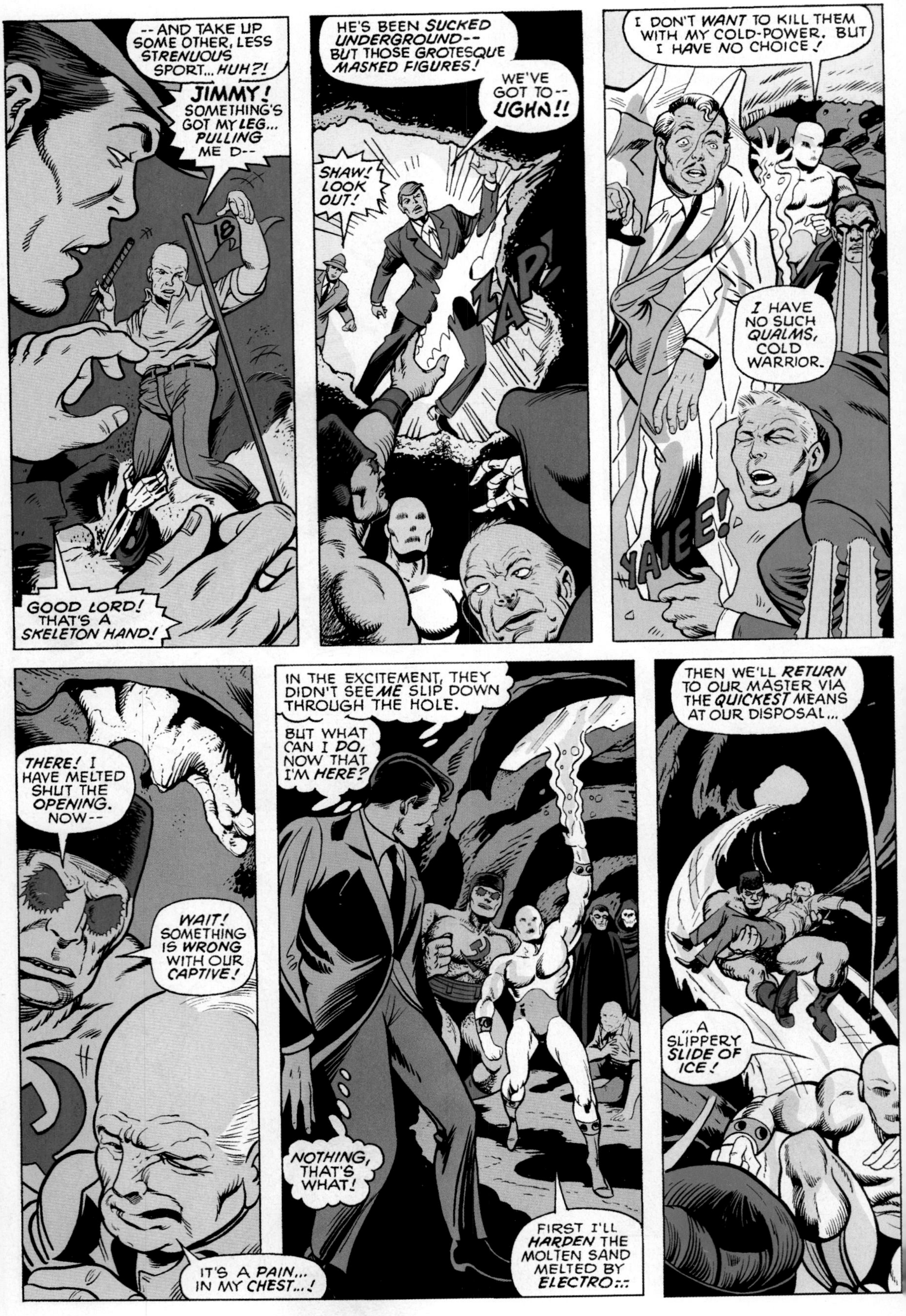
--AND TAKE UP SOME OTHER, LESS STRENUOUS SPORT... HUH?!
JIMMY! SOMETHING'S GOT MY LEG... PULLING ME D--
18
GOOD LORD! THAT'S A SKELETON HAND!
HE'S BEEN SUCKED UNDERGROUND-- BUT THOSE GROTESQUE MASKED FIGURES!
WE'VE GOT TO-- UGHN!!
SHAW! LOOK OUT!
ZAP!
I DON'T WANT TO KILL THEM WITH MY COLD-POWER. BUT I HAVE NO CHOICE!
I HAVE NO SUCH QUALMS, COLD WARRIOR.
YAIEEE!
THERE! I HAVE MELTED SHUT THE OPENING. NOW--
WAIT! SOMETHING IS WRONG WITH OUR CAPTIVE!
IT'S A PAIN... IN MY CHEST...!
IN THE EXCITEMENT, THEY DIDN'T SEE ME SLIP DOWN THROUGH THE HOLE.
BUT WHAT CAN I DO, NOW THAT I'M HERE?
NOTHING, THAT'S WHAT!
FIRST I'LL HARDEN THE MOLTEN SAND MELTED BY ELECTRO...
THEN WE'LL RETURN TO OUR MASTER VIA THE QUICKEST MEANS AT OUR DISPOSAL...
...A SLIPPERY SLIDE OF ICE!

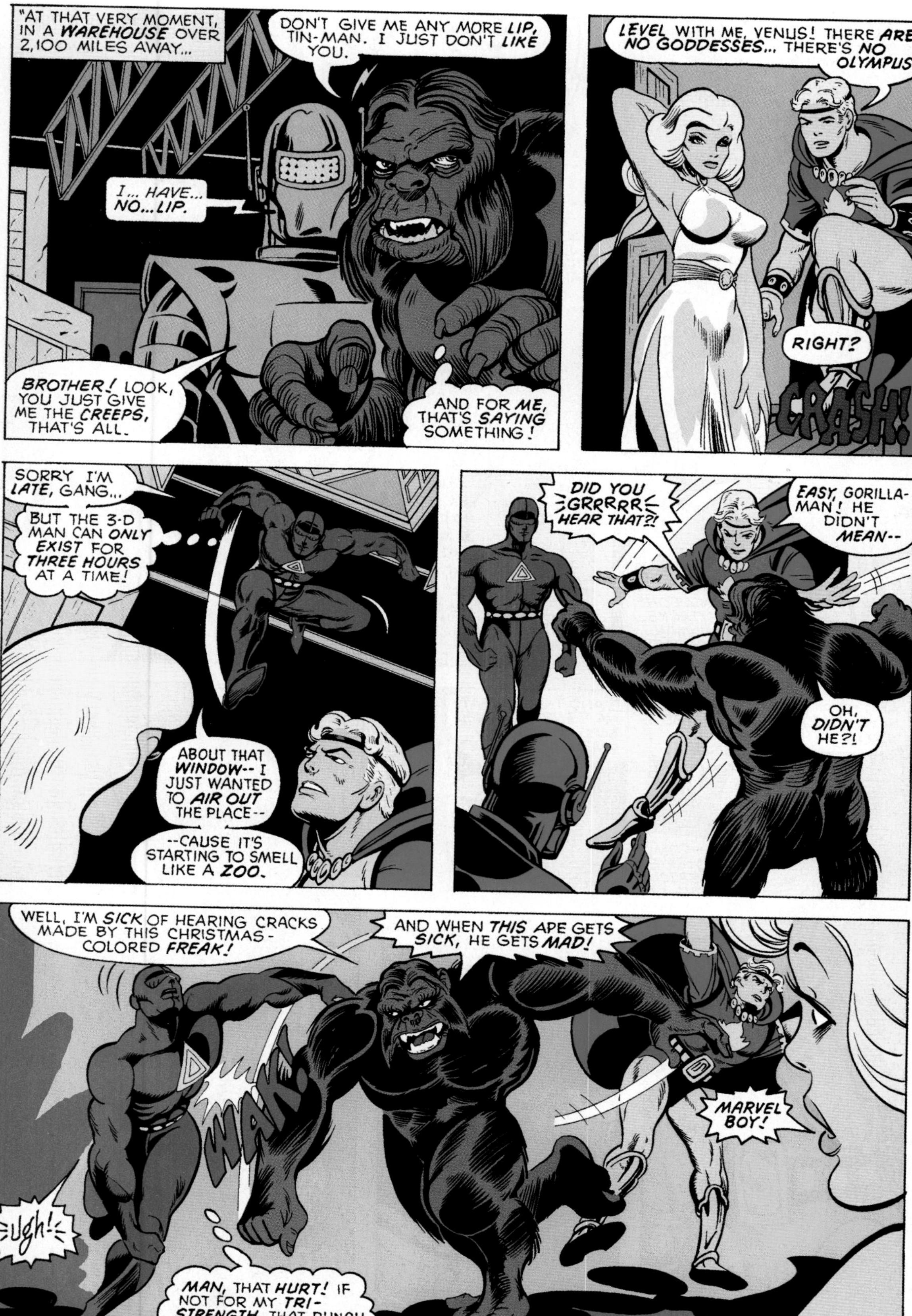
"AT THAT VERY MOMENT, IN A WAREHOUSE OVER 2,100 MILES AWAY...
DON'T GIVE ME ANY MORE LIP, TIN-MAN. I JUST DON'T LIKE YOU.
I... HAVE... NO...LIP.
BROTHER! LOOK, YOU JUST GIVE ME THE CREEPS, THAT'S ALL.
AND FOR ME, THAT'S SAYING SOMETHING!
LEVEL WITH ME, VENUS! THERE ARE NO GODDESSES... THERE'S NO OLYMPUS.
RIGHT?
CRASH!
SORRY I'M LATE, GANG...
BUT THE 3-D MAN CAN ONLY EXIST FOR THREE HOURS AT A TIME!
ABOUT THAT WINDOW-- I JUST WANTED TO AIR OUT THE PLACE--
--CAUSE IT'S STARTING TO SMELL LIKE A ZOO.
DID YOU GRRRRR HEAR THAT?!
EASY, GORILLA-MAN! HE DIDN'T MEAN--
OH, DIDN'T HE?!
WELL, I'M SICK OF HEARING CRACKS MADE BY THIS CHRISTMAS-COLORED FREAK!
AND WHEN THIS APE GETS SICK, HE GETS MAD!
WHAK!
MARVEL BOY!
UGH!
MAN, THAT HURT! IF NOT FOR MY TRI-STRENGTH, THAT PUNCH MIGHT'VE KILLED ME!

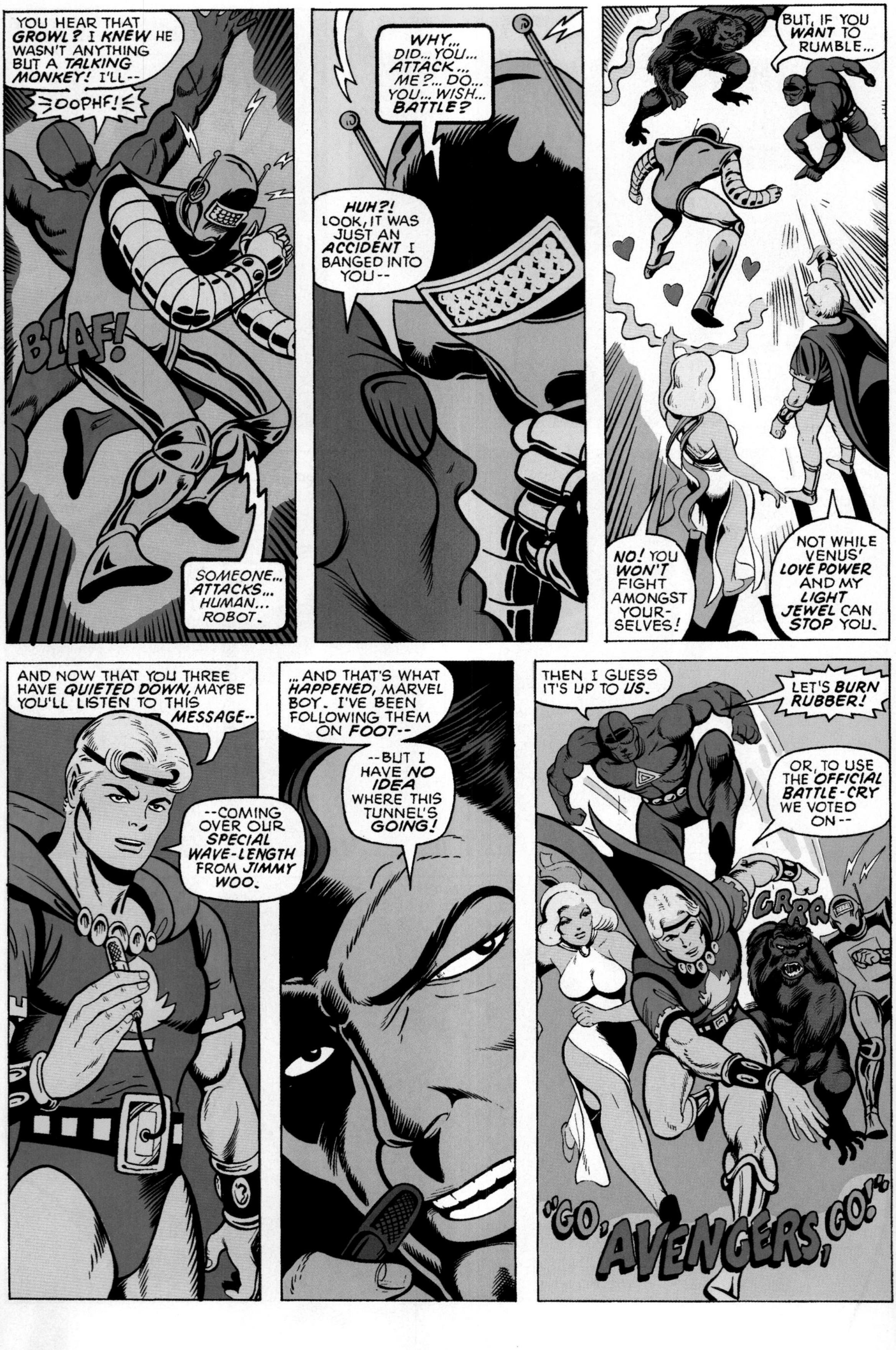

YOU HEAR THAT GROWL? I KNEW HE WASN'T ANYTHING BUT A TALKING MONKEY! I'LL--
OOPHF!
BLAF!
SOMEONE... ATTACKS... HUMAN... ROBOT.
WHY... DID... YOU... ATTACK... ME?... DO... YOU... WISH... BATTLE?
HUH?! LOOK, IT WAS JUST AN ACCIDENT I BANGED INTO YOU--
BUT, IF YOU WANT TO RUMBLE...
NO! YOU WON'T FIGHT AMONGST YOUR-SELVES!
NOT WHILE VENUS' LOVE POWER AND MY LIGHT JEWEL CAN STOP YOU.
AND NOW THAT YOU THREE HAVE QUIETED DOWN, MAYBE YOU'LL LISTEN TO THIS MESSAGE--
--COMING OVER OUR SPECIAL WAVE-LENGTH FROM JIMMY WOO.
...AND THAT'S WHAT HAPPENED, MARVEL BOY. I'VE BEEN FOLLOWING THEM ON FOOT--
--BUT I HAVE NO IDEA WHERE THIS TUNNEL'S GOING!
THEN I GUESS IT'S UP TO US.
LET'S BURN RUBBER!
OR, TO USE THE OFFICIAL BATTLE-CRY WE VOTED ON--
GRRR
"GO, AVENGERS, GO!"

YOU REACHED HERE *ALIVE.* GOOD! *DEAD* YOU'D BE *USELESS* TO ME!

WHAT DO YOU PLAN TO DO NOW, YELLOW CLAW-- *SURRENDER* ME TO YOUR "*COMRADES*"?

SO, MR. PRESIDENT, YOU *STILL* THINK I SERVE THE *COMMUNISTS!* BUT THE YELLOW CLAW SERVES *NO ONE...*

IS THAT NOT *SO,* HERR VOLTZMANN?

VOLTZMANN? YOU MEAN VON HORST-BADEN, DON'T YOU-- ONE OF THE WORLD'S MOST WANTED *WAR CRIMINALS?!*

HOW *FLATTERING!* AFTER ALL THESE *YEARS,* YOU *REMEMBER* ME

VAS I *SO* FAMOUS DURING THE *WAR,* HERR *GENERAL?*

YOU ARE A *BELOVED* PRESIDENT. AND SO I SHALL PUT YOUR LIFE UP FOR *RANSOM!* THE *PRICE*--

--COMPLETE *SOVEREIGNTY* OVER ONE OF YOUR *POPULOUS EASTERN STATES!*

YOU'RE *INSANE!* THE AMERICAN PEOPLE CAN'T BE *BLACKMAILED* LIKE THIS!

CAN'T THEY? FIRST, A SINGLE *STATE*-- AND, IN *TIME,* BY VARIOUS *MEANS,* YOUR ENTIRE *NATION,* MR. PRESIDENT.

THE *WEST* SHALL BE MINE... THEN THE *ORIENT...* AND FINALLY THE *ENTIRE WORLD!*

BUT HOW CAN I *STOP* HIM?

MY GRAND-UNCLE IS *MAD!*

I CAN'T BETRAY MY OWN *FLESH AND BLOOD!*

I'VE GOT TO THINK THIS THING *OUT,* IF--

Psssssst! SUWAN!

WHO--?

JIMMY! I THOUGHT I'D *NEVER* SEE YOU AGAIN! Mmmmmm...

THE *TUNNEL* BROUGHT ME HERE BUT IF I'M TO SAVE THE *PRESIDENT*--

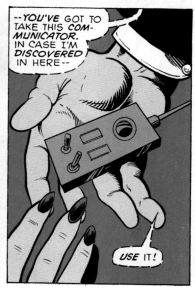

--YOU'VE GOT TO TAKE THIS *COMMUNICATOR.* IN CASE I'M *DISCOVERED* IN HERE--

USE IT!

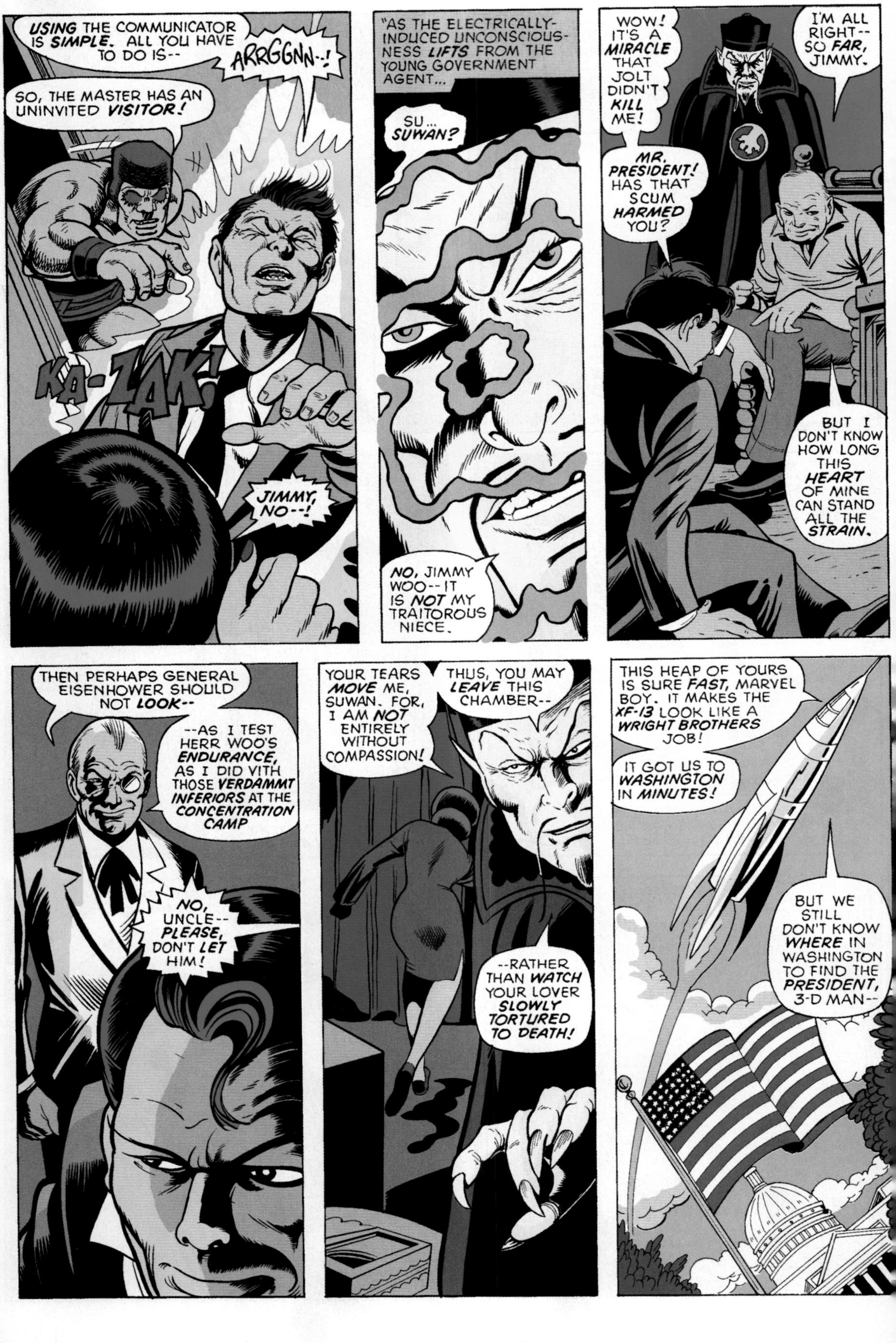
USING THE COMMUNICATOR IS SIMPLE. ALL YOU HAVE TO DO IS--
ARRGGNN--!
SO, THE MASTER HAS AN UNINVITED VISITOR!
KA-ZAK!
JIMMY, NO--!
"AS THE ELECTRICALLY-INDUCED UNCONSCIOUSNESS LIFTS FROM THE YOUNG GOVERNMENT AGENT...
SU... SUWAN?
NO, JIMMY WOO--IT IS NOT MY TRAITOROUS NIECE.
WOW! IT'S A MIRACLE THAT JOLT DIDN'T KILL ME!
I'M ALL RIGHT--SO FAR, JIMMY.
MR. PRESIDENT! HAS THAT SCUM HARMED YOU?
BUT I DON'T KNOW HOW LONG THIS HEART OF MINE CAN STAND ALL THE STRAIN.
THEN PERHAPS GENERAL EISENHOWER SHOULD NOT LOOK--
--AS I TEST HERR WOO'S ENDURANCE, AS I DID VITH THOSE VERDAMMT INFERIORS AT THE CONCENTRATION CAMP
NO, UNCLE--PLEASE, DON'T LET HIM!
YOUR TEARS MOVE ME, SUWAN. FOR, I AM NOT ENTIRELY WITHOUT COMPASSION!
THUS, YOU MAY LEAVE THIS CHAMBER--
--RATHER THAN WATCH YOUR LOVER SLOWLY TORTURED TO DEATH!
THIS HEAP OF YOURS IS SURE FAST, MARVEL BOY. IT MAKES THE XF-13 LOOK LIKE A WRIGHT BROTHERS JOB!
IT GOT US TO WASHINGTON IN MINUTES!
BUT WE STILL DON'T KNOW WHERE IN WASHINGTON TO FIND THE PRESIDENT, 3-D MAN--

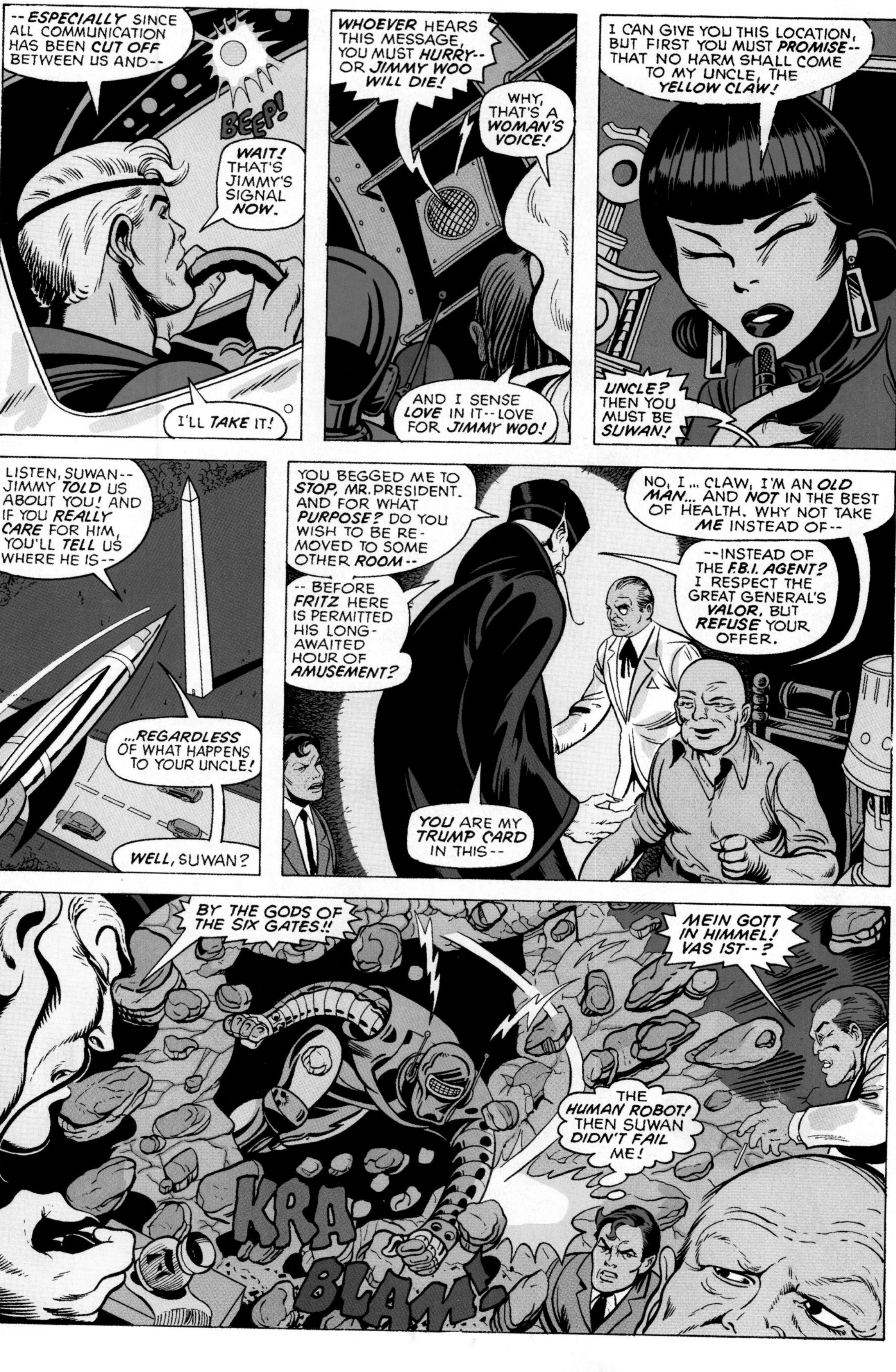

--ESPECIALLY SINCE ALL COMMUNICATION HAS BEEN CUT OFF BETWEEN US AND--
BEEP!
WAIT! THAT'S JIMMY'S SIGNAL NOW.
I'LL TAKE IT!
WHOEVER HEARS THIS MESSAGE, YOU MUST HURRY--OR JIMMY WOO WILL DIE!
WHY, THAT'S A WOMAN'S VOICE!
AND I SENSE LOVE IN IT--LOVE FOR JIMMY WOO!
I CAN GIVE YOU THIS LOCATION, BUT FIRST YOU MUST PROMISE--THAT NO HARM SHALL COME TO MY UNCLE, THE YELLOW CLAW!
UNCLE? THEN YOU MUST BE SUWAN!
LISTEN, SUWAN--JIMMY TOLD US ABOUT YOU! AND IF YOU REALLY CARE FOR HIM, YOU'LL TELL US WHERE HE IS--
...REGARDLESS OF WHAT HAPPENS TO YOUR UNCLE!
WELL, SUWAN?
YOU BEGGED ME TO STOP, MR. PRESIDENT. AND FOR WHAT PURPOSE? DO YOU WISH TO BE REMOVED TO SOME OTHER ROOM--
--BEFORE FRITZ HERE IS PERMITTED HIS LONG-AWAITED HOUR OF AMUSEMENT?
NO, I... CLAW, I'M AN OLD MAN... AND NOT IN THE BEST OF HEALTH. WHY NOT TAKE ME INSTEAD OF--
--INSTEAD OF THE F.B.I. AGENT? I RESPECT THE GREAT GENERAL'S VALOR, BUT REFUSE YOUR OFFER.
YOU ARE MY TRUMP CARD IN THIS--
BY THE GODS OF THE SIX GATES!!
MEIN GOTT IN HIMMEL! VAS IST--?
THE HUMAN ROBOT! THEN SUWAN DIDN'T FAIL ME!
KRA-BLAM!

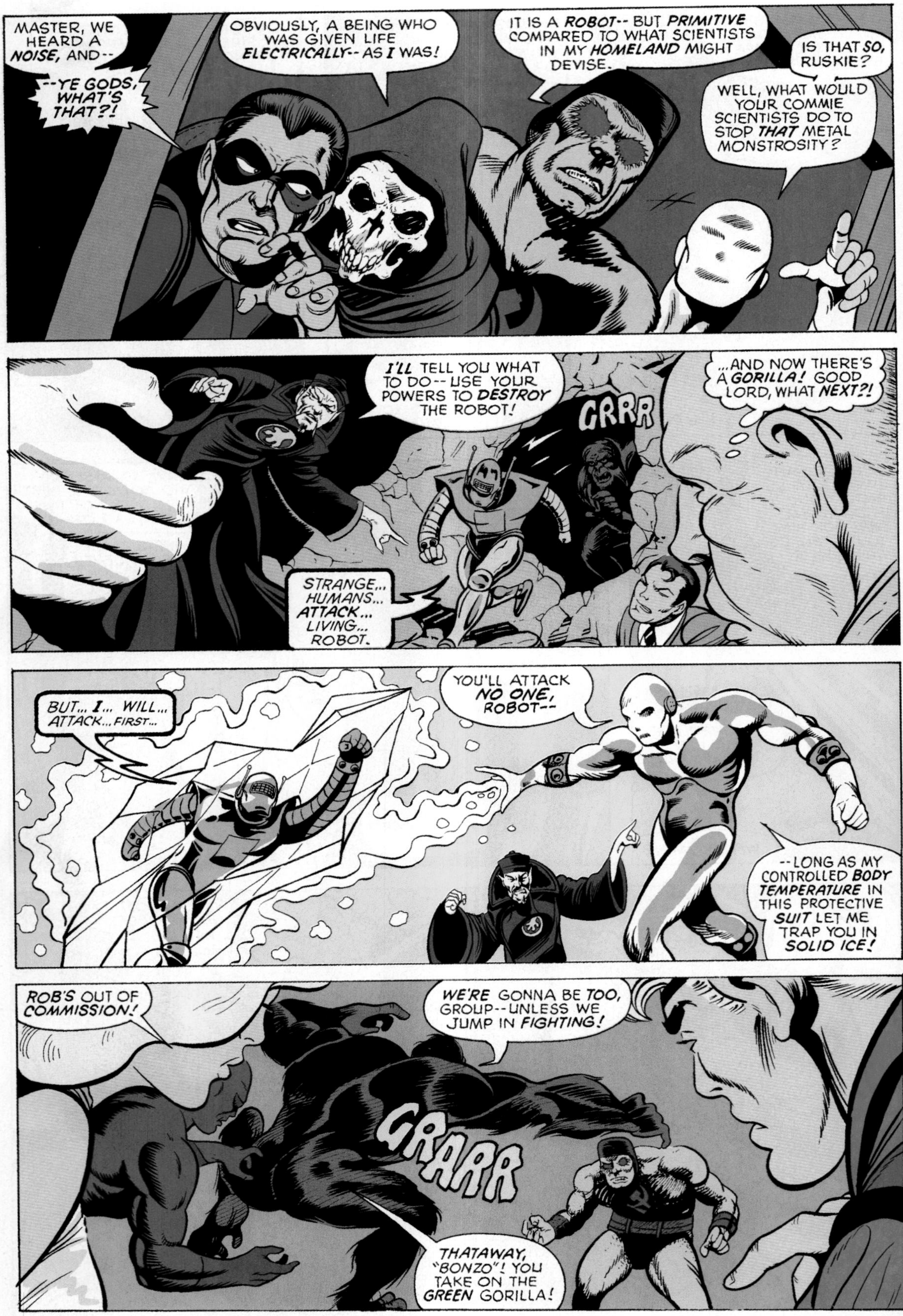
MASTER, WE HEARD A NOISE, AND--
--YE GODS, WHAT'S THAT?!
OBVIOUSLY, A BEING WHO WAS GIVEN LIFE ELECTRICALLY-- AS I WAS!
IT IS A ROBOT-- BUT PRIMITIVE COMPARED TO WHAT SCIENTISTS IN MY HOMELAND MIGHT DEVISE.
IS THAT SO, RUSKIE?
WELL, WHAT WOULD YOUR COMMIE SCIENTISTS DO TO STOP THAT METAL MONSTROSITY?
I'LL TELL YOU WHAT TO DO-- USE YOUR POWERS TO DESTROY THE ROBOT!
...AND NOW THERE'S A GORILLA! GOOD LORD, WHAT NEXT?!
GRRR
STRANGE... HUMANS... ATTACK... LIVING... ROBOT.
BUT... I... WILL... ATTACK... FIRST...
YOU'LL ATTACK NO ONE, ROBOT--
--LONG AS MY CONTROLLED BODY TEMPERATURE IN THIS PROTECTIVE SUIT LET ME TRAP YOU IN SOLID ICE!
ROB'S OUT OF COMMISSION!
WE'RE GONNA BE TOO, GROUP--UNLESS WE JUMP IN FIGHTING!
GRARR
THATAWAY, "BONZO"! YOU TAKE ON THE GREEN GORILLA!

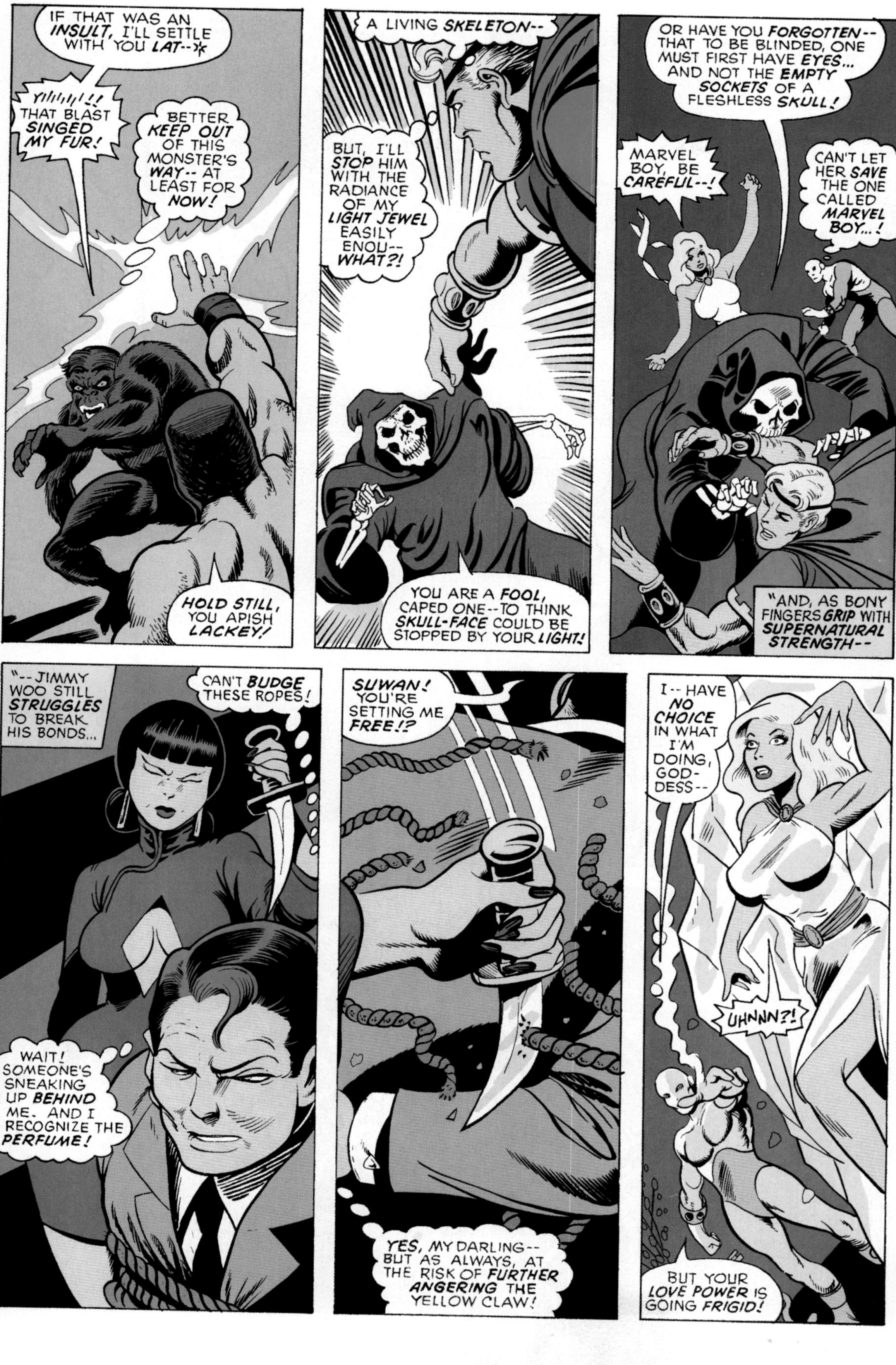
IF THAT WAS AN INSULT, I'LL SETTLE WITH YOU LAT--*
YIIIII!! THAT BLAST SINGED MY FUR!
BETTER KEEP OUT OF THIS MONSTER'S WAY-- AT LEAST FOR NOW!
HOLD STILL, YOU APISH LACKEY!
A LIVING SKELETON--
BUT, I'LL STOP HIM WITH THE RADIANCE OF MY LIGHT JEWEL EASILY ENOU-- WHAT?!
YOU ARE A FOOL, CAPED ONE--TO THINK SKULL-FACE COULD BE STOPPED BY YOUR LIGHT!
OR HAVE YOU FORGOTTEN-- THAT TO BE BLINDED, ONE MUST FIRST HAVE EYES... AND NOT THE EMPTY SOCKETS OF A FLESHLESS SKULL!
MARVEL BOY, BE CAREFUL--!
CAN'T LET HER SAVE THE ONE CALLED MARVEL BOY...!
"AND, AS BONY FINGERS GRIP WITH SUPERNATURAL STRENGTH--
"--JIMMY WOO STILL STRUGGLES TO BREAK HIS BONDS...
CAN'T BUDGE THESE ROPES!
WAIT! SOMEONE'S SNEAKING UP BEHIND ME. AND I RECOGNIZE THE PERFUME!
SUWAN! YOU'RE SETTING ME FREE!?
YES, MY DARLING-- BUT AS ALWAYS, AT THE RISK OF FURTHER ANGERING THE YELLOW CLAW!
I--HAVE NO CHOICE IN WHAT I'M DOING, GOD-DESS--
UHNNN?!
BUT YOUR LOVE POWER IS GOING FRIGID!

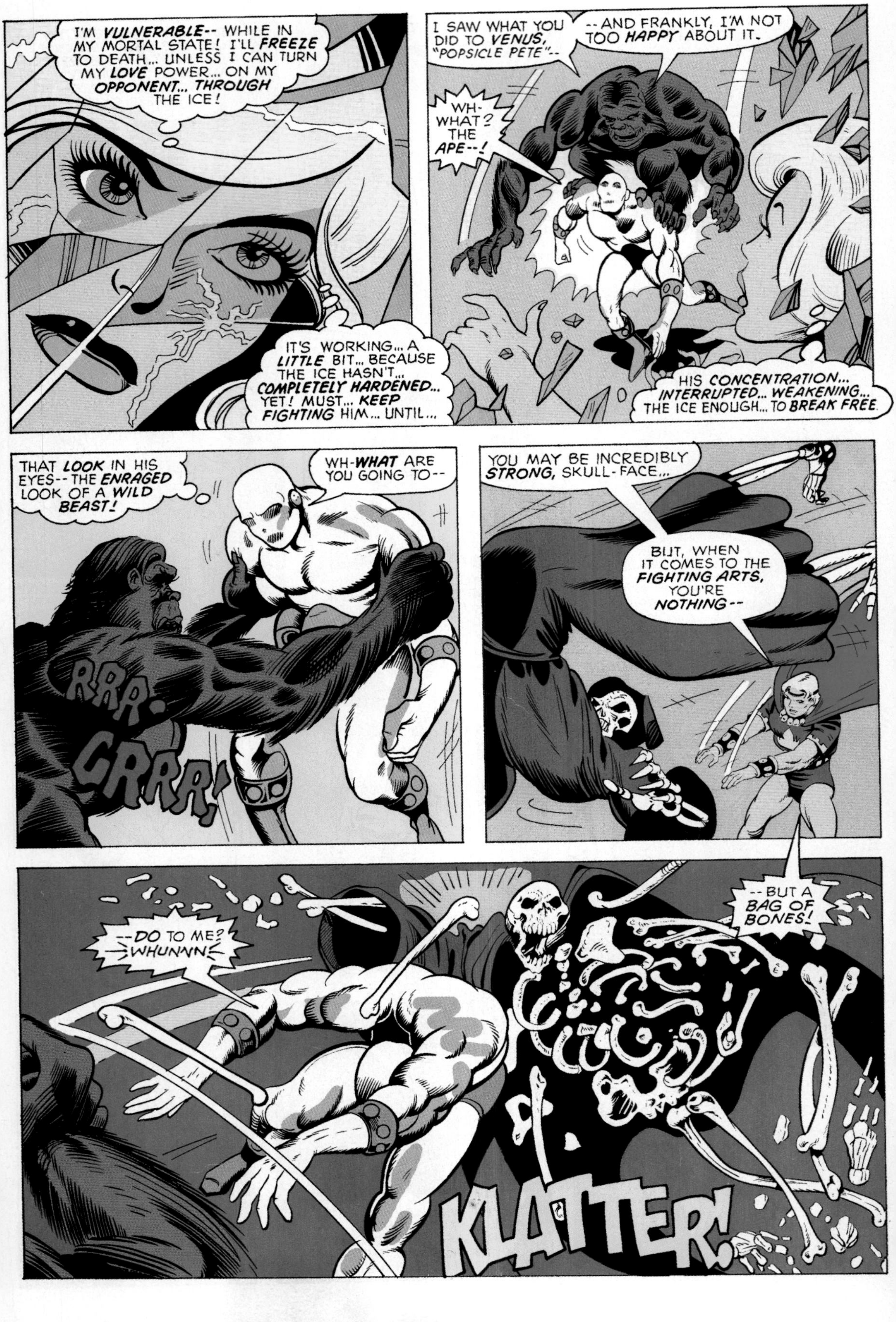

I'M VULNERABLE-- WHILE IN MY MORTAL STATE! I'LL FREEZE TO DEATH... UNLESS I CAN TURN MY LOVE POWER... ON MY OPPONENT... THROUGH THE ICE!
IT'S WORKING... A LITTLE BIT... BECAUSE THE ICE HASN'T... COMPLETELY HARDENED... YET! MUST... KEEP FIGHTING HIM... UNTIL...
I SAW WHAT YOU DID TO VENUS, "POPSICLE PETE"--
--AND FRANKLY, I'M NOT TOO HAPPY ABOUT IT.
WH- WHAT? THE APE--!
HIS CONCENTRATION... INTERRUPTED... WEAKENING... THE ICE ENOUGH... TO BREAK FREE.
THAT LOOK IN HIS EYES-- THE ENRAGED LOOK OF A WILD BEAST!
WH-WHAT ARE YOU GOING TO--
RRR-GRRR!
YOU MAY BE INCREDIBLY STRONG, SKULL-FACE...
BUT, WHEN IT COMES TO THE FIGHTING ARTS, YOU'RE NOTHING--
--BUT A BAG OF BONES!
--DO TO ME? WHUNNN!
KLATTER!

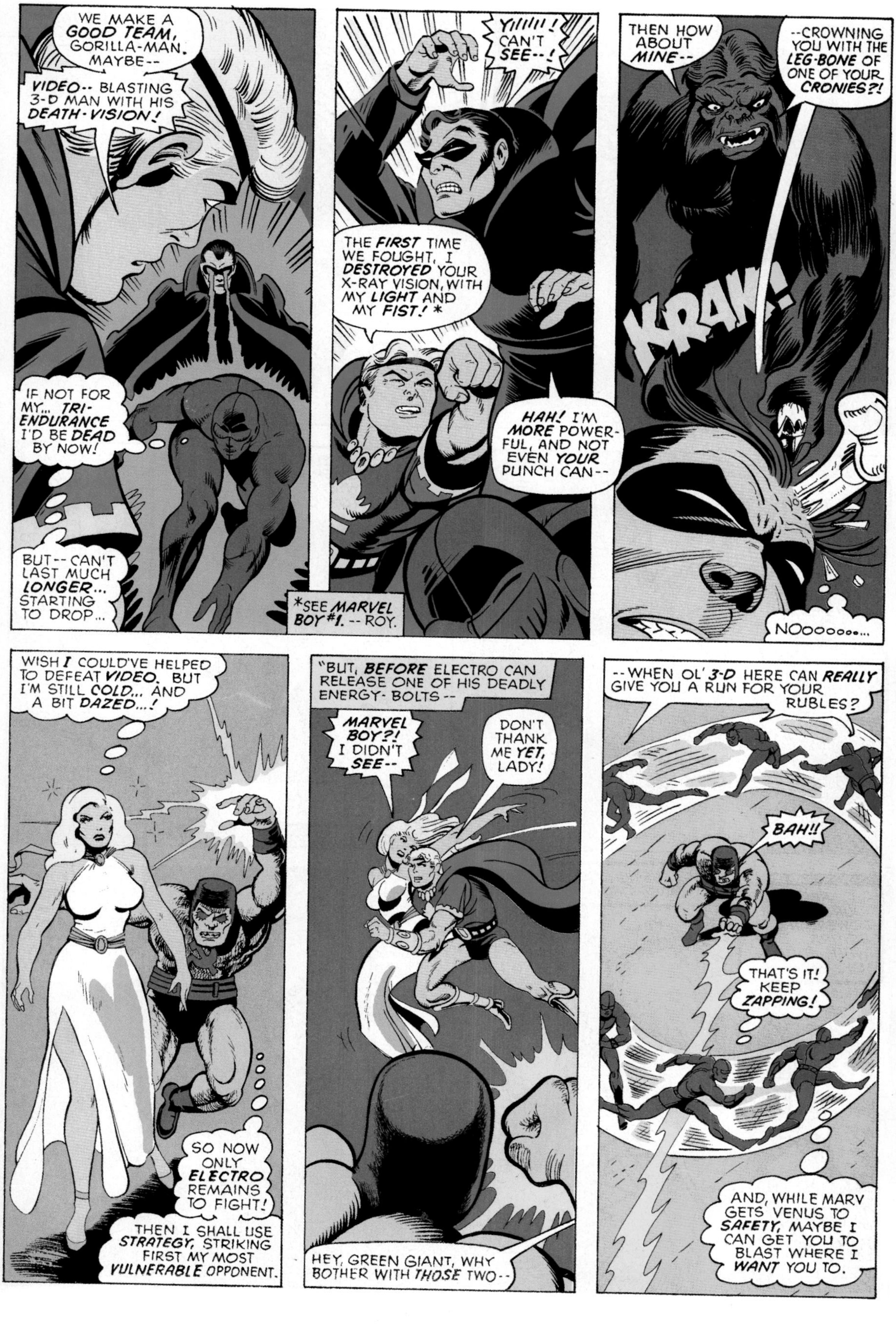
WE MAKE A GOOD TEAM, GORILLA-MAN. MAYBE--
VIDEO-- BLASTING 3-D MAN WITH HIS DEATH-VISION!
IF NOT FOR MY... TRI-ENDURANCE I'D BE DEAD BY NOW!
BUT-- CAN'T LAST MUCH LONGER... STARTING TO DROP...
YIIIII! CAN'T SEE--!
THE FIRST TIME WE FOUGHT, I DESTROYED YOUR X-RAY VISION, WITH MY LIGHT AND MY FIST! *
HAH! I'M MORE POWERFUL, AND NOT EVEN YOUR PUNCH CAN--
*SEE MARVEL BOY #1. -- ROY.
THEN HOW ABOUT MINE--
--CROWNING YOU WITH THE LEG-BONE OF ONE OF YOUR CRONIES?!
KRAK!
NOOOOOOO...
WISH I COULD'VE HELPED TO DEFEAT VIDEO. BUT I'M STILL COLD... AND A BIT DAZED...!
SO NOW ONLY ELECTRO REMAINS TO FIGHT!
THEN I SHALL USE STRATEGY, STRIKING FIRST MY MOST VULNERABLE OPPONENT.
"BUT, BEFORE ELECTRO CAN RELEASE ONE OF HIS DEADLY ENERGY-BOLTS--
MARVEL BOY?! I DIDN'T SEE--
DON'T THANK ME YET, LADY!
HEY, GREEN GIANT, WHY BOTHER WITH THOSE TWO--
--WHEN OL' 3-D HERE CAN REALLY GIVE YOU A RUN FOR YOUR RUBLES?
BAH!!
THAT'S IT! KEEP ZAPPING!
AND, WHILE MARV GETS VENUS TO SAFETY, MAYBE I CAN GET YOU TO BLAST WHERE I WANT YOU TO.

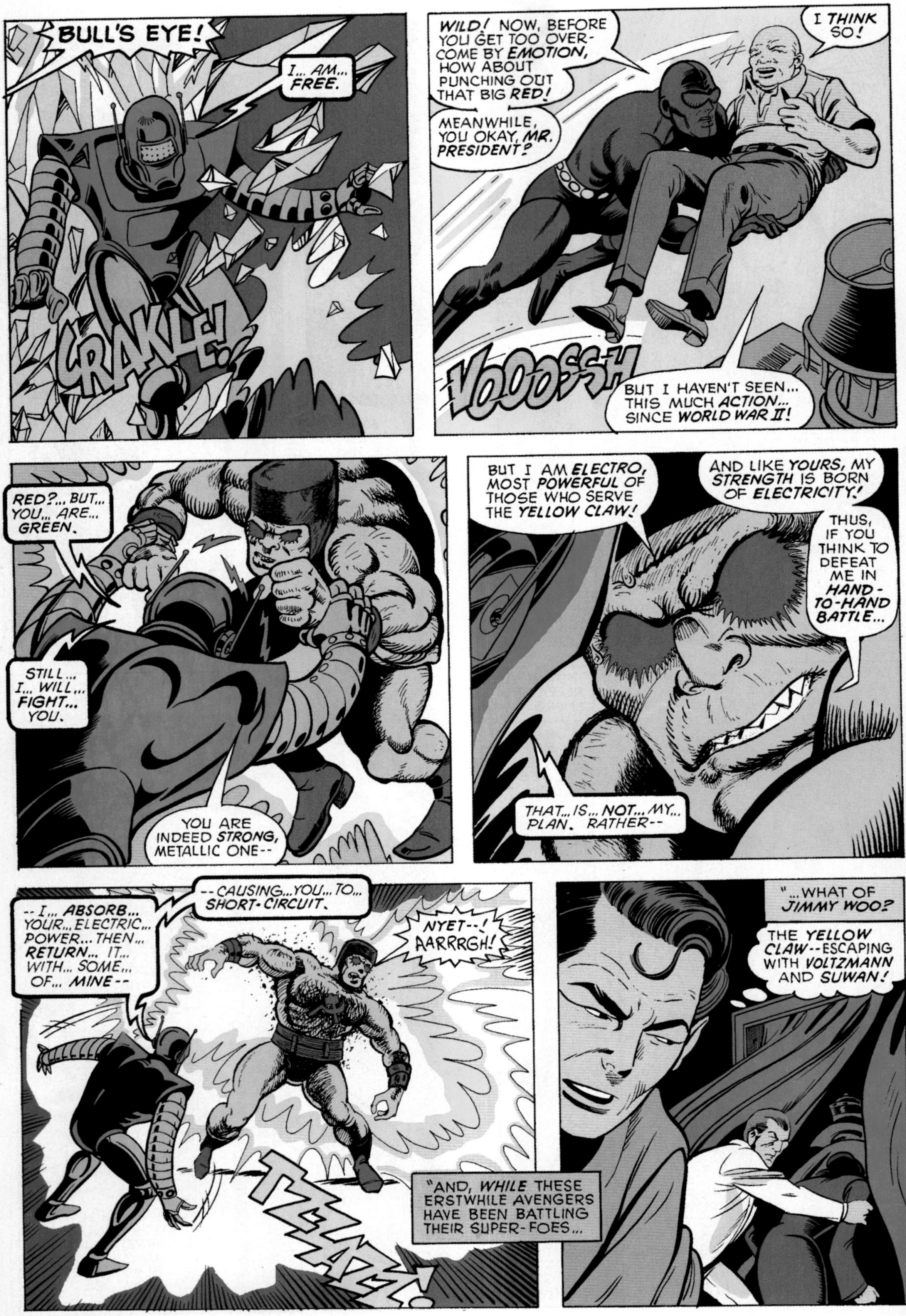
BULL'S EYE!
I... AM... FREE.
CRAKLE!
WILD! NOW, BEFORE YOU GET TOO OVER-COME BY EMOTION, HOW ABOUT PUNCHING OUT THAT BIG RED!
MEANWHILE, YOU OKAY, MR. PRESIDENT?
I THINK SO!
VOOOSSH
BUT I HAVEN'T SEEN... THIS MUCH ACTION... SINCE WORLD WAR II!
RED?... BUT... YOU... ARE... GREEN.
STILL... I... WILL... FIGHT... YOU.
YOU ARE INDEED STRONG, METALLIC ONE--
BUT I AM ELECTRO, MOST POWERFUL OF THOSE WHO SERVE THE YELLOW CLAW!
AND LIKE YOURS, MY STRENGTH IS BORN OF ELECTRICITY!
THUS, IF YOU THINK TO DEFEAT ME IN HAND-TO-HAND BATTLE...
THAT... IS... NOT... MY... PLAN. RATHER--
--I... ABSORB... YOUR... ELECTRIC... POWER... THEN... RETURN... IT... WITH... SOME... OF... MINE--
--CAUSING... YOU... TO... SHORT-CIRCUIT.
NYET--! AARRRGH!
TZZAK!
"AND, WHILE THESE ERSTWHILE AVENGERS HAVE BEEN BATTLING THEIR SUPER-FOES...
"...WHAT OF JIMMY WOO?
THE YELLOW CLAW--ESCAPING WITH VOLTZMANN AND SUWAN!

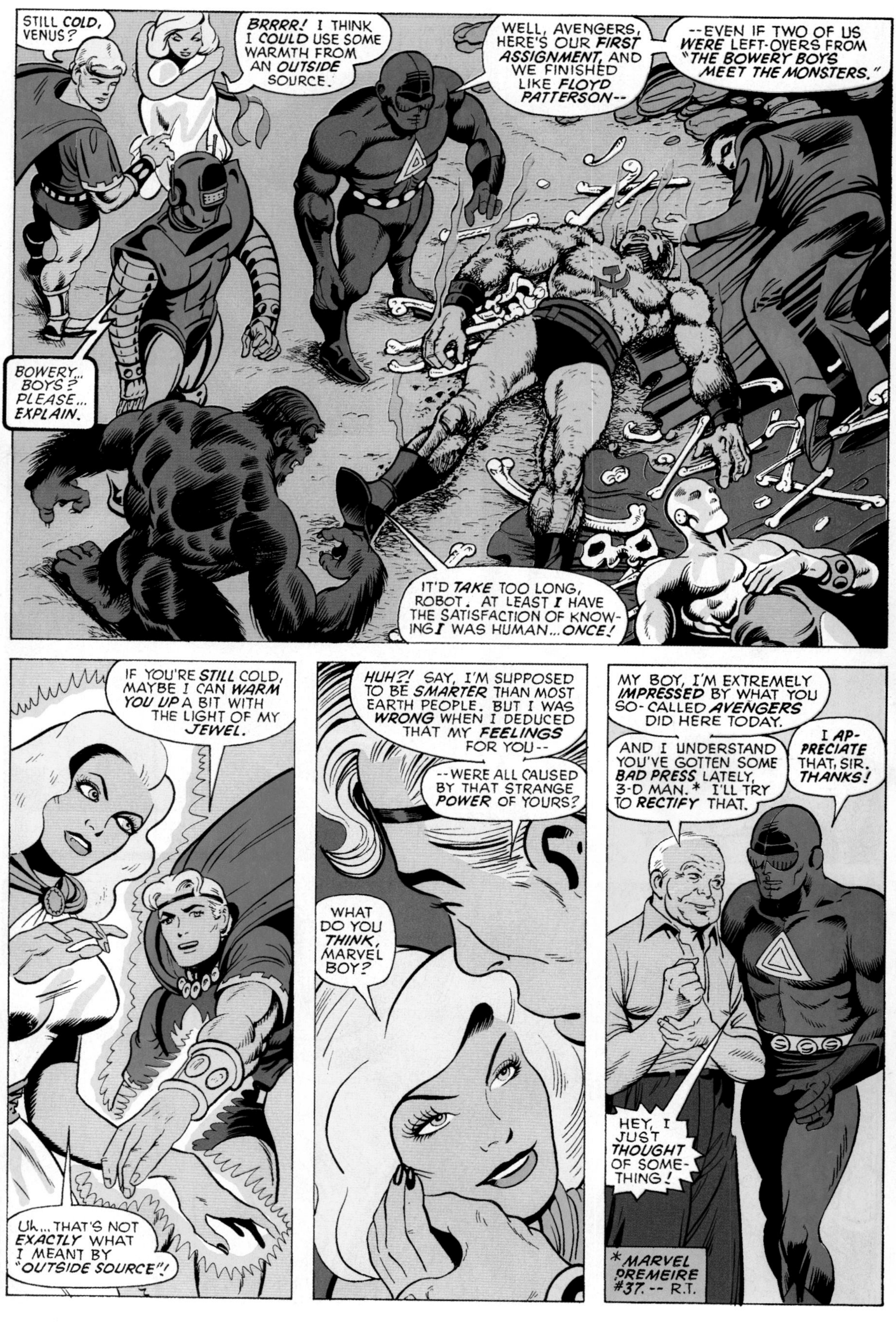
STILL COLD, VENUS?
BRRRR! I THINK I COULD USE SOME WARMTH FROM AN OUTSIDE SOURCE.
WELL, AVENGERS, HERE'S OUR FIRST ASSIGNMENT, AND WE FINISHED LIKE FLOYD PATTERSON--
--EVEN IF TWO OF US WERE LEFT-OVERS FROM "THE BOWERY BOYS MEET THE MONSTERS."
BOWERY... BOYS? PLEASE... EXPLAIN.
IT'D TAKE TOO LONG, ROBOT. AT LEAST I HAVE THE SATISFACTION OF KNOWING I WAS HUMAN... ONCE!
IF YOU'RE STILL COLD, MAYBE I CAN WARM YOU UP A BIT WITH THE LIGHT OF MY JEWEL.
Uh... THAT'S NOT EXACTLY WHAT I MEANT BY "OUTSIDE SOURCE"!
HUH?! SAY, I'M SUPPOSED TO BE SMARTER THAN MOST EARTH PEOPLE. BUT I WAS WRONG WHEN I DEDUCED THAT MY FEELINGS FOR YOU--
--WERE ALL CAUSED BY THAT STRANGE POWER OF YOURS?
WHAT DO YOU THINK, MARVEL BOY?
MY BOY, I'M EXTREMELY IMPRESSED BY WHAT YOU SO-CALLED AVENGERS DID HERE TODAY.
AND I UNDERSTAND YOU'VE GOTTEN SOME BAD PRESS LATELY, 3-D MAN.* I'LL TRY TO RECTIFY THAT.
I APPRECIATE THAT, SIR. THANKS!
HEY, I JUST THOUGHT OF SOMETHING!
*MARVEL PREMEIRE #37. -- R.T.

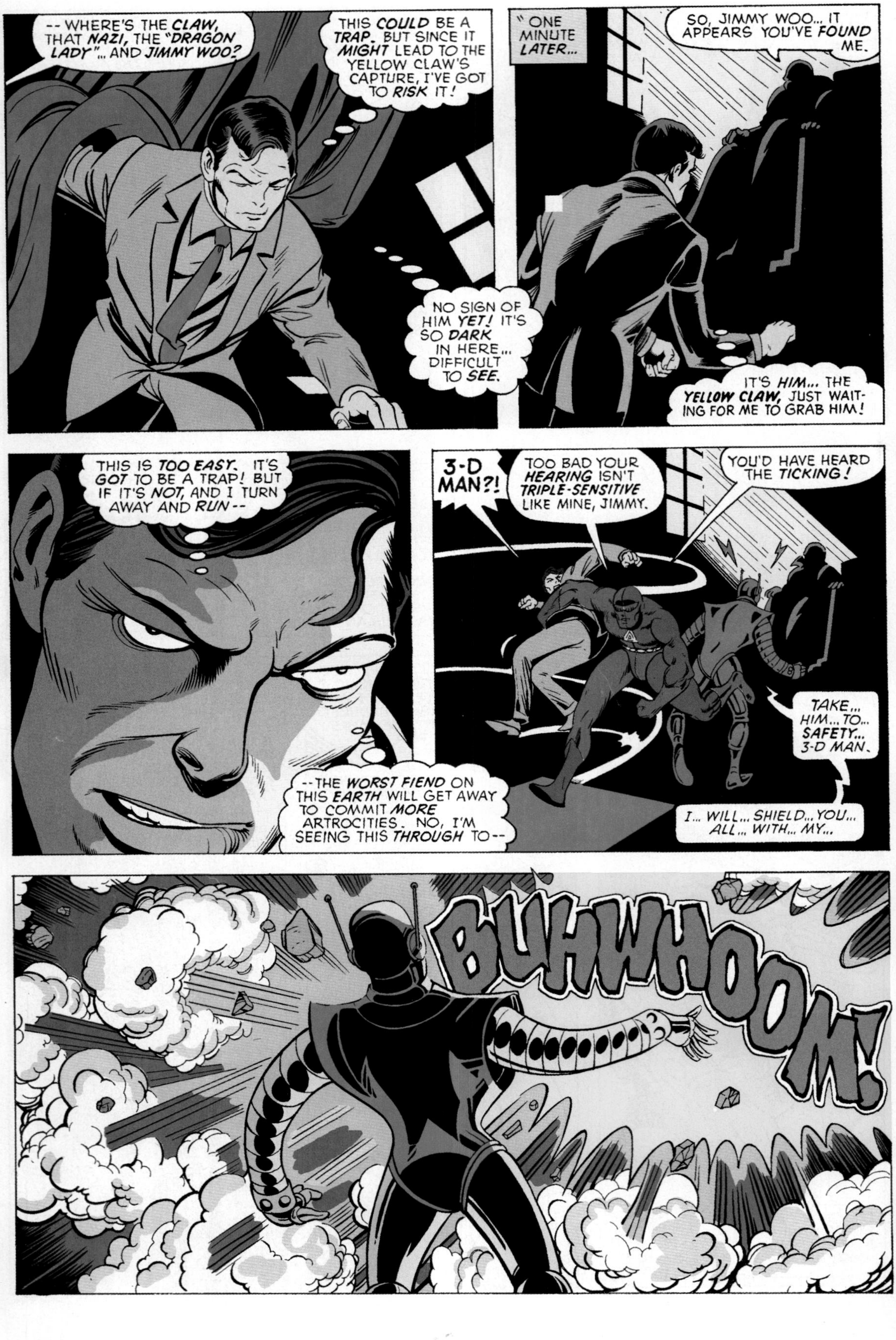

-- WHERE'S THE CLAW, THAT NAZI, THE "DRAGON LADY"... AND JIMMY WOO?
THIS COULD BE A TRAP. BUT SINCE IT MIGHT LEAD TO THE YELLOW CLAW'S CAPTURE, I'VE GOT TO RISK IT!
NO SIGN OF HIM YET! IT'S SO DARK IN HERE... DIFFICULT TO SEE.
"ONE MINUTE LATER...
SO, JIMMY WOO... IT APPEARS YOU'VE FOUND ME.
IT'S HIM... THE YELLOW CLAW, JUST WAITING FOR ME TO GRAB HIM!
THIS IS TOO EASY. IT'S GOT TO BE A TRAP! BUT IF IT'S NOT, AND I TURN AWAY AND RUN --
-- THE WORST FIEND ON THIS EARTH WILL GET AWAY TO COMMIT MORE ARTROCITIES. NO, I'M SEEING THIS THROUGH TO --
3-D MAN?!
TOO BAD YOUR HEARING ISN'T TRIPLE-SENSITIVE LIKE MINE, JIMMY.
YOU'D HAVE HEARD THE TICKING!
TAKE... HIM... TO... SAFETY... 3-D MAN.
I... WILL... SHIELD... YOU... ALL... WITH... MY...
BUHWHOOM!

IT WAS A *DUMMY*-- WITH A BUILT-IN *BOMB!* I SHOULD HAVE *GUESSED!*

YEAH-- AND THE *HUMAN ROBOT SACRIFICED* HIMSELF--FOR *ALL* OF US!

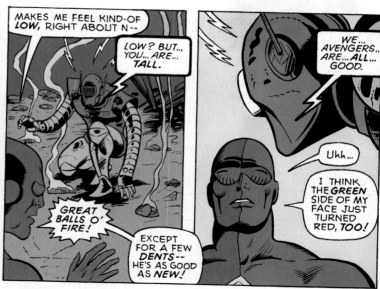

MAKES ME FEEL KIND-OF *LOW*, RIGHT ABOUT N--

LOW? BUT... YOU... ARE... *TALL.*

GREAT BALLS O' FIRE!

EXCEPT FOR A FEW *DENTS*-- HE'S AS GOOD AS *NEW!*

WE... *AVENGERS* ARE... *ALL...* GOOD.

Uhh...

I THINK THE *GREEN* SIDE OF MY FACE JUST TURNED RED, *TOO!*

... I MUST ADMIT THAT YOU FIVE ARE THE MOST *UNUSUAL* GUESTS I'VE EVER HAD HERE IN THE *WHITE HOUSE*...

... AT LEAST, ALL AT *ONE TIME.*

WE'RE *PROUD* TO HAVE DELIVERED YOU HERE *SAFELY,* MR. PRESIDENT.

THAT'S WHY I *HATE* TO ASK YOU... WHAT I *MUST.*

WHAT'S *THAT,* SIR?

THESE ARE *SUSPICIOUS* TIMES, MY *FRIENDS.* PEOPLE FIND *COMMUNISTS* UNDER THEIR BEDS-- AND *MARTIANS* IN EVERY WEATHER-BALLOON.

A FEW SIMPLISTIC SOULS EVEN FEEL THAT *COMIC-BOOKS,* AND ANYTHING *RESEMBLING* COMIC-BOOK CHARACTERS-- SUCH AS *YOURSELVES*-- ARE RESPONSIBLE FOR *EVERY SOCIAL ILL.*

THAT'S WHY I'M ASKING YOU TO *DISBAND THE AVENGERS*... WHILE I TAKE MEASURES TO *COVER UP* THE FACT THAT YOU *EVER EXISTED!*

THAT... DOES... NOT... COMPUTE.

WHAT!?

WON'T YOU *RECONSIDER,* SIR? WE--

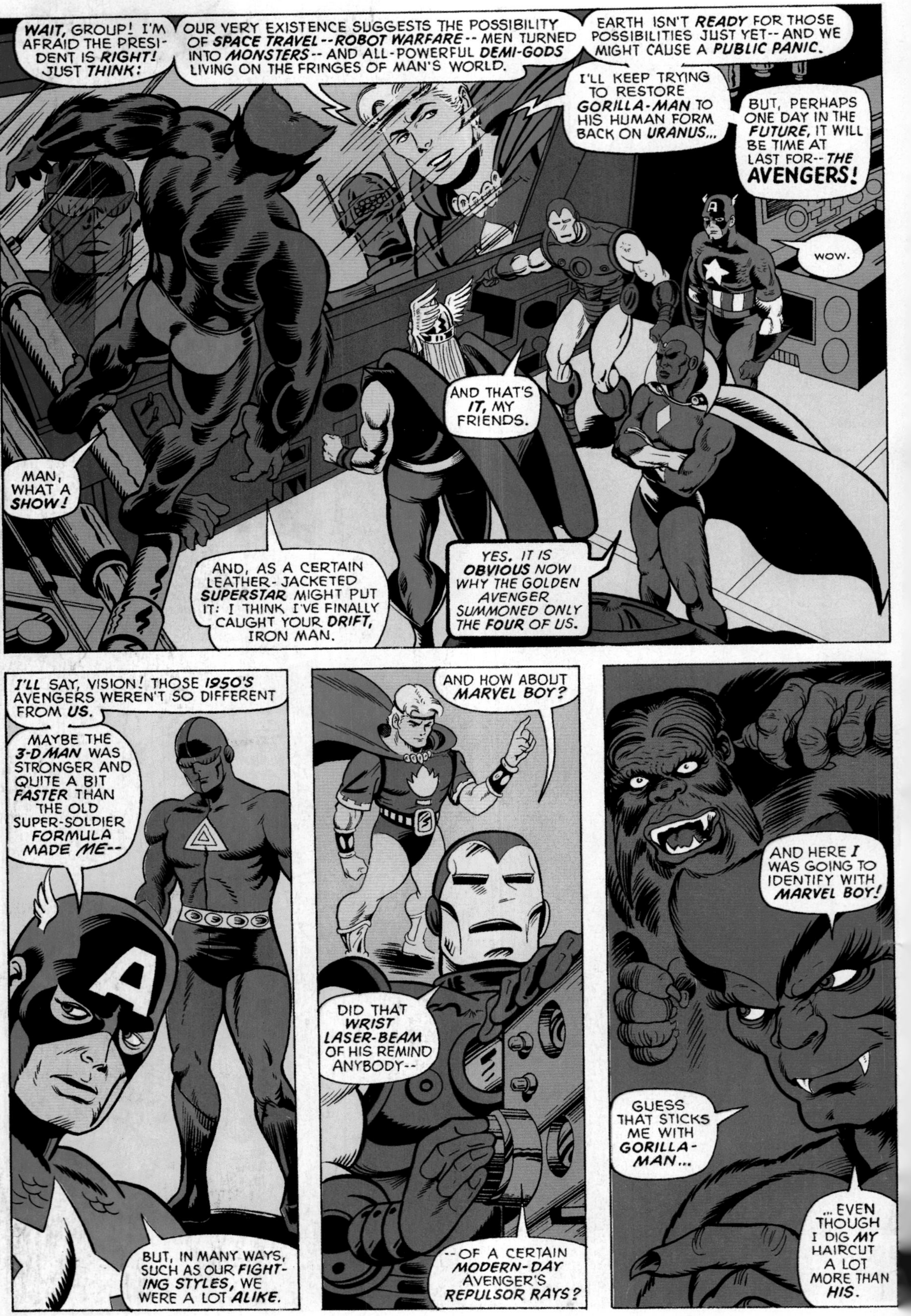
WAIT, GROUP! I'M AFRAID THE PRESIDENT IS RIGHT! JUST THINK:
OUR VERY EXISTENCE SUGGESTS THE POSSIBILITY OF SPACE TRAVEL--ROBOT WARFARE--MEN TURNED INTO MONSTERS--AND ALL-POWERFUL DEMI-GODS LIVING ON THE FRINGES OF MAN'S WORLD.
EARTH ISN'T READY FOR THOSE POSSIBILITIES JUST YET--AND WE MIGHT CAUSE A PUBLIC PANIC.
I'LL KEEP TRYING TO RESTORE GORILLA-MAN TO HIS HUMAN FORM BACK ON URANUS...
BUT, PERHAPS ONE DAY IN THE FUTURE, IT WILL BE TIME AT LAST FOR--THE AVENGERS!
WOW.
AND THAT'S IT, MY FRIENDS.
MAN, WHAT A SHOW!
AND, AS A CERTAIN LEATHER-JACKETED SUPERSTAR MIGHT PUT IT: I THINK I'VE FINALLY CAUGHT YOUR DRIFT, IRON MAN.
YES. IT IS OBVIOUS NOW WHY THE GOLDEN AVENGER SUMMONED ONLY THE FOUR OF US.
I'LL SAY, VISION! THOSE 1950'S AVENGERS WEREN'T SO DIFFERENT FROM US.
MAYBE THE 3-D MAN WAS STRONGER AND QUITE A BIT FASTER THAN THE OLD SUPER-SOLDIER FORMULA MADE ME--
BUT, IN MANY WAYS, SUCH AS OUR FIGHTING STYLES, WE WERE A LOT ALIKE.
AND HOW ABOUT MARVEL BOY?
DID THAT WRIST LASER-BEAM OF HIS REMIND ANYBODY--
--OF A CERTAIN MODERN-DAY AVENGER'S REPULSOR RAYS?
AND HERE I WAS GOING TO IDENTIFY WITH MARVEL BOY!
GUESS THAT STICKS ME WITH GORILLA-MAN...
...EVEN THOUGH I DIG MY HAIRCUT A LOT MORE THAN HIS.